RICKOVER

Norman Polmar

AND

Thomas B. Allen

SIMON AND SCHUSTER / NEW YORK

Copyright © 1982 by Norman Polmar and Thomas B. Allen
All rights reserved
including the right of reproduction
in whole or in part in any form
Published by Simon and Schuster
A Division of Gulf & Western Corporation
Simon & Schuster Building
Rockefeller Center
1230 Avenue of the Americas
New York, New York 10020
SIMON AND SCHUSTER and colophon are trademarks of Simon & Schuster
Designed by Edith Fowler
Manufactured in the United States of America

10   9   8   7   6   5   4   3   2   1

Library of Congress Cataloging in Publication Data

Polmar, Norman.
  Rickover.

  Bibliography: p.
  Includes index.
  1. Rickover, Hyman George.   2. United States.
Navy—Biography.   3. Admirals—United States—
Biography.   I. Allen, Thomas B.   II. Title.
V63.R54P64   359'.0092'4   [B]   81–14327
ISBN 0-671-24615-1   AACR2

To the officers and enlisted men of the U.S. Navy's nuclear program, especially those whom we have been privileged to call our friends.

Contents

Authors' Foreword   9
Authors' Note   13

THE RADIANCE OF A THOUSAND SUNS   15

1 The Unbeatable Man   17

THE PROMISED LAND   25

2 Father's Occupation: Tailor   27
3 The Class of 1922   41
4 Steaming as Before   60
5 Engineering Duty   90

UNDER WAY ON NUCLEAR POWER   113

6 The $1,500 Commitment   115
7 Building the *Nautilus*   135
8 The True Submersible   155

FATHER OF THE ATOMIC SUBMARINE   181

9 Passed Over   183
10 Congress Comes Aboard   206
11 Admiral of the Hill   222
12 Operation Sea Orbit   250

WHY NOT THE BEST?   267

13 A Fascinating Experience   269
14 The Men Called Nucs   294
15 The Day of the Nucs   317

THE RICKOVER NAVY   351

16 Building More Submarines   353
17 All Major Combatant Vessels . . .   377
18 Yesterday's Visionary   400
19 A Nuclear Submarine Is Missing . . .   423

ONE OF A KIND   447

20 A Day in the Naval Reactors Branch   449
21 Shooting the Admirals, Firing the Experts   463
22 Let Me Know, Promptly   486
23 Meeting the Press   514

IN THE PRESENCE OF MINE ENEMIES   533

24 The Highest National Priority   535
25 The Soviet Threat   552
26 The Ultimate Weapon—Again   564

HE NEVER WEARS A UNIFORM   583

27 Admiral of Education   585
28 From Shippingport to Three Mile Island   601
29 Danger: Radiation Hazard   616
30 The Admiral at Home   634

THE MAN WHO SHOUTS   651

31 The Unaccountable Man   653

Appendixes

    A. Rickover Chronology   669
    B. U.S. Naval Nuclear Reactors   675
    C. U.S. Nuclear-Propelled Ships and Submarines   677
    D. World Nuclear-Propelled Ships and Submarines   680
    E. U.S. Defense-Navy Leadership, 1947–1981   681
    F. U.S. Nuclear Submarine Accidents   683

Sources   689
Bibliography   707
Acknowledgments   721
Index   725

Authors' Foreword

When there are questions "involving the welfare or survival of the Nation," Admiral Hyman G. Rickover once said, "it is singularly unfitting to remain evasive. It is not only possible, but in fact the duty of everyone to state precisely what his knowledge and conscience compel him to say. A certain measure of courage in the private citizen is necessary to the good conduct of the State, otherwise men who have power through riches, intrigue, or office will administer the State at will and ultimately their private advantage."

It is upon this statement that we base this book.

Admiral Rickover made the statement while addressing a subcommittee of the Congress, a familiar occupation. He also said, "For the citizen, this courage means a frank exposition of a problem and a decrying of the excess of power. It takes courage to do this, for in our polite society frank speech is discouraged.... Only complete candor and frankness, deep respect for the facts, however unpleasant and uncomfortable, great efforts to know them where they are not readily available, and drawing conclusions guided only by rigorous logic can bring many of today's problems forward."

Inspired by Admiral Rickover's own attitude toward disclosure and frank words, we wrote to him immediately upon signing the publishing contract for this book.

The main thrust of the book, we told Admiral Rickover, "will be your impact on the Navy and the nation. Obviously, few naval officers have had a major impact on their navies or nation during or even after their lifetime.... Only a few names come to mind for the past one hundred years: Mahan, Fisher, Gorshkov, and, to a lesser extent, Fiske, Sims, and Scott. However, you have changed the nature of the U.S. Navy with respect to ship propulsion, quality control, personnel selection and training, and in several other areas. The impact of these changes has in-

9

fluenced the defense establishment, civilian nuclear energy field, and other national areas. . . .

"Your views on these and many other issues can be interpreted, in part, from your writings and Congressional testimony, as well as interviews with other persons. However, the subject would benefit greatly from your direct views. . . ."

A short time later, we received the following letter from Admiral Rickover's office:

> Admiral Rickover has asked me to reply to your letter. . . .
> Please be advised that he does not desire to have a book written about him. Therefore, he will not grant the interviews you requested.
>
> BARBARA J. WHITLARK
> Secretary to Admiral Rickover

Very few admirals have been able to bring about major change in their own navies, and even fewer have had major influence on their nation's structure and actions. At the start of the twentieth century Britain's Admiral Sir John (Jackie) Fisher did propel the world navies into the super battleship or *Dreadnought* era, in part due to the support of the First Lord of the Admiralty Winston Churchill. Fifty years later, after World War II, the Soviet Navy's Admiral Sergei Gorshkov pushed his navy into the guided-missile era, a fact that went largely unnoticed in the world until Trafalgar Day, October 21, 1967, when Egyptian missile boats fired four of Gorshkov's rockets to sink the Israeli destroyer *Elath*. Gorshkov's revolution in naval weapons was possible through the support of his national leaders, first Khrushchev, and then other men with strong naval leanings, Brezhnev, Kosygin and Romanov, among others.

Although Admirals Fisher and Gorshkov caused revolutions in their own navies and then on the world naval scenes, neither man significantly affected affairs in his nation outside the naval sphere. This is not to say that admirals could not change the course of history in battle. For example, Winston Churchill said of Admiral Sir John Jellicoe, the British commander in the 1915 Battle of Jutland, that he was the only man who could lose the war for Britain in one afternoon. But in peacetime few admirals can influence the course of a nation. Admiral Rickover has tried.

Admiral Rickover has affected both his navy and the nation. He has pushed the U.S. Navy into nuclear propulsion—a "revolution" in naval matters—and virtually took it upon himself to thrust the nation into civilian nuclear power.

In his attempt to propel the nation into nuclear power, he tried to show the need to replace the squandered resources, which, relatively long ago, he realized would eventually run out. He also attempted to change the face of American education, drawing heavily on Soviet educational concepts to force Americans to regain their leadership in a technological world. And he attempted to change the ethics of America—the concepts of right and wrong, of a full day's work for a full day's pay, of working for the common good and of striving for excellence.

Indeed, it is difficult to find another twentieth-century American who has striven so hard in so many areas of military and civil endeavor. And, especially, one who in doing so has, without elected office, without even accountability to his superiors in government, attained absolute and total control of a large segment of the American defense establishment. Probably no other military man and few civilians—even many of Cabinet rank—had in peacetime the personal responsibility for the expenditure of so much in public funds.

Admiral Rickover appears to have had his ideas and his methods shaped by three periods in his life. The first period was his four years as a midshipman at the Naval Academy in Annapolis, the school that for more than a hundred years has prepared almost all of the Navy's senior officers and many leaders in the nation's sciences and industry. The second phase in the education of Hyman Rickover was his service in the peacetime Navy of the 1920s and 1930s, mainly afloat in a succession of destroyers, battleships and submarines, and culminating in command of a small, aged minesweeper. Both ashore and at sea he constantly learned, with a year of postgraduate study at Annapolis and another year at Columbia University in electrical engineering. The third phase of his education was five World War II years in the Bureau of Ships in Washington, where Rickover was involved in the designing, installing and repairing of shipboard electrical equipment. From his Washington office, he ranged far and wide to deal with the fighting fleet and with industry—the contractors, who in time would be disparagingly referred to as "vendors," a dirty word in his vocabulary.

In all three periods of his education the Navy and ships were closely interwoven. The Academy was to prepare him for service in ships; for most of the 1920s and 1930s he was at sea; and in World War II all his efforts—in Washington, then briefly at Mechanicsburg, Pennsylvania, and on Okinawa—were directed toward putting ships to sea.

Thus, this book is in large part a book about the Navy and about ships. For once Rickover was exposed to the power and the appeal of the atom, it was to the propulsion of Navy ships that he sought to apply his genius for reaching a goal.

And it was the ships that he would appeal to Congress for funds to build, and it was the ships for which he would immerse himself into the development of power plants, the selection and training of their crews, and even the appointment of their commanding officers. In turn, his need to find brilliant young men to operate and command those ships would lead him into establishing his own educational system, and then into attempting to change the American educational process that provided him with students.

At the same time, the industry that built his nuclear reactors and his nuclear ships would become a target of his frenzy for efficiency. Except possibly General Leslie Groves during the brief period that he directed the American atomic-bomb effort and Admiral William Raborn for the brief period he launched the Polaris missile program, no American military officer has become so involved with the management and the managers of American industry. Indeed, in the opinion of some of his critics and the judgment of at least one court of law, Rickover and his lieutenants went too far into the domain of private industry.

In tallying Rickover's accomplishments, the one that appears to stand out—without question or debate—is that he did provide the United States with nuclear ships several years before they would otherwise have set to sea. This book, therefore, is about Admiral Rickover and the ships that Admiral Rickover built, the Navy that he changed, and those portions of the American society that he tried to change.

The authors are in debt to many individuals and organizations for their assistance in the writing of this book. Those who can be publicly acknowledged are listed in the back of this volume. Many could not be cited. Some could not be cited because they were or, in some cases, are still accountable to Admiral Rickover. Other persons simply would not speak to us, in part because they too are accountable to Rickover.

The authors also feel that they alone are accountable for all that is in this book. Much is not in this book. Material is lost, memories are dimmed, people die, and Admiral Rickover has kept material under lock and key. Within these limitations we have sought to make an accounting of Admiral Rickover—his life and his benefits both to the Navy and to the nation, and the costs.

NORMAN POLMAR
THOMAS B. ALLEN

Authors' Note

We have attempted to avoid the use of naval and nuclear jargon and acronyms. However, a few are widely used and we have used them as appropriate and as they have appeared in quotations. They are:

AEC   Atomic Energy Commission
BuPers   Bureau of Naval Personnel
BuShips   Bureau of Ships
CNO   Chief of Naval Operations
EB   Electric Boat Company (later a division of General Dynamics Corporation)
EDO   Engineering Duty Officer
FBM   Fleet Ballistic Missile
flag   reference to an officer of commodore rank or higher; usually an admiral
GE   General Electric Corporation
NRB   Naval Reactors Branch
Nuc   a nuclear-trained officer or enlisted man (pronounced as if spelled "nuke")
OLA   Office of Legislative Affairs (Navy Department)
OP-   part of the Office of the Chief of Naval Operations; followed by a number, as OP-31
OPNAV   Office of the Chief of Naval Operations
scram   automatic shutdown of a nuclear reactor, usually in an emergency situation (see page 151)
SLBM   Submarine Launched Ballistic Missile
SSBN   nuclear-propelled ballistic missile submarine
SSGN   nuclear-propelled guided (cruise) missile submarine
SSN   nuclear-propelled attack submarine
U.S.S.   United States Ship

THE RADIANCE OF
A THOUSAND SUNS

A few seconds before 5:30 A.M. on July 16, 1945, the desert sky over New Mexico erupted in a fire greater than the world had ever known. In the white heat of that fire the temperature was four times that at the center of the sun and more than ten thousand times the temperature at the surface of the sun.

At that moment, words from the sacred Hindu epic *Bhagavad-Gita* flared through the mind of J. Robert Oppenheimer, principal creator of the atomic fire that challenged the sun:

> *If the radiance of a thousand suns*
> *Were to burst at once into the sky,*
> *That would be like the splendor of the Mighty One ...*
> *I am become Death,*
> *The shatterer of the worlds.*

When that first nuclear weapon was detonated atop its tower at Alamogordo, our world entered what would be called the atomic age. It would be an age born as much in fire as in secrecy and dread. People, groping to understand this shatterer of worlds, would try to give the bomb a mythical quality, much as Oppenheimer had. From somewhere deep in the human psyche came the desire to call the first bomb Little Boy, the second one Fat Man. The bomb would be viewed as a creation, and Oppenheimer would be called the Father of the Atomic Bomb. Later, Edward Teller, another creator of this strange new force, would be called the Father of the Hydrogen Bomb.

And still later, there would be another: Hyman G. Rickover, Father of the Atomic Submarine. His creation would harness the thousand suns.

1 | The Unbeatable Man

One day, in mid-1967, Secretary of the Navy Paul H. Nitze arrived at the south entrance to the White House and was ushered in to see President Lyndon Baines Johnson. Paul Nitze was a distinguished member of the government, a lawyer whose military background dated from the intensive studies of the effects of strategic bombing on Germany and Japan that were made at the end of World War II. Before becoming Secretary of the Navy in late 1963 he had been Assistant Secretary of Defense for international security affairs.

As he entered the White House, Nitze's tenure as Secretary of the Navy was coming to an end, for he was moving up to become Deputy Secretary of Defense to Robert S. McNamara.

Nitze explained to the President how he had already discussed the subject at hand with Secretary of Defense McNamara. The subject was how to retire Hyman G. Rickover, a vice admiral of the U.S. Navy. "McNamara," Nitze told the authors, "had agreed that Rickover should go" but had said that "the matter was beyond his authority or mine." McNamara had compared Rickover to two older men whose tenure was beyond the control of reason or logic, J. Edgar Hoover, seventy-two, who had been head of the Federal Bureau of Investigation since 1924, and Major General Lewis B. Hershey, seventy-four, who had directed the Selective Service System since 1941. Rickover was, at least, sixty-seven years old at the time.

Nitze described the situation to President Johnson in detail. "I quite agree . . . we ought to get rid of him . . . but I don't want this to become a *cause célèbre*," Nitze recalls Johnson saying in reaction to his proposal. "I've got all sorts of trouble and don't need this," Johnson continued. The President said that Nitze should see the Joint Committee on Atomic Energy in Congress "and tell them I'm all for this . . . if you can get their backing, I'm all for it."

Thus armed with the backing of the President, who under the Constitution also functioned as Commander in Chief of the armed forces, Nitze went forward to Capitol Hill. The chairman of the Joint Committee on Atomic Energy was Senator John O. Pastore of Rhode Island. Pastore had served almost continuously on the committee since August 1952, and when Nitze entered his office Pastore was chairman of the committee for the second time.

Pastore, according to Nitze's recollection, listened as the Secretary explained the situation and his previous conversation with McNamara and Johnson. Then, as Nitze recalled, Pastore said, "I've got to talk to other members of my committee. Call me in three or four days." As Nitze remembered the meeting, Pastore also said, "I quite understand. I've thought for a long time that Rick's outlived his usefulness." (But Pastore, asked later about the incident, said he did not recall it—and he added that his admiration for Rickover had never dimmed.)

Nitze dutifully called Pastore and was asked to come up again to Capitol Hill. He probably made the fifteen-minute drive from the Pentagon to Pastore's office with some feeling of confidence. Attempts two years before either to have Rickover choose a deputy for himself or to simply have Rickover relieved as head of the Navy's nuclear propulsion program had been defeated by Rickover. Now, with Rickover again requiring Presidential action to keep him on active naval service for two additional years, Nitze felt more confident that 1967 could be Rickover's last year on active duty.

As he entered Pastore's inner office Nitze found assembled there Senators Clinton P. Anderson of New Mexico and Henry M. Jackson of Washington, and Representative Chet Holifield of California. All were long-serving members of the Joint Committee, and Holifield had been an original member when it was established in 1947. Including Pastore, one or the other had been chairman of the committee over the past decade.

There was one other man in the room. He was short, lean, almost anemic-looking in a plain gray suit. Vice Admiral Hyman G. Rickover.

Pastore opened the brief conversation with: "Admiral Rickover has a comment to make."

"I understand that you are trying to get me fired," said Rickover in a matter-of-fact tone.

Nitze was flabbergasted. He recalls that Jackson, in a short speech about Rickover, said, "Everybody agrees that at some time Rickover might be relieved—but that time has not come yet."

Nor had the time come a long time before, on July 2, 1951, when a Navy selection board met in Arlington Annex, the ugly, tan-colored buildings on Arlington ridge in northern Virginia, overlooking the Pentagon and, across the Potomac River, the Capitol. The selection board, consisting of nine admirals, would select eligible captains for promotion to the rank of rear admiral.

They would meet in secret. No minutes would be kept of their deliberations and no one was to discuss the details of their voting. If not selected by the 1951 board, Rickover would again be considered by the 1952 board—comprised of nine different admirals. Then, if "passed over" for a second time, within one year Captain Rickover would retire.

Rickover was not selected for promotion to rear admiral by the 1951 board nor by the 1952 board. By law, he would have to leave the Navy.

Laws, however, are passed by the Congress of the United States, and in 1952, then-Representative Henry Jackson of the Joint Committee on Atomic Energy flew out to the Pacific to observe nuclear tests. Also on the plane was Captain Rickover.

The two began chatting and soon struck up a conversation that launched an enduring friendship. Back in Washington, after Rickover's second pass-over, Jackson began to lobby for Rickover. So did Representative Sidney Yates, from Rickover's home town, Chicago. And so did other members of the House and Senate, both Democrat and Republican. At the same time, Rickover's immediate staff of naval officers and a man who had become "their representative" in the Time, Inc., organization, Clay Blair, Jr., began an unprecedented public-relations campaign. Blair wrote a book-length tribute to Rickover in Rickover's office with full access to his staff and unclassified files. Attempts were made to have nuclear contractors raise the promotion issue to their Congressional delegations. Attempts were also made to reach President Eisenhower, with one of Rickover's assistants, Commander E. E. Kintner having his brother-in-law raise the subject to John Eisenhower, son of the President. Kintner's brother-in-law had introduced John and Barbara Eisenhower and was a good friend of theirs. The fingers that "probed the system" seemed numberless, and Rickover—directly or indirectly—used all of them.

Finally, the Navy capitulated. Another selection board met. At the direction of the Secretary of the Navy it considered engineering captains who were specialized in nuclear propulsion. Captain H.G. Rickover was belatedly selected for promotion to rear admiral.

•

Nor had the time come even before that, when on August 6, 1945, a B-29 named *Enola Gay* took off from an obsure Pacific island and headed north, to Japan. Aboard was a crew of twelve men, including Captain William S. Parsons, U.S. Naval Academy, Class of 1922. Parsons, one of the few Navy officers involved in the creation of the atomic bomb, armed the bomb that *Enola Gay* dropped on Hiroshima that day.

On the day Hiroshima was destroyed, Captain Hyman G. Rickover, U.S. Naval Academy, Class of 1922, was newly arrived on Okinawa, as were some 95,000 Army and Navy construction troops. They were building a massive support base for the planned assault on the Japanese home islands, some 400 miles to the north.

Rickover and the other Navy officers on Okinawa believed that they were on a historic mission: What they built here would help to end the war. Rickover was commanding officer of the Navy base that would repair and send back into the war the ships damaged in those final terrible battles when Japan, in her death throes, would hurl *kamikaze* attacks against the invading fleet.

On August 9, a B-29 named *Bock's Car* followed the route of the *Enola Gay* from Tinian Island to Japan and dropped an atomic bomb on Nagasaki. Low on fuel on the way back to Tinian, *Bock's Car* landed on Okinawa. The aura of the atomic bomb thus briefly and secretly touched Okinawa. That would be the only role that Okinawa would play in the ending of the war. For Okinawa was already a backwater, a huge and useless monument to the conventional warfare that the atomic bomb had awesomely eclipsed. When *Bock's Car* landed, the war was effectively over. The fighting would cease in five days.

Captain Rickover had helped to win that war. He had worked hard and well in Washington as head of the Electrical Section of the Bureau of Ships in the Navy Department. But until he arrived in Okinawa he had no record in a combat zone. He had not served in a man-of-war. Men of his Academy class, men like Parsons, would earn combat commendations and glory. Eleven would die heroes. Rickover had not fought in the war. He had commanded only one ship in his naval career—the *Finch*, an ancient minesweeper pressed into use to move Marines to China, and even that had been four years before the Japanese surprise attack on Pearl Harbor. By December 7, 1941, Rickover was in Washington, where he would spend most of the war.

In July of 1945 Rickover finally got the orders that sent him to duty in the heart of the war: the Western Pacific, where once, long ago, he had briefly commanded a ship. The *Finch* was gone, sunk at Corregidor in the early days of the war. And since the *Finch* he had been part of the shore-based Navy, one of the men who planned, built, modernized, repaired and ultimately scrapped the ships of the Navy in war and in peace. Much of what Rickover did in war could have been done in peace. He was one of the unsung, one of the engineers who planned and built the ships that others would sail to battle and glory.

War and peace blurred in the BuShips navy, and in the engineer's mind of Hyman Rickover this was particularly true. Winning the war was not the only reason for working day and night, driving himself and his staff to exhaustion. Work, he believed, was the reason for existence. "Having a vocation," he would say years later, "is somewhat of a miracle, like falling in love."

On Okinawa he preached and practiced the gospel of work. He worked himself and his men as if the war were never to end. And when it did, he worked just as hard. His men did not understand how his sense of duty overpowered their sense of reality; the war was over; tens of thousands of men were leaving Okinawa, heading home to peace and leisure.

When Rickover arrived on Okinawa, there barely was a ship-repair base for him to command. The focus of war was on Okinawa's ports, where the invasion armada would assemble, and on her airfields, which were being prepared to accommodate hundreds of aircraft. On the table of organization of the Naval Operating Base, Captain Rickover's command at Baten Ko was one of the sixteen naval bases; it was four rungs down from the top Okinawa command.

The atomic bombs that ended the war also suddenly made obsolete all the plans that had centered on Okinawa, all the men working on Okinawa, and all the great piles of things on Okinawa. There was no need to do much more than close down and move out. Elsewhere in the Pacific, when the victors took off, much of the stuff of their war stayed behind to become rusting harbingers of a throw-away society. But where Rickover walked on Okinawa, there would be no waste. He insisted that whatever could be salvaged had to be packed up and shipped back to the United States. Heavy machinery and tent poles, bulldozers and blankets, whatever he could get crated and on a ship, left Okinawa.

During the long battle to take Okinawa, American planes had inadvertently bombed a leper colony. Not until Rickover heard about the incident and went to the colony did any American see the nightmare. The colony was in ruins. It had no electricity. Women who washed the ragged clothing and dressings did it by hand, and as they rubbed the soap into the rags, they wore their fingers away. Lepers hobbled by on makeshift limbs; one was made of the only material available—cement. A Japanese physician and his wife were struggling to keep the lepers alive. The couple could have left Okinawa with their three small children. But they chose to stay. Rickover befriended them and saw to it that they got food, medical supplies, blankets and clothing. The former head of the BuShips electrical section also managed to find a generator that restored electricity to the leprosarium.

But Rickover's main concern was his base, which he considered of vital importance despite the end of the war. Most of the base consisted of tents, but there were some metal quonset huts and other small buildings. Rickover had a command.

Then, on October 9, a typhoon named Louise whipped along the eastern edge of Okinawa, killing at least thirty-six persons and destroying nearly everything in its path. The piers at the main naval base at Buckner Bay disappeared. Nine small ships were sunk and more than one hundred and seventy-five other craft—from landing ships to small yard boats—were carried ashore on mountainous waves and left high and dry.

Many of the smaller bases were devastated. Some sixty to eighty percent of the tents and buildings were damaged or destroyed. The worst-hit was Rickover's. The official damage estimate put the amount of destruction at "ninety-nine percent."

At dawn, he began supervising the cleanup and the repair. But only a Rickover could have believed that the U.S. Navy still needed a ship-repair base at Baten Ko on Okinawa two months after the war had ended.

There had been typhoons before—one had struck on September 16—and courts of inquiry had followed, as much to assess human culpability as storm damage. Louise was declared an Act of God. This time there would be no board of inquiry. Nobody seemed to care any more. The war was over.

Rickover, with nothing to command, lingered on Okinawa until November 26. Two days later the Naval Repair Base at Baten Ko—which no longer existed—was officially expunged from the record and declared inactivated.

The only archival record of Rickover's duty on Okinawa is a report concerning postwar plans for the Okinawa naval base. The report is signed by Rickover as a member of the Okinawa Post War Advance Base Board. It recommended, among other things, that all future buildings "be of typhoon and earthquake proof construction." For Rickover the war had ended in ruins at a quiet cove on Okinawa.

·

In 1947, by Annapolis tradition, the Class of 1922 marked its twenty-fifth anniversary by publishing a small book of class biographies. The hero of the class was Deak Parsons, the man who had armed an atomic bomb and helped to bring a new weapon and a new power to the world. And, he had been a rear admiral since 1946. Another member of the Class of 1922 was W. J. Holmes, a former submariner, invalided out of the Navy just before the war but recalled to active duty in 1941. Not for almost forty years could Jasper Holmes reveal his part in the victory in the Pacific: He had spent the war years mostly in an underground intelligence center on Oahu, a key participant in the Ultra program—breaking and reading Japanese codes, and translating the information into useful intelligence for the fleet.* In 1946 he returned to the University of Hawaii. Later he would become chairman of the engineering department, and an engineering building would be named Holmes Hall.

H. G. Rickover was still a captain. The high point of his career had been his days on Okinawa—getting ready to help the invasion of Japan that never occurred.

Most of the men who sent in their biographies concentrated on their service in the war. For those who stayed in the Navy and for those who had become civilians, the war had been the peak of their lives. When their war began, members of the Class of 1922 were all about as old as the century. Many had already left the service, and some had retired. At the start of World War II, only 256 officers of the 539 graduates of the class were still on active duty in the Navy. Not many had an exciting war, and for those still in the Navy in 1949, Hyman Rickover's biography was typical. He wrote, "Spent most of the time during the war with the Bureau of Ships. During latter part of the war I was the Industrial Manager at Okinawa. At present I am assigned to the Atomic Energy Commission in connection with the development of mobile reactors for shipboard use."

By 1952, there would be only 160 members of the class on active duty. By 1964, there would be only one, the former commanding officer of the ship-repair base at Baten Ko.

Neither politician nor Navy selection board, nor war, nor even typhoon could stop him from reaching his destiny.

*Holmes's book about his wartime service, Double Edged Secrets, was published in 1979.

THE PROMISED LAND

"Our eyes beheld the Promised Land," an immigrant wrote of that moment when his ship passed through the Narrows and into the New York Harbor. There stood the Statue of Liberty, and just ahead lay Ellis Island.

More than sixteen million persons lived through that moment in the sixty-two years that Ellis Island served as the gateway to America.

One of those who passed through Ellis Island to the Promised Land was a young Polish boy who had cried when he saw his first ships along the waterfront of Antwerp. They frightened him because they were so big.

In the Promised Land he would grow up to join what he would call the "nucleus of martyrs," the doers of a nation's work. Fright far behind him, he would build a ship that would awe the world. And, looking back, he would say that "the present is the fruit of the past and the seed of the future."

To know him in the present, we must know him in the past.

2 | Father's Occupation: Tailor

By American standards, Hyman George Rickover was born into a medieval world, a Europe of emperor and peasant, a land of poverty, a place of fear. The empire was Russian, ruled by a tsar. The land was Poland, a conquered province within the empire. The place of his birth was a place for Jews, the Pale of the Settlement, the Jewish Pale.

Hyman Rickover was born one of about five million Jews of the Pale, a statelessness within a state, a way of designating aliens within a nationality. In the Pale there was daily uncertainty and occasional terror, the terror of the pogroms that came upon villages like a summer storm—all knew that the storm would come and come again, but no one knew what night. *Pogrom,* which once meant "riot" in Russian, arose from an ancient word that imitated the sound of thunder. By the late nineteenth century, *pogrom* meant not thunder or riot, but an organized assault on Jews by mobs urged on by officials. Around that time, *pogromist*—"one who takes part in or promotes organized massacres, as of Jews"—came into the vocabulary of Russians and Jews.

Rickover's father, born Eliachako but known as Abraham, had seen with the eyes of a child an outburst of pogroms in 1881 and 1882. His son would know of those pogroms by tale and, like his father, would himself know through inarticulate but indelible childhood memory, the days and nights of pogroms in the Pale.

Hyman Rickover was born in the village of Makow (now Maków Mazowiecki), about fifty miles north of Warsaw. The nearest town was Pultusk, eight miles to the south. Guidebooks of the time noted that in Pultusk there was a single inn "kept by a Jew." Most of the people who lived in Makow and in the towns and villages around were Jews. They thought of themselves as Poles, not Russians, for the Polish roots of most Jews went back to the middle ages. There was a touch of pride and much heritage in their Polish allegiance. In the early middle ages, Poland had

27

invited Jews who had been expelled by other countries, and the Polish rulers made use of and encouraged their great mercantile prowess. Even after Poland became Catholic there still was carefully calibrated tolerance for Jews. But never did Jews become a true middle class, never did they attain enough economic or social power to influence the country's rulers. By the late eighteenth century, after a continued increase in Catholic animosity, when Poland became part of the Russian empire, the tradition of toleration gave way to official anti-Semitism. With the empire came the Pale.

Polish freedom ebbed and flowed by the whim of the tsar, who offset each surge of nationalism with a reward of seeming independence or a punishment of sudden repression. In 1863 Polish nationalism flared into rebellion, Russian troops crushed the revolt, and imperial edicts interred it. Poles were forbidden to use their language in schools and universities, in the conducting of official business, in newspapers, in theaters and in their churches.

In the Pale, Polish Jews endured this and more. They could not own land, they were barred from most education, and always there was the fear of the pogrom. But in the little villages like Makow at least there was a cohesion, a sense of trust. There was a community, a place where people could love, marry, have children, and eke out a living. And, by the end of the nineteenth century, there was hope in the Pale. People were getting out. They were going to America.

Abraham Rickover was making a living as a tailor in Makow. He had married and was beginning to raise a family when the lure of America reached the Polish provinces of the Pale. Dates are often hazy in the Rickover family history, as they are in the histories of most immigrants. So it is not known for certain when Abraham and Ruchal Rickover started talking about America. But probably their planning began after the birth of their first child, Fanny, in the late 1890s.

The first great wave of immigrants from the Jewish Pale of Settlement arrived in America in previous decades, following an outbreak of pogroms. Most of these immigrants were White Russians and Lithuanians, people of villages and towns, not of the land. Most of them, both men and women, had worked in factories, and they had managed to save enough from their wages to make the journey. German Jews, beginning a generation before, had shown the way to America. Now there was a route, with dormitories run by German Jews, for those who had to make their way across Europe to the immigrant ships sailing from such ports as

Antwerp, Bremen and Hamburg. Passage to America from Hamburg cost about thirty dollars.

Many in the Pale could pay this sum with no great sacrifice. Throughout the towns of the Pale, in cigarette shops and in the needle trades, men and women were making steady incomes. Some even owned small factories or had converted their homes to shops. Some families could raise enough money to leave the Pale together, sail to America, and there establish themselves with a small stake of savings.

But for Abraham Rickover and others who had much smaller and less reliable incomes, there was only one way to finance an entire family's journey to America. First would go the wage earner and then, perhaps a few years later, he would send back enough money for the family to follow. Such a plan carried risks that man and wife both knew and rarely discussed. Many a husband and father had gone to America and there started a new family, leaving the other, as if dead. That was the worst that could happen. Even the best meant years of loneliness and then, in America, lifetimes out of phase: a husband and father of the New Land, a wife and mother of the Old; and children who would know the father as a stranger from a strange land. Or children who would know only America and who, as citizens of the New Land, would leave behind an Old that included much of what their parents really were.

How much of Hyman Rickover came from his parents and how much grew in his New Land? Those who may have answers, including Rickover himself, will not speak. Two who could have answered are dead. Abraham died in 1960; his age was eighty-five. Rachel (as she became known in the New Land) died in 1968; she was almost ninety-two.

From such sources as obituaries and school records, it is possible to sketch the early life of Hyman Rickover. And in this sketch can be seen hints, foreshadowings of the man. But the very records that should start the sketch are not in agreement. We do not know when Abraham Rickover came to America. We do not know when Abraham Rickover's family arrived in America. We do not know, as a certainty, when Hyman Rickover was born.

By Abraham Rickover's account in a 1958 interview with the *Chicago Sun-Times,* he left Makow in 1899, settled in New York City, and by 1903 had enough money saved to send for his family. By a *Time* magazine account based on interviews with family members, Abraham arrived in New York in 1904 and after "another two years of hard work, he saved enough to send for his family"—Ruchal; Fanny, eight; and Hyman, six.

Both accounts give Hyman Rickover's year of birth as 1900. His official Navy biography says he was born on January 27, 1900.

But Rickover's school records show that he was born in Makow on August 24, 1898. A discrepancy of two years in an immigrant's age is not unusual; immigration records are notoriously inaccurate. School records, however, usually are accurate, especially since they provide such a continuity that a mistake of several years becomes apparent and can be corrected. If Rickover were born in 1898, there might have been a problem—but not an insurmountable one—about his entry into the U.S. Naval Academy. Throughout his official life, he has recorded his birth year as 1900.

Sometime around 1904—when Hyman Rickover was four or six years old—he, Fanny and their mother set out for America in a ship that sailed from Antwerp. Abraham Rickover had made an investment in an apartment building in Brooklyn, and he had expected his family to settle in New York, among the thousands of Jews whose journey to America ended there. But Abraham lost his investment in the Depression of 1907. In 1908, soon after the birth of their third child, Hitel (her New Land name would be Augusta), the Rickover family headed for Chicago, the city that Hyman Rickover would always consider his home town.

Chicago's first Jews of the Pale had arrived in the 1880s. Many of them had been sent west by Jewish organizations in New York, Baltimore and Boston. These organizations were usually controlled by German Jews, who saw themselves as Americans a generation ahead of—and a social class above—the peasants from the Pale.

In Chicago, the established Jews had founded the Society in Aid of the Russian Refugees in 1891, when Jews from the Pale were getting off the immigrant ships in New York and being put on trains to Chicago. About fifty thousand Jews arrived in Chicago between 1880 and 1900. Many of them got no farther than a district near the station that became known as Maxwell Street.

The area, about a mile southwest of Chicago's downtown business district, got its name from a street that had become, with the influx of Jewish immigrants into Chicago, the center of pushcart commerce and tenement life. The Maxwell Street area, the first ghetto of Chicago Jewry, was the most densely populated slum in Chicago. By 1891, about sixteen thousand Jews were packed into its tenements and shacks, sometimes three and four to a single bed.

Here the Pale still could be seen and heard. Bearded men in black caps, black boots, and long black coats walked amid the kosher butcher shops, the matzo bakeries, speaking Yiddish, reading Yiddish newspapers. Beneath their coats each wore a tallis, the traditional prayer shawl. Here were three dozen Orthodox synagogues, many of them spiritual descendants of synagogues from the Old Land, formed by immigrants from the same town and still known as the synagogue of Kowner or Antipolier or Kalvarier.

There would come from this ghetto of the New Land men and women who would boast of their origins—"up from Maxwell Street"—sons and daughters of immigrants who bore the badge of "making it in America": I grew up in the slums. Like New York's East Side, Maxwell Street became famous as a place that produced a new breed of American, a new myth about the land of promise. "I know a Jew fish crier down on Maxwell Street, . . ." Carl Sandburg would sing. "His face is that of a man terribly glad to be selling fish, terribly glad that God made fish."

Abraham Rickover would not move his family to the tenements of Maxwell Street, where the pushcarts plowed through mud and garbage, where one hundred and twenty-seven people were found living in the six flats of a single building, where few people spoke English, and where children worked in sweatshops twelve hours a day.

Out of this ghetto of the New Land, out of "this very center of hard times," would come proud men, the sons of peddlers, cigar makers, storekeepers. They would include Supreme Court Justice Arthur Goldberg, whose father was a peddler with a blind horse because that was the only kind of horse he could afford; boxing champion Barney Ross, who, born Barney Rasovsky in New York and brought to Chicago as a youngster, saw his father shot to death in a holdup of his ghetto grocery store; William S. Paley, founder of the Columbia Broadcasting System; actor Paul Muni, whose father owned a Yiddish theater. There were also the many locally acclaimed products of Maxwell Street—the judges, political power brokers, civic leaders, and professional men who became members of the establishment that ran Chicago. And there were the men who left Chicago but always remembered Maxwell Street and claimed a common bond with others shaped and tempered there.

Hyman Rickover would not grow up to be one of those men. Knowing that the admiral was born Jewish and from Chicago, someone one day would ask Rickover about Maxwell Street, and he would reply that all he remembered was that "it was a street with pushcarts."

Abraham Rickover, wise to the ways of America—and just well enough off so that he would keep his family out of Maxwell Street tenements—settled his family in a section called Lawndale. The area, first developed by real-estate operators after the great Chicago Fire of 1871, had begun as a neighborhood of two-family homes occupied mostly by first- and second-generation immigrant families from Holland, Ireland and Germany. Many of the men worked at the new McCormick reaper plant. Some owned their houses and rented out half; other houses were owned by absentee landlords.

Around 1900, Jews who could get out of the Maxwell Street ghetto began trying to rent houses in North Lawndale, about one mile west of the ghetto. They were not allowed to rent, and so, many of them purchased houses—and even entire blocks. Abraham Rickover was among the newcomers, moving his family into their home at 3243 West Grenshaw Street around 1907, not "up from Maxwell Street" but out of New York and into the middle class.

Abraham Rickover was a tailor, and he would work at his trade—except for a brief attempt at retirement at age seventy-six—until he died. Eventually, the family would become at least moderately well off. Abraham would buy an apartment house, and he and Rachel would be blessed by the presence of both their daughters in Chicago.

But at the beginning, the family lived at the edge of poverty, and while men who grew up around Maxwell Street would tell of squalor, disease and death, the men produced by Lawndale would tell of jobs after school and how they had learned the value of money. In Lawndale, where congregations did not convert store fronts but built edifices, there would be fifty synagogues. Congregation Anshe Kneseth Israel, known as the Russian Shule in recognition of its members' origin, was dedicated in 1913. It had 3,500 seats. The former Jews of the Pale had built the largest synagogue in a city where a short time before they had been the charity cases of German Jews. Lawndale was being called the Chicago Jerusalem.

Hyman Rickover, growing up in Lawndale as an American Jew, would learn in the shelter of his neighborhood the values and lessons of his heritage, but rarely would he experience the prejudices and the terrors of that heritage. Jews were telling each other that they were Americans. Against the opposition of the Orthodox, but often with endorsement—or at least acceptance—by some Reform rabbis, Jews even were marrying gentiles. English-language Jewish newspapers, themselves a breakaway from the Yiddish tradition, thundered editorially at Jews who celebrated Christmas, even if only in fellowship. But one of these newspapers, responding to a letter about the correspondent's hard times in America, replied with a suggestion that sounded like the kind of remark an anti-immigrant, native-born American might make: "Go back to Russia if you don't like it here."

A Chicago Jewish newspaper, *The Sentinel,* said *The New York Times* had a new policy: "Unless from the context it is necessary to call attention to his religion . . . a person is not to be identified as a Jew." But if Jews were becoming Americans, there were always reminders of the dark side of the heritage. Hyman Rickover had just started eighth grade of Lawson Elementary School in 1913 when Chicago Jews staged a rally protesting an infamous event in Russia. On the eve of Passover in Kiev, a Christian boy had been found murdered. Police arrested Mendel Beilis and charged that he, as a Jew, had killed the boy as part of a Passover ritual. Booker T. Washington spoke at the Chicago rally protesting the arrest of Beilis, and Jews sent petitions in vain to Woodrow Wilson. Jews in Lawndale were outraged, but they felt that what was happening in Russia could never happen in America.

There were other Jews, though, who said that it was not far from Kiev to Chicago. In Atlanta, Leo M. Frank, superintendent of a pencil factory, had been arrested in 1913 for the murder of a fourteen-year-old girl. Between the time of his arrest and the beginning of his trial, Frank was pictured in the sensationalist press as a depraved Jew. Anti-Semitism continued to flare during the trial, which ended in his conviction and a death sentence. Then, on August 16, 1915, a mob broke into the jail where Frank was held and lynched him. The young men and women of Lawndale learned that a spasm of hate could kill a Jew in America as savagely as sustained hate could kill or banish the Jews of Russia.

We have no record of Rickover's memories of these events. He was a bright child raised in a literate house in a Jewish neighborhood, and it seems likely that he would have been aware of the issues that dominated the pages of *The Sentinel,* Chicago Jewry's most popular English-language newspaper. Rickover has spoken rarely of his youth, but what amounts to an authorized account of his childhood and adolescence is contained in *The Atomic Submarine and Admiral Rickover.* The book was published in 1954 during Rickover's struggle against the Navy's opposition to his promotion to rear admiral. The author of the book, Clay Blair, Jr., has acknowledged to the authors that Rickover was the source of the information about his childhood and that Rickover checked the manuscript, which was typed in Rickover's office by Rickover's secretary.

So it is safe to assume that Rickover was the inspiration for this, the only childhood incident recorded in the book: "Slight of build, he was a stubborn child. Once his father had to chip away his front teeth in order to force medicine down his throat." Rickover's willingness to reveal this incident makes it just as safe to assume that he did not look back upon a blissful childhood. His recollections, as recorded by Blair, are full of references to hard work, discipline, and a decided lack of good times.

The record shows that he went first to Lawson Elementary School near his home. According to his father's recollections, young Rickover delivered newspapers before school and worked in a grocery store after school. Lawson, along with its records, is gone. But something from that time endured. In a manual-training class there, Hyman Rickover built a small wooden table that was still lovingly displayed by his mother and father half a century later.

Rickover entered John Marshall High School in September 1914. The principal was Louis Block, a Harvard graduate who brought to the school his personal library and a deep commitment to educating the sons and daughters of immigrants. Records of his era, along with many of his books, still can be found at John Marshall, which now stands in the midst of a black neighborhood.

Rickover's records at John Marshall include one with handwritten entries that show he started attending in September 1914. His age on that form is given as *16-3*, which would indicate a birth date of about June 1898. A second record, written in a young hand that apparently is Rickover's, looks like this (handwritten entries in italics):

Rickover	*Hyman*			
Family name	Given name	Date of entering	*Sept.*	*1914*
			mo.	yr.

Address	*3243*	*Grenshaw St.*	*Chicago*
	St. No.	Street	City

Place of Birth	*Makow*	*Poland*
	City or Town	State or Country

Date of Birth	*24*	*Aug.*	*1898*
	Day	Mo.	Yr.

Last enrolled in *Lawson School*

Father or Guardian	*Rickover*	*Abraham*
	Family name	Given name

Business Address ⎯⎯⎯⎯⎯ Occupation *Maker of Men's Ready Made Clothes*

Birth Place of Father	*Poland*	Birth Place of Mother	*Poland*
	Country		Country

A third form contains typewritten entries (cited in italics): date of Birth *Aug. 24, 1898*. Place of Birth *Makow, Poland*. Date of Entry *Sept. 1914*. From *Lawson*.

Rickover himself, through the pages of the Blair book, implies that he worked so hard as a Western Union messenger "to contribute his share to the family income" that he did not do well in high school. "One year," says the book, "he failed two subjects because he had been too sleepy to absorb the material. (He made up the lost credits by attending summer school.)"

Detailed records show that he took algebra and an English course at summer school in 1915. His English had slipped, from a first-quarter *A* and semester grade of 88 in his first semester to *C* and 79 in the third semester, which ended in January 1916. His courses included Latin, which rose from *C* and 63 in the first semester to *A* and 90 in the third, and Drawing—*A* and 90 to *A* and 100.

His scholarship improved in his third year at John Marshall, and the record for the first semester of his senior year was outstanding:

	1st qr.	*Sem. Grade*
Typewriting	C	—
German	A	90
Physics	A	95
German	A	90
English	B+	94
Drawing	A	100
Gym	—	82

He took two semesters of German in one semester. He would always be proud of his ability to read German.

Another entry on the seven-semester record shows that for "Music" he studied the music of his graduation. He graduated early as a member of the February Class of 1918. At the graduation, he was the "mantle bearer," the member chosen for the symbolic passing of the mantle, "which represents the honors and achievements" of all previous John Marshall classes, to the next graduates, the June Class of 1918.

In his mantle-bearer's speech is a foreshadowing of the sardonic wit the adult Rickover would exhibit before Congressional commitees:

We can now truthfully say that this is the only class that has fulfilled the hopes, ambitions, and ideals of our school. When the mantle was given to us last year, it was actually covered with dust, caused by the neglectful handling of its last possessors. That class, as well as the one which follows ours, was large in number, but small in brains.

Under our guidance and care, the mantle has grown resplendent. We have brought it to its pinnacle of glory and height of fame . . . But alas and alack, its happy days are near the end! . . . Verily, fate has been unkind to this mantle. It must now suffer the indignity and insult of being forced to depart from the one class that has ever been worthy of it. . . . If there's a doctor in the house, will he please step forward, for in truth, this mantle is dying. Never mind, doctors, it is too late, no mortal power can save it from its doom. Ah, it is dead. An undertaker is needed now.

John Marshall High School officials treat Rickover as their most distinguished alumnus. Placed among the athletic trophies displayed in a case in the main corridor is a model of the U.S.S. *John Marshall*, a nuclear submarine. The model came from the U.S. Navy soon after the submarine was launched in July 1961. The connection between the model and Rickover is proudly explained to visitors. During one of the school's many renovations, someone found a large plaque that was salvaged only because Rickover's name was on it. The plaque lists members of the Student Army Training Corps and honors "Marshall's sons and daughters who took part in the World War 1914–1918."

Long before America's entry into the war in 1917, anti-German fervor had been rising. Americans shouted, "Kill the Kaiser!" at preparedness rallies. Sauerkraut became "liberty cabbage." Patronage fell off in German restaurants, and the music of German composers was rarely played. It is an early testament to Rickover's indifference to public opinion that the language he chose to study in 1917 was German.

For Hyman Rickover, Western Union messenger, the war meant black-bordered telegrams—"The War Department regrets to inform you . . ."—delivered to homes where the sight of a Western Union boy almost inevitably meant bad news. Home telephones were still relatively rare, and the only way to get a message delivered promptly was by entrusting it to the bicycling, neatly uniformed boys of Western Union.

Ordinary people usually sent telegrams only to inform family members of severe illnesses, imminent deaths, or funeral arrangements. But businesses and professional men used Western Union for routine commerce, and among these users of the service, messenger boys were often welcome—and occasionally rewarded in true Horatio Alger style.

One of Hyman Rickover's most frequent calls was on the Chicago office of Representative Adolph Joachim Sabath, a Democrat, who had been elected to Congress for the first time in 1906 and who would make a record in Congress by remaining there continuously until his death in 1952. The heart of Sabath's district was Lawndale, and, as an immigrant and a Jew, he was one with most of the people in his constituency. A powerful ally of President Wilson, he was in Chicago often, especially during the Presidential campaign of 1916. Some time between then and 1918, the young, hard-working Western Union messenger from Lawndale was introduced to Adolph Sabath as a fellow Jewish immigrant. Thus began a relationship between Rickover and the "Jewish Congressmen of Chicago," a relationship that would begin with his appointment to Annapolis by Sabath and would continue for decade after decade; Sabath's successor as the Jewish Congressman, Sidney R. Yates, would help to make Captain Rickover an admiral and would help Admiral Rickover make a nuclear navy.

Getting into Annapolis meant more than getting a letter from one's Congressman. The rules were set down in *Regulations Governing the Admission of Candidates to the U.S. Naval Academy*, published by the Navy's Bureau of Navigation (which handled personnel matters) in June 1918. Each Representative and Senator was allowed to nominate five midshipmen. One hundred enlisted men from the Navy and the Marine Corps were also admitted on the basis of a competitive examination. The Governor General of the Philippine Islands was allowed to place four Filipinos who would not be commissioned in the U.S. Navy, but went into Philippine service.

Regulation No. 16 stated: "All candidates are required to be citizens of the United States and must be not less than 16 years of age nor more than 20 years of age on April 1 of the calendar year in which they enter the Naval Academy." If Rickover were born on August 24, 1898, he would not have turned 20 by April 1, 1918. But it was possible to be appointed for a given year, flunk the tests for entry in that year, and then make another try the following year. A candidate born in 1898 might run out of time. And an overly cautious reading of the regulations might make a candidate believe that the fateful turning date was in September, when classes began. The safest—and most typical—year of birth for prospective members of the Class of 1922 was 1900.

Actually, if a candidate for the Class of 1922 was born in 1898, he had nothing to worry about. The oldest member of the class was, in fact, born on February 7, *1897*. (He had originally been in the Class of 1921.) Anyway, for those entering Annapolis in 1918, Regulation No. 16 had a hint of ex post facto, and the general interpretation was that the age restriction did not apply to the prospective members of the Class of 1922.

How much of this would have been known to a nervous, unsophisticated candidate? Probably not much. Would a candidate feel safe with a 1900 birthday? Yes. He would have nothing to worry about, except passing the entrance examination.

Examinations for admission to Annapolis were held in cities throughout the United States on the third Wednesday in February and the third Wednesday in April, under the supervision of the Civil Service Commission. If someone took the first test and flunked, he was not allowed to try for the second. The examinations covered English spelling, grammar and punctuation, geography, American history, arithmetic, algebra through quadratic equations, and plane geometry. The examinations were notoriously difficult, and everyone knew that there was only one safe way to pass them: by taking special courses at one of the prep schools in and around Annapolis.

The most famous of the schools was the U.S. Naval Academy Preparatory School, better known as "Bobby's War College." Bobby was Robert Lincoln Werntz, Class of 1884. Although the school was founded in 1887, Werntz did not resign from the Navy until 1890. He and his brother Jimmy are remembered as the only teachers, Bobby in his black alpaca jacket, Jimmy in his tweeds.

The school was in a brick building on Maryland Avenue in Annapolis, well outside the gates of the Naval Academy. Students paid in advance, found their own lodgings, and attended four hours of classes a day, Monday through Friday. Tuition was about $300, and there was no refund for dropping out or failing the examination. The curriculum was simple and effective. Students were given copies of entrance examinations from the previous ten years or so. On Saturday mornings, learning to work against the clock, they tried to answer questions from those old examinations. When they had mastered the answers, they were told, quite correctly, that the examinations they would be taking would be similar. There was nothing corrupt about the system. The examination questions did change every year, but the subject matter changed little and was well defined. If a student managed to learn how an examination was targeted, he had a good chance of spotting those targets when he took the actual examination.

There were no semesters. The school was open from about October 1 to May 30, but a student typically entered a few weeks before the scheduled examinations and began cramming. "If you don't learn," he was told, "we drop you from the school." A student usually studied at Bobby's until just before the nationwide examinations. He would then go home, or to a place of his choice, and take the examinations. If he passed, he would soon be given a physical examination, and if he passed that, he would report to the Naval Academy some time between June and September.

Werntz had remarkable success. By his account, more midshipmen entered from his school than from all the other cram schools combined. And of all the schools, his is the most fondly remembered.

In Rickover's approved version of his first fifty years, the name of his prep school is not given. Clay Blair's book says only that "after two weeks' study at the school, he quit, after deciding that the course was inadequate and that it would never boost him through the exams." He then "locked himself up in his boardinghouse room and for two months studied intensely." The account goes on to say that he did not get his $300 tuition back. And that is why old Annapolis hands believe that the school he so briefly attended was Bobby's War College.

The questions he had to answer in that entrance examination were formidable, and if decades later he railed against the lowering standards of American education, perhaps his memory went back to the sample questions that prepared him for the real thing:

> Draw a map to show how you might get by water from Duluth to Halifax. Indicate your route by dotted lines and name the bodies of water traversed.
>
> The diameter of a wheel is 3 feet 3 inches. Find the circumference, to thousandth of a foot.
>
> Compute the simple interest on $3,180 for 2 years 10 months and 16 days at 4 percent.
>
> History (two hours). Question 1 (a) In the Civil War, what battles did Grant fight in the West? (b) Explain the relations of the United States and England during the Civil War.
>
> A man walks from one place to another in 5½ hours. If he had walked ¼ of a mile an hour faster, the walk would have taken 36⅔ fewer minutes. How many miles did he walk, and at what rate?
>
> The sides of a triangle are 51 feet, 52 feet, and 53 feet. Find its area, and the radius of the inscribed circle.

Rickover passed the examination.

Members of the class began arriving on June 11, 1918. They would keep straggling in until September. Each one signed himself in, writing in a ledger his name, home town, address, birth date and birthplace, religion, and father's occupation.

Hyman G. Rickover   Chicago   121 South Spaulding Avenue
January 27, 1900   Makow, Russia   Hebrew   Tailor

But before Midshipman Rickover could begin classes, he began feeling feverish. He checked into sick bay, where his illness was diagnosed as diphtheria, still often fatal, still an epidemic disease. He was quarantined and kept under treatment long enough to miss assignment to a room in Bancroft Hall. He was put in the old Marine Barracks, isolated from most of the members of the Midshipman Regiment in Bancroft Hall. There, dwelling alone in a small room, was another midshipman who was also isolated, although not because of illness. Hyman Rickover would do well because of what he learned at the Naval Academy. The other midshipman, Leonard Kaplan, would do well despite what he had learned at Annapolis.

3 | The Class of 1922

Midshipman Hyman G. Rickover's days began at 6:30 A.M. and were supposed to end at 9:55 P.M., when tattoo was sounded. But his days went on longer, by secret lamplight, at first because he desperately needed to catch up, and later because he became obsessed with the need to learn.

Plebe courses were marine engineering and naval construction, mathematics, English, and Spanish or French. For every plebe the days were filled with study, and the days soon merged into a blur of books and blackboards and moving on the double. This was the life of the midshipman, and this was the world of the United States Naval Academy for the midshipmen who entered in 1918. In this life, Rickover could thrive.

There was another life—football games and hops, elaborate pranks and silly slang, a camaraderie that nurtured lifelong friendships. Men who graduated and those who bilged (flunked) out, men who succeeded in the Navy and those who did not, all of them would remember this life. A few of them would remember it bitterly.

Since 1906 Bancroft Hall had been home for midshipmen during their four years at Annapolis. The hall was named for Secretary of the Navy George Bancroft, who established the Naval Academy in 1845 with a stern admonition to the first superintendent: "In collecting them at Annapolis for purposes of instruction, you will begin with the principle that a warrant in the Navy, far from being an excuse for licentious freedom, is to be held a pledge for subordination, industry, and regularity. . . ." But for midshipmen in 1918, Bancroft's order was as much a thing of the past as sails and sideburns.

The war ended as Rickover began his first, or plebe, year in the summer of 1918. In the new era of peace, in the time that President Harding would call a "return to normalcy," Annapolis became less a place where a man studied war and more a place where young men prepared for an exciting, romantic, and socially acceptable career. The Academy was, for some, as much a part of the Ivy League as Yale or Harvard. They belonged to fraternities, took debutantes to dances (or, in the Academy dialect, dragged Four-O debs to hops), and stuck together. They called themselves "Our Set" and "blood." And many of the blood were truly that, for they were the sons and grandsons of naval officers.

There were more typical midshipmen, the young men of the farms and the small towns. And there were real sailors, the enlisted men who entered Annapolis from the fleet. All—the blood, the sons of Navy, the sailors, the ordinary and the undistinguished—lived in what appeared officially to be a classless society. But men of similar origins tended to stick together and tended to room together.

Bancroft Hall was the largest dormitory in the world; two new wings were being finished just as the Class of 1922 was entering in the summer of 1918. The huge building was designed to house all midshipmen, four plebes or two upperclassmen to a room. But not even Bancroft Hall, with its rooms for 2,200, could accommodate the entire regiment, which was growing toward 2,250. Most of the rooms were occupied by upperclassmen when the first of 898 plebes began coming through the gates of Annapolis in June 1918. Those in the first wave got rooms in Bancroft Hall. Latecomers were put up at the old Marine Barracks on the northern end of the Academy grounds. One of the latecomers was Rickover, who had spent his first weeks at Annapolis in sick bay.

What would become his unceasing dislike for Annapolis and its ways began in the Marine Barracks. Perhaps he would have had a different attitude toward the Academy if he had entered Bancroft Hall immediately and if he had begun his academic career in concert with his class. But his illness had put him behind and, though he later moved into Bancroft Hall, socially, at least, he never caught up.

His resentment could still be discerned decades later in his description of his days at Annapolis. The Rickover-approved pages of Clay Blair's book tell of how his late-night studying "irritated the other midshipmen." The book says that Rickover tried to make friends at the Academy, but "few of the middies seemed interested in making friends." The book blames this on Rickover's poverty—on two dollars a month, he could not afford to date and go to hops. The book also indicates that he was frequently hazed. Once, for instance, he was given demerits for smoking, though he did not smoke. Rickover did not supply details of the incident, but it apparently went beyond ordinary hazing, which was inflicted upon all plebes indiscriminately. He seems to have been framed because some individual or some group of midshipmen did not like him.

"Scornful of the juvenile rituals at the Academy," the Blair book says, "Rick finally withdrew to the privacy of his room. Dedicated to a life of hard work and scholarly pursuit, he read almost constantly, storing up odd bits of knowledge." That was all Rickover has to say about his days at Annapolis (though as Admiral Rickover, he would have much to say about what was wrong at the Naval Academy).

Most men would cherish their memories of the Academy. One member of the Class of 1922 did in fact preserve memories and presented them to the Academy. The memories of Midshipman Alvan Fisher tumble out of storage boxes in the archives of the Academy library—bits of paper that become a mosaic of life in Annapolis for the Class of 1922.

An orange rectangular "candy ticket." Around its edges are punched out the twenty five-cent squares that recorded a month's worth of purchases. Each midshipman had to deposit $350 to cover the cost of his uniforms and other clothing. He was paid $600 a year, but as a plebe he drew out only one dollar a month in cash. As a second-year man (a "youngster"), he received twice as much: he got the one dollar in cash and the one-dollar candy ticket.

A menu. For breakfast, bananas, shredded wheat, creamed codfish, cornbread. For lunch (called dinner), tomato-gumbo soup, roast pork, mashed potatoes, scalloped tomatoes, strawberry cake, bread. For supper, baked beans, potatoes, applesauce, bread, fruit jelly with whipped cream. Meals were served by black or Filipino mess boys. The blacks were called "mokes," and the Filipinos were called "Goo-goos."

A chit seeking permission for "late lights." Every minute of the day was covered by a set schedule, and every exception had to be authorized by a chit. A midshipman awakened to reveille at 6:30 A.M. and he washed, shaved, and ate breakfast in time to march to his first class at 8 A.M. Midshipmen marched in formation—plebes went on the double—from Bancroft Hall to class and from class to class. Morning studies ended at 12:15 P.M. Classes, including organized sports, resumed at 1:20 P.M. and continued until 3:20. There were usually drills from then until 5:30 P.M. After supper, midshipmen were expected to remain in their rooms, where they would study until 9:30 P.M. Tattoo came at 9:55, and taps five minutes later.

A handwritten request for Christmas leave. Subjects were graded on a 0-to-4 scale. Passing grade was 2.5. Midshipmen with less than 2.6 in any subject could not go on Christmas leave. They stayed at the Academy, where they were expected to engage in "earnest application to those studies in which they are in danger of being found deficient."

A copy of an annual examination. This one, on electrical engineering and physics, lasted two hours and twenty minutes. One of the questions: "Explain in terms of the ionization theory (a) the electrolysis of water, and (b) the neutralization of acid by a base, (c) illustrating the latter by two examples. (d) What is a colloid? Give one example including method of production." Annual and semiannual examinations were given in every subject until 1921. Flunking any of them meant expulsion (assignment to the U.S.S. *Outside*).

Sports page clippings. Rickover happened to be a member of what sportswriter Grantland Rice called "one of the greatest athletic classes in competitive history." The Academy's sports were baseball, basketball, boxing, crew, fencing, football, gym, lacrosse, rifle, soccer, swimming, tennis, track, water polo and wrestling. Every midshipman was urged to play on an Academy or class team. Rickover did try out for fencing, but his only athletic activity was swimming. He was a member of the Sub (for "submarine") Squad, which consisted of midshipmen who had a tendency to sink rather than swim. Thus began Rickover's lifelong loathing for sports, especially sports at Annapolis.

Notice of a smoker. For most of the term of the Class of 1922, smoking was forbidden to all but first-classmen (men in their last year). And they could smoke only in Bancroft's recreation room, known as Smoke Hall. At one end of the hall was a table bearing a large brass bowl that contained Bull Durham tobacco and cigarette papers. The bowl was watched over by the Keeper of the Bull. First-classmen did not go to this smoker just to smoke. They also went to discuss specific topics, one of which was of particular interest to prospective submariners: "The Submarine, on Trial before Humanity. Is it justified as a weapon? Should it be abolished? Limited in application? How?"

Bullfight poster. This was one of the many souvenirs of the summer cruise, the high point of a midshipman's life. Members of the class were put aboard ships—usually battleships—and sent off to such exotic ports of call as Gibraltar, Panama and its bullfights, Honolulu and its hula girls. On these cruises midshipmen discovered the sea and themselves. The cruise was a voyage of initiation into manhood, not one of those "juvenile rituals" mocked by Rickover. The cruise was a tradition, but it was also practical: The cruise taught men how ships worked and that the mission of the Navy was to go to sea in ships.

W. J. (Jasper) Holmes, also of the Class of 1922, kept a log during his youngster cruise in 1919. The log begins: "Last night was my first night in a seaman's hammock, a far different rig than the summer hammock slung under the old apple tree back home on the farm."

Holmes, with two dollars in his pocket, sailed aboard the battleship *Wisconsin;* first port, Guantanamo, Cuba. As a midshipman, he was barred from the wicked pleasures of that liberty port—except for ice cream, reputedly made of goat's milk. To earn money for other ports, he and another penniless midshipman scrubbed hammocks and sea bags for wealthier shipmates.

On the Fourth of July, the midshipmen were allowed to sleep until 6 A.M. and all classes were canceled. "We were supposed to have a turkey dinner at noon," says the log, "but when the turkeys were taken out of the freezer they smelled to high heaven. . . . The doctor condemned all the turkeys as unfit for human consumption and they were all dumped over the side. The sharks had a turkey dinner for Fourth of July, and we had boiled beef with thick curry gravy and boiled spuds, but we had delicious dried apple pie for dessert."

To read the log's description of the *Wisconsin*'s fireroom is to enter a Navy still in the coal age, a Navy that is old in a world that is modern. The Navy and the Academy still had a nineteenth-century air. The America outside the Navy was changing, going modern, as the flappers sang. Women's suffrage was on the way, and housewives were buying bread, not baking it. There was a new kind of telephone—it had a dial. And Henry Ford was putting electric starters in the Model T.

But in the firerooms of the *Wisconsin* and other ships of the training squadron,

> Shadowy figures staggered about shoveling coal, clanging tools and banging coal buckets. A furnace door opened, and in the sudden glare of light from the incandescent fire bed a fireman labored to feed coal into the insatiable maw. . . . I was the fireman for furnaces three and four, of which I was presently reminded by the water tender directing me to "Coal number three!" When I fumbled with the furnace door he realized how green I was and gave me a little instruction. He pushed open the furnace door of number three with the shovel, scooped up a big shovelful of coal, and with a mighty heave spread the coal over the back of the fire bed. . . .
> The coal we had taken aboard at St. Thomas [Virgin Islands] has a high ash content. Ashes fuse together under the heat of the furnace and form clinkers that lie on top of the grate bars and cut the air coming through the grate. Big clinkers become evident by dark

spots in the bright fire bed and shadows in the ash pit. They have to be broken up with the slice bar. The slice bar is an iron bar about two inches in diameter and seven feet long. At the business end it is flattened and pointed, and the handle end is an iron ring.

The fireman slid the slice bar over the top of the grate bars, under the fire, until it was in position under a clinker. He then pried it up to loosen and break up the clinker. The pointed end of the slice bar became red hot, and even the handle had to be muffled with a wad of dry rags to keep from blistering the hands that held it. . . .

This was the same Navy that had just learned to fly across oceans. A month before the cruise began the Navy's NC-4 seaplane flew the Atlantic to become the first plane to cross an ocean, albeit with stops in Newfoundland, the Azores and Portugal. The Navy's first aircraft carrier, a converted coal ship, would be commissioned as the U.S.S. *Langley* three months before the Class of 1922 graduated. But the Navy was still a battleship navy, and Midshipmen "Rickie" Rickover, Jasper Holmes, and several hundred comrades learned the duties of battleship sailors, from shoveling coal to standing watch in the crow's nest.

In the classrooms of the Academy, many in Mahan Hall, the Battle of Jutland—that classic clash of dreadnought battleships—was still fresh in the minds of faculty officers; and Jutland became the centerpiece of classes in strategy and tactics. Midshipmen studied more about battleships than any other kind of warship; most of the midshipmen, if not all, hoped that their first duty assignment after graduation would be to a battleship. The Navy was the Fleet, and the Fleet was a long, glorious line of battleships.

But many members of the Class of 1922 saw themselves never serving in a battleship or even going to sea. They called themselves the "Disarmament Class," for they knew that on graduation in the peacetime that came in the fall of the very year that they had entered the Academy, many would not be commissioned.

Competition for top standing in classes was always fierce at the Academy, and in the Disarmament Class the competition would become a duel. The winners would be commissioned and go to sea; the losers— those who stood lower in class standing—would simply be graduated and released to civilian life. Degrees were not awarded by the Naval Academy until 1933.

At the top of the Class of 1922 there was another kind of competition that, in many respects, was more deadly than the "cut" of being commissioned or not commissioned. Rickover was not one of the duelists in that deadly competition. But later in his career it would be incorrectly recalled, once even by a Chief of Naval Operations, that Rickover had been one of those duelists.

The duel was between Jerauld L. Olmsted and Leonard Kaplan. Olmsted was one of the most popular members of the class. Kaplan lived alone in an obscure corner of Bancroft Hall, and he lived alone in that room because he had been condemned to it by his classmates.

What happened to Leonard Kaplan at Annapolis would, through the years, become intertwined with what happened to Rickover at Annapolis. The awful truth about Kaplan's ordeal became eclipsed by tales of Rickover in which his name was substituted for Kaplan's. Navy people knew that hazing was unbridled in those days, and they knew that Rickover, as a grind, was a natural target of hazing. They also knew that Jews were often targets. So, when Rickover was fighting to be promoted to admiral, the Kaplan stories circulated as Rickover stories. The stories made sense, because Rickover had always spoken so bitterly about Annapolis. And they made sense because, in the social climate of Annapolis of the 1920s, the hazing of a Jew would seem to be inevitable, as would the failure of a Jew to become an admiral in the 1950s. In both cases, the truth was more complicated and was more deeply rooted in history than the easily concocted assumptions would suggest.

A few old grads of the Academy even maintain that Rickover was the first Jew ever to graduate—or the first Jew to become an admiral. The facts are that by the 1920s officers of the Jewish faith had been rare but certainly not unprecedented. Among the better known was Uriah Phillips Levy, who in 1860 attained the rank of Commodore, at the time the highest rank in the U.S. Navy.

Years earlier, while visiting in Brazil, Levy had rescued an American sailor beset by a mob. Afterward he was brought to the attention of the Brazilian emperor, who, after meeting Levy, offered him command of a new, sixty-gun frigate. Levy immediately responded, "I would rather serve in the American Navy as a cabin boy than as captain in any other service in the world." But Levy is best remembered for his crusade against flogging in the Navy. Indeed, the painting of Levy which hangs in the Museum of the Naval Academy at Annapolis shows the Commodore holding a scroll reading: "Author of the Abolition of Flogging in the Navy of the United States."

Another Jewish officer remembered at the Academy is Joseph Israel, who entered the Navy as a midshipman in 1801 and died less than four years later, when his ship exploded in Tripoli harbor while fighting North

African pirates. Israel and five other officers who died in that campaign are honored by a large statue next to the Academy's Museum.

In scientific history the Academy's most famous graduate is Albert A. Michelson. Born on the German-Polish frontier in 1852, Michelson was brought to the United States by his Jewish parents at age two. When he grew up, Michelson was determined to be a naval officer, and on his own he traveled to Washington to seek an appointment from President Grant. The ten Presidential appointments-at-large had already been made, but Grant's naval aide suggested the boy go to Annapolis on the chance that one of the ten might fail the entrance examination. All ten passed. Michelson, after waiting three days in the Commandant's office at Annapolis, announced that he would seek a meeting with Grant. Before the young man reached the White House, Grant ordered an additional appointment so that Michelson could enter the Academy.

When Michelson graduated from the Academy in 1873, the superintendent who handed him his diploma said, "If in the future you'll give less attention to scientific matters and more to your naval gunnery, there might come a time when you would know enough to be some service to your country." Nevertheless, because of his excellence in science and physics, he was was given the rare honor of being retained at Annapolis to teach. In that status, at the age of twenty-eight, he made the first measurement of the speed of light.

The young scientist left the Navy in 1881 to pursue his scientific studies and in 1892 was one of the outstanding American scholars and scientists to join the faculty of the newly endowed University of Chicago. Fifteen years later he became the first American to win the Nobel Prize. He subsequently served as president of the American Physical Society, the American Association for the Advancement of Science, and the National Academy of Physical Sciences. The celebrated Michelson-Morley experiment, carried out in 1887 to determine whether the velocity of the earth through the ether would demonstrate any effects on the velocity of light, served as the starting point for Albert Einstein's later theory of relativity. During World War I, at the age of sixty-five, Michelson rejoined the Navy with the rank of lieutenant commander to help develop optical equipment. He perfected the Navy's standard range finder of that time.

Closer in time to the Class of 1922 was another Jewish officer destined to become famous. He was Edward Ellsberg, the Number 1 man of the Class of 1914. Ellsberg was the first Jew to graduate at the top of the Academy class. He had led every class since plebe year, and it was commonly said that the Class of 1914 graduated in two sections—the one with Ellsberg in it, and the one with all the others.

Many of those other men were jealous of him, for in the highly competitive atmosphere of the Academy, high-ranking midshipmen often become obsessed about achieving number one. But Ellsberg always insisted that he had not experienced any anti-Semitism during his years at the Academy or during his years on active duty. He has also said that he had never noticed any acts of anti-Semitism directed toward the few other Jews in the Academy while he was there.

Ellsberg was graduated in 1914. After assignment to a battleship, Ellsberg specialized in ship construction. He gained national prominence when, in September 1925, the submarine *S-51* was rammed and sunk off the Atlantic coast. Ellsberg was named salvage officer for raising the stricken submarine from a depth of 130 feet. Never before had an effort been made to raise a submarine from so great a depth. A team led by Captain Ernest J. King as officer in charge, with Ellsberg as salvage officer, did succeed in the feat. Later, in writing about the epic salvage, King said of Ellsberg that "he was the embodiment of perseverance and determination."

In December 1927, Ellsberg—then a lieutenant commander—resigned his commission to enter private business. But a few days later another submarine of the infamous S-class—this time the *S-4*—sank with thirty-four crewmen still alive. Ellsberg immediately volunteered to come back on active duty and, with King again in charge, helped organize the rescue operation. The means available were too primitive, and the trapped sailors died long before the submarine could be raised.

Ellsberg left active service, but remained in the reserve, with a special act of Congress promoting him to commander in 1929. He resigned his reserve commission in 1940. Recalled to active duty again on December 8, 1941, Ellsberg served as the top Navy salvage officer in the Red Sea region and then North Africa during World War II. King—Chief of Naval Operations during the war—introduced Ellsberg to Eisenhower and they dined together at Algiers in 1942. When Ellsberg left the war zone in early 1943, Eisenhower wrote that it was with "the greatest regret" that he approved his transfer. Ellsberg finished the war as a captain, and was promoted to rear admiral upon his retirement in recognition of his many accomplishments.

Ellsberg has still another distinction: He is the most prolific author to graduate from the Naval Academy, eclipsing even the renowned Ned

Beach, Class of 1939. Ellsberg has more than a dozen historical and adventure volumes to his credit.

Ellsberg may not have experienced anti-Semitism at the Academy because of the force of his own personality. It took a determined man to defy tradition, for Jewish officers still were rare at the time. In the conservative Navy of those days, officers of the Jewish faith—in small numbers—were accepted, but their entrance into the Navy was not encouraged.

Plebes being admitted to the Academy had to sign a register that listed, among other things, their religion. Each man wrote down his religion in his own hand. Most wrote, "Protestant" or "Episcopal." The register is a good index to the number—and proportion—of Jewish prospective officers. (Some wrote "Jewish"; others "Hebrew.")

YEAR OF ENTRY	NUMBER SIGNING	NUMBER WRITING "JEWISH" OR "HEBREW"
1908	216	2
1909	212	0
1910	221	3 (including Ellsberg)
1911	244	2
1912	265	0
1913	308	4
1914	283	0
1915	254	3
1916	624	9
1917	722	9
1918	955	17 (including Rickover)
1919	698	10

For unexplained reasons, Leonard Kaplan, a Jew, never signed the register. (Various Navy records list his date of entry as July 15 or 16, 1918.)

Chapel was compulsory in those days, and so Protestant-oriented was the Academy that neither Catholics nor Jews could attend religious services on Academy grounds. They went to church or synagogue in the town of Annapolis. The overwhelming majority of midshipmen went on Sundays to the ornate domed chapel that has been called "the Navy's Cathedral." Beneath the chancel of the chapel lies the sarcophagus of John Paul Jones. When his body was laid to rest there in 1913 one of the midshipmen chosen for the guard of honor was Edward Ellsberg.

What happened to Kaplan did not happen to Ellsberg, and did not happen to Rickover. But it happened to a number of midshipmen, both Jewish and Christian. How many will never be known, for there is no record of such things. Kaplan was, in the saying of the day, "sent to Coventry" for all of his four years at the Naval Academy. No midshipmen could speak to him; no one could acknowledge his existence.

The idea of "Coventry" seems to have begun around the time of the civil war between Charles I and Parliament. Royalist prisoners were sent to Coventry, a redoubt of the Parliament supporters. Another theory holds that the townspeople of Coventry so disliked having troops quartered there that they ostracized women seen even speaking to the soldiers. So, being "sent to Coventry," for a soldier, meant isolation. By extension, the term came to mean being ostracized by one's peers.

The sending of a midshipman to Coventry was unofficially tolerated at Annapolis, although the practice was not officially acknowledged in any way. A member of the Class of 1915, who knew what happened to Kaplan, told the authors, "All Jews lived in Coventry" during their time at the Academy. The *all* has been denied by others, but there is no doubt that anti-Semitism was at times strong enough to exile Jewish midshipmen at least to a psychological ghetto and ultimately to Coventry.

Hazing, which could range from crude pranks and verbal abuse to physical torture, was also unofficially tolerated and rarely acknowledged outside Academy grounds. But in 1919—when Rickover and Kaplan were in their second, or "youngster," year—hazing was a matter of Congressional concern. Captain Archibald H. Scales, of the Class of 1887, became superintendent of the Academy in February 1919. Wartime commanding officer of the battleship *Delaware*, Scales was fifty years old, the youngest superintendent since the first, Commander Franklin Buchanan. He took over an Academy whose regiment of midshipmen had trebled in three years and now was far beyond the needs of a navy shrinking under the pressures of postwar disarmament. Many midshipmen decided to resign and get into the exciting world of civilians, where the twenties were about to roar.

One of the midshipmen who resigned was Worth Bagley Daniels, a member of the Class of 1922 and son of Secretary of the Navy Josephus Daniels. Many midshipmen believed that Daniels and others who were resigning had merely sought refuge in the Academy during the war years. When Daniel Vincent Gallery, of the Class of 1921, called Daniels a draft-dodger, Daniels challenged Gallery to a fight.

The day Daniels became a civilian he walked into Gallery's room and a preordained fight followed. Gallery knocked out Daniels, brought him to, and with time-honored chivalry the fighters shook hands. But the story leaked to the newspapers made it appear that a bully, in some kind of hazing ritual, had beaten up the son of the Secretary of the Navy.

Hazing was becoming a nightmare for Superintendent Scales and a source of sensational stories for newspapers. On two successive days in 1919 midshipmen attempted suicide because of hazing. Philip H. Seltzer, of the Class of 1923, slashed himself with a jackknife and drank ink and iodine. "I was hazed a little," he said to investigators. Academy officials took him to Washington and had him admitted to the Government Hospital for the Insane. The next day another member of the Class of 1923, Midshipman Henry C. Wetherstine, drank iodine in his room in Bancroft Hall. In a published statement he said, "I . . . didn't like the atmosphere of the whole place." Neither midshipman had listed himself as Jewish, although both could have been Jewish. Because of their names, some other midshipmen probably thought they were.

As letters of parental protest poured into his office—and into newspapers throughout the country—Scales dismissed two upperclassmen and wrung from first-classmen a promise to stop hazing. (The Gallery-Daniels fight was deemed a nonhazing incident, and Gallery went on to graduation and a full career; he retired as a rear admiral.)

The incidents inevitably inspired a Congressional investigation and reassessment of the traditional tolerance of hazing. Even in the handling of the two suicide attempts there was a hint that something was wrong with the victims, not their tormentors. Tradition maintained that men, *real* men, were supposed to be able to stand up to hazing. To many midshipmen, faculty members and alumni, hazing was a preparation for life. Plebes had to learn that their superiors ruled their lives. Their superiors in the Academy were first-classmen. If the plebes endured the lessons, they could someday expect to be first-classmen and teach the same lessons in the same ways.

The lessons were being taught with broom handles and, according to one description, upperclassmen "often stood on table tops and literally swung from the ceiling to deliver the blows." The victims of hazing could be just about anyone, but by custom plebes were hazed by all upperclassmen, particularly first-classmen. Most forms of hazing were relatively mild—teasing references to a plebe's accent or physique; an order to recite some doggerel on command. Some plebes, like Seltzer and Wetherstine, could not take it.

The level of anti-Semitism at the Academy in those days is difficult to gauge. The records show that the seventeen men who entered with the

Class of 1922 who were Jews became a microcosm of the class—seven, including Rickover, graduated; the rest dropped out, either voluntarily or by flunking out. Of the seven Jews who graduated, two, including Rickover, reached flag rank.

Out of loyalty to the Academy and to their class, men of the era usually decline to talk about anything but their pleasant memories. One member of the class who would speak about anti-Semitism was Holmes. "There definitely was an anti-Semitic attitude there," he recalled. "It was widespread, but not indiscriminate. Not every Jew was picked on. But if he were a Jew and also had any antisocial characteristics, then he might be singled out for special treatment." That, Holmes and others believed, is what happened to Kaplan. It is also the belief of some officers of that era that if Kaplan had not been there to absorb the anti-Semitism, Rickover might have been the victim of those efforts that pounded away at Kaplan.

Kaplan not only was a Jew, he was a grind, a striver for excellence. While Rickover too was a grind and shunned extracurricular activities, he could not attain the excellence that Kaplan strove for and achieved. Further, Rickover tried to help—"helping the other fellow"—at least with filling out their dance cards, as cited by his peers.

Although Rickover, to quote his peers again, "loomed large through the chalk screens" (blackboards), he was not an outstanding student at Annapolis. He graduated 106th in a class of 539. He was never in competition to graduate as Number 1. Kaplan was. The struggle would pit Kaplan against a single man, and their duel would become so notorious that it would make a dark mark on the history of the Academy.

Kaplan's chief competitor, Olmsted, had entered Annapolis from the ranks of enlisted men. Jerry Olmsted was one of the best-liked members of the class. In his graduation year he was the editor in chief of the yearbook, *The Lucky Bag,* and regimental commander. He was the supreme midshipman—handsome, self-confident, a born leader. He had a reputation for helping classmates known in Annapolis slang as "wooden" (those who struggled to reach 2.5). Grinds like Kaplan and Rickover had a reputation for working strictly on their own. Grinds also were accused of being intellectually snobbish and disdainful of such Annapolis traditions as hazing.

By the unwritten code of hazing (which persisted at the Academy until the 1970s), victims did not complain, and incidents were not revealed to outsiders. But the attempted suicides of 1919—and letters home from victims in the early fall of 1920—forced Superintendent Scales to issue unprecedented orders that segregated the plebes in the upper floors of two wings of Bancroft Hall. Guards were posted at stairways. The plebes ate in a segregated mess hall.

The segregation continued until Thanksgiving, when Scales, newly promoted to rear admiral, decreed that upperclassmen would have liberty only on Wednesday afternoon, and plebes would have liberty on Thanksgiving. After the order was read in the mess hall, upperclassmen mutinied by yelling and stomping. Twice they were marched out. Later they threw chamber pots—Bancroft Hall was still not completely modernized—and other crockery out of their windows. Finally, Scales forced the upperclassmen to again abandon hazing, and the segregation of the plebes ended.

But the unwritten code had been broken. The atmosphere was anti-victim, not anti-hazing. The majority of the midshipmen echoed the "Segregation Blues" written by John L. (Frazzles) Frazer, who would be the anchor man of the Class of 1922:

> For there's been disintegration
> Of the Navy's aggregation
> And the regiment is feeling mighty sore.

And in that atmosphere, the hazing of Kaplan gained enough support so that Olmsted, as editor in chief of the *The Lucky Bag*, could perform the ultimate act of Coventry.

Each biographical page of *The Lucky Bag* contained two large photographs of graduating midshipmen. Under each photograph was one or more nicknames—Beany, Shad, Windy, Nigger Boy (a dark-complexioned midshipman). Under the nicknames was a short biography that usually dwelt on the subject's physique, ancestry, or dating and study habits. There was much talk about "snakes and snaking," which translated as heavy daters and dating; "crabs," which were local young women; "bricks," "building materials," or "road paving," which all meant homely young women; and reference to the Academy as the Severn Seminary, Uncle Sam's Training School for Little Boy Blues, and the Naval Nursery. Midshipmen of Irish descent were called harps and micks, a class member of Italian ancestry was called a wop, and the study of French or Spanish was referred to as learning Dago. Coney Island was called a Hebraic haven.

Rickover, whose nickname was given as Rickie, had a biography that is somewhat typical, although there was about it a distant, restrained quality in contrast to the more intimate, more hearty tone of most of the other biographies, particularly of such popular members as Olmsted ("his earliest ambition was to enter the pearly gates of the Oyster College") and Frazer ("Long live the author of those 'Segregation Blues'! "). Rickover's biography said:

> Neither "from Iceland's snowy mountains or India's sunny clime" but from the Middle West comes the gentleman in question. As water seeks its level, so has "Rick" sought to bring himself up to the plane of a worth-while and credit-bestowing profession. Neither a star on the gridiron nor a terror in the pool, yet did he loom large through the chalk screens. He is a thorough Englishman in regard to humor, appreciating only Spanish jokes. Even the "No Soap" story failed to draw forth its much merited smile. For three entire nights before each large Hop, "Rick" used to be closeted in his boudoir with huge stacks of Hop Cards, engaged in his favorite pastime of helping the other fellow. We have rarely seen him drag, as he remains true to the O.A.O.* in "Chi," but some day we hope to see him putting his seamanship to practical use as he pilots HER in a gondola o'er the moonlit waters—of the Wabash.

The biographies were not presented alphabetically, but somewhat randomly. The two men portrayed on a page were usually roommates. Rickover shared his page with Louis Goodman, described in his biography as "a good-humored, poetic, unassuming Virginian." Goodman was Jewish, but not all Jews in the class were so paired.

Leonard Kaplan lived alone during his four years at the Academy, and so he was the only member of the class who had no one to share a page of *The Lucky Bag* with. Kaplan's photograph—the image of a dark-haired, dark-eyed, serious young man—appeared on the left side of the page. On the right side of the page, instead of a photograph, there was a crude cartoon of a pugnacious midshipman named P.A. List, with the nickname Porky. In midshipman slang, P.A. meant "positive action," and a P.A. list contained the names of midshipmen denied special privileges until they had performed what Superintendent Scales called positive actions, such as getting better marks. So the cartoon was not vicious; it merely symbolized an incorrigible midshipman. The biography below the cartoon, however, provided posterity with a window into the prejudices rampant at the Academy. The Irish and the Jews—and, indirectly, the

---

* *O.A.O. meant "one and only." In Clay Blair's book, by Rickover's account, he did not go to hops because he did not have money, not because he had a steady girlfriend back in Chicago.*

sailors from the fleet—all were targets in Porky's biography, which began:

> Born in the township of Zion, county of Cork, State of Ignorance, Sunday, the 17th day of March, 1900. Educated in the Convent of Zion, 1906–1911. Zion City Collech, 1911–1915. Department of Geological Engineering, School of Reductive Science, United States Naval Rock College, Portsmouth, N.H., 1915–1918 [site of a naval prison, where presumably an enlisted man would be prior to entering Annapolis].

The next paragraph uses the term "grease," which meant, as a noun, "Favor with anyone higher up" and, as a verb, "to boot lick, to curry favor," according to the slang glossary in *The Lucky Bag*. Porky, according to the biography, "has always maintained that the prime factor in good academic standing is grease rather than genius—grease, which includes first, the mental effort or coercive force to bone out of hours and before reveille; second, the knowledge of one's own importance."

Any doubt about the real subject of this mythical biography was dispelled by the listing of Porky's extracurricular activities. In other biographies, these listings were a combination of the true and the facetious. (Rickover's only activity was noted as "Sub squad.") Porky's activities included "Coventry (4, 3, 2, 1)."

Kaplan's own entry was called "An autobiography," and phrases in it were appropriated and twisted to make Porky's biography a parody of Kaplan's biography, which said:

> Born in the township of Weston, county of Lewis, State of West Virginia, Monday, the 26th day of November, 1900. Educated in the Public Schools of Weston 1907–1912; Weston High School 1912–1916; Department of Civil Engineering, School of Applied Science, Carnegie Institute of Technology, Pittsburgh, Pa., 1916–1917, and 1917–1918; Midshipman, U.S.N., July, 1918.
>
> A student above the average and a mathematician of marked ability, has always maintained that the prime factor in good scholastic work is application rather than genius—application, which includes first, the mental effort or coercive force to exert the brain; second, the knowledge of how to study.
>
> Unmarried. For further information, see "Who's Who in America, 1950–1952."

Kaplan's activities were listed as "Star," a standard reference to the star which could be worn by midshipmen who had a mark of 3.4, or 85 percent, for a year, and "Fifth Battalion," a snide reference to Kaplan's solitary status, since there were only four battalions in the regiment of midshipmen.

The nasty, isolated biography and photograph of Kaplan was not the end of Olmsted's efforts to humiliate his scholastic dueling opponent. The main portion of the 1922 *Lucky Bag* had 590 pages. But the numbering sequence missed a page, the last of the graduate descriptions, that between 326 and 327—Kaplan's page. Nor was his name in the index of graduates. And, as the ultimate insult, the page containing Kaplan's biography was perforated, so that it could easily and cleanly be torn completely from the yearbook.

The perforated page, the biography, the omission from the index of graduates, were all the idea of Editor in Chief Jerry Olmsted, who was Kaplan's competition for Number 1 in the class. Olmsted was a born striver. He had managed to get himself out of the enlisted Navy and into the Academy. He had fought against that prejudice—in fact, he seems to have exploited it and become one of the blood. (His brother George was also a striver; a member of the Class of 1922 at the United States Military Academy, he would graduate from there as Number 2.)

While Olmsted was making his plans to keep Kaplan out of *The Lucky Bag,* change was coming to the Academy. In July of 1921 Superintendent Scales had been succeeded by Rear Admiral Henry B. Wilson, Class of 1881, who described his mission as the molding of midshipmen "into educated gentlemen, thoroughly indoctrinated with honor, uprightness and truth, with practical rather than academic minds." He said he believed in "humane yet firm and just discipline," and he put that belief into practice by granting the first Christmas leave since 1848, by letting members of all classes smoke, and by trying to get rid of hazing. Although he did not do away with "rates"—such special privileges of upperclassmen as the use of certain walks and benches—he did forbid "the laying of hands on a junior . . . or requiring the performance of any physical or other exercise." He said there was "no place for either brutality or ridicule within these walls."

Wilson could be tough. He once expelled a midshipman six hours after receiving a report of misconduct. But he prided himself on being fair and on his ability to see the midshipman's view of life. A bilger once himself, he ordered the end of live-or-die annual and semiannual comprehensive examinations.

For the Class of 1922, he inaugurated the presentation of letters of commendation to the midshipmen who had contributed most to "the development of military spirit and loyalty within the Regiment." One of the midshipmen he selected was Jerry Olmsted.

Wilson apparently did not know about the plans for the perforated page, which was opposed by several yearbook staff members, one of whom was Jewish. Olmsted finally took full responsibility, and *The Lucky Bag* came out the way he wanted it. Never before had there been a yearbook with a perforated page, and never has there been one since. There are still venerable alumni of the Academy who insist that the perforated page never happened.

Olmsted graduated as Number 1 and received the cup for excellence in seamanship and international law. Kaplan was Number 2 and received the navigating sextant for excellence in practical and theoretical navigation.

Wilson's letters of commendation were to be awarded after graduation. By then *The Lucky Bag* had been published, and word of the perforated page got back to the Superintendent. He sent out letters of admonition to four midshipmen. Wilson decided to punish Olmsted for the perforated page by withholding the letter of commendation. No mention was made of Kaplan's ordeal of Coventry.

The story reached the *Baltimore Sun,* which reported, "The fact that Kaplan is a Jew is said to have had nothing to do with his unpopularity among his classmates. Some of the most popular, as well as the most brilliant of the institution, are members of the same race, and in the class of 1922 were several other Jews who were particularly well liked."

After graduation, Ensign Olmsted reported aboard the battleship *Wyoming.* Olmsted distinguished himself aboard ship, and he was one of those rare junior officers looked at early in his career as potential flag-officer material. But within a year of graduation he was struck down by poliomyelitis, which was then usually called infantile paralysis. On August 21, 1923, he died.

In October 24, 1924, a memorial tablet to Jerry Olmsted was dedicated in Dahlgren Hall. "Intellect placed him one in his class," said the bronze tablet at the head of the stairway, "character and disposition enthroned him in our hearts; erected by his classmates." Admiral Wilson made the major address at the dedication. He said that he had never met a young man of such all-around ability.

After graduation, Kaplan was one of nine new ensigns who reported to the battleship *Nevada.* Another from the Class of 1922 ordered aboard the *Nevada* recalled that when the orders were posted, several men going to the ship gathered to talk about their new duty and the subject of Kaplan was raised. All immediately agreed that he was one of them and arrangements were made for *all* to join for dinner before boarding. At sea, classmates recall Kaplan as being a good officer, always arriving to stand watch a few minutes early. Although remaining somewhat distant from his shipmates, he was liked. (Kaplan later became an engineering specialist, an EDO. He retired as a captain in 1949. His son, Leonard Kaplan II, graduated from the Naval Academy in 1972.)

Without special attention, Hyman George (Rickie) Rickover was also one of the 539 graduates of the Class of 1922. He had suffered during his four years at the Academy, mostly because of his already emerging reputation of being a "loner" and a grind; he probably did not suffer because he was Jewish. There was anti-Semitism in the Navy and at the Naval Academy, but neither the service nor the institution was anti-Semitic. If they had been, fewer Jews would have entered, Ellsberg could not have been Number 1 in his class, nor Kaplan Number 2 in the Class of 1922, nor would Rickover probably have graduated.

There were probably three specific periods of Rickover's life that shaped his adult personality. The Naval Academy was first. The four years at the Naval Academy—four years of his maturing process, four years of his intellectual development—would set the stage for his career in the United States Navy.

4 | Steaming as Before

Rickover's Class of 1922 graduated 539 young men, the largest single group to be graduated from the Naval Academy since its establishment seventy-seven years before. Actually, the previous class had been larger, but the shortage of junior officers in the fleet had led Secretary of the Navy Edwin Denby to graduate half of that class—the 285 midshipmen who stood highest in June of 1920—after a three-year course, and the other 259 midshipmen a year later, in June of 1921. There would not be a larger class graduating from Annapolis until World War II had begun.

Rickover and his classmates were handed their diplomas by Assistant Secretary of the Navy Theodore Roosevelt, Jr., who in his graduation address spoke words that, for Rickover, would be prophetic: "Your career is the sea, but your career is not simply the sea—for your career is the sea and public service. We speak of the man of the Navy as being 'in the service.' Those simple little words convey in themselves volumes. They constitute a tacit recognition of the fact that our Navy men are public servants."

When Rickover and his fellow hopefuls had arrived at Annapolis in the summer of 1918, the United States was at war and the Navy had a key role in the conflict. Being built on American shipways were scores of battleships, cruisers and destroyers, as well as numerous anti-submarine craft. Within four or five years of that sultry Annapolis summer, the U.S. Navy would have the world's largest and most powerful fleet and would provide career opportunities galore for the Class of 1922—or so it seemed.

But by June 1922, the war to end all wars had ended. And the United States, whose ships and divisions had tipped the balance in 1917–1918 in favor of victory for the democracies, took steps to insure that war would be less likely in the future. At an international conference convened in

Washington, D.C., on November 12, 1921, the United States Secretary of State, Charles Evans Hughes, had shocked the other representatives by proposing a moratorium on building battleships and the scrapping of hundreds of existing ships. Hughes declared that the United States was ready to demonstrate its good faith by breaking up thirty battleships and battle cruisers that were already built or under construction. He then called on Britain and Japan to make equivalent reductions in their fleets. It was the most radical proposal—other than absolute disarmament— ever put forward by a diplomat. One British observer is reputed to have remarked that Hughes sank sixty-six battleships and cruisers at the conference, "more than all the admirals of the world have sunk in a cycle of centuries."

If the Britisher was not technically correct, he was right in his observation of an attitude that permeated American society in the early 1920s. For the Class of 1922, the Washington Naval Conference and its resulting treaty, as well as the general austerity being applied to the Navy, meant disaster. There were rumors—some midshipmen of the time recall actual warnings—that fifty percent of the class might not graduate because of the reductions of the Washington Conference, and that those who did graduate would be lucky if they ever made the grade of lieutenant commander. Attrition at Annapolis from then on would be extremely severe.

Of the 539 graduates of the class, only 390 were commissioned as ensigns in the Navy and 24 as second lieutenants in the Marine Corps. Eight commissions were withheld pending physical examinations, while the rest of the graduates submitted their resignations because of the uncertainty of their future in the Navy. As was customary at the time, almost all new ensigns would become junior officers in the fleet, the hope being that they would put some of their newly minted knowledge to use, working with senior but now fellow officers, and directing enlisted men.

After graduation Rickover returned home to Chicago on leave with orders in his suitcase assigning him to the destroyer *La Vallette,* based at San Diego. Most new ensigns were assigned to battleships; a few went to destroyers and shore stations.

To reach San Diego, Rickover went east and boarded the transport *Argonne,** a brand-new ship on loan from the Army to the Navy. Ap-

---

* *That* Argonne *was named for a forest in France where, in September 1918, Americans participated in a major battle of the Great War. The ship was not named for the forest preserve southwest of Chicago that would become the site of a major nuclear laboratory in the next world war.*

parently without incident, Rickover and the other Navy passengers left New York on July 16, sailed south, transited the Panama Canal, and then steamed north. When Rickover reached San Diego on August 13, the *La Vallette* was at sea and he was temporarily assigned to the *Percival,* another destroyer. Rickover spent a week in the *Percival,* most of the time in his bunk or elsewhere, reading as the ship swung at a mooring buoy in San Diego. The ship was underway for drills and training for a few hours on August 18, but otherwise remained in the harbor.

The incongruities of Rickover's naval career begin during his brief stay aboard the *Percival.* An incident aboard the destroyer is recounted, apparently with Rickover's approval, in one way; the official records tell it in another. The first account comes from *The Atomic Submarine and Admiral Rickover.* It seems probable that the incidents in it were recounted by Rickover.

The book tells of a night when "a frame-smashing explosion echoed through" the *Percival,* "almost" jarring Ensign Rickover out of his wits. He is told that a whiskey still has blown up and a sailor has been thrown overboard by the explosion. Rickover helps pull the sailor out of the water, then discovers none of the *Percival*'s boats are alongside.

> Ensign Rickover made a command decision [the book says]. He told a signalman to flash the nearby *Charleston,* flagship of the destroyer squadron: "Send doctor immediately." The message went off. Shortly a message winked back from the haughty cruiser: "Send *your* boat and then we'll send doctor." Exasperated, Rickover fired back still another message: "Have no boat. Man seriously injured. *You* send boat and doctor." At length the cruiser dispatched a boat and doctor to care for the injured man.

The incident is used to show how early Rickover experienced "the sort of silly Navy shenanigans he abhorred," in this case a tradition that junior ships sent boats to senior ships.

The deck log of the *Percival,* the legal document that daily describes activities on board a Navy ship, tells a different story:

> About 10:45 fire occurred in the galley. The following man Truesdell, Harry Earl T.M.1c,*1047239, severely burned; clothes caught fire and man leaped over the side. First aid was given by chief pharmacist's mate and man rushed to Hospital via shore boat and ambulance. Mitzler, Alfred Jacob S.C.1c,†1432535, suffered minor burns

* *Torpedoman's Mate 1st class.*
† *Ship's Cook 1st class.*

when clothing caught fire. First aid was given this man and he was sent to [the tender] PRAIRIE for further medical attention. Fire was easily extinguished and no damage resulted to galley. Ensign H.C. [*sic*] Rickover, U.S.N. was this date detached from temporary duty on this vessel in accordance with Commander Destroyer Squadrons orders and ordered to report to Commanding Officer U.S.S. LA VALLETTE via. U.S.S. ARTIC [*sic*]

A.K. RIDGWAY,
Ensign, U.S. Navy

Of course, "galley fire" could be a euphemism for whiskey-still explosion. But there would be some mention of the boat and doctor from the *Charleston,* for officers from that ship would certainly be involved in any inquiry into the injury of a sailor aboard ship. But the aged cruiser *Charleston,* anchored nearby, has no suspicious entries in her log for August 21. The log contains neither a report of a problem in the *Percival* nor any reference about having to send a boat or doctor, the kind of information that normally appears in deck logs.

Perhaps the most fascinating aspect of the incident is the questionable chronology. The *Percival*'s log entry for the period 8 P.M. to midnight is quoted above. That meant that Rickover might have left within that time period—or he might have departed *sometime* during the day, and his departure was simply listed as the last item in the daily log. However, the log of the supply ship *Arctic,* which would carry Rickover up to San Francisco, notes that Ensign Rickover reported aboard at 4:20 P.M.—six hours and twenty-five minutes before the incident.

Was there a whiskey-still explosion? Was Rickover involved in the incident, whatever it was? Or was the incident merely an oft-told yarn inspired by a minor incident?

Regardless, the *Arctic,* a brand-new Navy refrigerated supply ship, steamed north with Ensign Rickover among her passengers. She stopped at various ports in the Los Angeles area, and then proceeded to San Francisco. On the evening of September 5, 1922, Rickover at last reported for duty aboard the U.S.S. *La Vallette.*

The *La Vallette* was one of 273 flush-deck, four-stack destroyers that had been mass-produced during the war. The *La Vallette* herself had been completed less than a year earlier at the Bethlehem Steel yard in San Francisco. The ship was long (314 1/3 feet) and narrow (31 feet in beam) so she could knife through the water at a speed of about 33 knots. At the time, battleships, by comparison, had a top speed of about 21 knots. To provide the 30,000 horsepower needed to drive her at 33 knots, most of the space inside the *La Vallette* was taken up with machinery and fuel. Under the four tall smoke stacks were four Yarrow boilers that filled the whole of the three-deck height of the hull.

The oil-burning boilers heated water into steam which was piped to two large General Electric-Curtis turbines in the engine rooms, located aft of the boilers. Extending aft from each turbine was a shaft which the turbine could rotate some three hundred times per minute. These twin shafts protruded through the hull and were capped with the steel propellers that could push the *La Vallette* through the water like a greyhound. When the engines were generating 30,000 horsepower and turning up 33 knots, the whole ship vibrated. Blower fans roared as they kept the firerooms under air pressure, seeming to add to the excitement and power that were felt as a destroyer raced along at full speed. Speed was a destroyer's main attribute.

Most of the ship's hull was taken up with machinery, and Rickover soon became a part of these crammed engineering spaces. Forward and aft, the lowermost decks were tanks for fuel or ammunition magazines. On the two decks above them there were shops, stowage spaces, and living spaces for the ship's eight officers and one hundred enlisted men.

The officers of the Navy were almost all "regulars," which meant they were graduates of the Naval Academy, a "band of brothers." White, Anglo-Saxon Protestant was the rule, although a few exceptions were tolerated and at times welcome in the wardroom of a warship, as they were at Annapolis. The adjective "Jew" did not automatically imply a derogatory term, but was merely an identifying term. Of course, there were no black officers (nor would there be in the U.S. Navy until World War II). There were a few "niggers" among the enlisted men—serving as deck hands and mess stewards—and "niggers" was what they were usually called.

Below the officers were four chief petty officers, one being the leading chief and senior enlisted man on board. The other chiefs and first-class petty officers ran their divisions of enlisted men and were the intermediaries between the officers and the enlisted men.

All of the Navy's enlisted men were volunteers. The enlisted spaces were filled with a heterogeneous group—drawling Texans, soft-spoken Southerners, muscular Midwesterners, a few Northeasterners, a few Jews and Italians (some not yet citizens). Some men were educated (in high school, that is) but most were not, and a number found that they could function effectively in the Navy of the 1920s although they could neither read nor write.

Destroyer sailors were of a different breed from the rest of the Navy. Their ships were faster and rolled more than the squat battleships and cruisers. And so the men rolled too, walking with a swagger on land, boasting of storms in which destroyers heeled so far that they took seawater in their stacks. Battleship sailors looked down at the ocean; destroyer sailors said they looked the ocean in the eye. Destroyers were tactically used like bullets. A man aboard a destroyer in battle knew that he and his ship were expendable. That kind of knowledge gave a man a certain bravado.

Most of the Navy's 100,000 officers and men—down from a World War I peak of over 530,000—went to sea, and most of the sailors were in the "destroyer navy" or the "battleship navy." Fighting was encouraged in the Navy in the name of competition and physical fitness, and smokers were held regularly, with ship's officers seated in the front row while sailors slugged it out. Regulation boxing rings were set up aboard the larger ships. Fighting was also encouraged, albeit unofficially, in bars, as pride ran high and an insult to one's ship or one's division officer—if made by a sailor from another division—would bring a fist to the jaw or a chair smashed down on a head. (Broken bottles were used mainly in the movies; the real fights were inspired by anger, not malice.)

When there was a Navy yard nearby with its Marine barracks or a squadron of battleships with their Marine detachments it would be a three-way competition—the battleship sailors, the destroyer sailors, and the Marines. The Navy's submarine and aviation communities were too small to really enter into these competitions.

The officers were above such goings-on, in part because they were virtually all graduates of the same school, and almost all had served or would serve in both battleships and destroyers at some time. It would be another twenty years when, because of the phenomenal growth of naval aviation in World War II, the flying Navy became known as a "union," and it would be still another twenty years until, in large part because of Rickover, the submariners would become a union.

In 1922 the power of the U.S. Navy was represented by battleships and destroyers. Above the *La Vallette*'s machinery-packed hull her narrow decks were crammed with the implements of war: four 4-inch-caliber guns, fired without the benefit of central or stabilized control systems, hence having a poor accuracy if the ship was rolling. Amidships were twelve long torpedo tubes, whose steam-driven torpedoes could sink any warship afloat. Aft was a single, slow-firing 3-inch gun, supposedly for anti-aircraft defense, and on the fantail were two racks of depth charges, or "ash cans," for attacking submarines.

The *La Vallette*'s wardroom consisted of her commanding officer, Lieutenant Commander Philip Seymour, a lieutenant, the destroyer division's medical officer, and five ensigns. A newly arrived ensign—often called George, as in "let George do it"—reported aboard a destroyer as the assistant communications, gunnery, or engineering officer, plus other duties. Ensign Rickover was assigned the duties of Assistant Torpedo Officer, Commissary Officer, Supply Officer, and a Watch Officer. Destroyer sailors—and officers—worked hard.

After Rickover reported aboard, the *La Vallette* steamed south, to her home port, San Diego. Most of the time the ship was spent swinging at a mooring buoy, because limited operating funds restricted time at sea to specific fleet exercises.

At sea the officers and enlisted men worked their ship as the *La Vallette* practiced making torpedo attacks against hostile warships or protecting the American dreadnoughts (and occasionally an aircraft carrier) from hostile destroyers, torpedo boats, or submarines. When the *La Vallette* swung at anchor, Rickover's multiple assignments plus studies plus paperwork kept him hard at work. Additionally, he rotated watch duties with the other ensigns. During his twenty-four months on the ship, he stood hundreds of watches aboard the *La Vallette*. When the ship was at anchor, he made a log entry every four hours that he was on watch as officer of the deck. A typical entry, that of Friday, October 22, 1922, for the period 8 A.M. to noon reads:

At 8:00 held quarters for muster—no absentees. Daily inspection of magazines and S.P. [smokeless powder] Indices made; conditions normal. Received the following stores for use in general mess: from M.K. Fisheries, 77 pounds halibut; from Snowflake Baking Co., 100 pounds bread; from San Diego Fruit & Produce Co., 50 pounds pears; from Sanitary Ice Cream Co., 4 gallons ice cream; from Wilson & Co., 93 pounds frozen veal; from Mason & Co., 83 pounds cabbage. Inspected as to quality and quantity by Ensign H.G. Rickover, USN. At 8:30 Division 37 underway. At 9:05 Division 12 underway. At 11:00 WOLFE, William C., (SC2c) (1649313) USN., was transferred to Naval Hospital, San Diego, California, for treatment.

[signed] H.G. RICKOVER, *Ensign, U.S. Navy.*

From December 19, 1922, until January 30, 1923, Rickover was sent north, to the Mare Island Navy Yard, north of San Francisco, across the San Pablo Bay, to attend an optical-instrument school. There he met Captain Thomas Jefferson Jackson See, one of the last officers in the Navy to be designated "professor of mathematics." Years later, Rickover would fondly recall the professor: It was the meeting of a young man who would become a character with a senior who already was. The professor, for example, did not give out an officer's traditionally staid calling card; his were engraved with the signs of the zodiac. "We had magnetic compasses . . . in destroyers in those days," Rickover remembered. "It was my duty, as a new ensign, to take the compasses ashore and calibrate them by measuring the earth's magnetic force. Professor took the trouble to assist me. I have always been grateful to this kindly gentleman." The professor was one of the few officers who would earn Rickover's lasting praise.

Rickover missed a sea exercise while he was at school. But there would be more. When he returned to the *La Vallette,* he fell into the peacetime Navy's routine. According to recollections of him at that time, he spent most of his off-duty hours curled up with a book or crawling through the ship's engineering spaces, studying the ship's steam plant. The ship sailed south, and on February 26, 1923, she stood off the western coast of Mexico and Central America with several other ships of the Pacific fleet. Periodically the ships would drop anchor at Balboa or Panama Harbor, at the southern end of the canal.

During one visit ashore at Balboa, Rickover reportedly had a few drinks and became tipsy. That evening, in the motor launch taking crews out to their ships, Ensign Rickover spied Lieutenant Commander Valentine Wood, who had been one of his instructors in the Marine Engineering and Naval Construction Department at Annapolis.

"Mistah Wood," shouted Rickover, as he careened across the launch toward the officer who was three grades his senior. "I knew you at the Naval Academy. You were so damned dumb. You were so damned wooden I put something on the blackboard deliberately wrong and you didn't know the difference. You were so *wooden,* Mistah Wood," shouted Rickover as he continued his verbal attack.

Lieutenant Commander Wood held his silence. Rickover staggered back to a seat, and that night his messmates put him to bed aboard ship. In the morning those same comrades in arms conspired to have at the young officer, telling him of the previous night's proceedings. And, they added sternly, Mr. Wood was filing charges and would ask for a court-martial. Wood was executive officer of the destroyer *Kiddler,* one of the six destroyers in the same division as the *La Vallette.*

But Rickover survived. There was no formal filing of charges and no court-martial. After that incident, Rickover's drinking took an immediate turn toward moderation. More significant, his interest in the ship's cramped, hot, noisy engineering spaces, which he seemed to leave only to find a better place in which to read and study, led to his being named assistant engineering officer and educational officer, in addition to his other duties.

That summer, when the *La Vallette* returned to San Diego, Rickover took a month's leave. Shortly after his return in mid-June he was appointed engineering officer of the ship. He was now responsible for the condition and operation of the ship's massive steam-propulsion plant, the numerous auxiliary components, and the third of the ship's crew that comprised the *La Vallette*'s "black gang" (a term that survived the coal-burning era and, with no racial overtones, still referred to engineers). As was the custom in a small ship with few officers, he would continue to stand watches both in port and underway at sea. After a year at sea, Ensign Rickover had responsibility. But, in the becalmed peacetime Navy, the *La Vallette* did not get up steam and go to sea under her new engineering officer until late on June 30.

In the *La Vallette*'s engineering spaces, where machinery almost crowded out the men who worked in them, and where the heat, the smell of fuel oil, the noise, the vibrations, were relentless, young Rickover found a place he loved. While other junior officers sought to emulate and become latter-day John Paul Joneses or Farraguts or Deweys, the Navy's engineers would become his heroes. In his vision of naval history, the line officers were aristocrats in white gloves while engineering officers were "men who are not afraid to get their hands dirty." One of his special heroes was Robert W. Milligan, engineer of the battleship *Oregon,* which had raced from Bremerton, Washington, around Cape Horn to reach Santiago, Cuba, in time to help destroy the Spanish fleet in the battle that ended the Spanish-American War. For Rickover the true victors were not Admiral Sampson, who commanded the American fleet that sank the Spanish at Santiago, or Admiral Dewey, who won victory at Manila Bay; rather, the victor was Engineer Milligan.

In Rickover's later telling of the tale, when the *Oregon* was blockading the harbor at Santiago, her skipper ordered Milligan to reduce the number of boilers being used to save coal. "Milligan replied," according to Rickover, "that he would obey such an order—provided it was made in writing, and provided he could submit a written protest. In Milligan's words, 'Damn the economy, efficiency is what we want.' The captain withdrew his suggestion. Milligan used his coal carefully and he kept fires lit under all boilers. When the battle came, the *Oregon* was one of the few vessels the Spanish could not outrun."

Rickover, in the *La Vallette*'s engineering spaces, saw himself in the spirit of Milligan. Years later, in a rare display of romanticism, Rickover would compare himself to Milligan. Both the engineer of the *Oregon* and a later engineer—be he Rickover in the *La Vallette* or, in the far future, an engineer in a submarine named *Nautilus*—"could walk through an engine room and, through the din and uproar, catch the slight sound of a component out of adjustment. They could touch a jacket of metal and feel from the vibrations whether the machinery inside was operating well. They could taste boiler water to see if it were pure, and they would dip their fingers into the lubricating oil to find out if a bearing was running hot."

An index to the extraordinary length of Rickover's career can be seen in his adoration of Milligan and the *Oregon*. The Spanish-American War and the *Oregon* were only about as far back in time for an ensign of the 1920s as the *Nautilus* was for an ensign in the 1970s. So, Milligan was as near in time to Rickover as Rickover would be to young officers of today. But to Rickover the legendary Milligan was a memory; to modern officers, Rickover is still there, still a day-to-day part of the Navy, a man who spanned time and seas from Admiral Dewey to Admiral Rickover.

Another Rickover hero, Admiral Joseph Mason Reeves, had been an ensign under Milligan during the race to Santiago. (In the wardroom of that great ship of that time were three other young officers who would become four-star admirals: Naval Cadet Harry E. Yarnell, who would, from 1936 to 1939, command the Asiatic Fleet, one of whose ships would be the only command Rickover ever held; Lieutenant (junior grade) Edward W. Eberle, Class of 1885, who would be Chief of Naval Operations from 1923 to 1937; and Engineer Cadet William D. Leahy, Class of 1897, who would serve as President Roosevelt's chief of staff in World War II.)

It would be Reeves—like Milligan, an exemplar—to whom Rickover would turn years later when he felt the need to show respect to an officer of the old, revered and traditional Navy. Testifying before a Congressional committee in 1972, Rickover said, "I was fortunate, as an ensign, to be present when Admiral Reeves, in 1925, addressed all the officers on duty at the Naval Air Station, North Island, San Diego. His address heralded the transformation of our naval air arm into an effective combat weapon. I was impressed by his vision."

What also seemed to impress the young Rickover and what would continue to impress the elder Rickover was the way Reeves believed in himself. And in later years, Rickover could take some comfort from the realization that Reeves was another officer who had been far along in his career when it had dramatically pivoted. Reeves was a fifty-three-year-old captain when he became Commander, Aircraft Squadrons, Battle Fleet.

As Reeves stepped up to give the 1925 lecture that Rickover mentioned, the admiral was thrust into a political crisis. Only a few weeks before, General William (Billy) Mitchell had charged that the loss of the Navy dirigible *Shenandoah* and the reported loss of a seaplane in the Pacific were caused by the "incompetency, criminal negligence, and almost treasonable administration of the national defense by the War and Navy Departments." Mitchell's sensational act of insubordination would, as he had expected, trigger the court-martial that would bring him notoriety, fame, and ultimately acclaim as a martyr. But, when Reeves gave his lecture, Mitchell—and the use of planes in warfare—were far from vindication.

Later the Rickover of the 1970s conjured up that Reeves lecture. Testifying about "his" nuclear navy, he told once more of the battles for what he believed was right. The "father of the nuclear submarine" invoked the memory of "the father of the aircraft carrier." Simultaneously, in his mind's eye Rickover sees a young ensign sitting in an auditorium and listening to Reeves's vision of the Navy's air age. Rickover and Reeves, one identifying with the other. Young Rickover and mature Rickover, the prophet as a young man.

Yet, curiously, the words Rickover cited in his 1972 testimony were not the words Reeves spoke in 1925 as a visionary of air power but his words a decade later when, now newly named Commander in Chief of the U.S. Fleet, Reeves summoned officers of every rank to the Naval War College in Newport, Rhode Island, and told them:

"In everything we do, we must ask ourselves: Does this directly advance preparation for war?

"Our fleet today is overorganized, overeducated, overtheorized, overinstructed, overadministrated, overcomplicated. . . .

"If war comes, this fleet must fight as is. You must fight at sea and not on paper. Victories are won by practical results. Practical results are obtained by application at sea of our studies, theories, and analyses on shore."

Young Ensign Rickover had not yet begun to rebel. Nor had the young ensign dashed from the San Diego lecture hall and signed up to become an aviator. What impressed the mature, testifying Rickover was not the remembered aviation lecture that Ensign Rickover attended but the 1935 paperwork lecture that Admiral Rickover recited in a Congressional hearing room. Merging the two lectures, and trying to summon up the young ensign, Rickover perhaps tells more than he intended.

For the admired Reeves was many things that Rickover was not. Reeves's family had been in America since 1640. Reeves, nicknamed Bull at the Naval Academy, had played right tackle on the Annapolis football team (which beat Army). And, according to *The U.S. Naval Academy,* published by the Naval Institute, as a naval cadet Reeves invented the modern football helmet (before, as an admiral, he "pioneered the development of carrier tactics"). He learned to play on a team and play by the rules. Reeves had not fixed upon a new and controversial Navy arm to build his career; he was a well-rounded naval officer, as loyal to battleships when he served aboard them as he was to carriers when he fostered them. He is known to people who know the Navy; he is not known to the general public. He never became a celebrity.

He would be virtually the only admiral of the pre-nuclear Navy ever praised by Rickover the elder. He would be, to the Rickover of the past and present, the kind of naval officer that Ensign Rickover had once hoped to become.

Exercises in 1924 took the *La Vallette* and the rest of the fleet south, along the Central American coast, through the Panama Canal, and up into the Caribbean for exercises. Following visits to ports along the Gulf Coast, including New Orleans, Rickover's ship returned to San Diego, arriving back at her home port in April. After local operations along the coast, Rickover was relieved as the ship's Engineering Officer in August 1924, and late the following month was admitted to the Mare Island Naval Hospital. The public records available do not specify why Rickover was hospitalized. While at the hospital Rickover "took up" the game of golf—which he played only once. According to his own account, Rickover and a classmate at the hospital found two clubs, a driver and a putter. They then found some balls that had been lost in the rough and went off to learn the game.

"I was learning to play that morning," Rickover later recalled during a Congressional hearing on government contracts, "when a rather stout lady who was behind us drove a golf ball right past us, nearly hitting my classmate. Of course, we got mad that anyone playing golf, a game I have been given to understand was played only by gentlemen and gentlewomen, could be so churlish as not to give the required signal. I waited until she passed, and then without saying 'fore' I drove off. The ball struck her in the bustle. That was enough for me. I said, 'Nick, let's get out of here.' And, we did, without apologizing to the lady—as required by the rules.

"That same day a notice appeared on all the navy yard bulletin boards. It warned of two ruffians who had hit the commandant's wife with a golf ball and asked all hands to inform the commandant of their identity. That ended my essay at playing golf—after one day and six holes. . . ."

After two months at the Mare Island hospital, on November 5, 1924, Rickover was detached. He took year-end leave, presumably spending most of it with his family back in Chicago, and then returned to the West Coast for his next duty assignment.

On January 21, 1925, Ensign Rickover boarded the battleship *Nevada* at Bremerton, Washington. The large dreadnought was quite different from the small, sleek destroyer that had been Rickover's first ship. At 28,400 tons the *Nevada* displaced more than twenty times the tonnage of the *La Vallette* and carried the powerful armament of ten 14-inch guns. Less than a decade old when Rickover reported aboard, the *Nevada* was one of eighteen battleships that formed the backbone of the U.S. Fleet.

While the *La Vallette*'s wardroom had been a small, close band of brothers, the *Nevada* had seventy-five officers on board, including *thirty* ensigns and a dozen warrant officers, most of the latter former enlisted men. The enlisted crew of the ship, counting the Marines, totaled almost 1,200 men. Shortly before Rickover had reported aboard, the *Nevada* had represented the United States in Rio de Janeiro for the Centennial of Brazilian Independence. The giant battleship was an impressive and mobile symbol of American technical achievement and military power. The *Nevada* epitomized Oliver Cromwell's view that "a warship is the best ambassador."

Rickover was assigned initially to the ship's engineering department. He had barely settled in when the Battle Fleet departed for Hawaii, the Navy's forward base in the Pacific. There, amidst the prewar splendor of the Islands, the U.S. Fleet prepared for a good-will cruise to Australia and New Zealand. The cruise, with battleships, cruisers and the destroyers and the fleet train of auxiliaries totaling forty-five ships manned by 23,000 sailors, officers, and Marines, sought to demonstrate American friendship and support for people called "our friends down under"—and to demonstrate the Fleet's cruising range to the Japanese. The distance from the battleship base at San Pedro, California, to Australia was about the same as from San Pedro to the Japanese home islands. After World War I, the Navy's leadership viewed Japan as the primary future enemy of the United States, and war plans and fleet exercises were intended to prepare the Navy for such a conflict.

Rickover did not make the fleet cruise to the southwest Pacific.

On the afternoon of May 20, while the *Nevada* and the rest of the Battle Fleet lay at anchor in Lahaina Roads, off the Island of Maui, Ensign Rickover departed the dreadnought and went aboard the hospital ship *Relief* for treatment. However, before the *Relief* departed on July 1 with the Battle Fleet for the South Pacific, Rickover shifted to another ship for return to the mainland, apparently for additional medical treatment at San Diego.

Thus, Rickover missed the Battle Fleet cruise to American Samoa, Australia and New Zealand. While ashore in San Diego, three years after his graduation from the Naval Academy, Rickover added the gold half-stripe to his single ensign's gold stripe to mark his promotion to lieutenant (junior grade).

He returned to the *Nevada* at Pearl Harbor in early September, reporting on board as the battleship's Electrical Officer. Rickover had charge of the ship's electrical systems, the power produced by four large turbo-generator sets built by General Electric, each rated at 300 kilowatts. Their electricity hummed through the ship day and night, powering the ship's radios, turning and aiming the big guns, energizing lights and refrigerators.

Many stories persist about Rickover's two years in the *Nevada*. As was already his style, Rickover passionately threw himself into his work. As electrical officer, he had an opportunity to further specialize within the engineering field. He learned everything that could be found out about his equipment, how it worked, how it was designed, and how it would fail. He had time for little else, except reading.

According to a favorite Rickover story, one day as he was working—or possibly reading—the captain's Marine orderly reported to Rickover that the captain would like the young officer to dine with him that night. In the larger ships of the Navy a commanding officer had his own mess, separate from that of the other officers in the wardroom. For company, and to better know his officers, sometimes a captain invited one or two other officers to be his guests for dinner.

Rickover astonished the Marine by asking him to please inform the captain that he was too busy with work to dine with him that evening.

A short time later the orderly returned, this time inquiring when it would be convenient for Rickover to dine with the captain. Rickover is said to have responded, "Thursday." The Marine again responded "Aye, aye, sir," and hurried back to the captain.

In general, Rickover shunned social activities. Once, when his captain directed that he attend a reception hosted by an admiral whose flagship was moored nearby, Rickover took a launch to the flagship, climbed the gangway on one side, paid his respects to the admiral and others in the official party and then, unobserved, crossed the deck. He descended by another gangway and, having previously directed the motor launch to meet him there, quietly returned to the *Nevada* for an evening of reading.

For the next year and a half the *Nevada* operated off the west coast of the United States. Then, in the spring of 1927 she steamed through the Panama Canal and up into the Atlantic for a two-and-one-half-year modernization at the Norfolk (Virginia) Navy Yard. Rickover, after five years of sea duty, was eligible to attend postgraduate school. He applied, was accepted, and left the *Nevada* at Norfolk on April 28.

Rickover first returned to the Naval Academy for a year's course in electrical engineering. This time at Annapolis he was an officer and a gentleman, saluted and "sirred" by all midshipmen he encountered and free to plan his own life around his classes. Following the year at Annapolis, the Navy's postgraduate program then enabled him to attend Columbia University's School of Engineering for another year of study. One of his professors, Dr. Charles Lucke, was a highly respected engineering teacher who had just published what would become a famous book, *Engineering Thermodynamics*. Lucke had trouble getting through to his students who were naval officers, including Rickover. Lucke could not understand why they were not able to absorb the principles he was teaching. After a while he told his students he knew what was wrong. They had memorized books, but had never learned to apply facts to a situation through logic. They were "an aggregation of photographic memorizers"—a phrase Rickover the admiral would recall in his perennial criticism of teaching methods at the Naval Academy.

His study at Columbia would lead to a master's degree in engineering. (Interestingly, Rickover did not then have a bachelor's degree, for the Academy did not begin bestowing a degree until the Class of 1933.) While earning his advanced degree at Columbia, Rickover was selected for promotion and became a "full" lieutenant in June of 1928. He also met Ruth Masters.

At Columbia, Rickover lived at the International House. A favorite topic of graduate students studying international affairs was naval arms limitations and the shipbuilding programs of various nations. Once Rickover gave an extemporaneous speech urging the United States to build more cruisers. One of those listening was Ruth Masters, who was doing graduate work in international law at Columbia. Afterward, Rickover and Ruth talked, and a friendship started. A native of Washington, D.C., she had lived abroad for several years and was at Columbia on a scholarship.

When Lieutenant Rickover completed his studies at Columbia, he was assigned briefly to the General Electric Company's plant at Schenectady, New York, for exposure to some of the latest electrical equipment being produced. GE, then a prime supplier of electrical equipment to the Navy, would have a key role in Rickover's later wartime assignment—and in the development of the nuclear submarine.

In 1929 Rickover received orders to report to the battleship *California* as electrical officer. Because he had already served in that position aboard another battleship, the *Nevada,* he asked that his orders be changed. He volunteered for submarine duty.

The submarine branch of the Navy was still small—the crews of all sixty-nine Navy submarines totaled slightly more than the crew of two battleships. Submarines were small, cramped, dirty from diesel oil, and they smelled. There were standing jokes about being able to tell a submarine sailor in the dark because of the stench of diesel oil that permeated his skin and even clean clothes. Popular nicknames for these undersea craft of the 1920s were "sewer pipe," which did not necessarily refer to their circular inside pressure hulls, and "pig boat."

But to Rickover the submarine branch offered an engineering challenge, especially with his new knowledge of electrical engineering, because all submarines were propelled underwater by electric motors. Another possible incentive was the early opportunity for command of a submarine. Most submarine commanders were lieutenants or newly promoted lieutenant commanders, the most junior among commanding officers of warships.

Rickover's request for submarine duty was turned down. At age twenty-nine he was considered too old to enter the submarine branch. He went to Washington, to the Bureau of Navigation, which then was responsible for personnel assignments. He was told he could not have his rejection changed. Then he chanced to meet Rear Admiral C. S. Kempff, who, as a captain, had commanded the *Nevada* during Rickover's second year in the battleship. Kempff, now Hydrographer of the Navy, listened to Rickover explain his problem. The admiral said he would do what he could. Rickover returned north.

A short time later he was accepted for submarine service. He reported to the submarine base at New London, Connecticut, and on October 10, 1929, went aboard the submarine *S-9* for temporary duty, awaiting the start of the next submarine-training course. Although Rickover's official Navy biography states "he had submarine training . . . and afterwards served consecutively in the U.S.S. *S-9* and U.S.S. *S-48*," he was aboard the *S-9* only until the end of the year, and most of that time the sub was moored at the submarine base.

In January of 1930 he started the submarine-training course, which was intended to teach men how a submarine runs, how all of its equipment works, how the piping systems lace through it, how to make a torpedo attack, and everything else anyone would want to know about submarines. The sub-school courses were relatively easy for Rickover, who was older, more mature, and more interested in studying than most of his classmates. In his spare time he played little, but read, studied and corresponded with Ruth Masters, then in Paris.

With his experience in the *Nevada* as electrical officer and a master's degree in electrical engineering, he was frustrated at the simplistic electrical courses being taught at the sub school. He complained, and had arguments with some of his instructors. After completing the six-month course, he was graduated and assigned to the New London-based submarine *S-48*.

The *S-48*, although of World War I design, was completed in 1922 and was one of the fleet's newest undersea craft. Like virtually all submarines of the era, the *S-48* had a shiplike hull enclosing the steel pressure hull which contained the crew, engines, and equipment. The outer hull was 267 feet long with a beam of 21½ feet, while the tubular inner hull was shorter and narrower. The pressure hull was designed for the submarine to have an operating depth of 200 feet, with an emergency or "collapse" depth rated at 300 feet. Thus, under normal circumstances the submarine could not dive as deep as she was long.

The tubular pressure hull had five main compartments. The foremost was the torpedo room, with the inner openings for four 21-inch-diameter torpedo tubes, several additional reload torpedoes, and bunks for sailors. Next came the battery room, subdivided into another area for bunks, the diminutive galley, and, below a false deck, the giant, 120-cell electric storage battery that provided energy for driving the boat while underwater. In the center of the submarine was the control room, with bunks for officers, and in cubbyholes within the compartment, the radio and an underwater acoustic device, a primitive sonar.

Aft the submarine was a mass of machinery, first the engine room with two giant diesels followed by the motor room with its two electric motors. On the surface the diesels drove the boat, with the *S-48*'s shiplike outer hull capable of cutting the water at just over fourteen knots—less than half of a destroyer's speed and slower even than a battleship of the same era. The diesels were also used to charge the batteries, which in turn provided power for the electric motors while the boat was submerged. At a few knots, the motors could propel the submerged *S-48* for perhaps a day; at higher underwater speeds—up to a maximum of 11 knots—the batteries would be exhausted in less than an hour, and the boat would have to surface to recharge her batteries.

At the stern of the *S-48* was a fifth torpedo tube, for a "stern shot" if a pursuing enemy destroyer could be caught in the right spot. Topside the *S-48* had a small conning tower topped by a miniature bridge, where the captain or officer of the deck and a couple of lookouts stood while the boat was on the surface. The structure also housed the retractable periscopes and mast. Forward of the tower was a 4-inch gun, specially designed to remain serviceable after being submerged. Some considered the gun to be the main battery, because small merchant ships and fishing craft, important to Japan in wartime, could be sunk by gunfire, and the torpedo capacity was limited. A maximum of fourteen "fish" could be carried—and torpedoes were expensive compared to the cost of a dozen or so 4-inch shells. Also, under existing international law, a submarine was required to surface and insure the safety of the passengers and crew of a merchant ship before sinking the ship. Thus, the gun was important for challenging and stopping the merchant ship before attacking. (The U.S. Navy, like the German and Japanese navies, ignored these niceties of international law once war began.)

The submerged displacement of the *S-48* was only 1,230 tons, slightly more than the weight of one turret of 14-inch guns in the battleship *Nevada*. Yet, such submarines could be potent if properly used in the right situation. Smaller U-boats had almost destroyed Britain in 1917 (as

Admiral Rickover would never tire of saying when he asked Congress for more nuclear submarines).

On June 21, 1930, Lieutenant Rickover crossed over the submarine *S-21,* moored to dock "H" at the New London submarine base, and stepped onto the *S-48,* his home and duty station for the next three years.

Submarine service could be exciting and dangerous. The S-boats could be especially dangerous: The *S-5* had accidentally sunk in 1920, the *S-36* and *S-39* in 1923, the *S-51* in 1925. On December 28, 1927, the fourth submarine in this ill-fated class, the *S-4,* collided with a Coast Guard ship and sank in Provincetown, Massachusetts, harbor in about one hundred feet of water. As the Navy tried to rescue the crew, some members of Congress actually proposed legislation that would ban submarines from the U.S. Navy. But one Congressman spent thirty-six hours aboard the *S-8,* a sister submarine, and returned to Washington, where he succeeded in convincing Congress that the *S-4* accident should not be used as an excuse to get rid of submarines. The Congressman was Fiorello La Guardia, later to be the colorful mayor of New York City.

Scores of submariners had been lost in these tragedies, and there could have been more, for there were several near-disasters for other S-boats, including the *S-48.*

As she submerged on her initial builder's trials, on December 7, 1921, water flooded in through a manhole plate of the *S-48* that was not properly secured. She sank in sixty feet of water. The submarine was ballasted down by the stern so that her bow projected up through the water. Her crew, builder's representatives, and Navy observers escaped through a torpedo tube. The submarine was salvaged, repaired, and belatedly commissioned on October 14, 1922.

Little more than two years later, on the night of January 29, 1925, the *S-48* was off the New England coast, making her way slowly on the surface during a heavy snowstorm. She ran aground; by midnight the waves were washing over the stranded submarine, rolling her as much as sixty degrees to starboard. Salt water apparently reached her battery and produced deadly chlorine gas. She had to be abandoned, with Coast Guard lifeboats taking off the crew. The *S-48* was refloated in February, but a lack of funds forced the Navy to decommission her for two years before she could be repaired, and even then money shortages slowed the work. It took almost two years to repair and modernize the *S-48.*

Rickover's skipper in the *S-48* was Lieutenant Commander W. J. Lorenz; another lieutenant and two lieutenants "jaygee" (for junior grade) completed the wardroom. There were few ensigns in submarines, because all Academy graduates first went to sea in a destroyer or battle-ship for a couple of years and attended the six-month sub school before going to a "boat."

Rickover, assigned as engineer and electrical officer of the *S-48*, was responsible for the sub's propulsion system and auxiliary machinery, and the maze of pipes and wires that permeated the craft and seemed to fill every nook and corner. There were forty-five enlisted men aboard the *S-48*, several more than the number called for on the sub's "allowance" list. So the *S-48* was even more crowded than she was supposed to be.

Mortal danger again came to the *S-48* on the evening of September 15, 1930, while she was anchored off New London, charging her batteries. Shortly after eight o'clock, fire broke out in the forward battery, a highly dangerous situation in submarines. There is the danger of short circuits; of improperly ventilated batteries generating odorless, tasteless, and invisible hydrogen gas, which, when accumulated, explodes; and should water have reached a battery and got into the sulfuric acid contained in the battery jars, highly poisonous chlorine gas would be generated.

As black smoke issued from the *S-48*'s battery, the compartment was evacuated; doors were closed to seal it off from the rest of the boat, and all lights turned off to reduce the possibility of sparking a hydrogen explosion.

The captain had the crew climb up onto the submarine's deck, to be ready to slip over the side should the submarine erupt in fire or explode. The hope was that with the compartment sealed and all pipes going into it shut off or gagged, the fire would die from lack of oxygen. At eleven o'clock, almost three hours after the fire had been discovered, Rickover, as engineering officer, donned a gas mask and entered the compartment. The fire was out. Frequent inspections were made throughout the night, and a portable air blower was set up on deck to make certain that no harmful gases built up.

The *S-48* safely returned to port. Rickover's name appeared regularly in the log. If at sea, the entry was often little more than "steaming as before" or if in port, "moored as before," followed by a list of other submarines and small craft moored nearby. On December 25, 1930, as was custom when Jewish officers were aboard a ship on Christmas Day, Rickover had the watch around the clock. The submarine was at the Portsmouth Navy Yard, and Rickover had the watch by simply remaining on board from midnight to midnight.

More operations off the coast followed during the winter of 1930–1931. Then, the sub loaded supplies, provisions and torpedoes, and late on the morning of February 20, 1931, the *S-48* got underway. In company with several other S-boats and shepherded by a large submarine tender, she sailed south toward the Panama Canal. The *S-48* would have a four-year stay in the Canal area as part of the force intended to defend the Canal against hostile naval attack. The submarine would also provide simulated opposition for U.S. surface warships exercising in the area.

On March 1 the *S-48* arrived at the hot, humid submarine base at Coco Solo on the Atlantic side of the Canal. She was at sea much of the time for coastal operations and cruised to Guantanamo Bay and Puerto Rico, and sometimes passed through the Canal to operate along the Pacific coast.

In mid-1931, Rickover was promoted to executive officer and navigator of the *S-48*, becoming the senior officer on board after the commanding officer. A short time later he completed the training requirements to qualify for submarine command. That meant that when his tour as exec of the *S-48* was completed, the Bureau of Navigation could assign him to command of a submarine.

While in Panama, Rickover had one of those encounters with a Navy chief that becomes a sea story. The chief, from another submarine, had a reputation as an expert acey-deucey player. So did Rickover. A game was arranged, and the chief beat Rickover, who remarked that he had beaten everybody in his own sub. "If I was on *your* sub," the chief responded, "you'd of beat me, too, *sir.*"

Rarely was there any excitement, although some came Rickover's way early one morning when a sailor, returning from liberty "in a very intoxicated condition," fell overboard. The sub was moored at Balboa and, because of the heat, Rickover was sleeping in a cot on deck. Although he had barely qualified as a swimmer at Annapolis, Rickover quickly went over the side and saved the sailor from drowning by holding his head above water until assistance came.

In July 1931, Lorenz turned over command of the *S-48* to Lieutenant Commander O. R. Bennehoff. In the fall, Rickover took leave and returned to the United States. His correspondence courtship of Ruth Masters ended successfully on October 8, when they were married in Litchfield, Connecticut, by an Episcopal priest, the Reverend William J. Brewster. During the four years since Ruth Masters and Rickover had first met at Columbia, she had studied at the Sorbonne in Paris and begun her studies for a doctorate in international relations. She would receive her doctorate in 1932. After their wedding, they traveled to Panama and a prolonged honeymoon, regularly interrupted by Rickover's leaving for short cruises in the *S-48*.

Rickover's relations with the submarine's new commanding officer were not good. The real causes of their problems are lost to memory. Perhaps Rickover had his own views, as executive officers usually did, of how the boat should be run and they did not coincide with his new captain's practices. Perhaps after his time in the *S-48* Rickover's mind sought new technical challenges that could not be met by the simple design of the submarine's propulsion plant.

After three years of submarine service, including two as executive officer, Rickover was eligible for assignment as commanding officer of a submarine. Although the newer submarines were commanded by more senior lieutenant commanders, the numerous S-boats changed skippers every two years or so, and opportunities for submarine command were available for qualified lieutenants. At the time, eleven of the S-boats and three older R-class submarines were commanded by lieutenants from the Class of 1922. (Another half-dozen officers from Rickover's class were in command of Navy minesweepers, tugs and other minor ships.)

Instead, Rickover was relieved as exec of the *S-48* on June 2, 1933, and three days later left the sub—and the submarine service—at the Broadway Pier in Baltimore. A month later he reported to the Office of the Inspector of Naval Material in Philadelphia. In his new assignment Rickover was responsible for inspecting supplies and equipment being produced for the Navy. The position, while demanding in some respects, did give Rickover time to take additional correspondence courses from the Naval War College and, as usual, do a considerable amount of reading. One book in particular said to have impressed Rickover during this period was *Peacemaking 1919* by Harold Nicolson.

Nicolson's behind-the-scenes accounts of the writing of the Treaty of Versailles gave Rickover an insight into a reality he would long abhor: Deals in politics were made by insiders—men who knew each other through old school ties, men who, self-licensed by privilege and heredity, acted as if they owned and ran the world. What had happened at Versailles would happen in the Navy, the young Rickover realized, for Annapolis bred a world of insiders as thoroughly as Eton and Oxford did.

Rickover would always retain the belief that personal honesty and integrity must be placed above old school ties and even ordinary friendships. This, then, to a great extent became Rickover's credo. He would demand full measure from all above him and below him. Forty-five years later one of his protégés, Vice Admiral Kinnaird McKee, declared that there are only two kinds of good people in the world: those who are dedicated and those who demand dedication from others. This was Rickover's philosophy even as a junior officer: full measure, always, regardless of conditions or circumstances.

Around this time in his career Rickover clearly revealed his feelings about favoritism. Commenting in the March 1934 issue of the Naval Institute *Proceedings,* he wrote on the problem of establishing a fair way for promoting of enlisted men. Criticizing the current method, which allowed a great deal of subjective judgment by an officer "possessing loyalty for his men," Rickover bluntly set down what he knew of the system; he said he was "impressed with its weaknesses and its injustices."

Conscientious young naval officers, then as now, tried to get their views published in the prestigious *Proceedings.* From a comment in 1934, Rickover advanced the next year to a full-fledged essay, written for the publication's annual prize essay contest. The essay, "International Law and the Submarine," combined two interests of the Rickover family—Lieutenant Rickover's views about the use of submarines in warfare, and Mrs. Rickover's special field of international law. (Rickover himself in this period took the correspondence courses from the Naval War College on international law as well as strategy and tactics.)

Ruth Masters Rickover had continued her studies after their marriage and had obtained her doctorate at Columbia, and in 1932 the Columbia University Press published her first major work, *International Law in National Courts.* The book is an exhaustive analysis of the relationship between international and national laws, based on her study of actual cases in the courts of Germany, Switzerland, France and Belgium. A linguist and a lifelong scholar, Mrs. Rickover also spent years in Europe studying how the obstacles of national laws had been overcome in the setting up of a European railroad system.

In his essay, Rickover used standard sources on international law, which his wife also had cited in her publications. Obviously, she shared with him her background knowledge of international law. But his essay was clearly his own, and in it he accurately predicted that Germany would soon begin rebuilding her submarine fleet and that the submarine practices of World War I would be continued in the future.

But the submarine's strategic concepts that Admiral Rickover would later set forth were not yet envisioned by Lieutenant Rickover, who wrote, "The submarine is the weapon par excellence of the weak naval power. Control of the seas can never be obtained through possession of a submarine fleet, no matter how large. But control of the seas can be effectively challenged and its exercise rendered hazardous by submarine operations."

Just before the essay appeared in the *Proceedings,* Rickover, after two years of shore duty, was again rotated to a shipboard assignment. On April 13, 1935, he reported to the battleship *New Mexico* anchored in Los Angeles harbor. The *New Mexico,* at 33,000 tons, was larger than the *Nevada* and, with an armament of twelve improved 14-inch guns, was more heavily armed than Rickover's previous battleship. Rickover, with graduate education in electrical engineering and his submarine experience, was ideally suited for assignment as the ship's assistant engineering officer.

As always, Rickover went at his work with a passion. The *New Mexico* was involved in the regular cycle of local operations off the coast and farther-ranging fleet exercises. When Rickover reported aboard the battleship, a division commander, a rear admiral, and his small staff were embarked in the *New Mexico.* Sometimes the ship served as flagship for the Commander in Chief of the U.S. Fleet, Admiral Joseph Mason Reeves, already a hero of Rickover's.

Reeves stressed accomplishment, and that was just fine for the assistant engineering officer in Reeves's flagship. In the peacetime Navy of the middle 1930s competition among ships and crews was keen, with coveted E (for efficiency) awards being given to ships that excelled in specific categories. The efficient use of fuel oil was a key factor in winning the engineering E, and Rickover set out to raise the *New Mexico* from her eighth place on the list of fifteen battleships. After careful investigation and analysis of the ship's fuel consumption, he took action. The evaporators which produced fresh water for the ship were oil-fired, so the water supply for washing and showers was reduced. Similarly, the ship's heating system was cut back to conserve oil. Rickover was also accused of walking along passageways unscrewing lightbulbs. The crew complained, officers complained, and even an admiral's staff officer is said to have complained, but Rickover, supported by the engineering officer, stood firm. The next year the *New Mexico* won the E award for engineering efficiency. Although he was only the assistant engineering officer, Rickover got most of the credit—or blame—because the engineering officer had turned over most responsibility to Rickover.

While Rickover was aboard, the *New Mexico* won three annual engineering E awards in a row. (She also won two gunnery awards in the same period.) Rickover was a dedicated officer in an extremely good ship. Her commanding officer at that time was Captain Frank Jack Fletcher, later commander of U.S. task forces in the battles of the Coral Sea and Midway.

The *New Mexico* soon became famous through tales about her fanatic assistant engineering officer. One of his junior officers, Joseph Barker (who would work for him again in the 1950s), remembered the problem of taking a shower aboard the ship. "He had special plugs made and inserted in the shower heads," Barker recalled, "and it cut the water down to a trickle. Then he fixed the valve that held the water on so that you had to use an awful lot of your strength just to get the trickle of water. And then he started timing junior officers' showers. If he thought you were taking too long, he would actually pull you out of the shower.

"I remember we were in Long Beach on Christmas day, and he turned off the heat. While he had the ship that way we got sudden orders to go to sea, and the captain and the admiral came aboard. They had walked into a deep-freeze. The captain said he wanted seventy degrees in ten minutes."

One of the junior officers pulled out of a shower by Rickover was Norman C. Gillette. He recalled the dim lights in the passageways aboard the battleship, the bumps and the curses and the cold. He also remembered how fuel-oil figures were manipulated: Rickover saw to it that the officer of the deck ordered "extra turns"—a speed-up of revolutions per minute of the propeller shafts—"two minutes before the hour, so that at the exact hour the ship's oil allowance would be greater than justified by the average turns for the hour."

Gillette did not get along with Rickover, and the young officer's fitness reports showed it. Gillette expected the poor reports would haunt him throughout his career. Later, when he was selected for rear admiral, he recalled, "One evening, about two months after my selection, I ran into a rear admiral who had been on the board which selected me, and told him how surprised I was that with those two poor reports from the Great Man, I survived. He said 'Those 3.1 reports were regarded as 5.0 by the board, when they realized who the real reporting officer was.' " (The highest possible mark is 4.0.)

Another junior officer in the *New Mexico* at the time, Kenneth G. Schacht, also remembered Rickover: "His knowledge of the plant was thorough. He tolerated nothing but above-average performance by his officers and men. If he didn't get this, somehow a transfer was arranged."

Commenting on Rickover's personality, Schacht noted that "He dedicated every waking moment to his job. He rarely went ashore. When he did he was alone. Aboard ship every hour was a duty hour. He'd wake up at night . . . at least once each 4 hour watch and call the Engine Room. He'd query the OOW [Officer of the Watch] about various readings: amounts of fuel consumed, water made, pressures, and temperatures. We learned that, when that phone rang, we should gather up all the clip boards of logs and carry them to the . . . phone. . . ."

Two years after joining the *New Mexico,* Rickover again received orders and a promotion. He was ordered to the Asiatic Fleet and would soon become a lieutenant commander.

As was customary at the time, Mrs. Rickover accompanied her husband to the Far East, and they sailed on a passenger liner to Japan before proceeding south to join the Asiatic Fleet in turbulent Chinese waters. By mid-1937, China and Japan had been at war intermittently for almost six years, following a Japanese-contrived "incident," a bomb explosion on a railway line in Manchuria. By the next morning Japanese troops had occupied the Manchurian capital of Mukden; Chinese troops marched north to occupy those portions of Manchuria that Chinese forces could hold, and Japan and China were thrust into an undeclared conflict.

Rickover would see the twilight of foreign rule in China. The Asiatic Fleet he joined was part of an international force formed by several nations to maintain order in the chaos of China. Those were still the days of Empire, when the British brought Sikhs from India to China to be traffic cops in Shanghai, when Highlanders in kilts, white spats, and sun helmets marched down Shanghai's Nanking Road, when the "Horse Marines"— U.S. Marines in dress blues, with sabers—rode about Peking on Mongolian ponies protecting American interests and guarding the U.S. Embassy. America, Great Britain, France, Italy and Japan maintained garrisons in Peking. And Shanghai was a city run by Europeans for Europeans.

A new Chinese leader was on the rise. Chiang Kai-shek, inspired by the principles of Confucius, was gaining support for his New Life Movement, which preached a doctrine of austerity: "Our clothing, eating, living, and traveling must be simple, orderly, and plain clean. . . . We must observe rules, have faith, honesty, and shame . . . Regard yesterday as a period of death, today as a period of life."

So the Rickovers were moving into a time when yesterday was becoming today, when China would be an exciting place for a naval officer and for a scholar whose field was international law and the mechanisms of peace.

While at sea, Rickover received orders naming him to command the

U.S.S. *Finch* on the Asiatic station. They were ominous orders. The *Finch* was a rundown, 188-foot wooden minesweeper, built in 1918 to sweep mines in the North Sea. Two decades later, when Rickover was ordered to command her, the *Finch* was employed to tow targets and carry supplies in the Far East. Rickover had possibly hoped for command of one of the old four-stack destroyers in the Asiatic Fleet or one of the large gunboats, or at least an important job on the staff of the fleet commander, that veteran of the revered *Oregon,* Admiral Harry E. Yarnell. The Asiatic Fleet at the time consisted of one modern cruiser, the *Augusta,* flagship of the fleet; a handful of four-stack destroyers and S-boat submarines, some gunboats, and two aged minesweepers. The gunboats varied in size and capability; some were shallow-draft river boats of the type immortalized in Richard McKenna's novel *The Sand Pebbles.*

The Rickovers spent two weeks sightseeing in Japan before they went on to China. Even as they were en route, on the night of July 7, 1937, Japanese troops were maneuvering at the Marco Polo bridge near Peking. The Japanese commander claimed that the Chinese interfered with his troops. A Japanese soldier was missing. Fighting erupted again, and full-scale war ensued.

Rickover had become a lieutenant commander on July 1, but word of his promotion would not be recorded in the log of the *Finch* until September 25. So, when he reported aboard early on the morning of July 17, the log would say:

> 00-04 Anchored in berth 9, Tsingtao, China, in 18 fathoms of water with 60 fathoms of chain to the port anchor. Target raft No. 113 moored alongside to starboard. Men-of-war present: U.S.S. AUGUSTA, ISABEL, PIGEON, PAUL JONES, Submarine Squadron Five; H.I.J.M.S. TENRYU, TATSUTA, FUYU, SARUSASE, R.C.S. YUNG HSIEN. 0010 U.S.S. PAUL JONES Underway and stood out. 015 Lieutenant Hyman G. Rickover, U.S.N. reported on board for duty in command with additional duty as Commander Mine Division Three, Asiatic Fleet, in accordance with Commander-in-Chief, U.S. Asiatic Fleet.*

Later that day Rickover relieved Lieutenant Joseph P. Rockwell, who, having served as commanding officer for less than a month, was hastily departing to become aide to the U.S. High Commissioner of the Philippines, which was then a United States territory. Rockwell had been

---

* *Mine Division Three consisted of the* Finch *and her sister ship* Pigeon. *As the senior commanding officer of the two minesweepers he additionally commanded the "division."*

put in command of the *Finch* at the specific direction of Admiral Yarnell, who had been impressed with the manner in which Rockwell had handled an ancient gunboat on a remote river in China. Yarnell wanted to observe Rockwell close at hand before sending him on to the Philippines with his highest recommendations and the additional half-stripe of a lieutenant commander. Rockwell grew fond of the lowly *Finch* during his brief command. He considered her the best of the five ships he commanded during his naval career.

One other commissioned officer was assigned to the *Finch,* a jaygee who served as executive officer, navigator and communications officer. The rest of what could hardly be called the "wardroom"—the term for both the ship's officers and the room where they ate, did paperwork and relaxed—consisted of three warrant officers, former enlisted men who shared the other officer duties and stood watch. Some fifty-five enlisted men were in the ship.

China was in turmoil as Rickover, a new commanding officer in the fleet, boarded the *Augusta* for the customary call on Admiral Yarnell. His diminutive minesweeper was dwarfed by the heavy cruiser as she swung at anchor a short distance away in Tsingtao harbor. Admiral Yarnell could spare little time for the commanding officer of one of his smallest and least important units. As Yarnell looked at his job of protecting American citizens and interests in strife-torn China, his two minesweepers were important only for towing targets and other utility work. Most of the *Finch*'s at-sea time was spent moving cargo and towing targets for other ships to practice shooting at—a humble mission that also meant she returned to her berth after the other ships. She did make a brief trip up the coast to Chefoo to carry sailors to other U.S. ships.

Tsingtao was crowded with several British and French ships, as well as those of the U.S. Asiatic Fleet, and even a couple from the warring parties, Japan and China. The Imperial Japanese Navy, like the others present, was still at peace. Every morning, at eight o'clock, most of the warships would parade their crews on deck, raise the national colors and, if there was a band on board, blare out a series of anthems—first that of the ship's own nation, then that of China, in whose waters the ships were anchored, and then the anthems of nations represented by the other ships present. It was an unreal situation, for nearby in the Chinese countryside soldiers and civilians were sometimes fighting and dying.

Then, on August 11, Japanese marines landed at Shanghai. This time the excuse was the shooting of a Japanese marine and sailor in Shanghai, China's largest city and principal port. Japanese ground, naval and air forces went on the offensive. Major battles raged around Shanghai. (The city itself would fall to the Japanese in November after a heroic and bloody defense by the Chinese.) The *Augusta* led the Asiatic Fleet south from Tsingtao at high speed to help protect Americans and other foreign nationals in the large international quarter of Shanghai. The target-towing minesweeper *Finch*, Lieutenant H. G. Rickover in command, trailed along.

Fighting raged ashore and "accidental" near-misses occasionally threatened U.S. ships (the first American casualty was a sailor killed aboard the *Augusta* on August 20; the U.S. gunboat *Panay* was sunk by Japanese bombers in December). The *Finch* went about her mundane work. For example, on August 26 she steamed down the Yangtze River to where the naval auxiliary *Gold Star* was moored, embarked one hundred and five U.S. Marines and carried them back up to Shanghai to help guard Westerners in the city. On her way back up the river the *Finch* passed two Japanese destroyers shelling Chinese positions in the town of Woosung.

Although the war flowed around her, the *Finch* was usually motionless. After her arrival at Shanghai on August 21, 1937, she lay at anchor, except to shift berth, until five days later when she was underway for seven and one half hours to pick up the Marines from the *Gold Star*. She was again anchored until September 19, when she was called upon to move more Marines and was underway for a few hours.

After less than three months in what would be his first and only command, Rickover was relieved on October 5, 1937, by Lieutenant Commander Donald S. Evans, a fellow member of the Class of 1922. Rickover's brief period in command of the *Finch* became controversial. Clay Blair, writing about the *Finch* from Rickover's recollections, said, "Disturbed at the poor morale and condition of the ship, Rick called the crew together one day and told them that he had begun a program to put the *Finch* shipshape once again . . . the Captain imposed hard duties on the crew: chipping and scraping rust and paint; overhauling machinery. The crew became more disgruntled. Rick replied by working them harder." The results of Rickover's working them harder may be found in the *Finch*'s deck log, which from mid-August until October 3 records that Rickover meted out punishment to crew members on numerous occasions, generally for fighting and for being absent from the ship for a couple of hours. Blair wrote, "During Rick's tenure as skipper, the *Finch* had been a taut ship."

Memories have been dimmed by more than four decades of time, a spectacular World War and many lesser conflicts, while the official records of such incidents—those that existed—have long since been lost in archives. But some officers on the Asiatic scene at the time vividly recall the *Finch*. Once, according to one officer, she was seen "steaming into port with a red flag flying from her mast and the crew had painted 'madhouse' on her side, in red." The red flag was a symbol of a crew in revolt—the "Bolsheviki," to use a popular term of the time, derived from the Russian revolutionaries. The words on her side were probably in "red lead," as the crew repainted the ship and made sport of their conditions under Rickover.

The situation in the *Finch* did not sit well with Rickover's contemporaries, and some officers later recalled Rockwell, her previous commanding officer, standing in the Army and Navy Club of Manila, bawling out Rickover. Although Rickover was shorter than the stocky, six-foot Rockwell, he was the senior of the two. That made no difference as Rockwell "came close to hitting him," the authors were told.

Evans relieved Rickover on October 5. At the time, the *Finch* was moored alongside the gunboat *Isabel,* at Shanghai. Evans, in turn, would command the *Finch* for only four months before he was relieved, carrying on the *Finch*'s tradition of changing commanding officers virtually with the seasons. (The *Finch* herself was not to survive for long. Late in 1941 she sailed to the Philippines and was sent to the bottom of Manila Bay on April 10, 1942, after a near-miss from a Japanese bomb opened her seams.)

Rickover remained aboard the *Finch* for almost three weeks after being relieved, until October 24, 1937, when he boarded the submarine tender *Canopus* for transportation to the navy yard at Cavite on Manila Bay. He departed the *Finch* to begin a new naval career.

Engineering Duty

Lieutenant Commander Rickover had seen more than his orders when he was told to report to the *Finch*; he had seen the writing on the rusty bulkhead, and he had asked the Bureau of Navigation in Washington to classify him for Engineering Duty. As an engineering duty officer—EDO in Navy jargon—he would be, for the remainder of his naval career, a specialist in ship design, construction and repair; he normally would not again go to sea, but would serve ashore, except possibly for a rare assignment on the staff of a senior admiral afloat.

Rickover's decision was fateful, for not only would it chart the path of his career; it would also be the reason for much of the controversy—and confusion—decades later when Congress challenged the Navy's decision not to promote Rickover to admiral. Relatively few people outside the Navy realized that Rickover was not a typical naval officer. He was different—in some ways very different—and this difference dated from his decision to become an engineering officer.

Leonard Kaplan, the man who had spent his four years at Annapolis in Coventry, had earlier changed to EDO status. Later Kaplan, while at the Brooklyn Navy Yard, met a younger officer—also Jewish—who expressed interest in becoming an EDO. Kaplan, still embittered, told the young officer that anti-Semitism was still rampant in the Navy and that, as a Jew, he would find it even tougher in the EDO community. Whether Rickover reasoned this way is not known, but he would become an EDO for there was no longer a place for him in the "line" navy.

By long tradition the Navy differentiated between line officers, who could command ships (line as "ships of the line"), and engineering officers who could design, operate and maintain ships. When engines were introduced into the Navy, they were dirty, undependable auxiliaries to glorious, reliable sails. Civilians were hired into the Navy to maintain the engines. As Rickover would remark bitterly years later, "Engineers were given no military duties as these were the preserve of the line officer, the aristocrat of the Navy." The line officer, by Rickover's assessment, "detested the greasy engineer and his smoking boilers that blackened the sails." Controversy continued despite several efforts to gain the acceptance of engineering specialists into the Navy. Finally, in 1916 Congress passed a law enabling officers to be designated as "engineering duty only," EDO, which later came to mean "engineering duty officer." An engineering officer would wear the star insignia of a line officer, but the EDO designation would make him a restricted line officer, the principal restriction being that he could not command ships.

When Rickover made his decision, there were only three EDO rear admirals in the Navy. All three were inspectors of machinery at major industrial concerns doing work for the Navy. No higher EDO rank was then possible. For Rickover to advance to full commander or captain would be difficult, because most engineering duty officers had become engineering specialists earlier in their careers. But Rickover believed that his postgraduate education, engineering experience at sea, and intensive study of machinery would more than compensate for his late entry into the EDO ranks.

He was ordered to the Cavite Navy Yard in the Philippines. He boarded the submarine tender *Canopus* at Shanghai on October 24, 1937, joining his wife, who along with many other American dependents had come aboard at Chefoo, about 300 miles north of Shanghai, on October 20.

Although not especially old, having been commissioned in 1922, the same year as Rickover, the ship was generally addressed as the "old *Canopus*." The old *Canopus* could officially steam at thirteen knots on paper, but her real sea speed was about eight knots. Another sailing characteristic was a list to port or starboard, depending upon the wind direction, caused by her towering deck house. The old *Canopus* reached Manila late on October 31. A few minutes after eight the following morning, the Rickovers went ashore.

He reported to the Cavite Navy Yard as assistant planning officer. Cavite was a relatively small shipyard, but highly important to the U.S. Asiatic Fleet. And, in the event of war, the U.S. Pacific Fleet based on the west coast of the United States was to steam across the Pacific to reinforce the Asiatic Fleet and defend the Philippines from Japanese assault. The stocks of ammunition, torpedoes, fuel and spare parts at Cavite plus the yard's overhaul and repair facilities, would be vital should war come to the Pacific.

But Cavite's facilities were far short of the capability that would be required when war came. The yard's ability to dry-dock or raise ships out of the water for maintenance or repairs was limited to the old *Dewey* dry dock, a floating contraption that had been towed from Chesapeake Bay to the Philippines on an epic 12,000-mile, six-month voyage back in 1905–1906. To supplement her lift capacity, the yard had a Spanish-built marine railway, and the ancient motor used to haul ships up out of the water proudly bore General Electric's serial No. 39.

Rickover had to work with other equipment that was equally antiquated and limited. The only heavy lift crane was a coal-burning steam affair on a barge that was towed from job to job in the yard. The crane belched forth smoke, which the yard commandant's wife complained spoiled her window curtains. Thus, use of the crane was scheduled when *la Senora Almirante,* as the workmen called her after the Spanish fashion, was off doing the Manila shops or at the Army and Navy Club across Manila Bay.

Even using powered hand tools such as rivet guns, chipping hammers, or power drills on the yard's piers was difficult, because the Japanese considered permanent air lines to be an infraction of the mutual agreement reached by the two nations that the United States would not strengthen the fortifications of the Philippines and Guam, and the Japanese would refrain from doing the same in their mandated islands. These included Tinian and Saipan, and a few atolls such as Kwajalein and Eniwetok, all of which would become the targets of bloody American assaults in World War II.

But war was far away from Cavite in the fall of 1937. Yard hours were from 7:30 A.M. to 3:30 P.M., to permit workers to escape some of the afternoon heat. Many of the workers were Filipinos, some of whom had even worked for the Spanish in repairing their ships prior to the dramatic arrival of Commodore Dewey in 1898. Filipino workers made up to forty cents an hour, a good wage for the time, especially in the islands.

Life was relatively easy for the sailors stationed at Cavite and excellent for the officers. An array of officer clubs ringed the bay area, both Army and Navy, plus the several civilian clubs that were available to the more senior officers. The officers of Destroyer Squadron Five had even purchased mounts and formed a polo team.

About a month after Rickover arrived at Cavite, the liner S.S. *President Hoover* went aground off Formosa with the commandant of the navy yard aboard. For years, this event and the events that followed would give Rickover a chance to show off his considerable skills as a raconteur.

"Cavite was then the jumping-off place insofar as duty in the Navy was concerned," he began as he once told the story to a Congressional audience. Cavite's status as the end of the line, he said, "was not so subtly indicated by its radio call sign—BARN. The call sign for the Bureau of Navigation in Washington, the Navy's choice duty station, was . . . STAR."

Getting back to the story of the commandant, Rickover recalled that he had called a meeting of all officers to "tell them of his concepts of leadership and efficiency." According to Rickover, the commandant told of the grounding of the *Hoover*. He said he was not surprised that this had happened, because, having been invited to the captain's mess he had noted that the latter did not wear garters to hold up his socks. At this point there was a loud thud as all the officers listening to the commandant dropped their feet from the backs of the chairs in front of them.

Rickover continued, "I was told later by the ship's service officer at the yard—who was charged with shopping for the admiral's intimate apparel in Manila—that he wore full-length stockings and used garters attached to his waist to hold them up."

As assistant planning officer at Cavite, Rickover was responsible for planning the repair and overhaul of machinery for ships coming into the yard. During the winter of 1937–1938 there were few customers for those services, as most of the Asiatic Fleet remained in Chinese waters to help protect American lives and interests during the war. The records are sketchy and memories hazy about the late 1930s period at Cavite. Rickover recalled that he "made considerable changes to the way of operating the navy yard at Cavite. . . . While I was there we drastically reduced the cost to repair ships and overhaul machinery. I thereby became known to the people in Washington." But one officer interviewed for this book, whose submarine was overhauled at Cavite in 1940, said that it "was the poorest-quality yard I have ever experienced." Another submarine officer then serving aboard the *S-38*, recalled that Rickover demanded a submarine turn in a part for each part drawn from the shipyard's stocks. "Sometimes, Rick himself would stand at the counter and make sure the sailor logged them in properly," the officer, later Vice Admiral F. J. Harlfinger, remembered. "But most times, the sailor would then put the piston, or whatever the part was, out in the area in back of the shed, and later some of our crew would march by and just happen to pick up what they had just turned in."

Neither the changes Rickover said he made at the yard—nor the records of those changes—survived the Japanese bombing and subsequent occupation of Cavite that came a few years later.

In their stay at Cavite, the Rickovers found time for sightseeing and touring. They purchased a car and traveled through much of the Philippines. Then, in the summer of 1938, while the Japanese forces continued to rape and conquer China, pushing all of Asia and the Pacific toward the war, the Rickovers undertook what was planned as a two-week cruise to Southeast Asia. They sailed to the Dutch East Indies, then continued to Singapore and into Thailand, going ashore frequently to visit towns, temples and ruins.

Years later, Ruth Rickover wrote an account of their travels, published under the title *Pepper, Rice, and Elephants.* Her detailed account of the trip told what they saw, whom they spoke to, what was said, and even how much was spent—"I cut it rather fine, arriving back home [Cavite] with only seventy-five cents in my pocket." The book provides a look and commentary on the world from the Celebes Sea to Siam, a world that would be changed dramatically and tragically in less than four years.

And the journal of Ruth Masters Rickover provides rare, fascinating insights into the ways of the middle-aged lieutenant commander she called "George." Here he is in Bali: "George saw some carabao or water buffalo, with tinkling wooden bells around their necks. We had seen these animals many times in the Philippines—in fact, George had ridden on one. He decided that he had to have the bells and made Abdullah [their driver] stop the car."

> Disdaining my help [she wrote] he went to interview the cowherd. Pointing at a carabao, George offered ten cents. (By this time he had learned to say in Malay: "ten cents"; "bring shave water quickly"; and "go away.") The cowherd, thinking George wanted to buy the carabao for ten cents, thought this a huge joke and shrieked with laughter. George then ran after the carabao and, catching the beast, pointed to the bells and repeated his offer. This seemed to the cowherd an even better joke, for the bells were not worth a tenth of the price offered. These doings had attracted the entire village which found our wanting to buy cowbells hilarious. The carabao didn't like the whole business and ran away, with George, the cowherd, and the village in hot pursuit. Finally, George got back into the car with the bells, which we draped in the windows. . . . I am sure everyone was more than ever convinced that all Americans were crazy.

When they reached Siam, which was to be the end of their odyssey, Mrs. Rickover had become "enamored" of Siam and "hated to leave." Rickover suggested that she continue sightseeing, for perhaps another two weeks or so. He caught a plane up to Hanoi, then capital of French Indochina, did some quick sightseeing, and went on to Hong Kong to catch an Italian-flag liner to Manila. Mrs. Rickover recorded an example of her husband's disquieting influence on his fellow passengers:

> In the dining room they had two pictures on the wall; one of Mussolini, at the right, the other of the king. George started seditious thoughts by asking whether the king's picture should not be to the right of Mussolini's since he was, after all, the number-one man. They were still debating the question when he left the ship at Manila.

And then, in a revealing conclusion to the passage, she added:

> George still uses this gambit when he visits a high-ranking official and observes pictures of superiors on the wall. He asks whether the senior ranking official should be on the right-hand side as the viewer faces the pictures or as the pictures face the viewer. Occasionally this has resulted in interchanging the pictures.

After Rickover left for Manila and the nearby Cavite yard, his wife, in the company of friends, continued onward to visit Hanoi and then made a brief trip up into the western Chinese province of Yunnan to see the Burma Road, newly opened although parts of it had existed as early as 1933. She returned to Hanoi and sailed from the nearby port of Haiphong aboard a steamer to Hong Kong, and then transferred to another ship for the return to Manila.

Rickover often wrote imaginative answers on the numerous forms he and Mrs. Rickover had to fill out in their travels. To the question of how he made a living, he once wrote "by work." He sometimes listed his religion as Mohammedan, and when a Japanese official registered surprise, Rickover said, according to his wife's account, "quite a few American naval officers were converting to Islam since this was a virile religion, and, what with Japan arming itself and acting warlike, it behooved American service personnel to be prepared." The jest was based on fact. Japan was arming, and agents, watching for espionage, had followed the Rickovers in Japan and perhaps elsewhere.

In mid-1939, the Sino-Japanese war continued on the mainland of Asia; Hitler's ministers negotiated with Stalin, seeking a pact that would permit the *Wehrmacht* to invade Poland, movements for which were already underway; and President Roosevelt, presumably fearing further

Japanese aggression, had just ordered the U.S. battle fleet back to the Pacific, canceling plans for its participation in the New York World's Fair.

That same summer, after two years in Cavite, the Rickovers departed the Philippines to return to the United States. Reportedly, he began his return by traveling back to the mainland, and then going by truck along the entire length of the Burma Road. His wife would later recall his letters to her during the trip—"fascinating letters" . . . which told how "the farther west he moved, the more medieval the country became. He observed the most extraordinary customs and a degree of poverty impossible for a Westerner to visualize. In many villages, mothers hid their children's faces in their laps when George's truck appeared for there—oh, horror—were two fearful creatures, one white, one black (the Hindu driver), and never had they seen anything so horrifying."

Rickover returned to the United States for assignment to the Bureau of Engineering, the home of the Navy's EDOs. The bureau was responsible for the propulsion plants and certain other features of ships, while the Bureau of Construction and Repair was charged with over-all design and building of ships. By the time Rickover reported to the Bureau of Engineering in July 1939, plans were being readied for consolidation of the bureaus. The actual consolidation began in October 1939, although the new Bureau of Ships (BuShips) was not legally established until June 20, 1940. This move placed full responsibility for the design, construction, maintenance and overhaul of the Navy's ships in a single organization.

Initially Rickover was assigned to the Design Division of the Bureau of Engineering (and then Bureau of Ships when the new organization came into being). Some of the Navy's best brains devoted to ship and submarine design were concentrated in that division: Lieutenant Commanders Andrew I. McKee, who would later be chief design engineer of the Electric Boat Company, the nation's leading submarine yard; Harry E. Eccles (Class of 1922), who would become the Navy's leading logistician; Harry Burris, who would be initially named to head the Navy's postwar group to investigate nuclear power at Oak Ridge; Armand M. Morgan, later director of Navy ship design; Lieutenant Elton W. Grenfell, who would become a three-star submarine force commander; and Commander Earle W. Mills, a veteran naval engineer who would have a major impact on Rickover's career. Indeed, much of Rickover's ability to survive and his success both in BuShips and the early Navy nuclear-propulsion program would be due to Mills.

A 1917 graduate of the Naval Academy, Mills had served in a cruiser during World War I and then in a succession of destroyers. Like Rickover, he earned a master's degree in (naval) engineering at Columbia University. Next, Mills served aboard battleships, on staffs, and as engineer of a cruiser. He was in the Bureau of Engineering as an EDO from 1933 to 1937 and was again assigned there in September 1939, just after Rickover arrived. A year later, as a commander, Mills went to England to study battle damage to British warships. He returned to BuShips in 1941. In another year Mills would become the Assistant Chief of BuShips with the rank of rear admiral, a position that he would hold throughout the war.

Rickover's arrival at BuShips occurred as the U.S. Navy was in the start-up of a massive shipbuilding program. In response to the gathering war clouds in Europe and Asia, Congress had authorized, and the Navy in 1938 and 1939 had ordered, large numbers of new warships. The start of war in Europe in September 1939 with the German assault on Poland, the German invasion of Norway and Denmark, and then France and the Low Countries in 1940, led to more warship orders. Still more were ordered after the Pearl Harbor attack on December 7, 1941, until within a month of the Pearl Harbor attack the Navy had on order or under construction almost seven hundred battleships, aircraft carriers, cruisers, destroyers, destroyer escorts and submarines. This was twice the number of ships in those categories in service on December 7, 1941. In addition, hundreds of mine, patrol and anti-submarine craft, along with auxiliary and support ships, were under construction. In every category the new ships were larger, more capable, and more complex than their predecessors. All ships—their design, construction, outfitting, maintenance and repair—were the responsibility of BuShips. A vital obligation of BuShips was the electrical systems in ships. Electricity was used to power radios, radars, guns, lights, refrigerators and freezers, and in some ships it was used for main propulsion.

Early in his BuShips assignment Rickover became head of the Electrical Section. Thus, when the United States entered World War II, Rickover was head of an extremely important division of a vital bureau in the Navy. It would be here, in BuShips, where Rickover would first learn bureaucratic warfare. He was in a power center, for to a great extent the Navy's technical bureaus ruled the Navy.

The bureaus traced their origin to 1842, when five were etablished to manage specific aspects of naval activities ashore. Although the bureaus were headed by naval officers, their chiefs were generally specialists (e.g., naval engineering, civil engineering, supply), and they reported directly to the Secretary of the Navy. Even after the establishment of the Chief of

Naval Operations in 1915, the bureaus continued to operate independently for another half century. Indeed, in 1924 the bureau chiefs openly fought the legalilty of a Navy regulation that implied that the CNO had jurisdiction over some of their activities. There were seven bureaus during World War II: Naval Personnel, Yards and Docks, Aeronautics, Ordnance, Supplies and Accounts, Medicine and Surgery, and Ships.

The Bureau of Ships was the largest of the bureaus and, in many respects, the most powerful. Ships were the Navy. And as the Navy expanded during the war, so would BuShips, until by the end of the conflict the headquarters of BuShips in the Main Navy building on Constitution Avenue in Washington would have 2,500 naval officers and enlisted men, and 3,800 civilians to oversee a program that involved 325 government and private shipyards with a peak labor force of one million workers, plus perhaps three times that number in related laboratories and industries that directly supported shipbuilding and maintenance. The ships that they designed, built and maintained ranged from large 60,000-ton carriers of the *Midway* class to small collapsible rubber boats for commando raids. New construction alone totaled 17 billion 1945 dollars.

Within BuShips Rickover built a large and efficient Electrical Section, which soon became known as one of the most effective branches of BuShips. Rickover made it that way by originating practices that would become his hallmark in the Electrical Section—and, years later, in the Naval Reactors Branch. His would be the only BuShips section that would ignore ranks among workers, that would make "education of personnel" an important task, that would develop autonomy, and that would employ few Navy men and many civilians.

Rickover also saw to it that a history was written about the Electrical Section, a history that looked forward as much as it looked back, because Rickover at the end of World War II did not want mistakes repeated in the World War III that he believed was inevitable.

"Other sections of the Bureau of Ships and other Bureaus utilized naval personnel throughout, or for the greater part of, their organizations," the history says. "This was purposely not done by the Electrical Section because of its foreseen drawbacks." These were, according to the Rickover-supervised history, problems that he still would be struggling with decades later: the continual rotation of naval officers and men—and the Navy's persistent placement of officers in assignments according to rank, though "an individual's qualifications as an officer" were "not necessarily indicative of his technical qualifications." The section quickly grew from a prewar staff of about twenty-five to nearly three hundred and fifty by the end of the war.

The Electrical Section was one of the first sections in BuShips to learn the realities of war. Electrical equipment designed for a peacetime Navy could not hold up against the effects of explosions and water-borne shock waves. Circuit breakers popped open or were jarred closed, paralyzing a ship's electrical equipment. Switches were tripped off, shutting down combat circuits at the precise moment when they were needed.

Rickover plunged into solving this problem with what would become legendary zeal. He fought with some industrial representatives and hired others, "borrowing" them for the duration. When a representative came to him with a piece of supposedly shockproof equipment, Rickover gave it his personal shock test: He threw it against the radiator in his office, or, on extreme occasions, out the window.

He personally prepared specifications and set deadlines for shockproof equipment and for mountings that could absorb shock. "He never took anyone's word for anything," Chancey Whitney, the senior engineer in the section, recalled. "He was pretty tough. He would take advantage of you if he could. He put you through a lot. But he did a hell of a lot for me, and I respected him. So did Admiral Mills."

What impressed Mills was Rickover's effectiveness: He got the work done. His methods were quite unusual, compared to the conventional and traditional bureau approaches to problems. Although unusual solutions became the norm during the war, Rickover always went one step beyond. He thought nothing of calling the president of an electrical parts company—or a major corporation—late on a Sunday night to locate a generator or reel of cable. When the corporate executive, after several hurried phone calls, would ring Rickover back and declare it was at such-and-such a shipyard or loading dock, Rickover would say he was standing in that yard or on that loading dock and the material was not there.

Whenever an executive or anyone else said that he would check in the morning, or whenever Rickover was asked why he was calling at 11 P.M. on Sunday, the reply would be that there was a war on or that the missing reels—or whatever it was that Rickover wanted—were holding up construction of a vital warship.

Rickover and his own key staff members worked continually; days, nights and weekends merged into simply long and then longer "days." Those who could not keep up the pace, physically or mentally, were shifted out of the Electrical Section. Those who remained, worked and traveled. Rickover and staffers shuttled across the country by plane and train, expediting, checking, badgering, directing.

In addition to visiting contractors and naval facilities, Rickover tried to visit damaged warships, to observe personally the effects of battle damage and to determine how electrical equipment had performed or failed. He visited many of the damaged ships, beginning with the carnage at Pearl Harbor after the Japanese attack of December 7, 1941. One of the ships sunk was the battleship *California,* which actually took three and a half days to sink as Navy men fought a losing battle to keep her afloat. But there were not enough pumps available.

Rickover told a Congressional committee many years later, "I was responsible for getting the U.S.S. *California* ready to go back to war about one-and-a-half years faster than had been previously estimated. I devised the system to get her repaired fast. Instead of having her towed back to the United States as planned, I devised a system where we could repair her using the capability at Pearl Harbor."

Writing about the *California,* then-Captain Homer Wallin, the fleet salvage officer, said, "There were a few optimists who felt that it would be possible to recondition the main [electric-propulsion] machinery of the *California* . . . at least sufficiently for return to a mainland and Navy Yard." Wallin took the word of the optimists and brought sixty General Electric employees out to Pearl Harbor to help the Navy men, with Rickover apparently having a key role. The effort was successful. "With respect to the success of this work," Wallin continued, "it might be stated that although a very optimistic understanding, the results were very satisfactory." The *California* was refloated after resting partly submerged on the shallow bottom of Pearl Harbor for three and a half months and then spent two months in the Pearl Harbor Navy Yard before returning to the mainland for a major reconstruction. She did not return to the fleet until early 1944.

Like many an officer kept in a vital though unexciting post, Rickover built as much as he could upon ventures away from his desk. He made trips to Pearl Harbor, and years later these trips would blossom into vital missions. "I visited practically every ship in World War II that was damaged," he once said, although several hundred ships were damaged and visiting them all was not physically possible. He also told of how he "happened to have visited the carrier *Franklin* two or three days after she was attacked." The *Franklin* was hit by Japanese bombs just fifty-five miles off the Japanese coast on March 19, 1945. The bombs had ignited fires among armed planes ready to take off. The resulting explosions and fires tore the carrier asunder, killing 724 men and injuring another 265. The ship, masterfully handled, was saved. Three days after her ordeal (when Rickover remembered having visited her) she was still at sea, only a few hundred miles from the Japanese coast, limping toward Pearl Harbor at fifteen knots. She stayed there briefly and then sailed for New York City.

"He liked to travel on Sundays," Whitney remembered, "and he always carried the pinks," referring to a practice Rickover originated. Later, even in the age of Xerox, Rickover would retain the "pinks system" he had invented in the Electrical Section.

The pinks were carbon copies of all correspondence, including memos and informal notes. Every secretary was instructed, under threat of dismissal, to give to Rickover at the end of each working day copies of all correspondence that had passed through her typewriter. Rickover read every word of every pink, and if he spotted a grammatical error or something else he did not like, he would call in the author and dress him down, sometimes punctuating the lecture by grinding the offending pink under his heel or balling it and tossing it in the general direction of the wastepaper basket.

On his trips he wore civilian clothes whenever possible, and this too would become a habit. So would his insistence on saving government money by staying in a contractor's or colleague's home instead of a hotel or by staying in the cheapest room in a hotel.

Those who knew Rickover then—and talked of him decades later—agreed that he was not trying to be merely exasperating. He had seen, from his vantage point in the Electrical Section, a Navy that had gone into war ill-managed and ill-prepared. He had seen electrical equipment put out of commission not only by the shocks of combat but also by mere moisture. He had seen how minor damage to a bulkhead could cripple a ship because behind the bulkhead lay unprotected cable and, when that was severed, fire-control systems or vital pumps were knocked out. He had learned that a system called battle lighting had failed in battle. Someone in peacetime had decided that in battle a ship's regular lighting should be automatically replaced by something called battle lighting— dim blue lights that paralleled the normal lighting systems. The battle lights were dramatic in drills. In combat, they were all wrong. The system was not designed to hold up under the sustained combat that frequently raged in World War II. The color blue was easily detected, and sailors going on watch had trouble adjusting from the darkness to the blue light. Rickover succeeded in getting the lights changed from blue to red.

But he had to fight to get this done, and to him it seemed as if he had to fight to get anything done. Rickover became mad at the Navy, and it would be an anger that would never cease.

One man who remembered Rickover's raging impatience was the kind of officer Rickover would always admire: an officer who had not graduated from Annapolis. He was John Fluke, a former General Electric Company engineer who was an officer produced by the Massachusetts Institute of Technology (destined to be a Rickover favorite) and the University of Washington Naval Officer Training Corps.

"Being a reservist between World War I and World War II gave me an insight into what Rickover disliked about the Navy," Fluke recalled. "I was told by a regular once that when war came the Navy would need *real* officers. He said that a bunch of shoe clerks couldn't stand up to an Academy graduate. That was the kind of thing Rickover hated."

The remark was particularly grating, for there was a shoe clerk in the reserve battalion that Fluke commanded in Bridgeport, Connecticut. He was Chief Machinist's Mate James S. MacBride, who had a distinguished seagoing career in World War I and then returned to duty for action in World War II. Two of his children, George and Muriel, also served in the Navy.

Fluke remembered that Rickover had personally edited the history of the Electrical Branch. He had considered the writing of the history an important task. Like so many activities spawned in the Electrical Branch, the written word—the getting of facts on record—would be part of the Rickover way of standing watch.

"He would tell me," Fluke continued, "that World War II was the second time we had got caught in a war with our pants down. He wanted to get that history written, get the facts corralled, so that what we learned might save the country. He was under the impression that the war was not just going to end in Germany and Japan. He foresaw an era of unsettlement and a need to enforce foreign policy."

Rickover already saw himself as a savior, even a martyr. In the Electrical Section he developed the patriotic grudge that years later he would summarize in these words: "Most of the work in the world today is done by those who work too hard; they comprise a 'nucleus of martyrs.' The greater part of the remaining workers' energy goes into complaining."

To solve the problem of electrical-system blackouts in combat,

Rickover had supervised the development of what amounted to plug-in "electrical casualty" units that by-passed damaged areas. According to Fluke, Rickover's championing of the units was opposed by Rear Admiral Edward L. Cochrane, Chief of BuShips. Outfitting of all warships with the system, as requested by Rickover, would make some ships unavailable for immediate combat duty. Cochrane believed it was more imperative to get the ships into action than delay them by adding extra equipment.

Rumors swept BuShips that Rickover was defying Cochrane by installing the equipment—and that Rickover was about to be court-martialed for insubordination. The rumor evolved into a legend that told of how, on the eve of the decision to court-martial Rickover, Cochrane's own son came home from a ship that had been saved by Rickover's electrical-casualty device.

The truth, treasured in Cochrane family lore, is that the cruiser *Helena* did sink in 1943, but the admiral's son, Lieutenant Richard L. Cochrane, survived. When he told his father about it, he reported that a Rickover device had saved him. That device was a one-cell flashlight attached to a life jacket. The light had been criticized by Rickover's superiors as expensive and unneeded. Young Cochrane's report is said to have helped the life-jacket light survive.

Rickover ran into resistance to change for many reasons. When he was putting fluorescent lights aboard ships, a captain looked up Rickover and confidentially requested that the light bulbs in the captain's cabin of his ship not be changed. Rickover probed until he got the reason for the captain's fear of fluorescent lights: He was afraid the new-fangled lights would make him sterile. "I told him," Rickover later recounted, "that not only was this not so, but, considering his age, I did not believe this eventuality would have any effect on the world's population."

Another mission for the Electrical Section was the development of countermeasures against magnetic mines. Rickover formed a subsection to deal with the magnetic mines by degaussing ships. The degaussing was accomplished by first determining a ship's magnetic pattern. Then the magnetic field was neutralized by introducing currents of various strengths into coils of electrical cable arranged around the ship. The solution was awkward for ship handlers and added both weight and bulk to the ship. Sometimes there would be miles of cable aboard.

Rickover had heard of another solution developed by the British—a floating electrical cable that could safely explode German magnetic mines. The cable, when towed in the water, produced an electrical "signature" similar to the magnetic field created by a large warship and would thus detonate the mine safely astern of a small minesweeper. Rickover inquired if anything was being done by the U.S. Navy in the field. Receiving no positive response, he took action himself.

According to naval historian Arnold S. Lott, "Rickover obtained a sample of the magnetic sweep used by the British. Working from that fragment, like reconstructing a dinosaur from a bit of tail bone, Rickover analyzed the cable, figured out power requirements, and drew up plans for the electrical generators needed to energize the finished cables. General Electric produced the generators, Anaconda Cable Company turned out the cables."

Possibly unknown to Rickover, the British Admiralty Research Laboratory had concentrated on countering the magnetic mine ever since that deadly weapon had been introduced by the British at the end of World War I. The U.S. military services had enjoyed close relations with the British from the outbreak of war in 1939 and many British "secrets" were being readily given to the Americans. In August of 1940, a group of radar experts came to the United States with all British radar data; during the winter of 1940–1941, Mills and Cochrane went to England to view battle-damaged British warships and were shown all. The first British jet airplane was displayed to U.S. officers before it even flew, and all plans and specifications were sent to the United States in the spring of 1941. Many other British military secrets were similarly shared before the United States officially entered the war.

Unquestionably, if asked through channels, the British would have provided full technical data—the plans for the magnetic minesweeping "dinosaur"—and possibly even a system for Americans to copy. But Rickover did not see it that way then or years later, when he gave his account of the incident to his Boswell, Clay Blair, who duly recorded it in these words:

> Rick set off on his own. He contacted a cable company and got them to begin making the secret cable (they were not told its purpose) in spite of British patent restrictions and a mountain of red tape. Then he went to General Motors [sic] and persuaded the company to start building a diesel-powered generator which would furnish electric power to run through the cable. In utmost secrecy, General Motors gave the project top priority and began ordering materials and parts. Soon they were almost ready to deliver the first generator, but they still had no contract from the Navy.
>
> All at once, the Navy's top purchasing agents realized that

something not quite cricket was going on. Rickover had made an unofficial contract with General Motors, amounting to some eight to twelve million dollars. No formal contract had been signed; it was still slowly milling its way through Navy red tape in the Bureau of Supplies and Accounts. When they learned all this, the Navy brass popped relief valves and hastily called Rick down for an explanation.

The Chief of the Electrical Section appeared before the officers and accepted full blame for the "deal" which was rapidly becoming famous among the fiscal experts in the Navy. He tried to explain that he was only attempting to expedite the delivery of equipment that was critically needed by the forces afloat. Admiral Claude Jones of the Bureau of Ships, who was in charge of the shipbuilding effort, quickly grasped what Rickover had done and at once settled the contract with General Electric [sic]. By the following day word of the goings-on got around the operating branch of the Navy, and people began to realize that Rick's foresight had really saved the Navy's day.

There were also other thoughts going around BuShips the following day and for many days after, and then again years after, when Rickover became head of the nuclear-propulsion program. Rickover had begun the expensive mine cable project "in utmost secrecy." But had it already been started—by the appropriate office, in secrecy, and with Rickover simply not being told, for security reasons, that the effort was under way? What other programs had Rickover started "in utmost secrecy"? In getting General Electric to assign "top priority" to the project, had other high-priority projects been starved or slowed for want of scarce men and material? What if other BuShips section heads were similarly starting clandestine, top-priority projects? At Rickover's level within BuShips there was also the interior communications branch, internal-combustion-engines branch, hull-arrangements branch, heat-transfer branch—a score in all. Did each one have such secret projects? If so, how much of the war effort was being drained off?

Rickover's results were impressive; many of his contemporaries—even critics—cite his effectiveness. The question was not in his results, but in his methods; what was the cost and could a bureau or even the Navy accept such methods without eventually producing a disaster?

Rickover himself might have answered this question in an address he delivered in 1974, but he did not do so. The 10,000-word account of the "role of engineering in the Navy" is a typical Rickover effort—scrupulously researched, clearly written, exhaustive in historical detail. He dwells for paragraph after paragraph on the Spanish-American War and other events of the nineteenth century. Yet, curiously, he skims over World War II except to remark that the Navy "was at its apogee at the end of World War II." In view of Rickover's penchant for using his actions as examples of the virtues he espouses, modesty could hardly account for his failure to mention the wartime record.

Rickover did not seem to want to relive those days. Those were days of many flaps and countless problems with Rickover and his methods. Many complaints concerned his use and assignment of personnel within the Electrical Section. He had commanders working for lieutenants or civilians, and he assigned people as he pleased, regardless of why they were ordered into his section. And there were the long hours, the phone calls at home late at night and on rare days off, often in the midst of Sunday dinner, with directions for the hapless officer or engineer to catch an imminent flight or train.

Rickover's impatience with delays, his distrust of seemingly plausible explanations, and his belief in the twenty-four-hour working day went beyond individuals and extended to corporations. He never would abandon the anticontractor attitude that he acquired in the Electrical Section, an attitude that always would be reciprocated. "All industry disliked him," Whitney remembered. "He loved to make enemies."

Although the official history of the Electrical Section does not mention Rickover's "secret" cable deal, it does tell how he handled cable contractors in general. The history was never widely distributed, and perhaps the reason why can be traced to its revelations about Rickover's handling of contractors, especially those who manufactured cables.

In April 1943, the history says, at Rickover's direction, "all outstanding purchase orders and contracts for Navy shipboard cable specified for delivery on or after 1 July 1943 were to be cancelled." The hundreds of abruptly canceled contracts were replaced by fourteen, each open-ended and each obligating the Navy to purchase a specified amount of cable. Delivery schedules were made part of the contracts. Rickover's system eliminated delays. By the last quarter of 1944, when 100 million feet of cable were purchased, 97 percent was delivered on time.

But the contracts made the Electrical Section the middleman between the manufacturers and the shipbuilders who purchased the cable. Any cable the shipbuilders did not need became the Navy's property. That would be a price paid for making schedules. Another price would be an emphasis on the big, efficient producers. This would all become a pattern—a symbiotic relationship between Rickover and such giants as General Electric and Westinghouse, a relationship that would continue for decades.

Now, too, another pattern would form. He bypassed channels. He and Fluke got to know two officers on the staff of Chief of Naval Operations Ernest J. King. The officers placed on King's desk letters of authorization for Rickover. King routinely signed them—giving power to a subordinate far down the chain of command.

Such tactics infuriated superiors who belatedly learned what he had done, but Rickover survived all flaps and problems, largely because of Rear Admiral Mills, the Assistant Chief of BuShips and Rickover's key supporter. Rickover was promoted to Commander on January 1, 1942, and in late June of that year he was made a temporary Captain. (Leonard Kaplan, the harassed Number 2 man in the Class of 1922, also an EDO, was similarly promoted on the same dates.)

Later, for "exceptionally meritorious conduct . . . as Head of the Electrical Section of the Bureau of Ships" during most of the war, Rickover was awarded the Legion of Merit, the highest Navy award for an officer outside a combat area. Because of the very close working relationship of BuShips and the British during the war, Rickover and many other captains as well as the admirals in BuShips were also presented the Order of the British Empire.

More important to the future of Rickover and the development of a nuclear navy, while in the Bureau of Ships from 1939 to 1944 he developed the management techniques that would later serve him well and developed his methods for dealing with industry. He would delegate responsibilities; the "pinks" and other procedures enabled him to keep close check on what was happening, but still he would test a man and, when he found him sufficiently dedicated and loyal, he would give important responsibilities to him. With respect to industry, Rickover developed his theory that all industry sought to make a profit at the expense of the government. Contractors—or vendors—could not be believed; they had to be watched and harassed. Rickover's various shipboard assignments of the 1920s and 1930s had been the second phase in his education in preparation for his future role. The period 1939 to 1944 in BuShips was his third phase.

Late in 1944, Rickover appealed to Mills: He had been in BuShips for five years. The war was drawing to its concluding, catastrophic phases in Europe and in the Pacific. Rickover wanted to get more directly into the war. As an EDO, he was not eligible for a command. He could go to sea on a fleet staff or, more likely, to a forward repair base.

Mills asked Rickover first to do a stateside job. Something had to be done about the sprawling Navy supply depot at Mechanicsburg, Pennsylvania, about three miles southwest of Harrisburg. The depot was inefficient. Tens of thousands of spare parts were to flow smoothly through Mechanicsburg to the ships of the fleet, but there were bottlenecks and too many delays. Straightening out Mechanicsburg was the kind of job Rickover relished. He enthusiastically accepted the assignment.

Rickover's systematic rehabilitation of the supply depot, like his administration of the Electrical Section, foreshadowed the way he would operate in the Naval Reactors Branch. At Mechanicsburg he gained a reputation that became known—and notorious—to the small circle of people he ruled over. When the interlude at Mechanicsburg ended, those people just chalked up their experience as an episode in the war. They had briefly encountered a man who, as Whitney had put it, loved to make enemies. They had met petty tyrants, zealous officers, clipboard-toting efficiency experts. It was all part of the rubric: "Don't you know there's a war going on?" But Captain Rickover was something special and extraordinary, and he would endure.

One of his major reforms in the Electrical Section was getting the mail organized. With his penchant for detail, he personally supervised the establishment of what he called "a central mail control system." The key to the system, typically, was in Rickover's hand—a daily list of what letters had arrived in the section and had not been answered on a previously assigned date. Thus Rickover each day possessed the names of miscreants to whom could be dished out the punishment he believed was warranted. In his mail-control system he encapsulated the essence of his management philosophy: Give a subordinate a well-defined responsibility and be in a position to judge the subordinate closely and frequently.

At the supply depot, Rickover found that the hard core of the inefficiency was in the mail system. He assigned people to track down what happened to pieces of mail, from the time a mail truck left Harrisburg, at 4:30 A.M., to the time a letter reached the addressee's desk. Sometimes the trip took days. Then the response was trailed with equal vigor.

Rickover also redesigned the mail room with a plan that included such details as the location of desks and chairs and the construction of mail-bag racks. He also produced for the depot an organization chart measuring eight inches in height and seventy-two inches in length.

Other teams of Rickover operatives examined Mechanicsburg's warehouses, checked the efficiency of the typing pool (too many typists,

Rickover decreed), and even learned that in the construction of numerous sheds at the depot the workmen had failed to recycle scrap lumber. Rickover set up a lumber-salvage operation.

Rickover completed his assignment with a report so scathing that the fifty copies of it were locked in a safe and could not be seen without specific approval of Admiral Mills or the admiral's aide. When Whitney last saw the reports, in January 1946, forty-two of them were still in the safe.

"He'd rather arouse a guy by saying something nasty than make a friend," Whitney told the authors in sad assessment. "I said something to him about it once when he yelled at a guy, and Rickover said, 'He is a son of a bitch. He deserved to be treated that way.' He was ruthless if he thought someone was trying to screw him or the Navy."

Fluke had a similar assessment. He talked of a man who "always took that last ten percent"—and yet a man who once suddenly turned to Fluke and asked, "Am I too tough?"

"We had a TOBR Club, Tossed Out By Rickover Club," Fluke recalled. "He would get mad at you and toss you out of his office. I had to take a couple of days' leave once when it happened to me. But some guys who were banned, they had it coming, trying to be deceptive or shading the truth. Some of them never got back in."

By the time Rickover turned in his report on Mechanicsburg, he was widely known as a "hard-headed" taskmaster. That report is still remembered by wartime officers at BuShips as the earliest example of a Rickover diatribe, much of it justified. But an officer who visited Mechanicsburg in Rickover's wake found one example of inefficiency that Rickover had overlooked in his report—warehouses full of electrical cable, ordered by Rickover. "There must have been tens of millions of dollars tied up in his stuff," the officer recalled. "He had simply ordered too much. The Navy would never be able to use it up." The officer who remembered the cable was Rear Admiral Ralph Kirk James; he would be Chief of BuShips when Rickover was fighting to build his nuclear navy.

James continued, "There were literally warehouses full of armored cable that he had purchased and stored in Mechanicsburg anticipating a war that had to go on for twenty more years in order for it to be consumed. When I learned this, I didn't think that he was a particularly qualified expert to judge the Supply Corps performance at Mechanicsburg. Most of his material later went on to the salvage-scrap sales. Not only Rickover's materials, of course, but that of many others who bought deeply and way beyond requirements."

Asked about Rickover's massive report, James responded, "His written report was a reference document which I used only when necessary." Then, referring to its size, James added, "I didn't consider it the greatest example of brevity I'd ever seen."

(James had also been a critic of Mechanicsburg from his viewpoint, directing repairs to battle-damaged warships in the Southwest Pacific. He went to Mechanicsburg—under protest—as second in command for just over a year, and then served for two years as commanding officer of the huge supply center.)

But Rickover's performance at Mechanicsburg earned him the war-zone assignment that Mills had promised. Rickover was ordered to Okinawa. Vice Admiral Albert J. Fay, then chief of staff of the Construction Battalion troops—the Sea Bees—on Okinawa, remembered Rickover from their days in the Philippines. Fay's men helped build Rickover's ship-repair base on Okinawa, and Fay was there when Typhoon Louise wiped out the base. "A more conscientious man never lived," Admiral Fay said of Rickover, "and on Okinawa he put his heart and soul into his job."

But not all of Rickover's associates on Okinawa praised the way he did his job. When he tried to establish his own organizational concepts, such as ordering a man to carry out an assignment regardless of rank, he ran afoul of the "real Navy"—the one beyond Washington. A few of his officers protested about their being bossed around by petty officers, and Rickover was ordered to conform to the "Navy way" of operating.

Although forced to run his own base according to Navy procedures, he still tried to deal with the rest of the Navy his way. An example was remembered by Edwin B. Hooper, a junior officer in 1945 on the staff of Commander, Service Force, Pacific Fleet, the command responsible for supplies, maintenance and repairs. "Without warning," Hooper recalled, "one day . . . Rickover came into my office with a number of sheets of long paper on which there was an extensive list of the ordnance items that he wanted added to the . . . repair parts he was to receive—although some of it may have been repair equipment as well."

Rickover was senior to Hooper, but Hooper recalls, "I felt a little irritated by his manner as he just insisted that I sign this . . . and all these items would be provided. After a rather heated period, I convinced him that we would go over this list in detail and would provide those things which he needed that were not already provided."

That answer did not suit Rickover. "I believe he complained not only to the Commander, Service Force, but the Commander of the Fleet Maintenance Office, and he even complained to Admiral Nimitz on that occasion," said Hooper. Fleet Admiral Nimitz was Commander in Chief of the Pacific Ocean Area, responsible for all air, ground and naval forces in the central Pacific and the fleets assembling to assault Japan.

Whatever the possible merits of the Rickover approach, it was impractical on Okinawa because the rest of the Navy was working another way. This was the seagoing Navy that was winning a war; these were men who had been there. Rickover was viewed by many as a desk man telling experienced warriors what to do and—worst of all—how to do it.

When the ship-repair base lay in ruins and was declared superfluous to the Navy, Rickover, as commander of the ruins, seemed equally so. He was a temporary captain with twenty-three years of active naval service. He was eligible for retirement, if he wished. The need for EDOs in the postwar Navy was limited. No new ships would be designed for at least several years, and after those hulls still on the building ways were completed (or, in many cases, scrapped without being completed), there would be few if any new ships built.

Although many innovations for naval warfare had been developed by the end of the war—guided missiles, jet-propelled aircraft, high-speed submarines—postwar austerity and the perception of lasting peace made it unlikely that there would be a large postwar fleet. And, as the *Enola Gay*'s atomic bomb had so dramatically demonstrated, if there were to be a conflict, the long-range bomber would be the immediate and final arbitrator.

What then could be the future of the U.S. Navy—and of temporary Captain Rickover?

UNDER WAY ON
NUCLEAR POWER

The captain of the *Nautilus,* describing his remarkable submarine to a visitor, explained the means by which the craft's propulsion machinery used "Bunsen cells instead of those developed by Ruhmkorff, which would have been useless. The Bunsen cells are few, but large and powerful, which in my experience is an advantage. The electricity passes back through big electromagnets, actuating a set of rods and gears which in turn transmit power to the propeller shaft. The propeller is twenty feet in diameter and can do up to twenty revolutions per second ... [giving a speed of] fifty knots."

The *Nautilus* was truly remarkable, the most spectacular undersea craft ever conceived. That description came from Captain Nemo, commander of the *Nautilus* in Jules Verne's novel *Twenty Thousand Leagues Under the Sea,* written in 1874.

For the next eighty years Jules Verne's fictitious *Nautilus* was the most remarkable undersea craft yet conceived by man. But then, in 1955, a new *Nautilus* went to sea, with performance in some respect superior to Verne's *Nautilus* and unquestionably superior to any undersea craft actually built since the earliest recorded efforts of submersible development, the diving bells of Alexander the Great.

Indeed, Commander Louis Roddis, a veteran of the Rickover Oak Ridge group, in 1954 presented the following comparison of two submarines called *Nautilus* to the Society of Naval Architects and Marine Engineers.

RODDIS'S "CHARACTERISTICS OF CERTAIN SUBMARINES"

	1874	1954*
DATE	1874	1954*
NAME	*Nautilus*	*Nautilus*
LENGTH	232 feet	(320 feet)
BEAM	26 feet	(27½ feet)
SURFACE DISPLACEMENT	1,417.6 tons	(3,530 tons)
SUBMERGED DISPLACEMENT	1,507 tons	(4,040 tons)
HULL CONSTRUCTION	double hull	(double hull)
HULL THICKNESS	2½ inches	—
PROPULSIVE POWER	sodium "bunsen" apparatus	thermal nuclear reactor
PROPELLERS	single; 20-foot diameter	twin screw
PROPULSION PLANT	electric	geared steam turbine
MAXIMUM SPEED	50 knots	over 20 knots
CRUISING RANGE	43,000 miles	thousands (62,562 miles on first core; 91,324 miles on second core; 150,000 miles on third core)
BUILDING YARD	a desert island	Electric Boat Division, General Dynamics Corp.
COST	£147,500	over $40,000,000 ($65 million)
ARMAMENT	ram	torpedo tubes (six with approximately 20 torpedoes)
OWNER	Prince Dakar of India	U.S. Government
CAPTAIN	Captain Nemo	Commander E. P. Wilkinson
COLLAPSE DEPTH	4,800 feet	(over 600 feet)

* Characteristics in parentheses were deleted in Roddis's article for security reasons.

6 | The $1,500 Commitment

What the distant future of the atomic research will bring to the fleet which we honor today, no one can foretell. But the fundamental mission of the Navy has not changed. Control of our sea approaches and the skies above them is still the key to our freedom and to our ability to help enforce the peace of the world. No enemy will ever strike us directly except across the sea. We cannot reach out to help stop and defeat an aggressor without crossing the sea. Therefore, the Navy, armed with whatever weapons science brings forth, is still dedicated to its historic task: control of the ocean approaches to our country and the skies above them.

These words of President Truman were broadcast on Navy Day, October 27, 1945, the day on which the Chief Executive stood on the deck of the superdreadnought *Missouri* and reviewed a long line of fifty U.S. warships in the Hudson River. Overhead flew twelve hundred Navy planes. Three hours before, at the Brooklyn Navy Yard, President Truman spoke at the commissioning ceremony for the U.S.S. *Franklin D. Roosevelt,* the second ship in the new class of large aircraft carriers. New York was a Navy town for the day; from "submarine" sandwich specials on menus to three-quarter-page ads for Bloomingdale's and Macy's in *The New York Times,* with "Greetings on Navy Day to all the men, 'Like Nimitz and Halsey and Me.' "

It was the Navy's proudest day, the capstone to a month-long Navy celebration of victory at sea. Earlier in October, Fleet Admiral Nimitz, commander of U.S. forces in the Pacific during the war, had addressed a joint session of Congress, and then led a parade up Pennsylvania and Constitution Avenues to the Washington Monument, to the cheers of a half million residents and visitors. Next, on the ninth, Nimitz led a ticker-tape parade up New York City's Broadway, with an estimated four

115

million cheering onlookers rivaling the size of the crowd that had turned out for General Eisenhower's triumphant return the previous June. Also in October, Admiral William F. (Bull) Halsey led fifty-four ships of his Third Fleet into West Coast ports for tumultuous welcomes. Halsey then asked for immediate retirement, but instead was ordered out on a five-week speaking tour—the nation was waiting to honor its naval heroes.*

But the sense of euphoria that the Navy enjoyed in October of 1945 would soon dissipate. Five factors were working against the Navy: (1) there was widespread assumption that the atomic bomb made surface ships and task forces obsolete; (2) there was a feeling that "push-button warfare," initiated with the German V-1 and V-2 missiles, might replace all conventional weapons, especially if they were married to nuclear weapons; (3) there was no other fleet afloat—especially not Soviet—that would require a large U.S. Navy; (4) the Army Air Forces, which would soon become the separate U.S. Air Force, sought to have the principal role in defense strategy, especially at the expense of naval aviation; and (5) there was the unconscious smugness of Navy leaders which assumed that the American people understood that World War II was won through Allied control and use of the seas.

In the coming months, the military budgets were cut, and the Navy would find itself fighting for survival. In that environment there would be little or no funds for new ship design or construction, the traditional roles of engineering duty officers.

The mighty armada that the United States had built during World War II was cut back until the active fleet was smaller than it had been before the war. After the war, many older U.S. ships were scrapped or sunk as targets, but hundreds more were "mothballed," laid up in reserve, for possible future use. Thus, there would probably not be any need for new construction even if there were—however unlikely—another crisis or war that required naval forces.

This was the situation when Rickover, now a captain with twenty-three years of service, left the typhoon-devastated repair facility on Okinawa and returned to the United States for duty. The Navy was being reduced to about one-tenth of its peak wartime strength. Rickover was ordered as Inspector General to the Nineteenth Fleet on the West Coast, an organization responsible for mothballing ships.

---

* Halsey began to raise a "bellow of complaint" at that order, but was silenced by a Gold Star in lieu of a fourth Distinguished Service Medal, and a month later he was promoted to the Navy's fourth Fleet Admiral (five-star rank). At the time the much larger Army had only three generals and the Army Air Forces one general at that level.

As ships arrived in West Coast ports to be laid up, Rickover insisted that their preservation be done properly. But most of the officers and enlisted men aboard the ships wanted only to get off, to go ashore, to leave the Navy for their long-awaited return to civilian life. While discipline did not break down in the Navy as it had in some Army units awaiting demobilization, most of the Navy was made up of reservists, and the hard professionalism of Rickover had limited impact now that peace had come.

Captain Rickover did his job in his standard professional, all-business manner. Unlike most captains assigned to the mothball fleets, he was not ready to sit behind a desk and merely give orders to subordinates. Rickover personally supervised the removal of perishable materials, the sealing-up of openings, the covering of exposed guns, radars and other equipment, and the installation of dehumidification devices. At times he donned dungarees and personally climbed through the compartments and bilges to make certain that the job was done right.

While Rickover was crawling through the now-still warships, events were happening in Washington and the new atomic city of Oak Ridge, near Knoxville, Tennessee. Efforts were already underway to determine the possibility of using Oppenheimer's "radiance of a thousand suns" to propel a ship, especially a submarine. The earliest U.S. submarines at the beginning of the century had primitive, dangerous gasoline engines to propel them on the surface and to charge the large storage batteries that gave energy to their electric motors when submerged. From 1912 on, U.S. submarines had diesel engines, which gave them more efficient and reliable surface propulsion, while there were advances in battery development. Still, underwater speeds were low, about ten knots maximum, and limited to only a few minutes at that speed or a couple of days at "creeping" speeds. American and foreign inventors looked at means for improving underwater propulsion, among them extending air-intake pipes to the surface to allow a shallow-running submarine to draw in air for diesel-engine combustion (later developed by the Dutch and used extensively by the Germans, who called it a *Schnorchel*).

Even before World War I was over the U.S. Navy was investigating the Neff propulsion concept for submarines, in which large amounts of compressed air were carried in the submarine to permit underwater use of the diesels. Later research involved carrying hydrogen peroxide, which, when broken down, could provide oxygen for engine combustion inside the submerged submarine (another concept brought to fruition by the German Navy in World War II).

This quest for improved submarine propulsion took a new turn in 1938, when German scientists Otto Hahn and Fritz Strassmann found that when uranium atoms are bombarded with neutrons a few of the atoms will split, releasing tremendous amounts of energy. This process of "splitting" atoms is called fission. The announcement of uranium fission by Hahn and Strassmann caused great excitement in scientific circles around the world, including that of physicists at the U.S. Naval Research Laboratory, located on the Potomac River in southwest Washington.

Under Dr. Ross Gunn, the Mechanics and Electricity Division of the Laboratory was seeking more effective underwater power plants for torpedoes and submarines. According to Gunn, "It was recognized immediately that perhaps here was an answer to the submarine propulsion problem ... [and] the problem of air conditioning the submarine would thereby be tremendously simplified and long cruising ranges assured."

Then, early in 1939, Dr. George Pegram of Columbia University, one of the nation's leading physicists, proposed to Rear Admiral Harold Bowen, Chief of the Bureau of Steam Engineering, which controlled the Naval Research Laboratory, that he meet with Navy researchers to discuss the practical uses of uranium fission. Pegram met with Bowen at the Navy Department buildings on Constitution Avenue on March 17, 1939. Also present at that historic session were Dr. Enrico Fermi, the world's leading authority on the properties of neutrons, who had come close to discovering uranium fission in 1934; Captain Hollis Cooley, head of the Laboratory; and Gunn.

The use of uranium fission to make a superexplosive bomb was discussed at the meeting. Fermi expressed the view that if certain problems relative to chemical purity could be solved, the chances were good that a nuclear chain reaction could be initiated.

"Hearing these outstanding scientists support the theory of a nuclear chain reaction gave us the guts necessary to present our plans for nuclear propulsion to the Navy," Gunn would recall. Three days later, on March 20, Cooley and Gunn called on Admiral Bowen to outline a plan for a "fission chamber" that would generate steam to operate a turbine for a submarine power plant. Gunn told the admiral that he had never expected to seriously propose such a fantastic program to a responsible Navy official, but here was a proposal for just that, and $1,500 was needed for initial research into the phenomenon of nuclear fission.

Bowen, himself an innovator who had fought many senior officers to get the Navy to adopt improved steam turbines for surface ships, approved the funds. The $1,500 was the first money spent by the U.S. government for the study of nuclear fission. That summer, after preliminary work, Gunn submitted his first report on nuclear propulsion for submarines. His report came four months before the famous letter urging that the United States undertake a nuclear-weapons program was signed by Albert Einstein and delivered to President Roosevelt.

In his report, Gunn noted that an atomic power plant would not require oxygen, "a tremendous military advantage [that] would enormously increase the range and military effectiveness of a submarine." Gunn's paper also pointed out the many problems and unknowns for such an effort, especially the need to develop means for separating lighter U–235 atoms, which would undergo fission when bombarded with neutrons from the heavier uranium atoms. The U–235 isotope was found to be present in mined uranium at the ratio of only 1 to 40.

Gunn turned his efforts to solving the separation problem. Several academic and research institutions were approached to work with the Naval Research Laboratory in the quest for a practical method of separating the elusive U–235 isotope. Beginning in January 1941, twenty-eight-year-old Philip H. Abelson of the Carnegie Institution worked on the separation problem. He already was codiscoverer of Element 93, neptunium. In July he joined the staff of the Laboratory and, together with Gunn, developed a relatively simple and efficient method of separating the U–235 isotope.

While these initial steps toward the development of nuclear energy were being taken in the Navy and in several civilian laboratories, the public was beginning to learn about the potential of atomic energy. In September 1940, science writer William Laurence, in a highly perceptive article in the *Saturday Evening Post*, wrote how "the world learned about the discovery of a new source of power, millions of times greater than anything known on earth." He described excitement over the German experiments and told how U–235 was "capable of liberating energy at such an unbelieveable rate that one pound of it was the equivalent of 5,000,000 pounds of coal or 3,000,000 pounds of gasoline. In explosive power one pound of the new substance would be equal to 15,000 tons of TNT."

After describing atomic developments up to that point, and the great interest in liberating nuclear energy from uranium, Laurence wrote that "such a substance would not likely be wasted on explosives." In a somewhat naïve proposal, he wrote: "A five pound lump of only 10 to 50 percent purity would be sufficient to drive ocean liners and submarines back and forth across the seven seas without refueling for months.

"And," he continued, "the techniques that would be required for its utilization would be even more simple than the burning of coal or oil. . . ."

Meanwhile, from October 1939 on, under top-secret conditions, the atomic-bomb program was underway in the United States, soon to be known as the Manhattan Project.* Subsequently placed under the direction of Brigadier General Leslie Groves, the Project took control of most of the fissionable material in the United States, and the Navy's atomic research efforts were effectively halted. Groves said that Admiral King, the Chief of Naval Operations, severely restricted the passing of atomic information to the Navy and, with a few notable exceptions, the American atomic effort was an all-Army program. Ironically, a uranium-separation process developed by Gunn and Abelson and built on a small scale in Philadelphia was adopted by the Manhattan Project and built on a massive scale at Oak Ridge. (Two days after Japan surrendered in 1945, Gunn and Abelson were each presented with the Distinguished Civilian Service Award for the process. They were cited for having shortened the war by a week or more through their contributions. Groves said it speeded up production of the Hiroshima bomb by "a few days.")

But the idea of propelling ships and submarines with atomic energy was not forgotten. In August 1944, Groves appointed a five-man committee to look into the potential nondestructive uses of atomic energy. Dr. Richard C. Tolman, the long-time dean of the California Institute of Technology's graduate school and chief scientific adviser to Groves, was head of the committee, which consisted of two naval officers and two civilians. The influence of the naval officers was considerable, because of both the significance of nuclear propulsion and Rickover's later participation. They were Rear Admiral Earle W. Mills, who, as Assistant Chief of the Bureau of Ships, was Rickover's boss. The other officer was Captain Thorwald A. Solberg, also in BuShips.

According to Groves, "One of the primary reasons why I appointed this committee was to have on the record a formal recommendation that a vigorous program looking towards an atomic powered submarine should be initiated when available personnel permitted. I wanted Mills on the committee to make certain of this, that he, Tolman, and Solberg did just that."

* *Manhattan Engineering* District *was the name within the Army's Corps of Engineers for the atomic-bomb effort.* Manhattan Project *was the over-all effort—including the District activities as well as political, scientific and operational aspects of the atomic-bomb program.*

That fall the Tolman Committee visited the Naval Research Laboratory and listened to Gunn and Abelson urge that a nuclear-powered submarine be given a high priority in the committee's report. The Tolman Committee made its formal report in December 1944, proposing that "the government should initiate and push, as an urgent project, research and development studies to provide power from nuclear sources for the propulsion of naval vessels."

A year later, with the war over, the subject of atomic energy for ship propulsion received public attention when the Senate established a Special Committee on Atomic Energy. In reporting the committee's hearings, *The New York Times* of December 14, 1945, quoted Gunn as saying that "the main job of nuclear energy is to turn the world's wheels and run its ships." The *Times* also mentioned the possibility of "cargo submarines driven by atomic power."

By the end of 1945, many scientists and engineers were discussing the possibility of nuclear submarines. At the Bikini atomic-bomb tests in 1946, Lieutenant Commander Richard Laning, skipper of the submarine *Pilotfish,* talked about the feasibility of an atomic-powered submarine with Dr. George Gamow. Gamow calculated that such a craft that could achieve underwater speeds of thirty knots would be twice the size of existing submarines, and could be developed "in ten years if we really put our heart into it." Laning immediately wrote a letter, through the chain of command, recommending a nuclear-propulsion program, and volunteering to serve in it. (He does not remember receiving a reply.)

After the war, both Gunn and Abelson turned their attention to the possibility of an atomic submarine. Abelson took an advanced German U-boat design and developed a scheme for a nuclear "pile" that could fit into the existing spaces with only minor changes in the basic submarine design. This approach, he felt, would accelerate the development of a nuclear submarine. Much of the Abelson report was vague or—from a technical viewpoint—questionable. For example, there was little information about the design of the nuclear pile, or reactor, except that it would use a sodium-potassium alloy as the means to transfer heat from the reactor to the steam turbine.

Abelson's report was submitted on March 29, 1946. Although in retrospect it had severe shortcomings, the report—"Atomic Energy Submarine"—would capture the imagination of many Navy men. His conclusions were:

A technical survey conducted at the Naval Research Laboratory indicates that, with a proper program, only about two years would be required to put into operation an atomic-powered submarine mechanically capable of operating at 26 knots to 30 knots submerged for many years without surfacing or refueling. In five to ten years a submarine with probably twice that submerged speed could be developed.

The twenty-seven-page report of the young physicist placed two "ifs" on the two-year timetable. These were that sufficient priority be given to the project by the Navy and the Manhattan Project, and that "cooperation between the Manhattan District and the Navy is expanded somewhat to permit greater emphasis on Naval participation in design and construction of a Uranium pile reactor of proper characteristics for this application."

There was prophecy in the Abelson report's comment that a high-speed, atomic-powered submarine would operate at depths of about one thousand feet and "to function offensively, this fast submerged submarine will serve as an ideal carrier and launcher of rocketed atomic bombs."

Abelson and Gunn began briefing the Navy's submarine community on the report. About thirty senior submariners were told about the atomic-submarine idea in March. Vice-Admiral Charles Lockwood, who had commanded U.S. submarines in the Pacific during the war, recalled one of those briefings:

> If I live to be a hundred, I shall never forget that meeting on March 28, 1946, in a large Bureau of Ships conference room, its walls lined with blackboards which, in turn, were covered by diagrams, blueprints, figures, and equations which Phil [Abelson] used to illustrate various points as he read from his document, the first ever submitted anywhere on nuclear-powered subs. It sounded like something out of Jules Verne's *Twenty Thousand Leagues Under the Sea*.

But much of what Gunn and Abelson were advocating, and what some officers in this submarine community were already supporting, was based almost entirely on theory and educated guesses. No engineering had yet been done. Further, Groves still would not share nuclear information with personnel who were not under his direct command unless specifically directed to do so by the Chief of Naval Operations. Groves felt that sharing would violate the President's directive on the security of atomic information. Groves was also aware of the very limited amounts of enriched uranium available and realized that there was too little for a separate Navy program. Finally, knowing that there would soon be some form of civilian agency to control atomic matters, Groves was reluctant to commit the Manhattan Project to a possible long-term policy concerning naval nuclear propulsion.

To increase Navy participation in postwar nuclear-energy development, Admirals Bowen and William (Deak) Parsons prepared a letter for Secretary of the Navy James V. Forrestal to send to the Secretary of War. Bowen had been appointed by Secretary Forrestal in May of 1945 to head the new office of Research and Inventions, set up to continue close Navy cooperation with the scientific community and to encourage research into areas not being explored by the technical bureaus. Bowen's office, later to become the Office of Naval Research, had jurisdiction over the Naval Research Laboratory. Parsons, a classmate of Rickover at Annapolis, had been the senior Navy participant in the Manhattan Project, and flew on the Hiroshima mission to arm the atomic bomb while in flight. He was selected for promotion to rear admiral by Secretary Forrestal's express direction to the Navy selection board. The Forrestal letter, dated March 14, 1946, stated that the Navy wished to undertake the engineering development of atomic power for ship propulsion. Secretary of War Robert Patterson responded, in agreement with Groves, that the Navy would best benefit by assigning personnel to the power-pile program being set up at Oak Ridge. Patterson—with Groves's recommendation—was willing to have a group of naval officers begin participating in the program in preparation for eventual development of a seagoing reactor plant. Groves later wrote that his "goal in power reactor development was not a stationary power plant but a power plant with full knowledge on my part that the most attractive use for atomic power was the military one of submarine propulsion."

In discussing the Navy's participation in the Oak Ridge pile project, Admiral Cochrane, Chief of BuShips, advised the General Board, the principal advisory body to the Chief of Naval Operations and the Secretary of the Navy, "It is the Bureau's opinion that the action being taken by the Manhattan District to develop an experimental power pile is the soundest possible approach to the problem and will produce the fastest results." Addressing the time factor, Cochrane noted that "at least 4–5 years will elapse before it will be possible to install atomic energy in a naval ship for propulsion purposes."

Separate from the Navy interest, several industrial firms that had participated in the Manhattan Project began to express interest in power reactors and even in ship propulsion. In particular, the General Electric

Company, which had taken over operation of the plutonium-producing plant at Hanford, Washington, and had established the Knolls Atomic Power Laboratory at Schenectady, New York, proposed the development of a nuclear plant suitable for powering a destroyer. BuShips reacted favorably to the idea and asked that Groves authorize GE to begin design studies. This was done in August. GE was focusing on the possibility of using liquid sodium as a means of transferring heat from the reactor (the "atomic boiler") to the steam turbines that would actually propel the ship.

BuShips also let contracts in mid-1946 to commercial firms to conduct research into the properties of sodium-potassium alloys and their possible use as a heat-transfer medium. The Bureau of Ships was thus involved in several nuclear-power projects by mid-1946.

Now qualified naval personnel had to be selected and assigned to these projects. Parsons and most of the naval officers who had participated in the Manhattan Project were ordnance specialists. Engineering officers would be needed in nuclear ship-propulsion projects. The selection of those officers to participate in the propulsion programs fell to Captain Albert G. Mumma, head of the Machinery Design Division in BuShips. Mumma, who would later head the Bureau, chose five naval officers and three civilians to go to Oak Ridge to observe the Daniels nuclear-pile (reactor) project, and two officers to go to Schenectady to work with GE in designing a nuclear plant suitable for destroyer use.

The Oak Ridge list consisted of Lieutenant Commander Louis H. Roddis, Jr., twenty-eight, who had stood first in his 1939 class at the Naval Academy, achieved distinction in graduate studies at the Massachusetts Institute of Technology, and was on the planning staff for the 1946 atomic-bomb tests at Bikini atoll; Lieutenant Commander James M. Dunford, thirty-one, who had been Number 3 in the Annapolis Class of 1939, had attended MIT, and was a most promising engineer; Miles A. Libbey, also a lieutenant commander, twenty-nine, an Annapolis and MIT graduate, who was already investigating the use of radioisotopes, particularly in determining the characteristics of materials; Lieutenant (j.g.) Raymond H. Dick, twenty-four, a graduate of Ohio State University, who had done graduate work in metallurgy, and had won a combat promotion; Alfred Amorosi and George B. Emerson, both BuShips engineers; and Everitt P. Blizard, a physicist in BuShips.

Captain Harry Burris, who had done an outstanding job in expediting the production of steam plants for destroyer escorts during the war, was chosen by Captain Mumma to be the senior officer in the Oak Ridge group. This list of candidates was submitted to Rear Admiral Mills, the deputy chief of BuShips. At about the same time, the Bureau was also assigning Captain Rickover as one of two naval officers who would work with GE at Schenectady in developing a nuclear plant for destroyers. Mills, who had been Rickover's wartime boss, knew well the ability of Rickover to take on difficult tasks and quickly absorb technical material. His electrical section had been the most technically competent section of BuShips during the war.

Mills approved Mumma's recommendations with one change: Rickover was ordered to Oak Ridge and Burris to Schenectady. Mumma had felt that Rickover's attitudes would antagonize fellow officers as well as the Army and civilian communities at Oak Ridge. Mills understood fully the "personality problems" of Rickover, but also knew his single-mindedness could overcome the interservice, interagency,* and Navy bureaucratic problems that would arise as the Navy moved toward nuclear propulsion. Roddis said later that Mills knew the Oak Ridge job "would take a guy of great determination."

When Rickover received his orders in May of 1946 he was probably happy to leave his uninspiring task of mothballing ships. He is said to have gone out and gathered all the texts on math, physics and chemistry that he could put his hands on and, until his departure for Washington, spent his evenings studying. Upon arrival in Washington, Rickover checked in with Admiral Mills and others in BuShips, returning to the same World War I "temporary" on Constitution Avenue, where he had worked during World War II as head of the electrical section. He then went through the BuShips files—meager as they were—to review all that existed on nuclear matters: the various Gunn and Abelson reports and proposals, the Tolman Committee report advocating an "urgent project to study nuclear propulsion," and a proposal to establish a separate Navy laboratory specifically to develop nuclear propulsion for ships. While in Washington, Rickover also met with officials from GE who were discussing their nuclear destroyer proposal with BuShips leaders. But his most important meeting in Washington was with Groves.

After their discussions of the Navy's participation at Oak Ridge, Colonel Kenneth D. Nichols, Groves's deputy, who was leaving for Oak Ridge the next day, offered Rickover a ride in an Army plane and he immediately took up the offer. Nichols provided not only transportation but

---

* After the war there were immediate discussions on how to bring the nation's atomic-energy efforts under civilian control. On January 1, 1947, the civilian Atomic Energy Commission took over control of the entire Manhattan Project from the Army.

Rickover's first of a series of lengthy discussions with the key participants in the Oak Ridge efforts. Nichols had served continuously as the deputy chief of the Manhattan Project since its beginnings in June 1942.

When Captain Rickover arrived at Oak Ridge in late June 1946, he was part of a flood of military and industrial engineers, scientists and planners who would participate in or work on the Daniels project. Present were several of the men from Westinghouse, General Electric and Allis Chalmers who would later have a role in the development of the nuclear submarine.

By September the remainder of Rickover's team had assembled. Rickover was the senior Navy man at Oak Ridge. Each officer had been told that he was going down to Oak Ridge to learn—they were not going down there as a unified group, nor were they to report to Rickover. Each was to send back reports directly to BuShips. But Rickover soon established that he was the de facto head of the Navy group by arranging to write the "fitness reports" of his fellow officers for the Army command. Those reports were the annual evaluations on which an officer's future promotions would be based.

Rickover organized his "team" so that at least one attended each of the lectures and courses being given in nuclear physics and chemistry at the Clinton Laboratories at Oak Ridge. Dr. Teller and some of those who remained at Oak Ridge after the war called the reactor classes DOPE, for "Doctors of Pile Engineering." Every aspect of nuclear technology, especially the Daniels project, was examined and studied by the Navy team, with evenings and weekends, in the Rickover fashion, being simply time for more studies and reviews.

The results of these studies and reviews were written up, in clear, concise reports. Rickover, realizing that their efforts would become the base for future Navy participation in atomic energy, demanded that the reports not be written in jargon and that they be readily understandable by persons with limited technical backgrounds. And, all were submitted to Washington by Rickover.

As important as the classes, lectures and informal discussions were to Rickover, the contacts were perhaps more significant. Many of the original Manhattan Project scientists and technicians left Oak Ridge after the war, but a small group stayed. Rickover talked with those who remained, and he traveled to other atomic-research facilities to meet with the experts. Writing about those who were at Oak Ridge after the war, Teller would later note, "One DOPE was an unknown Navy captain who put his education (at Oak Ridge) to good use, developed the nuclear submarine, and became an admiral: Hyman Rickover." Teller also recalled Rickover's self-introduction when they met: "I am Captain Rickover. I am stupid." But as Teller began "educating" Rickover, the pupil became the teacher, explaining the value of nuclear energy for ship propulsion.

Rickover also talked his way into a meeting of the Atomic Energy Commission's General Advisory Committee. He took Lieutenant Ray Dick with him. Eventually, the deliberations turned to the question of developing useful nuclear power. After lengthy discussions, the committee arrived at the consensus that perhaps in twenty years there would be a real demonstration of the generation of useful power, and perhaps sometime later it could be made available for specific purposes.

Turning to Dick, Rickover said: "Jesus! Twenty years! By that time you'll be an admiral and I'll be pushing up daisies." Then Rickover stood and proceeded to berate the distinguished scientists for taking a scientific approach to an engineering problem. With that the meeting broke up.

While Captain Rickover and his team were learning all that could be gleaned from the experts at Oak Ridge, Captain Mumma, who had drawn up the original list of Navy attendees for Oak Ridge—minus Rickover—arrived at Oak Ridge accompanied by Captain Burris, now assigned to the GE Schenectady effort. Rickover learned that Mumma was being placed in charge of BuShips' nuclear-power efforts. To quote an earlier writer, Rickover "was dumbfounded." In response to Mumma's request that Rickover send all reports on nuclear propulsion directly to him, Rickover "exploded." He pointed out that the Manhattan Project was still under the Army, and that if Mumma wanted the reports he should ask the Chief of the Bureau of Ships to ask the Secretary of the Navy to request them from the Secretary of War. Rickover simply continued to send his reports directly to Admiral Mills, who would soon (on November 1, 1946) become Chief of BuShips.

Although Rickover seemingly had won in this encounter with Captain Mumma, there were serious implications in Mumma's having been selected to become Coordinator for Nuclear Matters within BuShips. Rickover already had envisioned that he would become the head of any Navy effort in nuclear propulsion. Also, others were becoming the principal spokesmen for nuclear propulsion. Rear Admiral Bowen, who had been interested in nuclear research since 1939, presented a major paper on nuclear energy as a power source to a 1946 meeting of the American Society of Mechanical Engineers. His paper, subsequently published in

Mechanical Engineering and the Naval Institute *Proceedings,* pointed out six aspects of Navy responsibility in atomic energy:

> 1. The maintenance of a vigorous program for the propulsion of ships, submarines, and aircraft by nuclear energy.
> 2. The development of nuclear munitions, and the vehicles to launch and carry them.
> 3. The utilization of nuclear studies for the medical sciences.
> 4. The exhaustive exploration of all possible countermeasures to nuclear munitions and their carriers.
> 5. The maintenance of a broad program of research in nuclear physics and the allied fields of science.
> 6. The education and training of naval personnel in nuclear energy and its applications.

In his 1946 paper, Bowen also wrote:

> The Navy is not only the greatest single user of power, it is also the largest single technical organization in the world. In the Bureau of Ships are many highly trained and competent power engineers who are available to develop and perfect atomic power. . . . The use of atomic energy as a source of power for war vessels is justified now from military considerations.

Bowen was confident of the Navy's nuclear future. Although he had Secretary Forrestal's full support, he was unable to bring about a unified Navy position. Gunn and Abelson, who had been kept out of the mainstream of nuclear research, were leaving the Naval Research Laboratory. Admiral Parsons was now fully involved in gaining a viable role for the Navy in the nuclear-weapons field.

Captain Rickover thus saw Bowen, Mumma, and others as becoming the Navy's principal spokesmen and leaders in the field of nuclear propulsion. At the same time, the probability that Rickover and his team would be involved in developing a power reactor, the Daniels pile at Oak Ridge, was rapidly disappearing as that project died. Teller attributed the problem to security:

> There can be no doubt that this secrecy harmed our reactor development. Science thrives upon freedom of discussion, and scientists—given a choice—almost always prefer to work on open rather than secret projects. When it became clear that reactor work was to be conducted in strict secrecy . . . many scientists returned to the freedom of university laboratories.

AEC historians have written about the "technically ambitious plans for the [Daniels] reactor, but . . . little evidence of a systematic effort to define engineering problems."

Rickover pointed out that building the reactor was five percent theory and ninety-five percent engineering, and that there was too little engineering and there were too few engineers for the project to suceed. He was correct. The Daniels pile would never be completed.

Rickover's fortunes continued to decline in the fall of 1946. But he gave no indications of despair. He saw nuclear power as an opportunity for the Navy—and for himself. And he launched a memo-writing campaign designed to keep his Oak Ridge group intact, to make him the Navy's expert on nuclear power, and to produce a nuclear-powered ship within a schedule that was already taking shape in his mind.

Rickover's campaign began when he received a request from Nichols, now a brigadier general and head of the Manhattan Project in its final days as an Army activity. Nichols wanted the new Atomic Energy Commission to have a position paper on the Navy's atomic-power interests. Rickover's four months at Oak Ridge had established him as the Navy's authority on nuclear power, at least as far as Nichols was concerned.

As Louis Roddis recalled those hectic days, the request from Nichols came just before Rickover was scheduled to have a hernia operation at the Bethesda Naval Hospital, in a Maryland suburb north of Washington. Rickover decided to write the report at the hospital. He brought Roddis with him to Bethesda. The operation was postponed, secretaries were borrowed from BuShips and the hospital, and Rickover and Roddis went to work.

Rickover prefaced the report with a detailed memorandum—"Nuclear Energy Propulsion for Naval Vessels"—which he sent to Mills. The memorandum first outlined the advantages of nuclear propulsion in ships and then listed the problems that had to be solved before the revolutionary power source could become a reality.

The report itself, which was signed by both Rickover and Roddis, took two days to write. The report, which went into more detail than the memo, also predicted that the first nuclear-propelled ship could be produced within five to eight years. The report added that in ten to sixteen years' time the Navy could produce nuclear-propelled warships of all major types. But much engineering work was required in that period, Rickover and Roddis predicted. The reactors produced during the war, mainly to manufacture material for weapons, had no weight or space constraints, which would be required for shipboard reactors, and new metals had to be found to operate in the very high-temperature environments of power reactors. Their report left little doubt that ship-propulsion plants were feasible. One hour after the report was completed, Rickover entered surgery for his operation.

When the report reached BuShips, forty minutes by car from Bethesda, there was surprise and concern. Mills formally sent the report to Nichols via the Chief of Naval Operations. Mills's covering letter said that the report had only been "hurriedly reviewed," but it was "a reasonable evaluation of the Navy's interest in nuclear-energy developments." In fact, the report was far more ambitious than most officers at BuShips who saw it were willing to concede was feasible. In his covering letter to Nichols, Mills reflected this concern and caution, noting that the report "represents the thinking of two individuals, and has definite limitations as such."

Still, the report went forward, raised eyebrows everywhere it was read, and in doing so opened the eyes of many more people to the possibilities for nuclear propulsion.

Once discharged from Bethesda, Rickover led his team to Schenectady to look over the GE efforts at developing a nuclear power plant for a destroyer-type ship—that is, a warship of about 3,500 tons or less. With the encouragement of Captain Burris, GE was making significant progress—more than at the ill-fated Daniels pile effort at Oak Ridge. Also, GE was studying the fascinating concept of a "breeder reactor," which produced fissionable material as well as power. The breeder reactor offered the promise of independence from future fuel worries.

Rickover apparently attempted to interest GE in developing a small reactor plant, one suitable for a destroyer escort, a warship of about 2,000 tons, or even a smaller plant for a submarine. Rickover, like several others before, realized that the most useful application of nuclear propulsion would be to submarines, to free them from their dependence on the oxygen of the earth's atmosphere for long periods of time. Also, submarines would be an efficient user of nuclear propulsion, providing higher speeds for a given horsepower because the submarine would not have to push through waves at the surface of the sea.

After their discussions with Rickover, GE looked at submarine-propulsion possibilities, leading to initiation of a series of GE submarine-reactor plants. (The destroyer escort concept was retained for "cover" purposes long after GE dropped that program.)

The encouraging progress that Rickover observed at GE at the end of 1946 was not of his doing. Coupled with Mumma's appointment at BuShips and the failure of the Daniels pile project, Rickover's future in nuclear propulsion continued to appear dim. Back at Oak Ridge, Rickover and his group had little to do. He and the others remained there as the AEC organized and sought to develop a national nuclear program. Rickover returned to Schenectady in the spring of 1947 to find GE emphasizing the breeder-reactor effort and downgrading the submarine-reactor effort. As an engineer, Rickover felt this meant that GE was being controlled by the scientific community rather than the engineering community. The latter would emphasize the practical—building a near-term reactor plant for shipboard use.

Three memos Rickover wrote in that frustrating summer of 1947 reflect his impatience with the Navy. The memos also provide an insight into what would become the Rickover technique of hammering at superiors and telling them what they did not want to hear. One officer who knew Rickover long and well once said, "He thinks like a communist—like Lenin." Perhaps Rickover recalled Lenin's admonition: "A reasonable strategy is to stick to the operation so long that the moral dissolution of the enemy makes a deadly strike possible."

On June 4 Rickover wrote to Mills about the future assignment of the Oak Ridge group. He began by telling Mills that he had taken charge of the group at the request of the Manhattan District, not the Navy. Mills probably knew better. Rickover also reviewed his efforts at training the men of his group. Each of them, he said, had been assigned a specialty in the broad field of nuclear power, and all of them had written on their specialites. He listed the titles of twenty-eight papers.

Then Rickover lectured Mills on the economics and politics of nuclear energy. He wrote, "Since there is no economic or other reason which would impel the electric-power industry to invest in the development of atomic power, and since the AEC has other immediate primary concerns [weapon development], it would appear that if we are to have atomic power plants in naval vessels the inspiration, the program and the drive must come from the navy itself.... When the navy will have a practical nuclear power plant depends almost entirely on the amount of effort expended."

He reiterated the problems that had to be solved, noted the lack of qualified engineers to do the solving—and pointed out how lucky the Navy was to have on hand five officers "probably as well trained a group ... as there is in this country today." The group "offers an opportunity for the navy to take the lead in developing atomic power."

He recommended that he and the other four officers be assigned to the AEC in Washington with additional duty at BuShips. "The Bureau would then be in a position," he wrote, "to effectively carry forward a development program with adequate liaison between the navy and the AEC and with such contractors as are working in the field.

"The possibilities offered by nuclear power plants in naval vessels, particularly in submarines, are so meaningful that we cannot afford to miss any opportunity which may further its progress. The five BuShips officers have been trained and have been operating as a team to exploit atomic power as rapidly as is possible."

Rickover got no encouragement about the preservation of his "team." But he did manage to maintain the image of a team by getting permission for his group to visit the nation's nuclear activities, to meet with any scientists who would talk to them. Such a review of the nuclear program and people could also perhaps identify what hopes existed for Navy nuclear propulsion. The tour was taken in the summer of 1947.

Along with the others he could contact, Rickover sought out Dr. Teller, one of the few senior nuclear physicists who continued to work for the government. The AEC had selected Teller as the first chairman of its Committee for Reactor Safeguards. In that role, he and his committee colleagues "attempted to help various groups working on reactors to share their knowledge," according to Teller.

When Rickover and the other four officers entered Teller's office on August 15, 1947, the physicist listened attentively while Rickover briefly and concisely told Teller why there should be a nuclear-submarine program, and why the Oak Ridge group had sufficient knowledge to direct such an effort. Then, for several hours, the naval officers and Teller continued in vigorous discussion.

Dr. Teller put a key question to Rickover: "What sort of official backing do you need for the atomic-submarine project in the Navy?" To this Rickover explained his views on how to move the Navy into the nuclear program.

When the Navy group left, Teller wrote a letter to Dr. Lawrence R. Hafstad, his close friend and the executive secretary of the Joint (Defense) Research and Development Board. Hafstad, who would soon become director of reactor development for the AEC, favored an accelerated program of reactor construction.

Teller's letter, dated August 19, 1947, was the strongest recommendation for nuclear ship propulsion yet presented by someone outside the Navy. Teller noted that he was "very much impressed" by Rickover and his four officers, and "by their enthusiasm and enterprise and also by their detailed knowledge which they picked up during their stay at Oak Ridge."

> I have the feeling [he wrote] that such people as these should thoroughly be made use of and that they should be encouraged to go ahead with an extensive program working toward tangible results within a short time. I do not know whether they can get a first model in working order in two years' time, but I think they should be encouraged to try. I think what they are trying to do has a very good chance of being feasible. . . . Our greatest shortage is that of capable men, and I don't think we can afford not to encourage a group of people like Captain Rickover and his friends.
>
> Perhaps I am over enthusiastic but I think that we have lots of good long-range plans—what we really lack is the push toward short-range objectives of which there was so much during the war, and of which there is so little now.

Despite Teller's interest expressed directly to Rickover and his letter to Hafstad, five days after the session with Teller, Rickover wrote to Admiral Mills that "it is significant that during our entire tour, of the many scientists contacted, not one was found who had a definite interest in and was working on the problem of furthering nuclear power." In his next long memo to Mills, Rickover also noted that the Navy and the Air Force were the "only logical customers for an atomic power plant." The Air Force, he said, had several projects under way, "but it is believed that the achievement of the goal will not come until long after the first successful nuclear pile for propulsion of a naval vessel. . . . It has already been pointed out that industry and science if left alone will not produce nuclear power rapidly since the driving force is not there." Rickover urged that his Oak Ridge team be established in the Bureau of Ships as the group that would be that driving force.

Rickover waited a week and, having received no response, wrote another memo to Mills. He repeated that "the impetus must come from the Navy itself" and that the Navy already had the people in Oak Ridge to develop nuclear power. If the "team" were disbanded, he wrote, "much of the ground which has been gained in the past year will be lost; the task of keeping abreast of nuclear-power developments will become difficult, and the potential help such as this group could be to other interested agencies of the Navy will not be fully realized."

He then recommended specific duty assignments. All five officers would work at the Bureau of Ships, with Rickover "in charge of nuclear matters as they pertain to ship propulsion" and the others concentrating on their specialties. The team would also have additional duty with the AEC and the Military Liaison Committee. He also foresaw the expansion of his team, for he suggested that "we should commence the education of additional officers as soon as possible." Significantly, Captain Rickover further recommended that none of the prospective trainees have a rank higher than lieutenant commander.

Mills did order Rickover and the others back to BuShips headquarters, in the temporary buildings facing Constitution Avenue. But the Oak Ridge group was no longer a group, and it was not directing the Navy's nuclear-propulsion program. Lou Roddis was assigned to Captain Mumma—who was in charge of the nuclear-propulsion effort; Ray Dick joined the metals section of BuShips; Miles Libbey was ordered to the Military Liaison Committee (between the Department of Defense and AEC); and Jim Dunford went to the military applications branch of the AEC.

The main question was what to do with Rickover. Some BuShips officers did not want Rickover in Washington at all. Apparently, orders were actually written at one point for Rickover to go to Oak Ridge to help declassify information on atomic matters. Admiral Mills, long Rickover's patron, was not prepared to establish Rickover as head of a nuclear-propulsion group, an action which would replace or be in conflict with Mumma's activities.

Support for Rickover then came from Rear Admiral Solberg. He had been on Groves's Tolman Committee, had organized the Navy's participation in the 1946 atomic-bomb tests at Bikini, and had served on the Military Liaison Committee since 1946. Solberg urged Mills to keep Rickover at BuShips and in nuclear work. Mills directed that Rickover become his special assistant for nuclear matters.

Rickover, having served his internship in the world of the atom, was now assigned to the Bureau of Ships and had an official assignment in the field of nuclear propulsion. He was now in a position to begin to build a nuclear submarine.

Building the Nautilus

Abelson, Bowen, Gunn, Mills, Rickover, Solberg, and many others in the Navy believed that nuclear propulsion was feasible for ships and possibly even for submarines. But approval to pursue a realistic nuclear-propulsion program, one that could result in the construction and operation of nuclear-propelled ships, had to come from the highest levels of the Navy, from the Secretary of the Navy and the Chief of Naval Operations.

Fleet Admiral Chester W. Nimitz, the wartime commander of United States forces in the Pacific, became Chief of Naval Operations in December 1945. Nimitz was a submariner, had specialized in diesel propulsion, and had been involved in submarine design as a junior officer, although he remained a line officer during his entire career.

Admiral Nimitz was immediately impressed by the promise of nuclear propulsion for the postwar Navy. However, Rear Admiral Parsons and others on the OPNAV staff believed that the Navy's primary efforts in atomic energy should go into weapons.* In general, they believed that the resources and knowledgeable people available to the Navy were too few to initially approach both nuclear weapons and nuclear propulsion, and that the Navy must enter the nuclear-weapons field if it was to compete with the Army Air Forces for major missions or, indeed, to even survive as a major military service in the postwar period.†

In the fall of 1946, Admiral Nimitz asked the Submarine Officers'

---

* OPNAV is the term for the Office of the Chief of Naval Operations, with specific staff functions being designated as OPs. From September 1945 to November 1946, the senior OPNAV office concerned with nuclear matters was the Deputy Chief of Naval Operations (Special Weapons) or OP-06; it was then designated Atomic Warfare Division (OP-36) until 1949, when it became the Atomic Energy Division (still OP-36). Parsons was the deputy of OP-06 and then head of OP-36 while simultaneously a member of the AEC Military Liaison Committee until May 1949. He then served as deputy chief of the Bureau of Ordnance from March 1952 until his sudden death on December 5, 1953.
† The U.S. Air Force was established as a separate service in September 1947.

Conference to address the subject of nuclear propulsion. The Conference was an almost monthly meeting of senior submarine officers and others involved in submarine-related matters in the Washington area. Dating back to 1926, the Conference was the CNO's principal advisory group on submarine matters, with many of its members having major submarine responsibilities. After the war the meetings were chaired by Rear Admiral C. W. Styer, the Assistant Chief of Naval Operations for operations and coordinator of undersea warfare (OP-31).

As a result of Nimitz's request, nuclear propulsion was discussed by the Submarine Officers' Conference in 1946 and in a major report completed on January 9, 1947, and given to Nimitz, the submariners noted:

> Present anti-submarine techniques and new developments in submarine design have rendered our present fleet submarines obsolete, offensively and defensively, to a greater degree than any other type [of warship]. The development of a true submarine capable of operating submerged for unlimited periods, appears to be probable within the next ten years, provided nuclear power is made available for submarine propulsion.

The report then recommended a multiphase program, including the construction of advanced conventionally propelled submarines pending the design and development of nuclear power plants. The Conference had already recommended that the Navy build eleven to thirteen submarines in the fiscal year 1948 program, the Navy's first postwar new construction effort. It was recommended that two of these have atomic propulsion and four to six others have conventional propulsion, but be suitable for later conversion to atomic propulsion. Thus, the Navy's senior submariners asked that half of the first postwar submarines have nuclear engines. They would be ready for service in the middle 1950s. The submariners identified the major requirements for applying nuclear propulsion to submarines as: (1) development of an operable power "pile" (reactor); (2) development of an effective and safe control system for releasing energy from the pile; (3) finding suitable fluids for transferring heat from the pile to propulsion engines; and (4) adapting the pile, with the necessary shielding, to shipboard installation.

Rickover had spoken at the Conference's meeting in November 1946, telling about the nuclear program—what there was of it. Rickover was highly enthusiastic about the possibility and promise of nuclear propulsion for submarines. A few naval officers were not so enthusiastic and urged caution. Vice Admiral Robert B. Carney, at the time Deputy Chief of Naval Operations for logistics, hoped for a worldwide ban on nuclear propulsion for warships, fearing that if the United States had them at a future time so would its enemies.

Significantly, it is difficult to find U.S. naval officers, especially submariners, who did not urge the development of nuclear ship propulsion, and the Submarine Officers' Conference report recommending to Nimitz that the Navy give high priority to "design and develop nuclear power plants for eventual installation in submarines to give unlimited submerged endurance at high speed" was approved by the CNO on the following day.

Still, Admiral Nimitz's actual future actions related to nuclear propulsion could not be predicted. Nimitz had been made CNO over the objections of Secretary of the Navy Forrestal (soon to be the first Secretary of Defense), and a compromise had been agreed to whereby Nimitz would serve only two years. He might not wish to commit his successor to the cost and technology risks of a nuclear propulsion program. Further, the establishment of the new Atomic Energy Commission on January 1 meant that the civilian side of the picture was not yet clear enough to support a ship-propulsion program.

The potential lack of direction for such a program was compounded in BuShips, where Vice Admiral Mills had several officers at different "desks" addressing the question. However, the seeds of future control of the program were planted early in the year, when Mills had Rickover and Roddis evaluate General Electric's nuclear-power plans for the coming year. Although they had originally been working on a destroyer-size plant, the GE engineers now felt that a reactor using liquid metal as the heat-exchange medium could be installed in a submarine. Liquid metals had a much higher efficiency than water as a heat exchanger, hence a smaller reactor plant could be developed for a specified horsepower.

Rickover reportedly liked the idea and sought to have Admiral Mills approve GE development of a test reactor using liquid metal for a destroyer escort and then, incorporating improvements that were deemed necessary, installing a modified liquid-metal plant in a submarine—possibly by the end of 1950! But Mills was simply not ready to commit BuShips to such a program, in part because of the OPNAV priorities for nuclear weapons and the disarray of the Atomic Energy Commission. Finally, in late July, Mills approved continuing research by GE (some of which would be funded by the AEC).

An alternative reactor concept, using pressurized water as coolant and heat exchanger, was also being pursued by the AEC at the Navy's urgings. This effort, being started at the Argonne National Laboratory near Chicago, had apparently been first proposed in April 1946 by Dr. Alvin M. Weinberg, who had also been at Oak Ridge when the Rickover group was there.

This was the situation in October 1947 when Rickover addressed an AEC-sponsored conference at the Clinton Laboratories at Oak Ridge. Rickover charged that the AEC was making too little progress on reactor development because too many physicists and not enough engineers were involved. He asked Robert Oppenheimer whether he had waited until all the facts were available when he built the atomic bomb. Unfortunately, from Rickover's point of view, Oppenheimer responded that he had had all the facts, but he admitted that it would probably not be possible to reach that point before building anything as complex as a power reactor. Rickover's arguments and demands helped lead to formation of an AEC reactor development group with emphasis on engineering. Subsequently, Mills himself addressed the reactor group, stressing the value of submarine nuclear propulsion.

Also in October, with Admiral Mills coming around to his point of view, Rickover and Ray Dick began to draft correspondence for Admiral Nimitz and Secretary of the Navy John L. Sullivan that would provide the needed top-level Navy approval for an all-out effort. Rickover made arrangements to short-circuit the normal, relatively slow procedures for such action. Two of the Navy's outstanding submariners came to Rickover's aid, Captain Elton W. Grenfell and Commander Edward L. Beach.

Grenfell, who had served with Rickover in the Bureau of Engineering in 1939-1940, had been a top-scoring submarine commander in World War II. He had sunk the first Japanese warship—another submarine—to be destroyed by American forces. Beach too had had distinguished submarine combat service in the war and, like Grenfell, was awarded the Navy Cross, second only to the Medal of Honor for heroism in wartime. Beach was better known to some Americans as a novelist, with his *Run Silent, Run Deep* acclaimed as the best war story about submarines written by an American.

In October 1947, when Rickover sought help from these submariners, Grenfell was in the office of the Assistant CNO for operations (OP-31), and Beach was the submarine officer assigned to the Atomic Energy Division (OP-36). Grenfell and Beach prepared a memo dated October 30, 1947, which was signed by Rear Admiral Styer (OP-31) and became the genesis of the Navy's nuclear-submarine program. On December 5, 1947—ten days before the end of his tenure as CNO—Admiral Nimitz forwarded the OP-31 memo to Secretary of the Navy Sullivan. The second paragraph of the secret memo stated: "The most secure means of carrying out an offensive submarine mission against an enemy is by the use of a *true* submarine, that is, one that can operate submerged for very long periods of time and is able to make high submerged speeds . . . it is important that the Navy initiate action with a view to prompt development, design, and construction of a nuclear powered submarine."

The Nimitz memo predicted that by the middle 1950s, when such a submarine could be completed, it would be possible for a submarine to launch a guided missile with a nuclear warhead to a range of about 500 miles. That weapon, already under development, was the Regulus guided or cruise missile.

Secretary Sullivan immediately responded, sending memos to Secretary of Defense Forrestal and the Defense Research Board, headed by Dr. Vannevar Bush, strongly endorsing the Nimitz letter. The board was a blue-ribbon assembly of prominent civilian scientists. Bush had been president of the Carnegie Institution in 1940 when President Roosevelt had asked him to head the National Defense Research Committee, wartime version of the subsequent Defense Research Board. In his wartime post Bush had been intimately involved with the Manhattan Project and had a deep personal commitment to nuclear power. Secretary Sullivan signed and sent the letters forward to Secretary of Defense Forrestal and the Defense Research Board.

On December 8, Sullivan also named BuShips as the Navy agency responsible for developing an atomic submarine, with the assistance of the newly established Office of Naval Research. This was all that Rickover had hoped for, and it had come more promptly than he had believed the bureaucracy could move. It also demonstrated that there were many within the Navy who fully supported the development of a nuclear submarine, a fact that would often be overlooked in future Rickover lore.

With this high-level backing, Rickover was able to take a strong stand in soliciting—and cajoling and badgering—various AEC laboratories to begin work on the nuclear-propulsion effort. Rickover, only a staff assistant to Admiral Mills, still had no direct authority. He and Roddis drafted a letter from Mills to the AEC stating that "the problems to be solved are so intimately connected with both the Atomic Energy Commission and the Navy that neither activity can make separate engineering decisions regarding them." The letter then proposed a single, working-level organization that would direct the project under the dual sponsorship of the AEC and the Navy. The proposal also suggested specific support by AEC laboratories. Mills signed the letter and sent it to the AEC on January 20, 1948.

The initial reaction from the key members and advisers of the AEC was less than enthusiastic. The main problem was simply the lack of AEC organization and goals. However, in January 1948, the AEC—only one year in existence—was faced with major problems in the reactor field. Among them were the increasing difficulties with the Soviet Union, leading to overwhelming interest in "breeder" reactors that could produce plutonium and other fissionable material for nuclear weapons. The AEC was also being pressured to allocate resources to developing nuclear-powered aircraft.

The AEC offered the Navy a counterproposal: naval officers would be assigned to work with the AEC staff and take back to the Navy specific recommendations for studies and development. At a formal meeting, an attempt was made to hammer out a mutually acceptable plan. The Navy participants in the Navy-AEC discussion were Vice Admiral Mills and Rear Admiral Solberg. Rickover's role was behind the scenes, prompting and advising, ably assisted by two members of his Oak Ridge group— Dunford, who was a member of the AEC staff, and Roddis in BuShips.

In the Navy-AEC meeting, Mills and Solberg agreed to the AEC's establishing the nuclear submarine as a formal program, with the Argonne National Laboratory near Chicago being responsible for the reactor design and the Navy participating in the design, engineering development and construction of the submarine. This was much less than Rickover had wanted.

As AEC historians Richard Hewlett and Francis Duncan observed, "Because Admiral Mills himself had negotiated the agreement with the Commission's staff, Rickover could not oppose it directly. Instead he chose what for him was an uncharacteristic strategy: inaction. He elected not to follow up the agreement to work out the details of the agreement with [Walter] Zinn," the head of the Argonne Laboratory, who had negotiated the broader agreement with Mills.

Argonne was unable to take the lead in so specialized a project as a submarine reactor. Mills, soon frustrated by the inactivity, accepted a recommendation by Rickover that Mills give a hard-hitting speech on the subject of nuclear submarines at an Undersea Warfare Symposium in Washington that April. The several hundred naval officers and civilians attending the symposium included Lewis L. Strauss and several other

AEC commissioners, with Strauss chairing the session. A banker by profession, Strauss had served in the Navy during World War II, subsequently becoming a member of the Interdepartmental Committee on Atomic Energy, and attaining the rank of rear admiral in the Naval Reserve. Strauss thus seemed predisposed to Mills's recounting of the Navy's interest in nuclear propulsion, which dated back to 1939.

Reading from his prepared speech, Mills became more and more critical. He attacked the Atomic Energy Commission for its failure to develop nuclear power, especially for the Navy. At one point in his speech the giant Mills turned to Strauss and said, pointedly, "Mind you, the Navy isn't griping, but we do want atomic power."

After Mills finished, Strauss, surprised at Mills's demands for AEC action, responded: "I never thought an old friend would do that to me."*

The AEC was in disarray, incapable of effectively organizing a submarine-reactor program. Rickover now had gained the full support and commitment of Admiral Mills, who had great personal prestige and directed the most powerful of the Navy's technical bureaus. Mills was now willing to go directly to industry to advance progress in nuclear propulsion. The AEC representatives dealing with the Navy approved such action, in part probably because of the Manhattan Project and AEC experience in using private industry and research institutions to operate nuclear facilities. The major Navy programs were the Westinghouse study of pressurized water as a reactor heat-transfer medium (Project Wizard) and the GE use of liquid sodium for heat transfer (Project Genie). In addition, the AEC was to begin a study at Argonne on the feasibility of gas for heat transfer. This parallel approach to the heat-exchange problem was similar to the technique used in the atomic-bomb development and appeared necessary for the submarine-propulsion effort.

Despite the agreements with the AEC and the allocation of research, the Navy felt that the AEC was not moving fast enough or organizing to carry out the effort. Again, part of the problem was the high priority of nuclear weapons, which took most the the AEC's attention, and the desire to develop a balanced nuclear-research program.

Again, frustrated, Admiral Mills sought and obtained a formal meeting with the AEC commissioners on June 16, 1948. Mills was ably backed up by Captain Grenfell and Rear Admiral Charles B. Momsen, the Assistant CNO for undersea warfare (OP-31). Momsen and Grenfell

---

* *Strauss served as one of the five AEC commissioners from 1946 to 1950, when he resigned after gaining President Truman's support for the hydrogen bomb. He subsequently returned to the AEC as chairman from 1953 to 1958.*

stressed the need for high-capability submarines to counter the predicted increases in quality and quantity of Soviet submarines. Naval Intelligence estimated that the Soviet Navy could be building a fleet of modern submarines to sever the United States from Europe. If the Soviets attained the maximum German wartime production rate of twenty-five submarines per month, the Soviet submarine fleet could reach a thousand undersea craft in just over three years. Naval Intelligence estimated that such a number of submarines could be produced.

The submariners with Admiral Mills stressed the need for nuclear propulsion in submarines to help redress the predicted imbalance between U.S. anti-submarine forces and the Soviet submarine fleet. Then, addressing the issues at hand, Mills argued for specific AEC commitments to develop a submarine power plant. The session had the result of making the AEC leaders personally aware of the Navy's situation.

A month after these meetings, on July 16, 1948, Mills appointed Rickover as the BuShips liaison to the AEC. According to Hewlett and Duncan, the failure of the AEC to respond to Navy proposals had convinced Mills "that the task needed the kind of hard-headed, even ruthless, direction which he knew Rickover would give it."

"But," continued the AEC historians, "the decision was not an easy one for Mills. Some of the qualities which Rickover would bring to the job troubled Mills and many of his fellow officers in the Bureau. Rickover flouted Navy tradition and ridiculed a system that seemed to him to give more weight to an officer's social accomplishments and willingness to conform than to his practical ability and industry. Mills could guess that once he gave Rickover a free hand, he would outwork, outmaneuver, and outfight the Commission, its laboratories and the Navy. He would threaten, cajole, and even insult those who stood in his way. In the process he would no doubt embarrass Mills and the Navy, but Mills was ready to do what the situation demanded. He wrote [AEC Chairman David] Lilienthal that Rickover would be his liaison with the Commission's headquarters."

This action by Admiral Mills put Rickover at the helm of the Navy's nuclear-propulsion program. Technically, Captain Albert Mumma and Captain Armand Morgan were responsible for nuclear matters within BuShips. Admiral Mills corrected this situation on August 4 with his establishment of a Nuclear Power Branch within the research division of BuShips.*

---

* For organizational purposes, branches within BuShips were designated by "codes." The Nuclear Power Branch was first designated as Code 390. Later, because of reorganizations, the code number would change—primarily to 1500 and later to 08.

This move gave Rickover a considerable degree of freedom, and he rapidly began to reassemble his Oak Ridge group in the branch.

Rickover immediately drafted correspondence for Mills and Secretary Sullivan to Secretary of Defense Forrestal protesting what Rickover saw as AEC inaction. Again demonstrating the Navy's interest in nuclear propulsion, the documents were pushed through the Navy hierarchy in just two days. The Navy offensive led to a series of Rickover-AEC staff meetings, with some progress being made. At the same time, Rickover was clarifying the participation of GE and Westinghouse in the development of nuclear reactors.

The AEC belatedly established a Division of Reactor Development in January 1949 under Hafstad, who was suggested to the Commission by Mills himself. Hafstad, who would head the division from 1949 until 1955, immediately accepted the Navy's Nuclear Power Branch as his own Naval Reactors Branch. Rickover was thus effectively "double hatted" in both the AEC and the Navy. This dual-agency situation was ideal for Rickover, permitting him immediate and direct access to both organizations, while he could take advantage of either agency's letterhead to bring pressure on the other. Further, Rickover had access to both AEC and Navy field activities (laboratories and shipyards) and their industrial contractors. Immediately a Navy team was set up at Argonne. The members included several civilians from BuShips and one officer for temporary assignment, Lieutenant Commander Eugene P. Wilkinson, a submariner but not a Naval Academy graduate.

Rickover mobilized the Argonne Laboratory and the new Westinghouse-operated AEC Bettis laboratory at West Mifflin, Pennsylvania, to develop a pressurized-water reactor; the heat-transfer feasibility of a gas-cooled reactor using helium was assigned to Allis Chalmers; and both Argonne and the GE Knolls Laboratory at Schenectady (Project Genie) were working on sodium as a liquid-metal heat-exchange medium.

By the spring of 1949 it became evident that the pressurized-water reactor design offered the highest probability of success, and Westinghouse and Argonne were given the task of developing the "Mark I" reactor plant. This would be a full-scale prototype, constructed on dry land, to demonstrate the feasibility of the concept, to "work out bugs" before it went to sea, and to serve as a training facility. This Mark I Submarine Thermal Reactor (STR) would be constructed in the remote Idaho desert, at the newly established AEC reactor test station near the town of Arco.

Rickover was also able to turn the primary General Electric effort from a breeder reactor to development of a sodium-cooled submarine reactor. This would be developed by GE and the AEC Knolls Laboratory, which GE operated. Subsequently, the decision was reached to construct the prototype Mark A sodium-cooled Submarine Intermediate Reactor (SIR) at West Milton, New York.

The parallel development of "intermediate" and "thermal" reactors would provide a backup plant, if either proved unsuccessful, and would allow for both a conventional and a highly advanced approach to reactor development. In the submarine plant, the pressurized-water, or thermal, reactor serves as a boiler, producing heat without the need for oxygen. The reactor uses water flushed through the reactor to moderate or slow down the neutrons created in fission. The water is also used as a coolant for the plant, absorbing the reactor heat as it goes through the fuel core, and carrying that heat to the steam generator.

The steam generator is a shell-and-tube heat exchanger. The primary (reactor) coolant flows through the tubes to heat the secondary (boiler) water surrounding the tubes. This form of heat exchanger keeps the radioactive primary coolant separate from the boiling water that produces steam for use in the turbine engine that turns the propeller shaft.

The primary coolant is kept under high pressure—about 2,000 pounds per square inch—and at a temperature of some 475 degrees F. (not high enough to boil under pressure). Within the steam generator, this primary coolant heats the boiler water to steam at about 400 degrees F.

The rationale for pursuing the alternative, the sodium-cooled intermediate reactor, began with General Electric's interests in a breeder reactor that would produce more fissionable material than it consumed. As a submarine plant, the sodium intermediate reactor could be more efficient and simpler than the pressurized-water reactor. For example, the sodium, which serves only as a primary coolant and not as a moderator, needs to be kept under pressure of only about 75 pounds per square inch. However, the heat-absorbing qualities of sodium result in the primary coolant reaching a temperature of some 850 degrees F. as it flows through the reactor's fuel core. Then, in the heat exchanger, the boiler water is heated to just over 600 degrees F. Thus, a much more efficient steam-producing system is possible without the problems of a very-high-pressure primary coolant. But as would be demonstrated, liquid sodium is highly corrosive.

When Admiral Mills retired from the Navy, at his own request, on March 1, 1949, Rickover was running the Navy's nuclear-propulsion program. Mumma and Morgan, Rickover's chief rivals within BuShips in the nuclear-power field, had been disarmed by Mills (although Mumma would continue to advance, becoming the Chief of BuShips in 1955). The only real rival to Rickover as head of the nuclear-propulsion program had been Rear Admiral Solberg, a friend and colleague of Mills, whose experience in nuclear matters dated back to the Tolman Committee. Solberg was a member of the AEC Military Liaison Committee from November 1946 until June 1948, when he became Chief of Naval Research. As such, he was removed from consideration for directing the nuclear program.

Rickover's relations with Hafstad, head of AEC reactor development, while not always cordial, were effective. Possibly as significant, there were many former naval officers, several of them Academy graduates, at Westinghouse and GE, as well as on the professional staff of the Atomic Energy Commission itself, at all levels. Through these people, on whom he could impress the urgency of his submarine-reactor program, and with men from his own Naval Reactors Branch assigned to both the contractors and laboratories, Rickover established candid and immediate sources of information, and close control over the entire program.

At the same time, Rickover's office—NRB as it came to be known—grew, and with the growth came guidance and direction for the program. Numerous technical handbooks and reports issued forth, with NRB publications becoming the standard works in their field. These, coupled with the training programs that Rickover instituted at various facilities, also meant that he was establishing the basis for the nation's civilian and military reactor development.

Meanwhile, the submarine community itself was pushing for approval of the actual submarines which would be nuclear-propelled. Ship requirements originated in the Office of the Chief of Naval Operations and not in the technical bureaus. Admiral Louis Denfeld, who had succeeded Nimitz as CNO in December 1947,* and who would soon be "fired" by President Truman in the carrier–versus–B-36 controversy, in March of 1949 had directed the Submarine Officers' Conference to review submarine opportunities and requirements. Rickover, among others, briefed the submariners, and their report was highly favorable. The Conference recommended that "the Navy very strongly support the early development of a nuclear propelled submarine for evaluation purposes."

With Rickover's help, the OPNAV staff converted the Submarine Officers' Conference recommendations into a memorandum for Admiral

*See Appendix E for a listing of senior Navy and Department of Defense officials.

Denfeld. Signed on August 19, 1949, the document called for a nuclear-propulsion plant to be ready for installation in a submarine by 1955. Preliminary design and development by both BuShips and the shipyards that would build the submarines had to begin at once for inclusion of the actual submarines in the fiscal year 1952 shipbuilding program, then under discussion. Further, with parallel Westinghouse SIR reactor and General Electric STR reactor efforts, two nuclear submarines would initially be built.

Early selection of the shipyards was necessary for fabrication of the submarine sections of the land prototypes for the reactors, and for the yards to undertake the necessary preparations, including developing the detailed drawings and plans. The two leading submarine-building yards in the nation were the Portsmouth Naval Shipyard, on an island in the Piscataqua River between Maine and New Hampshire, and the Electric Boat Company on the Thames River in Groton, Connecticut.* After World War II the few orders for new submarines were divided between the two yards. Rickover approached Electric Boat to construct the submarine for General Electric's Sodium-cooled Intermediate Reactor (SIR) plant. On December 6, 1949, Rickover discussed the project with O. Pomery Robinson, general manager of EB, and Andrew I. McKee, the firm's chief design engineer. Robinson had started with the firm as a boy in 1915, and, except for a four-year break, had been with the company ever since, becoming general manager on the eve of the massive World War II submarine-building effort. McKee had served as officer in charge of submarine design at the Bureau of Ships during the 1930s and the design superintendent at the Portsmouth Navy Yard from 1938 to 1945. Men with the experience and intelligence of Robinson and McKee had made EB the nation's most competent submarine yard.

The few new submarines being built and the obvious potential of nuclear submarines led Robinson and McKee to immediately accept Rickover's proposal that the firm build one of the atomic subs. A week later, Rickover and representatives of General Electric visited the EB yard, beginning a mutual education process that would lead to EB's construction of both the "hull" for the land sodium-cooled SIR reactor plant and the actual SIR-propelled submarine.

Next, on January 12, 1950, Rickover went to the Portsmouth yard with the intention of teaming it with the Argonne Laboratory and Westinghouse for the water-cooled STR submarine project. Rickover is said

* In 1952 the firm became the Electric Boat Division of the General Dynamics Corporation.

to have demanded that the shipyard personnel assigned to the nuclear submarine project report directly to him as well as through their normal chain of command. But the Portsmouth commander balked. Portsmouth was the lead yard for the new *Tang*-class diesel submarines and was involved heavily in the GUPPY program to modernize war-built submarines. Shipyard officers told Rickover that they could give little attention to his demands for a priority nuclear-submarine effort.

The story is told that without hesitation Rickover reached across the desk of the shipyard commander, Rear Admiral R. E. McShane, and placed a call to Robinson at Electric Boat. Robinson immediately informed Rickover that his yard would be able to construct both of the planned nuclear submarines.

The incident, which would assure EB's role as the nation's principal nuclear-submarine yard, was an advantage for Rickover, because the civilian yard had more flexibility than a government yard enmeshed in the Navy bureaucracy. Also, there could be some benefits in having both submarines constructed in one shipyard.

That same evening, January 12, Rickover and two of his staff arrived at Robinson's home and began detailed planning of the effort. Westinghouse and General Electric would be fully responsible for the design and construction of the reactor plants. Electric Boat, under subcontracts to each of those firms, was to assist in design—to make certain the reactor plants would fit in the submarines—and construct the hull portions of the respective land reactor plants.

The next step would be to obtain Congressional funding of the submarines themselves. In January 1950, Rickover's office prepared a memorandum for Rear Admiral David Clark, the Chief of BuShips, to the Chief of Naval Operations, Admiral Forrest P. Sherman, who had replaced the fired Denfeld two months earlier. At the same time, Rickover initiated his now-famous end-run tactic of going directly to the Congress to gain support for his program.

On February 9, 1950, Rickover appeared as the sole witness before the subcommittee on reactor development of the powerful Joint Committee on Atomic Energy. In this, his first official appearance before the Joint Committee, Rickover impressively described the advantages that nuclear-propelled submarines would have over the Soviet Union's increasing submarine force. The Congressmen, surprised by and concerned over the first Soviet nuclear explosion five months earlier, were receptive to Rickover's urging for a high-priority nuclear-submarine program.

Shifting back to the Navy system, on March 28, Rickover testified before the Navy's General Board, mostly captains and rear admirals who collectively served as the principal advisory group to the Secretary of the Navy and the Chief of Naval Operations. The General Board was soon to be abolished, having never recovered from its downgrading by Admiral King, the wartime Chief of Naval Operations. But in 1950 it still had considerable prestige and some influence.

Rickover was called into the secret General Board session only after other officers representing BuShips and OPNAV were unable to answer specific questions about costs of the first nuclear submarine. The austere defense budgets of the period had severely limited new ship construction, and a key issue was how much of the cost of a nuclear attack submarine would be paid for by the Atomic Energy Commission. The four postwar shipbuilding budgets had averaged only four ships per year, and an aircraft carrier, which would have been the largest and most costly warship yet built, had been canceled by President Truman a few days after being started.

In discussing the funding of a nuclear attack submarine in the fiscal year 1952 budget, Rickover was careful to speak as a representative of the Atomic Energy Commission. He explained that up to 1950 the Atomic Energy Commission had spent about $15 million for nuclear propulsion, and the Navy abut $10 million. He estimated that another $32 million— most of it AEC funds—would be spent through mid-1952. Those funds, he said, were for research and engineering, and they would not include the construction of either the reactor land prototypes or the submarines themselves. The construction cost to the Navy for the first atomic submarine was estimated at $40 million plus the reactor's cost, compared to about $20 million for each conventional submarine of the new *Tang* class. (The final *Navy* cost for the first nuclear submarine would be $65 million.)

"The Atomic Energy Commission, due to frequent pressure on them, has given this reactor the highest priority," Rickover continued. "The Navy will have to say, 'We are sorry. We don't have the submarine to put it in.' " A month after Rickover's testimony, the members of the General Board endorsed construction of the first nuclear submarine; their recommendation meant that it would be included in the proposed Navy shipbuilding program for fiscal year 1952. The Board also directed that the submarine have torpedo tubes, thus ending speculation that the first nuclear submarine might be an unarmed propulsion-test craft. If built without torpedo tubes, the submarine would require a later, costly conversion to provide weapons, or would force a delay until a combat nuclear-propelled submarine could be approved and constructed.

Late in April, Admiral Sherman formally proposed the fiscal 1952 shipbuilding program to Congress. It included one SS(N)—submarine, nuclear propulsion.

Meanwhile, at the National Reactor Test Station, near the town of Arco in the Idaho desert, ground was broken for the prototype pressurized-water STR reactor plant. Normally, engineers built a prototype in a spread-out, or "breadboard," manner to facilitate watching how equipment works and making changes. If that prototype works, then the next step would be the building of another in the compact shape required for the factory, aircraft or ship.

Rickover, a submariner as well as engineer, fully understood the constraints of a submarine hull as well as the time delays in changing complex "breadboard" systems from prototypes to operational hardware. He insisted that the Mark I reactor be both an engineering prototype and a shipboard prototype, completely sized to fit in a submarine's hull. This approach would cost engineers some flexibility, but with it Rickover could speed up the development schedule. So certain was Rickover of his approach that by late 1949 he had predicted the date when the first nuclear submarine could be ready to get underway: January 1, 1955. His prediction turned out to be remarkably accurate.

This shortcut—which Rickover described in the catch phrase "Mark I equals Mark II"—was a major factor in the rapid development of the nuclear submarine. The Navy, including many officers who believed that Rickover had usurped their prerogatives, closed ranks and moved cooperatively to help to keep that schedule, as did the AEC's Argonne Laboratory, Westinghouse, Electric Boat, and scores of smaller firms. At the head of this impressive team stood Captain H. G. Rickover.

The Mark I submarine plant at Arco began as a wood-and-cardboard mock-up containing dummies of every pipe, valve, switch, and other component. Electric Boat assembled this mock-up at Groton yard and, according to official AEC history, it "held a special fascination for Rickover. During visits to Groton he would climb through the simulated compartments in the drab shedlike structure . . . studying the configuration from several angles to make certain that there was enough space for men to maintain and replace equipment at sea and to make sure that a valve handle would not project dangerously into the walkway."

The Navy had long used scale models in ship construction. The full-scale mock-up that Rickover insisted upon further speeded up the project and helped to assure success. Meanwhile, for the more complex sodium-cooled STR reactor, General Electric's Bettis Laboratory produced a full-scale model of the plant, missing only the radioactive core. This model permitted realistic work on the sodium-handling problem, and parts of it were later installed in the Mark A, the sodium-cooled land-prototype reactor.

Slowly the Mark I water-cooled reactor plant took shape at Arco. An actual steel section of a submarine hull was constructed and fitted with the STR reactor plant, including the steam generator and a submarine turbine. A sea tank was constructed around the hull section. The tank, about fifty feet in diameter and almost forty feet high, held some 385,000 gallons of water. With this arrangement, tests with the reactor compartment at sea could be simulated.

Meanwhile, the *Nautilus*—the actual submarine that would have the Mark II reactor plant—was started at the Electric Boat yard. President Truman spoke at the June 14 keel-laying ceremony. He sought to place the *Nautilus* in historical perspective, stating:

> As we celebrate this Flag Day, it marks one of the most significant developments of our time.
>
> We are assembled here to lay the keel of a Navy submarine, the U.S.S. *Nautilus*. This ship will be something new in the world. She will be atomic powered. Her engines will not burn oil or coal. The heat in her boilers will be created by the same source that heats the sun—energy released by atomic fission, the breaking apart of the basic matter of the whole universe. . . .
>
> The day that the propellers of this new submarine first bite into the water to drive her forward, will be the most momentous day in the field of atomic science since the first flash of light in the desert seven years ago [when the first atomic bomb was exploded at Alamogordo].

These were strong words, but that was the Truman style. After the President finished his remarks, Gordon Dean, Chairman of the Atomic Energy Commission, made a brief speech. Dean said, "There are many persons who have played a role in the events which have led to this ceremony, but if one were to be singled out for special notice, such an honor should go to Captain H. G. Rickover, whose talents we share with the Bureau of Ships and whose energy, drive, and technical competence have played such a large part in making this project possible." Rickover, in civilian clothes, stood nearby, as did his wife, Ruth, and their twelve-year-old son, Robert.

Then, as the *Nautilus'* keel plate was placed on the building way by a large overhead crane, President Truman declared the keel of the world's first atomic ship to be "well and truly laid," and his initials were welded into the steel plate. As the crowd dispersed, Electric Boat workers went to work on the *Nautilus*.

Work also rushed ahead two thousand miles away in the Idaho desert, where the Mark I reactor plant was being built. In late March of 1953 the STR reactor control rods were slowly raised out of the core. These rods absorbed neutrons, preventing them from splitting uranium atoms and causing a chain reaction. As the rods were raised, there were periodic shutdowns, or "scrams,"* as the reactor's sensitive instruments detected possible problems and automatically dropped the rods back into the core. The engineers and scientists would carefully check to determine whether there was a real problem or an adjustment was needed in the controls. Criticality could be started or stopped by a difference of only one or two inches in the distance that a control rod was inserted or withdrawn.

At 11:17 P.M. (local time) on March 30, 1953, the STR Mark I reactor attained sustained criticality. The reactor worked.

Slowly and carefully during the next few weeks, the reactor was checked and tested, and minor modifications were made. Two months after the initial start-up, Rickover flew to Arco from Washington with Thomas E. Murray, the first engineer to serve as a member of the Atomic Energy Commission and the commissioner with whom Rickover developed the closest rapport.

On May 31, 1953, Rickover, ever the politician, showed Murray the throttle and, as he opened it, the reactor plant fed steam to the main propulsion turbine for the first time. More tests followed. The number of safety circuits was reduced; there were too many and they were too sensitive. A man clumping past would scram the reactor.

Full power was achieved for the first time with the Mark I on June 25. Everything worked perfectly. The Westinghouse engineers began a forty-eight-hour, full-power run, primarily to obtain nuclear-physics

---

* *The word dated to the earliest days of reactor development when controls were so crude that engineers joked about the only solution to a runaway reactor: Everybody should scram. Later, in the acronym era, nuclear-power trainees were told that in the first reactor, the Fermi pile outside Chicago, control rods were suspended by rope from the ceiling. A man with an ax stood ready to cut the ropes if the reactor went super critical. According to the story, he was the SCRAM—the "Super-Critical Reactor Ax Man."*

data. After twenty-four hours at full power the engineers decided that sufficient data had been collected, and preparations were made to shut down the plant. When Rickover heard of the decision he immediately overruled it. He directed that the plant be kept wide open. Rickover reasoned that if the plant could simulate a submerged submarine's full-power run across the Atlantic Ocean it would convince all doubters and skeptics.

Lieutenant Commander Edwin E. Kintner, in charge of the Mark I plant, objected strenuously. He later recalled: "I felt that extension of the run was unwise considering the many uncertainties, and told Rickover that beyond forty-eight hours I could not accept responsibility for the safety of the $30,000,000 prototype." Rickover ordered the throttle kept open.

Charts were put on the wall of the reactor control room, and a great-circle route was plotted from Nova Scotia to Ireland. The Navy men at the Mark I for training began regular four-hour shipboard watches. Tension increased as the turbine's whirring monotone filled the building. Each watch tried to outdo the previous ones, pushing the mark on the charts farther and farther across the Atlantic. The hours clicked off as the very real reactor plant drove the imaginary submarine eastward at top speed. Never before had an actual submarine traveled so far—underwater or on the surface—at full power. As Rickover would often point out, surface ships need maintain full power for only four hours to be accepted by the U.S. Navy.

The Mark I plant reached the two-day mark without problems. But at sixty hours carbon dust from the brushes in the electric generators caused instruments to become erratic. Then one of the pumps that forced water between the uranium fuel rods in the core began to whine. Without the flow of water to carry away heat the reactor would burn up. Was "crud" collecting, despite the use of highly purified water, and clogging the pump? Or was radioactivity corroding metals within the reactor and clogging the pump? The pump began to work smoothly again.

A few hours later a tube in the main steam condenser failed. Steam pressure dropped. The Westinghouse technicians recommended an immediate halt to the run. The Navy personnel also urged a halt. Rickover was undaunted. He gambled and won. Twice the plant had to be throttled back to half power, and once to two-thirds power, but it was never stopped.

At the end of ninety-six hours the line on the charts reached Ireland. In theory, the Mark I plant had driven a submarine some 2,500 miles across the Atlantic at an average speed of 26 knots without stopping or refueling.

After the Mark I had cooled down and could be inspected, no "crud" was found nor was there any defect or damage that could not be corrected with minor improvements. This did not mean, however, that the Mark I plant was trouble-free. A short time later Rickover reported, "We still have a lot of trouble. It would be far-fetched for me to say we are not having many difficulties at Arco." He continued, "We are having trouble with valves and with controls, but we are solving every one of them, and as fast as we learn anything that needs modification, we are incorporating it into the *Nautilus*."

This Rickover achievement in late June 1953 came as debate was raging in Washington over his second "pass-over" for promotion to rear admiral by a Navy selection board. Word of the Mark I success was flashed back to Washington. Secretary of the Navy Robert B. Anderson directed that a special board be convened to select one engineering duty captain experienced and qualified in the nuclear field for the rank of rear admiral. On July 1, 1953, Rickover was selected and donned the two-star shoulder boards of a rear admiral.

He was quickly immersed in still another controversy. The first naval officers assigned to nuclear propulsion at the working level were those in his Naval Reactor Branch, whom Rickover had selected himself. Those men and their successors naturally became the men who ran the Mark I and would later be assigned to the *Nautilus*. But who would command the revolutionary submarine? Many Navy men favored Commander Ned Beach, an early supporter of Rickover, to command the *Nautilus*. Beach had been second in his Academy class, was a highly decorated sub-mariner, and in January 1953 had become naval aide to President Eisenhower.

The man Rickover nominated to skipper the *Nautilus* was Commander Eugene P. Wilkinson. He was not an Academy man; he had graduated from the University of Southern California. He had taught high-school mathematics and chemistry before entering the Navy. He had served in submarines during World War II. In the late 1940s he had joined Rickover in NRB and worked at various Navy-AEC activities. He returned to sea from 1951 to 1953 to command one of the new *Tang*-class submarines, a highly prized assignment.

Beach gave his support to Wilkinson and, with Rickover's hard-line on the matter, in August 1953, thirty-five-year-old Wilkinson was named prospective commanding officer of the world's first nuclear submarine.

Wilkinson was an excellent choice to command the *Nautilus* for many reasons. But perhaps most significantly, his selection left little doubt that Rickover, who was already choosing the key enlisted men and junior officers for nuclear submarines, would also choose their commanding officers. That had long been the prerogative of the Chief of Naval Personnel.

Meanwhile, work continued on the *Nautilus* at Electric Boat. Overall supervision of the *Nautilus'* design and construction was vested in various branches of the Bureau of Ships. To be sure, Rickover maintained complete and absolute control and direction of the submarine's reactor and propulsion machinery, and all personnel selection and training related to the nuclear portions of the ship. However, he had neither the organization nor the time to become involved deeply in other aspects of the *Nautilus'* construction. But because of his special relations with Electric Boat, and because only he could discuss propulsion, shielding requirements, and many other matters that affected aspects of the submarine, he became involved in the design and construction procedures for virtually all of the *Nautilus*.

In September 1953, on a building way adjacent to where the *Nautilus* was being built at Electric Boat, the keel was laid down for the second nuclear-propelled submarine, the *Seawolf*. There, on the bank of the Thames River, the world's first two nuclear submarines were being built. They were frequently visited by Rickover, who considered them merely the harbinger of his nuclear navy.

8 | The True Submersible

"A larger boat [more than three hundred feet long] will never be feasible unless we discover some better system of storing electricity than exists today—a contingency which is exceedingly doubtful, . . ." declared John P. Holland in 1900. Holland, an Irish-born schoolteacher, had planned several submarines, originally for use against the British rulers of his homeland. He came to the United States in 1873 and continued his efforts, building several experimental submarines. In April of 1900 the U.S. Navy formally accepted its first submarine, and subsequently named the fifty-foot craft *Holland* to honor its builder.

Fifty-four years later the successor to the John P. Holland Torpedo Boat Company, the Electric Boat shipyard, launched the U.S.S. *Nautilus*. This latest submarine was 320 feet long and, as Holland had predicted, her propulsion was a "better system"—nuclear propulsion.

Heavy fog rolled along the Thames River and swathed the *Nautilus* on the morning of January 21, 1954. But just before the launching ceremonies began, the fog lifted and the sun beamed down on the First Lady, Mamie Eisenhower, the assembled VIPs, and the 12,000 spectators crowded in the shipyard and along the river. They would witness not only the launching of a historic ship but also the launching of an era.

Chief of Naval Operations Admiral Robert B. Carney said in his speech that the fleet was "hungry to put [the *Nautilus*] to work," and that he looked beyond the *Nautilus*, "marvelous a product as she is," to "succeeding generations of atomic-powered submarines and surface ships powered by nuclear fission."

The CNO credited the teamwork of men in science, industry, labor and government with the conception and building of the submarine. He mentioned only one man by name, newly promoted Rear Admiral Hyman G. Rickover. The other major speaker, AEC chairman Lewis L. Strauss, also cited Rickover by name.

Rickover was on the speakers' platform but said nothing. He was in uniform, for the first time in the memory of some of those assembled on the platform.

Then, speeches finished, Mrs. Eisenhower stood ready to christen the submarine. A workman on a nearby catwalk shouted, "Hit it good and hard, Mrs. Eisenhower." Mamie smiled and got a good grip on the traditional bottle of champagne. Captain Ned Beach, President Eisenhower's naval aide, signaled "all clear," and at 10:57 A.M. she yelled, "I christen thee *Nautilus,*" and swung. The submarine easily slid down the building ways into the Thames River. On the deck of the unfinished submarine stood Commander Eugene Wilkinson and several of his crew, at attention, saluting smartly. Representative W. Sterling Cole, chairman of the Joint Committee on Atomic Energy, also was on board to demonstrate Congressional support for the *Nautilus.*

The launching ceremonies over, tugs nudged the *Nautilus* alongside a pier at EB, and while the VIPs went off to luncheon, workmen continued construction of the submarine.

As the *Nautilus* was being completed at Electric Boat, Rickover's organization was going through a generational crisis. Of the four officers who had started with Rickover at Oak Ridge, only two were still with him in the Naval Reactors Branch—Louis Roddis and James Dunford, who with Ned Beach had held the top three spots in the Naval Academy Class of 1939. Miles Libbey had left the Navy; Ray Dick, the brilliant reserve officer, who had been a metallurgist and frogman before entering the nuclear program, had died in January 1953.

A new generation of engineers was coming into the Naval Reactors Branch. Most were young naval officers, just out of graduate school. There were also a few experienced men who had seen war service, among them Joseph Barker, Willis Barnes, John Crawford, John Hinchey, Theodore Iltis, Edwin Kintner, David Leighton, Sherman Naymark, Robert V. Laney, Eli Roth, Milton Shaw and William Wegner. One officer, Vincent Lascara, was a supply specialist. He went on to become a vice admiral, the only officer, with the exception of Rickover, who had a long tour of duty—not for training—in NRB (from April 1953 to September 1960) and went on to attain flag rank.

Rickover wanted the officers he selected to stay in NRB for indefinite periods, regardless of the Navy's officer-rotation policy. Whereas the Navy's intent was to give officers a variety and breadth of experience that would qualify them for more and more responsible billets, Rickover was building a retinue of people with long tenure in his own service, dependent on him, but increasingly competent, as his power increased, to do battle themselves with the "transient management" of the rest of the Navy.

One of the first officers to run head on into this policy was Eli Roth. Like Beach, Roddis and Dunford, then-Commander Roth had been a top member of the Class of 1939. Following graduation and through nearly all of World War II he had served in surface warships, run convoys in the North Atlantic, and commanded a destroyer escort in combat, for which he received two personal awards and his ship a Presidential Unit Citation. Before the war he had considered becoming an engineering-duty officer. After the war he attended postgraduate engineering school and went to work for Rickover in 1948. In early 1951, while in NRB, he joined the EDO ranks. Except as part of a ship's company during outfitting or overhaul, he had never had any shipyard experience.

While in the Naval Reactors Branch, first at Argonne and later in Washington, Roth helped to affect some of the technical innovations that created the *Nautilus* reactor plant. He worked on two major technical problems: the development and manufacture of zirconium for the *Nautilus'* reactor fuel core and the transfer of heat from the reactor to the submarine's propulsion system.

On July 27, 1953, not quite a month after the keel laying of the *Nautilus*, Rickover signed a memo assigning himself, Roth, and Roddis, and several other NRB staffers to the "PWR Project." The PWR (pressurized-water reactor) had been under development for use in what was expected to be the world's first nuclear aircraft carrier; the reactor was later designated the CVR, and Roth was made project officer for the reactor.

Roth had had a proprietary interest in the PWR. Even before his assignment to the CVR, in several hectic weeks of traveling, interviewing and report-writing, he had put together the basic document that showed how a slightly enriched light-water-cooled reactor—a PWR—would be the best type of reactor for carrier propulsion. When the PWR evolved from the CVR program, Roth was named its project officer by Lawrence R. Hafstad, chief of the AEC's Division of Reactor Development, with Rickover's concurrence. But a political battle over the PWR erupted when the Department of Defense, in one of its recurrent economy drives, said it would not support a nuclear carrier. (See Chapter 28.) When the political struggle was resolved in the late fall of 1953, the reactor was destined to end up as a civilian power station, not in a warship, and while Roth felt that such a use might be important for nuclear power, he was a naval officer and did not want to be sidetracked into a civilian assignment.

Roth's commitment to nuclear power was indisputable. He endorsed its use for naval ship propulsion and its civilian potential in an article he wrote for the Naval Institute *Proceedings* in 1953. Because at that time description of the NRB program would have been a breach of security, Rickover's name did not appear in the article. When Roth showed the article draft to Rickover for comment, the Admiral grumbled, "Now *you'll* be the expert."

On October 22, 1953, the AEC announced that the first civilian nuclear plant would be built under Rickover's direction, using a design "inherited from a naval project." With the civilian designation now official and public, on November 23, after two difficult interviews with Rickover, Roth requested assignment for a tour of duty to a naval shipyard. It seemed the perfect opportunity.

In his request Roth noted that he had been working on "the development and construction of a large-ship nuclear power plant" and now that the project had been canceled, he wanted shipyard experience. He felt that in terms of his future use to the Navy as well as of his own professional career, he needed to make up for his deficiency in shipyard training, to get experience that others in his EDO peer group had undergone during the years he had spent at sea. What he was asking was, in the Navy tradition, logical to ask. But what happened next made him a typical victim of Rickover's attitude toward those who sought to leave NRB on their own initiative, even temporarily. On December 4, Rickover passed the request on to the Chief of Naval Personnel. He did not add the customary endorsement, but—his objections implicit—he tersely marked, "Forwarded."

Roth had requested orders to the Portsmouth Naval Shipyard. He became shop superintendent there after a six-month waterfront indoctrination in submarine repair. Within two years he qualified for production officer, the number-two job in the yard and an assignment that in normal rotation took several tours of duty, about ten years, to achieve.

Coincidentally, Portsmouth had become another battlefield in Rickover's war against the Navy. The civilian Electric Boat yard would build the first three nuclear submarines; the fourth, the *Swordfish,* would be constructed at Portsmouth. Rickover's representatives, who had been treated as valued customers at Electric Boat, would find themselves merely part of the ordinary, regular Navy at Portsmouth. Rickover would fight to extend his hegemony over Portsmouth, as he had done over Electric Boat. BuShips would fight back.

Although Roth well knew that he had displeased Rickover by requesting a transfer, not until May 1954 did he become aware of what it meant to be Rickover's victim. At about that time he learned that Rickover had been accusing him of disloyalty, claiming that he had talked a young officer out of joining NRB. On June 5 Roth wrote a friendly letter to Rickover and tried to set the record straight. When the officer first heard about the assignment to NRB, Roth wrote, "he asked me about it. I spent about a half hour encouraging him to be happy about the forthcoming assignment and telling him what an excellent break it was for him. When the conversation ended, I had no idea that he would later request release from the assignment. June 2 was the first I heard of his change of plans."

But Rickover had already begun what seemed to Roth to be a vendetta. Roth, although at the time the only nuclear-experienced officer at Portsmouth, did not get the nuclear-submarine project officer's post at the yard—a job that Rickover, not the shipyard commander, controlled. When Rickover assembled a group at Portsmouth in mid-1954 to discuss arrangements related to building the *Swordfish,* Roth, because of his nuclear background, was asked by the yard commander to attend the meeting. But Rickover specifically excluded him. A petty matter, perhaps, but disturbing enough to prompt Roth, later in Washington on other business, to call on Rickover and ask why he had been going out of his way to punish him.

Roth came out of that meeting more disturbed than ever. Wondering whether at some future time he might come to question his own recollections, he got what he could of it down on paper and filed the memorandum away among his private records. According to that memo, Rickover said that he "was sorry that I looked at it that way, i.e., that he was trying to hurt me. But that he would do everything in his power to keep me out of nuclear power. I had requested 'out' of nuclear power and he would 'see that I stayed out.' "

When Roth tried to explain that he had simply felt it necessary to get a few years' shipyard experience, Rickover would not listen. Rickover "made statements to the effect that I had joined the 'other' crowd—the 'BuShips crowd'—and it would do me no good. That I had little chance

of being selected for promotion to captain 'because of my religion.' "
(Roth had never discussed religious beliefs—or whether indeed he had
any—with Rickover.)

Rickover then, according to the memo, "made disparaging remarks
about the fitness reports he gave me, indicating he should not have given
me as good reports as he did. When I left I was quite puzzled about the
association that Admiral Rickover seemed to have made between the
statements that I would not make Captain (said very positively) and the
remarks that tended to deny the accuracy of the good fitness reports he'd
made out on me. The only interpretation that fitted with the tone of these
remarks and my knowledge of six years' association with him was that he
intended to do everything in his power to keep me from being promoted
as well as from returning to nuclear power."

In 1956 Roth narrowly missed being selected for captain, a disap-
pointment that scarcely surprised him. As usual, the reasons for such a
pass-over undoubtedly were complicated. For example, Roth had had
less than two years' shipyard experience in his EDO record at the time the
selection board met. But how much influence, if any, Rickover exerted
will probably never be known.

Roth did make captain in September 1957, but he was never permitted to return to the nuclear navy. In March 1958, when his Portsmouth
assignment was ending and he was preparing to transfer to BuShips in
Washington as ordered, he received a private letter of warning from
Dunford, who was then handling NRB personnel matters for Rickover
and who had never found occasion to write Roth a letter before. Dunford
told of Rickover being very upset with him. So puzzling and disquieting
was the tenor of Dunford's letter that on March 26 Roth again called on
Rickover, and again made notes of the meeting after it was over. "He
greeted me with the statement that he had let me in only because he had
something he wanted to clear up," the notes say. "He stated that I had
been broadcasting to many people that he had ... caused my being
passed over for captain by his fitness reports on me and that he wanted
that stopped."

Roth told Rickover that he had said no such thing, that the reports
had in fact been very good—too good to warrant the clearly intentional
treatment Rickover had given him since. Rickover then named the prospective commanding officer of a nuclear submarine as his source and
challenged Roth to say the man was lying. Roth repeated that the fitness
reports themselves had never been in question. "Then he said, 'I'll call
him on the telephone right now.' I said OK and he placed the call." The

submarine officer confirmed that while Roth had indeed remarked on having made captain "in spite of Admiral Rickover," there had not been any mention of fitness reports. Rickover's only concession to accuracy was to say, "So I was wrong."

The meeting had not ended. Roth repeated his objection to Rickover's harassments. Rickover said, "Yes," and he added that whatever he had done *was not* on the record. Then, according to Roth's notes written immediately after the meeting, Rickover said "in a threatening manner that he was going to contact the Chief of Naval Personnel and get a written statement" on the fitness reports "and force me to stop circulating any statements.... He added, 'You know I can get it done.' I replied I supposed he could if he chose.

"He then added that he did not want ever to hear of me doing anything about Atomic Energy. I asked what he meant by that, did he figure he had some sort of monopoly—that all of it was his province? He then modified it to say he did not want me in any way in his affairs.... I told him I did not choose to work there.... I left with another warning from him to keep out of nuclear power...." Following a three-year tour of duty as director of the Naval Radiological Defense Laboratory in San Francisco, not a Rickover-controlled job, Roth retired from the Navy in 1963.

Roth had admired Rickover in many ways, to begin with, and during Rickover's fight for promotion to admiral, Roth, risking the severe displeasure of the Navy hierarchy, had tried to influence his home-state Senator, Herbert Lehman, on Rickover's behalf. (Roth was disconcerted when he later learned that his father, in his innocence and on his own initiative, had written a letter to President Truman appealing for Rickover's promotion.) Discussing his fate with the authors, Roth admitted that in the end he viewed Rickover on two levels—"He was a national asset and a human failure."

The duel between Rickover and Roth foreshadowed the emergence of "two navies." While Roth was at Portsmouth, for example, any of his ideas or observations about nuclear submarines could not be transmitted from one navy to the other, because of the barrier between him and Rickover. In the Navy's first nuclear decade, such barriers divided individuals. In the next decade the barriers would divide the U.S. Navy.

But for the moment it was still one Navy, and nine months after her launching, on September 30, 1954, the *Nautilus* was placed in commission. Like other postwar U.S. submarines, the *Nautilus* incorporated several design features of the German Type 21 U-boat, including a rounded bow, straight deck lines, and a streamlined "sail" structure to house the periscopes and retractable masts. There were no deck guns, a feature that further enhanced her underwater speed.

The foremost compartment of the *Nautilus* was the torpedo room, with the inner doors of the submarine's six torpedo tubes. The tubes fired torpedoes almost twenty-one feet long, weighing some two thousand pounds.

The next compartments on the uppermost level were the crew's quarters and "officers' country." One *Nautilus* skipper would write that "two things impressed me almost as much as the [nuclear] plant. One was the crew, the other the comfort or habitability. . . ." In the crew's quarters each sailor had an individual bunk with foam rubber mattress, and adjacent storage for personal items. The officers had small, shared staterooms (except for the captain, who had a private room), and a large wardroom, where the ship's dozen officers could eat, do paper work and relax.

Below these rooms were the submarine's galley, where all food was prepared, and the large crew's mess, which doubled as a classroom and movie theater. Thirty-six men could sit at one time for meals, or fifty could be accommodated for lectures or movies. This was the first submarine to have an ice-cream machine, Coke dispenser, and a nickle-a-play juke box connected to a built-in hi-fi system, which, coupled with bright interior colors, made the *Nautilus* seem unreal to veteran submariners. At the lowermost level the *Nautilus* had storerooms and a large electric storage battery for emergency power.

Amidships, below the sail structure, were the attack center and control room. Nearby were the small radio and sonar rooms. The sail structure was too narrow for the traditional conning-tower compartment from which submarine commanders directed underwater attacks. Other than shafts for the periscopes and masts, the sail, as in later submarines, had only a ladder in a pressure tube opening to a small exposed bridge atop the sail.

Most of the after portion of the *Nautilus* was devoted to the propulsion plant. Behind heavy shielding was the reactor, more than two stories high, with a narrow deck running atop the reactor to the engine and machinery rooms. Twin geared steam turbines, fed with steam from the reactor's secondary coolant system, turned the submarine's two propeller shafts. The *Nautilus'* reactor plant, originally designated Submarine Thermal Reactor (STR) Mark II,* was identical with the Mark I plant

---

*See Appendix B for a listing of Navy reactor designations.

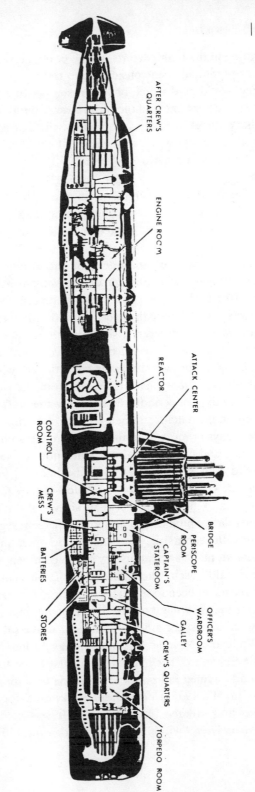

AFTER CREW'S QUARTERS

ENGINE ROOM

REACTOR

ATTACK CENTER

CONTROL ROOM

CREW'S MESS

BATTERIES

STORES

CREW'S QUARTERS

GALLEY

CAPTAIN'S STATEROOM

OFFICER'S WARDROOM

PERISCOPE ROOM

BRIDGE

TORPEDO ROOM

Cutaway drawing of the *Nautilus*.

U.S. NAVY

operating in the Idaho desert. At one point, according to Rickover, a twin reactor plant had been considered, to reduce the possibility that the submarine would be disabled or lost at sea because of a reactor failure. But size was a constraint, and the *Nautilus* was built with only one reactor. An auxiliary diesel generator, complete with snorkel installation for submerged operation, was also installed. It could bring the *Nautilus* home in an emergency at a few knots' speed.

The *Nautilus'* power plant, in the opinion of many experts, was crude. But it was a power-producing plant and it was in a submarine, and Wilkinson and his hand-picked, carefully trained crew could make it work.

The aftermost compartment of the *Nautilus* was the after crew's quarters, where the remainder of the submarine's ninety-odd crewmen were berthed. There were no stern torpedo tubes as in earlier submarines; there was just not enough space. Stuffed into corners were an automatic clothes washer and dryer, a small machine shop, a photographic dark-room, a library with several hundred volumes, and a small laboratory.

The *Nautilus* was fully air-conditioned with a carbon-monoxide "scrubber" to remove harmful gases from the submarine's atmosphere. With fresh oxygen periodically bled into the craft from storage tanks, the *Nautilus* could remain submerged with a completely closed atmosphere for sixty days or more. Certain items, such as some types of cooking fats, soap suds, and oil-based paints, could not be used aboard because they produced contaminants that could be harmful in a closed atmosphere. But the crewmen could smoke as much as they liked. The air-conditioning kept the temperature between sixty-eight and seventy-two degrees and the relative humidity at about fifty percent regardless of what area of the world the submarine happened to be operating in. These features of the *Nautilus* made ancient history of the comment of German U-boat historian Harald Busch, who, in his classic *U-boats at War,* wrote: "To those who have never been to sea in a submarine, it is hard indeed to convey an adequate idea of what it means to live, sometimes for months on end, in a narrow tubular space amid foul air and universal damp."

While the *Nautilus* was still alongside her fitting-out dock at the Electric Boat yard, her nuclear plant first came to life on December 30, 1954, and attained full power in dockside tests four days later. At 11 A.M. on January 17, 1955, Commander Wilkinson stood on the bridge of the *Nautilus* and ordered lines cast off. "It was cold," recalled Wilkinson some years later, "with a strong January wind blowing in over the piers.

In the summer it is pleasant, but in winter naval officers always think of the New London Submarine Base in terms of icy wind."

"Take in number one line. . . . All back two thirds. . . ." Wilkinson's commands were almost drowned out in the noise of helicopters hovering overhead with newsmen filming the historic event and the shouts of hundreds of persons on the nearby escort ship and ashore. Slowly the big submarine pulled away from the pier. Standing alongside Wilkinson, Admiral Rickover quietly looked on as his protégé calmly and confidently gave commands.

As the submarine cleared the pier, the engineering officer reported that there had been a loud noise in the starboard reduction gear and that he had switched to electrical propulsion. The nuclear plant had been disengaged. Wilkinson was tempted to bring the submarine back alongside the pier, but the press and hundreds of others were looking on. Rickover was determined to carry on unless there was more evident danger.

In a few minutes the problem was found—a loose locking pin on a retaining nut—and corrected, and the *Nautilus* shifted back to nuclear power. As the *Nautilus* slipped down the Thames toward Long Island Sound, the signal lamp on the bridge blinked out the historic message: UNDERWAY ON NUCLEAR POWER.

Wilkinson heard a sailor remark, "You can only be first once."

Several short runs off the Atlantic coast followed during the next few weeks to test the submarine's systems and equipment. Then in May the *Nautilus* made her shakedown cruise from New London to San Juan, Puerto Rico. The cruise was made entirely submerged—1,381 miles in ninety hours. The trip to Puerto Rico set a host of records: the distance was greater by a factor of ten than any previously traveled by a submarine without using a snorkel; it was the first time that a combat submarine had maintained a speed as fast as sixteen knots submerged for more than an hour; and it was the longest period that a U.S. submarine had remained completely submerged. Later, an even faster submerged passage was made from Key West, Florida, to New London, a distance of 1,397 miles at an average underwater speed of twenty knots.

Although later nuclear-propelled submarines would significantly exceed these records, those of the *Nautilus* were overwhelmingly impressive when one considered that the German Type 21 submarine that went to sea only a decade before had revolutionized submarine warfare. That submarine had a maximum speed of just over 17 knots for sixty to eighty minutes, after which the craft's batteries would have to be recharged (by operating on diesel with the snorkel mast raised out of the water).

Officially, the top speed of the *Nautilus* and all other U.S. nuclear-propelled submarines is listed as "over twenty knots" and their operating depth at "over four hundred feet." The *Nautilus* apparently did not meet her design speed of some twenty-seven knots, but did reach an impressive twenty-three knots submerged. Also, while she was the world's fastest combat submarine, she still followed the conservative American trend in operating depth. Unofficial statements have indicated an operational or "test" depth of some 750 feet for the *Nautilus*. In comparison, during World War II the U.S. Navy's submarine had a 400-foot depth capability, while several contemporary German U-boats had survived more than double that depth; the Type 21 was designed to operate down to 850 feet.

While nuclear propulsion gave the *Nautilus* unprecedented high-speed underwater endurance, she did not have all the advanced military features available. Rickover would later stress that he resisted incorporating advanced features in the *Nautilus*. One submarine officer who heard him at a briefing recalled Rickover stressing that he made sure the only thing innovative in the *Nautilus* was the propulsion plant and that the submarine was not a test bed "for every crazy idea." Indeed, Rickover had to fight off some of his staunchest supporters. For example, Melvin Price and Clinton P. Anderson, the latter chairman of the Joint Committee on Atomic Energy, strongly recommended advanced weapons for the *Nautilus*. Price found it ironic that the *Nautilus* had only torpedoes; he and Anderson both called for arming the ship with missiles carrying nuclear warheads.

In 1954, such weapons were becoming available, particularly the Navy's Regulus cruise missile for attacking shore targets. (Although the *Nautilus* would never be given a missile, a toy company did produce a plastic model kit with a Regulus missile on her deck, no doubt to the consternation of Soviet intelligence analysts.) In retrospect, keeping the *Nautilus* highly conventional except for her power plant was the proper approach, for difficulties with any new or radical system incorporated in her would be construed by critics as having been related to her nuclear plant.

Still, the *Nautilus*, with an underwater endurance measured in months rather than hours, was unquestionably the world's first true submersible. The secret to her great underwater endurance was complete independence from the earth's atmosphere afforded by her nuclear reactor, producing heat, and hence steam, without combustion. Oxygen for the crew could be obtained through the electrolysis of sea water, using electricity produced by the heat of the reactor core.

The crew of the *Nautilus*—more than one hundred officers and enlisted men—were protected from the "hot" radioactive core and primary coolant water by heavy shielding that surrounded the reactor. Moreover, because of the protection afforded by sea water, the Navy said, the crew was exposed to less radiation than that received from sources in space by a person on the earth's surface. In one year aboard the *Nautilus,* the Navy said, a crew member received less radiation than the maximum allowable dosage for one week as then set by the National Bureau of Standards.

Rickover was quick to show off the fantastic *Nautilus.* A parade of Congressmen visited her; on March 20, 1955, while the submarine cruised under the Atlantic off the New England coast, several members of the Joint Committee on Atomic Energy held a formal meeting aboard the submarine, a remarkable and impressive political coup. Other political figures and government officials, including AEC commissioners, as well as scores of senior naval officers, visited the *Nautilus.* Among the admirals was Arleigh Burke, whose May 1955 cruise in the submarine came three months before he was sworn in as Chief of Naval Operations. Burke would become the first CNO to oppose Rickover—but he would also be one of the Navy's strongest proponents of nuclear power.

Royalty also visited the *Nautilus.* On the afternoon of November 16, 1958, while the submarine lay tied up at a New London pier across the Thames River from the Electric Boat yard, Queen Frederika of Greece, accompanied by her daughter, Princess Sophie, and her son, Prince Constantine, and escorted by Admiral Rickover, boarded the *Nautilus,* toured the submarine, and dined on board.

When not carrying VIPs, the *Nautilus* was undergoing tests and trials, or participating in anti-submarine exercises, usually playing the part of a high-speed enemy submarine. In February 1957, after traveling 62,562 miles during her first two years of operation, the *Nautilus* entered the Electric Boat yard for her first "refueling." More than half of her at-sea time had been spent submerged. The Navy estimated that a conventional submarine of comparable size would have used three million gallons of fuel oil. Her "refueling" consisted of replacing her nuclear core, a delicate and complex process. (Afterward the used core was tested in the Arco reactor plant to determine how much effective life remained in it.)

The *Nautilus,* fitted with a new, longer-life core, departed from the Electric Boat yard on April 11, 1957, and the following month steamed into the Pacific for exercises. She also conducted a series of port visits and the unending VIP tours. The *Nautilus* took a total of eleven hundred visitors to sea during this series of brief cruises along the West Coast.

The pioneer nuclear submarine gained even greater international prominence by her remarkable voyage to the top of the world. The U.S. Navy developed an interest in under-ice submarine operations after World War II, spurred on largely by Dr. Waldo Lyon, a physicist at the Naval Electronics Laboratory, and Commander Robert D. McWethy, a submariner. If a submarine could travel under the polar ice pack, the Navy could shift submarines between the Atlantic and Pacific fleets without having to transit the vulnerable Panama Canal; hide missile submarines in the ice (which could fire up through the ice or through openings in the ice pack); and seek out enemy submarines that might seek cover under the ice.

Another expression of interest in under-ice operations came from Senator Henry M. Jackson, who, after an arctic flight, asked the Navy if it would be feasible to operate a nuclear-propelled submarine under the arctic ice. Even Navy men at the *Nautilus* reactor prototype in the Idaho desert talked of their land-locked "submarine" being able to cruise to the North Pole submerged (course 318° true from Arco).

On June 18, 1957, Commander Eugene Wilkinson was relieved as skipper of the *Nautilus* by Commander William R. Anderson, also a personal selectee of Admiral Rickover. Anderson, unlike Wilkinson, was a Naval Academy graduate (Class of 1943). He previously had succeeded Wilkinson in command of one of the new *Tang*-class diesel submarines.

Before taking command of the *Nautilus,* while in training at NRB, Anderson had met with Lyon and McWethy to discuss the feasibility of a nuclear submarine trip to the North Pole. Rickover had some hesitation about the *Nautilus* going under the ice, Anderson later recalled. But the Atlantic Fleet submarine commander, strongly influenced by McWethy, ordered a preliminary trip under the ice pack.

The *Nautilus* was provided with special equipment for her initial probes of the ice pack, including five inverted Fathometers and special compasses. The Fathometers, normally used to tell the distance from the submarine to the ocean floor, would look *upward,* at the bottom of the ice, to show how much clearance the *Nautilus* had under the ice. The special compasses, it was hoped, would counter the problems of normal magnetic compasses, which are erratic within a thousand miles of the magnetic pole, and gyro compasses, which become unreliable near the geographic pole. Should the *Nautilus* become lost while under the ice she might travel around in endless circles or run aground on an ice-locked coastline.

Sailing from New London on August 19, 1957, the *Nautilus* was accompanied part way by a diesel-electric submarine. A number of minor mechanical problems plagued the *Nautilus,* but she continued north and down under the ice. The *Nautilus* initially sought to penetrate a distance of only fifty or sixty miles under the ice to test equipment and get a feel for under-ice operations.

As the submarine reached the turn-around point, her ice-detecting equipment indicated an opening in the frozen ceiling above. With a periscope extended upward, the *Nautilus* rose slowly toward the surface. Suddenly, the periscope blacked out and the submarine shuddered to a halt.

The scope had collided with a chunk of ice floating in the open sea. The ice was in a blind spot not covered by the inverted Fathometers mounted on the *Nautilus'* deck. The damaged *Nautilus* cautiously went deeper and then headed out toward the edge of the ice pack. She surfaced in the open sea and her two periscopes were inspected. One was damaged beyond repair and the other was badly bent. These "eyes" were needed for the forthcoming NATO exercise. The submarine could race back to New London for repairs, but she would then be unable to continue her polar probes before the exercise. Anderson and his men wanted to continue their polar exploration.

The periscopes were made of stainless steel. When jacks were used to try to straighten the bent scope, the aluminum structure of the sail began to bend but the scope remained rigid. Finally, through the use of cross bracing, the scope began to give—and then it cracked. The only solution now was to weld the broken scope. Welding stainless steel is difficult under the best of conditions. It is much more difficult on the open bridge of a submarine in rough seas with gale winds and freezing temperatures. It also takes specially trained men, but the *Nautilus* had a host of specialists on board, among them Machinist's Mate 1/class Richard T. Bearden and Engineman 1/class John B. Kurrus, both expert welders.

For twelve hours on the open bridge of the *Nautilus* the two sailors, assisted by Anderson and others, worked on the periscope. They fixed it—"well enough anyway," according to Anderson. He later described this as "the most amazing repair job at sea I have ever witnessed."

Once again the *Nautilus* turned her rounded prow northward and slipped down into the depths and then under the arctic ice. Anderson felt that this time he could reach the North Pole. He estimated that the *Nautilus* could make the 660-mile under-ice trip and return to the open sea in four or five days. With every turn of her twin propellers through the icy waters the big sub moved closer and closer to her goal. Inside her steel hull, the crew enjoyed comforts never before accorded to human beings this far north.

Soon the magnetic compass and then the standard gyro compass began to behave erratically. More trouble loomed up suddenly when the special northern-latitude gyro compass began to act up and became useless. Within seconds the cause of the trouble was found: a fuse had blown. For six hours more the *Nautilus* moved northward beneath the ice at ten knots, steering by averaging the sweeps of the erratic magnetic compass's fluctuating needle. But finally, Anderson had to admit defeat. Cautiously the *Nautilus* turned around and headed south, away from the North Pole. She had reached latitude 87 north, about 180 miles from her destination.

Steering with the erratic magnetic compass, the *Nautilus* almost ran onto the ice-choked coast of Greenland. Finally, the submarine broke through the surface outside the ice pack. She had been submerged under the ice for seventy-four hours and covered almost one thousand miles. With some time remaining before the NATO exercise, the *Nautilus* made a third short foray under the ice. On this trip she logged 200 additional miles of under-ice navigation and surfaced in a "water hole" in the ice.

Anderson felt that if he had had more time the *Nautilus* could have reached the North Pole on her third under-ice effort. "By the third trip we had all the compass problems pretty well analyzed and could have ourselves fixed the circuitry in the gyro compass to make sure it wouldn't go out again," he said. The submarine then participated in the exercise, impressing U.S. and allied commanders. But the North Pole remained uppermost in the minds of many *Nautilus* crewmen.

After the exercises, the *Nautilus* returned to New London, and Commander Anderson traveled to Washington to brief the Navy's leadership on the NATO exercises and the abortive polar operations. Leaving the Pentagon's River entrance, he encountered Captain Evans P. (Pete) Aurand, naval aide to President Eisenhower. They had met before, when Ned Beach, former White House aide, had brought Aurand to visit NRB's offices. Aurand offered Anderson a ride into downtown Washington, and the *Nautilus* skipper told Aurand about his boat's polar probes. The next day, Anderson gave him a complete briefing.

So impressed was Aurand with both the political and military implications of a polar voyage by the *Nautilus* that a week later he arranged for Anderson to brief some thirty White House staffers, among them Presidential assistant Sherman Adams and Press Secretary James Hagerty. "Can you take that ship of yours around the world submerged?" asked Hagerty. "Yes, sir," was Anderson's immediate response. Thus began White House support for both the voyage to the top of the world and the later around-the-world nuclear-submarine cruise.

When President Eisenhower had heard over the radio about the earlier, secret probes under the ice by the *Nautilus*, he was upset. He had told Hagerty that he wanted to announce such submarine exploits. When the full plan to reach the Pole was explained to the President, "He bit on it like a piece of fresh trout," Hagerty told Anderson. But this time the project would be *top* secret and the President himself would announce the success.

Admiral Burke—the CNO—and Rickover subsequently gave quick agreement to Anderson's response and, with maximum secrecy, planning went forward in the White House and the Pentagon, and in New London and San Diego. Special inertial navigation equipment was fitted in the *Nautilus*. Developed for missile guidance, the inertial navigator could measure the submarine's movement to provide precise submarine navigation that would permit the later development of the Polaris missile submarine. A special compass was installed for high-latitude operations, a steel plate was fitted to provide additional protection to the periscopes and masts housed in the sail structure, and additional sonar equipment was provided for under-ice navigation.

A story to cover the true purpose of the voyage was planted in the press: the *Nautilus* was to proceed to the Pacific in April for a two-month cruise to familiarize Pacific Fleet personnel with the operations of nuclear submarines. The west-to-east Arctic route was planned to put the difficult, shallow waters of the Bering and Chukchi Seas at the beginning of the trip. Obviously, the press assumed that the submarine would go west and return east via the Panama Canal.

On the night of April 25, 1958, the *Nautilus* put to sea and turned her prow southward, toward the Panama Canal. As the submarine raced toward the canal, a small salt-water leak developed in one of the steam condensers. The dripping water fell into part of the submarine's machinery not designed to resist the corrosive effects of salt water. Despite efforts by the crew, the source of the leak could not be found because of the complexity of the condensers. At about the same time, fumes of unknown origin began to drift through the craft.

The *Nautilus* stopped at Panama for two days and than transited the canal and entered the broad Pacific. As she headed down into the Pacific depths, the fumes that had wafted through the submarine gave way to billowing smoke. The lagging, or insulation, around one of the craft's turbines, which had become oil-soaked during the submarine's three years of operation, had caught fire. In the confined engineering spaces, filled with smoke and heat, the men pulled the burning lagging from the engine as comrades carefully fought the open flames with fire extinguishers. The fire was put out with minor injuries. But the *Nautilus* had had to surface. Such a casualty under the ice—where the submarine might not be able to surface—could easily have led to disaster.

Recovering from her ordeal, the *Nautilus* sailed into San Franscisco. Repairs were made at the Mare Island submarine yard, and emergency breathing devices were installed for the men at controls in the event another accident introduced toxic fumes into the submarine while submerged. (Later, enough masks were installed to insure that the entire crew could survive such an emergency.)

While the *Nautilus* was at Mare Island, technicians from throughout the nuclear community went over the steam condenser; they were seeking the source of the sub's minute salt-water leak. The search was futile. Rather than lose more time, Commander Anderson took the *Nautilus* back to sea and headed north. The next stop was Seattle, Washington. As the *Nautilus* plowed through the depths, Anderson met again with his officers to discuss the elusive leak. Suddenly, he hit on an idea: use the same type of additive that was sold for leaky automobile radiators. Anderson, who had never had a leaky car radiator himself, brought up the idea as a last resort. But wasn't the condenser just a big radiator? Nearly everything else had been tried in vain.

When the *Nautilus* reached Seattle several crewmen went ashore and started buying the radiator additive. One hundred and forty quarts were brought aboard the submarine. Half of them were opened and poured into the cooling system. The rest were held in reserve. The plant was started up. The leak stopped.

As the *Nautilus* rested at Seattle, Anderson was joined by Dr. Lyon, and the pair boarded an airliner for Alaska. From there a Navy plane flew them out over the Bering Sea for a last-minute ice reconnaissance. Anderson returned to the *Nautilus* on June 8, and just before dawn the following morning the submarine put to sea (with Lyon and an assistant having come aboard covertly to prevent onlookers from spotting the Arctic specialist).

Again the *Nautilus* headed north. While still on the surface, the white numerals *571* on her bow and sail were painted out in case she was sighted. Only then was the entire crew briefed on the *Nautilus'* true destination.

The *Nautilus* slipped beneath the waves, then passed through the Aleutian Islands and entered the Bering Sea, which separates Alaska from Soviet Siberia. At the northern end of the Bering Sea is the Bering Strait, the narrow entrance to the Chukchi Sea and the ice-covered Arctic Ocean. After being blocked from one entrance to the strait by large ice floes that extended deeper into the water than expected, Anderson tried another route, and on June 17 the *Nautilus* entered the shallow Chukchi Sea. More ice floes were encountered in that open sea, and the *Nautilus* went down to one hundred and ten feet, about the maximum operating depth possible in that area. As the submarine passed through the Arctic Circle, the water became shallower. Luckily, the ice above opened up and the *Nautilus* came to the surface. After several hours of running on the surface, she encountered the relatively solid polar ice pack. She submerged to creep along slowly under the ice.

Suddenly, the submarine passed under ice projecting sixty-three feet down from the surface; there was a scant eight feet of water between the top of the sail and the bottom of the ice. Anderson immediately ordered the boat as deep as possible. She dropped to one hundred and forty feet, leaving only twenty feet of water between the *Nautilus'* keel and the ocean floor. Soon the submarine was passing under still deeper ice; one ice projection came within five feet of the sail. The men watching instruments that showed the ice formation instinctively ducked their heads as the submarine squeezed under the ice.

They could not proceed farther. Again the *Nautilus* had to admit defeat, and the painful message of failure was transmitted to Washington. As she slowly probed her way south, she encountered unexpected ice floes, adding dangers to the injury of thwarted hopes.

On June 20 the *Nautilus* reached open water and set off at high speed for Pearl Harbor. All material referring to the aborted transpolar cruise was classified "top secret," and the crew was ordered not to mention the operation. Eight days later the *Nautilus* arrived at Pearl Harbor. Four hours after the sub was secured, Anderson, Lyon, and several members of the crew were on their way to Washington in a Navy plane. After a briefing in Washington and quick visits home, the submariners headed back to Pearl Harbor. All but one, that is. Lieutenant Shepherd M. Jenks, the *Nautilus'* navigator, was "transferred" to duty in Washington. He was officially given a job in the Pentagon but was actually enroute to Alaska without submarine insignia or any other indication that he was connected with the *Nautilus*. There, Navy patrol planes flew Lieutenant Jenks over the proposed track of the *Nautilus'* next polar attempt for up-to-date ice reconnaissance. He was then flown back to Pearl Harbor to rejoin the ship.

Meanwhile, the *Nautilus* continued with her own cover-up story by taking local naval personnel to sea in demonstrations. Also, the additional emergency breathing devices were installed, along with a closed-circuit television set with its camera lens pointing upward to give a view of ice above the submarine.

On July 23, 1958, the *Nautilus* glided out of Pearl Harbor with Lyon and an assistant again smuggled aboard to make scientific observations, her identifying *571* again painted out, and her blunt, black prow again pointed north. This time Anderson planned to enter the Bering Strait by heading between St. Lawrence Island and Siberia, a track that Lieutenant Jenks's air reconnaissance had found was now free of ice.

The Aleutians were passed, and as the *Nautilus* prepared to enter the strait, there was no ice in sight. In the Chukchi Sea floating ice and fog were encountered, forcing the *Nautilus* to surface and move cautiously. A piece of ice found on deck was placed in the sub's deep freeze, as an important souvenir.

Soon the *Nautilus* was confronted with solid ice that covered the shallow Chukchi Sea. Anderson turned the *Nautilus* eastward and headed for Point Barrow, Alaska, and an underwater "valley," which could now be reached because of better ice conditions. The surfaced submarine's radar warned of an approaching aircraft and she went down, but she soon surfaced again and on August 1 reached the Point Barrow valley. She then dived and headed due north. Ahead was the North Pole, about one thousand miles away and some eight hundred miles beyond the open Atlantic ocean.

As the *Nautilus* barreled along, the tension grew inside her steel hull. At 11:15 P.M. (Washington time) on August 3 the *Nautilus* crossed the North Pole. The pioneer nuclear submarine was the first vessel in history to reach the top of the world, and she had brought more men there than had ever been assembled there at one time. On board were fourteen officers, ninety-eight enlisted men, and four civilians—Dr. Lyon and his assistant, and two civilian technicians caring for the intricate inertial navigation system.

After the *Nautilus* crossed the North Pole, there was a cake-cutting ceremony, a sailor was reenlisted, and eleven others were "qualified" as nuclear submariners. Then Santa Claus appeared and rebuked the submariners for using their garbage disposal unit in his private domain.

The *Nautilus* did not stop at the North Pole, but continued across the top of the world and down the other side. A change in course aimed the ship at the Greenland Sea, between Greenland and Spitsbergen. Soon the *Nautilus* entered ice-covered waters that she had probed during her 1957 Arctic cruise.

The edge of the ice pack was reached, and the submarine rose slowly. The navigator "shot" the bright sun with a sextant, and the *Nautilus* was found to be exactly where Anderson thought she was. After a submerged transit of 1,830 miles in ninety-six hours, the *Nautilus* had surfaced to within a few miles of where her captain had intended her to be—a tribute to the remarkable craft, her amazing instruments, and the officers and enlisted men who sailed her.

But now the *Nautilus* was faced with a new problem: how to tell the White House of her accomplishment. No radio station was acknowledging the radio signals that the *Nautilus* had been transmitting since surfacing. Arctic atmospheric conditions play tricks with radio communications. One of the crew quipped, "We should have brought some carrier pigeons with us." Finally, a Navy radio station in Japan picked up the message and seconds later it was being relayed to Washington. It read: NAUTILUS NINETY NORTH. Latitude ninety north is the top of the world. Then a longer message was sent giving details of the cruise.

Having told Washington of her achievement, the submarine headed south and at dawn on August 7, the *Nautilus* surfaced off the coast of Iceland. An Air Force helicopter hovered over the submarine to hoist Anderson aboard. In a matter of hours he was in Keflavik, Iceland, and then a Navy plane flew him to Washington and the White House. There, in front of a battery of television and newsreel cameras, the announcement of the *Nautilus'* polar crossing was made. Then President Eisenhower presented the *Nautilus* the first Presidential Unit Citation ever awarded in peacetime.

To the skipper of the *Nautilus* the President awarded the Legion of Merit. The award was made to

Commander Anderson who by foresighted planning, skilled seamanship and thorough study of the Arctic Area, succeeded in cruising the *Nautilus* across the top of the world from the Bering Sea to the Greenland Sea, passing submerged beneath the geographic North Pole. Under his intrepid leadership, *Nautilus* pioneered a submerged sea land between the Eastern and Western Hemispheres. This points the way for further exploration and possible use of this route by nuclear-powered cargo submarines as a new commercial seaway between the major oceans of the world.

Conspicuous by his absence at the ceremonies was Rear Admiral Rickover. After the presentation, Anderson and his wife, Bonny, whom the Navy had flown in for the ceremony, drove to Rickover's office to pay their respects. Immediately after seeing the Andersons, Rickover rushed off to visit the pioneer civilian reactor plant he was building in Pennsylvania. Asked about not having been invited to the White House ceremony, the Admiral responded, "Ah, we haven't got time to worry about things like that." But reacting to the snub in a rare—and uncharacteristic—public outburst, Ruth Rickover called some of the Navy's senior officers "stupid windbags" who were out to "hurt my husband for his independent and free spirit."

But the snub may well have been accidental. In typical Navy fashion, the invitations had been made according to the chain of command: Secretary of the Navy, Chief of Naval Operations, Commander Atlantic Fleet, Commander Submarine Force Atlantic, and the skipper of the submarine. Rickover was simply not in the operational chain of command. Rather, he was above the chain.

The Secretary of the Navy quickly issued a public apology for the oversight, pleading that the Admiral had been inadvertently overlooked in the preoccupation of arranging the White House ceremonies. Next, the White House announced that the Admiral would be the President's personal representative at the welcome-home ceremonies for the *Nautilus* in New York.

There was still more to the incident. The press asked why Mrs. Rickover had not christened one of the nuclear submarines (a total of six had been launched by that time).* There were reports that she was angry because she had not been asked to preside at a launching. The Navy re-

---

* *The sponsors of the first six nuclear submarines were Mrs. Eisenhower (Nautilus); the wife of Representative W. Sterling Cole of the Joint Committee on Atomic Energy (Seawolf); the wife of former AEC chairman Lewis L. Strauss (Skate); the wife of a World War II submarine hero (Swordfish); the wife of Rear Admiral Frank T. Watkins, Commander, Submarine Force Atlantic (Sargo); and the wife of Admiral Robert L. Dennison, Commander in Chief Atlantic Fleet and an early nuclear-submarine supporter in OPNAV (Seadragon).*

sponded that Mrs. Rickover's name had been on the list of future sponsors since the month before. However, in fact, she would never be called upon to smash a bottle of champagne against a submarine.

On August 19, Anderson flew to England and was then taken by helicopter out to the *Nautilus*. The submarine docked at Portsmouth for a six-day stay in England, the first foreign-port visit by an American submarine. Back at sea, the *Nautilus* headed west and shattered another submarine speed record by crossing the Atlantic in six and a half days, an average speed of twenty-one knots for the 3,350-mile trip.

Upon arrival in New York the submarine was given a tumultuous welcome. Rickover came on board and was presented with the chunk of ice that had been trapped on the deck in the Chukchi Sea on July 30 and kept in the freezer since then. In the opinion of some present in the *Nautilus* wardroom, that memento was to Rickover the most important prize of the entire cruise.

The *Nautilus* swung up the East River and moored at the naval shipyard on the Brooklyn shore. Except for the duty watch—about one fourth of the crew—the *Nautilus*' sailors climbed into a score of jeeps. The vehicles crossed over to Manhattan and began a ticker-tape parade up Broadway.

There were bands and marching units from the Army, Navy, Air Force, Coast Guard, and New York Fire Department. The cavalcade—led by massed colors of the services and other organizations—consisted of Rickover, Anderson, and a city official in the first car; Mrs. Anderson, son Michael, age thirteen, and another city official in the second car; and then jeeps loaded with *Nautilus* sailors and officers.

As the cavalcade moved up Broadway, an estimated 250,000 persons lined the streets to cheer the first Navy men so honored since Nimitz's visit thirteen years before. The sailors were inundated with ticker tape, while the crowd cheered and screamed. By the time the vehicles reached City Hall there were additional passengers, young women who had clambered aboard the sailors' jeeps.

At City Hall Mayor Robert F. Wagner officiated at a brief ceremony, and then all moved to the Waldorf-Astoria Hotel for a stag luncheon. At the same time, Mrs. Wagner was the hostess at a luncheon for Mrs. Anderson and seventy-seven other *Nautilus* wives. Mrs. Rickover was invited but did not attend.

In the Empire Room, the *Nautilus* crew were treated like royalty, receiving accolade after accolade. Admiral James Russell, the Vice Chief of Naval Operations, paid tribute to Rickover, calling him a "distinguished leader in engineering and science." When Rickover stood—in a rare appearance in uniform—he told the luncheon guests that he was proud to serve in an organization "that can inspire such courage and devotion" as that demonstrated by the men of the *Nautilus*.

The *Nautilus* was in New York from August 25 to 28, when she headed back to her home base, New London. It was the first and last time that the *Nautilus* or any other nuclear submarine would visit New York. The city was put "off limits" for nuclear ships, even though many city officials have stated that they have no objection to such visits. The Naval Reactors Branch has consistently refused to explain why New York is different from other cities such as Charleston, Norfolk, San Diego, Vallejo (near San Francisco), Bremerton or Seattle. The issue did not fully become public until 1979, when there was a proposed visit by the nuclear submarine *New York City*. (See Chapter 29.)

The *Nautilus* remained in active service for the next twenty-one years, making operational cruises and serving as a target in anti-submarine exercises. She was soon overshadowed by the exploits of later nuclear submarines, and by the late 1960s she was referred to as a "second-line" warship.

The *Nautilus* was decommissioned in March 1980 after twenty-five years of operation. Her voyage to latitude 90 north was the triumph of her career. Although many U.S. and Soviet nuclear submarines subsequently reached the North Pole, and in 1977 the Soviet icebreaker *Arktika* became the first surface ship ever to reach the top of the world, the *Nautilus* was the first vessel and, as the sailor had said when the submarine first got underway, "you can only be first once."

In the same way, the *Nautilus* was Rickover's greatest triumph. Although many more nuclear submarines have been built, and they can go farther, travel faster, dive deeper, and carry more sophisticated weapons, none can ever again be *first*. And, nuclear propulsion, personified by the *Nautilus*, was one of the few nonstrategic naval innovations that flowered during this period, and virtually all credit for it went to Rickover. After Admiral Mills's retirement in early 1949, Rickover became the most vocal and most visible symbol of the Navy's drive for nuclear propulsion. His efforts, his control, and his single-mindedness of purpose overshadowed those of all other individuals, regardless of their contributions or advocacy.

Earlier naval-engineering innovations—the ironclad warship, breech-loading gun, submarine, radar, and dreadnought—had become the "property" of the navy to which they belonged once they were operational, and their designers and builders for all practical purposes lost all control and influence over them. But not so the *Nautilus*. She remained Rickover's, with his choice of men commanding her, with her entire crew selected and trained by him, and with her commanding officer at one end of a direct line of communications to Rickover. The *Nautilus* was far from flawless. She did not meet all her design goals, and she had serious problems, such as the reactor leak and flammable lagging around her pipes. But when the submarine failed, her crew came through—Rickover's crew, men who were intelligent and well trained.

The *Nautilus* belonged to Rickover, even more than to the nation that had paid for her, more than to the Navy that operated her, more than to the shipyard that built her. And that submarine was the world's most revolutionary undersea craft to go to sea since the end of the previous century. The *Nautilus* was the world's first "true submersible."

FATHER OF THE
ATOMIC SUBMARINE

We have with us this afternoon Admiral Rickover of the U.S. Navy, in my considered opinion the most valuable, the most effective man who has ever been honored with the exalted title since John Paul Jones. He has accomplished the impossible, at least he has achieved what the authorities and experts said was utterly visionary.

So we are particularly fortunate in having the counsel and advice of a man of his ability and capacity and experience. And in view of his achievements we would like to inquire of him as to his recommendation of our fiscal program in this important feature of national defense.

—Representative Clarence Cannon,
Chairman of the House Committee
on Appropriations, June 25, 1959

9

Passed Over

To understand what happened to Hyman Rickover while the *Nautilus* was being built in the early 1950s, it is necessary to go back a few years, to that point when Rickover and nuclear propulsion were not major issues in the Navy. That point is 1949, when, thanks to the efforts of Admiral Mills, Captain Rickover was wearing two hats—one as the head of the nuclear-propulsion program in the Bureau of Ships and the other as the Navy representative in the Division of Reactor Development of the Atomic Energy Commission. He had a good record behind him and was intimately involved in an important program. Rickover could certainly believe that there was opportunity for still further advancement.

Although the number of EDO rear admirals was small, Rickover felt that his record would stand well against the other EDO captains with whom he would be competing for selection to flag rank. As an EDO rear admiral, Rickover could expect to command a major shipyard or be named an assistant chief in BuShips. Then, after one or two flag assignments, Rickover could have a shot at the top EDO position in the Navy—Chief of the Bureau of Ships. Then, after perhaps four years as Chief of BuShips, at about age fifty-seven, he would retire on his admiral's pension.

Officers who knew Rickover at the time believed that in 1949 he had this traditional view of his future career. As proof, some could point to the manner in which Rickover handled the grooming of his successor. Rickover in 1949 assumed that he would need to demonstrate that he had a qualified relief if he were to be selected for rear admiral and move up to a more important position. The man Rickover selected to succeed him was Robert Lee Moore, Jr.

Captain Moore had been the senior assistant to Rickover in the electrical section of BuShips during most of World War II. Moore, who graduated from the Naval Academy eight years after Rickover, had also attended postgraduate school and served in surface ships and submarines (both an S-boat and a larger submarine in the 1930s). Unlike Rickover, however, Moore had seen combat early in World War II aboard the new destroyer *Dale*. He was executive officer of that ship on December 7, 1941, but like most officers from ships at Pearl Harbor that Sunday morning, Moore was ashore. (During that Japanese air attack a young ensign, the senior officer aboard, got the *Dale* underway and out to sea.) As executive officer of the ship, Moore was in combat in the southwest Pacific during the early days of World War II as the *Dale* escorted carriers in strikes against the expanding Japanese Empire.

Moore returned to Washington in April 1942 as a lieutenant commander to work for Rickover in the electrical section of BuShips. After the war he did a tour of duty as design superintendent at the Portsmouth Naval Shipyard, returning to BuShips for duty in July 1949. On September 2, 1949, in a memorandum to Rear Admiral David H. Clark, Mills's successor as Chief of BuShips, Rickover recommended Moore as his successor, laying out a training program that included a year's graduate work in nuclear physics.

Rickover's memo also set up a timetable that would put Moore in the position to assume Rickover's nuclear-propulsion job in September 1951—just when Rickover believed that he would rise from captain to rear admiral (lower half),* a key step on the rungs up the ladder to Chief of BuShips.

In his memo Rickover recommended that a "new senior officer" be introduced to nuclear propulsion "as an ultimate relief for me." The memo was in typical Rickover style—a style that would never vary: to the point, in plain English, not bureaucratese. The memo said:

1. In the assignment of Engineering Duty Officers to nuclear propulsion billets, nearly all efforts to date have been devoted to obtaining younger officers. Recently, a plan was placed into effect for the education of new younger officers. An adequate input of younger officers into this important field of work is now established. However, there still remains the considerable gap in seniority between myself and the other Engineering Duty officers assigned to this field. The nuclear propulsion field is quite distinct from other aspects of atomic energy work and should be regarded separately.

* *The one-star rank of commodore was abolished for the Navy in peacetime in 1899. Instead, the two-star rear admiral list—the rank corresponded to that of one-star brigadier general in the other military services—was divided into an upper and lower half for purposes of pay and protocol. In 1981 the one-star rank was reintroduced in the U.S. Navy as Commodore Admiral.*

2. The introduction of a new senior officer actively into the nuclear propulsion field should be done only after he has devoted a considerable period of time to familiarizing himself with the very complex technical and administrative arrangements. My own estimate, based on seeing several officers introduced into this field during the past two years, is that about two years is required before a capable officer can become a really effective agent.

3. I recommend that one senior Engineering Duty officer be assigned in the near future to nuclear propulsion work for education and familiarization in this field and then assigned as an ultimate relief for me. This officer should fulfil the following requirements:

(a) Be qualified to command submarines, as familiarity with their operating and technical characteristics is essential.
(b) Desire assignment to this type of duty and believe in the future it affords.
(c) Have a seniority in the general range 1928–1932. A more senior officer would have less long-time availability for assignment. A more junior man would be too close to several capable officers who have already had three years' experience in this field.
(d) Be experienced in machinery design, especially in submarine machinery.
(e) Have had experience in the Bureau in a technical position.
(f) Be sufficiently mentally alive to readily learn a field that is quite new and unusual both technically and administratively.
(g) Be able to deal effectively with civilian scientists, some of whom do not have a strong liking for military men.

4. The officer selected as my relief should be given one year's instruction in various phases of Nucleonics. Such a course is presently available at Massachusetts Institute of Technology. Upon completing the year's work at Massachusetts Institute of Technology, he should spend about six months at various Atomic Energy Commission installations, such as Oak Ridge, Argonne, Schenectady, and Westinghouse. An additional six months duty in Washington should fit him to take over the job.

5. The question of an officer to take my place has given me considerable concern during the past two years. I consider that the attainment of nuclear propulsion for naval vessels is of utmost, and perhaps crucial importance to the future of the Navy. For this reason, I have carefully reviewed the list of Engineering Duty officers includ-

ing those senior and junior to the seniority range mentioned above. I have talked and corresponded with several likely possibilities. My considered opinion is that Captain R. L. Moore, Jr., best possesses the qualifications and capabilities of doing the job. He is intelligent, far-sighted, hard working, and has that degree of energy and persistence which is necessary in the formative stage of a venture of this sort.

Admiral Clark approved Rickover's tacit recommendation of Moore, who began his prescribed training. Rickover, meanwhile, continued on his timetable. As he seems to have then viewed his career, he, Moore, and the *Nautilus* would reach their fateful dates at the same time. In 1950, while Moore studied advanced nuclear engineering at Massachusetts Institute of Technology, the building of the *Nautilus* remained on schedule, and, as far as Rickover was concerned, so did he. But in 1951, when the Navy signed a contract with the Electric Boat Company for construction of the *Nautilus* and when Rickover, getting his first taste of national publicity, was featured in *Time* and *Life* in the same week, the Rickover timetable was destroyed. A Navy selection board met in Washington to choose captains for promotion to rear admiral.

The selection board is the means by which the Navy selects officers for promotion for the grades of lieutenant up to rear admiral. (Beyond selection to rear admiral, promotions are based on the job to which the officer is assigned.) The selection boards have before them the files of all officers who have a specified number of years of service as officers and are eligible for promotion. The boards meet in secret, following the guidance of the Secretary of the Navy. Their selection lists are then approved by the President and confirmed by the Senate. Officers who are in the "zone" with respect to length of service and who are not selected for two successive years are normally retired from the Navy.

On July 2, 1951, a selection board under Admiral William M. Fechteler, commander of U.S. and NATO forces in the Atlantic, met in Arlington Annex buildings on Arlington ridge in northern Virginia, overlooking the Pentagon and, across the Potomac River, the Capitol. The board—Fechteler, three vice admirals, and five rear admirals—met to consider captains for selection to rear admiral.* The board separately considered line captains and EDO captains. The board's focus was on the eleven EDO captains of the class of 1921—the year before Rickover's—who were completing thirty years of service.

* *In August 1951, Fechteler was suddenly named Chief of Naval Operations following the death of Admiral Sherman.*

They kept no minutes of their deliberations, and no one would officially discuss the details of their voting. The Navy had used boards since the late 1800s to "pluck" officers who were less qualified than others, a form of selection that made space within the Navy for junior officers. In 1916 Congress passed the first selection law, which provided for the selection of qualified officers to serve in the grade of rear admiral as well as in some lesser grades.

When the board's selections were announced, there were two EDO captains on the list. Rickover was not one of them. He had been passed over.

When he learned of the first pass-over, Rickover seems to have made the most momentous decision of his career: He would henceforth not rely on the Navy system. Already he had developed a degree of independence because of his Atomic Energy Commission appointment. Now, in the opinion of an officer who worked with him then, Rickover began to show not just independence but isolation, a "me-against-them" attitude.

The officer is Ralph K. James, who knew Rickover as a fellow officer in BuShips and later, in tumultuous years for both of them, was Rickover's ostensible boss. Looking back over those years, James, a retired Chief of BuShips, told the authors that the change in Rickover was obvious to all who worked with him.

"When Rickover was first passed over," James recalled, "it was a brand-new ball game. From then on, it was apparent that he took no steps to prepare for a successor. Suddenly, Moore and Rickover were estranged. The situation was explosive."

Moore, the man Rickover had hand-picked, suddenly had become a potential rival rather than a successor. Moore, the man who did things the Navy way and who had been moving up the ladder, was no longer a man Rickover wanted at his side. Rickover, an officer known only in the Navy as a loner, now was publicized in *Time* and *Life* as a loner and a nonorganization man. And, to those around him, he seemed to have believed he had got the Navy's payment for that behavior: no promotion. He is also said to have believed that by playing the Navy's game of naming a potential successor he had even set himself up for routine retirement—without admiral's stars.

Rickover knew that he could not afford to be passed over twice. The second pass-over was virtually a layoff slip. The Navy system was inexorably in motion. There was normally no possibility for a third chance.

When Moore reported back to Rickover's nuclear-power group in September 1951, he was no longer a protégé. "It was apparent," Moore said later, "that there was no place in the inn for me. From the first day he took no action to recognize my status or in any way to prepare me for relieving him. In fact, he did everything he could to make my life miserable, my work assignments almost impossible, and in every way to show me I was no longer wanted."

Moore asked the Chief of BuShips for a change in assignment, and on August 8, 1952, he was transferred to Groton, Connecticut, as supervisor of shipbuilding at the Electric Boat yard. In that role he was still part of the nuclear program, helping to supervise the construction of the *Nautilus* and the *Seawolf*. After successful service at Electric Boat, in early 1956, Moore became commander of the Portsmouth Naval Shipyard, the Navy's leading submarine yard, where the first Navy-built nuclear submarines were being started. While at Portsmouth, Moore was selected for promotion to rear admiral. And, in April 1959, he returned to BuShips as Deputy and Assistant Chief—the penultimate position for an EDO at the time.

After Moore, there is no record or indication that Rickover ever even contemplated the selection of another successor. Many officers who were on active duty in the later 1950s and early 1960s believe that the 1951 turning point in Rickover's career came because of a cluster of events: the pass-over, the return of Moore, and the sudden rash of publicity, especially from the presses of Time, Inc. The man who fostered that publicity was Clay Blair, Jr.

Blair, an enlisted submariner during World War II, was a persistent, twenty-five-year-old *Time-Life* reporter in 1950, when he first heard about the nuclear-powered submarine Rickover was building. But not until September 1951, after the Navy announced the signing of the contract for the submarine, did Blair get his chance to write a major story, loaded with details that no other reporter had.

He got many of those details from Ned Beach. Another source was Commander James M. Hingson in the office of the Chief of Naval Information. "If there was any person who should get the credit for making Captain Rickover an admiral," Hingson told the authors, "it was Clay Blair."

In September 1951, Clay Blair did not know that he was going to have that much influence. He was only after an exclusive story, which was still called a scoop. Robert Sherrod, the regular Pentagon correspondent for *Time,* had been assigned to work on the *Life* picture history of World War II, and so when young Blair got his scoop, he had the Pentagon beat to himself.

"One night last month," his story in *Life* began, "a slim, sparrow-faced Navy captain wearing a gray civilian suit hurried unnoticed into Washington's Union Station and boarded a northbound train." From that opening paragraph there was no doubt that Blair and *Life* had found a hero: "Wiry, beady-eyed, frugal, Captain Hyman George Rickover may be destined to go down in naval history as the man who exerted as much influence on naval shipbuilding as Robert Fulton."

The 2,700-word story (and a similar one in *Time*) told little about the as-yet-unnamed nuclear submarine. It did tell quite a bit about the "hard-driving" captain who had "declared war on naval indifference"—and eventually convinced the Navy that it needed an atomic submarine. Most of the facets of the Rickover personality and most of the enduring Rickover techniques were laid out in that story, which would be the source of most of the Rickover stories and legends to come.

In *Life*, too, came the first major publicity photograph of Rickover: standing straight, in a civilian suit, behind his desk. One of the early legends had it that Rickover declined to be photographed because, as he would periodically tell one of the authors of this book, "I am too busy building nuclear submarines." *Life* photographer Hank Walker finally prevailed through the auspices of the Navy's Chief of Information, who called Rickover. Grudgingly, Rickover agreed. But when the lights were set up and Walker had taken his specified photographs, Rickover relented and allowed Walker to shoot away as he pleased—on the condition that Rickover received prints to give to his staff.

Rickover was already making publicity by seeming to avoid it. Blair had had to dig for his scoop. He had not been encouraged by Rickover; Blair had never even met Rickover. For the most part, the *Time-Life* stories were recognized by the Navy as fine publicity for the nuclear-submarine program, for the Navy and for Rickover. There certainly was abundant animosity in the Navy toward Rickover, but the stories could have inspired little more than additional jealousy. Two intertwined issues that soon would erupt did *not* arise in Clay Blair's story: the selection board's passing-over of Rickover and the possibility of anti-Semitism.

And, it would be Clay Blair who would, as he later said, "keep Rickover from being thrown out of the Navy."

On Flag Day 1952 an overhead crane had lifted the keel plate of the world's first nuclear submarine and laid it on a building way at the Electric Boat yard. President Truman had officiated at the *Nautilus* keel laying. Rickover, who had gone to the ceremony with his wife and their young son, Robert, had hovered in the background in a gray civilian suit. After the ceremony, as he sat in one of the official cars, President Truman spotted him and walked over to shake his hand. The President's train of uniformed, beribboned naval officers looked on in horror as Rickover remained seated in the car. News of the incident—for that is how it was viewed—soon began making the rounds of the Pentagon. Rickover, it was said, was embarrassing the Navy. But there were officers who pointed to the calendar and said that the Navy would not have to put up with Rickover much longer.

About this time—Blair remembers it as a Sunday afternoon in early summer—Blair received a telephone call at his home from Ray Dick, one of Rickover's officers. With a sense of immediacy in his voice, he told young Blair that it was vital that they "meet privately on a matter of utmost urgency about the nuclear-submarine program." Dick, with a touch of the dramatic, suggested that they meet within the hour at a large rock on Beach Drive in Rock Creek Park, a meandering, path-laced woodland that runs through the middle of Washington.

Dick had been with Rickover since the earliest days in Oak Ridge. Dick was a passionate man, a loyalist whose belief in Rickover transcended all—even the friendship of men who fell out of favor with Rickover. One of those friends, fellow Oak Ridge alumnus Miles Libbey, said of Ray Dick, "He was brilliant, an idealist seeking a cause, and he really latched onto that cause." The cause was a complex one: it was Rickover; it was nuclear power; it was a nuclear-powered submarine. But most of all it was Rickover.

When they met, Dick told Blair that Rickover was in trouble—and so was America's nuclear-submarine program. A Navy selection board was to convene shortly, and if Rickover was again passed over, not only would the Navy lose an outstanding officer but the United States would lose years in the race to get nuclear submarines before the Soviet Union. Dick unburdened himself about the sufferings of Rickover—the anti-Semitism, the snubs by haughty officers, the conspiracy not merely to deny him promotion but, much more importantly, to break up his team. The Navy was destined to lose Rickover and, very possibly, nuclear submarines for years to come. . . .

For hours Dick talked while Blair listened. So hurriedly had the meeting been called that Blair had rushed from his house without a notebook. According to Blair, Dick said, " 'If Rickover goes, the project is going to die. Only the team can pull off this miracle of nuclear power.

The young Rickover in his role as "mantle bearer" at high school graduation, as photographed for the John Marshall newspaper.

"Rickie" as he appeared in the 1922 *Lucky Bag,* yearbook of the Naval Academy. Although that year *The Lucky Bag* contained a unique unnumbered, perforated page for another Jewish midshipman, Rickover and his classmate Louis Goodman shared a numbered, permanent page in the yearbook.

OPPOSITE TOP   Rickover's first assignment after his June 1922 graduation from the Naval Academy was to the flush-deck, four-stack destroyer *La Vallette,* based at San Diego. Most of the ship's internal volume was taken up with machinery and fuel. Rickover soon became enamored with the "plant."

OPPOSITE BOTTOM   The battleship *Nevada,* seen here at Guantanamo Bay, Cuba, launching a manned observation balloon, was Rickover's second ship. After only four months on board, he was transferred off for medical reasons and missed the Battle Fleet's cruise to the South Pacific. He later returned to the *Nevada,* continuing his early interest in engineering.

ABOVE   After his duty in a destroyer and a battleship, and two years of postgraduate studies, Rickover sought more challenging duty in the submarine service. He served three years in the diesel-electric submarine *S-48,* and although he "qualified for command" aboard her, he did not become commanding officer of a submarine or ever again serve in submarines.

Ruth Masters Rickover, at home.

The U.S.S. *Finch* was Rickover's only ship command. The minesweeper had been launched in 1918, the year Rickover entered the Naval Academy, and was well overage in 1937 when Rickover commanded her in Chinese waters for two and a half months. At that time, the *Finch* was used mainly to transport American troops protecting American interests during the Sino-Japanese conflict.

Rickover, in uniform, astride a carabao, or water buffalo, while in Bali, apparently photographed by his wife, Ruth Masters Rickover. Their extensive tour of Southeast Asia in 1938 led to her writing of a charming and perceptive book, published after her death under Rickover's sponsorship.

Mrs. Dwight D. Eisenhower christens the U.S.S. *Nautilus,* the world's first nuclear-propelled vehicle, at the Electric Boat yard on January 21, 1954. Assisting her is Commander Edward L. Beach, Presidential naval aide; at left are John J. Hopkins, president of General Dynamics, EB's parent firm, and Mrs. Eugene P. Wilkinson, serving as matron of honor for the ceremony.

Artist's concept of the nuclear plant in the *Nautilus.* The reactor serves as a "boiler" to produce steam for the submarine's steam turbine, which actually turns the propeller shaft. Radioactive water is shown with dark arrows and the nonradioactive steam (produced in the steam generator) is shown with shaded arrows. The reactor and steam generator are contained within the "coolant system shield," and personnel cannot enter that area while the reactor is in operation.

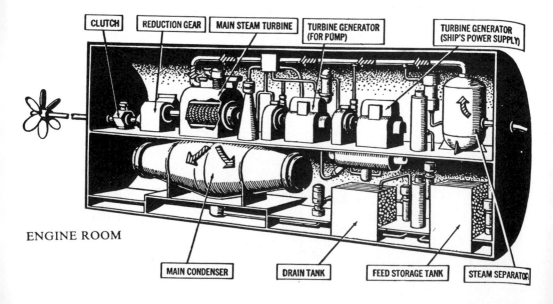

CLUTCH   REDUCTION GEAR   MAIN STEAM TURBINE   TURBINE GENERATOR (FOR PUMP)   TURBINE GENERATOR (SHIP'S POWER SUPPLY)

ENGINE ROOM

MAIN CONDENSER   DRAIN TANK   FEED STORAGE TANK   STEAM SEPARATOR

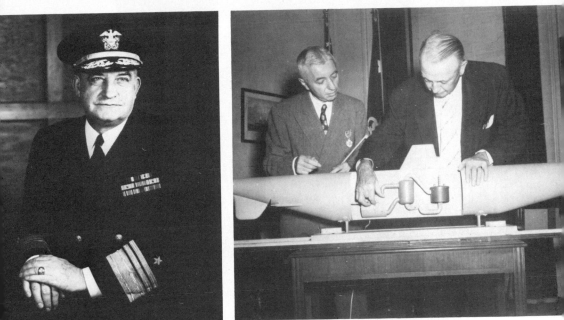

Vice Admiral Earle W. Mills, photographed shortly before his retirement in 1949. Mills was Assistant Chief of the Bureau of Ships during the war and supported and encouraged Rickover. After the war, as Chief of BuShips, he made Rickover his liaison to the Atomic Energy Commission, an appointment that led to development of the atomic submarine.

Secretary of the Navy Dan Kimball and Rickover show off a simplified model of a submarine nuclear power plant on July 7, 1952. Kimball had just presented Rickover with his second Legion of Merit award. The following day a Navy selection board met to consider captains for promotion to rear admiral. Rickover was not selected.

REACTOR ROOM

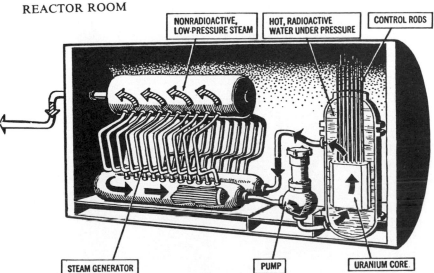

NONRADIOACTIVE, LOW-PRESSURE STEAM

HOT, RADIOACTIVE WATER UNDER PRESSURE

CONTROL RODS

STEAM GENERATOR

PUMP

URANIUM CORE

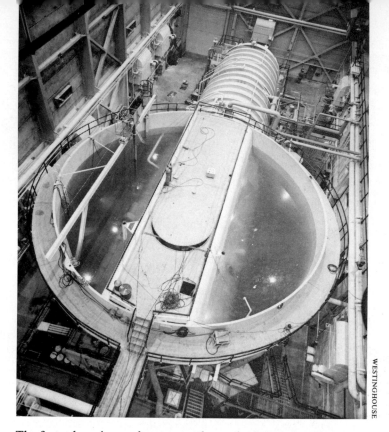

The first submarine nuclear power plant—the Submarine Thermal Reactor Mark I—constructed in the Idaho desert at the National Reactor Test Station. The prototype plant is within the submarine-hull-like structure that passes through the sea tank, which is some 50 feet in diameter and 40 feet high and holds about 385,000 gallons of water. Use of the prototype speeded up construction of the similar STR Mark II for the submarine *Nautilus*.

Commander Eugene P. Wilkinson at one of the periscopes in the *Nautilus*. He was the first commanding officer of the first nuclear submarine and later the first nuclear surface warship, the *Long Beach*.

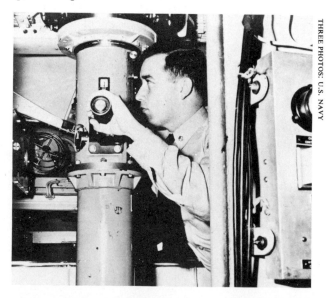

The *Nautilus* steams in triumph up the East River toward the navy yard in Brooklyn while fireboats salute and crowds along the Manhattan shoreline cheer. Her visit to New York—the only time a nuclear ship has visited the city—came after her voyage to the North Pole. Although the *Nautilus* had a streamlined appearance, her hull design was based on the German Type 21 U-boat of World War II.

A heroes' welcome was given to the crew of the *Nautilus* when the submarine reached New York after her arctic exploit. Here Commander William R. Anderson (left), then commanding officer of the *Nautilus,* Richard C. Patterson, Jr., New York City's Commissioner of Commerce and Public Events, and Rear Admiral Rickover, representing President Eisenhower, travel to City Hall through a ticker-tape parade. Their car was followed by a convoy of jeeps carrying the crew of the submarine plus some female friends acquired along the parade route.

U.S. NAVY

This cartoon strip in *Mad* magazine of July 1959 was a takeoff on the controversy that arose because Rickover's wife had never been invited to christen a nuclear submarine.

HYMIE RICKOVER AND HIS ATOMIC SUBS

OPPOSITE, TOP LEFT   Pentagon reporter Clay Blair, Jr., whose articles, both published and unpublished, were a major influence toward the selection of Rickover for promotion to Rear Admiral and his retention in the Navy. Blair's biography *The Atomic Submarine and Admiral Rickover* was written in Rickover's offices and reviewed and edited by Rickover, Rickover's wife, and several members of his staff.

OPPOSITE, TOP RIGHT   Edward L. Beach was an early supporter of Rickover while in several Washington assignments, including naval aide to President Eisenhower from 1953 to 1957. He subsequently commanded the nuclear submarine *Triton* during her remarkable around-the-world cruise. But the giant *Triton* and her achievement were overshadowed by the downing of Francis Gary Powers' U-2 spy plane over the Soviet Union and the massive Polaris submarine program.

ABOVE LEFT   Rickover never achieved success in the world of television, despite his introduction to that medium by Edward R. Murrow on "See It Now" in 1957. Here Murrow and a dour-looking Rickover explain to the TV audience the nation's first nuclear-power-generating plant, at Shippingport, Pennsylvania.

ABOVE RIGHT   Robert L. Moore, Jr., was Rickover's deputy in the Electrical Branch of the Bureau of Ships during World War II. After the war, Rickover hand-picked Moore to succeed him as head of the Naval Reactors Branch. But after Rickover failed to be selected for flag rank, he took steps to get Moore out of the nuclear program. This photo shows Moore as a rear admiral and deputy chief of the Bureau of Ships.

OPPOSITE TOP U.S. and then Soviet nuclear-propelled submarines became regular visitors to the polar reaches. Here the U.S.S. *Sargo,* the third American submarine to achieve the North Pole, is shown surfaced through the arctic ice pack on February 9, 1960. During that cruise she spent almost 15 days under ice.

ABOVE The U.S.S. *Skate,* the second American submarine to reach the North Pole, is shown during her second cruise to the top of the world. She surfaced at the pole on March 17, 1959, 50 years after Commander Robert E. Peary reached the North Pole.

LEFT The atom at sea: Task Force 1, the world's first all-nuclear task force, consisting of the cruisers *Bainbridge* (foreground) and *Long Beach* and the aircraft carrier *Enterprise.* Although their weapons were similar to those on conventionally powered warships, their nuclear power plants gave them essentially unlimited high-speed cruising ranges.

GENTLEMEN— WE MAY BE ABLE TO BEAT RUSSIA ANY WEDNESDAY BEFORE LUNCH— BUT WHAT CAN WE DO ABOUT RICKOVER?

OPPOSITE TOP   The nuclear-powered merchant ship *Savannah* was designed and constructed outside Rickover's regime by the Maritime Administration and the Atomic Energy Commission. Although the *Savannah* was expensive to operate and had a relatively short service life, she demonstrated the potential for peaceful use of nuclear propulsion at sea.

OPPOSITE BOTTOM   Rickover has been the continued subject of jokes within and outside the Navy. This expression of official frustration, from the *San Francisco Chronicle* of June 20, 1961, typified the concern he periodically caused the Navy's top brass.

ABOVE   The sleek "tear-drop" hull form of the *Skipjack* and later classes of nuclear attack submarines is evident in this view of the *Scorpion* launching on December 9, 1959. Note the narrow sail structure and the diving or control planes mounted on the sail. Compared with earlier submarines, the deck is narrow and is actually covered with water when the submarine runs at high speed on the surface. But nuclear submarines spend virtually all their at-sea time submerged. The *Scorpion* was the second U.S. nuclear submarine to be lost at sea.

Rickover during the 1960s, at the time a vice admiral, returns to the *Nautilus,* his first success.

Save the team.' Never was it a matter of Rickover's being promoted. Dick was hypertense as he explained the whole selection process to me."

Blair then began "working the story around the politics of Time, Inc.," which, he recalled, "was like a branch of the Pentagon. The whole *Time-Life* organization was very militaristic." James R. Shepley, chief of the Washington Bureau, "was anti-Navy and pro-Air Force." The bias against the Navy, according to Blair, also was fostered by Roy Alexander, the managing editor, a former test pilot for Grumman, and Charles J. V. Murphy, a *Fortune* writer working out of the Washington Bureau. Murphy, formerly of the Air Force, was an influential interpreter of Time, Inc., policy.

Blair finally convinced these champions of the Air Force that the nuclear submarine would doom the Navy's aircraft carriers, then the principal target of the Air Force. "And, so, I told them the Air Force should support Rickover. I got carte blanche," said Blair.

While Blair started writing a piece on Rickover and the problems of Rickover and the nuclear submarine, what Dick had predicted was coming true. On July 7, 1952, three weeks after the keel-laying of the *Nautilus*, Secretary of the Navy Dan Kimball presented Rickover a gold star, in lieu of a second Legion of Merit, for Rickover's work on the development of the *Nautilus*. The citation even noted, without details, Rickover's struggle with the establishment—"He has held tenaciously to a single important goal through discouraging frustration and opposition. . . ." The award was affixed to Rickover's earlier medal, which was pinned under the breast pocket of a civilian suit. Even to get a medal Rickover would not put on a uniform. Nor would he allow himself to be impressed. "One star instead of two," he reportedly said of his medal, referring to the two-star insignia of rear admiral.

A day after Kimball made the presentation, another nine-man selection board met to consider captains for promotion to rear admiral. Four EDO captains were selected. Rickover was not. He had been passed over for a second time. The Navy had spoken. Now he would surely be retired by the end of June 1953.

Rickover's subordinates immediately began a campaign to save their chief. At least one of them, in violation of Navy regulations, contacted a home-state Senator. The staff man who did that was Eli Roth. The Senator was Herbert H. Lehman, a Democrat and, like Roth, Jewish. Lehman's name would bizarrely figure in the rumors about the campaign to keep Rickover.

Two of the Oak Ridge originals, James Dunford and Raymond Dick, were particularly active. There is not much of a record about what they did to help Rickover. Dunford declined to be interviewed for this book; Dick died in 1953. From Blair's recollections, however, it is possible to piece together the main thrust of Dick's campaign: the recruiting of the press, mainly through Blair.

The August 4, 1952, issue of *Time* launched the Dick-Blair campaign. After describing Rickover's accomplishments, the story said:

> Two weeks ago a 15-man Navy selection board met in Washington to choose 30 new rear admirals. Rickover's name was passed over. Selection boards work in secrecy and never give reasons for such actions. In Rickover's case, people who know how the Navy's mind operates believe that the Navy was expressing a deep-seated prejudice against technical specialists. Both the Army and the Air Force have partially broken down similar prejudices. The well-rounded officer in those services is still regarded as the ideal, but they recognize that in a technological age specialization is so valuable and so unavoidable that specialists cannot be barred from high rank.
>
> The Navy's failure to recognize this in Rickover's case promises to cost it a brilliant officer who developed the most important new weapon since World War II. . . .

The story was headlined "Brazen Prejudice," and although the prejudice referred to was against specialists, people in and out of the Navy read it as a signal that something more was involved. There was no mention that selection boards have always met in secret and that the Navy had many technical specialists in its admiral ranks. There was no mention in the Blair story that Rickover was Jewish; by this time Rickover considered himself an Episcopalian.

The theory of anti-Semitism did surface at this time, however, and it was never to be laid to rest. In *Nuclear Navy,* the official history of nuclear propulsion from 1946 to 1962, authors Hewlett and Duncan, with some access to Rickover's files, examine the promotion fight assiduously. They confine their feelings about anti-Semitism to a note in the back of the book. The note says: "Although none of the naval officers, including Rickover, interviewed by the authors would acknowledge that religious prejudice was an influence in the Navy during these years, the authors concluded on the basis of all the oral evidence that Rickover's Jewish origins did in some instances fuel the antagonism between Rickover and his fellow officers. Religious prejudice was in our opinion a reinforcing but not a controlling factor in Rickover's unpopularity in the Navy."

The word "origins" was accurately used—not "religion" or "belief" or some other word to indicate that Rickover considered himself a Jew at the time.

Blair perceived prejudice deeper than this cautious note would suggest. After his August 4 piece was published, his quest for a good story on Rickover had become a patriotic quest to keep Rickover in the Navy.

"There was a lot of nervousness at *Time* about the 'Brazen Prejudice' story," Blair remembers. "We were taking on the Navy, looking anti-Navy. Shepley, Roy Alexander, and myself had a strategy meeting. I was convinced by then that if Rickover were not kept in the Navy, the team would break up. The meeting took up the question of how to save Rickover.

"It was Roy's suggestion that I write a huge story, giving the whole history of Rickover, the stupid Navy, the whole thing. It was a scheme. We didn't intend to publish the story, but we would turn it into the Pentagon's voluntary censorship office—the office of security and review—and just see what happened."

As word got around the Pentagon that Blair was crusading for Rickover, Blair started hearing reports that he, Blair, was part of a "Jewish cabal." The source of the rumors, Blair recalled being told, was Vice Admiral James Fife, a Deputy Chief of Naval Operations when the *Nautilus* was begun. Fife, who had held major submarine commands during the war, was no fan of Rickover. Blair told the authors that Fife himself believed, until his death in 1975, that Blair was married to a daughter of Senator Lehman. Blair, who was Catholic, was actually married to a Catholic, the former Agnes Kemp Devereux, niece of former Congressman James Devereux, the famed Marine hero of Wake Island.

Fife himself said in his memoirs, "I didn't think the feeling about Rickover was anti-Jewish. . . . I knew him for a long time before I ever knew that he was a Jew, and I think that was the reason that was used for getting him a lot of attention, that he was discriminated against, but I don't think that had anything to do with it."

Nevertheless, Blair heard himself being called "Rabbi Blair," and he took the rumor campaign seriously enough to wonder whether it would affect his pending membership in the Chevy Chase Country Club, one of Washington's most exclusive and most gentile clubs. (He was accepted.)

Certainly there are many tales about Rickover that are openly anti-Semitic or at least insensitive to the religion of his birth. At least one member of the Class of 1914 went to his grave convinced, as he repeatedly told his son, that the promotion of "that little Jew" had ruined the Navy. Admiral James L. Holloway, Jr., who, as Chief of Personnel would help Rickover in many ways, nevertheless referred to him as "a little Jew." The reference is made in Holloway's memoirs, where Holloway suggested that "Rick had his heart on his sleeve a long time because, a little Jew in the Naval Academy, [he] probably got kicked all over the place, and he had to be over-aggressive to overcome it, which he was."

Rear Admiral William Thompson, a former Chief of Information, remembered hearing a discussion of Rickover between two admirals: Elton Grenfell, an early supporter of Rickover and at the time Commander of the Pacific Fleet's submarine force, and Ruthven E. Libby, commander of the First Fleet. Libby, a classmate of Rickover, had graduated Number 3—behind Olmsted and Kaplan.

Grenfell was briefing Libby on a recent visit by Rickover. Grenfell, according to Thompson, said "That SOB told me I wasn't even qualified to command a nuclear submarine."

"I know Hyman, too," Libby reportedly remarked. "When they circumcised him they threw the wrong end away."

There is no evidence that Rickover himself raised the anti-Semitism issue. Evidence of what Rickover did to help himself is difficult to find. He did have discussions with members of Congress on nuclear issues during this period. It is a matter of record that he met in the White House with President Truman on February 9, 1952, to brief the President on the *Nautilus*. Later, Rickover suggested to Senator McMahon, founding chairman of the Joint Committee on Atomic Energy, that he invite President Truman to the keel-laying. McMahon, dying of cancer, telephoned the President. That is how President Truman got to McMahon's home state for the ceremony that, to Navy eyes, had been spoiled by the sitting-handshake incident. However, President Truman—who liked feisty people and disliked stuffy institutions—did not interfere again with the Navy's selection process, possibly because he was nearing the end of his term. (Earlier, when the Secretary of the Navy had allegedly dropped Arleigh Burke from the selection list because of his participation in the "Admiral's Revolt," and later, when Robert L. Dennison, Truman's naval aide, was not selected, Truman had both men added to the list. Both Burke and Dennison later reached four-star rank.)

Dick became the director of the save-Rickover campaign. He worked his full day on Rickover's staff and then, at night, with his colleagues he gathered around his kitchen table and mapped out the strategy. The most important project soon became the book that Clay Blair would write on Rickover.

As Blair recalled the sequence of events, Ned Beach, long a supporter of Rickover, had written a novel, *Run Silent, Run Deep*. The editor was William F. Buckley of Holt and Company. Beach put Blair in touch with Buckley, who offered Blair a contract with Holt. Blair talked to Dick, and soon received not only approval but also promises of extraordinary cooperation. By now it was late in 1952.

Blair, meanwhile, had written some 10,000 words on Rickover for *Time*. This story, designed to smoke out the Navy's opposition to Rickover, was swirling through the Navy, ostensibly for security clearance. "It was there for about ninety days," Blair says, "and it was that unpublished material—not what eventually *was* published in *Time*—that caused such consternation in the Pentagon."

Time had officially submitted the hoax story to the Navy's Chief of Information, or CHINFO, on December 9, 1952. (Lewis S. Parks, the CHINFO, was a new rear admiral; he had been selected by the same board that had passed over Rickover.) When the story was still being held up more than two months later, *Time* leaked news of the hold-up to *The Washington Post*, which was enough aware of the plot to have a reporter call the anonymous author of the *Time* story, Clay Blair. In this way the news behind the news—the suppression of a pro-Rickover story—finally was made public.

The story, the *Post* said on February 18, 1953, "was given a Defense Department security okay in two days, it was contended. The subsequent weeks of delay were due to an effort to change the magazine's slant on the story and meanwhile to plant counteracting friendly stories in other magazines, *Time* reporters feel . . ."

The *Post* said that the Atomic Energy Commission had circled in red and labeled "delete—not true" a part of the story that said that "the atomic submarine program has been going to hell in a handbasket. Where morale was once top-notch, where work was once carried on at a frenetic pace, the office of Rickover's special Washington task force is now beset with trials and tribulations."

Rear Admiral Homer N. Wallin, Chief of the Bureau of Ships, was also shown Blair's story. Wallin ordered an aide to write a memorandum that would refute Blair's claims. *Time* got a copy of the memorandum and passed it to the *Post*. The memo said that "perhaps 90 percent of the raw factual data appear to be accurate, but the story itself was 'biased.' " The memorandum suggested that CHINFO, "with extreme delicacy," plant a refuting story "more friendly to the Navy" in *Newsweek* or *U.S. News & World Report.*

Wallin then wrote Parks a five-page letter that called the story "a scurrilous and uninformed emotional appeal to sympathy for a supposed underdog." That was the heart of it. Wallin spoke for many officers in the Navy when he said that he disliked Rickover's role as "a supposed underdog." What the Navy had against Rickover was the way he operated on his own; the way he sat down, in civilian clothes, when he shook hands with the President; the way he sought to use Congress and the press; the way he did not go off stage when the Navy told him to; the way he tried to undermine the selection-board system.

The system itself would next come into public view. Wallin, who was Rickover's boss, suggested to Rickover that he retire but stay on the job, as a passed-over captain until the *Nautilus* was completed. That offer was mentioned in a story in *Time's* competitor, *Newsweek,* on March 23. That story seems to have been part of the Navy's counterattack against Clay Blair's unpublished story. *Newsweek* described Rickover as "a man who believes the shortest distance between two points is a straight line even if it bisects six admirals." By the time *Newsweek* published its story, though, the battle was nearly over.

The Navy had apparently forgotten that Rickover had another job: He also worked for the Atomic Energy Commission, and there he had more friends than enemies. Clay Blair had been called to the AEC for "conferences" on his story, as he had been called before the Navy. AEC's public-information officials had evaluated the story on its own terms and circulated a memo to AEC commissioners. The memo said:

> The writer's premise seems to be that if the Navy does not make Capt. Rickover an Admiral the AEC atomic submarine projects will collapse. This is false and represents gross distortion. The atomic submarine projects are too far along and have gathered too much momentum to be more than temporarily slowed down by any change in personnel, no matter how important that personnel may be. However, if Rickover is forced to resign from the Navy on retirement schedules, these things probably will happen: (a) morale of the AEC Naval Reactors Branch will be affected; (b) some of Rickover's staff will leave; and (c) there will be a time lag that usually occurs when there is a change in a key post.

The AEC had found the terms—*morale, time lag*—that would trigger a response from another institution where Rickover was gathering far more friends than enemies: the United States Congress. The atom was popular in Congress at that time. On November 1, 1952, the AEC had exploded the world's first hydrogen bomb at Eniwetok. The Soviet Union followed with its H-bomb a short time later. The AEC was about to begin its fifth round of nuclear-weapons tests in Nevada. Atmospheric testing of atomic nuclear bombs had been an issue in the Presidential election; Adlai Stevenson had been against it; Dwight D. Eisenhower had been for it, and he had won.

Anything that was affecting the morale of people in the nuclear business, and anything that was delaying the United States nuclear effort was a political issue in 1952 and 1953. In Congress, "national security" had become a patriotic phrase that could be invoked by anyone who believed that something was being done that would hurt the United States in the cold war with the Soviet Union. While the Rickover retention fight was quietly being discussed in Congress, he and his career secretly became part of a sensational national-security case.

William L. Borden, who had served as executive director of the Joint Committee on Atomic Energy, in November 1953 wrote a letter to J. Edgar Hoover, director of the Federal Bureau of Investigation. Borden charged that atomic scientist J. Robert Oppenheimer, "the father of the atomic bomb," was "more probably than not . . . an agent of the Soviet Union." This letter, which launched the Oppenheimer case, aired the claim that would bring down the scientist: that he "worked tirelessly . . . to retard the United States H-bomb program." The letter also contained what would be, in the shadow of the hydrogen bomb, a minor issue—but the issue that would greatly help in rounding up conservative and right-wing support for Rickover in Congress. Oppenheimer, Borden told Hoover, had "used his potent influence against . . . the nuclear-powered submarine. . . ."

In those days of the hunters and the hunted, to be aligned against Oppenheimer was to be on the side of patriotism. Rickover eventually would find himself safely on the side of Dr. Edward Teller, a witness against Oppenheimer, and AEC Commissioners Lewis L. Strauss and Thomas E. Murray, who would be in the majority that stripped Oppenheimer of his security clearance because of the cloud cast over him by Borden.

Borden himself had been a key Rickover operative on Capitol Hill since 1950, when Rickover first met with Senator Brien McMahon, chairman of the Joint Committee, to brief him on the nuclear submarine. At the time Borden wrote the letter to Hoover, Borden was no longer executive director of the committee because he was a Democratic appointee and the Republicans had taken control of the committee in 1953. Rickover found Borden a job in 1953. Though Borden was a lawyer, not an engineer, he was made, on Rickover's recommendation, special assistant to Charles H. Weaver, Westinghouse vice-president in charge of atomic-power development. The long-lasting relationship between Weaver and Rickover—and Westinghouse and Rickover—had begun when Rickover was in charge of BuShips' electrical section during World War II.

Borden's work on Capitol Hill is not as well known or documented as the work of another man who also deeply believed in the atom, Henry M. Jackson, who in November 1952 was elected to his first term as a United States Senator. Jackson had been involved with nuclear matters almost as long as Rickover had. As a Democratic representative from the state of Washington, he was appointed to the Joint Committee on Atomic Energy in January 1949. He met Rickover occasionally on committee business. Then, on a plane carrying observers to nuclear tests in the Pacific in 1952, Representative Jackson talked for hours with Captain Rickover. Their enduring relationship began on that plane, where Jackson first heard from Rickover of his fight against the Navy.

Now, in early 1953, the new Senator Jackson learned that the Navy and the nation might lose Rickover. He went to work in the halls of Congress. So did Congressman Sidney R. Yates, the Democratic representative from Rickover's home town, Chicago, where Rickover's naval career had begun when Representative Adolph Joachim Sabath appointed him to Annapolis. Sabath had been Chicago's "Jewish Congressman" in his time, and Yates had succeeded him in that role. Yates, like Sabath, was a Congressman who listened to his constituents. He listened to entreaties from Rickover's staff, and he also listened to Rickover's relatives still living in Chicago.

Dick and the others on Rickover's staff rounded up published documents that had praised Rickover and his work—magazine articles, statements by AEC commissioners, speeches by Senator McMahon, and President Truman's remarks at the *Nautilus* keel-laying ceremony. Yates obligingly put the packet of praise into the *Congressional Record.*

The Navy tried to hold off and then fight off Congressional inquiries about Rickover. A memorandum—classified as "Confidential"—was circulated by the Bureau of Naval Personnel to explain the selection process and to show how unlikely it was that any EDO captain would be selected for rear admiral. The Navy tried to make its case objective, with figures and appeals to tradition: "Members of a board ... take an oath which through some 30-odd years of the application of this system has been taken as one of the most serious of the duties which they perform. Traditionally, the integrity of our selection boards has never been challenged by individuals who were selected or not."

Once again, Rickover was being portrayed by the Navy as the sorehead, the self-proclaimed underdog.

The memo ended on "philosophical points" made by the memo's author, Rear Admiral Roland N. Smoot, an assistant chief of Naval Personnel. "I do not believe," he wrote, "that the layman understands that we do not promote as a reward for long and faithful service or for any single outstanding accomplishment."

From another quarter, the Bureau of Ships, the Navy tried a similar argument, this one aimed at Senator Leverett Saltonstall, chairman of the Senate Armed Services Committee.

> The Bureau of Ships [Saltonstall was told] has several specialized Engineering Duty Officers in the grade of Captain who are deemed qualified to fill the nuclear power billet now held by Captain Rickover, which, incidentally, is a Captain's billet. . . .
>
> The Navy has had the foresight to conduct a program of education and training in nuclear matters for many years. As a consequence, we have a strong group of officers and civilians actively engaged in nuclear matters . . . we depend upon teamwork rather than solely upon individual performance.

The letter also noted that nuclear propulsion "was not the idea or hope of any one person" and had been "under discussion in 1939–1940." So the Navy even denied the paternal claims of the father of the nuclear submarine.

The Navy, through the Bureau of Ships, the Bureau of Personnel, and the Chief of Information, had tried to establish the facts and the justice of the system. History and good sense is on our side, the Navy was saying. But Congress was not listening to the Navy.

Clay Blair had been writing his book. For nearly a month he had been holed up in an office adjacent to Rickover's. One of Rickover's most trusted staff men—Louis Roddis, an Oak Ridge original—was passing Blair everything that could legally be shown to him. Blair was introduced to Rickover's famous "pinks," the flimsy carbons that poured out of secretaries' typewriters. Rickover had ordered the secretaries to make a pink of everything they typed, and Blair says he looked at every unclassified pink while he was working at Rickover's headquarters.

"The book was written almost exclusively in Rickover's office," Blair recalled. "They gave me an office and a typewriter, and I had total access to all but classified information."

Mrs. Rickover, a scholar and a fine stylist, read the manuscript. Blair said she did not like it. He felt that she had toward him and the manuscript the special kind of disdain that scholars often have for journalists. Blair had typed the book on cheap copy paper, triple-spaced "with lots of changes and inserts penciled in." He handed this to Dixie Davis, Rickover's own secretary, who typed the final manuscript on her typewriter, just outside Rickover's door.

Dixie Davis told the authors that Rickover himself worked over the typed manuscript. "He edited it to make sure it was factual," she remembered. "He seemed to like the book. He bought lots of copies."

Blair said that Rickover checked the smooth typescript. "He and Mrs. Rickover read it over. She made a lot of corrections, changes in grammar and punctuation. She was very intelligent and well read. I remember she gave me a file folder with a well-written, thoroughly researched piece on the history of selection boards."

In the transition from President Truman to President Eisenhower, Secretary of the Navy Dan A. Kimball would be replaced by Robert B. Anderson. There was some talk that President Truman would, in effect, order Kimball to promote Rickover in an eleventh-hour move. At Kimball's final press conference, Blair and Lloyd Norman of the *Chicago Tribune* persistently questioned the outgoing secretary about the Rickover promotion. Kimball said nothing, and he and President Truman left office in January 1953 with Rickover still a captain and his forced retirement scheduled for June.

When Anderson became Secretary of the Navy, Blair's book was finished but still in manuscript form. What happened next, according to Blair, was that Beach, President Eisenhower's new naval aide, told Anderson about the book and Anderson called in Blair. "Rickover has been dumped in my lap," Anderson said, according to Blair. "May I read your Rickover book?" Blair said he then gave Anderson a copy of the manuscript.

On Capitol Hill, meanwhile, Jackson went to Saltonstall and pressed for a more thorough examination of the "Rickover Case" by the Senate Armed Services Committee. Admiral Wallin was brought before the committee, and the Chief of BuShips reiterated the Navy's basic claim: Rickover is in a captain's billet, and "we now have on hand a number of Engineering Duty Captains who are well qualified to assume this post." By this time, members of the committee, along with members of the Joint Committee on Atomic Energy, were getting angry at the Navy's insistence on making the issue whether Rickover could be replaced. That was no longer the point. Rickover's staff, along with Jackson and Yates, were convincing Congressmen that the point was the one that had been made by the AEC: the loss of Rickover would delay and have a demoralizing effect on a vital defense operation.

Yates, introducing a bill that would add civilians to the selection board, said that the Navy was jeopardizing the future of nuclear propulsion. Then Yates, a Jew, raised another issue. He said that the Navy was not promoting Rickover because many officers in the Navy personally disliked him. Anti-Semitism had not been openly raised, but now it simmered. So did apprehension that the Rickover Case would somehow be pulled into the vortex of anti-Semitism and McCarthyism.

In ways too subtle to monitor publicly, the two *isms* had become entwined. In the witch-hunting climate, they thrived on each other. Republican Senator Joseph R. McCarthy was at the height of his power, and anti-Semitism had been rising. Julius and Ethel Rosenberg were awaiting execution in the electric chair in Sing Sing Prison for passing atomic secrets to the Soviet Union. A witness at a futile hearing to appeal the death sentence said, "When I look in that courtroom I see no [Judge Irving R.] Kaufman but McCarthy." The Rosenbergs were labeled by the anti-Semitic pamphleteers as "Jew-Communist-atom-spies"—a label that summarized the fears and hates of the times.

McCarthy himself had embarrassed the Senate Armed Services Committee by fostering a blatant case of anti-Semitism. In 1950 President Truman nominated Mrs. Anna Rosenberg (no relative to Julius and Ethel) for Assistant Secretary of Defense. Soon McCarthy got "evidence" that she was a Communist. The informant was the Reverend Wesley Swift, later described as "an anti-Semite who had refused to believe that Christ was a Jew." Mrs. Rosenberg was soon cleared of the baseless accusation, and the Armed Services Committee learned that the man behind the charge was Gerald L. K. Smith, notorious for his anti-Catholic, anti-black, anti-Semitic campaigns.

McCarthy had been regarded as a pro-Navy Senator ever since he, as an ex-Marine, lined up against the Air Force in the bomber-versus-aircraft-carrier debate. He had also spoken out against the "usurpation of

Congressional prerogatives by the brass in the Pentagon"—a theme that soon would be Rickover's. But there was an uneasiness about McCarthy, a fear that the free-swinging Senator might be able to manufacture a case against Rickover. In that era when guilt-by-association often triumphed over justice and reason, McCarthy could make a sensation out of a Russian-born Jewish naval officer who possessed the nation's most precious secrets—and was married to a woman employed by an organization headed by Alger Hiss.

Of such stuff were McCarthy's charges often made. Mrs. Rickover had worked for and written for the Carnegie Endowment for International Peace, a pillar of the foreign-service establishment. John Foster Dulles and Dwight D. Eisenhower had been members of the board of directors of the Endowment. But when Alger Hiss was indicted for perjury in 1948, he had been a president of the Endowment, and he and the institution became part of the shorthand used to describe supposed plots of the Communist conspiracy. There also was the potential problem of Drew Pearson, the muckraking Washington columnist who regularly attacked McCarthy in print and was himself physically attacked by McCarthy in a fight broken up by Senator-elect Richard M. Nixon in December 1950. Pearson had been cultivated by Rickover's staff, and it was feared that Pearson's sympathy for Rickover might turn McCarthy against Rickover.

In such a climate of hysteria, staff man Ray Dick mapped his kitchen-table strategy. He got word to McCarthy that Rickover was an independent-minded patriot and worthy of McCarthy's support. At the same time, backing for Rickover was recruited by Senator Lehman and his Democratic colleague Senator Estes Kefauver, both of them political foes of McCarthy. Dick's strategy seemed to tilt Rickover toward Republicans but not offend the Democrats. It turned out to be a masterful winning strategy, and it earned for Dick a well-deserved reputation as a sagacious politician.

Jackson, though a freshman Senator, was already on the rise because of his experience as a Representative and a member of the Joint Committee on Atomic Energy. Among his fellow Democrats and among members of the Armed Services Committee he spread the word that he knew what was really going on. There is a record of what Jackson said—or what he meant when he told Senators—that he "knew the full story of the Rickover case." That fragmentary quotation is in the archives of Rickover's Nuclear Reactors Division in the form of a memo, "Rickover to the Files, March 3, 1953." Existence of the memo, noted in *Nuclear*

Navy, is a rare bit of documentary evidence that Rickover was well aware of the backstage political maneuvering over his promotion. He himself remained publicly aloof from the issue.

Holloway, Chief of Naval Personnel, admired Rickover and worked behind the scenes. Exactly what he did he revealed for the first time in his unpublished reminiscences. Discussing Rickover, he said:

> He's got plenty of G-U-T-S. . . . I think his compatriots in the EDO group were probably jealous as hell of him. So he was passed over. [He] got the *Nautilus* built five years ahead of what it would have been without him, just by being a little ornery pusher and fighting and giving them hell. . . .
>
> Well, they passed him over, and there was a hell of a roar on the Hill. I talked to Henry Jackson, whom I know very well, and he said, "Admiral, I know he's probably obnoxious to a lot of people, but that fellow's got a following." And I said, "I . . . agree with you." So I went to Bob Anderson, the Secretary of the Navy, and I said, "There is machinery in the law which is very strict about the promotion and the Secretary can't dictate, but there is a way that you can write in a precept a certain qualification that you want, and we can write it so strongly that they can't accept anybody but Rickover." So I wrote a precept for a board of 6 line [officers] and 3 EDOs and . . . tied it up so that the qualification was such that only Rickover could qualify.

The end came abruptly on February 26, 1953, when the Senate Armed Services Committee announced that it was holding up the promotion of the thirty-nine captains picked by the selection board while the committee arranged for the launching of an investigation of the operation of selection boards. The Navy almost immediately surrendered. On March 6, Secretary Anderson wrote to Saltonstall that the Navy would empanel a selection board to "recommend engineering duty captains for retention on active duty for a period of one year with a requirement in the precept that one of those recommended for retention be experienced in the field of atomic propulsion for ships."

The battle was over, with Rickover clearly the victor. He would remain on active duty until the next specially instructed selection board was convened in July. Somehow, Holloway learned what happened at this supposedly secret meeting. All three of the "stupid" EDOs, Holloway later wrote, "didn't vote for him. The line gave him six votes and did [select him], and made him by two-thirds [majority] an Admiral, a Rear Admiral."

Later, Holloway recalled, one of his friends said, "This is the end of the selection system." "No, it isn't," Holloway replied. "It isn't the end . . . because we've used a law to promote him . . . to make the will of the Secretary felt. When we're too highbound and reactionary, there's room in the law for the Secretary to get his way. If you don't do that, you'd have a special law in Congress which would *really* be the end of the selection system."

No ceremony attended Rickover's promotion. His name was merely one on a list of officers formally nominated for promotion by President Eisenhower on July 30. At the same time, Wilson D. Leggett, Jr., Rear Admiral, became Chief of BuShips, succeeding Wallin, who had been opposed to Rickover's promotion and, apparently, to Rickover himself. Wallin's replacement could be explained away as an example of the Navy's traditional rotation of officers—a tradition grandly ignored in Rickover's retention. But there was also the feeling of a purge, a feeling that Congress was, as McCarthy had put it, fighting "the brass in the Pentagon." (McCarthy soon would take on the Army in his most celebrated hearings.)

The Navy was reeling. An old tradition had been publicly disregarded for one man. Congress had brazenly waded into the Navy's private promotion system. Rickover supporters had swarmed to Capitol Hill like lobbyists. Attempts had been made to get defense contractors to put pressure on Congress to retain Rickover. Nothing like this had ever happened before. Never had a captain made a spectacle out of being passed over. Never had a single officer so openly used Congress for his personal purposes.

Some speeches and the appeals were on the record. Off the record was at least one approach through what President Eisenhower would one day call the "military-industrial complex." The approach was made by Isaac Harter, chairman of the board of the Babcock & Wilcox Company. Though not a household name, Babcock & Wilcox was a manufacturer well known in the Department of Defense and the Atomic Energy Commission. The company, which built large equipment, had been in the nuclear business from the beginning, producing reactor vessels. (Its name would be heard again in 1979, for Babcock & Wilcox built the reactors at the Three Mile Island power plant.) Harter tried to recruit the influence of David E. Lilienthal, former chairman of the Atomic Energy Commission, but Lilienthal declined. "I did this," Lilienthal later wrote, "because I didn't like the idea of a political approach to promotion, but also because I never had been sympathetic with a fellow who got things done by beating the hell out of others, as I felt he had."

Rickover had broken all the rules, and yet here was Rickover—*Rear Admiral* Rickover now—suddenly one of the most well-known men in the Navy. The ultimate proof of this came on January 11, 1954, when Rickover—a week after Man of the Year Konrad Adenauer and a week before Vice President Richard M. Nixon—made the cover of *Time*. If there was one moment when the official, traditional Navy lined up against Rickover it was during that week.

For there was more. Not just *Time* but also Clay Blair's book, *The Atomic Submarine and Admiral Rickover*. The book was plugged in a footnote to *Time*'s laudatory cover article. Much of what was in the magazine article was in the book. The simultaneous publication of the book and the cover story was a triumph of publicity management, and a testament to the power of Time, Inc., which had made Rickover an official hero of Time, Inc. He would be one of only three military officers on *Time* covers in 1954. The other two would be Air Force generals, an indication that Blair's original thesis, back in 1951, had been correct: Time, Inc., liked the Air Force. And now Time, Inc., liked not the Navy but the Navy's chief antagonist.

Rickover even put on a uniform for *Time*. He stood on the page in full glory, next to words that were making of him a savior and a prophet: "Admiral Rickover is convinced that nuclear submarines will save the Navy from near-complete elimination as a fighting arm of the nation." This was not the thinking of the Chief of Naval Operations; this was the thinking of a very new and very junior rear admiral. Senior admirals who read the story saw that Rickover had not learned a lesson from the promotion fight. He was not merely feeling lucky, or even grateful. He was talking like someone who planned to take over the Navy.

10 | Congress Comes Aboard

In Rickover's struggle to get his admiral stars, he had been pictured in Congress as a brilliant, embattled captain being deprived of what he had earned by a jealous, hidebound, and possibly bigoted Navy. That view of Rickover had given him not only support but also sympathy. On Capitol Hill support is a commodity and, like any other commodity, it can be bought and sold, or traded. Sympathy is far more enduring and dependable. It is also rare.

Congressmen could sympathize with Rickover, the underdog fighting bureaucracy. In their offices, endless hours were devoted to "case work"—attempts to solve the problems of constituents entangled with federal bureaucrats. To most Congressmen, a bureaucrat was a bureaucrat, no matter in which agency or department he or she worked. Even the most patriotic of Congressmen felt free to berate officials of the Department of Defense—the largest of the bureaucracies—including those in uniform.

In their skillful politicking during the promotion campaign, Rickover and his staff had sensed that he had to work at developing a strong, personal relationship with Congress. He had to become a lobbyist. And, characteristically, he strove to be the best lobbyist on the Hill.

When Rickover started out, his cause was nuclear propulsion and a Congressman could easily support the nuclear submarine, especially if equipment producers or related activities were located in the Congressman's district or state. When Rickover himself became the cause, he too received support. Cynics have difficulty finding the obvious political motive for that support. But a deeper search turns up sympathy. Rickover was not a mere petitioner—the lowest and shortest-lived form of lobbyist. He was an advocate, an ideologue, something of a rebel. Upon Jackson and Yates, upon the Joint Committee on Atomic Energy, and upon other defense-related committees, with his *Time*-reinforced image, Rickover

206

began to build a power base on Capitol Hill. It would not be long before Rickover would get what he wanted for himself—retention, promotion— and what he wanted for what was beginning to be known as his navy, the Rickover navy, the nuclear navy.

Not until the *Nautilus* was a success would Rickover himself be secure. He treated the *Nautilus* as a vindication—although he was painting a somewhat surrealistic picture when he portrayed himself as the underdog battling the mossbacks of the Navy. Through a political chemistry that is very hard to document but can be strongly sensed, many Congressmen came to think that they had helped Rickover build the world's first nuclear-powered submarine. They felt they had been part of the process that gave not just money but encouragement—and perhaps even guidance—to a man who would be out of the Navy if it had not been for them. Congress admired Rickover's image, his style, his apparent honesty, and especially his assaults against what vaguely was the "system."

Soon after he got his admiral stars he began sharing with Congressmen his vision of a nuclear-powered navy. He began to make personal presentations—sometimes they were merely "chats"—before Congressional committees. He sided with and supported the views of the Congressmen; he rarely if ever argued. And Rickover gave as well as he received. Previously, admirals would arrange a VIP visit for a few Congressmen aboard an aircraft carrier or a cruiser, a ship with plenty of room and scores of stewards to assist them, and lots of aircraft or missiles to go streaking overhead and impress them. Rickover did better. On March 20, 1955—just two months after the *Nautilus* went to sea for the first time—the atomic submarine submerged into the Atlantic carrying members of the Joint Committee on Atomic Energy. While the submarine cruised under the waves, the Representatives and Senators held the first Congressional committee session in history to meet underwater. Similar hearings would be held aboard other nuclear submarines and, of course, nuclear surface ships. Later, the wives of Congressmen would largely replace the spouses of naval officers as the principal sponsors of submarines when it came time to break bottles of champagne over their bows. And, in the ultimate of largesse, Rickover would arrange to have nuclear submarines and ultimately a supercarrier named for members of Congress, alive as well as deceased.

By the time the *Nautilus* put to sea, Rickover fully realized that the Navy system had tried to be his nemesis. Only by Congressional intervention had he been promoted to rear admiral and retained in the Navy. He would have to look to Congress, not the Navy, for further retention.

(Promotion beyond two stars for an EDO in peacetime was rare.) There was even the threat of reassignment by the Navy, as EDOs were regularly reassigned every few years, albeit less frequently than line officers, who generally held a position for only about two years. Even if retained on active duty, Rickover would need Congress to keep him in charge of the nuclear program.

"I am a creature of Congress," he would say, encapsulating reality, as usual, in the fewest possible words. There is no specific date when Hyman Rickover finally did become a creature of Congress rather than of the Navy. But the turning point came in 1958.

On February 28, 1958, at a meeting of commissioners of the Atomic Energy Commission, the promotion of Rear Admiral Rickover was on the agenda. The AEC, of course, had nothing to do with the promotion of naval officers. But the Commission was also a creature of Congress, on the leash of the Joint Committee on Atomic Energy, and the AEC commissioners were told that Capitol Hill had discovered a new Navy plot against Rickover.

The situation was this: As a rear admiral at age fifty-eight (or possibly sixty) Rickover once again faced the possibility of forced retirement. If he were not promoted to vice admiral by June 30, 1959, he automatically would be retired under the existing laws. The Navy could intervene. A retention board, scheduled to meet in July 1959, could extend his duty for a year. Such annual extensions could be bestowed until he reached the mandatory retirement age of sixty-two.

The Navy's leadership certainly had not intervened to retain him in 1954, and it seemed highly unlikely that any official attempt would be made to retain Rickover this time. In the four years since the earlier promotion battle, he had become even more obstreperous, more outspoken in his attacks on the Navy and the Defense Department. The Navy was also becoming more outspoken about Rickover. During this escalation of hostilities, *Our Navy,* a private magazine but one which took pride in having its finger on the Navy's pulse, could say in a profile:

> Hyman Rickover isn't quite *Navy.* He just doesn't look the part. There's nothing bluff or salty about him. He's probably the smallest man in the service. He weighs 125 pounds, barely comes to five feet six. . . . Rear Admiral Rickover isn't *Navy* in another way too. He isn't very pliable or sociable. Cards, small talk, golf, dancing—they're all too frivolous for him. Even more important, he is not a team man. Tradition and protocol mean very little to him. The only thing that counts with him is getting the job done. . . . Going through

the regular, accepted channels means nothing to the dehydrated-looking admiral. . . . He's a lone wolf in a sea where *togetherness* is a key word, an egghead within an institution that does not particularly greet some with open arms and may even regard such species with some suspicion.

The magazine inadvertently said quite a bit about the Navy. So did the comments of Rickover's boss, at BuShips, Rear Admiral Albert G. Mumma, who many years before had been in competition with Rickover for head of BuShips' nuclear program. In a newspaper interview, Mumma said, "Rickover . . . works like a dog himself, but he's not a happy, pleasant individual. People feel rebuffed by someone exceptionally tough, and Rickover makes a fetish of that." The Navy charges against Rickover seemed to be that he just did not get along with people who insisted on obeying the Navy's rules, regulations and, most importantly, traditions. Also, he increasingly was arguing against Navy positions put forth by the Secretary of the Navy and Chief of Naval Operations.

The Navy was maneuvering for a battle it expected to win, for the Commander in Chief seemed to be on the Navy's side. President Eisenhower was not a Rickover fan. In Congress, the Admiral's passionate pleas for funds were threatening Eisenhower's equally passionate hope for a balanced budget. And time seemed to be on the Navy's side, too; a flurry over Rickover in 1958 would die down by 1960. Or so it seemed to Pentagon strategists who, once again, were underestimating their enemy.

Around the time of the February AEC meeting, James T. Ramey, staff director of the Joint Congressional Committee on Atomic Energy, began preparing a portfolio of pro-Rickover information for members of the committee. Ramey, a lawyer, had been a Rickover man since the late 1940s. He had moved through several of the boxes on the AEC side of Rickover's Navy-AEC table of organization. In 1958, Ramey was in an important Congressional box and, so, was in a perfect place to set up the Capitol Hill counterattack against the Navy.

All the looming battle needed was an incident to set it off. The Navy and the White House obligingly provided the incident—the snubbing of Rickover through his not being invited to the White House ceremony that celebrated the North Pole voyage of the *Nautilus*.

The Joint Committee aide called members of the committee and gave them the promotion-for-Rickover material. Ramey told them that the snubbing of Rickover was a sure sign that the Navy once more was plotting to dump him. Reporters were soon told the same story. Clay Blair, who had gone from *Time* to the *Saturday Evening Post,* had been at the ceremony, had seen the array of Navy officials, and had missed Rickover. "I called every newspaper bureau in Washington—the *Times, Herald Trib,* the wire services," Blair recalled, "and told them that Rickover had been snubbed. It caused a furor." Within a few days, twenty-one Democratic and Republican Senators agreed on a bill that would award a special medal to Rickover.

The Navy and the White House tried to stop the Rickover offensive. Secretary of the Navy Thomas S. Gates issued a public statement of apology for what he insisted had been a regrettable oversight. President Eisenhower announced that Rickover would be the President's personal representative at the forthcoming welcoming-home ceremonies for the *Nautilus* in New York City.

But it was too late. The press and Congress had established the story of the snub. Even Mrs. Rickover, in a rare appearance in print, spoke up. She told a Hearst reporter, "Navy brass was out to hurt my husband for his independent and free spirit." She also let it be known that she had been snubbed, too. During August two submarines were launched and she had not been asked to sponsor either of them by smashing a bottle of champagne against the prow. Pointedly, Rickover had been "too busy" to attend either launching, although his absences from such events, at which politicians—often Congressmen—would speak, were very rare.

Rickover did not say anything publicly about the reputed snubbing. In fact, he seems not to have said anything, even in a private meeting, after the ceremony, with Commander Anderson and his wife. They visited Rickover in the shabby, plasterboard offices, where Anderson had worked for a year after being picked by Rickover to be the second skipper of the *Nautilus*.

"We found him in a very happy mood," Anderson later wrote. "[He] was not anxious to dwell on the feat. His mind was preoccupied with the details and planning of nuclear submarines of the future."

Years later, people who thought they knew Rickover were still wondering just how genuine the uproar had been. Rickover always insisted that he hated ceremonies and usually tried to avoid them. One aide recalled how, when Rickover was invited to the Nixon White House, he called the President personally to inquire whether the "Military Full Dress" instructions on the invitation was obligatory. The President told him it would be all right for him to appear in a tuxedo.

Whether the snub had been exaggerated or not, the effect of the reaction was that Rickover almost immediately was out of danger. Rumors of his impending retirement ceased. And the Navy withdrew to carry out an ignominious task: Some way had to be found to make Rickover a vice admiral even though his boss—the Chief of BuShips—was a rear admiral. The Navy would have to countenance what Rickover had consistently done since Oak Ridge days; rank would have to be ignored.

Mumma, Rickover's nominal chief in BuShips, was a rear admiral. They were barely coexisting at equal rank. But there was ample precedent in the Navy for such an arrangement. For a strict seniority system made it possible for officers of the same rank to know where each stood in the naval hierarchy; the man longer in the rank was senior. So, under the system, Mumma had still been over Rickover. Promotion of Rickover to vice admiral, however, would painfully wrench the system, but there was no doubt that the system had to be wrenched.

Congress had chosen Rickover over the Navy. The Navy's sense of tradition, of system, of how to operate—all this suddenly had to go by the boards. Yet, it was far better to lose this battle over Rickover than to bring down upon the entire Navy the wrath of the most powerful men in Congress.

Power in the Congress is concentrated in specific committees, and that power has a way of being transmitted back to certain states. No power was more visibly transmitted than that handled and dispensed by the Joint Committee on Atomic Energy. Membership on, say, the House Appropriations Committee might mean that a member's district would be a likely candidate for some of the many boons—from an irrigation project to a military base—that the committee could bestow. Because the committee's benefices were so varied, however, it was often difficult to discern in a committee decision the immediate benefits to a specific member's district. The Joint Committee on Atomic Energy had only one concern—the incredibly powerful, well-publicized, and extremely expensive phenomenon that the committee controlled. So, to see a relationship between what that committee did and whether a member's constituency prospered, it was only necessary to see where the principal nuclear facilities were located.

Senator Brien McMahon was a freshman Senator from Connecticut when, in December 1945, he introduced a bill that would pass control of atomic energy from the military to civilians. He became the first chairman of the Joint Committee and also one of Rickover's earliest supporters. His political career was tragically cut short by his death from cancer in 1952, but he lived to see the *Nautilus* being built—at the Electric Boat yard in Connecticut.

Henry M. Jackson of the state of Washington had been on the Joint Committee as a Representative and he would serve on it as a Senator. He was also one of Rickover's first admirers and was his champion in the promotion fight. The nation's key nuclear processing plants, built to produce plutonium for weapons, was located in Richland, Washington.

The most powerful of the atomic Congressmen was without a doubt Senator Clinton P. Anderson. His state, New Mexico, proudly called itself the birthplace of the atomic bomb. Anderson helped to preserve that birthright by his membership on, and in the late 1950s domination of, the Joint Committee. The capital of his nuclear fiefdom was Los Alamos, site of the nation's most secret nuclear research. No man in the Senate had more political dependency on nuclear energy than Anderson when, in August 1958, he revealed to the Senate the new threat against Admiral Rickover. No man in the Senate had more political clout in a discussion that touched in any way on nuclear energy.

"In the past," Anderson said, "the old guard attempted to force this man out of the Navy. Congress saved him before and it is my opinion that, if necessary, Congress can save him again."

The campaign had officially begun. The medal-for-Rickover resolution sped through both the Senate and the House. Despite the press of other, high-priority items on the agenda in the rush to adjournment, the unanimously endorsed resolution went to the White House on August 18.

President Eisenhower could do little more than sign, smiling his famous smile and undoubtedly wondering as he did so what it was about this man that put him in such exclusive company.

Good engineers always build redundancy into the system, and Rickover acted like a good engineer. He backed up the medal with hand-tooled publicity. He allowed himself to be interviewed by Associated Press reporter Frances Lewine and, although he had little to say on the record—"Forget the personal stuff," he told her—he did emerge as a hero: "He has been offered many lucrative civilian jobs—some paying more than 10 times his Navy salary and allowances of $1,568 a month— but Admiral Rickover is intent on doing a job for his country."

He also allowed himself to be interviewd by *Life* magazine and, curiously, the lucrative job-offer reference occurred in that laudatory piece, too, though in another context. To show how respected Rickover was on the Hill, *Life* quoted Congressional statements made earlier that year. At issue was $35 million to develop a nuclear power plant for a destroyer. Members of the House were debating the allocation—if debating is the word for what went on.

Representative Chet Holifield of California, an author of the original atomic-energy act and by then a confidant of Rickover, started the paean:

"Mr. Chairman, I rise in support of the bill. . . . I have a great deal of confidence in the man who is in charge of this particular program, Admiral Hyman Rickover. . . ."

Representative John W. McCormack responded with, "Admiral Rickover appeared before the special select committee of which I am chairman in connection with outer space the other day. He made an outstanding witness and made a profound impression. . . ."

Holifield added more praise: "I do not believe there is a man in existence that has the composite knowledge which is embodied in Admiral Rickover . . . there are many industrial companies that would pick this man up and pay him five times as much as the Navy. . . ."

"I would say ten times as much," McCormack remarked.

That hypothetical remark apparently was the basis for the assertion in the AP story that Rickover could do so much better financially if he left the Navy and took a job in private industry. Rickover, of course, had no control over what was said in the AP story or the *Life* article. But he apparently was the source for the Holifield remark, made in Congressional debate, and for the statement in the AP story.

The hint that Rickover might quit could only have been the work of a public-relations genius. Rickover himself was certainly that genius, although he publicly postured against the very idea of such activities. He once was asked, "How many public-relations officers do you have?" "Zero," he replied; and then he candidly added: "I think I am my own best public-relations officer."

August 1958 belonged to Rickover. The whole month, *Life* said, amounted to a "National Be-Nice-To-Rear-Admiral-Hyman-G.-Rickover Week"—and in a long story, its adulation reminiscent of Clay Blair's book, *Life* again told the underdog-against-the-Navy story and raised the issue of "prejudice against Jews at Annapolis" during Rickover's days there. (This time the issue of anti-Semitism seemed even less likely than before. More persons knew of Rickover's break with the Jewish faith some years earlier. Republican Senator Jacob Javits, himself Jewish, said, "It's more a Billy Mitchell case then a Dreyfus case.")

He was in the halls of Congress now, taking his plea for a nuclear navy to people like Senator John F. Kennedy, who quoted Rickover as saying that he needed five years more to complete his "monumental work"; and to Senator Lyndon B. Johnson, who called him "an uncommon man"; and to Vice President Richard M. Nixon, who would take Rickover along on the highly publicized Nixon tour of the Soviet Union. Each of these future Presidents would face in the White House the choice between retiring Rickover or pleasing the Navy. Each would choose Rickover.

The 1958 crisis over Rickover's retention ended in October with a four-paragraph Navy press release that said Rickover would be promoted to vice admiral "to fill a newly created three-star rank authorized by President Eisenhower for the Chief, Naval Reactors Branch, Atomic Energy Commission." The Navy withdrew from further challenges—for a while. But in a "fact sheet" the Bureau of Naval Personnel noted that Rickover faced a mandatory retirement in seven years "unless the Secretary of the Navy determines that the needs of the service are such as to warrant his retention on active duty. An officer so retained continues on active duty on a yearly basis, but must be reconsidered each year for continued retention on active duty."

For the next seven years, the Navy would try, with diminishing effect, to convince Congress that Rickover should be retired. At the same time, Rickover's relations with Congress grew until he was, next to J. Edgar Hoover, probably the most firmly entrenched bureaucrat in the federal government. Looking back to those years, it seems impossible for the Navy not to have realized that Rickover had become a power independent of all conventional restraints.

The Navy's assessment of Rickover had started with an understanding that a zealot could go only so far, and then he must acknowledge that the Navy was more important than his own particular program. If this was, as Javits said, a Billy Mitchell case, then the Navy did not intend to expose the case with a court-martial or public nastiness. When the zealot Rickover had gone too far, the Navy had seen this and had tried to stop it by not selecting him for promotion. That was the quiet, Navy way. It was Congress that had pinned admiral stars on him, and it was Congress that kept giving him its attention—and money for his nuclear ships and submarines. But that did not mean he would have any real power in the real Navy.

He had some power. He was, in a phrase popular in the wardrooms of the 1960s, establishing an organization that was mildly irritating and somewhat subversive. The Rickover Mafia, it was called. But what, after all, could a Rickover really do? In Navy terms, Rickover in the 1960s was a fourth-echelon officer in a technical bureau. His Atomic Energy Commission post was at least three levels down from the AEC's ultimate commissioners. The Navy's system was designed so that a third- or fourth-echelon *mafioso* could not cause any real trouble.

But, as Admiral Elmo R. Zumwalt, Jr., would recollect, Rickover "was a master at blurring the line, pretty fuzzy to begin with, between the two jobs." Long before Zumwalt became Chief of Naval Operations, he saw the way the line blurred. About 1963, while Zumwalt was an aide to Secretary of the Navy Paul Nitze, the Dutch made a request that could have resulted in Holland having some access to U.S. Navy nuclear-reactor technology. Nitze felt that the request should be turned down. But, routinely following the Navy's chain of command, he asked for an opinion from Rickover, as the admiral in charge of nuclear propulsion. "He sent back a strong negative reply, not on Navy stationery as it should have been but on AEC stationery, " Zumwalt wrote in his memoir, *On Watch*. "That was his standard practice whenever a Navy request irked him, since it enabled him to distribute copies of his reply to his Congressional friends without going through the Navy chain of command. . . . Rick doffed his admiral's suit whenever he found himself in conflict with Navy policy, and sniped at the Navy in his civvies."

Rickover's civilian uniform—usually a dark, baggy suit, white shirt with oversized collar, nondescript tie—became his symbol of independence, his show of disdain for the Navy of Annapolis and tradition. In Congressional appearances, the slight, acid-tongued man in the baggy suit became the antithesis of tall, flattering naval officers, wearing dazzling blue and gold. Rickover's posture was a natural to him as Charlie Chaplin's was to him. Neither image was artificial. Rather, both were created by their owners, both effectively produced public recognition, and both were scrupulously maintained to keep that recognition sustained over the years.

In that era, when Presidential aides were beginning to discover a secret called "image," Rickover had already invented and perfected his own. It was vastly different from a public-relations man's idea of image. Rickover's image was a projection of something real, something total. It did not spring out of some hired flack's imagination. It did not have the trappings of an institution. Here was a man—alien to the traditional naval officer—who was more than a cog in an institution. Here was an individual, a singular man who could attract politicians because they saw in him traits that they saw (or wanted to see) in themselves.

Many Congressmen genuinely liked Rickover and there was a camaraderie among them. The reality of that feeling shone forth on April 15, 1959, when, the latest promotion dispute behind him, Rickover walked into the new House Office Building to receive his gold medal from Congress. The Navy probably would not have minded if on that day Rickover, as usual, had worn civilian clothes. But he wore a uniform, its cuffs gilded with the stripes of a vice admiral.

A few days before, Rickover had taken members of the Joint Committee on Atomic Energy aboard the nuclear submarine *Skipjack* for a voyage below the Atlantic. Senator Anderson, the committee chairman, recalled that he and three other members of the committee had been on a similar voyage aboard the *Nautilus* four years before. In the intervening four years there had been, as usual, changes in Congress. But there had been no real change as far as Rickover and his mission were concerned. A continuity had begun: Congressmen would come and go; Rickover would stay.

Television cameras had been set up in the hearing room on that April day. It was the first time that stands for the cameras had been allowed by the Architect of the Capitol. In the glare of the lights, Rickover presented Anderson with a gift—a bottle of "North Pole water," collected by a nuclear submarine.

Anderson had decided to frame the award ceremony within a hearing staged for testimony from Rickover. The hearing started, as such Rickover hearings usually did, with a standard opening question: How many nuclear submarines, ships and power plants are under construction and in operation? There might be questions beyond that area, but this is where the committee focused its attention: Here was the nuclear navy, captained by Rickover and supported by the Joint Committee.

The opening question that day came from James E. Van Zandt of Pennsylvania, a captain in the Naval Reserve. Soon after Van Zandt had become a member of the Joint Committee in 1947, he had met Rickover, mentioned their mutual Navy background, and asked Rickover what to do. "Just keep quiet and get reelected." Rickover had replied.

Rickover launched into his testimony, which usually started out with a listing of the strength of the nuclear navy and homage to what was producing that navy: ". . . Congress has authorized a total of . . . " Rickover rattled through the statistics of the nuclear navy, brought the committee up to date on the problems of the Naval Reactors Branch, and then broke off from his recitation to remark upon an incident aboard the *Skipjack* on the recent Congressional voyage. He recalled that when members of the committee were working on the press release that would describe their voyage, they had asked Rickover what figures would not violate security regulations. He instructed the Congressmen to say in their release that they had "traveled at a depth in excess of four hundred feet, and that you traveled faster than any submarine has ever traveled." Anderson wanted to say something more specific, and Rickover relented. The press release could say "in excess of twenty knots"—but only because President Truman had used that in his remarks at the keel-laying of the *Nautilus*. (Over twenty years later, "over twenty knots" would still be the maximum speed officially attributed to U.S. nuclear submarines.)

Now, as he testified, he again referred to President Truman's revelation and noted that since then the Navy had not been authorized to disclose a higher figure. "I hope that the Republican Administration will permit us to give a new figure." The remark was blatantly made to curry favor with the Republicans of the Administration. This was something Navy witnesses did not do. But Rickover did it, and precipitated no immediate harm. For, soon after Rickover testified, Lyndon B. Johnson, the Democratic majority leader, spoke.

Johnson recalled that "about the time of my birthday last year, Clint Anderson came to me in a hurry and said that he had a little resolution that didn't cost much money but would bring great results to this nation, which he wanted passed by unanimous consent. Before I had a chance to call it up, I found that he was going to pass it by unanimous consent, because he had practically every member of the Senate as sponsor of it."

Johnson went on to say that when Congress launched "this uncommon man on this uncommon venture, we had to renovate a restroom to provide him with an office." Johnson turned to Rickover, who, standing, barely reached Johnson's shoulder. "You are our secret weapon," Johnson said. "You are a symbol of the 'can do' man."

Symbolism had not been lost on Rickover. He and his assistants were originally placed in jerry-built offices behind the Main Navy building in Washington. The offices had been thrown up to house the rapid expansion of Navy headquarters in World War II. One of them, the T-3 Building, was where Rickover was put. The plasterboard offices were so poorly converted for use by Rickover's staff that visitors could easily discern what some of Rickover's spaces had been in earlier days: a ladies room. The ladies'-room-cum-office would become an important part of Rickover's image. He would long remind Congressmen and others that the Navy had assigned him a ladies' powder room in which to build a nuclear submarine.

The gold medal that Rickover received—"on instructions of the Congress of the United States, in behalf of the American people"—was remarkable evidence of just where he stood in the hearts of Congressmen. The first such medal was struck for George Washington in 1776. Other recipients were few and unquestionably distinguished: Cornelius Vanderbilt, Cyrus Field, the Wright brothers, Thomas Edison, Charles Lindbergh, General George C. Marshall, General John Pershing, General Billy Mitchell, Army Surgeon General Walter Reed. The two medals just prior to Rickover's were awarded to Vice President Alben Barkley in 1949 and polio-fighter Jonas Salk in 1958. Anderson said Rickover was the third admiral to get a gold medal by act of Congress. The others he cited were Richard E. Byrd for his polar explorations and Ernest J. King for his service in World War II.

Anderson noted that John Paul Jones had received a medal, "but he was never an admiral in the Navy of this country. He was an admiral in the Russian Navy."* Looking further into Congressional records, one finds a large number of naval heroes were given gold medals by Congress—Truxtun, Preble, Hull, Jacob James, Decatur, Bainbridge, Matthew Calbraith Perry (who opened Japan to the West), and Oliver Hazard Perry ("We have met the enemy and they are ours"), among others. At least one, Victor Blue, cited for his intelligence work in the Spanish-American War and as captain of the battleship *Texas* in European waters in World War I, later became a rear admiral.

Still, on that day in 1959—a day that was relatively early in Rickover's incredibly long career—Congress had shown the Navy just where Rickover stood in Capitol Hill's hierarchy of heroes. But the Navy persisted in thinking of him merely as a violator of the system, a disturbing, arrogant misfit who would be gone in a few years, while the Navy and its system lived on.

In 1961, perhaps with a view toward beginning Rickover's graceful departure, the Navy awarded him its highest peacetime decoration, the Distinguished Service Medal. The ceremonies took place aboard the *Nautilus,* moored at the Electric Boat shipyard. There, six years to the day after the *Nautilus* signaled "underway on nuclear power," Rickover watched as the keel was laid down for the *Lafayette,* first of a new class of Polaris submarines. The French ambassador to the United States was among the guests. Officials were so concerned about protocol that the

---

* *Jones attained the rank of commodore in the American Navy. From 1787 to 1789 he served in the Russian Navy of the Empress Catherine with the rank of rear admiral.*

Chief of Naval Operations reportedly ordered Rickover to wear a uniform. He did.

Five days after the ceremony, the Navy seemed to confirm the "goodbye medal" theory by leaking a story that said Admiral Rickover had to retire before July 1, 1962, according to regulations. But in less than a month Secretary of the Navy John B. Connally announced that he had asked Rickover to stay on. "In the absence of this special action," Connally said, "Admiral Rickover would have retired on February 1, 1962, because his sixty-second birthday is January 27, 1962. The limit of the legal power to extend the active duty of such officers is to age sixty-four."

Age sixty-four was the mandatory retirement age for military officers. But, obviously, some exceptions were on record, generally by Presidential directive, as the classic case when, in October 1942, CNO Ernest J. King wrote to President Roosevelt:

> My dear Mr. President
>   It appears proper that I should bring to your notice the fact that the record shows that I shall attain the age of 64 on November 23rd next—one month from today.
>   I am, as always, at your service.
>
> Most sincerely yours,
Ernest J. King
Admiral, U.S. Navy

Roosevelt's response, penned to the bottom of King's note, was simple and direct: "So what, old top! I may even send you a Birthday present! F.D.R." Rickover, the Navy should have realized, could similarly make use of his relationship to the President—even if he wasn't Chief of Naval Operations and Commander in Chief of the Fleet and there wasn't a war going on.

But the Navy kept leaking speculative stories about Rickover's retirement. In February 1963, after one such story, Rickover slipped into a side door of the White House, spoke to President Kennedy and was photographed with him. Shortly afterward, Secretary of the Navy Fred Korth announced, "The Navy will continue to avail itself of Admiral Rickover's services beyond his statutory retirement date next year." In June 1963, Rickover won from Korth a commitment to recall Rickover to active duty immediately upon his scheduled retirement in February 1964. Then, in December 1963, President Johnson nominated Rickover for permanent rank as a vice admiral (his permanent rank was rear admiral, his temporary rank vice admiral) and announced that he would be kept on active duty after retirement. President Johnson followed this up in September 1965 with announcement of a two-year extension of active duty.

That would be the pattern: Every two years the President—Johnson, Nixon, Ford, Carter—would extend Rickover's active duty. From 1965 on, there rarely would be any drama, although a partisan note was occasionally sounded. Soon after President Nixon's appointment of Melvin R. Laird as Secretary of Defense, for example, the Joint Committee on Atomic Energy expressed the hope that "the Navy will act swiftly to announce their intention to reappoint Admiral Rickover when his present term expires in January 1970 so as to avoid any conjecture to the contrary that might arise again this year based on the poor record of their predecessors in this matter for the past 16 years." Thus went on the record the implication that Rickover's problems had something to do with the Democrats' being in power.

But Rickover always had bipartisan support. Such powerful Democrats as Senators Henry Jackson, Lyndon Johnson, Clinton Anderson, and, in the House, Chet Holifield and Melvin Price had been there from the beginning. In 1962, during one of the early biennial melodramas about Rickover's continuity, Anderson, Holifield and Price were among the members of the Joint Committee taken aboard the nuclear-powered carrier *Enterprise* by Rickover. As the world's largest ship steamed off Guantanamo, Cuba, Holifield interrupted the floating hearing to ask Rickover: "How many years do you have ahead of you before mandatory retirement?"

"Until January 1964," Rickover answered.

There was a discussion—off the record. Then Holifield, once more on the record, told of his concern about the future of nuclear propulsion. He added, "I would not want anything to destroy what you have built up."

"As long as I am able and both I and others feel I can do a useful job, I would like to stay on."

"I don't think Congress is going to stand idly by and watch you put on the shelf," Price interrupted to say. "Congress has expressed itself before on this matter, and if further action is required, we are not reluctant to act. We will have to get into this thing."

Congress indeed did get into it, until, as Rickover's two-year reappointments became almost automatic, the Secretary of Defense was expected to send letters to the leading members of Congress to advise them in advance of Rickover's continued tenure. And, in 1973, when Congress

recommended, by resolution, that the Navy name an engineering building at the Naval Academy Rickover Hall, the Navy meekly accepted the
resolution.

Rickover's fourth star came that same year, by vote of Congress with
no formal recommendation from President Nixon. The resolutions were
introduced by Democrats—Jackson in the Senate, Samuel S. Stratton in
the House. "Admiral Rickover himself protested rather characteristically
against my introduction of this legislation," Stratton said. "He told me
when it was being considered by the subcommittee that if he had been a
member of the subcommittee, he would have voted against it."

Just as characteristically, Rickover was quoted as saying, "Hell, what
difference does it make, as long as I do my job? I could do my job as a
seaman second-class. Nature knows no rank. Rank is like jewelry—the
old women are the ones who get the jewelry, and it really is the young
ones who should get it."

But Congress had spoken, and the former captain, whom the Navy
had tried to retire, became a four-star creature of Congress, no matter
what he or the Navy had to say.

II | Admiral of the Hill

In July 1959, Vice President Richard M. Nixon flew to the Soviet Union, officially to open the American National Exhibition in Moscow and unofficially to launch himself as a Presidential candidate who could talk face to face with Soviet leader Nikita Khrushchev. The highly publicized trip was billed as Nixon's "Mission to Moscow," and although he did not wish to share that publicity with anyone, he did take along a small entourage that included Admiral Rickover.

Rickover went as a vague gesture of technical exchange, since a party of Soviet officials had visited the United States and had been escorted by Rickover. He also was an exhibit in response to Sputnik. The Soviet satellite had gone into orbit nearly two years before, and the Eisenhower Administration was still smarting from having been "beaten by the Russians." Rickover's presence was a way of pointing out that at least we had built a nuclear submarine before the Soviets.

Nixon got his publicity; Rickover was hardly noticed at the time. But the Admiral had also launched himself on that trip. He would gain, in those days, the power to speak to Congress on subjects beyond nuclear power. Rickover did manage to receive limited attention on the trip. He made a fuss when his Soviet hosts hesitated about allowing him to look over their unfinished nuclear-powered icebreaker. And, when Nixon went to Poland, Rickover was shown off as a Pole who had emigrated to the United States and made good. "Admiral Rickover, an outwardly unemotional man," Nixon later wrote, "was greatly moved by the reception given him in Poland."

But the most significant aspect of Rickover's trip to the Soviet Union was what happened when he got home. Within days of his return he went before the House Committee on Appropriations and gave a "Report on Russia." More requests would come for copies of that report than for any report previously published by the committee. Rickover overnight had become more than an admiral, more than an engineer. He was now a witness—*the* witness—for much that the Congress wished to hear about. Not only did he talk for hours about the Soviet Union (his testimony covers eighty single-spaced pages), but he also embarked on long dissertations about what was wrong with American education and the American people—why the Russians were pulling ahead. "If the father works a five-day week," Rickover testified, "if he wastes his leisure time, if he goes on long vacations, how can he expect to convince his children they ought to go to school six days a week for more than one hundred and eighty days a year? Almost all Europeans go to school for six days a week for two hundred and forty to two hundred and eighty days a year and in addition study many hours at home, so that the total time almost always exceeds what an American father puts in on the job."

And so it went—what was wrong with foundations, with boards of education, with the American spirit. It was a lecture, a warning about "the Russian educational menace" and the need for our post-Sputnik society to reform. He talked on and on, issuing personal proclamations based on his few days abroad, reeling off statistics on education in America, the Soviet Union, and wherever else he wished to draw comparisons between our decadent society and more sensible, more spartan European societies. "For example, when you compare the years spent at school by a Danish child . . ."

He said he was compelled to testify. "I have to take off time from my real work to be here," he told the Congressmen. "I do not have a minute's time."

Then why was he there, lecturing Congressmen on Russian education? Why was he not testifying about his prime area of expertise, nuclear propulsion? The answer is complicated. He was reacting, as many Americans were, to the national embarrassment caused by Sputnik. He was articulating a hysteria—"we would not wish our children to know less than the Russians." He was also setting himself up as a savior. If Congress, if America, would only listen to him, he could show the way to save the country. Much of his way would be through drastic changes in American education. He would make a separate crusade of that. (See Chapter 27.) But it would be from the pulpit of Congressional hearing rooms that he would try to save America because he was a patriot and because, being Rickover, he knew no one else who could do a better job as a savior.

Congress just could not get enough of him. His first significant testimony was as a captain at a Senate defense appropriations hearing in

1953. He continued to testify regularly through the 1950s, increasing his number of appearances as he and the Congress waxed in their mutual admiration. By 1966 he was sitting at a witness table several times a year, and his total number of appearances had reached about eighty-five. By the time he went before committees of the Ninety-sixth Congress in 1979, he had been an official witness more than one hundred and fifty times. He had spoken to members of Congress informally on innumerable other occasions.

Each time he walked into a hearing room and sat at the witness table before a Senate or House committee, he had scrupulously prepared himself—often with learned quotations and epigrams, a tool very few of his admiral colleagues ever employed, and one that tended to add credibility to his conclusions. He could testify as an expert witness on practically anything.

On management systems: "Blaming deficiencies in management systems for problems that exist in real unknowns, or in the deficiencies of people, is mere foolishness. In a poem called 'Bagpipe Music,' by Louis MacNeice, the final couplet is:

> *The glass is falling hour by hour,*
> *The glass will fall forever,*
> *But if you break the bloody glass,*
> *You won't hold up the weather."*

On mediocrity in society: "... the full recognition and encouragement of talent is not inconsistent with general social harmony among citizens of a free society. Without such encouragement, our society will find itself burdened as in Goethe's apothegm: *'Was uns alle bandigt—das Gemeine.'* " (Rickover graciously translated the remark for any Congressional listeners who might not be proficient in German: "That which hampers us all—the commonplace.")

On treaties: "Bismarck once said to an Austrian diplomat: 'Austria and Prussia are both states too large and important to be linked by the text of a treaty. They can be guided only by their own interests and by their own convenience. . . .' "

In a single dazzling Congressional performance, Rickover once referred to or quoted Aristotle, Bismarck, Edmund Burke, Lewis Carroll, Rachel Carson, Catherine the Great, Winston Churchill, Hercules' cousin Eurystheus, Frederick the Great, Galileo, George Gallup, Adolf

Hitler, Sherlock Holmes, Langston Hughes, William James, Thomas Jefferson, Carl Jung, Robert E. Lee, Douglas MacArthur, Thomas Babington Macaulay, André Malraux, George Marshall, William Mc-Kinley, Gregor Mendel, Count Metternich, Billy Mitchell, Napoleon, Richard M. Nixon, Hyman G. Rickover, Elihu Root, Matthew Ridgway, Herbert Spencer, Josef Stalin, Voltaire, Max Weber and Woodrow Wilson.

Rickover did not hesitate to lecture Congressional committees on foreign relations, on morality and—continually—on education. ("In its education, to paraphrase Lord Haldane, the soul of a people mirrors itself.") And on man's purpose in life.

That topic went into the record, as so many other topics did, after the question had been served up by a Congressman, in this case George H. Mahon of Texas, chairman of the House Committee on Appropriations.

> MAHON: Admiral, you have at times in your testimony before the committee expressed your concept of man's purpose in life. Could you add to that this year?
>
> RICKOVER: This is a difficult question to answer. But, perhaps I can start by quoting what Voltaire once said: "Not to be occupied and not to exist are one and the same thing for a man." With those few words, Voltaire captured the essence of a purpose in life: to work, to create, to excel, and to be concerned about the world and its affairs.

The answer went on for some three thousand more words—some of them from other people ("As Robert Browning wrote, 'Ah, but a man's reach should exceed his grasp, or what's a Heaven for.' . . . Sherlock Holmes once told Dr. Watson, 'Watson, mediocrity knows nothing higher than itself. It takes no talent to recognize genius.' ")* But most of the words were from Rickover, including his conclusion, "To struggle against these enemies, and against apathy and mediocrity, is to find the purpose to life."

"I am sure," Mahon said reverently, "all of us here are touched by these sentiments."

The Rickover Lecture, as it came to be called, would be set down in official records as "Views" of Admiral Rickover, in contrast to, say,

---

* *Arthur Conan Doyle, in* The Valley of Fear, *actually wrote:* "Mediocrity knows nothing higher than itself, but talent instantly recognizes genius."

"Testimony" of a Chief of Naval Operations or a "Statement" of a deputy Secretary of Defense. The implication was that others spoke directly to specific issues and testified in the traditional way by giving answers to questions, while Rickover from a loftier vantage point dispensed his views.

There was always more to the Rickover Lecture than a voyage through his remarkable mind. No matter how far he might tack, he always stayed on course—what Rickover thought about the U.S. Navy.

Rickover was doing more than fighting the system. He was building his own. His system was, in its crudest form, an antithesis to the U.S. Navy system that had developed over two hundred years of war and peace. Wherever the Navy was on any issue, Rickover almost inevitably was 180 degrees away. He never publicly stated that he did this deliberately; nor is he known to have remarked privately that he had opposed merely for the sake of opposing. But an analysis of his actions—and, particularly, of his Congressional testimony—leads inescapably to the conclusion that Rickover's strategy was based almost entirely on his need to convince the money-dispensers in Congress that he was on their side—against the "bureaucracy"—regardless of the issue.

Shrewdly, Rickover had sensed something that few others in the Defense Establishment had ever realized. He had discovered that Congressmen preferred to give money to people rather than to institutions. The Navy, like the Army or the Air Force, is only an abstraction. Congressmen have to be patriotic and "support" the Army, Navy and Air Force. But they do not have to *like* these institutions. Indeed, it is very difficult for many Congressmen to support actively all the services as institutions because of the competition for defense appropriations. It may be difficult for a Congressman to support, for example, the B-1 manned strategic bomber the same year that he has advocated construction of additional Trident missile submarines, because the two weapons are to some extent in competition for the strategic mission and hence for the funds. Further, once a Congressman voices support for a specific system, he often perceives that his credibility demands that he continue to support it to justify his original position. Thus, once a Congressman is committed to a specific weapon or system, he will generally support it long after the need or even feasibility has diminished or, in some cases, ended. The manned bomber and the supercarrier have often been cited as examples of this situation.

Rickover thoroughly understood the Congressional preference for supporting individuals. He knew that loyalty, once given, could be captured. Rickover accordingly came before Congressional committees as an individual, not as a Navy official. He gave the strong and convincing impression that he spoke as a man speaking truth and right.

He knew his Constitution, and he knew his audience. He frequently reminded his listeners in Congressional committees that they, not the Executive Branch, were charged by the Constitution to "provide and maintain a Navy." But Rickover carefully did not urge them to support *the* Navy; he asked for support of *his* nuclear navy. Unlike other admirals who appeared before the committees and urged support of essentially all Navy programs, Rickover could attack any and all other programs— while supporting his own efforts. No other admiral on active duty could realistically attack another flag officer or a Navy program. Rickover could and did.

He did more than attack the Navy. He went far beyond, telling Congressmen things they wanted to hear; things they said to each other but rarely heard from a government witness at a hearing: "Those of us who have an objective, a desire to get something done, cannot possibly compromise and communicate all day long with people who wallow in bureaucracy, who worship rules and ancient routines."

And he did not merely attack. He advocated. He came before hearings as an expertly prepared witness. Rickover knew how to tune his presentations to climates of the House and Senate. In the House, where the members have to face the voters every two years and tend to be closer to the folks back home, Rickover became the down-home philosopher, the "folksy" witness. Before Senate committees he tended to assume the role of statesman and behave with the dignity that Senators have come to expect in their chamber.

From the beginning, his testimony was characterized by outstanding preparation and delivery. His performance was almost flawless. He knew when to be profound and when to reach for the headline. At Rickover's whim he could command space in the press by inspiring such headlines as GIVE THE ADMIRALS COLORING BOOKS and IDEAL WEST POINTERS SHOULD BE PARENTLESS—RICKOVER.

The latter headline came from his testimony before the House Appropriations Committee, when he fell to talking about the Military Academy at West Point. Rickover said that he had just read a study by a psychiatrist who wanted to find out why so many West Pointers had been failing. The psychiatrist, according to Rickover, had reported that unsuccessful West Point plebes had identified with their fathers and also had been loved by their mothers. Rickover then leaped to a headline-making

conclusion—"the ideal West Pointer should have no father or mother"—
and, vaulting even further, reached another point:

> I view with horror the day the Navy is induced to put psychia-
> trists on board our nuclear submarines. We are doing very well
> without them because the men don't know they have problems. But
> once a psychiatrist is assigned, they will learn they have lots of prob-
> lems. . . . The Navy is getting in this sort of act.
>
> They recently reported—it was in the newspapers—that they
> had completed a study of submarine sailors at New London, Con-
> necticut, to determine the psychological differences between sailors
> who had been tattooed once, sailors who had been tattooed more
> than once, sailors who had never been tattooed but wished they had,
> and sailors who didn't get tattooed and didn't want to be.
>
> As you might suspect, the sailor's love life or lack of it and his
> attitude toward mother and father were all deeply involved. Of
> course it is a very complex subject and will require more study; in
> other words, more money.

Rickover's rambling words were not uttered offhand. Rickover
wanted to get across the impression that he and he alone knew which men
to put aboard nuclear submarines and nuclear surface ships—and that he
and he alone knew how to train them. While criticizing the outlay of pal-
try sums for psychological research, he was implicitly asking for vast
powers and vast amounts of money. He would make the Navy all-
nuclear, at enormous cost, and he would personally direct the training of
nuclear officers and crews, also at enormous costs. In some part, those
goals were built on the ruins of programs that he attacked—some soft, as
the tattoo study, and some hard, as Navy efforts in the 1960s to adopt
aircraft-type gas-turbine engines for warships.

The British and Soviet navies already had gas-turbine–propelled destroyers, but Rickover urged Congress not to spend money on such a
program. Such expenditures, he explained, would detract from developments in conventional steam-propulsion systems and nuclear-steam
plants for surface ships. He successfully delayed competition until, in the
early 1970s, Admiral Zumwalt as Chief of Naval Operations pushed gas
turbines for new classes of destroyers, frigates and missile craft. So, for
several years the Navy did not seriously consider gas-turbine engines,
largely because of Rickover's opposition, expressed to Congress as well as
to the Navy's leadership. The subsequent success of U.S. gas-turbine

warships—with almost one hundred in service or under construction by 1981—proved Rickover wrong.

What is read as the testimony of Admiral Rickover may well be the second thoughts of Editor Rickover improving upon the words of Witness Rickover. He was given carte blanche in the amending of his testimony. He was not the only one. Friendly witnesses before Congressional committees are routinely allowed to edit the transcript of their testimony before it is published as a hearing report. But Rickover went further than witnesses traditionally did, according to a former staff director of a committee that frequently heard Rickover. "There were ground rules," the former director told the authors. "You could improve your syntax, correct mistakes in grammar, correct misspelled names, answer queries. But Rickover went way beyond that. He would change whole sections of testimony."

Rickover's editing was ostensibly for security reasons, as well as for answering questions for the record. But he also changed numbers: The Soviets "are spending about 35 percent of their naval budget on submarines" was changed to 40 percent; asked how many nuclear ships and submarines the Navy had operating, he responded "we have 107 operating," which was changed in the written record to "we have 115 operating, sir." Rickover has always added lots of "sirs." Small changes, perhaps, but numerous—and sometimes significant.

After a discussion of Defense Department policy on nuclear surface ships for the benefit of Representative Bob Wilson, new to the House Armed Services Committee, Rickover noted: "Mr. Wilson, I think this is a good introduction for you to the Navy." But the printed record, as "corrected," has Rickover saying: "I think this is a good introduction for you to the Defense Department." Wilson was from San Diego—a "Navy town." Rickover apparently thought it might hurt Wilson to have his constituents believe he was new to the needs of the Navy.

Some changes were to keep the Rickover image within bounds. At one point, discussing the President's National Security Council, Rickover declared: "In my opinion, the most prestigious part of that organization is their name." That entire sentence was stricken. Probably the National Security Council, which includes the Secretaries of State, Treasury and Defense, was too much even for Rickover.

Other changes to Rickover's actual testimony have been even more political. In one exchange, Representative Charles Bennett, chairman of the powerful sea-power subcommittee of the House Armed Services Committee, apologized to Rickover: "Admiral, I cut you off. It is not really the question and answer period. It was my fault." Rickover's quick reply—"I am sorry. I am glad that it was your fault"—was carefully deleted from the printed record.

In contrast, examples of Rickover's humility are never deleted. Representative Charles Wilson once declared: "I have been critical of you in the past, as you may know, because I felt that you, in turn, had been critical of our top people and I was critical of you without really knowing anything about it, I am afraid. I have learned a lot today in hearing you present your case before the subcommittee." Rickover's response remained in the record of the hearing: "Mr. Wilson, if you knew more about me, you might be even more critical." A few minutes later, Bob Wilson commended Rickover with: "You have always had the courage and the opportunity to state your personal opinion." To this Rickover appropriately responded: "It is not courage, Mr. Wilson. It is my duty."

Commendations have always come fast and heavy when Rickover has appeared before a Congressional committee. He is invariably introduced with fulsome praise from Congressional stocks usually reserved for eulogies and epitaphs: "We have with us this morning not only one of the most indispensable men in national defense but one of the most remarkable men in our history and in world science." ... "I would like to say that it is indeed a pleasure to have this illustrious man before us, one of the real great Americans of all time." ... "For many years, the committee has had the privilege of meeting with Admiral Rickover. ... This has always been one of the highlights of the year." ... "We have great respect for you because of your dedication and because of what you have done and are doing for the United States."

Rickover would give as well as he received. In response to one of these introductions, a Rickover "off the cuff" response went along these lines: "I would like to start by telling you how deeply I appreciate the opportunity to appear before this committee. You have made me feel so at home that I almost feel like an ex-officio member. It is a genuine honor to be able to talk to you and the members of the committee in a personal way because I know of no group of men in Congress who are more patriotic or who have so many onerous duties to perform." Periodically he cited other Congressional groups in the same manner.

Once the hearing was underway, there were laudatory interruptions as Rickover testified—or lectured—in a voice devoid of inflection. A typical interruption occurred one day when Rickover made one of his curiously arrogant attempts at modesty: "If I am an 'expert' in anything, it is in naval design and construction and in the Navy's requirements for modern technology. . . . "

Representative John J. Rhodes: "Admiral, may I suggest also that you are expert in getting along with people?"

"That is very simple, Mr. Rhodes," Rickover replied. "You can easily get along with people if you know what you are talking about. That makes it much easier to get along with people."

The seeming give-and-take of his Congressional testimony was often an illusion. He seldom let himself be a witness under interrogation. He came before a committee well prepared and unsurprised. When he spoke, he spoke as a superb practitioner of the English language, reading premeditated responses to friendly inquiries, generally sent over to his offices days or even weeks before his appearance. These questions may have been originally prepared by Congressional staffers or by his own staff. He has exercised a great deal of control over what Congress has asked him.

At one point in a hearing Rickover was talking about a favorite subject, the evils of regularly rotating naval officers to different jobs. The Navy wants its line officers to be broad-gauged and has generally rotated them at intervals of eighteen months to about two years, through tours of duty afloat and ashore. This gives them experience in a number of ship and shore assignments, maintains morale, and helps the peacetime Navy family. Taking his usual antithetical position, Rickover said he believed in putting a man in one place, letting him develop a deep, although perhaps narrow, knowledge of the subject, and then keeping him at that task.

He once summed up his criticism of the Navy system in these words: "To remain inexpert by frequent emigration from one's job, to leave one's mistakes and one's past, to start out for a new life—this is what the short tour of duty does. One can be carefree forever. True responsibility for one's actions is not ever comprehended. Life becomes a series of disconnected events to which one is a paid observer." After letting it be known once again that he did not like the Navy's rotation scheme, Rickover told the Congressmen, "Perhaps the reason I can talk with a little more cogency on the subject is that I stick around. The other people come and go as on a conveyor belt."

Representative Daniel J. Flood, a power on the House Appropriations Committee, responded: "The only reason you stick around is because we insist you stick around or you would have been a dead duck long ago."

Sympathetic, long-term Congressmen like Flood time and again reminded Rickover how well he got along with Congress. And just as frequently he reminded Congressmen that he got along with them because he did not get along with the Navy. From the time he first started testifying before Congressional committees he had portrayed the Navy as a kind of bumbling, benevolent foe of the Congress and of Rickover. *We* (he and the Congress) were aligned against *Them* (the Navy and the Department of Defense). The bureaucracy was delaying, slowing, retarding the development of a nuclear navy, and it was Congress that was seeking to build *that* Navy under Rickover's leadership.

Rickover frequently reminded his Congressional listeners of this situation: "If it weren't for the fact that my organization was in the Atomic Energy Commission, . . . " he told a House committee in 1960, "I doubt we would have a nuclear navy today. If we had to depend entirely on the Navy, I doubt there would be nuclear-powered ships at sea today." Whatever his doubts, one of them certainly was not whether Congress would think that his actions were insubordination, for he openly (and proudly) admitted disobeying orders. "I have been importuned year after year by the Navy to undertake very expensive developments in nuclear power. I have refused to undertake them because I could not see real promise in them."

The "I have refused" statement is interesting because those who "importuned" Rickover were his legal superiors—the Secretary of the Navy and the Chief of Naval Operations. Despite the words of his oath and commissions—"to obey the orders of those placed over me"—Rickover could freely tell the Congress, which granted him those commissions, that he would refuse such orders.

He also prided himself on not following Navy policy on how to testify before Congressional committees. "I have never followed any directive in testifying to Congress," he said. "Once one of my seniors called me before I was due to testify and told me what his policy was. I said, 'Fine, thank you very much. When I testify I will say that this is what you told me to say.'

"He said, 'Oh, no! You mustn't do that.'

"I said, 'Didn't you tell me?'

"Since that time I have never been directed."

But at least one Navy official, Paul Nitze, who was Secretary of the

Navy from 1963 until June 1967, when he became Deputy Secretary of Defense, could tell a different version of how Rickover followed orders when he testified before Congress. The issue was aircraft-type gas-turbine (jet) engines, which Rickover strongly opposed because some officers considered them a potential alternative to nuclear propulsion in surface ships.

In late April 1967, Nitze recalled, "I thought the case was just wholly solid" in favor of adopting gas turbines. "I decided we were going to do this. McNamara was for it, the White House was for it, and the Bureau of the Budget was for it." Then, "one day I heard that the House Appropriations Committee was going to hold hearings and they had invited Admiral Rickover to come in and testify. Rumor had it they were going to ask him about gas turbines for ships, and Rickover was going to destroy it, if he could."

Nitze called in Rickover. "Rickover said it is true. . . . 'I wouldn't be surprised if they asked me about this,' " Rickover said, according to Nitze, " 'and I will in all honesty tell them my thoughts.' "

"Rick," Nitze remembered saying, "let's get it straight about what the rules and regulations of the Pentagon are. In the first place, you understand, that when a program has been approved—and is an approved government program—then no one will testify against it, no one will *volunteer* testimony against it.

"On the other hand," Nitze continued his directions, "if you are asked questions about it, then you will give your honest, unbiased judgment from a technical standpoint with respect to the merits of the case, even if they are quite contrary to the Executive Branch's viewpoint. *But you will also explain to the Congress where it differs from the Executive Branch's view so it will get both sides of the case.*"

Rickover said, "Mr. Secretary, I don't know what the Executive Branch's position on this is."

"Damn it, Rickover, you do know," Nitze snapped back.

"No, I don't know. I don't know what the Executive Branch's position is. I would be only too pleased to give the Executive Branch's position on this if I understood it."

"All right. Today is Friday," said Nitze. "I will spend hours this weekend putting together in a memorandum the Executive Branch's case and I will give it to you on Monday."

That Monday morning, May 1, 1967, the scene was again Secretary Nitze's office. Rickover read the memorandum. "Rick, tell me, is there anything that is technically incorrect in my memorandum?" Nitze asked.

"No," said Rickover. "It's very clear and technically wholly correct. There is nothing wrong with it."

"Then, Rick, I assume that you now understand the Executive Branch's position and agree therewith."

"No, I do not."

"*Why not?*" appealed Nitze.

"The entire argument is based on the assumption that cost-effectiveness is a merit. And I don't believe in cost-effectiveness. I believe that the Navy should have the best ships that can be bought, and I believe that nuclear-propelled ships are better than gas-[turbine]–propelled ships, and I believe that the Congress will give the Navy whatever money it requires to build the best ships, and as far as the Navy is concerned, the issue of cost-effectiveness does not arise," replied Rickover. "The only issue is which is the best ship," concluded Rickover.

"I wish you wouldn't take the outrageous position," Nitze tried again, to which, he remembers, Rickover responded, "I must."

Later that morning, Rickover entered the hearing room of the House Committee on Armed Services.

Representative George H. Mahon of Texas, chairman of the committee's Department of Defense subcommittee, obviously was fully aware of what was about to happen. "We realize that witnesses generally support the programs which have been approved by higher authority in the Government," Mahon said, in introducing Rickover, "but when requested by the committee for their own personal views it is traditional that witnesses and officials give us their personal views. We feel in the Congress that we are entitled to have the personal views of witnesses who appear before us even though they may conflict with the views of the administration in power at that time."

After a few polite words of greeting between Rickover and the Congressmen, Rickover began to talk in general about what was wrong with the Navy. "Some in the Navy," he said, "are afraid of this new world that seems to have descended upon us so suddenly."

When he launched into the testimony he had discussed with Nitze, he began by noting that the Secretary of the Navy "asked me to give you his statement, his views about the nuclear Navy. His views are quite different from mine. There are basic differences in our concepts. In accordance with his request, I would like to turn his statement over to you."

"Admiral Rickover, you are now beginning your response to my first question," Mahon said, "that is, what are your views with respect to the nuclear Navy and nuclear propulsion, major fleet escort ships, and what should we do this year with respect to the nuclear-powered ships?"

Then Mahon tersely added: "Off the record." (The published record shows: *Discussion held off the record.*)

For the record, Rickover summarized Nitze's statement as saying that "for the same investment cost we can get more conventional ships by not going to nuclear power than we can by going to nuclear power."

After some more discussion, Rickover was asked by another member of the subcommittee, Glenard P. Lipscomb (who posthumously would have a nuclear submarine named after him), "I don't understand why you have to present a statement of Secretary Nitze before you testify."

Rickover said that he was directed not only by Department of Defense instructions but also by Nitze's own personal instructions. He then soared into a denunciation of the directives.

> In ways which officers themselves perceive only dimly or not at all [he said], they are compromised or manipulated into conforming to the official line. . . . Dissent is welcome, as long as it is irrelevant to the existing policies of the DoD. For example, when I criticize U.S. education no one in the DoD is at all concerned—because someone else is being criticized.
>
> An example of inability or fear to dissent and where it can lead is that of General Wilhelm Keitel who was Adolf Hitler's Chief of the Combined General Staff. Time after time, when he knew Hitler to be wrong, he failed to speak out, and so became one of the architects of German defeat.
>
> What proved fatal to Keitel was not his weaknesses, but his virtues—the virtues of a subordinate, a man with the mentality of a sergeant major, dressed up in a general's uniform. Duty, obedience, loyalty, were the code he clung to, by which he exercised all sense of responsibility. And, like patriotism, they were not enough. In a world like ours you cannot afford not to ask questions, or else you may end up as the leader of disaster. Keitel lived to sign Germany's unconditional surrender in 1945, and was subsequently hanged in accordance with sentence of the Nuremberg war crimes trial.

The hearing went off the record again. (Inferences in subsequent open testimony strongly hinted that Nitze and McNamara had been attacked as nonelective officials who were charting the course of national defense, duties that were more rightly those of the Congress—and of Rickover.)

The Navy's plans for gas-turbine destroyers were aborted by that hearing. Not until almost a decade later, largely due to the efforts of a Nitze protégé, Elmo R. Zumwalt, did the U.S. Navy join those of Britain, the Soviet Union, and other nations in building gas-turbine–propelled surface warships.

Rickover's personal feelings about "the Navy" have been more difficult to fathom. Once, in a hint of uncharacteristic introspection, he said the Navy believed "that with my personality and my looks I could not get along with Congress. In order to get along with Congress, you had to be good-looking and you had to be able to talk the way you were instructed to talk. I must confess that by Navy rules I don't know what it takes to get along with Congress."

The Navy rules included the clearing of testimony through the chain of command. The appearance of a Navy witness before Congress is handled by the Office of Legislative Affairs (OLA), which is part of the office of the Secretary of the Navy. OLA is where the strategy for dealing with Congress is as studiously developed as is the strategy for fighting the Soviet Navy. Coordination and teamwork are the keys to Congressional strategy in that admirals (and generals) are required to testify before several committees of Congress. Their statements are reviewed. Probable questions are developed, and answers for them are prepared. Reams of statistics are readied as backup. There may even be a practice Q & A session to prepare a witness for the ordeal.

On the day of the hearing an OLA aide usually escorts the witness to the hearing room. The witness is resplendent in uniform and is accompanied by a convoy of assistants loaded with backup data. Someone from OLA sits in the hearing room to monitor what the witness says. His notes are immediately sent (or in some cases telephoned) to the Chief of Naval Operations so that there can be up-to-date awareness at the highest level of Congressional actions and reactions.

"It's a big Navy, you know, and keeping track of it is the CNO's job. One thing he always wants to know is what's going on with the Navy and Congress," a former OLA Chief told the authors. "It was vital to know that everybody was at least trying to stay inside the framework."

It was different for Rickover. His prepared testimony—always well written, clear, and free of jargon—was sent to OLA, but too close to Rickover's appearance on the Hill for any review or comment. He was accompanied by no OLA aides, only by his trusted AEC lieutenants; in the 1960s and 1970s they were usually David Leighton and William Wegner.

No other officer called on to testify before Congress—including the Chief of Naval Operations—is given the privilege of independent, untutored and, from a security viewpoint, uncleared testimony. Not only does Rickover defy tradition, he has made his own—a unique tradition of independence.

Weeks or months might pass between the time Rickover testifies and the publication of the laundered transcript. During that interval, except for some leaks from friendly Congressmen or the notes taken by a Navy observer, the Navy often does not know exactly what Rickover has said. Yet what he has said would have a profound effect on the Navy's budget, for in some years nuclear-ship construction cost over two thirds of the annual shipbuilding budget.

Rickover almost always told tales, with great detachment, about the evil ways of his enemy—the Navy. His self-awarded independence from Navy control dates to about the time that he won his retention and promotion through Congressional intercession. On the basis of that independence, he could picture himself as aloof from the Navy—yet continually harassed by it. "My primary duty is in the Atomic Energy Commission" was a frequent statement before Congressional subcommittees. "I have additional duty in the Navy to help me to do my job. This is where I get fouled up. . . ."

To Congressmen who listened to Rickover's complaints, he seemed to be working against terrible odds, unable to get anything done—his way. The fact was that he was running his organization just about the way he wanted to run it.

But a key difference between Rickover and the solons was that they had to be concerned about elections every two or six years. Some would suffer defeat in elections; some would retire from politics; and some would die. Rickover would go on, to hearing after hearing, year after year. The flavor of his testimony would never change, as his monotone droned on.

Before the defense subcommittee of the House Committee on Appropriations in 1960: "Several years ago the Atomic Energy Commission was building a diffusion plant at Paducah, Kentucky. The company responsible for the work was not doing a good job, so the Commission placed another contractor in charge. The first thing the new contractor did was to lay off about five thousand men; the job immediately started going faster."

Before the same subcommittee ten years later: "About fifteen years ago the Atomic Energy Commission was building a large diffusion plant and construction was falling way behind. The AEC fired the contractor and hired a new one. The first thing the new contractor did was to fire five thousand people because of the gross inefficiency. Immediately the work started to improve."

Before the Joint Committee on Atomic Energy about the same time: ". . . when the contractor for this project was replaced, the new contractor dropped several thousand people; the work immediately speeded up."

No one seemed to notice—or at least to mind—that Rickover was repeating himself. No one seemed to notice that the captain fighting the system in 1949 was, thirty years later, a full admiral who was the head of his own system, a veritable bureaucrat himself.

No one seemed to notice that what the Admiral said did not always square with the facts. His most persistent claim—in similar words, year after year—was that the Navy had opposed *him* and nuclear submarines from the beginning. "Without the support of Congress, particularly this committee," he was still saying in 1980, "there would not be a nuclear Navy as we know it today." Another regular claim was that "analysts" (a pet hate) "concluded that nuclear power was not worthwhile. . . . This argument was similar to a view held by the Navy at the end of the nineteenth century. President Theodore Roosevelt said that the Navy feared to push submarines lest Congress would withhold appropriations for building battleships. Fortunately, in the case of nuclear power, Congress prevailed, and the *Nautilus* was built."

Much of that statement—the very heart of Rickover's anti-Navy thesis—is simply not true. The Navy bought its first submarine, the *Holland,* in April 1900. It is a matter of record that from 1900 to 1910 the Navy did buy twenty-eight submarines, an average of three a year. Roosevelt, president from 1901 to 1908, was primarily a supporter of a bigger-battleship Navy, not submarines.

More factual errors tended to occur when Rickover discussed foreign navies, especially the Soviet Navy. In seeking support for his submarine programs, Rickover often cited the Soviet Navy, especially the Red submarine force, which, in his opinion, "is superior to ours." He once testified that "the other night I met with the Russian Vice Chief of Naval Operations Admiral Kasatonov, who is in charge of submarines." Rickover erred in that although Kasatonov was a veteran submariner, from 1949 onward he had major staff- and fleet-command assignments, becoming First Deputy Commander in Chief in 1964, a post in which his responsibilities extended far beyond the Red submarine force.

Rickover then stated that "both the Chief and the Vice Chief of Naval Operations in the Soviet Union [are] members of the Presidium. I discussed this point with Admiral Kasatonov. Both are thus members of the highest ruling body in the Soviet Union. That is equivalent to being members of the Presidential Cabinet except that in Russia the 'Executive Branch' controls the parliamentary and judicial bodies as well." Here too Rickover was in error. The highest ruling body of the Soviet Union is the Politburo, which was called the Presidium from 1952 until 1966. During the entire history of the Soviet Union only two professional military officers have achieved membership in the Politburo, Marshal G. K. Zhukov, in 1956–1957, and Marshal A. A. Grechko, from 1973 until his death in 1976. No admiral aspired to that select body.

Rickover, who frequently cites historical examples to support his positions before Congress, has also erred in his knowledge of German and British naval history. He noted to one committee that "if Admiral von Tirpitz had had his way and had not been required to spend so much money on surface ships, the Germans would have had more submarines and probably would have won the war [of 1914–1918]." This discourse on German submarines in 1914, unfortunately, does not agree with von Tirpitz's own views. The German admiral wrote in his memoirs that at the start of World War I, "The significance of the high-seas submarine was fully recognized by us, and its development as energetically and quickly pursued as was consistent with efficient equipment and the safety of the personnel. So soon as the high-seas submarine was practicable for war purposes we procured in peacetime as many as our manufacturers could deliver. . . ." Indeed, von Tirpitz also quoted Commander Bartenbach, his leading submarine expert, who wrote, "The reasons why at the beginning of the war there were not more submarines with the fleet lies in the failure of the builders, who were not in a position to deliver the boats contracted. . . ." Thus, Rickover was misinformed in his theory that von Tirpitz had to invest in surface ships rather than submarines; more submarines simply could not have been constructed in Germany.

Errors—major and minor—crop up frequently in Admiral Rickover's testimony. He has often referred to Winston Churchill as the First *Sea* Lord of the Royal Navy. The indomitable Churchill served as First Lord of the Admiralty at the start of both World Wars, but First Sea Lord was the title of the senior naval officer, a position which Churchill, a civilian, could not hold. And almost amusing is Rickover's continued reference to his own service in both World Wars: "I am a veteran of World Wars I and II, and I have seen more naval developments than any officer now on active duty." True, Rickover was admitted to the Naval Academy on June 29, 1918, with the Armistice still four months and several days away. But more than a veteran of World War I, Rickover was a "veteran" of a stint in the U.S. Naval Academy hospital, plebe summer, and a few classes along the banks of the Severn River, which was where he was when the war ended.

Once, at a reception in the Washington Navy Yard, a Marine general walked up to Rickover and introduced himself. Rickover scanned the several rows of ribbons on the Marine's chest, ran his finger along them, and said, "I have two that you don't have." Rickover paused and then added, "The World War One victory medal and the Atomic Energy Commission medal." He said he got the latter merely by signing a book in the office of General Leslie Groves. He did not explain where he had earned the former.

Such has been Rickover's reputation for knowing practically everything ("I happened to have translated for the War College the definitive book on World War I German submarine experience") that his testimony rarely has been interrupted or argued over. But at least once his knowledge of the Soviet Navy was challenged. Rickover was rattling off his familiar litany of statistics when the mustachioed Daniel J. Flood, a veteran Pennsylvania Representative, broke in, asking, "Do the Russians have a history of fighting submarines against anybody?"

"Yes sir," Rickover answered. "They did some minor fighting in World War II."

"Minor?"

"Yes, sir."

"They have no tradition or experience fighting subs," Flood persisted.

"They may not have had the tradition—"

"They don't."

"They do not have the tradition," Rickover finally admitted, and Flood needled him: "Or the experience?"

Rickover would not concede: "But the people who man our submarines today don't have much tradition either."

"Now wait a minute," Flood said sharply. "Wait a minute. The U.S. Navy has an experience, a history, a tradition of submarine warfare since the Civil War." Flood sometimes affectionately called Rickover "Skipper." He did not call him that now.

They argued some more, Rickover finally saying, "I would rather have a lot more submarines and less tradition. . . ."

"I don't care what you would rather have," Flood concluded. "I just asked the question."

Rickover ended the exchange meekly, saying, "You are right, sir."

He could also put a Congressman down. When Representative Morris K. Udall interrupted Rickover's testimony to talk at length about what was wrong with the Social Security system, Rickover listened with obvious impatience and then finally said, "I only hope that when it comes time to do something about it, your feet follow your mouth." And, when Senator John O. Pastore confessed, "Maybe I am out of my ball park on this," Rickover snapped back, "I think you are, sir."

But humility and obsequiousness usually characterized his performances before Congress. His *sirs* were liberally sprinkled, along with references to a Congressman's "charming wife" or to the "beautiful Southern girls" and the fine chicory-flavored coffee in a Senator's office. Once, testifying before Senator Charles H. Percy, he asked the Senator if he would join in singing "Illinois," the state song, "in homage to the home state we share." Percy declined, but not without praising Rickover and recalling what a hero he was when Percy was an apprentice seaman.

Rickover continued the currying, saying, "I hope you will emulate a former Congressman from Illinois. Do you know who I mean?"

"Senator Dirksen spent some time in Congress," Percy coyly responded.

"I mean Abraham Lincoln," Rickover said, "I am setting for you a higher standard."

From the beginning, Rickover realized that the ego and vanity of politicians were larger and hungrier than those of other mortal men, and he made offerings—submarine-collected bottles of polar water and chunks of polar ice; submarine-postmarked letters written "At Sea, North Atlantic"; and, to L. Mendel Rivers, chairman of the House Armed Services Committee, a gavel made of oak from the historic frigate U.S.S. *Constitution.*

Rickover even dispensed immortality to the dead and the living. After the death in 1957 of California Congressman Carl Hinshaw, an early member of the Joint Committee on Atomic Energy, Rickover told the committee, "I talked to the chairman of the board of Combustion Engineering. They have their new plant at Windsor, Connecticut, and I think they would be very happy to name it the Carl Hinshaw Laboratory." Combustion Engineering in Windsor has no such laboratory. But Rickover had better luck with the United States Navy. He managed to set aside Navy traditions by getting ships named after Congressmen.

Once tradition held that warships be named categorically: submarines after fish and marine life; battleships for States of the Union; cruisers for cities; destroyers for men (and one woman) who benefited or served in the Navy and Marine Corps; and aircraft carriers after historic ships or famous victories (or after such *very* famous men as John F. Kennedy). When the new category of Polaris missile submarines was created in 1958, President Eisenhower himself reportedly decided that the ships would be named for famous Americans. *George Washington, Patrick Henry,* and *Theodore Roosevelt* were the first three.

This naming scheme began to falter in 1968 when the Navy's leadership took the unprecedented step of naming the new nuclear carrier after one of its own—the *Nimitz.* The following year, with strong White House support, the Navy began naming cruisers for states; there was some psychology behind this, since the Navy was reclassifying all of its "frigates" as "cruisers," a term more in accord with their size and missile capabilities. The first renamed frigate-to-cruiser would be the U.S.S. *California,* honoring the home state of the incumbent President, Richard Nixon. When the *California's* keel was laid down on January 23, 1970, it was "authenticated" by the wife of Glenard P. Lipscomb, ranking Republican member of the House Appropriations Committee's defense subcommittee. A week later, on February 1, 1970, Lipscomb died. Rickover named a submarine for him.

Traditionally, ship names are chosen by the Secretary of the Navy, based mainly upon recommendations of his Director of Naval History, with awareness of the current political climate. (One did not name a battleship for the state of the President's political opponent.) Rickover changed that.

William H. Bates, representative from Massachusetts, had served on the Joint Committee on Atomic Energy since 1959 and was a strong Rickover supporter. When the carrier *Kennedy* was launched in 1967, it was Bates who, on the floor of the House, had declared: "It is a sad commentary for those who have worked for the development of nuclear propulsion in our Navy to see a ship which will be with us in the year 2000 will be propelled by conventional means, and not nuclear propulsion."

In 1970 a nuclear attack submarine begun at the Ingalls shipyard in Pascagoula, Mississippi, was named *William H. Bates.* It broke a seventy-year tradition, for not since the Navy's first submarine, the *Hol-*

land of 1900, had a torpedo-armed or "attack" submarine been named for a man. More followed, as time took a toll of Rickover supporters and he was able to dispense a new kind of largess. Asked by the authors about the reason for the change in the tradition of naming submarines, an admiral put it in three words: "Fish don't vote."

Rickover, wishing to give Congressmen honors once reserved for fish, engineered the change without any officially documented approval. "We've gone farther afield for names," another admiral said, obviously embarrassed by the crumbling of another tradition. But, reaching for a rationale, he noted that battleships, which were named for states, are being replaced as capital ships by Trident submarines, which receive state names.

In February 1971 the Navy announced that attack submarines being constructed at Newport News, Virginia, would be named *L. Mendel Rivers,* for the late chairman of the House Armed Services Committee, and *Richard B. Russell* for the chairman of the Senate Armed Services Committee, who had passed away a few days earlier. Next was the *Glenard P. Lipscomb,* an attack submarine laid down at Electric Boat in June of 1971. Speaking at the *Lipscomb* keel laying, Secretary of Defense Melvin Laird recalled their service together in the House—describing Lipscomb as "the hardest working member of the House of Representatives ... to whom," Laird recalled, "I turned for counsel whenever I encountered a tough problem in the field of national defense."

The Ford Administration in 1976 introduced state names for the new Trident missile submarines, beginning with the *Ohio,* and then *Michigan* (thank you, Mr. Ford), followed by the *Georgia*—named out of alphabetical sequence—which Mrs. Rosalynn Carter proudly christened with the name of the President's home state.

Of course, at virtually all ceremonies for these nuclear carriers, cruisers and submarines—which occurred every couple of days when one considered that each warship had a festive keel laying, launching, and commissioning—Rickover would be on stage, front and center. Always, at the last minute, he would rearrange the seating, bow graciously and say just the right words to the ladies, and to their children or grandchildren when present, joke with the Congressional delegation, and avoid most of—or all—the Navy and shipyard officials.

One officer's wife recalled how Rickover behaved when he was at Pascagoula for a ship event at the Ingalls shipyard. Rickover was being introduced to the wives of the submarine's senior petty officers when he spied an arriving Congressman. "Without an 'excuse me' or 'thank you' to the wives of the men who would go to sea and make his submarine operate, he promptly turned away and hurried over to the arriving Congressman, who was already being met," she recalled. It was *always* Congress first—and at times Congress only.

By the 1970s Rickover was practically an honorary member of Congress. In fact, as Capitol Hill experts noted, "Congress doesn't really think of Rickover as an admiral at all, but kind of as a Senator." Rickover himself was proud of his longevity, even touched by it. When he walked into the Joint Committee's hearing room on February 25, 1974, he carried a list of members who had been on the committee in previous years. With his usual precision, he named them in alphabetical order: William Bates, Harry Byrd, Tom Connally, John J. Dempsey, Everett Dirksen, Henry Dworshak, Aime Forand, Bourke Hickenlooper, Carl Hinshaw, Thomas Jenkins, Edwin Johnson, Lyndon B. Johnson, Paul J. Kilday, Bill Knowland, Brien McMahon, Eugene Millikin, Richard B. Russell, Albert Thomas, J. Parnell Thomas, Arthur Vandenberg. He had known them all. And they all were dead.

While members of the committee listened, hushed, Rickover listed former committee members who had left Congress. He began with Clint Anderson and, by the time he had reached James Van Zandt and Jack Westland, he had named nineteen men and women who had also passed through his long life and now were no longer part of it.

Then Rickover looked across the witness table to those who sat before him: Senator George D. Aiken, who was eighty-two years old and had come to Congress in 1940; Representative Chet Holifield, seventy-one years old and a member of Congress from California since 1953; Craig Hosmer, another Californian who was fifty-nine years old and was in his twenty-first year on Capitol Hill. Aiken, Holifield and Hosmer were hearing Rickover for the last time; they would be retiring, he noted, as were two other Joint Committee members not there—Senator Wallace Bennett, a member of Congress for twenty-three of his seventy-six years, and Senator Alan Bible, who, at sixty-five, was leaving Congress after twenty years.

As he began his testimony—The Rickover Lecture—with his familiar reel of statistics, he sat before men who must have felt that he would outlast them, too. He was a man so old, so long in office, that he was seemingly defying a fundamental law of nature: Here was a man who was somehow older than Congress.

Rickover made no editorial comment about the number of men who had come and gone from the Joint Committee, except to praise them and implore the committee to do more toward building *their* nuclear navy. Nor would he comment on the changes of the officials in the Atomic Energy Commission from his first dealings with that body in 1947 until its demise in 1974. In that period the five AEC commissioner seats had thirty-seven incumbents; some such as Francesco Costagliola, who served for nine months, had relatively short terms.

But when discussing the Department of Defense, Rickover was quick to point out to his Congressional colleagues the rapid changeovers in the Pentagon. For example, in 1977, looking back at three decades of his serving as head of the nuclear-propulsion program, Rickover named fourteen Secretaries of Defense, sixteen Deputy Secretaries of Defense, thirteen Directors of Defense Research and Engineering, eight assistants to the Secretary of Defense for atomic energy, fifteen Secretaries of the Navy, eighteen Under Secretaries of the Navy, eleven Chiefs of Naval Operations, fourteen Vice Chiefs of Naval Operations, five Chiefs of Naval Material, and eleven commanders of the Naval Sea Systems Command (and its predecessor organizations).

"On the average," he said, "each of these one hundred and twenty-five key officials in the Department of Defense approval chain held his position a little over two years. In any given year, about four of these ten top positions had a new incumbent. Since my own tour of duty . . . spans this entire period, I undoubtedly have a different view of the events that have occurred than do the officials I have mentioned and their numerous subordinates whose approval had to be obtained before I could proceed with my work. . . ."

And so here was *the* secret of his success on Capitol Hill: Hang on. It was not really a secret, though. At a naval aviation luncheon in Washington, he was asked publicly, "How do you get things done?" He answered: "You just outlive them."

His supreme achievement as Admiral of the Hill was passage of the unique piece of legislation that stipulated that all major combat ships of the strike forces of the Navy had to be nuclear-powered. This made the creation of an all-nuclear navy—a Rickover navy—a matter of law. Under this law there could be only one way a nonnuclear ship could be built: The President would have to go to Congress and say that a certain ship had to be powered by something other than a Rickover reactor because such a nonnuclear ship was "in the national interest." Such a ship, to the lawmakers, was unimaginable, and such a humiliating act by the Commander in Chief was also unimaginable.

The law had been long in coming. Mention of an all-nuclear navy had been made by Congressional supporters of Rickover as far back as his first promotion fight in 1953. In the 1960s the concept of a nuclear navy came up again and again in Rickover's Capitol Hill bastions—the Joint Committee on Atomic Energy and the House Armed Services Committee. Men whose names would be on submarines showed up again and again as champions of the nuclear navy. They passionately orated in Congress. They tirelessly wrote long, and often angry, politically threatening letters to the President, the Secretary of Defense, and high Navy officials.

But their most important battle, the one that rallied them, was one they lost. That was in 1967 when the carrier *John F. Kennedy* was launched. She was not nuclear-powered, and the nuclear-power zealots in Congress vowed that this would never happen again.

"Godspeed to all who sail in *Kennedy*," cried Chet Holifield, vice-chairman of the Joint Committee, on the floor of the House. "Our freedom depends on the brave men who will man such ships, but I wonder if we are doing, as a nation, what we should to provide these brave men with the best to do this job. *Kennedy* ... was obsolete when it was launched. It is a second-best aircraft carrier."

Daniel Flood attacked Secretary of Defense Robert McNamara and "Mr. McNamara's Band at the Pentagon" for making "one of the most shocking errors and mistakes in the history of our Military Establishment. . . ." Flood said that never again would he vote for a combat ship that was not nuclear-powered. Armed Services Committee Chairman Rivers said that as long as he held that post there never would be a carrier that was oil-powered. To underscore its concern, Congress ordered the Secretary of the Navy to design and build as soon as possible two nuclear-powered missile frigates. "If this language constitutes a test as to whether Congress has the power to so mandate," the report said, "let the test be made and let this important weapons system be the field of trial."

Under McNamara and his immediate successors, the Navy continued to advance proposals for large nonnuclear surface ships as well as those propelled by nuclear reactors (although from fiscal 1963 to 1966 no frigates or cruisers were authorized for the Navy). The now-nuclear, now-not-nuclear weaving and dodging of the Navy exasperated Rickover's Congressional supporters and in April of 1974 a bill was introduced to mandate nuclear power for *all* "major combatant vessels." The "nuclear navy" bill became law, incorporated as Title VIII, entitled "Nuclear Powered Navy," in the Department of Defense Appropriation Authorization Act of 1975. Title VIII stated:

> It is the policy of the United States of America to modernize the strike forces of the United States Navy by the construction of nuclear powered major combatant vessels and to provide for an adequate industrial base for the research, development, design, construction, operation, and maintenance for such vessels. New construction of major combatant vessels for the strike forces of the United States Navy authorized subsequent to the date the enactment of this Act becomes law shall be nuclear powered, except as provided in this title.

The law was an open-ended commitment to an all-nuclear Navy, a Rickover navy. Rickover, when he wished, could deny that the law mandated an all-nuclear Navy; ships of "strike forces" were the only ones covered by the law. But the law, in fact, did define those ships as combatant submarines, "combatant vessels intended to operate in combat in aircraft carrier groups (that is, aircraft carriers and the cruisers, frigates* and destroyers which accompany aircraft carriers)" and any of these ships that were "designed for independent combat missions, where essentially unlimited high-speed endurance will be of significant military value." In other words, small anti-submarine ships could slip through a loophole in Public Law 93–365, but the impact of the law clearly put Congressmen—and their favorite admiral—in the business of building a nuclear navy.

The effects of the law, though, were not unlike the effects of the admiral's favorite form of energy—much heat over a long period of time, fallout in predictable and unpredictable patterns, and a steadily growing controversy about its efficacy. In its immediate impact, however, the law did what Rickover wanted it to do: It proved that he was correct.

The Title VIII was Congressional legislation, not merely a resolution passed by the Joint Committee on Atomic Energy or one of the others in which Rickover had influence. Armed with Title VIII, given the entire Congress as a platform from which to air his grievances, and possessing

---

* Missile frigates (designated DLG or, if nuclear-powered, DLGN) were mostly reclassified as cruisers in 1975 (CG or CGN). Subsequently, the term "frigate" was applied to smaller, anti-submarine escort ships, as was common usage in foreign navies.

the never-worn four stars of a full admiral, by the middle 1970s it appeared that Rickover was truly at the zenith of his power.

Then, with little warning, his power base was cut deeply. The energy crisis had been building for several years, exacerbated by the Arab oil boycott after the 1973 war in the Middle East. In part as a result of the energy situation, the Atomic Energy Commission was abolished, and the Joint Committee on Atomic Energy was dismantled. In January 1977, the House Armed Services Committee was given authority over national-security programs of the Energy Research and Development Administration (ERDA, the predecessor to the Department of Energy and the Nuclear Regulatory Commission). The Armed Services Committee formed a Subcommittee on Intelligence and Military Applications of Nuclear Energy, and it was before this committee—this mere shade of the powerful Joint Committee—that Rickover appeared for the first time on April 27, 1977.

Rickover began testifying in his age-old way, answering perhaps a few more questions than he had been used to, hearing some mild contradictions to his answers. There was just the slightest hint that some of the new names—the names that were not on submarines and probably never would be—did not quite feel about Rickover the way their predecessors had felt.

The testimony suddenly ended when a Congressman told Rickover, "We have a vote here."

"Are you coming back, sir?" Rickover asked.

"No, Admiral," said Representative Charles H. Wilson of California, a member of Congress since 1962. "I think we are going to recess the committee now and we want to express our great appreciation to you for coming and assisting us today. . . ."

"I hope I have your permission to extend my remarks and to complete my testimony," Rickover said.

"Absolutely. Your entire statement and any accompanying material that you may want to submit in connection with it, backup material, will be made a part of the record."

"Thank you, sir."

"We appreciate it very much," Wilson said. He appeared nervous, perhaps embarrassed. "The budget resolution is on, and the defense part of it, national security part—we are anxious to be on the floor and participate. And I appreciate your understanding. Thank you very much. We will recess the hearing."

As the subcommittee members began to shuffle out, Rickover said, "Thank you, Mr. Chairman, for your very courteous treatment and being willing to listen to me. And I hope I have helped to inform you to some extent."

Wilson tried to be friendly. "I ran that picture of you and me in my last newsletter, Admiral," he said.

"Yes, sir, but I have not seen it."

"I will get it to you," Wilson said, and Rickover was left to put the rest of his statement into the printed record.

It began, "As you know I have been responsible for directing the naval nuclear propulsion program for over twenty-eight years. . . ."

He was still Admiral of the Hill, although perhaps he was not viewed that way by as many members as once he had known. He was an admiral whose major battles were behind him, and most of them he had won.

Title VIII had been a mandate to build a nuclear surface navy that would complement the nuclear-submarine navy. The first three ships of that surface navy had, over a decade before, demonstrated the unequivocal advantages of the nuclear propulsion he had brought to the Navy. That demonstration, called Operation Sea Orbit, had taken place while most members of the Ninety-sixth Congress were still growing up.

Operation Sea Orbit

Rickover's increasing constituency on Capitol Hill, coupled with the demonstrations of the effectiveness of nuclear power by the *Nautilus* and other early atomic submarines, would lead to the construction of nuclear surface ships. By the end of 1962 the Navy had at sea an entire nuclear-powered carrier task force—a giant aircraft carrier and a missile-armed cruiser and a large destroyer to escort her.

In a most dramatic example of the power of their atomic furnaces, the all-nuclear task force sailed around the world in just sixty-five days without replenishing fuel or provisions—except for some food for a young kangaroo taken aboard when the task force visited Australia. The nuclear warships, designated as Task Force 1, averaged just over twenty knots continuous steaming for the two months, with only short visits to three ports, another unprecedented record. (At several other locations, dignitaries were flown on and off the carrier for brief, highly impressive ship tours while the ships remained at sea.)

This headline-grabbing cruise was called Operation Sea Orbit by the Navy. Like the nation's orbital space flights that garnered funds for the Apollo moon project, the around-the-world cruise was staged to demonstrate the value of nuclear ships and the need for more of them. For Rickover, more nuclear ships would mean still more power, for there would be more Rickover-influenced shipyards engaged in building them, and more Rickover-selected and Rickover-trained men to sail them.

Congress had been intrigued by the possibility of nuclear-powered ships almost since the dawn of the nuclear era. The Senate set up a Special Committee on Atomic Energy and held hearings in December 1945. The committee, which would evolve into the Joint Committee on Atomic Energy, was under the chairmanship of Brien McMahon, then the freshman Senator from Connecticut. McMahon, who frequently declared that the bombing of Hiroshima was the greatest event in world history since the birth of Jesus Christ, sought to establish his claim to legislative leadership in this new field. Although the first hearings of the committee, for thirteen days between Thanksgiving and Christmas, had little real value for the future of nuclear energy, they did give many scientists an opportunity to air their views. Several witnesses, among them Ross Gunn of the Naval Research Laboratory, testified that, in the future, nuclear energy should be used for peaceful purposes. "The main job of nuclear energy is to turn the world's wheels and run its ships," Gunn said.

To many in Congress and to the American public this was the first indication that nuclear energy could be used to propel ships across the seas. Virtually all Navy personnel and civilians who were aware of the propulsion possibilities of nuclear energy realized that the greatest advantages would come from applying nuclear propulsion to submarines, freeing them from air-consuming combustion, and making them true submersibles. But there were indications that nuclear propulsion might be better suited for surface ships. Nuclear reactors would require heavy shielding to protect the crews from radiation, and the vast array of piping, pumps, controls, heat exchangers, and turbines might be too large to be crammed into a submarine's small, tubular hull.

But to the credit of Rickover and others, the first nuclear ship to be developed was a submarine. The concept of a nuclear-propelled aircraft carrier soon followed. Admiral Nimitz, the first postwar Chief of Naval Operations and the man who had approved the first nuclear submarine, was succeeded after two years in office by Admiral Louis Denfeld. A naval aviator and former carrier commander, Denfeld argued strongly for an increased role for carrier aviation and gave total support for the planned U.S.S. *United States,* the first "super-carrier." That ship was laid down in April 1949, only to be canceled a few days later, thus touching off a massive debate between the Navy and the Air Force on service roles and missions. Dubbed the "admirals' revolt" in the press, the battle raged in the services, the press, and the halls of Congress. Denfeld, forced to resign, was succeeded by another aviator, Forrest P. Sherman.

Admiral Sherman, who had a reputation as an intellectual, was a strategic planner, and in 1948–1949 had developed the Navy's position on military unification. He became CNO in November 1949, at age fifty-three, the youngest until that time. Sherman immediately backed Navy efforts to get large carriers back into the budget.

The outbreak of the Korean War in June 1950 made the value of carriers immediately apparent as all airfields in South Korea were quickly overrun, and bases in Japan were too far from the peninsula to permit effective fighter operations in the war zone. There was immediate Congressional support for more carriers.

Less than two months later, Admiral Sherman wrote a secret memorandum to his principal deputies and the Chief of BuShips: "I believe that the time has come to explore the feasibility of constructing a large carrier with an atomic power plant to determine time factors, cost factors and characteristics."

Despite earlier skepticism over nuclear power for surface ships, Rickover's Naval Reactors Branch responded quickly to the CNO, asking the AEC laboratories at Argonne, Knolls and Oak Ridge to prepare feasibility studies of a suitable reactor plant. Their reports were in Washington within two weeks, and a short time later BuShips had the recommendations on Admiral Sherman's desk. By December 1950, Sherman judged the time was right to broach the subject in a memorandum to the Joint Chiefs of Staff, then the policy-making group within the Department of Defense. "I have investigated the possibility of constructing a replacement fleet aircraft carrier with a nuclear power plant, . . ." he wrote. "Such a carrier would have no stack or exhaust gas problem, would be capable of operation without refueling for very long periods of time, and would have other important advances in the military characteristics. . . . I therefore recommend that the Joint Chiefs formally request the Atomic Energy Commission to consider undertaking now the construction of a shore-based prototype for aircraft carrier propulsion."

The Rickover submission to the CNO in the fall had proposed a land-based reactor prototype to be operational by 1953, with a shipboard plant in 1955, but Admiral Sherman's memorandum to the Joint Chiefs mentioned only the prototype. Further, the AEC assigned responsibility for monitoring the effort to another group in the division of reactor development—not to Rickover's NRB. Lawrence R. Hafstad, director of reactor development in AEC, feared that Rickover would simply scale up the submarine-reactor design to produce the carrier reactor.

AEC studies continued, but at a slow pace. Rickover, meanwhile, was increasing his influence over all Navy-related reactor projects through his relations with AEC Commissioner Thomas E. Murray and McMahon, chairman of the Joint Committee on Atomic Energy. Disturbed by the slow progress of the large-ship reactor, these men probably influenced the Joint Chiefs, who in October 1951 approved a formal requirement for "a single shore-based prototype of a nuclear-powered propulsion unit suitable for driving one shaft of a major warship such as an aircraft carrier, and for use after completion of the shore installation for the production of plutonium and electric power."

Thus, the proposed carrier reactor could meet several goals—large-ship propulsion, plutonium for use in weapons, and a prototype for civilian power reactors. And, Rickover took control of the program into NRB.

Rickover, after reviewing six Westinghouse designs for a large-ship reactor plant, did favor one similar to the pressurized-water plant being developed for the submarine *Nautilus*. Now Rickover would have three reactors under development: the pressurized-water reactor for the *Nautilus*, the sodium intermediate reactor for the *Seawolf*, and the large-ship reactor. The Westinghouse-run Bettis laboratory was assigned development responsibility for the third. Rickover estimated that the land prototype could be built and operating by 1956.

During this time, large conventional carriers were being constructed at an impressive rate. But the slowdown of the Korean War and the election of President Eisenhower led to a reappraisal of defense expenditures. Eisenhower, appalled at spiraling defense costs, sought a reduction in federal expenditures and a balanced budget.

On March 31, 1953, Lewis L. Strauss, Eisenhower's special assistant on nuclear energy, suggested to a meeting of the National Security Council that more than $200 million annually could be saved by eliminating an Air Force nuclear aircraft project and the Navy's nuclear carrier. Strauss, a retired rear admiral in the Naval Reserve, a former AEC commissioner, and a staunch supporter of military programs, carried considerable weight in the discussions. (Strauss would become chairman of the AEC in July 1953.)

Rickover still tried to have the carrier reactor funded, but failed. Admiral Sherman had died in office in July of 1951, and there was no strong advocate of nuclear carriers in the Pentagon's senior ranks. Rather, the naval-aviation community was simply seeking more carriers of any kind.

Later, Rickover would pointedly blame the 1953 cancellation of the nuclear-carrier project on the Department of Defense. But the initiative seems to have come from Strauss, whose background and experience as a Navy budget specialist and officer during World War II gave him excellent credentials. After the National Security Council meeting, the Department of Defense proposed an indefinite postponement of the program, but Strauss and the President both wished for a full stop to the effort.

AEC Chairman Gordon Dean then argued that the action would

end the Commission's plan to develop civilian nuclear power, to which Eisenhower responded that he would consider any recommendation that the AEC would make for converting the program to the civilian role. Through this opening the AEC and Rickover pushed a proposal for the large-ship reactor design to become the prototype for a civilian power reactor. It was built at Shippingport, Pennsylvania, in record time. (See Chapter 28.) Strauss, in his new position of AEC chairman, directed Rickover to supervise its construction. Rickover would only temporarily lose the carrier reactor, while gaining a whole new area of responsibility.

On the national strategy level, the Eisenhower attack on defense spending caused a revision of basic national-security policy, placing emphasis on massive atomic-strike capability or, as it was called after Secretary of State John Foster Dulles' address on the subject in January 1954, a policy of "massive retaliation." The Navy's leadership had long viewed with apprehension an overreliance on bombers with nuclear weapons. Admiral Robert Carney, who became CNO in July 1953, stressed the need to include aircraft carriers as well as land-based bombers in the national strategic arsenal. (The first carrier-based aircraft able to drop nuclear bombs were deployed in 1951 to the Mediterranean; this first squadron of Navy nuclear bombers was commanded by Captain John T. Hayward, who had been one of the naval officers in the Manhattan Project.)

Prodded on by Rickover and his Congressional supporters, Secretary of Defense Charles E. Wilson in mid-1954 advised the AEC that on the basis of technological developments during the past fourteen months, "it is now timely and highly desirable from the military standpoint to undertake active development of a practical working prototype of a reactor . . . for the propulsion of large ships." The AEC responded in the affirmative, with the Westinghouse-operated Bettis laboratory being assigned the task of developing the large-ship reactor, while continuing its work for the Shippingport civilian reactor. And the new effort was placed under the auspices of NRB.

By 1954, Rickover's thirty-second year in the Navy, he could celebrate not only his hard-won promotion to rear admiral but also the fact that he had *seven* reactors under the control of NRB. He had accomplished this despite the retirement in 1949 of his greatest—and at times only—supporter, Vice Admiral Mills; despite the enemies he was making at all levels in the Navy; and despite the fact that there was still not even one nuclear ship at sea.

A few weeks after Secretary Wilson's letter to the AEC, the Commission approved funds for the development of a land-based prototype of the large-ship reactor, to cost an estimated $26 million over a five-year period. The prototype for the large-ship reactor would be erected near the *Nautilus* prototype at the National Reactor Testing Station in Idaho. The carrier plant would have two pressurized-water reactors powering one steam turbine that would produce some 70,000 horsepower. This was one quarter of the propulsion plant required for an aircraft carrier, which would have eight reactors to produce an estimated 280,000 horsepower, the amount of power generated by eight high-pressure, oil-fired boilers in the later *Forrestal*-class carriers. According to estimates at the time, the plant would propel a nuclear carrier for a theoretical 120-day trip at a speed of 32 knots, while the *Forrestal* could steam at that speed for only seven days. Similarly, at 20 knots the nuclear ship could cruise for several hundred days, compared to twenty-two days for the *Forrestal*. The nuclear carrier was expected to travel over 200,000 miles—eight times around the world at the equator—without refueling. (On its initial fuel cores the nuclear carrier actually traveled 207,000 miles.)

Construction of the prototype in Arco, Idaho, began in April 1956, and engineers for the Newport News Shipbuilding and Dry Dock Company in Virginia were assigned to BuShips to help develop plans for a nuclear carrier.

Still there was no nuclear carrier approved for construction. The one-per-year approval of large carriers was continuing in the Department of Defense and in Congress, with the oil-burning *Kitty Hawk* in the fiscal 1956 budget and the similar *Constellation* in fiscal 1957. The fiscal 1957 budget provided long-lead funds for the start of procurement of nuclear reactors for an aircraft carrier. The funds were necessary because of the length of time it took to fabricate the reactors.

Already the Navy was campaigning publicly for a nuclear carrier. Admiral Arleigh Burke, who succeeded Carney as Chief of Naval Operations in August 1955, and Secretary of the Navy Charles S. Thomas and other Navy leaders were stumping for nuclear surface ships. Thomas told a Navy League conference in October 1956, "Nuclear power is now conventional for all new submarines and soon will be for cruisers and carriers." A Navy propaganda booklet published a short time later had this title:

C   arriers are
V   ital to the
A   tomic
N   avy

The pamphlet called for six attack aircraft carriers—nuclear, or CVAN in Navy jargon—to be built at the rate of one per year. Admiral Burke signed the booklet, noting, "The future is limited only by our imagination and zeal." Some Navy leaders would even go so far as to say that they were willing to sacrifice "some ships" in the building program to fund nuclear carriers, although such statements were rare and carefully qualified to deter the loss of any ships from their plans. Burke, known as "31-knot Burke" for his destroyer exploits in World War II, was ready to fully support the development of nuclear propulsion and, as will be seen, other advanced weapons systems, such as the Polaris submarine missile.

When the Eisenhower Administration sent its 1958 budget request to Congress, it asked for funds for a nuclear carrier. In general, Congress was favorably disposed; only superficial hearings were held on the nuclear carrier. But some questions were raised. The House Appropriations Committee, for example, in an otherwise favorable report, said, "In approving the funds requested the Committee wants it clearly understood that it is not approving the entire program for the Navy for five additional nuclear-powered carriers in future years."

More vociferous were the remarks of Clarence Cannon, the chairman of the committee and a long-time opponent of naval forces. Despite the Korean War and a score of cold-war crises, Cannon and others failed to comprehend the role of navies in the postwar period. "If war should come," Cannon asked, "could the Navy protect us? Ridiculous. Enemy bombers would fly right over them. With the exception of our submarines the Navy would cease to exist in a matter of hours. . . . A carrier is the most expensive machine the world ever saw. It consumes more skilled labor, more strategic material, and more than any human contrivance the sun has ever shone upon. And yet in war it would be worse than useless. . . .

"They propose to power this carrier with atomic energy. [They] have not a very definite idea of just how it will be done—but they will not wait for that. They will spend the money now."

Even after the Congress approved funding for the first nuclear carrier, Cannon continued his opposition. In January of 1958, Cannon initiated efforts to have the funds already allocated for the nuclear carrier shifted to nuclear submarines. He failed, but—significantly—the subcommittee vote on the issue was an eight-to-eight tie.

The Department of Defense was still not a key player in the nuclear-surface-ships debates and would not be for another few years, until

Robert S. McNamara would use an earlier (1958) defense reorganization as a launching pad to impose himself and various Defense agencies as a "super staff" between the President and the armed services. In later years Rickover would make the pre-McNamara Department of Defense a scapegoat for the casting-off of the sin of being against nuclear power; he could not afford the risk of reminding his Congressional supporters that some of their most revered colleagues had been against forms of nuclear propulsion.

Also, as Rickover rose in rank, he had more difficulty in pointing to "the brass" as obstructionists to nuclear power. In the eyes of some Congressmen, Rickover himself, as an admiral, was by definition one of the brass, although he was only rarely seen in his gold-laden uniform, with four rows of ribbons and the submarine dolphins he had won in 1930.

The aircraft carrier would not be the Navy's first nuclear-propelled surface warship. The fiscal year 1957 shipbuilding program, which provided the long-lead funds for the carrier reactors, included a guided-missile cruiser that was nuclear-powered. There was exceedingly little debate over this ship, as starting with the fiscal 1956 budget the Navy had begun building many surface ships to provide missile-armed escorts for the new aircraft carriers. In fiscal 1956 the Administration asked for six large missile destroyers (designated DLG), followed in fiscal 1957 with a request for four large (DLG) and eight small (DDG) missile destroyers, plus a nuclear ship. Congress approved all—nineteen missile escorts in two years.

The *Long Beach,* the first nuclear surface warship, would use the reactor plant developed for the carrier—but with only two reactors providing some 80,000 horsepower to two propeller shafts. Moving rapidly, in October 1956 the Navy awarded a contract to the Bethlehem Steel shipyard at Quincy, Massachusetts, to construct the *Long Beach.*

Originally the ship had been proposed as a nuclear-missile–armed large destroyer or "frigate" (designated DLGN) with a standard displacement of 7,800 tons. Reactors for small ships had been considered almost since the end of the war, with General Electric having proposed a reactor plant as early as 1946. (Of course, submarines are also small, but less power is needed for a specified weight and speed because submarines do not meet the resistance that surface ships encounter from waves and rough seas.)

The principal problem of a nuclear ship was the concentration of reactor-plant weight in a small area, relatively high up in the ship. Thus, the larger the nuclear ship, the easier to handle internal arrangements. Before the contract for the *Long Beach* was awarded, the Navy, deciding to capitalize on the capabilities of nuclear propulsion, enlarged the ship. Three antiaircraft missile launchers would be installed instead of one, and provisions were made for advanced radars, with space being provided for Regulus land-attack missiles (neither these nor subsequently proposed Polaris missiles were ever actually installed). CNO Burke said that "the ship should have the maximum capability that can be built into her, and the limitations imposed on her should be only those imposed by our lack of knowledge."

The *Long Beach* would finally emerge with a standard displacement of 14,000 tons; fully loaded with all munitions and stores, she would be a 17,000-ton warship. With the increases in size and capability, there were major increases in costs—from just over $142 million when ordered to over $320 million when completed.

The carrier authorized in the fiscal 1958 budget, which would be named *Enterprise*, was ordered from Newport News on November 15, 1957. With a full-load displacement of 89,000 tons, the 1,123-foot *Enterprise* would be the largest ship yet built. She would be similar to the improved *Forrestal*-class ships in design, but about 9,000 tons larger. More space was needed for the eight reactors and shielding than was required for the steam plant in a conventional carrier. Then, after the ship was enlarged for a nuclear plant, the hull was lengthened to maintain a high speed with the greater displacement.

Like the *Forrestal*-class carriers, the *Enterprise* would have some ninety of the latest jet-propelled planes, including several attack aircraft weighing thirty-five tons each. The nuclear ship could handle a few more aircraft than the *Forrestals*, but her main advantages were the much larger stores of aviation fuel (because ship fuel was not carried), more weapons for aircraft, and, of course, the virtually unlimited cruising range.

While the two nuclear ships were being built, at Arco the two-reactor A1W plant reached criticality at 10:30 A.M. on October 21, 1958. But not until September 15, 1959, would the large-ship plant operate at full power.

With the cruiser *Long Beach* scheduled to serve as an escort ship for the carrier *Enterprise*, nuclear-power advocates began to seek additional screening ships. Normally, four to six cruisers and destroyers "screened" each aircraft carrier against hostile aircraft and submarine attacks. One proposal at the time called for six nuclear cruisers plus sixteen nuclear destroyers to escort the six carriers. But the *Long Beach* was obviously too large, had too many complicated systems, and was too costly to be replicated in large numbers.

The Navy proposed, and the fiscal 1959 budget funded, a nuclear-propelled destroyer leader. There had been several proposals by industry and BuShips for destroyer-type ships with nuclear propulsion, but the real impetus for this ship seems to have come from the fleet. The admiral commanding the Atlantic Fleet's destroyer force, Joseph C. Daniel, began arguing for nuclear destroyers with his World War II boss, Arleigh Burke. Daniel, reportedly writing weekly letters on the subject, convinced Burke that nuclear propulsion was vital for destroyers, which normally refueled every other day during high-tempo fleet operations. Burke finally concurred, and the large destroyer or frigate (DLGN) was included in the 1959 budget.

Various Congressional committees questioned the merit of the nuclear destroyer, but despite her much higher cost—$108 million, more than twice the cost of an oil-burning DLG—the ship was easily approved. Rear Admiral Albert Mumma, Chief of the Bureau of Ships, became a principal spokesman in favor of nuclear surface warships, pointing out to Congressmen that, in addition to an increased high-speed range, the nuclear surface ships would have their weapons and radars in better positions because they had no smoke stacks, and they were more resistant to atomic and chemical attacks because their engines did not require air for combustion. At this time, Rickover only infrequently appeared before the armed services and appropriations committees of the two houses of Congress; that was left to the "real" Navy. Rather, Rickover's arena was the more sympathetic Joint Committee on Atomic Energy.

Not addressed in most of the nuclear-frigate discussions was the fact that such a small ship (8,500 tons fully loaded, or half the size of the *Long Beach*) could not accommodate the reactors developed for the larger nuclear cruiser and carrier. A whole new destroyer reactor plant was being developed for the ship. That project had been started in the Naval Reactors Branch in 1956, but had been immediately in trouble with the AEC leadership. An alternative approach had been proposed to the Navy by industry, which had hoped to set up a surface nuclear-propulsion project independent of Rickover. But he was soon able to squash that effort, and the NRB-managed destroyer reactor became a reality.

The frigate's reactor would be developed by the General Electric-operated Knolls laboratory in Schenectady. A prototype would be installed in the structure that previously housed the *Seawolf*'s sodium prototype. The actual ship, which would be named *Bainbridge,* was to have a two-reactor plant generating some 60,000 horsepower for two propeller shafts. The Bethlehem yard at Quincy, Massachusetts, where the *Long Beach* was being built, would construct this first nuclear "destroyer." (Rickover also initiated a single-reactor propulsion plant for destroyers at the Westinghouse-Bettis laboratory in 1960. However, this concept did not prove feasible and was soon scrapped.)

Construction of the three nuclear surface ships was undertaken with high priority, despite the resources being given at the time to nuclear attack submarines and, subsequently, to Polaris missile submarines. In yards where nuclear ships were being built, the top priority was always given to nuclear-propulsion plants. The attention that Rickover demanded—and received—from the yards reduced the attention given to other parts of the ships. Officers responsible for the nonnuclear systems often felt that they were stepchildren.

Commander Todd Blades was such an officer. He was one of the original commissioning crew of the *Long Beach.* Her main battery consisted of Talos and Terrier antiaircraft missiles, and Blades was the main battery officer.

> Sometime in the spring of 1961 [Blades recalled years later] I was the in-port officer of the deck on the forenoon watch, observing dockside preparations to load the ship's spare main coolant pump. Each of the two nuclear reactors has four of these high-precision pumps in its primary loop, and because of their vital role in the plant, the ship carries one spare. . . .
>
> Things seemed to move ever so slowly during the evolution. The precise and delicate positioning of the pump on its pallet at just the right place on the pier and the slow, precise and gentle positioning of the dockside crane's lifting block above the pump were in total contrast to the way the shipyard's riggers usually went about their business. The pier seemed to be swarming in supervisors. . . . Finally, the pump was lifted, raised, and slowly and gently moved over the access hatch on the ship. I'm sure it took much longer before it was resting securely in its stowage below, but by that time I had been relieved of the watch.
>
> Watching the care taken with that pump made me angry. Just a couple of days before, we had had our first Talos test missile delivered. It was a fully operational one except for a dummy warhead. . . . Despite an equally thorough and adequate preparation by our ship's force, we could not get the same careful attention from the

shipyard. The missile had, in fact, suffered some stove-in damage while being lifted aboard.

The "problem"—Blades mildly called it a problem of emphasis— had begun when the *Long Beach* was born. On the ways in the Quincy shipyard, more than a dozen nuclear-propulsion supervisors watched over the installation of her nuclear plant, but only four or five supervisors paid attention to the complex warship's multitude of other needs.

> The upshot of all this [Blades recalled] was that the ship's nuclear power plant and all its auxiliaries were completed, tested, and ready to go to sea before the rest of the ship. For whatever reasons, justifiable or not, no matter what organizations were responsible, portions of her combat system had not even been installed, much less readied.

The *Long Beach* was commissioned on September 9, 1961, without her advanced radars or tactical-data system, which correlated radar data to help the ship's captain make split-second decisions in firing the ship's guided missiles against high-speed enemy aircraft. But Rickover could claim that the world's first nuclear surface warship was on schedule. (The *Long Beach* went to sea in December; the Soviets' nuclear-powered icebreaker *Lenin* already was at sea.) On her forty-three-day, 11,600-mile "good will" trip, the *Long Beach* visited Bremerhaven, Le Havre, and Bermuda. Her commanding officer was Eugene P. Wilkinson, who had been the first skipper of the *Nautilus*. She was a truly peaceful ambassador, for, according to Blades, her only "fully operational weapon subsystem" was her anti-submarine rocket launcher.

When she returned to the United States in late April 1962, the *Long Beach* entered a shipyard for installation of her radars and tactical-data system. Not until eight months later did she emerge ready for combat.

The *Enterprise*—the "Big E"—followed the *Long Beach* into active service on November 25, 1961. Her building cost, like her size, exceeded that of the *Long Beach*, with the Navy listing her price tag at $444 million, or almost $200 million more than the two conventional carriers completed the same year, the *Constellation* and the *Kitty Hawk*. The *Enterprise* was larger and, driven by the power of eight nuclear reactors, much more impressive. Under Captain Vincent de Poix, the 4,600 officers and enlisted men of the "Big E" sailed a ship that had a flight deck longer than three and a half football fields, that was twenty-three stories high from keel to top of her "island" superstructure, and was a mobile airfield that could operate ninety jet aircraft. The ship's self-sufficiency begged superlatives. The four galleys could produce 13,800 meals per day (plus snacks), the salt-water evaporators could distill a quarter of a million gallons of water a day, the ship's air-conditioning could cool four hundred homes, and there were 1,800 telephones and 25,500 light fixtures, plus four ladies' powder rooms (for the use of visitors in port—women were not yet allowed aboard warships at sea).

After her trials, the CNO said the ship's performance "exceeded by far" the predictions of her designers. On board for those trials were Rickover, Rear Admiral Ralph K. James, Chief of BuShips, several other flag officers, representatives of the Newport News shipyard, and AEC commissioner Loren K. Olson.

The initial operational assignment of the "Big E" was to the Project Mercury recovery force off Bermuda, serving as a tracking ship for Astronaut John Glenn's orbital flight. Further at-sea operations followed off the East Coast, with members of the Joint Committee on Atomic Energy spending two days aboard the flattop as she cruised off Guantanamo Bay, Cuba. Members of the committee previously had met aboard three nuclear submarines; and with the "Big E" cruise, Admiral Rickover again demonstrated his expertise in handling the lawmakers.

Chairman Chet Holifield opened the session in the admiral's cabin with a brief review of the committee's hearings aboard nuclear ships, and then gave the now-traditional accolades to Rickover as "a man who, more than any other person, is responsible for the tremendous advancements that have taken place and revolutionized our Navy during the past seven years."

For two hours Admiral Rickover, Captain de Poix, and Lieutenant Commander R. E. Smith, the ship's engineering officer, explained to the committee members the advantages of the *Enterprise* compared to conventional ships, lauding the importance of nuclear propulsion. Then Rickover made his plea for more Congressional support of nuclear ships. Recalling the first committee hearing aboard the *Nautilus* in 1955, Rickover said:

> At that time we had definitely proved that nuclear power was feasible for underwater ships, and due to the efforts of the Joint Congressional Committee the Navy was finally persuaded to go extensively into construction of nuclear submarines.
>
> The objection to building nuclear submarines at that time was

this: Congress was appropriating about $40 million per year for one conventional submarine. The people in Naval Operations were afraid if we changed to nuclear submarines they might get two every three years instead of one every year. So they were opposed to building nuclear submarines.

While the accuracy of that statement may have been merely questionable, Rickover's next statement was highly misleading and self-serving:

> As it turns out, fourteen nuclear submarines have been requested [by the Administration] in the fiscal 1963 shipbuilding program, so it is clear the Navy didn't suffer as a result of having a better, though more expensive ship. Exactly the same situation prevails today with regard to the surface Navy as existed in 1955 with the submarine Navy. You get hurled at you figures showing nuclear power for surface ships . . . costs 30 to 50 percent more than a conventional one. So I thought it would be interesting to quote a few cost figures on other improved weapons.
>
> In comparing World War II costs with costs today for various items of military equipment, an Army rifle went up from $31 to $100. Conventional destroyers have gone up from $9 million to $35 million; four times. . . .

Rickover's list of comparisons continued. But he ignored two vital factors in his comparisons. First, the fourteen nuclear submarines requested in fiscal year 1963 included six Polaris missile submarines, a type unknown a decade earlier, and in no way related to the Navy's pre-Polaris submarine requirements. Similarly, the eight non-Polaris (i.e., torpedo attack) submarines in the budget were wanted to help compensate for the heavy allocation of funds to Polaris submarines during the previous few years.

No one in the Navy of the 1960s proposed building more World War II ships, even assuming that they could be built for their previous cost. At issue was whether to build another oil-burning carrier at $265 million— Rickover's estimated price—or to build another nuclear flattop like the *Enterprise* at $444 million. Or, whether to build an oil-burning frigate for $49 million or a nuclear ship like the new *Bainbridge* for $108 million. True, the costs of nuclear ships would decline as more of them were built, but the cost difference—forty percent more for carriers and sixty-five percent more for frigates—was becoming a major factor as the number of major surface warships being built started to decline rapidly in the 1960s.

But Rickover made his point. As the two-hour formal session continued, to his most supportive audience Rickover revealed: "The reason I said earlier that this meeting tonight is historic is because I think the Joint Congressional Committee can be just as influential for our surface Navy as it was for the submarine navy. You are the ones who forced the nuclear submarine navy. I think without your forcing we will not have a nuclear surface navy."

Three nuclear surface warships—the carrier *Enterprise,* missile cruiser *Long Beach,* and missile frigate *Bainbridge*—were a long way from the nuclear surface navy that Rickover sought. Still, the ships were impressive and, for the U.S. Navy in the cold war, very useful. During her first year at sea the *Enterprise* made a six-week deployment to the Mediterranean, then played a major role in the Cuban quarantine of 1962, and early in 1963 returned to the Mediterranean, this time for seven months with the U.S. Sixth Fleet.

Similarly, the *Long Beach* and then the *Bainbridge* operated with U.S. and NATO task forces in the Atlantic and Mediterranean. They drew high praise, from fleet and task force commanders, allies and, of course, the ships' own commanding officers. Rickover, in a manner unprecedented in the military lobbying of Congress, quickly turned these words of praise into powerful weapons in his quest for more nuclear surface ships.

Captain Raymond Peet, first skipper of the *Bainbridge,* was one of several nuclear-trained witnesses Rickover paraded before the Joint Committee in its more familiar Capitol Hill setting. "Nuclear power in a destroyer does give you another dimension," he said. Another witness was Vice Admiral John T. Hayward, an early supporter of Rickover in the Pentagon. Hayward had taken a reduction in rank, to rear admiral, to command a carrier task force built around the *Enterprise.*

Hayward continued his backing of Rickover and a nuclear navy in a letter to the Secretary of the Navy, which Rickover made part of the Congressional testimony. The letter declared that "the *Enterprise* outperforms every carrier in the fleet."

The praise went on and on.

And it had the intended effect. During those 1963 hearings before the Joint Committee, when Dr. Harold Brown, head of research for the Department of Defense, took his place at the witness table, he was addressed by John O. Pastore, committee chairman. After listing the previous witnesses—the Secretary of the Navy, the Chief of Naval Operations, and commanding officers of the first three nuclear surface ships—Senator Pastore told Brown: "They have all taken an unequivocal position that there is no question at all about it, that nuclear-propelled surface ships are much superior and have tremendous military advantages over conventional [ships].

"Now," continued Pastore, "will you tell me how that can be disregarded by the Department of Defense?"

Much of Congress was now squarely in Rickover's camp, obviously against Robert McNamara's Department of Defense. And within the Navy, Rickover's men—his "nucs"—were moving into positions of importance and were exerting more influence for the creation of a nuclear navy.

WHY NOT THE BEST?

I had applied for the nuclear submarine program, and Admiral Rickover was interviewing me for the job. It was the first time I met Admiral Rickover, and we sat in a large room by ourselves for more than two hours, and he let me choose any subjects I wished to discuss. Very carefully, I chose those about which I knew most at the time—current events, seamanship, music, literature, naval tactics, electronics, gunnery—and he began to ask me a series of questions of increasing difficulty. In each instance, he soon proved that I knew relatively little about the subject I had chosen.

He always looked right into my eyes, and he never smiled. I was saturated with cold sweat.

Finally, he asked me a question and I thought I could redeem myself. He said, "How did you stand in your class at the Naval Academy?" Since I had completed my sophomore year at Georgia Tech before entering Annapolis as a plebe, I had done very well, and I swelled my chest with pride and answered, "Sir, I stood fifty-ninth in a class of 820!" I sat back to wait for the congratulations—which never came. Instead, the question: "Did you do your best!" I started to say, "Yes, sir," but I remembered who this was and recalled several of the many times at the Academy when I could have learned more about our allies, our enemies, weapons, strategy, and so forth. I was just human. I finally gulped and said, "No, sir, I didn't always do my best."

He looked at me for a long time, and then turned his chair around to end the interview. He asked one final question, which I have never been able to forget—or to answer. He said, "Why not?" I sat there for a while, shaken, and then slowly left the room.

—JIMMY CARTER,
Why Not the Best?

13 | A Fascinating Experience

First Classman Joseph H. Barker III, a high-ranking member of his class at the Naval Academy, was summoned for an interview with Admiral Rickover in the late fall of 1966. Barker had been tapped for consideration for nuclear training, and the interview was the launching of a midshipman's nuclear career.

Rickover's interviews were notorious. They had begun when he probed the minds and attitudes of almost every potential officer and crewman of the *Nautilus*. And they had continued as the nuclear fleet expanded.

Barker's interview ended when Rickover asked him if he was willing to give up his Christmas vacation, his spring vacation, and every weekend until graduation in order to study in preparation for entering the nuclear program. Barker thought for a moment and politely told the Admiral that he did not think that so much study was necessary or reasonable. Rickover angrily ordered Barker out of his office and called in the next candidate.

Back at Bancroft Hall, Barker and his classmates exchanged reports about their interviews with Rickover. Many had been asked to make the same sacrifices and many had agreed to do so. They had so wanted to enter the nuclear program that they would do nearly anything that Rickover demanded. Barker had no such yearning. He would, in fact, enter what was then called the "real" navy, and he would enjoy a fine career.

When he and other midshipmen began streaming out of Annapolis for their Christmas leave, they left many comrades behind. On the nearly deserted grounds of the Academy, the intensive, sacrificial study of nuclear power had begun for members of another class. So had an unprecedented headache for Superintendent James Calvert, himself a graduate of Rickover schooling.

The phone calls began coming into his office soon after the nuclear initiates had called or written home to say that they would be missing Christmas with their families. So many complaints came in that Calvert ordered a quiet inquiry. He soon learned that Rickover was the man who had stolen Christmas. Indirect pressure was put on Rickover to relent. But not until Chief of Naval Operations Thomas Moorer intervened did the prospective nucs head home for the holidays. The CNO had ordered them home. Or at least he had ordered Rickover to stop playing Scrooge. All that can be accurately stated on the basis of memories of the event is that the midshipmen did go home.

Christmas was just another day that, in Rickover's opinion, belonged to him if the man was in the nuclear program. So could the man's love life.

"Do you have a girl friend?" he asked an NROTC graduate applying for Rickover's own elite staff in 1963. The candidate, a young, soft-spoken Midwesterner, was embarrassed. He had easily fielded the technical questions in the interview and had not expected this one. He had a girl friend and planned to propose to her. A typically cautious engineer, he was holding off on his proposal until he was sure he had a job. The young officer told Rickover that he had a girl friend.

"Are you prepared to sacrifice her for the program?" Rickover asked.

Fifteen years later the candidate would shake his head and remember clearly what he had answered: "That sort of puts a fellow on the spot, Admiral."

The Admiral did not press the question. Instead, he went on to other standard questions—such as "What ten books have you read in the last six months?" and "What does your father do for a living?"—and soon ended the interview. The candidate got the job, incidentally. (He did indeed propose to the girl. He became the father of two children—that, to Rickover, was being a "bird hatcher." Long since gone from the nuclear program, he talked about that interview as if it had occurred the day before. He was still astounded at his calm response to Rickover's question.)

Stories of Rickover's bizarre interviews became the most frequently heard yarns in the wardrooms of the nuclear navy. Some were apocryphal. Many were basically authentic, but embroidered with details borrowed from other interviews. All had a common image: Rickover the sardonic, pitiless inquisitor who often spouted obscenities and foul insults. From accounts of the interviews emerged a portrait of an irascible, often raging Rickover whose bullying manner and outrageous questions either shattered the candidate's outer shell, laying bare his essence for Rickover's instant analysis, or hardened that shell so that not even Rickover could penetrate it. Whatever the result, Rickover would make a judgment that seemed to have no obvious logic; a man who cracked might be accepted; a man who fought back might be rejected. Or vice versa.

Most of the early interviews had a standard theme: Put a man in an imaginary stress situation and then ask him how he would get out of it. A man might be asked this one: The people of Washington have decided to execute either the young candidate or a street cleaner. Who should be executed? If the man being interviewed thought Rickover wanted false modesty, he would say, "Save the street cleaner and execute me." *Wrong!* Rickover would slam his fist down on the desk and shout, "No! Anyone can sweep streets, but the street cleaner cannot do the job of a naval officer!"

Or this one. The candidate was told to imagine that he was on a sinking boat with five other men. "The conditions are that one, and only one of you, can be saved," Rickover told him. "Are you resourceful enough to talk the other five into letting you be the one?"

When the candidate said he could, Rickover called five members of his staff into the room and said to the candidate, "Start talking."

Rickover apparently looked for quick responses and would tolerate, to a varying degree, antagonistic reactions to his questions. When a candidate was told, "Piss me off, if you can," the candidate unhesitatingly swept everything off Rickover's desk. The candidate was accepted. Apparently word of this incident got around, and the next time Rickover tried it, so the story goes, he had a valuable ship model on his desk. Again the question; again the sweeping off of his desk—but this time there was battle damage to the model. Still, the candidate was accepted.

When Lieutenant Paul Tomb was granted his interview, Rickover pronounced the lieutenant's name as *Toom* rather than *Tom.* Tomb corrected Rickover's pronunciation, but Rickover ignored the lieutenant's remark and, keeping to the *Toom* pronunciation, asked, "Mr. Tomb, when were you first interested in the nuclear-submarine program?" The lieutenant replied, "Right after the atomic *boom,* sir." He got into the program, later won command of a nuclear-powered ship, and became Rear Admiral Tomb.

As the years went on, the stories became less funny. Midshipmen told of cruel tricks. One said that he had been asked whether he had a fiancée and whether he could reach her at that moment. According to his story, Rickover then handed the midshipman the phone and ordered him to call his fiancée and tell her that the engagement was off because of the needs of the nuclear-power program. The young man said that, as he began to dial, Rickover cursed him and ordered him out of the office.

Another highly qualified midshipman said that he was told during an interview that he would be accepted only if he would delay his wedding for a year. He refused and was rejected. Members of Rickover's staff were appalled because they realized the potential value of the young man and saw his rejection as a loss. According to pro-Rickover sources, the story had a happy ending. The staff members made a rare attempt at intercession and succeeded in getting Rickover to change his mind—an even rarer event. He reportedly relented and accepted the midshipman into the program, but only after making the bridegroom wait a year.

Several survivors of the interview told of trying to maintain balance and dignity in a chair whose front legs had been shortened. Others said that their interviews had been interrupted by inexplicable, hours-long banishments to a broom closet. These were only stories, oft-told, usually anonymous, and difficult to verify thoroughly.

One of Rickover's secretaries who was interviewed for this book cleared up the rumor about the chair, which was not consistently present for the infamous interviews. Its use, she said, apparently depended upon Rickover's mood. "I had to sit on that, and this was in my interview, too," she said, remembering being sent to Rickover from Navy yeoman's school. "It sits at an angle, and you're just about ready to fall out. He doesn't put it in his office except on days when he is interviewing midshipmen—or other days. It caused quite a few laughs. One guy fell out of it once."

She also recalled how insistent Rickover would be in determining the marital and prospective paternal status of a candidate. "One man came in," she recalled, "and he said he had a girl friend and she was pregnant. The Admiral said, 'Are you going to marry her?' The man said, 'No.' The Admiral just looked at him and said, 'How far along is she?' The man said, 'She's about six months.' " The interview soon ended. The candidate was accepted into nuclear power.

Stories of the "broom closet" seemed to be sea stories, the product of panicked imaginations. One, for instance, was told by a successful candidate. He said he refused to enter the closet, and Rickover said, "OK. Just go over there and let the other three out." The candidate, according to his oft-told tale, opened the door and did find three other candidates cowering inside.

But the authors were able to establish the existence of the "closet," or at least one or more small, dark rooms, which served as props in the staging of the interviews. The revelation came in a detailed reminiscence from a man who had been in the Naval Reserve Officer Training Corps.

When he arrived at Rickover's office, around 7:15 A.M., he and other members of his group were all given keys to unlock a certain door. They were briefed, and in the briefing assured that Rickover did not have a chair with sawed-off legs. (Its use apparently declined in the 1970s.) They were told about the floor plan of the Naval Reactors Branch, and the probable state of Rickover's mood; they were also informed that each would be given three interviews before The Interview.

In the preliminary interviews, the candidate recalled, he knew he was being prepared for Rickover. He was told to answer all Rickover questions—"to give him numbers—any numbers—when he asked for an answer that needed numbers, and simply 'yes' or 'no' when that would do." Pressed on this by the authors, he insisted that he had been told, in effect, to lie, or at least dissemble, by giving any number to questions that asked for numbers.

When he entered Rickover's office, the Admiral was reading through papers. He did not look up. "I had been told exactly where the Admiral's desk would be, the armchair for me, and the chair for the commander—the witness," the candidate recalled. "There was no greeting from me. I had been told to say nothing. He asked me why I wanted to be in the nuclear program. I told him so I could serve in nuclear submarines."

"Are you trying to snow me?" Rickover asked.

"No."

"Why do you want to be in the nuclear program?"

"I want to be in the nuclear program because—"

"Damn it. Don't repeat the question. Get him out of here!"

The commander escorted the candidate from the room to the infamous broom closet. "Actually," the candidate remembered, "it was a storage room, because for a while people came in to get things. I became concerned. After a while, people stopped coming in. Then someone came in with a broom, cleaning up. I had been in there for an hour and a half." He wondered if anyone ever got left there overnight. He thought he had heard a story about someone who had. But he was soon led out and returned to Rickover's office.

The interview resumed. Suddenly, Rickover interrupted the dialogue, exclaiming: "Stop drumming your fingers. Why are you drumming your fingers?"

"Because I'm nervous."

"Where would you be more nervous—here or on a sinking nuclear submarine?"

"On the submarine."

Rickover turned to the commander, asked the same question and got the same answer. He called in a female yeoman, asked the question, and again got the same answer. Then he turned back to the candidate and asked, "Even if *I* were on the submarine, too?"

"Yes, sir. On the submarine."

"What was the original question?" Rickover asked of the commander, who said, "Why does he want to be a nuclear submariner?" Rickover then repeated that question.

Thinking back, the candidate remembered deciding he would say the first thing that had come to his mind. "So I can command one," he blurted.

"You want to command a nuclear submarine? A midshipman? [As an NROTC student, he was a midshipman.]"

"No, sir. After I have training."

"Suppose I threw you out of the Navy, and the only way that you could get back in was to command a battleship. Would you?"

"No, sir."

The commander broke in: "Stop trying to snow the admiral."

Rickover said, "Get him out of here."

This time the candidate was taken to another room, this one larger. After a short while, the commander came in, and the candidate tried to explain that he had been confused by the question. "Look," he said, "I'm here because I'm just trying to get into the program. I could have volunteered for naval air."

"You're wearing glasses," the commander said. "You couldn't fly."

"I could become an NFO [Naval Flight Officer; the physical requirements are lower than for pilot.]"

The commander exploded and asked whether the candidate knew the NFO promotion rates, compared to those of the nuclear-submarine force. The candidate then was taken back into Rickover's office for the third time. Rickover began asking about the candidate's grades, which had dropped somewhat in his last year. Asked why the decline, he explained: "I was counseling students. I was a para-professional."

"What the hell is that?" Rickover asked. "What do you advise them on? Their love life? Their love affairs?"

"On their normal problems."

"How much time does it take?"

The candidate remembered to always give Rickover a number: "Thirty hours a week."

"What! That's twice as many as you study. The Navy is paying you. BuPers will find out about you. I want you to write down the name of every person you have counseled. I'm going to check on every one of them. Who is in charge there?"

The candidate gave Rickover the name of the officer in charge of the university's NROTC program, and Rickover instructed one of his secretaries to get the officer on the phone. Within a few minutes Rickover was barking into the phone at the startled officer, who praised the candidate and his extracurricular work. Rickover hung up on the officer and told the candidate to get out.

It was after 8 P.M. He had been in the building since seven-fifteen that morning. As he was being processed out, a representative from the Navy's Military Personnel Command—the organizational successor to the Bureau of Naval Personnel—asked him whether he had been mistreated and if the pre-Rickover interviews had been helpful.

"I said that if I made it I would have a different view than if I didn't. I thought I had really flunked out. Then a secretary came into the room, asked my name, and when I told her, she said that I had been accepted."

Why had the candidate been interviewed about "mistreatment" by a representative of the Navy's Military Personnel Command? The authors put that question, in a formal query, to the Navy. The presence of such representatives was confirmed, but the reason for their presence was explained officially in these words:

> The purpose of this meeting is to verify that the midshipmen understand their selection status and to talk to them in detail about convening dates at Nuclear Power School, possible temporary assignments and service selection information. Additionally, it is time to welcome selectees into the program. The meeting is short and no prescribed questions are asked. No records of their meeting are maintained.

Records of almost anything to do with the Rickover interview are indeed impossible to find. But the account of one particular interview was destined to become an official document and a published record. The only interview known to have been made such a record was preserved by former Chief of Naval Operations Elmo R. Zumwalt, Jr., who was a commander when he faced Rickover.

Zumwalt recorded his recollections of the interview—he called it a "fascinating experience"—soon after the interrogation in May 1959. Zumwalt has made it a practice to write down important events in his life, relying on a trained memory. His description of the fascinating experience reads as if it had been tape-recorded. But it is a written recollection, and its tone is similar to other such recollections, which he wrote while he retained the words of conversations. This is noted here to emphasize the high probability of his verbatim accuracy. What was written down by Zumwalt and what is presented here is, in the opinion of the authors, a true record of an interview with Rickover. Zumwalt's original account is in the form of a thirteen-page, single-spaced document marked PRIVATE—OFFICIAL. He later used part of the material in his memoir, *On Watch.* The authors have drawn on the "private official" document for what follows.

The interview took place when Zumwalt was on the executive staff of Richard Jackson, Assistant Secretary of the Navy for Personnel. Zumwalt had been informed earlier by Rickover's office that he was a member of a group of commanders selected as candidates to command a large nuclear destroyer (then called a frigate) or to become executive officer of the nuclear cruiser *Long Beach.*

Zumwalt was told to stand by on a certain Friday to be interviewed by Rickover. "I appeared at about ten o'clock," Zumwalt wrote. "A receptionist sat in a barren corridor of the very austere cubicles assigned to Admiral Rickover and his people. Having been identified, I stood at the desk until she obtained telephoned permission to have me enter the waiting room." There Zumwalt found some chairs, a table, nothing to read, and six or seven other officers. "Responses to questions gave one the feeling that at least some of the officers felt their conversations were being recorded or that their general demeanor was being photographed by a hidden camera." A sign in the waiting room warned that anyone returning to the room after an interview with Rickover was to pick up personal possessions and leave without talking about the interview.

After waiting for an hour and half, Zumwalt was led from the room and escorted to the first of three preliminary interviews. His escort was Captain James M. Dunford, who had been associated with Rickover from the earliest Oak Ridge days. Dunford conducted one of the pre-Rickover interviews. The other two interviewers were also long-time associates of Rickover. These three interviews, Zumwalt wrote, were conducted "in accordance with the finest administrative procedures and psychological techniques."

The preliminary interviews ended about five o'clock in the evening, but Zumwalt was told to wait for Rickover. Zumwalt waited until about seven-thirty, when he was informed that Rickover had left about five-thirty and that the interview would take place the following day, Saturday. Zumwalt waited—by special dispensation, in his own Pentagon office, rather than in a Rickover office—all day and then, late in the day, was told that he would be interviewed by Rickover at some time the following week.

Nearly a month later, at about eight-fifteen on a Friday morning, Dunford called Zumwalt to ask whether he would be available for the interview on that day. Zumwalt had just started his office day. He glanced at his calendar and said he would be able to get away at any time after 10 A.M. At eight-thirty Zumwalt was called again and told that Rickover wished to see him immediately. Zumwalt, stunned by the game, rushed into Assistant Secretary Jackson's office and asked permission to go to the interview. Jackson, aware of the weeks of anxiety, gave permission, and Zumwalt bolted out of the office. He stopped only long enough to remove his aiguillette, the gold shoulder cords that marked him as an aide. For Zumwalt had been warned that Rickover did not like aides, and Zumwalt saw no reason to distract Rickover by flaunting a symbol that could inspire a diatribe. Zumwalt knew about Rickover's likes and dislikes because earlier, as a BuPers assignment officer, he had sent many young officers to Rickover interviews and had listened sympathetically to their tales when they had returned.

Zumwalt was interviewed briefly in Dunford's office. Then Dunford stood, opened a swinging door, and took Zumwalt into "a narrow, ugly office consisting of a desk, behind which sat the gnomelike figure, and in front of which were two chairs."

Zumwalt was motioned to an apparently even-legged chair; Dunford took a chair at a table behind Zumwalt. Dunford would remain in the room throughout the interview, as a witness. (Rickover had started the practice of keeping a witness in the room some time before, when the first wave of interview horror stories had begun circulating. Apparently many of the witnesses were of a special breed—PCOs or Prospective Commanding Officers of nuclear ships. While they were in the Naval Reactors Branch for training, Rickover would use them in the interviews, as witnesses, to keep them under observation, and to give them an opportunity to watch how candidates reacted under pressure. Occasionally, Rickover would turn on the witness and give him a dose of the same kind of abuse being dispensed to the interviewee.)

Rickover shuffled through the records of the previous Zumwalt interview. Then he looked up and said, "Everyone who interviewed you tells me you are extremely conservative and have no initiative or imagination." Rickover paused, apparently waiting for an answer. Then he asked: "What do you have to say about that?"

"I need a few seconds to reflect on that, Admiral," Zumwalt replied. "It is the first time I have received a charge like that about me."

"This is no charge, goddamn it. You're not being accused of anything," Rickover said, "You are being interviewed and don't you dare start trying to conduct the interview yourself. You are one of those wise goddamn aides. You've been working for your boss so long you think you are wearing his stars." (Jackson, a civilian, of course did not wear stars. Zumwalt did not point that out.)

"You are so accustomed to seeing people come in and grovel at your boss's feet and kiss his tail that you think I'm going to do it to you," Rickover continued.

Rickover looked past Zumwalt and motioned to Dunford. "Now, get him out of here. Let him go out and sit until I think he is ready to be interviewed properly." Turning to Zumwalt, Rickover said, "And when you come back in here, you better be able to maintain the proper respect."

The tales Zumwalt had heard often mentioned a room called the "tank," and it was to this room that Dunford took him. All that was in the room was a table and a chair, turned toward a blank wall. Sitting in this chair and facing the wall, Zumwalt, at the edge of his vision, could see people walking down a corridor, and he suspected that they were peering at him. After about thirty minutes, he was taken back to Rickover. But the phone rang, and Rickover, despite Zumwalt's top-secret clearance, said to Dunford, "Get him out of here. I don't want him listening to this."

Ten minutes later, Zumwalt was summoned in again, and the interview was resumed.

RICKOVER. Now, what is your answer to my question?
ZUMWALT. I think that my record shows—
RICKOVER. Answer the question.
ZUMWALT. I believe I have—
RICKOVER. Answer the question.
ZUMWALT. I have initiative, imagination, and I am not a conservative.
RICKOVER. Humphhhhhh! Where did you go to high school?

ZUMWALT. Tulare Union High School.

RICKOVER. Where did you stand in high school?

ZUMWALT. I was the valedictorian.

RICKOVER. I said where did you stand.

ZUMWALT. Number one.

RICKOVER. How many in the school?

ZUMWALT. About—

RICKOVER. Answer the question, approximately.

ZUMWALT. Three hundred.

RICKOVER. Aside from the summers, did you work or did your family support you?

ZUMWALT. I worked in the summers—

RICKOVER. Listen to my questions, goddamn it. You've been an aide too long. You're too used to asking the questions. You are trying to conduct this interview again. I said, "Aside from the summers." Now, do you think you can answer the question or do you want to stop the interview right now?

ZUMWALT. My family supported me.

RICKOVER. What did you do after high school?

ZUMWALT. I went to prep school for a year.

RICKOVER. Why? To learn what you should have learned in high school?

ZUMWALT. I didn't have an appointment to the Naval Academy yet.

RICKOVER. Why didn't you go to college?

ZUMWALT. I had a great awe of the Academy and wanted to have a better background.

RICKOVER. In other words, you did go to prep school to learn what you should have learned in high school. Where did you stand in the Naval Academy?

ZUMWALT. In the top three percent.

RICKOVER. Did you study as hard as you could?

ZUMWALT. Yes, sir.

RICKOVER. Do you say that without any mental reservations?

ZUMWALT. Yes, sir.

RICKOVER. Did you do anything besides study?

ZUMWALT. Yes, sir.

RICKOVER. In other words, you didn't study as hard as you could.

ZUMWALT. I gave my answer in the context of what I thought was the balance between academic and extracurricular—

RICKOVER. Stop trying to conduct the interview. You're acting like a damn aide. I told you for the last time, I am conducting this interview. Now shall we go ahead on that basis or do you want to get out of here?

ZUMWALT. I'm ready to go ahead on that basis.

RICKOVER. Now, what were these extracurricular affairs you are so proud of?

ZUMWALT. I was a debater, an orator, and—

RICKOVER. A debater! In other words, you learned to speak equally forcefully on either side of a question. Doesn't make a damn bit of difference what you believe is right. Just argue the way someone tells you to. Good training for an aide.

ZUMWALT. No, sir. I consider that debating taught me logical and orderly processes of thinking.

RICKOVER (*shouting*). Name one famous man who was able to argue on either side of a question.

ZUMWALT. Clarence Darrow.

RICKOVER. Darrow. Darrow. What case?

ZUMWALT. Leopold and Loeb case.

RICKOVER (*shouting*). You are absolutely wrong. I warn you here and now: You better not try to talk to me about anything you don't know anything about. I know more about almost anything than you do, and I know one helluva lot more about Darrow than you do. I warn you, you better stop trying to snow me.

ZUMWALT. In my mind, Darrow believed in the right of every man to have counsel, and, believing that, he could take either side of a case.

RICKOVER. You're wrong. Absolutely wrong. Darrow believed in the fundamental dignity of human life, and there was only one side of any case that he could take. [*Turns to* DUNFORD] Get him out of here. I'm sick of talking to an aide that tries to pretend he knows everything.

Dunford returned Zumwalt to the "tank." About an hour later, a friend on Rickover's staff opened the door and handed Zumwalt a sandwich. A moment later, Zumwalt was summoned back to Rickover's office. The Admiral's first words were: "Don't you even have enough sense not to chew gum when being interviewed?" And the interview was resumed.

ZUMWALT. I am not chewing gum, sir.

RICKOVER. Then what the hell are you chewing?

ZUMWALT. I had a bite of sandwich in my mouth when sent for.

RICKOVER (*trace of a smile*). All right. Now, are you ready to talk sensibly about Clarence Darrow?

ZUMWALT. Yes, sir.

RICKOVER. Do you still think he could take either side of a question?

ZUMWALT. Yes, sir, having in mind his fundamental belief that everyone deserves counsel.

RICKOVER. I give up. [*Pause*] Suppose you were the superintendent of the Naval Academy. What would you do with the curriculum?

ZUMWALT. In these troubled times, with the midshipmen's course as crowded as it is, I would eliminate some English and history to provide more math and science.

RICKOVER. Thank God you are not the superintendent! It's just the kind of stupid jerk like you who becomes superintendent. That's what's the matter with our curriculum today. Do you mean that you would graduate illiterate technicians?

ZUMWALT. No, sir. I would expect the midshipmen to acquire their extra history and English on their own, after finishing school. In fact, I would insist on it.

RICKOVER. Did you ever read anything after you graduated?

ZUMWALT. Yes, sir.

RICKOVER. Any philosophy?

ZUMWALT. Yes, sir.

RICKOVER. Name one.

ZUMWALT. Plato.

RICKOVER. Now, I warned you not to try to impress me. I told you I was sick of having an aide trying to impress me. I proved how stupid you are on Darrow. I know more about this subject and almost any other subject than you do. Are you sure you want to go on about Plato?

ZUMWALT. Yes, sir.

RICKOVER. What did he write?

ZUMWALT. *The Republic.*

RICKOVER. Did you read it?

ZUMWALT. Yes, sir.

RICKOVER. What's it about?

ZUMWALT. The ideal man or the ideal democratic state.

RICKOVER (*addressing* DUNFORD). You see what kind of a stupid jerk this guy is? Trying to pretend he knows about *The Republic*. [*Turns to* ZUMWALT] I can tell you what *The Republic* is about. It's about justice. How long did you study *The Republic*?

ZUMWALT. About twenty hours.

RICKOVER (*shouting*). Twenty hours! You mean to tell me that a guy like you could learn all about one of the great works in twenty hours?

ZUMWALT. No, sir. I am sure I could have put more time in it.

RICKOVER. How many?

ZUMWALT. Probably one hundred.

RICKOVER (*shouting*). One hundred! Much more like one thousand for a guy like you. Do you think Plato would have advocated eliminating history and English from the curriculum?

ZUMWALT. No, sir. But Plato was postulating a perfect world, and we don't have one.

RICKOVER. Stop trying to conduct the interview. [*Turns to* DUNFORD] I am getting sick of this guy. He is trying to act like an aide again. Get him out of here.

This time Zumwalt stayed in the tank about forty-five minutes. When he was summoned back to Rickover's office for the fourth time, the interview was not immediately resumed. Rickover once again told Zumwalt that he was acting too much like an aide who was used to seeing people act cravenly before his boss. Rickover asked him if he thought there was any sense in continuing the interview. Zumwalt said that he thought there was, and so Rickover once more began asking questions.

RICKOVER. How long have you been interested in nuclear power?

ZUMWALT. Five years.

RICKOVER. What have you done to prepare yourself for nuclear power?

ZUMWALT. I have watched for various—

RICKOVER. Answer the question.

ZUMWALT. Very little.

Rickover suddenly called in his secretary. She entered carrying a pad and pencil. Rickover turned to her and began dictating a letter to a bank president. "Dear Mr. President: For five years I have wanted a million dollars. Please send me a check for same today. Yours very truly. H. G. Rickover. P.S. I have done nothing whatsoever in the last five years to earn the money. But send it anyway." Rickover dismissed his secretary and then asked Zumwalt, "Do you get the idea?" The interview was resumed.

RICKOVER. Why haven't you done anything?

ZUMWALT. My modus operandi has always been to study intensively the background of the specific area in which I am currently operating.

RICKOVER. What is your current area?

ZUMWALT. Personnel.

RICKOVER. How much do you study?

ZUMWALT. I average four hours per night.

RICKOVER. Just on personnel?

ZUMWALT. Two hours a night on the important papers of my office and two hours a night on background studies.

RICKOVER. God help us! That's what is wrong with our personnel—when we have guys like you working on it. How long have you known that you were going to be interviewed?

ZUMWALT. About four to six weeks.

RICKOVER. Four times seven is twenty-eight. Times four is one hundred and twelve. That's one hundred and twelve hours at least since you've known—that you've had available for study, by your own admission. Now, why haven't you studied anything about nuclear power in this period?

ZUMWALT. I have.

RICKOVER. What?

ZUMWALT. The BuPers booklet on nuclear physics.

RICKOVER. Are you ready to take a test on it?

ZUMWALT. No, sir. But I think I could pass.

RICKOVER. I doubt it.

Rickover then veered to a quick interrogation about Zumwalt's concept of leadership. Sneering, he asked Zumwalt if he had learned about leadership from a book.

"No, sir," Zumwalt said.

Rickover veered again, remarking, "Well then, you must have been born with it. Was your father a great leader?"

For the first time in the interview, Zumwalt later recalled, he began showing his temper. Tight-lipped, he replied, "Yes, sir," and, when Rickover asked what Zumwalt's father did for a living, the answer flowed from Zumwalt with an intensity he had not felt before. Though he knew that Rickover preferred answers expressed in six words or less, the words now tumbled out:

"He is a country doctor. He has practiced for forty years in his small town. He has been mayor, a member of two school boards, the president of Rotary, Scout chairman, and he ran as Republican nominee for Congress. He has been the kind of outstanding citizen that makes a small community go."

As Zumwalt recalled this moment, Rickover nodded, showed a trace of a smile, and started asking questions in a staccato that guaranteed his six-word minimum.

RICKOVER. Where did you stand in math?

ZUMWALT. About the top three percent.

RICKOVER. In science?

ZUMWALT. The same.

RICKOVER. English?

ZUMWALT. Within the top seven.

RICKOVER. And you want to eliminate it?

ZUMWALT. Curtail it.

RICKOVER. What did you do when you graduated from the Naval Academy?

ZUMWALT. Went to a Pacific destroyer.

RICKOVER. Which one?

ZUMWALT. *Phelps.*

RICKOVER. What did you do?

ZUMWALT. Assistant engineer.

RICKOVER. Assistant engineer. Are you sure?

ZUMWALT. Yes, sir.

RICKOVER. How many in the engineering department?

ZUMWALT. Three officers.

RICKOVER. Oh. Then you weren't the assistant engineer. You were just a flunky. There you go again, trying to act like an aide again. Trying to impress me. The assistant engineer is the number two officer.

ZUMWALT. We called all officers assistants, other than the chief engineer.

RICKOVER. Don't start trying to conduct this interview.

And so it went; question after barbed question; answer after routine answer—even though Rickover already had available to him almost all the answers. They were a matter of record in Commander Zumwalt's file. So were the answers to the questions Rickover next asked.

RICKOVER. Are you married?

ZUMWALT. Yes, sir.

RICKOVER. Children?

ZUMWALT. Yes, sir.

RICKOVER. How many?

ZUMWALT. Four.

RICKOVER. What ages?

ZUMWALT. Thirteen, ten, five, and one.

Rickover shook his head from side to side, sadly, Zumwalt thought, as if the Admiral did not approve of the commander's nest-building and bird-hatching. Then he asked, "What are you going to do when you get back to the Pentagon, run up and down the E-ring and tell everybody about this interview?"

"Admiral," Zumwalt replied, "I'm going to say it was the most fascinating experience of my life."

"Now you're being greasy," Rickover said. He ended the interview with an order: "Get out of here."

Zumwalt returned to his Pentagon office and called his detailer in BuPers to report that he was sure he was not going to get a nuclear assignment. An hour later, BuPers called back to say that Rickover had selected Zumwalt. Commander Zumwalt was on his way to becoming a nuc.

Zumwalt realized he was at a crossroads in his career. He could become part of the nuclear navy. But he also could turn down the chance to work for the man who had hazed him. Before Rickover had summoned him, Zumwalt had been told that he had been selected to be commanding officer of the guided-missile frigate *Dewey,* which was conventionally powered by fuel oil. If Zumwalt accepted the nuclear navy, he could become the commanding officer of the *Bainbridge,* the same kind of ship as the *Dewey,* but larger and nuclear-powered.

Zumwalt chose the *Dewey* and continued his career through the "regular" Navy of conventionally powered ships. His classmate Ray Peet accepted the nuclear navy at the same time that Zumwalt rejected it. Peet would get his captain's stripes a year ahead of Zumwalt, as would other classmates who chose the nuclear navy. But Zumwalt would go on to become one of the first two members of his class to make admiral. (The other would be a nuc: James F. Calvert, first commanding officer of the *Skate.*) And Zumwalt would go on to become the youngest officer ever to be appointed Chief of Naval Operations.

In 1959, officers could choose to turn down assignments to the nuclear navy. But in the years beyond Zumwalt's decision, more and more officers—including all submariners—would find that the most promising path to admiral began in Rickover's office. Over the years the essence of that interview would never change: Rickover; a barren room; a witness; harsh questions; demeaning tactics; sometimes foul language.

The interview was notorious through the Navy, but the real Navy did nothing to moderate the ordeal. Even the chief of what was then known as the Bureau of Naval Personnel, Vice Admiral William R. Smedberg, admitted that during his watch, from 1960 to 1964, he was powerless.

"I had numerous instances of young officers coming to me after their interview with Admiral Rickover and stating that they didn't want to stay in a Navy that had an officer like Admiral Rickover as a flag officer," Smedberg said in his unusually candid reminiscences, which were part of the Navy's semiofficial oral-history program. The indictment of the interviews was there on the record. But none of Smedberg's successors did anything about it.

"He was insulting to them, degrading in their interviews," Smedberg recalled. "I remember the son of a classmate of mine who came in, Hugh Webster, whose father, Hugh Webster senior, was in my class and a captain in the Navy at the time.

"He made fun of this boy's father, said he was one of those dumb football players at the Naval Academy who didn't have sense enough to come in out of the rain, didn't once admit that he knew that Hugh Webster was one of the star men in my class, one of the most brilliant fellows, a brilliant naval constructor with a fine career. He made that young man so mad he said he'd never go in that nuclear program as long as they had people like Admiral Rickover in it."

Smedberg said that he often wrote down what the young men told him and confronted Rickover with the reports. But Smedberg recalled that Rickover always said, "Oh, I'm just trying to irk them and see what responses I get, see if they're fighters. This is my method. You know I'm kind of a psychiatrist in a way; I'm an amateur psychiatrist. I want to see what responses I get out of them and in order to do it I have to make them mad. That's why I do this."

"I said, 'Well, Admiral, you're wrecking the morale of a lot of these young people. A lot of these young people, as a result, don't want to stay in the Navy if it has you in it.'

" 'Well,' he said, 'I'm sorry I have that effect on them but I've got to find the best men for my program.' "

By the 1960s the Rickover interview had become a ritual, for very practical reasons. The nuclear navy was growing. The need for officers was desperate. No longer could Rickover conduct a rambling, time-consuming interview. There simply was not time for one. But he insisted on continuing the ritual, and occasionally he would drift back into the luxury of interminable interviews paced by seemingly illogical questions.

There was some persistent logic, though—as was noted by retired submariner Dick Laning. "These interviews," Laning said, "were a very effective way or method of leadership. Once someone had been through the stress of an interview, he never forgot who the boss was.

"But what he found out about people in these interviews is question-

Nuclear propulsion added a new dimension to strategic weapons in the Polaris project. This photograph shows a rare surface launching as the nuclear submarine *Henry Clay* fires a Polaris A-2 test missile off Cape Kennedy on April 20, 1964. Minutes earlier the submarine had fired a missile while submerged, the normal launching mode. The tall mast is a telemetry antenna installed only for the test firings.

The recently completed Polaris submarine *Sam Rayburn* waits with her 16 missile tube hatches open while workmen complete the finishing touches on the craft. Although diesel-electric propulsion is feasible for strategic missile submarines, nuclear propulsion adds to their effectiveness an enhanced capability of surviving against enemy forces.

ABOVE   Admiral Arleigh A. Burke, who served as Chief of Naval Operations from August 1955 to August 1961, tours the engineering spaces of the *Nautilus* shortly before assuming that office. An astute and perceptive officer, he was an advocate of nuclear propulsion while seeking to curb Rickover's influence on the Navy.

OPPOSITE TOP   Soft-spoken William F. (Red) Raborn, Jr., was the "father" of the Polaris submarine. At the direction of the Chief of Naval Operations Admiral Arleigh A. Burke, Rickover was largely excluded from development of the Polaris submarine. Here Rear Admiral Raborn (center) apeaks with another officer and a sailor aboard the Polaris submarine *George Washington*. Minutes before, the submarine had successfully fired two Polaris test missiles.

OPPOSITE BOTTOM   The U.S.S. *Thresher* was the first nuclear submarine to be lost. The lead ship of a new class of deep-diving, anti-submarine craft, she was on post-overhaul sea trials off the New England coast on April 10, 1963. That morning, carrying 129 officers, enlisted men, and civilians, she plunged out of control into the depths of the Atlantic. An implosion tore her apart, killing all on board. It was the worst submarine disaster in history.

BELOW Rickover—in khaki uniform with black tie—stands on the portside diving plane of the nuclear submarine *Barb* as she returns from her initial sea trials. The *Barb,* a *Thresher*-class submarine, has a narrow sail structure to house retractable periscopes, antennas, and masts. There is no "conning tower" familiar from World War II submarines. The commanding officer, Commander Charles D. Grojean, stands on a small platform atop the sail. Rickover would change to civilian clothes before going ashore.

OPPOSITE TOP The first President to become directly involved with Rickover and the atomic submarine was Harry S. Truman, here inscribing the keel plate of the *Nautilus* at ceremonies on June 14, 1952. Behind the shipyard official to the President's right (in light suit) stands Rickover, partially hidden, also in civilian clothes. His 12-year-old son, Robert, is behind him.

OPPOSITE BOTTOM Dwight D. Eisenhower, whose wife christened the *Nautilus,* was the first President to go to sea in a nuclear submarine. His first such cruise, aboard the *Seawolf,* was done quietly and without publicity. On his second trip, aboard the Polaris submarine *Patrick Henry* in 1960, he was accompanied by reporters and admirals. Here the President poses for photographers at the controls of the *Patrick Henry.*

LITTON/INGALLS SHIPBUILDING

GENERAL DYNAMICS/ELECTRIC BOAT

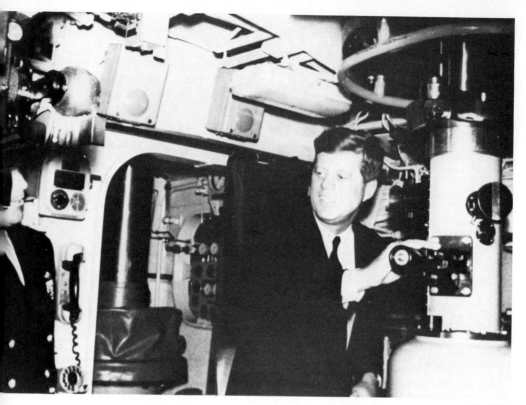

OPPOSITE TOP   President John F. Kennedy after looking through the periscope of the Polaris submarine *Thomas Edison.* Kennedy was highly impressed with the Polaris program, and an increase in the number of submarines being built was one of his priorities upon entering the White House in January 1961. A few days before he was assassinated in November 1963 he watched a Polaris missile firing off Cape Canaveral.

OPPOSITE BOTTOM   Lyndon Baines Johnson approved the proposals of Secretary of Defense Robert S. McNamara and Secretary of the Navy Paul H. Nitze to "retire" Rickover, but the plan was thwarted by several members of Congress. President Johnson, deeply involved in the Vietnam controversy, could not take on the Rickover issue at the time.

ABOVE   Richard M. Nixon congratulates Rickover on his promotion to full admiral at White House ceremonies on December 3, 1973. Rickover still wears the gold stripes of a vice admiral on his sleeve. He was only the second Engineering Duty Officer to reach the rank of full admiral, the first having been Jackson D. Arnold, Rickover's nominal boss, who as Chief of Naval Material was given four-star rank in 1970.

PHOTOGRAPHER'S MATE 2/CLASS DAVE LONGSTREATH, U.S. NAVY

OPPOSITE TOP   Gerald R. Ford, U.S. Representative from Michigan, stands next to Rickover as other members of Congress operate the controls of the nuclear-powered submarine *Nautilus* during a Rickover-arranged VIP cruise on February 24–25, 1956. At Rickover's direction, the startup of land-based submarine reactor plants, submarine keel layings, launchings, commissioning ceremonies, and cruises at sea all became important political events, unmatched in any other military program.

OPPOSITE BOTTOM   Jimmy Carter listens attentively as his onetime mentor explains a point during the President's cruise aboard the attack submarine *Los Angeles* on May 27, 1977. Although selected for the nuclear program—he later called himself a nuclear engineer during his Presidential campaign—Carter is not believed to have been aboard a nuclear submarine until his visit to the *Los Angeles*.

ABOVE   Rickover takes the limelight at the press conference following President Carter's cruise aboard the *Los Angeles*. Carter had titled his campaign biography *Why Not the Best?* after the question that Rickover had asked him during his interview for admittance into the nuclear power program.

PHOTOGRAPHER'S MATE 3/CLASS D. H. ROEHL, U.S. NAVY

OPPOSITE TOP   Commander Eleonore Bednowicz, Rickover's second wife. A career Navy nurse, she retired shortly after their marriage.

OPPOSITE BOTTOM   Dynamic and intelligent, Admiral Elmo R. Zumwalt was a most tenacious opponent of Rickover's during Zumwalt's tenure as Chief of Naval Operations, from July 1970 to June 1974. Here Zumwalt discusses his personnel policies with officers aboard the nuclear-powered submarine *Ray* shortly after becoming CNO. He was the youngest U.S. Navy officer to attain the rank of rear admiral (at age 44) and the youngest Chief of Naval Operations (age 49).

BELOW   The Rickovers at ease with the Carters at a White House luncheon on February 5, 1977. President Carter appears to have been the first President to engage in a social relationship with Rickover. "Admiral Rickover had a profound effect on my life—perhaps more than anyone except my own parents," Carter wrote in his autobiography, *Why Not the Best?*

LEFT The large, fast nuclear attack submarine *Los Angeles* on sea trials in the Atlantic in late 1976. In the previous decade the fastest combat submarines at sea had been the Soviet Victor class. A few years after this photo was taken the Soviet Alfa-class SSN became operational, with a much higher reported speed (43 knots) and deeper diving depth than the *Los Angeles*.

OPPOSITE BOTTOM The nuclear attack submarine *Los Angeles* glides into Hong Kong harbor. Modern nuclear submarines are much faster submerged than on the surface, because of their modified "tear-drop" hull design. Most of the submarine's hull is underwater even when the craft is on the surface.

BELOW The only known occasion when Rickover appeared in the uniform of a full admiral took place on March 29, 1974, when Rickover Hall was dedicated at the U.S. Naval Academy. From left are Mrs. Rickover (in commander's uniform), Rickover, Congresswoman Marjorie Holt, Captain Howard H. Haynes, Academy Superintendent William P. Mack, and Secretary of the Navy John Warner. Warner, later a United States Senator, had directed Rickover to wear his uniform for the ceremonies.

U.S. NAVY

OPPOSITE TOP   Four giants: The Electric Boat yard at Groton, Connecticut, is the largest submarine construction facility in the West and one of only two American yards now building submarines. The 360-foot nuclear attack submarine *Phoenix* has just been "side-launched" in this photo taken on December 8, 1979. At the top of the photo the bow of the Trident missile submarine *Florida* is visible protruding through the construction building; in the center is the Trident submarine *Michigan* (note missile tubes); and at right is the Trident submarine *Ohio.*

OPPOSITE BOTTOM   Rickover at a submarine launching at the Newport News (Virginia) Shipbuilding and Dry Dock Company. He was a regular attendee at nuclear ship ceremonies until the late 1970s, when animosity between him and the Newport News and Electric Boat yards began causing major problems in the nuclear ship program.

BELOW   The U.S.S. *Ohio*—the first of the giant Trident missile submarines—at sea for the first time in June 1981. Because he had not personally approved publication of this photo, Admiral Rickover had the Navy charge that its publication in a General Dynamics advertisement "represents both a serious breach of security and willful violation of terms of the contract [to build the submarine]." Similar photographs were taken by scores of persons as the giant submarine headed down the Thames River to reach Long Island Sound.

GENERAL DYNAMICS/ELECTRIC BOAT

Rickover aboard the *Nautilus*.

able. He'd get an impression, but he could not get much more. And the BuPers selection system got him the right people to start with. Of course, he also had to almost arbitrarily turn down some of these people to put the fear of God in all the people who take the interview."

Other officers agree with Laning. A persistent rumor in recent years has it that the candidates are selected—or turned down—*before* the interview, which is merely a ratification of a decision already made. That decision was increasingly made in light of harsh demands for men in a part of the Navy that was experiencing a chronic shortage of qualified officers.

What once had been a sometimes enlightening, always memorable encounter between high priest and initiate would become a mere moment of presentation of initiate to the high priest. He still held the power of dispensing nuclear power upon the initiate, but both he and the initiates knew that he no longer could afford to withhold that power as frequently as he had in the past. He needed more warriors than ever before. And so arrived the quickie interview.

Many warriors would have to come directly from the Naval Academy, which Rickover professed to despise. Because he so frequently and vehemently denounced the Academy, midshipmen were given the impression that they had little chance of entering the nuclear navy. Rickover's reputed preference was for NROTC graduates.

Those midshipmen selected for the Admiral Rickover Interview were run through the procedure—or ordeal, depending upon their viewpoint—in three days. Rickover's office calculated that the average interview would last less than one minute.

Each of the three days began in the same way. Buses rolled out of Annapolis early in the morning and arrived an hour and a half later in the Crystal City complex in Arlington, Virginia, where Rickover maintained his headquarters from 1970 onward.

More than 250 members of the Class of 1978 made the trip. One of them was so impressed with the event that he wrote down his experience and, some time later, shared what he wrote with the authors. What follows is his recollection, which was subsequently verified by other members of the class who were interviewed by Rickover in the same period.

It started off just fine [he began]. We had to get in long lines to be processed—about 80 guys in a line. And I was walking around trying to find out where I was supposed to go, and I nearly stepped on a little man in civilian clothes. A small man. You guessed it. Admiral Rickover. He didn't say anything, but it was an awful way to start the day.

We were first of all shown the rooms and the hallways where we could and could not go. It was a high-security place. That was really emphasized. Then our 80-man group was taken to a briefing room. We sat there for a while, feeling nervous, wondering what was going to happen.

A commander came in and introduced himself. He was easy-going and tried to put us at ease, too. He acted as if he was going to be our friend for the rest of the day. But, well, you'll see. . . .

About 40 of us were taken to another room, a much smaller one, about 25 by 12 feet. There were chairs arranged along the four walls and in two rows, back to back, in the center of the room. By the door was a small desk, and a petty officer sat there, I guess to watch our comings and goings. He was in uniform, as of course, we were. But nobody else was.

We sat in the room about 20 or 30 minutes telling jokes, writing letters, and killing time. Then, about 8:45, the preliminary interviews began. Each of us was told when to leave and was given the room we were supposed to go to. To get there, we needed a map and a key. The key was to open two or three doors. You had to go through some hallways and up and down staircases a couple of times. The key in one hand, the map in the other. It was like a maze.

The interviews were being conducted by high-level assistants to Admiral Rickover. When I entered the office, there were two men in it. One was the interviewer, and the other was somebody who was being trained to conduct interviews.

They had a dossier of my high-school math and science courses. They were not interested in grades on nontechnical subjects. They asked low-key questions about my marks, which were not all that good in all subjects.

Then I went back through the maze to the first room. Other guys were coming in and we gave each other what we call the "gouge"—inside information—about the interview. It wasn't turning out to be much of an ordeal.

About 9:45 there was a second round of interviews. It was pretty much the same drill with the key and the map. Again I had to go through a couple of doors and up and down stairways. This inter-viewer was also training somebody.

They asked me to work out some physics problems. One was to figure out the velocity of something falling from the Washington Monument. And they asked me about my extracurricular activities.

That second interview took about 20 minutes. Then I went back to the little room. And they gave me a key and a map and I went off to the third interview. The interviewer began asking me questions about why I wanted to get into nuclear power and why I majored in oceanography. It turned out that oceanography is a pet peeve of Admiral Rickover's.

He asked me questions about buoyancy, the principle of the Archimedes screw, and basic questions about physics. I had to give the wave lengths of certain elements, for instance. I thought I did pretty well.

The preliminary interviews ended about 10:30 or 10:45. Then we were taken to a waiting room outside Admiral Rickover's office. We told jokes and ate our box lunches. We kept telling each other jokes and fooling around because we were feeling terrified by now. It was about 12:30 before anything happened.

We were given a diagram of Admiral Rickover's office and shown exactly where his desk was, and where he sat, and where we were supposed to sit. And we were given our orders. When our names were called, we were to march in a straight line—it was shown to us on the diagram—to the chair in front of his desk, not say anything, and answer his questions.

My name was called and I marched straight in. It was a very small office, covered with books that were piled all around him. It looked like the office of an editor for a small newspaper. The window was open. There was a conference table in the room that about four people could sit around.

At the table was the commander I had thought was my friend, the one we met at the beginning of the day. I had been told that the average time for an interview was 59 seconds, and I expected that I would be in and out fast.

But Admiral Rickover began a tirade and so did the commander who was sitting behind me. Admiral Rickover said that oceanography was a foolish waste of time and worthless to the Navy.

"How can it possibly help the Navy?" he asked me. "Turn around and convince the commander you haven't been worthless."

I turned around, and the commander really began yelling at me, too. I tried to say that there was some value to a submariner in the knowledge about currents and underwater sound—I mean, I *knew* that you're blind under water without being able to *hear*. And I said that. And then Admiral Rickover stood up and said, "You're worthless to me." And he walked out.

But the commander kept hazing me—that was what he was doing, hazing. And he kept saying *worthless*. The word was being used all the time.

Then Admiral Rickover came back in, and he and the commander began talking over me.

The commander said, "Anything he knows, I could get a seaman to look up. He's worthless."

"Yes," Admiral Rickover said, "worthless. Oceanography is worthless."

Then he turned to me and said, "How many oceanographers are there in the Navy?"

I said, "Enough to fill the billets." And he exploded. He swore a lot in the interview—"goddamn, hell, son of a bitch," nothing more than those.

He asked me for numbers, and I said I thought there were probably 2,000 oceanographers in the Navy. I don't know where I got that figure.

And he exploded again. He called in his secretary and he gave her the name of some admiral in BuPers and said to find out how many oceanographers there were in the Navy. She came in and said that admiral wasn't available and he exploded again and gave her the name of another admiral. She came back in and said that *that* admiral wasn't in, either, and he exploded again.

"How many oceanographers were there in World War II?" he asked me. And, I don't know why, but I said 2,000 again.

He really blew up. "Goddamn it," he said. "You son of a bitch. There were only two in the whole goddamn war."

All of a sudden he asked me if I was engaged. I said I was. He asked me the name of my fiancée, and I told him. He was slicing me up good, and I didn't know what to expect. All I could think of was, *Worthless to the Navy.* But he was asking me if my fiancée and I had decided how many children we were going to have. I said yes, three.

"Three children?" he said. And I said yes. And all of a sudden he was saying things like, "Well, you could tell her to have triplets twice or twins three times or she could have a litter of six—a litter of six." I didn't even think right then that he was insulting my fiancée. And right then he told me to get out.

I had been in his office about 15 minutes. And then I realized that he hadn't even asked me to sign the paper.

The paper is a kind of contract between Rickover and midshipmen whose marks in difficult subjects, such as engineering and mathematics, are not up to Rickover's standards. The midshipman is asked to agree to study thirty-five hours a week—about ten more than the Academy expects—and send a written report to Rickover each month. One midshipman thought he would amuse Rickover by enclosing a valentine with his February report. The Admiral was not amused. Rickover called the superintendent. The midshipman was called into the superintendent's office and censured. He was not accepted into the nuclear program.

Incidentally, the "worthless" oceanography major with the insulted fiancée was accepted. Why? He and his mates do not know. Perhaps his answer, "Enough to fill the billets" struck Rickover as having just enough snap and not too much disdain.

The Rickover interviews began in the early 1950s and never stopped and never changed except, in recent years, in duration. They became inane and an embarrassment to the Navy and even to members of the nuclear navy. But they went on, and only Rickover seemed to know exactly why. In 1979, testifying before a Congressional committee, Rickover admitted that his interviewing "has been criticized for years by many senior naval officers." He said, however, that he would continue the interviews because through them he was "able to detect an individual who may have good school grades but who is really incapable of passing the course" or intelligent individuals who "may have absolutely no capability to be put in charge of the operation of a reactor plant." He said that the decision to accept a candidate for nuclear training rested entirely "in his own mind."

The interview resembles a ritual whose purpose has been forgotten but whose incantations must be uttered. The interview pits a twenty-one- or twenty-two-year-old midshipman, who has spent his last four years relatively cloistered on the banks of the Severn, against a team of experienced and hostile interviewers led by the venerable Rickover. Indeed, the very idea of a midshipman doing verbal conflict with an aged, aggressive, four-star admiral, who has debated Congressmen and secretaries of defense, is nothing short of ludicrous.

Probably because there was no better way to treat the ordeal than as a ludicrous event, a member of the Class of 1980 decided to do just that. His English professor had given him an assignment: write a sample of "conflict dialogue," The midshipman knew just where to turn for inspiration. He wrote an essay called "The Rickover Solution." The essay follows.

"Sit down!"
"Aye, aye, sir."
"How old are you?"
"I'll be twenty-one on 20 November."
"Answer the question!"

"Twenty, sir."

"So you're an operations analysis major. I'll tell you something—I hate operations analysis majors! I bet you think you're pretty smart, don't you?"

"Well, I—"

"Don't 'well, I—' me, mister! 'Yes! No! Maybe! I don't know!' Which one is it?"

"Yes, sir!"

"What do you do in your spare time?"

"I play my guitar, swim, and play touch football."

"Don't you study at all? You want to get into my program, yet you don't study. What have you read recently?"

"I've read *Fields of Fire, Shogun,* and *Confessions,* sir."

"You read gossip magazines?"

"No, sir. It's about Saint Augustine and his con—"

"What! Are you trying to teach me something? Do I look like I need a literature lesson? I know about Saint Augustine. What do you know about his book, *The City of God?*"

"Well, sir, I haven't read *The City of God.*"

"You haven't read the book, and yet you feel qualified to give me a lesson on Saint Augustine. It's obvious you don't know anything about literature! Tell me why you joined the Naval Academy."

"Well, I—"

"Blast it! A well is a deep hole in the ground filled with water!"

"Yes, sir! I joined the Naval Academy because I want to serve my country as a naval officer."

"Why did you choose your major?"

"I enjoy mathematics."

"Why did you get the C in plebe chemistry?"

"I didn't study hard enough."

"How many hours per week do you study now?"

"Twenty hours, sir."

"Forty hours—if you want to get into my program, you have to study forty hours. You didn't study enough plebe year—you don't study enough now. Do you write letters home?"

"Yes, sir, every week."

"I don't care how often you write home. You'll write me every Friday to tell me how many hours per week you've studied—if I decide to take you. You have a girlfriend?"

"Yes, sir."

"Where does she live?"

"Alexandria, Virginia, sir."

"Do you see her often?"

"Every weekend, sir."

"No! Telephone her. Tell her you won't be able to see her every weekend from now on. There's the telephone. Call her."

"Hello, honey. I'm going Navy Air!"

14 | The Men Called Nucs

While Rickover was propelling the idea of *Nautilus* through the Navy hierarchy, he was also insisting that he select and train the officers and crew of his nuclear submarine. He won that right with little opposition, for he was not doing anything particularly radical. The men he selected had already been trained in traditional ways, and if Rickover wanted to give them additional technical training, he would not be violating that most sacred of laws, tradition. But Rickover, no fan of tradition, was looking far beyond the mere manning of a single submarine. He was planning a virtual takeover of what could become a large part of the Navy.

His first move was to pluck officers and enlisted men from the fleet. Candidates were screened by BuPers—the Bureau of Naval Personnel— in customary ways through recommendations from commanding officers, academic and service records, and experience in the nearest engineering specialty. But Rickover added what he would diplomatically describe as "the advice and assistance of the Atomic Energy Commission's naval reactors personnel." This meant that for the first time in history an outside agency was looking over the shoulders of BuPers. Rickover, as an officer in BuShips, could not have moved into BuPers territory. So he moved as a "civilian." In a typical bureaucratic maneuver, he used his AEC credentials to face down BuPers.

As a student of history, Rickover could draw upon historical examples with the ease of a biblical scholar quoting chapter and verse to win an argument. He could explain his need to train officers by pointing to what happened to the gunboat *Bennington* in San Diego harbor in 1905. A boiler exploded, killing sixty-five men. Why? Because, as Rickover would grimly point out to his critics, the chief engineer "was an ensign who had never stood an engine-room watch before being assigned to the billet. He knew nothing of machinery, and he did not have the technical knowledge to stop the chain of events that led to the tragedy." Other acci-

294

dents would be similarly cited by Rickover to prove his point.

Under Rickover doctrine, such accidents could not happen aboard a nuclear-propelled submarine or ship because there could not be an inexperienced man on watch. Rickover required all captains and subordinate officers to be qualified as "operators of the propulsion plant" before going to sea in the Rickover navy. But before stepping aboard a nuclear submarine, an officer had to be trained, the Rickover way. At first, the prospective commanding officers and executive officers spent a year at Naval Reactors Branch. Eventually, as the nuclear navy grew, the training evolved into a formal course, with eight-hour written examinations and three-hour oral examinations. The examinations were given in Rickover's headquarters, and Rickover himself would sometimes decide who passed.

By 1960, Rickover each year would be skimming the top-ranking graduates of the Naval Academy and colleges whose Naval Reserve Officer Training Corps programs had Rickover's approval. And by that time he would be selecting and training not only line officers and crew members but also medical officers and enlisted hospital men assigned to nuclear-powered ships, and all naval personnel in the shore posts of the nuclear navy—from engineers and Wave secretaries in his own headquarters to key personnel in shipyards.

The training of the officers and crew of the *Nautilus* began in 1951, and the training soon became ritualized. The structure—and many of the details—of training would little change across more than a quarter of a century. By the 1970s, when Rickover once again was attacking the traditionalism of Annapolis, his own schools were being run under directives that he had set down twenty years before.

During a 1962 hearing before the Joint Committee on Atomic Energy, Rickover, in his prepared testimony, set forth the broad outlines of his training program: "The course at the nuclear power school lasts for six months and consists of approximately 700 hours of classroom instruction. The operational phase of training takes another six months and is conducted at one of the five land-based naval reactor prototypes. . . ."

Ten years later, again before the Joint Committee, Rickover reported on training: "The course at the nuclear power school lasts for six months and consists of approximately 700 hours of classroom instruction. The operational phase of training takes another six months and is conducted at one of the the six land-based naval reactor prototypes. . . ."

Except for the number of prototypes increasing by one, not a word in this passage of his testimony had been changed in a decade. In fact, there was no change, line after line, detail after detail—"the quality of the trained product" . . . "by surveillance and by repeated written and oral examination". . . "familiar with both theoretical and practical aspects of safe reactor operation. . . ." Nearly all the 2,500 words in the 1962 statement were repeated exactly a decade later in the 1972 statement.

To Rickover, the task of selecting and training nuclear sailors was a problem in engineering. The emphasis was on the engineering plants, not the ships, and so men were trained in Idaho or other places far from the sea, at land prototypes identical with the reactors and engine rooms in nuclear warships, from submarines to carriers. A graduate of that school, a reactor officer aboard the carrier *Enterprise,* said of the prototype, "if you make a mistake, the ship does not run into the dock. . . . You get more out of it. It is worth many, many ships."

A prototype in a school is an enginer's concept: what matters is learning to work on the machine, regardless of where that machine may be. A mock-up in a school is an educator's concept: what matters is learning to work in the environment of the machine. From the beginning, Rickover and the Navy clashed over this basic argument. On his side was the need to produce highly skilled crews to operate the most complicated—and dangerous—propulsion system that men have ever been asked to master. On the Navy's side was tradition and faith in an educational system that ultimately focused on one mission: the preparation of men for sea.

Rickover could put his machine in a building in an Idaho wasteland because he saw his machine as the centerpiece of the ship it would someday propel. The Navy saw the reactor as a mechanism in the evolution from sail to improved propulsion; what counted was the warship, not the machinery that moved it. And what counted to the Navy was that the men serve the ship, not the machine.

The stage for the clash over the educating of the men called *nucs**
was to be the submarine base at New London, Connecticut, a place where Rickover did not feel comfortable. He saw New London, along with Charleston, San Diego and Pearl Harbor, as social centers—"clubs," he called them—for the submarine community. There are veterans of that community who say that Rickover's bitterness went back to the *S-48,* the venerable "pig boat" he served aboard in the 1930s. Rickover never became part of the submarine navy's society, just as he had not become part of the Naval Academy's society. He had become executive officer of a submarine; but he had never been given a submarine command. In the

---

*A term, not originally of endearment, used extensively inside and outside the nuclear navy. It is pronounced as if it were spelled "nuke."

words of a contemporary officer, "Rickover just never fit in. He couldn't get along with people. He was passed over for CO because of his abrasive personality."

Rickover might not have fitted in the old submarine navy, but as he built and manned the *Nautilus,* he was creating a new submarine navy, and his would not have social clubs.

The old submarine navy had produced officers in an informal, custom-laden way that Rickover abhorred. Volunteer officers took six months of classroom training at New London sub school and then were ordered aboard a submarine for on-the-job training, in the grand old Navy tradition. The new officer was dubbed "George" and treated as a kind of plebe while he learned his way around the submarine. Much of his education was informal, passed along as experience and lore, rather than as precise instruction. In his year or so aboard he had to learn how to perform every officer's duties.

He could qualify as a submarine officer only after three senior submarine officers had examined and passed him. Then, in a rite that would symbolize what Rickover despised about tradition, the new officer would get the sign of his entry into the submarine navy, his gold dolphins. The coveted insignia lay on the bottom of a ten-ounce glass filled with whiskey and he had to drink his way to it.

Rickover's first nucs, the officers and crew of the *Nautilus,* were trained by civilians—employees of Westinghouse at the Bettis Laboratory in Pennsylvania. The men of the second nuclear submarine, the *Seawolf,* were trained by civilians from General Electric at the Knolls Atomic Power Laboratory in Schenectady, New York. There was no nonsense, no building of traditions. Just day after sixteen-hour day at the controls of a reactor prototype, virtually memorizing piping systems, reading manuals over and over, taking written examinations.

Navy officials had to accept such training by civilians; after all, there were no nuclear submarines to put a prospective "George" aboard for training. The submarine school at New London had no facilities for teaching submariners about the new type of propulsion, and no Navy personnel were qualified to instruct the first crews. But the Navy was planning to take over the training of officers and men for later nuclear submarines. When Rickover learned about the plans of what he would call "the other Navy," he initiated the battle for the nucs.

After the first crews were in training for the *Nautilus* and the *Seawolf,* Rickover started a more formal program. The Naval Reactors Branch became an interview, reporting and control center for prospective nuclear submarines. The actual training, however, would be done at Navy schools.

Historically, the source of power in the submarine navy had been ComSubLant—Commander, Submarine Force Atlantic Fleet—who controlled not only all the submarines in the Atlantic area but also the submarine school at New London. Rear Admiral George C. Crawford was ComSubLant in mid-1954, when the bureaucratic struggle began for control of nuclear education.

Crawford planned to put nuclear-submarine training at New London, where submarine training had been carried on since 1917. Word of this plan reached Rickover through what would become his own intelligence network—nuclear-trained officers loyal to him and often operating outside the Navy's chain of command. In July 1954, Dick Laning, as Rickover's choice to be the first commanding officer of the *Seawolf,* was interviewed by a BuPers officer who, in the course of conversation, revealed that Crawford was planning to set up a nuclear-training school in New London. Laning went to New London, confirmed the report, and sent a memorandum to Rickover in what was one of the first uses of his nuc spy network.

Rickover was informed that the school Crawford was planning would eliminate the use of prototypes, the heart of the Rickover training method. Rickover moved fast. Two days after Laning made his report, Rickover had a representative from his group meet in New London with Navy officials. They worked out an agreement that put basic nuclear training in New London (taking that task away from the Westinghouse and GE civilians), transferred responsibility for the school from ComSubLant to BuPers, and made the use of prototypes a permanent and official matter. The six-month training at the prototype sites would be under the control of the Atomic Energy Commission (meaning Rickover, in his AEC role), but BuPers would at least theoretically administer the training.

The Chief of Naval Personnel at the time was Vice Admiral James L. Holloway, Jr., who had taken over BuPers in 1953 and had already given Rickover what amounted to veto power over officers proposed for nuclear-submarine duty. That power would broaden to include the selection and training of officers for nuclear-powered surface ships. (One of those officers would be Admiral Holloway's son, James L. Holloway III. He would command the *Enterprise*; he became the Chief of Naval Operations in 1974.)

The ComSubLant plan would have used mock-ups and simulators at the school in New London. Students would be trained not at prototypes in Idaho but, following tradition, aboard submarines. The prototypes would be ignored—as would Rickover. In the official historical account of the submarine-school dispute, ComSubLant officers are accused of proposing the use of mock-ups and simulators because "these devices . . . epitomized the issue of control, not only in an organizational sense (which was important) but also in terms of the longer-range objectives that Rickover had in mind. If New London could impose its standards on nuclear training, there would be little hope for creating the new type of naval officer Rickover envisioned."

To create this new type, Rickover needed more than an adjunct school at New London. The main submarine school and the establishment itself were still under control of ComSubLant. Although Rickover could develop an intensive curriculum at his school, he would still have to endure an atmosphere that he felt was hostile toward his nuclear students. He needed more than what he had got in the New London agreement, and he set out to get more—characteristically by turning not to the Navy but to the Atomic Energy Commission.

On August 5, 1958, a letter was prepared by the Commission's advisory committee on reactor safeguards. It is reasonable to believe that Rickover had a hand in the creation of that letter. He long had had close relations with the committee and, indeed, had used his influence in Congress to give the committee's recommendations the impact of law. In 1957 Rickover's friend Senator Clinton P. Anderson of the Joint Committee on Atomic Energy had introduced a bill that gave the safeguards committee the power to speak with statutory authority. Anderson's bill became an amendment to the Atomic Energy Act. Because of Rickover's close ties to the committee, the amendment had the effect of giving the Admiral, as a civilian, greater control over "safety," and, by his interpretation, safety was all.

The committee's letter was transmitted through the AEC to Admiral Arleigh Burke, Chief of Naval Operations. One paragraph became the perpetual authority for Rickover's sweeping powers in training the men of his nuclear navy:

> The committee reiterates that the prime assurance of safety during building, operating, and repairing nuclear ships at various locations depends upon the proper prior evaluation of potential hazards. This must be done for each new situation and at present, on a case by case basis, by persons having a detailed knowledge of the

factors influencing reactor safety. This requires that the training of officers and crews of nuclear ships must continue to emphasize knowledge of reactors and reactor safety. It also means that the experience and technical judgment of the Naval Reactors Branch (Division of Naval Reactors) must be utilized to the maximum extent on evaluating such operations. The problem assumes increased importance as the number of nuclear-powered ships increases.

The "judgment of the Naval Reactors Branch" was, of course, the judgment of Rickover the civilian. The letter was the foundation upon which he built the schools run by Rickover the naval officer. For, after getting the virtual mandate from the advisory committee, Burke issued orders that said, "All aspects of the operation of naval nuclear propulsion are to be treated with special care. This includes selection and training of personnel. . . ."

Rickover opened an independent nuclear-power school in January 1959—a continent's breadth away from New London—at the Mare Island Naval Shipyard in California. The second Rickover school, opened in July 1962, was at the Bainbridge Naval Training Center in Maryland. "By the time I entered [the school at Mare Island] in January of 1959," a veteran submariner wrote to the authors, "we all thought that the Admiral had the only say in what was taught and how it was done. Dean Axene was the director of the school then, and I had the feeling that his previous position as executive officer of *Nautilus* had been a determining influence in Admiral Rickover's upgrading of the nuclear school. I had always felt that *his* school started in 1956 in New London, but it was moved to get away from corrupting influences. Remember, starting in about 1960 he had run out of acceptable submarine officers from the fleet and was taking ensigns directly out of the Academy."

In the required six months at one of the schools, a prospective nuc received 700 hours of formal instruction in mathematics, physics, reactor theory and engineering, electrical engineering, heat transfer, chemistry, materials, nuclear plant systems, and radiological control. The curriculum was prepared by Rickover's staff, not by BuPers. As Rickover described the course of studies, officers were on the graduate level, enlisted men on an undergraduate college level.

The six months of formal training were followed by six months at one of the prototypes. No matter where the students went they walked halls bearing copies of the same sign. It said: "In this school the smartest work as hard as those who struggle to pass. H. G. Rickover."

From the beginning, Rickover's control of the making of a nuc has been total and exhaustive. He has supervised the writing of the text-book—he calls it a "topical guide"—required for each subject taught at his nuclear-power schools. (There is now only one, in Orlando, Florida; the Bainbridge school was moved there in 1976, and the Mare Island school in 1977.) Each topical guide specifies exactly what should be taught and how much time should be devoted to each aspect of the topic. The guide contains lesson plans the instructor must follow. He is also told when he must give examinations. The instructors are regularly monitored in the classroom by superiors.

The monitoring of an instructor is certified by a kind of ritual. The instructor signs the completed and graded examination sheets and sub-mits them to his superior. Then the superior opens a locked desk drawer or filing cabinet from which he takes an "embosser" similar to the sealing device used by a notary public. The superior then initials the instructor's signature and embosses the initial and the signature. Everything now certified to the ultimate degree, the superior places the embosser back in its container and locks it.

By Rickover's orders, no examinations can contain multiple-choice or true-or-false questions. Each question must "involve single and multi-ple concepts which require essay answers, definitions, statements of facts, or calculations." Each examination is written and reviewed by two mem-bers of the faculty. The examination is then given to another faculty member, changed if necessary, and reviewed again through a chain of command that ends with the commanding officer of the school. For every subject there is a weekly quiz, a two- or three-hour examination every ten days, and a final four-hour examination. There is also daily homework.

Because the homework often involves classified material, a student cannot actually do all of his homework at "home." Classified documents cannot be removed from the school or reactor facility. So the student must log his study time in order to have access to the documents. The number of hours he spends at his homework can thus be monitored.

The control of each student, in the words of one nuc, "is relentless." Any indication of a falling-off results in an interview with an "advisor" from the faculty. He can order a student to sign in and out when he goes to a specific place to study. This is another way to monitor the student's study time. The advisor may also hand out "weekend review packages," which contain questions calculated to keep a student at his books throughout the weekend so that he can turn the answers in on Monday morning. Besides the study package, he may spend Saturday morning on additional review—designated as makeup work, not homework. A failing student is given a final chance before an academic board, which subjects him to an oral examination. On the basis of his performance, the board can put him on probation or drop him from the program.

After six months in the classrooms of the nuclear power school, the successful student goes on to reactor-prototype training at a land-locked reactor site. The prototypes are owned by the Department of Energy (formerly the Atomic Energy Commission); the instructors are both civilian and Navy, and the places themselves are monastic. There are no television sets and no officer clubs. Much of the food consumed comes from vending machines. At the prototypes, where life is spartan and the days and nights are drenched in study, was born the nucs' reputation as crusaders against frivolity.

Much of the training takes the form of standing watch at the reactor plant. Officers and enlisted men actually operate the plant. Under the eyes of instructors, the students man controls that directly affect the reactor. There is no simulation; this is in keeping with a fundamental Rickover principle: "You have to train people to react to the real situation at all times. But if they are trained with a simulator, they tend to expect there will be no consequences as a result of their actions."

Before he stands his first watch, the student spends five weeks listening to lectures and taking examinations. The lectures are at the reactors, which are located some distance from the living quarters (an hour's bus ride away, at Arco, Idaho). His day at the reactor site ends after about seven hours of lectures and on-site training, and five to six hours of misnamed "homework." When he actually does get home, the student often falls asleep studying. By now he is well on his way to becoming a nuc, and he is beginning to realize that there is not much room in his life or career for anything but work and duty. For, as the master of the nucs himself has said, "Man's work begins with his job or profession. Having a vocation is always somewhat of a miracle, like falling in love."

The on-site instruction prepares the student for his watch-standing. Officers and men are assigned to crews and begin a rotating schedule of eight-hour shifts, twenty-four hours a day, seven days a week. A student works about sixty hours a week, either on his shift, at the site, or at his studies.

Surveillance is now even more intensive. A daily record is kept on each student. And the student himself carries a document called the Qualification Standard, a thick book of bits of information that he must know. The Standard consists of a series of instructions—such as "explain the functions of the electrical system" and "draw a one-line sketch of the system from memory." Each such bit must be performed and approved by an instructor, who verifies the performance by signing his name alongside a checkoff list. By the time a student completes his prototype training he will have collected more than one thousand signatures.

A student gets a grade for each watch he stands. He is even more closely monitored when he performs a task on watch, not only because he is operating real, valuable equipment but also because he is experiencing the essence of the Rickover system of learning by doing. Now, as he makes every move, he is scrutinized by a member of the prototype staff. At a certain point on his watch, for example, a student may have to start up a pump. The staff watch-stander steps up and fires a series of questions and orders: "How are you going to start up that pump? Show me the procedure. Discuss each step with me. What is the purpose behind that step? What would happen if you did not do that step? What else in the propulsion plant will be affected by it?"

As the student goes through his watches, his performance is being constantly rated on a complex system involving points and an "expected progress curve." If the points plot out a curve that falls below the expected one, the student is given extra hours of remedial work at the prototype. He earns his points by following the book—or by virtually memorizing it. The "book" exists in the form of volumes of written procedures covering every aspect of reactor operation. The students' prototype manuals are as true as possible to shipboard manuals.

An officer's final watch has a special audience: a three-man board of evaluators. Each watcher of the watch-stander grades performance on a pass-or-fail basis. All three must pass the student in order for him to continue his training. If he does not pass, he will be given remedial training and another chance. If he flunks one more time, he usually is, in the language of the nucs, "disenrolled."

The year-long training ordeal begins to end with a four-hour final examination for enlisted men and an eight-hour one for officers. The eight-hour examination covers five areas—fluid systems, radiological controls, chemistry, electrical and instrumental systems, and operational procedures. If a student flunks one of those areas he is given one chance to take the examination again. Another failure virtually guarantees disenrollment.

One lieutenant (junior grade) who flunked nuclear training at this juncture was given the usual option of another try at the test in three months. He knew the record of a previous group; eight out of twenty failed the first time, four out of eight the second time. He decided the odds were against him and he transferred out of the nuclear navy. His decision was based in part on the belief that his examination failure would dog his career even if he did pass the second time. A student's detailed records—including all reports on any "counseling sessions" he has had with his advisors—are maintained for five years. A summary of his training record is maintained in his personnel file for twenty years.

A student who passes the written examination is not quite through with his training. To qualify as a nuclear officer—and to get on the career path toward commanding officer—he must be accepted by all members of a four-man oral board. The oral examination is almost as formal as a court-martial. Each board member has a copy of the student's training record. And, using that, the board members seek weaknesses in the student's knowlege so they can concentrate their probing in those areas. For an officer, the inquisiton usually lasts from two to three hours. The questioning of an enlisted man may take less time. His career also pivots on the decision of the board.

A student turned down by the board may ask for another hearing. He may get it, but he must agree to remedial training. The second board consists of higher-ranking officials. Failure the second time around means disenrollment unless Rickover personally steps in.

About twelve percent of the officers and twenty percent of the enlisted men flunk out of nuclear training. Those who survive know their business. And in the words of a veteran of that training, they learn three important lessons: make sure you understand the orders, keep your cool, and be conservative. The third lesson came from the master: ". . . in an advanced field such as nuclear power, conservatism is necessary so as to allow for possible unknown and unforeseen effects." This conservatism, epitomized in the education of nucs, would take Rickover into direct and sustained conflict with the Navy over the administration of the Navy's most cherished institution, the United States Naval Academy.

Until 1960, the nuclear power schools drew most of their students from the ranks of submariners. From then on, the nuclear-submarine fleet grew so rapidly that men had to be taken directly from the Naval Academy, Officer Candidate School, and the Naval Reserve Officer Training Corps. Rickover welcomed the opportunity to take the untrained—to him, the unspoiled—into his schools. And he welcomed the chance to assess, on his terms, "the quality of the trained product." Compared to graduates of Annapolis, he said, "the young men from the civilian colleges are more adult in their attitudes, and they are generally better qualified academically."

Rickover had begun his public attacks on the Naval Academy in 1959. In Congressional testimony he told his inevitably friendly questioners that Annapolis graduates were "about two years behind graduates of our good engineering schools." He contended that "the Naval Academy does not develop or even encourage the kind of professionalism which is absolutely necessary if we are to build and maintain an officer corps capable of meeting the challenge of nuclear power and the coming space age."

Rickover's 1959 attack came as the Academy was expanding and improving curriculum. What he did not tell the Congressmen was that academic standards were rising. Of the 2,540 midshipmen in the three upper classes, 750 had grades at or above 3.0 (4.0—"four oh"—was long the Navy's traditional mark of perfection; a mark below 2.5 was failing).* Of those 750 students, more than half were voluntarily carrying extra subjects as part of a newly enacted "overload" curriculum. Most of the overload courses were in mathematics—probability and statistics, differential equations, or matrix theory.

Rickover delivered his most detailed attack on the Academy in 1961 when he was asked by Congressman Daniel J. Flood, a leading member of the Rickover-Congress mutual admiration society, what the Admiral would do if he were named superintendent of the Naval Academy. It was a typically soft, preplanned question for a typically long and polished answer.

The Admiral said that he would institute ten reforms. The first had to do not directly with scholarship but with age. Perhaps looking back to his own concerns about entrance requirements in 1918, Rickover said he would lower the maximum age for entrance from twenty-one to nineteen. He said that the higher age limit allowed midshipmen to enter the Academy after having been out of high school for four years. He suspected that the age rule might have been set up to help the football team rather than to improve scholarship. Younger midshipmen, he said, tended to do better scholastically than older ones.

Rickover's special prejudices against Annapolis, dating to his own midshipman days, seem to have inspired some of his reforms. He would, for example, tighten scholastic entrance requirements by making certain examinations mandatory. In his Annapolis, there would be more Rick-

* In 1964 the Naval Academy's passing grade was lowered to 2.0, the equivalent of a C.

over-like grinds and fewer men who got by on personality. He would also lower physical-fitness requirements. Rickover, the midshipman who had such trouble learning to swim, had become an admiral who said, "Modern warfare no longer calls for some physical qualifications that were once considered necessary." As for football and the claims that the sport developed initiative and leadership, he could not see how this could be when what the players do is carry out "plays which are selected by the coach and which require precise movements laid out in advance by him. With sadness, I must predict that when the day finally dawns when football has disappeared from all better colleges, its last stronghold will be the three Service Academies."

He would drastically change the curriculum, eliminating "practical courses, which train technicians" and adding "theoretical and liberal courses, which are required to educate professional men." He would also get rid of "the apparatus and machinery" used for "practical instruction" and install "laboratories and equipment needed to teach subjects of a more fundamental nature." Rickover's emphasis on learning, not drills, would extend the curriculum to include more elective courses. And, these would be taught by a faculty that would include many more civilian professors and far fewer naval officers—who tend to "create a less academic approach, which is reflected in the attitude of the midshipmen."

In the Rickover Academy, emphasis would be on study and not on such time-honored notions as military formations and the hazing of plebes by upperclassmen. By carrying out unquestioningly the often whimsical orders of their superiors, the young midshipmen get the idea that "a person in authority can issue an order of almost any kind on any subject. Time spent in carrying out many of these orders is wasted. More serious is the danger of training young minds in the belief that the substitution of powers of authority for thought constitutes good leadership." At the Academy, he said, there is no "freedom to argue and dissent in what concerns ideas and knowledge. . . . And yet the freedom of ideas, and the implied freedom to dissent, are at the very foundation of a true system of education."

Rickover's midshipmen would be free to argue, but they would not be free to engage in many extracurricular activities—one of Rickover's hates. He reached for his pet example by telling of a midshipman whose grades had plummeted in his final year because he had spent one week with a group of classmates who were escorting Miss America candidates, and another week on a junket to Mexico.

In Rickover's ideal Academy, the academic departments would prevail over the executive departments, which control the students' hours outside class. Essentially, Rickover would transform Annapolis into an educational institution that would resemble a graduate-level university, not a service academy.

Yet, in the area where he had complete control of education—in his nuclear power schools—he seemed to be another kind of educator: harsh, inflexible, determined that his students learn by rote. In the school of the nuc, there was no questioning of authority, no emphasis on educating the professional man. The nuclear power schools turned out technicians, whether they were officers or enlisted men. The only resemblance between them and Rickover's ideal Annapolis was a disdain for Navy ranks, rules and traditions.

The possibility that the Naval Academy—the home of the naval aristocracy since 1845—could actually change into the type of school that Rickover desired was raised when Vice Admiral Kinnaird R. McKee became the forty-eighth superintendent on August 1, 1975. McKee, himself an Academy graduate of 1951 as well as nuclear-trained, had served in the *Skipjack,* the first of a class of high-speed nuclear submarines.

McKee went from the *Skipjack* to Rickover's staff to handle personnel and training. After a subsequent tour as commanding officer of another nuclear attack submarine, he had joined the personal staff of Chief of Naval Operations Elmo R. Zumwalt. McKee could thus claim a membership in both the Zumwalt and Rickover cliques.

McKee was not the first nuc to become superintendent. That honor belonged to Vice Admiral James Calvert, who, in becoming the Academy's forty-sixth superintendent in 1968, was at age forty-seven the youngest admiral to head the Academy until that time. When Calvert took over the Academy, his appointment was not considered a victory for the nuclear navy. In fact, the term *nuc* was only starting to become significant. Calvert, a decorated World War II veteran, commanded a submarine in the 1950s, and in May 1955 was accepted into the Rickover program. He became the first skipper of the *Skate,* the third nuclear submarine and the first to surface at the North Pole.

Calvert seemed to have been awarded the Annapolis position because of his intellect and leadership abilities. Few outside the nuclear navy would cite Calvert's appointment as an indication that Admiral Rickover was taking over the Naval Academy. (Calvert later served as a three-star fleet commander, another first for a nuc, before retiring. At one point he was considered a contender for CNO.) During Calvert's term as superintendent, Rickover's criticism of the Academy seemed muted, as if he did not want to question the ability of one of his hand-picked nuclear officers.

Calvert was succeeded in 1972 by Vice Admiral William P. Mack, a well-decorated officer fresh from duty as commander of the Seventh Fleet in the war zone of Southeast Asia. Mack had never been part of the nuclear navy. And, since his plebe days at Annapolis, he had been the kind of naval officer Rickover had never been.

Mack, Class of 1937, had been a member of the plebe baseball, basketball and football teams. His official Navy biography notes that he was a "member of the varsity baseball team but because of injuries was forced to give up football and basketball." From the Academy his career was that of an officer who was obviously moving up, including combat in a four-stack destroyer in the Far East at the start of World War II, commands at sea, service with both Navy and Defense Department staffs in the Pentagon, including duty as a senior aide and chief of Navy information. His appointment as superintendent placed him, at the end of a distinguished career, in a place that he loved.

Mack believed that Annapolis produced men who had learned, in mind and *body*, to become not merely technicians but leaders. One way he decided to demonstrate his belief was to emphasize athletics at the Academy. "Just studies were not enough," he would remark as he recalled his days as superintendent. "Sixteen percent of the men we graduated were going to be Marine officers. They don't need differential equations. Football would help them. And we were graduating aviation officers. They needed good eyes and reflexes. Fencing and baseball could help them."

Rickover did not like athletics. But he did like differential equations. And that, at least in metaphor, was the basis for the dispute that flared between Rickover and Mack. They looked at the Academy from opposite poles—one an old grad who cherished his Academy years; the other a man who unfondly remembered the Academy as a place where, as a member of "an aggregation of photographic memorizers," he "had memorized all the textbooks on ordnance and gunnery." To Midshipman Rickover, Annapolis was textbooks, not June Week and hops; hydraulics, not football and fencing.

Rickover should have had no grievance against Mack. Although Mack had been very much a part of the Navy establishment that Rickover had so often scorned, Mack had not been known as an anti-nuc. He had never hesitated, officially or unofficially, to praise the performance of the nuclear-powered ships in his command. As the commander of a task force, he had often volunteered praise for the nuclear ships' high speed and unlimited range. He liked the ships, and he even seemed to like the man who had fostered them.

One of Mack's Washington tours was duty as chief of Navy legislative affairs. He had seen Rickover in action before Congress and had been impressed. "He gave them attention, but not flattery," Mack recalled. "He never did anything improper, and he did not lie. But sometimes it was hard to differentiate between what he had done for the Navy and what he had done for Rickover."

By the time Mack became superintendent in June 1972, many nuclear officers were on the Academy campus as battalion and company officers—the young Navy and Marine Corps officers assigned to supervise the activities and life-style of the midshipmen. Like the nucs in the fleet, the nucs at Annapolis had two loyalties: one to the command and one to Rickover. Nucs on the Academy staff were reporting not only through the chain of command to the superintendent but also by mail and even at times by phone to Rickover.

They kept him posted on the gossip. (He delighted in telling of the visitor to the Academy who had confused it with—or at least rated it on the level with—another tourist attraction. Somehow Rickover had picked up the visitor's comment: "I'm happy I was able to take advantage of my visit to the east coast to visit Disneyland, too.") The serious news Rickover also picked up concerned what he saw as the failure of the Academy to provide him with enough officers suitable for nuclear training.

Although the number of nucs selected from Academy graduates had been rising steadily year after year—and it was totally voluntary until 1980—the number of nucs from Naval ROTC colleges had drastically dropped off. The antiwar movement on campuses had cut back or even closed down many Navy and Army ROTC units. More and more, Rickover had to turn to Annapolis for his officers, and he often said that he did not like what he was getting.

Mack was just ending his first year as superintendent when Rickover attacked the Academy more vehemently than ever before. As usual, he chose as his pulpit a seat in a Congressional hearing room. He began with a tale of a fallen nuc, an Academy man just dropped from a nuclear power school for academic failure. A physics major who stood in the top three percent of his class, the young man had been the pride of the Academy—a Trident scholar. These midshipmen, because they are "exceptionally capable," are allowed to carry out independent study and reduce their formal course load during their senior year.

Several Trident scholars have become nucs. But to Rickover, such scholarship was nonsense, for it produced a man "subtly trained to be a college professor rather than a naval officer." The Academy, he proclaimed, "has only a few more years to live a useful life unless it is radically reformed. . . . Instead of concentrating on teaching the basic subjects such as history, geography, English, literature, physics, engineering, seamanship, and ordnance, they are being taught system analysis, management, international law, and other similar subjects. . . ."

He also criticized the building of "large new expensive facilities, such as a large model basin which will be of little use to the midshipmen." (This building would be named Rickover Hall, and Rickover, reportedly under the direct orders of the Chief of Naval Operations, would go to Annapolis—for the dedication of the hall's foundation—in his uniform. After the ceremony, he would ask Superintendent Mack for the white overalls his wife wore when, with a welder's torch, she inscribed her name on a metal plate that was part of the foundation.)

The facts did not support Rickover's criticism of the Academy's curriculum. At the time he testified, a midshipman had to earn a minimum of 140 credits for graduation. He had to take 53 credits—about 40 percent—in technical subjects; 28 credits (20 percent) in professional subjects; 25 credits (17 percent) in communications, English, humanities and social sciences. A midshipman's 38 other credits went toward developing a major. An analysis of the curriculum in comparison with those of the U.S. Military Academy and the U.S. Air Force Academy showed that the ratio of "math-science-engineering" to "social science-humanities" was 70:30 at Annapolis, 55:45 at West Point, and 50:50 at the Air Force Academy.

Mack weathered Rickover's criticism. He endured the nucs-to-Rickover loop outside his chain of command. He tried to fulfill what he saw as his quotas for Marines, aviators, and nuclear submariners. In speeches to midshipmen, he told them that the nuclear navy looked like the wave of the future. He ran his command firmly, as he had run all his commands. He was pleased about his institution's academic record: the home-grown Trident scholars, the exported Rhodes and Fulbright scholars. And the athletic record. The Naval Academy's twenty-one sports, ranging from football to golf, are tabulated on an over-all win-loss-tie scoreboard.

Under Mack, the "win" percentage rose from .648 to .671 (162 wins, 79 losses, 2 ties), the highest record in ten years.

Mack did not respond to Rickover by making changes. Mack was in charge, and by tradition he was relatively independent. But that tradition was to end.

Rickover, uncharacteristically, had suggested that the Navy bureaucracy be placed in closer control of the Academy. Superintendents, he believed, had too much independence. He said that Academy graduates needed to be in touch with the world and the Navy, but he was also apparently hoping that more pressure from Navy brass could create changes that would help solve his now-chronic problem: a shortage of volunteers for nuclear training.

When nonnuclear Mack was replaced by nuclear McKee in 1975, nonnuclear Zumwalt had been succeeded as Chief of Naval Operations by nuclear James L. Holloway III. And three months after McKee took over as superintendent, Holloway issued a "Naval Academy Policy Statement" and an order: "I have determined for matters of broad policy establishment and review, and in keeping with the pattern of other Service chiefs, to have the Superintendent of the Naval Academy report directly to me."

Parts of the policy statement had a Rickover ring:

> . . . Although many academic disciplines have peripheral application to naval matters, not all are well suited for the central role in this regard. The modern Navy and Marine Corps, whose material foundations are so strongly based on technology, require that their officers be provided with a technically oriented educational foundation. . . .
> The present distribution of disciplines—a minimum of 80 percent science and engineering with the remainders in the humanities—is considered valid for the present but the 80 percent figure may be subject to further *upward* adjustment. . . ." [Emphasis added]

There were other, subtle changes under McKee. He installed what he called "a realistic military environment," which, with its gun-toting watch officers and blizzard of paper orders, convinced even the dullest midshipman that he was marching around a military base, not a campus. *The Log,* the Annapolis humor magazine, even began publishing some serious matters between its pages of cartoons and snapshots of midshipmen's girlfriends.

The Log traditionally has assigned to it an "officer rep" who tries to keep the magazine from straying too far beyond the boundaries of good taste. To the nonnuc who was the rep when McKee took over, good taste included wisecracks about nucs, a comic strip about "Captain Hymo and his fantastic nuclear realm," and a cartoon which showed a Rickover-like character standing in front of a "Hymie's new and used nuclear cores" sign. The caption asked: "Would you buy a used nuclear core from this man?"

Then blanks began appearing in *The Log*. Censorship, the editors explained. *Nuked,* said the italicized line inserted in the blanks. A humor column in one issue suddenly became serious for a sentence: "The administration must have decided that since the *Log* was writing so much about nuclear trained officers they'd better give us one to act as a stellar example." A nuc had replaced the nonnuc as officer rep.

One of the items he snatched from *The Log* just before it went to press was a "ransom note," classically prepared with newspaper-headline paste-ups: WE HAVE ADMIRAL RICKOVER. DELIVER $5,000,000 PLUS A HAM FRANCISCO SUB [a popular snack-bar sandwich] TO THE 4-1 HEAD [bathroom] IN A LEAD SEA BAG BY O-DARK 30 [12:30 A.M.] TOMORROW OR WE GIVE HIM BACK!

In the nuclear atmosphere, certain midshipmen were feeling like second-class citizens. They were "Bull majors," in Annapolis slang "Bull" being the designation given those midshipmen who had chosen to be part of the twenty percent of the student body (brigade) enrolled in the non-technical curriculum. The eighty percent non-Bull quota had been set in the 1977–1978 academy catalog: ". . . the needs of the Navy require that at least 80 percent of the midshipmen in each class be enrolled in engineering, scientific, or mathematics majors. Other midshipmen may major in the humanities or social sciences."

Some officers in the "real" Navy began to joke about the 80–20 program—Annapolis was "training eighty officers for every twenty that were being educated." One midshipman said in 1978 that he had been told by a nuc officer that Bull majors did not belong at the Academy. Bull majors, of course, did not usually volunteer for the nuclear-power program.

Members of the Class of 1978 who had entered the Academy of Mack and would be graduated from the Academy of McKee were particularly vulnerable. Since their plebe year they had been subtly and brazenly recruited by faculty members and other officers who boosted their own branches. Marine officers tried to get those "few good men" the recruiting posters were asking for, and naval aviators would seek out the students with 20/20 vision and good looks and extol the romance of the skies. (And would-be aviators with a touch of astigmatism would be told by Marine officers and naval aviators that there was a "back seat" in the airplane available for them.)

But the strongest recruitment was done by the officers of the nuclear navy. One was a battalion officer whose job was to keep watch over the academic and military life of 720 midshipmen, most of them in the senior, or first class, year. He kept his valuables in his battalion office, secured by a combination lock. Among them was a stack of booklets containing the official 196-page transcript of Rickover's 1973 testimony to a Congressional subcommittee—the testimony that included his fiercest attack on the Naval Academy. The nuc battalion officer could quote parts of that testimony by heart.

He and the other Annapolis nucs had helped to recruit many of the 240 men who entered the nuclear navy from the Class of 1978. The goal had been almost double that—400. The following year only 191 went into the nuclear navy, which was by then desperate for men. Then came the Class of 1980—they were not merely *asked* to be nucs; they were *drafted*.

First-classmen are allowed to choose their branch of specialization. In the months before graduation, this process builds toward "Selection Day," when first-classmen file into an auditorium where representatives of the branches have set up tables—aviation, surface weapons, and so forth—for the signing-up of prospective ensigns. Prior to Selection Day, the Marine Corps has already found its men, and so has the nuclear navy.

From about mid-January to mid-February, the busloads of volunteer candidates for the nuclear navy are transported from Annapolis to Rickover's headquarters in Crystal City, Virginia, for the ritual of the Rickover interview. Year after year, Rickover has found the men he wanted and rejected the ones he did not want, usually with no explanation given and always with no explanation asked by the Navy. Drawing from Academy volunteers, along with volunteers from Naval ROTC units at favored colleges, and Officer Candidate School, he made his quota—until 1980; that was the year when the Navy drafted midshipmen into the nuclear navy against their will.

The goal that year was 250 volunteers for the nuclear navy. A total of 344 first-classmen of the Class of 1980 volunteered and were interviewed by Rickover. He selected only 152 candidates. "The interviews and the selection seemed more arbitrary than ever before," an Academy faculty member told the authors. "There didn't seem to be any rhyme or reason." The Number 28 and Number 29 men in the class, for example, were among the volunteers. Both were political-science majors; their academic records were virtually the same. Number 29 was chosen; Number 28 was rejected. No reason was given.

As word was passed about the high number of Rickover rejects, Academy officials realized that the nuclear-navy quota would have to be met by drafting midshipmen. Young men who had spent years planning to fly in the Navy suddenly were told that they would spend their careers in submarines instead. One of them called retired Admiral Arleigh Burke, former Chief of Naval Operations. Burke and the midshipman's father had been friends. Never before had the midshipman or the father tried to use that friendship.

"I told him there was nothing I could do," Burke said. "But I called up BuPers and asked, 'Is this true?' They said, 'Yes.' I said, 'My God, what happens to those people?'

" 'I know it's wrong,' the man in BuPers said, 'but they are being ordered there.'

" 'You know what you're doing, don't you?' I said. 'There will be some of them who will resent it to beat hell. Some of them will resign before graduation. And some of them will stay in and get out just as soon as they can and will be bitter all their lives. You don't make good officers that way.' "

Philosophizing on what happened, Burke told the authors, "That was a dreadful thing to do. It's perfectly all right to assign people now and then, but it shouldn't be a usual thing. They're taking top people who are fully capable, at the expense of all the other programs—and then losing a large percentage of them in their damn program. You get people not by giving them things. You get people by making them want to serve."

A Naval Academy faculty member said, "We spend about $100,000 to produce a graduate. I'll bet that eighty of our draftees don't stay in the nuclear navy after the required few years. That means $8 million down the drain."

By the time the Class of 1980 was graduated, the quota still had not been filled. Of the 250 wanted, only 237 had been found, and 76 of those were drafted. The Marines had made their quota of 159 male officers and were short only one of the nine female officers asked for—all were volunteers. Naval aviation wanted 210 male pilots and five female pilots; aviation got 208 male pilots and four female pilots—all volunteers. (All of the nuclear-power billets had to be male, because of the law that allows women to serve for only up to one hundred and eighty days aboard combatant ships; a duty tour aboard a nuclear submarine would be longer than that period. Unofficially, Rickover did not want any women even to volunteer. There were fifty-five women in the Class of 1980, the first to include female midshipmen).

The concept of volunteerism was important to the Navy and to the Naval Academy. In time of war the Navy and Marine Corps have always been the last to draft. Naval aviation and submarines were traditionally volunteer branches of even those services. Now, with the draft into the nuclear navy, still another tradition—and motivation—was shattered by Rickover.

Rickover saw nothing wrong with drafting his nucs. In fact, during his 1980 testimony before a House committee, he complained about the draftees' "childish" attitudes. "It was clear," he said, "that, in some cases, non-volunteers from the Naval Academy did not understand that they were on military orders to be interviewed for the nuclear power program and because of this, it was their duty to do their best to answer the questions put to them in the interviews at Naval Reactors. . . .

"The one area in which I think Congress should be firm," he later said, "is in not allowing lower standards of acceptances. I have been chided that we could meet our officer and enlisted goals if I would just lower the standards. The lessons of the Three Mile Island accident have reinforced the importance of maintaining high standards in the selection, training and qualification of personnel.

"I have no intentions of lowering these standards. . . ."

In finding and training his nucs, Rickover has inevitably set and kept his own standards. He has sought and has found men who were different from—and, often, better than—their peers in Annapolis and NROTC classes.

A captain interviewed for this book was perhaps the most articulate spokesman for the nuclear navy the authors heard in scores of interviews. A 1954 graduate of the Naval Academy, he became a nuc in 1958, served in and commanded submarines, and assumed other responsibilities. At the twenty-five-year mark in his career, he confidently expected to achieve flag rank. Like many nuclear-trained officers of his time, he believed that he could someday become Chief of Naval Operations.

He assessed Rickover's accomplishment as an engineer: "He saw a wave of technology coming towards us, and he saw how to apply that technology—nuclear power—to the Navy. There was a certain inevitability to what he did. He administered new technology, and he found ways to get that technology into the Navy. I'm not saying that nobody could have done that. But it took a good engineer and someone who understood how the Navy worked. Don't forget the *Nautilus* was built inside the rules, not outside.

"His real genius, I believe, lies elsewhere. He infused into the Navy the idea of excellence. He had to. You don't just fool around with nuclear energy. He said that the *standard* would be excellence and he made that happen.

"Look around. Do you see excellence anywhere? In medicine? In law? Religion? Anywhere? We have abandoned excellence, sometimes wrongly, in the name of civil rights or equality. Don't get me wrong. I know our country is going in the right direction, in the main. We can't make demands on our citizens that go beyond what society as a whole is demanding.

"But in the Navy, Rickover showed we could make the demand of excellence. It's a proud word for us.

"He did his job as an engineer. He never did much more than that. Certainly he was no strategist, no expert beyond his specialty. But he was the genius who gave a generation of naval officers the idea that excellence was the standard. They learned that he would tolerate mistakes—even if a mistake resulted in a collision at sea.

"If you made a mistake, there would be no bloodletting. But a short-coming, a failure to work toward the standard of excellence, that was not tolerated. Of all he did, this may be the most significant: He taught us the difference between making a mistake and falling short of the standard of excellence. He taught that to a whole generation of naval officers."

15 | The Day of the Nucs

At first the Navy's leadership saw little difficulty in assigning personnel to Rickover's nuclear training and to subsequent assignment aboard nuclear-propelled submarines. Even if the young men assigned were among the best in the Navy, they would, after finishing Rickover's schooling, serve aboard nuclear submarines that were part of the "real" Navy, and eventually go on to shore duty and higher positions in the fleet. From the earliest *Nautilus* cruises it was evident that many more nuclear submarines would be built. Still, the submarine force was traditionally a small part of the Navy, and few submariners rose to the uppermost ranks of the Navy's hierarchy. By the time a submariner pinned on the shoulder boards of an admiral he would have long since left the "boats."

Indeed, since the establishment of the position of the Chief of Naval Operations in 1915, only two submarine officers had risen to that top uniformed position in the Navy, Ernest J. King and Chester W. Nimitz. King, who was also an aviator, had not even entered the submarine service until he was a captain, and had served more time in battleships and aircraft carriers than in submarines; Nimitz, who as CNO sponsored the funding of the nuclear-submarine effort after World War II, served in a battleship, a cruiser and a destroyer (which he briefly commanded until he ran her aground) before he entered the submarine service. Nimitz returned to surface ships for several years, again served briefly in submarine commands as a captain, and then went on to major commands in the surface fleet.

Thus, exposure to the nuclear-propulsion program and service in the "submarine navy" were accepted and, by some senior officers, even encouraged. But, well beyond the boundaries of tradition, Rickover was creating his own navy within the submarine navy.

By the end of 1960 the nuclear navy consisted of thirteen submarines in service with another thirty-five in various stages of construction or authorized for construction. There were also three nuclear surface ships being completed, an all-nuclear task force—the supercarrier *Enterprise* and the missile-armed cruisers *Long Beach* and *Bainbridge*.* Rickover supervised the propulsion system for every ship and increasingly had influence on other parts of the ships. And, perhaps what was more important, he personally interviewed, selected and supervised the training of virtually every submarine officer, many of the senior enlisted men, and the captains and engineering officers of the surface ships.

An order to report to the Naval Reactors Branch—always as a part of the Atomic Energy Commission, not the Navy—was less than appealing to many officers as Rickover's methods and reputation began to spread, first through the fleet and then to the Naval Academy and college campuses. John Paul Jones had preached, "give me a fast ship, for I intend to sail in harm's way." For many naval officers, to go to work for Admiral Rickover was to sail in harm's way without a ship under his feet. Duty with the Naval Reactors Branch on the concrete and tile of the Main Navy building meant that the officer was immediately suspect by the rest of the Navy or, as it was sometimes called, the "real" Navy.

Once in the nuclear program—after the infamous Rickover interview sessions—it was work, study, exam, in an endless cycle. Compliments for hard work were nonexistent. At the reactor prototypes, extra work was encouraged . . . and easily monitored. "Special confidence and trust," the traditional words on United States military commissions, had no relevance in the nuclear-power program. Everything and everyone was checked and checked again, and still again.

Many of the men who were assigned to NRB in the early days of the nuclear program were pushing forward in a new technology that was to revolutionize navies. After they had served in a nuclear submarine, their shore duty or other fleet assignments were in a world far different from the halls of the prototype reactor schools or NRB offices. Until the middle 1960s—that is, for the first full decade of nuclear ships—NRB nucs were too junior to affect the careers of their fellow nuclear officers. Selection boards for captain and rear admiral were controlled by the "real" Navy, and only the best of Rickover's best could expect preferred assignments and promotions once they left his nuclear navy.

But Rickover had the best of the Navy to choose from, and flag promotions were inevitable. Captain Eugene P. Wilkinson, the non-Academy first skipper of the *Nautilus*, was selected for admiral in 1963. Al-

---

* *When built the* Bainbridge *was classified as a guided missile frigate (DLGN); the ship was reclassified as a cruiser (CGN) in 1975.*

though Wilkinson was an ardent supporter of Rickover, the selection board had not produced a Rickover triumph. It had selected the hero of the *Nautilus*, not simply a nuc. The day of the nucs was not yet at hand.

As the nuclear fleet grew, Rickover had to go beyond the ranks of submariners to pick his men. Maintaining his AEC-endorsed claim that he had control of the safety requirements for reactors in nuclear ships, he moved from control of submarine personnel to surface ships without pause or apology. But there was some significance, not lost on the Navy's Rickover-watchers, when he took four captains, all Academy graduates and none submariners, into his nuclear program.

Earlier, in January 1958, Captain Ned Beach had been assigned to the Naval Reactors Branch in preparation for his commanding the giant nuclear submarine *Triton*, the only two-reactor U.S. submarine. Beach, a veteran submariner and former Presidential naval aide, as a captain was spared the traditional Rickover interview and some other humiliations. (All other submarines were skippered by lieutenant commanders or commanders.)

Next, the three nuclear surface ships also would need captains. The first would go to submariner Eugene P. Wilkinson. The first skipper of the *Nautilus*, he had gone on to command a submarine division. Then, as a captain, he was ordered back to the Naval Reactors Branch in preparation for his becoming skipper of the world's first nuclear surface warship, the *Long Beach*. It then was routine for submarine officers to hold cruiser commands when they became captains, but the *Long Beach* was indeed a plum for Wilkinson, especially since he was non-Academy. And he had not had the auxiliary ship command, normally prerequisite, to get him accustomed to handling a large-size and large-crew ship. (Beach had spent a year in command of a large oiler.)

But the next four line captains in the program established the precedent for nonsubmariners: Vincent P. de Poix, Frederick H. Michaelis, William H. Harnish, and Raymond E. Peet. Under a law passed soon after the Billy Mitchell controversy of the early 1920s, all aircraft carriers had to be commanded by aviation officers. Of course, even without the law Rickover at the time would have had no other submarine captains available who were qualified or experienced for major ship commands.

De Poix, an aviator, became the first captain of the nuclear carrier *Enterprise*. He would later reach three-star rank. Harnish, also an aviator, was executive officer of the *Enterprise*, while Michaelis trained to provide a later relief for de Poix and, as another admiral put it, "to be ready to take over if de Poix broke a leg." Mike Michaelis did command the *En-*

terprise, and go on to four-star rank. Ray Peet was a surface officer, with much service in destroyers. When selected for training in the Naval Reactors Branch, he was a commander and aide to Chief of Naval Operations Arleigh Burke. He became the first commanding officer of the cruiser *Bainbridge*. Later Peet achieved three-star rank.

All four of these officers were among the "best and brightest" of the Navy's captains. However, most of the officers entering the Rickover program in the late 1950s and early 1960s were far more junior, usually ensigns just out of the Naval Academy, Naval ROTC, or Officer Candidate School. These young officers—about five hundred of them a year—would no longer be considered "typical" naval officers. Rickover did not like the typical naval officer anyway. He said so in Congressional testimony, and officers assigned to the nuclear program were bluntly told that they had to be "re-educated." If re-education did not work, they could not expect to stay very long. As Rickover boasted, "We take . . . very few officers who have had over two or three years of commissioned service" (and no enlisted men with over four years of service).

In the days when he was recruiting extensively from Naval Reserve Officer Training Corps at universities, he usually found the young men of the new nuc breed that he was looking for. Almost invariably they had no family ties to the Navy. They believed in engineering—if not as a religious occupation, at least as a profession. They seemed to enjoy work and little else. And they had never seen the inside of Bancroft Hall and cared little for class standing.

An NROTC graduate who joined the nuclear navy in 1963 told the authors how the recruiting worked. "During my senior year," he recalled, "I was given what we called a 'wish list.' I was supposed to be able to pick what I wanted—a destroyer, a carrier. Or the nuclear program. We got a lot of literature on that. And I decided that the nuclear program was what I wanted. I wanted to work with Admiral Rickover.

"I filled out the form and it was sent to him. His staff screened the application and sent it back to the NROTC unit. A little while later—not long before graduation—those of us who wanted to join the program and were acceptable were sent to Washington.

"We met with three or four staff members who asked a lot of questions and took notes. One big question was whether I wanted to serve on a ship or in Rickover's office—on his staff. I said staff. They said that their notes would be reviewed by Admiral Rickover and he would then interview me."

The usual interview took place: caustic, insulting questions from

Rickover; stumbling answers from the terrified young man. One exchange, though, perhaps provided an insight into Rickover's attitude about the difference between a man's essence and his job:

"What does your father do for a living?"

"My father is an industrial engineer."

"I didn't ask you what he *is*. I asked you what he *does*."

As so many interview victims had believed before and since, the young man thought that he had flunked his inquisition. But the hand of Rickover moved in mysterious ways. The young man was accepted and was assigned to Rickover's staff, bypassing the usual cycle of nuclear power school and reactor prototype. Just before he left for duty in the Naval Reactors Branch, an older officer on the NROTC faculty told him, "If you want a normal career, don't go on Rickover's staff." He did not have a normal career. In his six years in the Navy he never wore a uniform.

Rickover's independence from the Navy, which began when he forged a Congressional alliance in his first promotion battle, was at first expressed by hat-juggling. "My primary duty is in the Atomic Energy Commission," as he often testified. "I have additional duty in the Navy to help me to do my job. This is where I get fouled up, because of constant changes in senior military personnel. Instead of their realizing my duty in the Navy is for the purpose of helping me get naval support, they try to take over. That is the trouble."

Despite these statements, Rickover was running NRB just about the way he wanted. And he was running more than the Naval Reactors Branch. He was defying superiors and supervising the transformation of the Navy into a nuclear navy, regardless of the expense and regardless of the wide spectrum of national interests involved in such a transformation. Here was one man and his small group in the Navy making major decisions—and successfully lobbying the appropriations to finance these decisions—without regard to the priorities and strategic plans of the Pentagon and the White House.

But because he appeared to be at the height of his power in his sixties, those who took the long view in the Navy and elsewhere in government believed that the Rickover era would soon end, if not with his retirement at or near the age of sixty-five, then certainly before the 1970s. They were wrong, of course; his power in the 1960s was not yet at its height. It would not crest until the late 1970s—years after many of those who had anticipated his demise were themselves long in retirement.

The organization he had built in the 1950s would remain basically the same, year after year. His BuShips staff consisted of about 135 people, most of them "technical," as he labeled them, or "professional," as they usually referred to themselves. Naval Reactors managed the Bettis Atomic Power Laboratory in Pittsburgh and the Knolls Atomic Power Laboratory near Schenectady. Bettis, owned by the AEC and operated by the Westinghouse Electric Corporation, had about 3,300 people. Knolls, also owned by the AEC and run by the General Electric Company, had about 2,000 employees. Rickover referred to the laboratories—and the people—as "ours," meaning Naval Reactors', not the Navy's and not the AEC's. He also had his prototype reactors for training and experimental purposes in Idaho, New York, and Connecticut. And, of course, there were thousands of nuclear-navy men in schools and in the Fleet, and his inspectors at a score of shipyards and branch offices.

He acted as if he were answerable to no one except the Congress and hence to the American people. He was the ultimate antiorganization man in the age of the opposite. And he was a man with an image: He was plain, humble. When he lunched with the Secretary of the Navy, for example, it was the Secretary of the Navy who went to Rickover's dingy offices and got what cynics in the "real" Navy called "the austerity act." The Secretary or, on other occasions, a high-ranking officer or a powerful Congressman would lunch with Rickover on canned soup, crackers, cottage cheese, and skimmed milk. Lunch would be at his desk or at the end of a partly cleared conference table. The food came from a scant larder maintained by Rickover's secretary. It was well known that Rickover did not leave his office for lunch, that its ingredients rarely varied, and that he spent at lunch just enough of his valuable time to consume the food.

Such dedication was expected not only of the people around him but also of the thousands of people in the outposts of the Naval Reactors Branch. If there were any doubt about who was in charge of these people—and who could fire them if they failed to emulate his dedication—then Rickover was always ready to set the record straight. He did this several times a year in his annual performances before Congressional committees.

"I am the head of this organization," he told his friendly inquisitors in a typical statement. "I am responsible for all the research and development that goes on. . . . I have nuclear plants to design and build; ships must be completed on schedule; officers and crews must be trained; complex safety features must be observed. The nuclear plants must be right. . . ."

"But," he complained, "my job is being slowed"; and for a moment the Rickover view of the U.S. Navy shone through in brazen clarity: "The people who interfere with me are not familiar with the technical aspects of my job, nor are they responsible for obtaining results. Nevertheless, they have authority to take actions which affect my work, without consulting me."

One Congressman asked him, "Of what rank are these folk who clog the work?"

"The people who cause most of the trouble," Rickover answered, "are above commander in rank."

"You get very little from the lieutenants?"

"No, sir."

"And not so much from the lieutenant commanders?"

"No, sir. It is mostly the people of higher rank."

Rickover never portrayed himself as one of those men of higher rank, an admiral and a top-level bureaucrat in two federal bureaucracies. But in fact there was a table of organization, and Rickover not only was part of it; he had constructed it. While he was complaining to Congress about the way the U.S. Navy interfered in the work of his small, dedicated band of brothers, he was in fact operating out of a self-made, impregnable bureaucratic maze that was able to interfere with much of the naval establishment. And it was he who, in fact, as a routine matter, was interfering with the work of thousands of people in laboratories, industrial firms and shipyards.

A table of organization usually is fascinating only to a bureaucrat or a historian. But the one Rickover created has a certain intrinsic beauty that anyone can appreciate. (See page 324.)

Rickover did not build this marvelous table privately in his plasterboard office in T-3 building. Congress knew what he was doing and had tacitly endorsed his double-barreled control over nuclear reactors. And the Navy had stood by helplessly as Rickover not only flaunted his power but also humiliated officers and ruined careers. One of the most flagrant displays of power came one day in 1955, when Rickover, testifying before a Congressional committee in executive session, was idly asked if there were any specific officers who were giving him any trouble.

What happened next is based on the recollection of officers in BuShips. At least two of them recorded their recollections, and they later expanded on them in interviews with the authors. Rickover testified that he had no problems with the Chief of BuShips, Rear Admiral Albert G. Mumma, but that he had been having unspecified difficulties

NUCLEAR REACTOR PROGRAM ORGANIZATION
Early 1960s

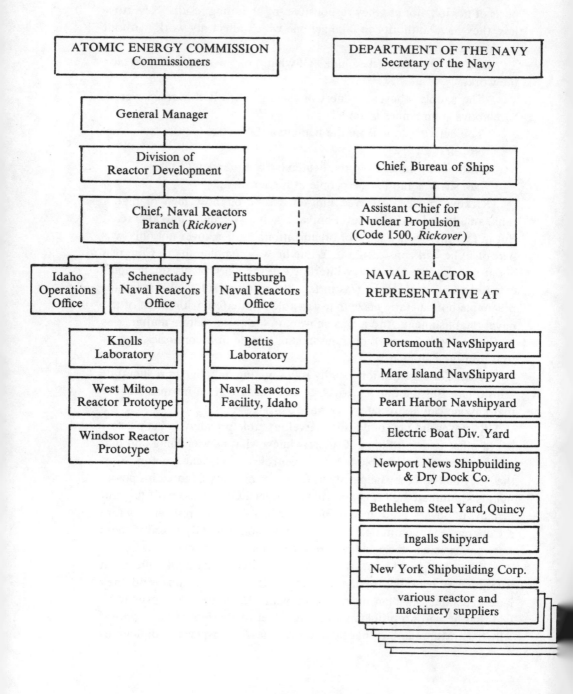

with Rear Admiral Robert Lee Swart, an officer who was, indirectly, a superior.

That very day—by one estimate, within an hour of the conclusion of the Congressional session—Secretary of the Navy Charles S. Thomas called Mumma and told him to move Swart out of any position of responsibility over Rickover.

Subsequently, Rear Admiral Ralph K. James, who later would become Chief of BuShips, was called into Mumma's office and told that he would be sent to command the Long Beach (California) Naval Shipyard by the end of the week. James had been slated to command the San Francisco Naval Shipyard. He asked about the swift change in assignment and was told, "Rickover has popped out again." Mumma then disclosed the phone call from Secretary of the Navy Thomas.

James simply was caught up in a flurry of transfers that were "all to happen virtually overnight, because Mumma had to report to the House of Representatives committee—Carl Vinson was its chairman then—and advise that he had taken steps to remove the burr from under Rickover's saddle."

Years later, looking back to the early rise of Rickover, Admiral James said, "There were those, and I surely number myself among them, who thought Rickover needed intelligent burrs periodically under his saddle to keep him from becoming too much of a demagogue."

Rickover's widening influence over the Navy spread from two sources, Capitol Hill and BuShips. There was little the Navy could do about Capitol Hill, but BuShips was directly under the control of the "real" Navy, and theoretically it was here that the Navy could fight the key battles for the control of the nuclear navy. But BuShips, where Rickover had originally established himself, would be his citadel, even though he would never command it or rise into its upper echelons beyond the nuclear-power role.

As Admiral Mumma's term as chief was ending, he narrowed his choice of a successor, ultimately tapping James. But there was one test James had to pass before he could be chosen. Mumma took James into the office of Secretary of the Navy Thomas S. Gates. The Secretary asked James how he got along with Admiral Rickover. James tactfully said that, although he did not know Rickover very well, he believed they could get along. James, having passed the test, was nominated by President Eisenhower, approved by the Senate, and sworn in on April 29, 1959.

Perhaps James could have been named without the overt approval of Rickover, but James certainly could not have been made Chief of Bu-

Ships if Rickover had opposed him. For 1959 was one of Rickover's vintage years: He accompanied Vice President Nixon to the Soviet Union; the Polaris missile program—based on nuclear submarines—was being accelerated; and he would weather another promotion fight. He would be the hero of every influential and most noninfluential Congressmen on Capitol Hill. No one in the Navy would challenge him, from Chief of Naval Operations Arleigh A. Burke on down. Burke had assumed office in the year of Swart's humiliation and would remain CNO until 1961, an unprecedented six years. During Burke's watch as CNO, Rickover would consolidate his influence on the real Navy and would install his nuclear navy. Burke's biographer, Dr. David A. Rosenberg, would later say that in his opinion Burke's only major mistake while CNO was in not stopping Rickover.

At a reception for James on the day he took over as Chief of Bu-Ships, Rickover approached him in the receiving line and said, "Just remember one thing: I am not your shipbuilding assistant. I am your boiler-maker assistant. It's a nuclear boiler, to be sure, but I make your nuclear boilers."

In his recollection of that meeting, James said, "This was just part of his customary smoke screen. He no more intended to be just the Bureau of Ship's nuclear boiler maker than I intended to become an elf in fairy tales."

Like many theoretically superior officers before and since, James had to put up with Rickover as a price for staying in business. As long as James managed to keep Rickover out of the mainstream of BuShips work, Rickover and his Naval Reactor Branch stayed in its own nuclear navy, and the routine of BuShips was rarely disturbed. But when Rickover and certain other officers happened to cross paths, the war between the real navy and the nuclear navy suddenly became a duel between two men. Once, according to James, the clash became something very close to an actual duel.

One of James's outstanding officers was Robert L. Moore, Jr., the man who had been supervisor of shipbuilding at Electric Boat when the *Nautilus* was being built. Moore had been in Rickover's electrical section during World War II and was the man who at one time had been Rickover's hand-picked successor. All that was well behind Moore and Rickover by the time James took over as Chief of BuShips and selected Moore as his deputy.

"Bob Moore's feelings for Rickover are not fit to print," James said of those days. "It even broke out one day in my office when I had all the assistant chiefs—Rickover was one—in my office for discussion of ship-building efforts."

One of the participants in the meeting was Rear Admiral James M. Farrin, assistant chief for design, shipbuilding and fleet maintenance. Not until he attended the meeting, Farrin recalled, did he find out that Rickover had given a submarine-design contract to Electric Boat without having gone through Farrin's office. Farrin, according to James, "was a rather short-fused officer. He took on Rickover and challenged some of his statements. Bob Moore joined in with him.

"Rickover, in a moment of distress, which is seldom characteristic of his attitude, turned on Bob Moore and said something to the effect, 'Don't ever come to my office. Ever since you chased me around New London with a knife in your hand I've got a .38-caliber revolver in my desk, and I'll use it if you ever set foot in my office.' " Farrin recalled that threatening remarks were made "by Rickover and Moore," but Farrin did not remember Rickover's mentioning a gun.

James, in his recollections of working with Rickover, said that Rickover was continually purging Naval Reactors. This process—mentioned by several others who worked with him—ostensibly was inspired by Rickover's mania for perfection. But, as James viewed it, "anyone who began to challenge him . . . wasn't long for the program. He's arranged for the transfer out of the program, never to be re-entered into it, any number of senior engineering-duty officers who had tremendous technical capability, greater by many measures than Rickover ever possessed."

James described Rickover as "an expediter, a person who knew how to twist people's tails and get the maximum out of them by threatening, more than by leadership. . . . I have in mind at least four possible successors . . . who might have carried on the program with equal, if not greater, success because they wouldn't have been so brutal and wouldn't have achieved their pinnacle of success by stepping over the recumbent bodies of their associates, which was typical of the Rickover approach."

Rickover's tactics may have seemed like bloody bureaucratic vendettas inside the little world of BuShips. But beyond, in the greater Navy, Rickover was fostering a grand strategy—the nation must have an all-nuclear navy.

Although Rickover did get Congress to endorse his strategy by getting a law that mandated a nuclear navy, the real Navy and eventually Congress itself would resist the mandate. This was not mere resistance to a new form of propulsion; nor was it only a matter of money, considerable as that money might have been. Even if the architects of the Navy's future decided that a nuclear navy was needed, the price was too dear. The price was Rickover's domination of the entire U.S. Navy, and not just his nuclear navy.

In the *Nautilus* days, Rickover had set up his own communications structure, outside the existing Navy chain of command. After the *Nautilus* was built and after the concept of a nuclear-submarine force had been accepted by the Navy, Rickover's command structure burgeoned. Numerous times, in statements made by nuclear officers, the term "Rickover back-channel" appears. Commanding officers of nuclear-powered submarines and surface ships, as a matter of routine, communicated directly with Rickover. The NRB representatives in field offices, in contractors' plants, at shipyards, in nuclear schools, and at reactor prototypes were also under orders to report to him, in writing, every week.

The Navy already had two chains of command: tactical, by which ships and aircraft were organized for forward operations and combat; and administrative. For example, a task-force commander was normally tactical, having command of ships and aircraft for a combat task, while the "type" of commander, such as Commander, Cruiser-Destroyer Force, Pacific Fleet (ComCruDesPac), was administrative, being responsible for the material condition and training of cruiser and destroyers for assignment to operational commanders.

Rickover's chain of *communication* superseded both Navy chains of command, for in his AEC hat, as the man responsible for nuclear safety, all commanding officers of nuclear ships reported directly to him. Their reports were both routine and *in extremis.* For example, on June 14, 1960, while at Pearl Harbor, the nuclear submarine *Sargo* was rocked by an explosion as fire erupted in her after torpedo room. Conventional firefighting methods had little effect on the oxygen-fed flames. Commander John Nicholson ordered the after torpedo room sealed off from the rest of the ship and submerged in the shallow berth with the torpedo room's deck hatch open, flooding the compartment. The flames were soon extinguished. Reportedly, Nicholson raced ashore and telephoned Rickover before reporting details of the incident to ComSubPac or the other officers in his chain of command.

Rickover's routine communications with his commanding officers and other key personnel were in the form of a "personal letter." By his directive, the letter had to describe "all recurring nuclear-propulsion-plant training"—subjects covered, dates of training sessions and examinations, the names of the trainees, the instructors, *and* the monitors of the instructors; and, also, the grades on examinations, and how the instructors were prepared to give the training and the tests. Every one of these thousands of letters, throughout the entire history of nuclear propulsion, according to his testimony to Congress, has been read by Rickover.

One young officer who served aboard a Polaris missile submarine told the authors that the training and examinations added about three hours a day of what he saw as extra duty for himself and the more senior officers and enlisted men involved. "The CO, the exec, the engineering officer—they're all training themselves, too," he said. "Training is continual—exams, lectures, casualty drills, and interviews with the CO and the engineering officer. But that's all hardly nothing compared to the ORSE."

ORSE is the annual Operational Reactors Safeguards Examination of every nuclear-powered ship, her officers and her crew. This examination became part of standard Navy procedure on March 13, 1967, when Admiral Thomas Moorer, the Chief of Naval Operations, set up naval nuclear-propulsion examining boards on the staffs of the commanders in chief of the Atlantic and Pacific Fleets. Each board is headed by a senior captain who has served as the commanding officer of a nuclear-powered submarine or surface ship. Each board has teams that conduct the actual examinations. A team consists of four nuclear-trained officers—one a man who has been a commanding officer; the other three, men who served as engineering officers.

One aspect of the examination is called a crew quiz, a drill that usually lasts a day. "The pressures are almost indescribable," a ship's weapons officer wrote in a letter to a fellow officer. "The nucs have been working 12 to 16 hours per day, seven days a week for the past month conducting drills, seminars, class-room training and critiques. Everything the past week has been geared to this one inspection which lasts one day. All the nuclear-trained officers, from the CO on down to the most junior nuc, were walking around like zombies by the time the inspection team arrived yesterday."

The team stays aboard two to five days, working night and day to determine, by their Rickover-directed reckoning, whether there is anything wrong with the ship herself or with the way her crew and officers are operating her. Every record they ask for must be handed up, and their range of inquiry is so wide that hardly any aspect of the crew's behavior is beyond the team's mandate. When the team calls a casualty drill for, say, a reactor "discrepancy" (naval reactors do not have "accidents"), the performance of each person in the drill is methodically compared to the step-by-step procedures outlined in one of the countless manuals prepared by Rickover's staff. Any deviation is noted.

On the basis of the examination, the board gives the ship a grade—something called a "trend," a label that shows that things were worse or better than during the previous examination. The grade and trend are sent to Rickover and to the Chief of Naval Operations. Rickover later telephones the commanding officer and discusses the examination.

Rickover has always claimed that the examinations were for the purpose of safety and training, the only official basis for his interference in ship operations. But the sending of the examining board's report to the CNO indicates the report's true significance. For a bad grade from Rickover's team can mean that a nuclear-powered warship can be pulled from fleet operations and kept in port. It has happened. And, since Rickover's men have the power to take a U.S. Navy warship off the line, they—and he—have powers far beyond the original intentions concerning training and safety.

Information about ORSE is scarce. Reportedly, much of what goes on involves highly classified matters. Rickover himself stopped talking to the press years ago, and his nucs, for the most part, have emulated him. But two years after the birth of ORSE, a Congressman, in an unusual public chastisement of Rickover, said that he knew of four nuclear-submarine officers who were resigning because they had been harassed by Rickover's inspectors. "They were subject to what one called an inquisition and a third degree—incredible demands for perfection and demands interpreted by a single man." The statement was made during a hearing; Rickover did not respond to the Congressman's charge, and the hearing went on.

Complaints rarely emerge from the tight-lipped nuc-community, which is not encouraged to generate publicity.

Rickover was not above using nuclear inspections—or anything else—as a weapon against people. Ned Beach, the brilliant and talented captain of the giant nuclear submarine *Triton,* tells how he once accepted an invitation to give a high-school graduation address near his Connecticut home town. When Rickover learned of it, he invited Beach to do something else at the scheduled time. Instead, Beach went ahead with the graduation commitment.

Later, a Boy Scout group in Philadelphia asked the Navy to provide a nuclear submarine commander to address a major dinner. Beach was designated to attend, and he duly prepared his speech for the Saturday evening affair. The night before the scheduled event, he was called from

Washington and told that a surprise nuclear inspection was to be held on his ship the following day . . . and would last well into the evening.

The admiral who had directed Beach to speak had to name a last-minute substitute. According to Beach, "the Boy Scouts of Philadelphia never forgave me, nor did the local businessmen sponsors."

Writing about the incident later, Beach noted that "Saturday was a grim day, alleviated only by the facts that first, we passed the inspection handily, and second, it obviously had been made up not long previously, and third, the improvising inspection team had to be there too, including Rickover."

Nuclear-powered submarines and ships are run by the book, and the book was written by Rickover. The book takes the form of thick manuals published and continually updated by NRB. The manuals line book-shelves in reactor rooms and other compartments, where men on watch must follow NRB procedures to the letter. Any variation in these proce-dures must be reported in an "incident report" that goes to Rickover. A report may cover a technical problem, such as a valve malfunction. NRB responds with technical solutions that find their way into revisions of the manuals. For engineers, this is a standard procedure—a feeding back of information to improve performance.

Rickover, the reigning engineer of a navy within the Navy, has ex-panded the coverage of incident reports to include anything that, in his opinion, may constitute a deviation from his standards. This could mean an incident report on the obesity of crewmen. Or, in Rickover's own words, incident reports may "describe cases where, had the individual been better trained, he might have avoided an error in the performance of his job."

When one of the authors was invited to visit a nuclear submarine, still in the building yard and hence especially under Rickover's control, the Admiral "blew his stack," according to one nearby nuc. One of the officers involved with the invitation, naturally, wrote an "incident" report about the aborted visit. Like all incident reports that the authors have seen, this one was self-effacing, with the officer recalling that Rickover had told him he "would not be smart enough to know what's going on until he was 100 years old," and that the officer's performance during the incident "certainly bears out the wisdom of the Admiral's analysis."

The ultimate Rickover inspection is "the monitor watch," which is defined by its creator as "a surveillance conducted by someone, knowl-edgeable in a given area, to observe and detect deficiencies in perform-ance that occur during the period of observation." The monitoring is almost always at night, when routines may slacken. During the two hours a monitor has a subject under surveillance, the monitor supposedly fades into the shadows so that, according to Rickover's theory, the crewman forgets he is being watched. One young nuc who was monitored several times did not remember it that way. He said that on his submarines the NRB monitors were conspicuous: they did not wear uniforms and they carried notebooks. He also said that just the mention of "Naval Reactors" was enough to inspire fear in the crew.

The fear is not paranoia. In the intensely monitored world of the nuclear navy there are no trivial misdeeds. One day, a sailor going on watch in the engineering spaces of the nuclear submarine *Tautog* was handed a letter from his wife. Without opening the letter, he jammed it into his dungarees' pocket and entered the reactor control room. He became the subject of a discrepancy report—for taking "unauthorized literature" on watch. The nuclear navy's policy stemmed from the realization that in the real Navy sailors often had been observed reading while on watch. There could, of course, be no idle reading while on watch in nuclear-engineering spaces. But the rules could not be stretched. The unopened letter was literature, and it had been taken on watch, although it had never left the sailor's pocket.

Rickover's no-nonsense approach is based on the unassailable premise that there is no room for error aboard a nuclear submarine—or, to only a slightly lesser extent, aboard a nuclear-powered surface ship. He has said that, as an engineer, he did not subscribe to the faddish notion of "zero-error" machinery. All that is left is people, and by his decree, all that is needed is a system guaranteed to make people behave intelligently. Most nucs seem to believe that the so-called Rickover system is as simple as that. The nuclear navy lived by its own rules. An officer familiar with anti-submarine warfare once offered a particularly vivid example. He recalled seeing an ASW device classified as "confidential" aboard a Navy plane, where twelve crew members "had knowledge of its place in the total ASW picture and at least three of the crew members could operate it correctly." Aboard a nuclear submarine, this same piece of equipment was classified as top secret "and only the commanding officer fully knew what it was."

Nucs are often accused of being humorless and more interested in working overtime than in having a good time. That was the talk in the other Navy in 1975 when Commander Connelly D. Stevenson, the commanding officer of the nuclear submarine *Finback,* was relieved of his command for allowing a topless go-go dancer to perform on the submarine's deck as the ship went to sea.

Stevenson was a "mustang," to use the slang term for his accomplishment—he entered the Navy as an enlisted man and became an officer. (Enlisted men in the nuclear program become officers at about twenty times the rate of enlisted men in the other Navy.)

Stevenson not only had to be bright enough and industrious enough to get out of the enlisted ranks; he also had to work his way into nuclear training. And then he managed to climb to the pinnacle—command of a nuclear submarine. Once, during an overhaul, he and his officers worked eighty-five hours a week and his enlisted men sixty-five—this ashore, in a shipyard, where the work routine is traditionally eased. At sea the *Finback* spent more than half of one year at sea submerged.

Stevenson was skipper of the *Finback* that year and two other years. No one in the nuclear navy is watched more closely than a commanding officer. He had to be an outstanding officer, by Rickover's standards. Stevenson's fitness reports reflected his quality.

Then, in a matter of minutes, his career was over.

Stevenson's troubles began when some of his officers and men suggested that the *Finback* pull a stunt to impress the crew of the *Alexander Hamilton*, a neighboring nuclear submarine in Port Canaveral, Florida. The *Finback* is an attack submarine; the *Alexander Hamilton* is a missile-carrying submarine, a "boomer" in nuclear-navy parlance. Attack and boomer submarines traditionally are rivals.

Stevenson agreed to let a topless go-go dancer, known as Cat Futch, appear on the deck of the *Finback* as she sailed out of port—past the *Alexander Hamilton*—before submerging to begin a months-long patrol. Cat Futch did perform, and, after about ten minutes of topless go-going, she donned her white robe, got a kiss on the cheek from Stevenson, climbed into the accompanying pilot boat, and waved goodbye.

Although Cat Futch was an unusually dressed female visitor, she was technically a visitor and, as such, could be aboard the submarine, even when under way. But the book said that such visitations must be authorized by higher authority. Stevenson had not exactly followed the book. When word of what Stevenson had done began circulating in the Navy, many responsible officers—nuc and nonnuc—believed that he had hazarded his ship and should be disciplined. An admiral, still exasperated years later when he discussed the case, said, "What he did had nothing to do with a nuclear submarine. He was underway in a crowded harbor. His crew was paying attention to the dancer, not their duty. And besides that, he had solicited the money for that dancer from the crew. He was very much responsible. But the point is," the admiral continued, "that it was not a nuclear-navy matter. It was a *Navy* matter."

The *Finback* was somewhere in the Atlantic when the radio message came: Return to port. Stevenson was relieved of command and exiled to a desk in Norfolk while the *nuclear* navy decided what to do with him.

"He was close to being court-martialed," his lawyer, retired Navy Captain Joseph K. Taussig, Jr., recalled. "One of the charges being contemplated was conduct unbecoming an officer. He was advised to come to me. I told him I wanted to know what kind of an officer he was, and I asked for his last six fitness reports. His record was incredible. He was obviously of great value to the Navy."

Taussig managed to stave off the court-martial, although Stevenson's superiors were holding out for a charge that would have had Stevenson detached from command "for cause"—a death-blow to an officer's career. Stevenson's career was doomed anyway; he had embarrassed the nuclear navy.

Rickover himself did not appear publicly in the case, but, as Taussig remarked, "his hand was everywhere." At the order of the Chief of Naval Operations, Admiral James L. Holloway III—himself a nuc—a "punitive letter of admonition" was put in Stevenson's record. The Navy officially maintained that he had completed "a normal three-year command," and therefore he was not sent back to the *Finback*. He was dispatched to the Navy Research Laboratory's office in London—traditionally, sometimes a Siberia for officers who distress Rickover. Soon afterward, he left the Navy.

A man who had served with Stevenson told *The Washington Post* that Stevenson, by the standards of the nuclear navy, was not a model skipper. "He wasn't one of those technocrats who just breathed neutrons," the former shipmate said. "Why, he turned the wardroom table into a ping-pong table; would sometimes watch the movies with the crew in his pajamas—I mean those things were unheard of in the nuke submarine Navy."

In the other Navy, the use of marijuana had become an issue treated with about the same tolerance found on a typical college campus. By Rickover's rules in the nuclear navy, prospective candidates for nuclear power schools must get a waiver from the Chief of Naval Personnel and the Naval Reactors Branch if they had used marijuana even before entering the Navy. Anyone who is found to have used any illegal drug after enlistment is barred from entering the nuclear program. And any nuc who is caught using marijuana is instantly transferred to the other Navy. NRB relentlessly investigates reports of illegal drugs. After one such investigation, the Navy pulled thirty-three men (out of about one hundred) from the crew of a nuclear attack submarine.

But, oddly, Rickover sometimes will tolerate performances that would not be accepted in the other Navy. By long tradition, for example, a commanding officer who seriously hazards his ship never gets another chance to imperil another ship and crew. Many a commanding officer has a sign on his desk or bulkhead that reads, "A collision at sea can ruin your entire day." More to the point, a collision almost always means the ruin of an entire career.

But at least one submarine commander in the nuclear navy was given a second chance. Commander Ernest R. Barrett, an Academy graduate, after more than a year of NRB training, was named prospective commanding officer of the nuclear attack submarine *Permit,* being built at the Mare Island yard in California. On May 9, 1962, while the submarine was on precommissioning sea trials some thirty miles off the California coast, the *Permit* collided with a freighter. Both ships were damaged, but no one was injured.

Barrett was immediately relieved of command and given shore duty until an investigation could be held. After the investigation, he was assigned to a submarine tender. Then in January of 1964 he was given prospective commanding officer's training for nuclear-missile submarines, and in May he took command of the U.S.S. *Ethan Allen,* which carried sixteen Polaris strategic missiles and was bigger than his previous submarine. He successfully skippered that submarine until January 1965, when it collided with a merchant ship in the Mediterranean. He was again relieved of command and served ashore for the remainder of his Navy career, retiring six years later as a captain.

By 1972, Rickover was able to boast that he had trained 4,000 officers and 22,500 enlisted men. In that year the nuclear navy mustered 2,000 officers and 10,000 enlisted men—a navy, as Rickover put it, "larger than the entire Navy in the Spanish-American War."

Not all the men aboard nuclear ships were part of the nuclear navy. In the missile submarines, for example, because officers were hard to retain, the missile and supply officers, and sometimes others, were not nuclear-trained. Although they were qualified in submarines, none of them could ever become commanding officer or executive officer of a nuclear submarine. Similarly, in nuclear carriers and cruisers only in the engineering and reactor departments (650 and 250 men, respectively, on the *Enterprise*) are the crew nuclear-trained. Except for the commanding officer and the exec, the rest of the officers and men of nuclear carriers and cruisers generally are not nucs.

As the numbers of nuclear-trained crewmen and nuclear ships increased, the nucs rose higher in rank and command status. After his selection as rear admiral in 1963, Wilkinson became head of the Submarine Warfare Division in the Office of the Chief of Naval Operations, at the time the senior submariner on the OPNAV staff. His successor in the *Nautilus*, William R. Anderson, did not seek flag rank. After serving as aide to the Secretary of the Navy, Anderson left the Navy to enter politics. He served one term in the House. Dick Laning, the outspoken first skipper of the *Seawolf,* did not make admiral, nor did Ned Beach of the *Triton.* But James Calvert, first skipper of the *Swordfish,* and George P. Steele, first skipper of the *Seadragon,* and William W. Behrens, first skipper of *Skipjack,* all made vice admiral. Of the ten men who were first skippers of the first ten nuclear submarines, seven became admirals. So did many of their successors. Laning probably failed because he alienated Rickover by continuing to push for the sodium plant in the *Seawolf* long after the decision was made to scrap the project; Beach, former Presidential aide and novelist, was, in the words of a colleague, "too well known" and too outspoken. Still, the record for flag promotions among the men who as lieutenant commanders and commanders had been skippers of nuclear submarines was extraordinarily high.

The day of the nuc was drawing near.

The first dramatic recognition of the nuc's power came in 1971 when the CNO, Admiral Zumwalt, established the position of Deputy CNO for Submarine Warfare. Heretofore, dating back to World War II, only the aviation community had enjoyed its own deputy CNO—a so-called "E-ring baron," denoting an office on the Pentagon's prestigious E-ring and one of the principal advisors to the CNO. In his 1971 reorganization, Zumwalt set up deputy CNOs for submarines and surface ships at the same three-star level as the deputy for air. In the previous setup the surface community essentially had a deputy, who was senior to the two-star director of submarine warfare.

According to Zumwalt, "Setting up the Deputy CNO for Submarines made it easier to deal with the submarine community and with Rickover. It also gave me a senior submariner on my immediate staff." But discussing the new position in the terms of representing the nuclear navy, Zumwalt described the officer as a "papal representative."

The first Deputy CNO (Submarine Warfare)—or OP-02 in Navy jargon—was Vice Admiral Philip A. Beshany, a nonnuc. A year later Wilkinson, already a vice admiral, stepped into the deputy CNO billet. All subsequent OP-02s have been nucs.

By 1972 no fewer than ten of the Navy's forty-three vice admirals were nuclear-trained: Wilkinson and two others were in OPNAV, three had commands in the fleet, while de Poix, first skipper of the *Enterprise,* was head of the Defense Intelligence Agency; Peet, first skipper of the *Bainbridge,* was in the Department of Defense staff; and Behrens, the first skipper of the high-speed *Skipjack,* was assistant deputy administrator of the National Oceanic and Atmospheric Administration, a civilian agency in the Department of Commerce; and James Calvert was Superintendent of the Naval Academy. (Vice Admiral Rickover, on the retired list, was not counted as one of the forty-three vice admirals.)

The next year Holloway, the third commanding officer of the *Enterprise,* was the first nuclear-trained officer to reach the rank of full admiral, becoming Vice CNO to Admiral Zumwalt. While some observers predicted that that job made him the obvious successor when Zumwalt completed his four-year term in July 1974, others noted that no officer had ever moved from that assignment into the CNO's position. But Holloway did just that, becoming the Navy's twentieth CNO on June 29, 1974. By that time there was another four-star nuc as well, this one a submariner, Harold E. Shear, who had been skipper of one of the early Polaris submarines. In May 1974, as a full admiral, Shear became the Navy's senior officer in Europe.

Holloway's vice chief initially was Worth H. Bagley, a surface officer and strong critic of Admiral Rickover. Bagley retired in mid-1975, and his post was taken by Robert L. J. Long, a nuclear submariner and very strong supporter of Rickover. Long established still another nuc tradition, as probably only the second line officer in U.S. Navy history to achieve four-star rank without having commanded a surface ship.* He had commanded a diesel submarine and two nuclear Polaris submarines, and as a rear admiral commanded a group of auxiliary support ships. Long had also been the first nuc to command the Atlantic submarine force, replacing Vice Admiral Elton Grenfell in 1964. (In 1978, when Holloway retired, Long was considered a leading contender for the CNO position, but

---

* *Admiral Arthur W. Radford, Chairman of the Joint Chiefs of Staff from 1953 to 1957, never commanded a ship. He was executive officer of a carrier and was scheduled to become her captain in 1941, when recalled to Washington to direct the massive Navy pilot-training program. He was promoted to rear admiral in July 1943 as a carrier division commander.*

was instead named in 1979 to the post of commander in chief of all U.S. forces in the Pacific.)

Still another victory for the nuclear navy came in 1975 when Rear Admiral Kinnaird R. McKee—a former *Nautilus* officer and thus a member of a revered fraternity within a navy within the Navy—became superintendent of the Naval Academy. McKee was possibly unique in being both a full-fledged nuc and a trusted and respected assistant to Zumwalt, heading the CNO Executive Panel during much of Zumwalt's tenure.

McKee's appointment showed that nucs no longer were merely grim-faced "submarine jockeys" in their own little nuclear undersea world. *Nuc* became a familiar word in the passageways of Bancroft Hall and other buildings of the Naval Academy. In the midshipman's humor magazine, *The Log,* McKee became "Big Mac" and his changes in the curriculum inspired a vision of the "United States Naval Vocational and Technical School" of tomorrow. But McKee's curriculum changes would be overshadowed by a far more historic event—the admittance of the Academy's first female midshipmen. McKee managed the event with the no-nonsense authority of a nuc and the grace of an old-fashioned professional.

Many other nuclear-trained officers moved up into key Navy flag positions. Mike Michaelis, second skipper of the *Enterprise* and one of the best-liked four-star admirals of the modern Navy, became Chief of Naval Material in 1975. He had responsibility for all of the *systems commands* (which the bureaus had been redesignated in 1966). Michaelis, in turn, was succeeded as head of Naval Material by a nuclear submariner, Admiral Alfred J. Whittle, while Long was succeeded as Vice CNO by nuc James Watkins. Thus, nucs—always the best and the brightest—rose naturally into the top positions of the Navy from the middle 1970s onward.

Rickover's boldest thrust toward power in the other navy came when, with hardly a ripple of hostile reaction, he founded his own graduate school—a kind of remedial course for admirals and other senior officers not fortunate enough to have been nucs. The school was established in 1976 at the Naval Reactors Facility in Idaho Falls, Idaho, one of the least naval of sites and, to Rickover, one of the most cherished of historical places, for here the *Nautilus* reactor prototype had been born. Perhaps as importantly, here could be found the three basics for a Rickover operation: isolation, control, and secrecy. The isolation was not only geographical but also psychological, for Idaho Falls was not a traditional duty station—such as San Diego or Pearl Harbor—where old shipmates might turn up, where an admiral might fondly recall days as an ensign. Idaho Falls was strictly NRB country, a place under total Rickover control. Because the students would be dealing with highly classified matters, Rickover also had a built-in guarantee of secrecy. Although graduates might indignantly swap sea stories about the place, there was little likelihood that much would be written about it.

The Idaho program was called the Senior Officer Ship Material Readiness Course. Its official purpose was "to provide senior officers with the knowledge and understanding necessary to improve the Navy's material readiness."

A nonnuc destroyer officer, Commander David C. Clark, was one of the "senior naval officers being dragged to the Naval Reactors Facility" for the course. But he saw the course as offering possible solutions to problems besetting the post-Vietnam Navy, not merely the nuclear navy—a decline in the number and quality of personnel, the increasing complexity of modern ships. These problems, Clark believed, were severely impairing the material condition and operational readiness of the fleet.

That was Rickover's perspective exactly.

Besides the fourteen weeks of "classroom and practical instruction" in Idaho Falls, the students received two days of class work at the Propulsion Engineering School at the Navy's Great Lakes Naval Training Center; two days of practical instruction at a naval shipyard, and four days aboard a ship, where the students were to apply what they had learned.

The first class consisted of nine admirals and sixteen captains, all of them headed for sea commands, many of them having no direct involvement with nuclear-powered ships. Naval officers can best appreciate the spectacle. For a civilian, an analogy might be a situation in which members of the board of, say, U.S. Steel spend sixteen weeks in steel mills being told about steel by instructors from Republic Steel. The potential for affronts was explosive, especially since Rickover had long proclaimed a disinterest in the protocol of rank and privilege. The director of the course was a civilian from NRB. The tone of the course was set by Rickover.

That tone resounded in the room when he spoke to the first graduating class. Rickover strode onto stage, where an official of the school had set up a chair and a table. On the table was a bowl of fruit and nuts (a standard item on the standard list of what to have available when Rickover appears).

"What is this *shit!*" Rickover shouted, according to one student who later shared his recollections with the authors. "Get rid of this garbage. . . . Get me another chair."

His startled audience heard a speech remembered as a tirade of jagged, disconnected phrases and proclamations: "There never was professionalism until I brought it to the Navy. . . . I am the best engineer . . . the best historian . . . in the Navy. . . . The Navy was never professional until I came along. John Paul Jones and other naval heroes just stood in the rigging. . . . A warrant gunner fought the ship and a warrant sailing master sailed the ship . . . [Jones] was just a figurehead. . . . Only when I came into the Navy did it become professional—when I put engineers in command of nuclear ships and submarines. . . ."

The senior officers looked at each other with embarrassment if they were nonnuc; with stoicism if they were nucs. In deference to Rickover's own dislike of uniforms, they had appeared in civilian suits. But even their wardrobe inspired a pointless comment: "I'm glad you're in civilian clothes. . . . You don't deserve to wear uniforms."

What was the purpose of such a speech? What was the purpose of the course? How did those senior officers get into that room in Idaho? The Navy gives this official answer: such training "is considered to be extremely beneficial for officers enroute to major sea commands and certain staff assignments who have not had the opportunity to develop a strong engineering background. The Chief of Naval Personnel makes the determination of who will attend."

The school was the brain child of a man who despised the Naval Academy, who was contemptuous of the Naval War College, and who for decades had been attacking conventional methods of education both in public schools and in the Navy. Some critics of Rickover's own educational philosophy have suggested, off the record, that the Senior Officer Ship Material Readiness Course, at best, provided Rickover with a platform for indoctrinating officers into the ways of the nuclear navy, and at worst, gave Rickover an arena where he could act out his hates and frustrations.

Retired Vice Admiral John T. Hayward, a longtime supporter of Rickover, openly ridiculed the school as the "height of Admiral Rickover's foolishness." Writing in the Naval Institute *Proceedings,* Hayward, a former president of the Naval War College, said, "The educational requirements of a modern professional naval officer have little relationship to his idea of what a 'nuke spook' should be."

Graduates who shared their school experiences with the authors were asked whether anything they had learned in Idaho had helped them to run their commands. One thought back carefully to classes that included lessons on a prototype of a nuclear carrier's propulsion system and hours of mathematics review. He said, "Yes. It did help. The course showed me how to get much more from my ships and my men. But to do that I needed Ph.D. chemists, and what the nonnuclear surface navy gets are ghetto dropouts."

And he had a good word for nucs. "The surface navy loves to get nuclear-submarine dropouts because they are highly qualified and well trained." In contrast, enlisted men in the nonnuclear navy learn from training films that often are mere cartoons and from training manuals pegged to sixth-grade reading levels.

The nuclear navy was, by the 1970s, becoming the better navy. It was receiving considerable money and brains, more of the best and the brightest. Nucs were running large areas of the Navy and, in many ways, remaking it. The 1970s were the years of the nucs. And if one day could be circled as the Day of the Nucs it would be Inauguration Day, 1977, when former Lieutenant James Earl Carter, Jr., became President—and Nuc One.

Carter and Rickover had been linked from the day in 1974 when Carter announced his candidacy in a speech that ended with these words: "It is now time to stop and ask ourselves the question which my last commanding officer, Admiral Hyman Rickover, asked me and every other young naval officer who serves or has served in an atomic submarine. For our nation—for all of us—the question is, 'Why not the best?' "

The question became Carter's campaign slogan and the title of his campaign autobiography. Rickover's question, according to Carter's account, was in response to Carter's admission that he did not always do his best. (Rickover asked, "Why not?"—using two words, rather than the four that became famous.)

In his uneventful Navy career, Carter had only briefly encountered Rickover. When Carter was the man known as "Jimmy Who?," Rickover was one of the millions of Americans who asked that question. During Carter's ascendancy—some accounts put the time as late as Carter's nomination—Rickover reportedly had Lieutenant Carter's personnel file pulled so he could refresh his memory about the man who had written: "He may not have cared or known it, certainly not at that time, but Admiral Rickover had a profound effect on my life—perhaps more than anyone except my parents."

Such sentiments have been expressed by countless nucs. Many of them are hero worshipers with only one lifelong hero. Yet, like Carter, they had little or no close contact with their hero. Carter tried to explain in *Why Not the Best?* that the lack of a relationship was, in some way, the bond. "It was an impersonal demand of a perfectionist," Carter wrote. Rickover "demanded from me a standard of performance, and a depth of commitment, that I had never realized before that I could achieve."

Carter, wanting to describe himself to the American people, chose to emphasize that he had been trained in the nuclear navy. He obviously believed that by displaying this facet he would show qualities appealing to voters. Early in his campaign he called himself "a nuclear physicist and peanut farmer." When some reporters questioned the nuclear half of that description, Carter began describing himself as "a nuclear engineer."

Carter's actual nuclear career consisted of eleven months at the Knolls Atomic Power Labortory near Schenectady, where he was assigned to the crew being trained for the second nuclear submarine, the *Seawolf.* Richard Laning, the first commanding officer of the *Seawolf,* said later that Carter "never finished the first part of the course."

Nucs, then as now, saw themselves as very special people. Lieutenant Carter believed that if he stayed in the Navy he would become Chief of Naval Operations. Such is the evangelical faith of the nuc in himself and his mission. Nucs knew they were vital to the Navy—even though the Navy did not appreciate them or their special qualities. Carter, in transforming his quest for CNO into a quest for the Presidency, carried to the ultimate level the message of a Rickover disciple: For a good President, vote for a nuc.

On levels below Presidential, the message is merely this: We can do it not just better but best. Nucs are taught to think that way. Throughout his candidacy and Presidency, Carter publicized the thoughts of a nuc. If we look at what he wrote, not as the words of a Presidential candidate but as the words of a naval officer, we can gain some insight into the type of men who made it to high posts in the Navy and spread the gospel of the nuclear navy.

"He was unbelievably hardworking and competent," Carter wrote of Rickover,

and he demanded total dedication from his subordinates. We feared and respected him and strove to please him. I do not in that period remember his ever saying a complimentary word to me. The absence of a comment was his compliment; he never hesitated to criticize severely if a job were not done as well as he believed it could be done. He expected the maximum from us, but he always contributed more.

A compliment in the Navy is formally a "well done"; informally, it is an "atta-boy." One consistent criticism of nuclear officers is that they rarely give their men "atta-boys."

Carter told of flying to Seattle with Rickover—characteristically at the end of the day, for days were for work and nights were for travel. "It was a long flight in the commercial propjet plane," Carter wrote.

He began to work when the plane took off, and we were determined to do the same. After a few hours the rest of us gave up and went to sleep. When we awoke, Rickover was still working.

Hard work twelve or eighteen hours a day, six or seven days a week—that is how nucs give testimony to their devotion to Rickover's principles.

Carter admitted, and both critics and supporters agreed, that his working style resembled Rickover's. A politician in Georgia once said Carter tried to run the state the way he would run a submarine. Carter's White House staff director, Hamilton Jordan, eventually was won over to the Rickover-Carter way because Carter "expects us to be like him—well-disciplined, well-organized perfectionists."

When Carter became President, word was passed in the Navy that Rickover would enter the White House inner circle. The first display of Rickover's potential influence came a month after Inauguration Day. The occasion was only a lunch, but it was in the residence wing of the White House. As an intimate social event, it did not appear on the President's daily schedule. That luncheon was publicized, complete with an official White House photograph of the Rickovers and the Carters. But visitors a President does not want publicized can be slipped in unseen and unchronicled via the social route, and reporters wondered if future meetings would be hidden in that way. Rumors persisted that Rickover would become a gray eminence, a cherished White House elder in the tradition of Bernard Baruch and W. Averell Harriman.

As the new administration organized itself, a public relationship between Rickover and the President seemed to be developing. It remained to be seen whether Rickover would become a Presidential adviser. But at first Carter certainly did allow himself to be used as a publicity-harvesting celebrity for the Rickover navy.

In late May, with a great flourish of media coverage, the President and Mrs. Carter joined Rickover for a nine-hour voyage aboard the new nuclear submarine *Los Angeles*. Rickover, an old hand at underwater symbolism, saw to it that the President received red-carpet treatment. Carter later said the submarine's crew "acted as if I was not there. They didn't stand at attention when I came into their compartments. . . . I didn't go aboard to be treated as a high official." (Perhaps Carter should have recalled some of his own Navy training; men working in a ship do not come to attention when a senior enters the compartment.) Carter was spared the sight of five *Los Angeles* crewmen judged to look too fat; the five were transferred to another submarine for the day.

Carter went aboard the submarine bareheaded; he emerged wearing a Navy baseball cap with "Commander in Chief Jimmy Carter" in gold letters. Like numerous Congressmen and Presidents who proceeded him on Rickover-sponsored underwater junkets, President Carter ate with the crew, operated the submarine controls (posing for photographs side by side with Rickover at the control consoles), and handled the throttle of the nuclear plant.*

Rumors persisted that Rickover would play a role in the new administration. But no documentation of his presence came until October 1977, when *Los Angeles Times* political writer Robert Shogan revealed that Rickover had given a supposedly secret background lecture to members of Carter's domestic-policy staff. Although the White House would not comment on Rickover's hour-long lecture, Shogan managed to get the gist of what Rickover said—"Liberally salted with 'hells' and 'damns.' "

The story said that, in Rickover's view, the country "is basically 'oligarchical'—that is, dominated by wealthy businessmen and other special interests." Rickover said he saw himself in adversary relationships with federal bureaucrats and greedy defense contractors. He said that he never backed away from a fight. "Of course," he added, if he has any problems, "I can just go in and see the President."

---

* *Rickover took Presidents Eisenhower, Kennedy, and Carter aboard nuclear submarines while they were occupants of the White House. Rickover made up for an apparent oversight by taking former President Nixon aboard the attack submarine* Cincinnati *in November 1980. The submarine went to sea and Nixon had dinner underwater with the crew. The Navy gave the trip no publicity. (President Ford had gone to sea in a nuclear sub as a Congressman.)*

"He was grinning when he said it," Shogan reported. "But some in the audience were not sure he was kidding."

"Some policy staffers," Shogan wrote, "regarded Rickover's performance not only as an intriguing glimpse of the Admiral but also as an illuminating insight into the personality of their own boss in the Oval Office."

One staffer explained. "You could see something of the same black and white attitudes that Carter has, the same sense of conviction on a broad range of issues, and the same sense of being an outsider."

Regardless, many White House staffers left the historic Rickover briefing feeling that Rickover had wasted their time. "Some people were upset because he kept referring to people, to everybody, as 'civilians.' What he had to say was almost totally useless to us," one staffer complained. Never again did Rickover publicly surface inside the White House. And no further stories appeared about off-the-record appearances of Rickover with Carter or Carter's advisers.

It was truly the "day of the nucs" as Rickover stood in the White House conference room lecturing to his protégé's chief advisers. Four miles away, across the Potomac River, in the Pentagon another Rickover-trained officer, James Holloway, was holding forth as Chief of Naval Operations, assisted by a platoon of three- and four-star admirals who were nucs—Long, his Vice CNO; Doyle, his surface deputy; Watkins, his chief of personnel; Griffiths, his submarine deputy; Michaelis, his chief of material; Kaufman, his director of command and control; Bryan, his chief of shipbuilding; Petersen, his head of aircraft procurement; and many lesser deputies and aides.

At the same time, plans were being laid down for further Carter participation in the nuclear shipbuilding program, Rickover's *raison d'être.* The President himself would be the guest speaker at the commissioning of the nuclear cruiser *Mississippi,* named for the home state of John Stennis, powerful chairman of the Senate Armed Services Committee, while Rosalynn Carter would preside at the keel laying for a nuclear-missile submarine named for the Carters' home state of Georgia.

But to some observers, the Rickover-Carter axis was an obvious façade that was cracking. Perhaps the President looked to the nuclear submarine as a link to his past; or even justification for his striving to be "the best." Or, to be unkind, strictly for political points that Rickover could gain for him with a Congress and press sympathetic to Rickover.

More obvious, a few days after the informal Carter-Rickover private luncheon, President Carter sent his first defense plan to Capitol Hill for

Congressional approval and funding. The defense plan, put forward by Dr. Harold Brown, the new Secretary of Defense, called for cancellation of a planned nuclear-strike cruiser, no funds for upgrading the cruiser *Long Beach*'s weapons to the new Aegis air-defense system, and no plans for building additional nuclear carriers. The Carter-Brown budget even reduced the number of nuclear attack submarines from the two requested in the Ford proposal to only one.

Rickover himself went to the Hill on February 22 to personally appeal for more funds for his nuclear ships. As usual, his testimony—15,000 words—was well organized, well articulated, and highly persuasive. Calling attention to the threats posed by the Soviet Union and Pentagon systems analysts, he again pointed out that "Congress has had to step in many times . . . to keep the nuclear-submarine program going."

As the special hearing before the House Armed Services Committee's sea-power subcommittee drew to a close, Representative Charles Wilson, confused over the Administration's cuts in nuclear ships, noted, "I know that there are games being played, Admiral. I thought you were a good friend of President Carter's, I read that in the papers. You can't believe everything you read in the newspapers."

"We are," Rickover said.

"But it looks like the staff has made up his budget for him," Wilson continued.

"The President and I are good friends," Rickover replied. "But I never take advantage of my position for any special pleading. I will never do that."

If Rickover did not plead with Carter, he also didn't plead with Admiral Holloway, the CNO. The next day, February 23, Holloway told the same subcommittee that he supported the Carter-Brown program, in part because he was concerned with maintaining the current fleet as well as building for the future. Rather than building either nuclear-strike cruisers with Aegis or converting the *Long Beach,* Holloway supported spending the funds on oil-burning DDG-47 destroyers armed with Aegis.

The Carter-Brown Administration would never again ask funds for nuclear-powered surface ships. Indeed, when Congress did vote over two billion dollars for a fifth nuclear carrier in 1978, Carter vetoed the defense procurement bill, saying that he had more important programs for the funds. The following year the Congress again voted another *Nimitz*-class nuclear flattop. This time Carter approved the ship, but only because of increasing national concern on defense issues stemming from the Panama Canal and SALT debates, and the status of the 1980 Presidential campaign. Clearly, Carter and Brown were not responsive to Rickover's wants.

Amid the controversy over Carter's decision to veto the nuclear carrier and cut back on other nuclear ship construction, Carter appeared on the same platform with Rickover. The occasion was the commissioning of the nuclear-missile cruiser *Mississippi*. Carter assured the Navy, especially the nuclear navy, that he would continue to support "the submarine-launched ballistic missile component" of America's strategic defenses. Rickover hailed Carter as "one of our finest leaders and a prophetic thinker who will be recognized for his true value as a great legislator." Great legislators, of course, do not live in the White House and rule the Executive Branch. Rickover, a master of words, seemed to have found a mischievous way to twit his commander in chief. But if his odd praise was given in wit, no one publicly made note of it.

Rickover's influence on the Hill was noticeably waning, but he still had enough power to fight against what his commander in chief wanted, just as he had under every President since Truman. Rickover did not succeed in getting Congress to override the 1978 carrier veto. With the carrier doomed, Washington and the Navy knew that Rickover did not have crucial influence over "Nuc One." And so, only a short time after its promising dawn, the Day of the Nuc passed.

A relic remained. On President Carter's desk was a plaque that read: *O God, Thy Sea Is So Great And My Boat Is So Small.* The plaque had been presented to him by Rickover, on the day of the famous luncheon.

In the Navy itself, Rickover now would be criticized more openly than ever before. A second wave of rumors buoyed the criticism: Carter would not reappoint Rickover; Carter would move Rickover into some obscure spot in the Department of Energy. Counteracting rumors appeared—Rickover would be made Secretary of Energy; Rickover would be called in to solve the energy crisis; Rickover would police the nuclear industry in the wake of Three Mile Island.

None of this happened. But the criticism of Rickover in official and unofficial channels did continue. And nowhere was that criticism more potent than in the pages of the Naval Institute *Proceedings.* Where critical remarks about the nuclear navy had been few and then usually muted, a young nuclear-trained officer exposed what he believed was wrong with the nuclear navy. Significantly, the officer's criticism was adjudged by the Naval Institute's editorial board to be the prize essay on leadership for 1978, winning the annual Vincent Astor Memorial Contest. The editorial board, chaired by an active rear admiral, with six other active Navy, Marine and Coast Guard officers as members, awarded the author a cash prize and published his essay in the *Proceedings,* the Navy's professional journal.

The author, Lieutenant Ralph E. Chatham, had entered the Navy through Rickover's favorite gate, Naval ROTC. He had a doctorate in physics, had served in a diesel submarine, attended the Submarine Officers Advance Course at New London, and, when his essay was published, was about to go aboard a nuclear submarine as navigator. Although not trained as a nuc, he obviously had the credentials to address the nuclear navy.

"Each nuclear submarine," Chatham wrote, "is commanded by two people: its captain and the Director, Division of Naval Reactors [NR]." The revelation, so stark in print, had been spoken numerous times down through the years. Ever since the *Nautilus,* nuclear and nonnuclear officers had been telling each other sea stories about Rickover's control. Never, though, would a naval officer go into print with anything directly critical of Rickover.

Chatham broke the taboo. Rickover, said the essay, "has been known to place a call to a submarine's engineering space telephone and then personally direct the commanding officer how to organize his watch bill. . . . The Director of NR personally controls everything. . . . This chain of command has the power to stop the operations of a ship without warning."

The "tunnel vision" of nucs, Chatham wrote, keeps the junior officer tied to the power plant. He does not see his submarine as a weapons system. Chatham, who had served on a diesel-powered submarine, apparently drew from his own experience to wryly note: "this tunnel vision can result in such situations as the only operating diesel submarine in a squadron firing well over half the total number of exercise torpedoes launched by all the ships in the squadron."

The essay focused on an overwhelmingly important issue—trust—by looking at the question of "rudder orders" and at the seemingly trivial matter of "attaboys." Because "initiative is not a well-rewarded trait" in the nuclear navy, Chatham wrote, "the most successful nuclear officer is one who can justify his every action with specific requirements of higher authority. . . .

"A leader who does what he is told and ensures that he is told everything he must do does not make mistakes. . . .

"The need for rudder orders also leads to a bizarre situation in which form and ritual are more important than the safety they are intended to promote. The question that is asked is not 'What is safe?' but 'What will NR think?' "

In the nuclear navy, "if you can show somebody else is wrong, that is a mark for you. It appears to be a general policy of NR that no one should be permitted to know that he has done well: hubris causes mistakes. . . . The significance of not giving deserved praise is obvious, yet the policy persists. . . ."

The logic of the nuclear navy holds, according to Chatham, that the key to success is never to make a mistake, that a "leadership habit of trust inevitably leads to some mistakes," and therefore "a leader on a nuclear submarine cannot afford to trust his people."

Among those who reacted to Chatham's essay was retired Vice Admiral Ray Peet, first commanding officer of the nuclear-powered cruiser *Bainbridge*. Peet said that Rickover "never attempted to interfere in the military operations of the ship." But, while denying that there were two chains of command, Peet did say, "As CO of a nuclear-powered ship, I was always comforted to know that NR was available and willing to help whenever I had material or personnel problems." Peet's denial inadvertently proved Chatham's charge that the nuclear navy operated outside the regular Navy, for the CO of a nonnuclear cruiser would be supported operationally by his fleet or force commander; only if testing a new piece of gear or about to go into a shipyard for overhaul or modernization would a nonnuclear-ship CO discuss receiving help or support from a "bureau" or systems command in Washington. The nonnuc had only the U.S. Navy's chains of command for support; the nuc had them *and* NRB, and not always in that order.

By July of 1978, when Lieutenant Chatham's essay appeared, the Day of the Nuc had passed. Indeed, 1978 became the year in which the *Proceedings* opened its "forum" to many of the problems perceived in the nuclear navy. While Chatham's essay had the distinction of being cited by the editorial board of the Naval Institute, two other highly significant articles also appeared that year. First, a Marine captain on the Academy staff, K. W. Estes, in a letter published in the *Proceedings,* addressed the "typical . . . nuc breed, which sees enemies in virtually every corner mostly because of its lack of breadth in military knowledge and unfamiliarity with defense requirements at large." And, in the same issue that contained Chatham's essay, Robert M. Chapman, a civilian, wrote about the Navy's attack-submarine problem. Chapman's article, based on a secret paper he had prepared two years earlier while in the Department of

Defense, directly challenged the nuclear-submarine designs as dictated by Admiral Rickover.

The criticism led to many thousands of subsequent words of commentary in the *Proceedings*. Never again would the nuclear navy—and Rickover himself—be safe from adverse comment in the pages of the Navy's professional journal.

The Years of the Nucs had peaked. The triumphantly Presidential Day of the Nuc had come and gone. But the nuclear navy itself had surfaced as a reality that had to be acknowledged. It would not go away. Its power, once concentrated in one man, had spread throughout the Navy. More than thirty-five percent of the major warships were nuclear, and nucs had spread permanently through the hierarchy of the Navy. They would not go away.

Neither would Rickover. In 1979, five of his civilian deputies retired, and rumors of his retirement again glimmered. But in that year the funds for his nuclear carrier reappeared, and this time President Carter had to surrender; he signed the nuclear-carrier authorization that he had vetoed the year before. And in October, three months before Rickover's latest biennial appointment expired, the office of the Assistant Secretary of Defense issued a three-sentence press release that announced what the Pentagon had been announcing every two years since 1963: Admiral Rickover had been reappointed "Head of the Nuclear Propulsion Program for an additional two years."

THE RICKOVER NAVY

This ship and her sisters are the finest products of the naval shipbuilding art ever fabricated. The officers and men who run her are the most carefully selected, the best-trained and educated, and the most highly motivated naval seamen the world has ever know. Crew and ship together represent the furthest advance of naval power in all history. Each is a fitting match for the other. . . .

These men make this ship effective as one of the basic components of United States national power. And that power, to my way of thinking, is one of the few guarantees of peace and freedom left for mankind anywhere on this small planet. . . .

The size of our Polaris fleet, forty-one ships, and the projected size of our nuclear-powered attack-submarine fleet, about sixty-eight ships, was in the making as long as a decade ago. The numbers were picked to meet the threat of those years. They were fixed long before the Soviet Union expanded its naval operations around the world and before it accelerated its nuclear-submarine construction program. They were fixed before the Chinese posed a nuclear threat, before France undermined NATO and before Great Britain abdicated as a world power.

Many in Congress share my concern that these numbers have not been reevaluated in terms of the changing threat. It is absolutely incredible to me that our nuclear-submarine building program should be grinding to a halt at the very moment the dangers around us so obviously multiply. It must be comforting to the Russians—though somewhat puzzling to them as it is to me—that we should stop competing just as they start to compete.

In closing let me pay tribute to a great American patriot who is more responsible than any other for the excellence of both the ships and the men of our Nuclear Navy. He is the man whose "close but benevolent supervision" for many years has made it possible for these strong ships to sail swiftly and for their magnificent crews to sail safely on their missions. This nation owes deep gratitude to Vice Admiral H. G. Rickover.

REPRESENTATIVE CRAIG HOSMER,
Joint Committee on Atomic Energy,
at commissioning ceremonies for the
U.S.S. *Gato,* Groton, Connecticut,
January 25, 1968

Building More Submarines

Twenty-five years after the *Nautilus* went to sea Admiral Rickover could proudly boast to Congress that the Navy had—primarily because of Congressional support—a nuclear fleet of 126 warships: 74 attack submarines, 41 strategic-missile submarines, 3 aircraft carriers, and 8 missile cruisers. Also powered by atomic energy was the unarmed research submersible NR-1. A formidable fleet indeed, comprising in 1980 over one third of the Navy's warships.

The attack submarines—two thirds of the nuclear navy—were built for the specific purpose of hunting and killing Soviet submarines. According to Rickover, "the single most effective weapon for detecting, localizing and killing the nuclear submarine has been and will continue to be the high-speed, quiet, highly capable nuclear attack submarine."

The anti-submarine role was a radical departure for American undersea craft, which in the Pacific during World War II had been used mostly for attacking merchant ships. This was the same anti-shipping role that German U-boats had had in the Atlantic during both World Wars. In the postwar era the Soviet Union had neither a surface fleet nor a large merchant marine. However, the Russians did have a tradition of large submarine forces. This tradition, coupled with the Russians' appropriation of German U-boat technology and the internment of German scientists and engineers, gave them the potential for building a large fleet of advanced undersea craft. In a future war these might try to sever the United States from Europe, as the U-boat flotillas had sought to do. And, at some future date, Soviet missile-firing submarines—again based on German developments during the war—could threaten American cities. The U.S. Navy thus sought to justify advanced submarines on the basis of the anti-submarine or "hunter-killer" mission.

The U.S. Navy developed a two-phase approach for getting advanced submarines: First, large numbers of recently built wartime submarines were modernized to incorporate late-model U-boat features, including large batteries, streamlined hulls and conning towers, recessed deck fitting, and no guns. This program was known by the acronym GUPPY, for Greater Underwater Propulsion Power. Submerged speed had not been important in World War II, because U.S. submarines had long distances to travel to the combat zone in the Far East and could do so on the surface at high speed, day and night, for most of the way. In the combat zone they tend to operate submerged. But in the submarine-versus-submarine war, underwater speeds higher than the fleet boat's maximum of ten knots were needed.

The naval shipyard at Portsmouth, New Hampshire, undertook the first two GUPPY conversions on a high-priority basis in 1946. Electrical systems were a major consideration in the conversion, and these were worked out by the newly arrived design superintendent at Portsmouth, Captain Robert L. Moore, Jr. He had served most of World War II as senior assistant to the head of the BuShips electrical section, H. G. Rickover.

The second method of obtaining advanced submarines was through new construction. In the fiscal 1947 budget the Navy was able to gain funds to start a new class of attack submarines. These two long-range, 2,100-ton *Tang*-class submarines were based largely on German U-boat technology and could attain sixteen knots submerged. For fiscal 1948 there were funds for two more large *Tang*s, plus the *K-1*, a 1,000-ton prototype for small "killer" submarines that were to lie in wait off Soviet ports and in narrow straits to ambush Soviet submarines going to sea.

At that time the U.S. Navy's leaders felt that six new submarines should be built every year to provide a force of not fewer than one hundred modern submarines. But funds for new ships were limited, and the fiscal 1949 budget had only four undersea craft, two more *Tang*-class boats plus two more of the diminutive K class. Increasing postwar austerity plus emphasis on strategic bombers, at the expense of Navy programs, cut back even this small submarine effort, and the fiscal 1950 budget—which President Truman sent to Congress in 1949—provided for only one submarine, an unarmed research craft, the *Albacore*, to evaluate an improved underwater shape. Similarly, the fiscal 1951 budget—voted before the outbreak of the Korean War—contained funds for only a small, unarmed training submarine.

The flood gates for naval construction opened when the Korean War, in large part a naval war, began in late June 1950. Defense spending was also spurred by fears that Korea was only the prelude to monolithic

Communist aggression in Europe as well. Most of the new-construction funds were for aircraft carriers and their escorts, plus amphibious ships and minesweepers. Older destroyers and submarines were modernized for anti-submarine warfare.

Three combat submarines were funded in fiscal 1952—two radar pickets (conventional submarines with large radars to provide early warning of air attacks against carrier task forces) and the *Nautilus*. The Navy, responding to Rickover's two-pronged pressure—from within Bu-Ships and through the AEC—requested the nuclear submarine in the budget. A year later, the fiscal 1953 budget funded a diesel-electric submarine that could carry the Regulus (a surface-launched cruise missile that evolved from the German V-1), and the second nuclear submarine, the *Seawolf.*

The *Seawolf* would test the sodium-cooled reactor, using liquid sodium as the heat exchanger between the nuclear reactor and the steam propulsion plant. The *Seawolf* would be similar in over-all design to the *Nautilus,* but slightly larger because of the size of the sodium plant.

The plant was designed and built, under Rickover's supervision, by the Knolls Laboratory, which was operated by General Electric. Originally designated SIR (for Submarine Intermediate Reactor), the SIR Mark A reactor would be a test and training plant ashore, in West Milton, New York, and the Mark B would be installed in the submarine. The submarine, constructed at Electric Boat, would be launched on July 21, 1955.

Rickover had pushed for two alternative reactor plants, the pressurized-water plant of the *Nautilus* and the sodium-cooled plant of the *Seawolf.* Liquid sodium was to carry the heat from the reactor to the heat-exchange system, where the secondary water-steam loop would be separated from radioactive sodium. Subsequently, a third fluid system, using sodium-potassium, was also used to separate the sodium loop from the water-steam loop, adding complexity to the plant. According to Moore, who became Navy supervisor of shipbuilding at Electric Boat in 1952, the shift to sodium-potassium was made "without paying any attention to the NRL [Naval Research Laboratory] reports on catastrophic failures of stainless steel in superheated steam with as little as ten parts per million of potassium present."

The *Seawolf*'s reactor plant reached a self-sustaining chain reaction (became critical) for the first time on June 25, 1956. Dockside tests began and leaks were discovered on August 20, as one of the superheaters and some of the steel piping failed. The plant was shut down, and during that process additional leaks of the sodium-potassium alloy were found.

More than three months were needed to modify the *Seawolf*'s steam-generating plant to correct the problems and resume dockside tests. The plant superheaters were bypassed, meaning that full power could not be achieved. A few days after testing was resumed, more sodium-potassium leaks were detected, and further repairs were needed.

Rickover hovered around the *Seawolf* as much as possible, but at times he had to be away. One of his trips took him to Rome, where he was to receive an award. He would miss a crucial series of component tests prior to the starting-up of the entire reactor system.

One Sunday afternoon, as tests were being conducted, the phone rang on a barge alongside the *Seawolf*. It was a long-distance call for Commander Richard B. Laning, her prospective commanding officer. He instinctively knew who was calling. As Laning remembers the call, Rickover began by asking: "Guess where I am."

"Obviously in the Vatican," Laning replied.

"Guess where in the Vatican."

"I don't know."

"In the basement, helping to repair a Raphael painting. Did you know I am the only U.S. naval officer qualified to help repair a Raphael painting?"

Laning side-stepped with an offhand remark—"I just read an American Institute of Management study on how the Vatican is run."

"I read that," said Rickover, who was known by his subordinates to have read "everything." "I told one of the cardinals here that I could take this place over in six weeks."

The *Seawolf* belatedly went to sea for trials on January 21, 1957. She could operate at only eighty percent of her designed power. Finally, on March 30, 1957, the world's second nuclear-propelled submarine was placed in commission.

Her first skipper, Dick Laning, had graduated from high school at fourteen and gone to Berkeley for a year before entering the Naval Academy. He graduated from there in 1940 and served aboard an aircraft carrier and two submarines in World War II. After the war he had extensive training in nuclear engineering and physics as well as nuclear weapons. He was a Pentagon planning officer dealing with nuclear weapons, which then included torpedoes and the Regulus submarine missile, when he was designated a prospective nuclear commanding officer.

He was in NRB only briefly and then ordered to the *Seawolf* prototype reactor at West Milton. When, early in the development of the prototype, mercury was used as a heat-exchange liquid between the sodium and water loops, a leak developed in the primary system. Mercury mixed with sodium and was carried into the reactor itself. Rickover flew up to the prototype, was picked up at the airport by Laning, and asked for a briefing as they drove to the site. "I have some good news, Admiral," Laning said. Rickover looked at him quizzically. What good news could there be? "As the mercury goes through the reactor, it is bombarded by neutrons—and guess what it gets turned into? Gold!" Rickover showed a rare response—excitement.

"How much gold have we made?" an astonished Rickover asked.

"Thirteen cents' worth a day," Laning replied.

Rickover, who did not appreciate very many jokes, enjoyed this one enough to repeat it in Congressional testimony.

Laning showed more flair and independence than most of Rickover's early nucs. When NBC's "Today" show arranged for an on-board program about nuclear submarines, the *Seawolf* was substituted at the last minute for the *Nautilus*. On his own, Laning invited William R. Anderson, skipper of the *Nautilus,* aboard the *Seawolf* so that Anderson could be on the show. It had been Laning who had first told Rickover about Anderson, who was once Laning's executive officer in a diesel submarine.

As the *Seawolf* put to sea on the day of the show, the show's director suddenly asked, "Is it safe?" Laning told him, "There's a better chance that this sub will make a successful submerged telecast than there is that you'll get back to New York by highway."

The show was about to be filmed when the *Seawolf* received a message from ComSubLant: The Atomic Energy Commission—meaning Rickover—had decided to stop the televising for fear that classified information would be revealed. Laning sent back a message saying he would take full responsibility for what was shown. When an officer warned him, "Dick, your career will be in jeopardy," Laning said, "I don't have a career. I just have a job to do." The show went on and was a success.

As skipper of the *Seawolf,* Laning had the job of handling a submarine known from the very beginning to be unique. Sometimes, for example, her hull would glow in the dark. The glow was a phenomenon called Cerenkov radiation (named after a physicist). The bluish glow is emitted by high-speed charged particles as they pass from one medium to another. The radiation, more commonly observed in the water around a nuclear reactor, was not dangerous. But it was novel.

One submarine officer who missed the opportunity to serve in the *Seawolf* was Lieutenant Jimmy Carter, who spent some time at the reactor prototype, but left the Navy without having gone to sea in a nuclear submarine. He would go aboard his first nuclear boat many years later as President of the United States. The first President to go to sea in a nuclear submarine was Dwight D. Eisenhower. Wearing his golf clothes, he was picked up by the *Seawolf* at Newport, Rhode Island. At sea he had lunch with the crew, was shown around the submarine, and then returned to shore. Rickover, who personally supervised future Presidential visits to nuclear submarines, did not accompany President Eisenhower on this historic trip. (Later, Eisenhower went to sea in another nuclear submarine accompanied by Rickover and the press.)

The *Seawolf* operated for almost two years, primarily in anti-submarine exercises. She demonstrated the underwater endurance of nuclear submarines when, in the fall of 1958, Laning took her on a record-breaking submerged run of 13,761 miles, not surfacing for sixty days. Then, "overriding technical and safety considerations indicated the abandonment of the sodium-cooled reactor as a means for propelling naval ships," according to Rickover. The *Seawolf* returned to her birthplace in late 1958, where she was torn open, her sodium plant was removed, and a duplicate of the *Nautilus*'s reactor plant was installed.*

For some time before the conversion Laning had known that a change was going to be made. When there was still a little more than one year's supply of fuel left, Laning had suggested that a pressurized-water reactor be built in a module the size of that portion of the *Seawolf* hull that housed the sodium reactor. When that was completed, the submarine could be taken into the yard, her old plant cut away, and her new one installed. Laning estimated that the operation would take about six weeks. He believed that this form of conversion would dramatically demonstrate the advantage of modular submarine construction and would give the submarine more time in the fleet.

Laning's idea was vetoed, as was an earlier one when he had proposed that the *Seawolf* go around the world submerged in seventy-nine days and arrive at London in time for the premiere of the film *Around the World in 80 days.*

The "re-engineering" of *Seawolf* took one and a half years. She entered the Electric Boat yard when the first Polaris missile submarines were being started. The *Seawolf* was a low-priority job.

Although the *Seawolf* sodium plant was abandoned as a program,

* *The* Seawolf *reactor, with fuel core removed but still radioactive, was subsequently dropped into the Atlantic in April 1959 to a depth of some 9,000 feet at a point 120 miles due east of the Delaware-Maryland state lines.*

many felt that she should have been kept in service as a test bed for the sodium-reactor plant. Rear Admiral Albert Mumma, an early participant in the nuclear propulsion effort and Chief of BuShips when the *Seawolf* went to sea, said that there were several reasons for keeping the submarine in service, among them the potential of sodium reactors. With heat-exchange properties higher than those of pressurized-water reactors, the sodium reactors might be better for aircraft and commercial power use, and for application in surface ships where more horsepower was needed than in submarines. But Rickover would not tolerate the substandard performance of the *Seawolf.*

To Admiral Rickover's credit, as soon as the *Nautilus* and *Seawolf* plants were designed he began work on more advanced pressurized-water plants. The *Nautilus* plant was relatively crude, while the *Seawolf*'s sodium limitations were evident. At the Bettis laboratory run by Westinghouse and the Knolls facility operated by General Electric, scientists and engineers were available for new design work. There was interest in nuclear-powered surface ships, but submarines were still the obvious and immediate payoff for nuclear power.

The submarine community wanted smaller submarines. The *Nautilus* and *Seawolf* displaced half again as much as the *Tang* class and were almost 50 and 70 feet longer, respectively. Bettis was assigned the task of designing the submarine fleet reactor. It would be a pressurized-water plant similar to that of the *Nautilus,* but smaller, with improved operation and easier maintenance. Because of the new reactor's similarity to the *Nautilus* STR plant, a land prototype was not needed.

Obtaining funds for submarine construction, however, was difficult. The arrival of the Eisenhower administration in early 1953, and the end of the Korean War that summer, brought new Presidential scrutiny of defense programs. There were also questions about the usefulness and cost of nuclear propulsion. Neither the *Nautilus* nor the *Seawolf* had yet gone to sea. Admiral Arleigh Burke, at the time a senior Navy planner, later recalled, "Nuclear power was untried, and the proponents of nuclear power said, 'Let's go whole hog.' The people who felt that this was dangerous said, 'It is not proven yet—let's take it easy because the goddamn thing won't work.' . . . There was a lot they didn't know about the good things about nuclear power." And nuclear submarines were expensive; one of them cost twice as much as a diesel-electric boat.

The defense budget made up in 1953—that is, for fiscal 1954—provided funds for only one submarine, an improved, conventionally powered *Tang*-class boat. But the following year the Navy obtained funds for two nuclear attack submarines of a new class, plus a second new Regulus missile submarine with conventional propulsion.

The new nuclear submarines, with the improved submarine fleet reactor based on the *Nautilus* design, would be the first "production" nuclear submarines. Like the *Nautilus* and *Seawolf,* they would be fully capable of combat, but they would be smaller and slightly slower. Two different reactor arrangements would be used, the S3W and S4W.* The lead submarine in this class, the *Skate,* would be built at Electric Boat, like the two previous nuclear submarines. The subsequent submarines of this class would introduce two naval shipyards to nuclear submarines, the Portsmouth yard and the Mare Island yard in California. In all, four of the *Skate* class would be built: the lead ship at Electric Boat; the *Swordfish* and *Seadragon* at Portsmouth; and the *Sargo* at Mare Island.

As the nuclear-submarine program expanded, the chief of BuShips decided that the assistant chief of BuShips—supposedly Rickover's immediate superior—would direct all design work and administer all contracts, including those for the propulsion plant. Rickover objected, wanting more voice in the decisions affecting future nuclear submarines. After several conferences, it was decided that all hull and other submarine-design work would be done by other branches of BuShips, while Rickover would retain responsibility for future reactors *and* the propulsion system, from the reactor through the heat exchangers and turbines, to the propeller shaft.

There were still more questions about how the nuclear submarines would be handled at Portsmouth. The shop superintendent at Portsmouth was Eli Roth, fresh from six years in Rickover's office and the only officer at Portsmouth with nuclear experience. But Rickover refused to allow Roth to be involved with his project. Instead, Commander Marshall Turnbaugh, who had been with NRB since September 1948, went to Portsmouth to serve as nuclear-power superintendent, the first of Rickover's representatives at a shipyard. Such representatives in some respects would have more power and authority than the shipyard commander. (In February 1956, Captain Robert Moore became commander of the Portsmouth yard, thus taking the yard through the construction of its first nuclear submarines. It was an interesting bit of irony for Rickover, who had several years before sought to expel Moore from all connection with nuclear propulsion.)

The situation at Mare Island was different. Commander Edwin

---

* *See Appendix B for an explanation of reactor designations.*

Kintner reported to Mare Island in 1955 as nuclear power superintendent. An EDO, Kintner had been assigned to NRB since 1950 and had been in charge of the *Nautilus* prototype plant (Mark I) at Arco when it was started up and made its historic one-hundred-hour run. Mare Island was far different from Portsmouth. Perhaps it was the Californian environment; perhaps it was more flexible than the older Portsmouth yard, or perhaps the shipyard commander at Mare Island was simply less authoritative.

Kintner reported to both the planning and production officers at the Mare Island yard, but Rickover arranged for him to formally see the shipyard commander every week—alone. Kintner, of course, reported directly to Rickover weekly by letter and whenever he wished by phone.

More to the point of how the *Sargo* would be built at Mare Island, Rickover visited the yard a few weeks after Kintner arrived. As Kintner drove him from the airport, Rickover asked who ran the yard. Kintner's initial reaction was to name the shipyard commander. But Rickover wanted to know who *really* ran the yard, who got things done. "That," Kintner later recalled, "was Irv Whitthorne, head of the pipe shop at the yard." Whitthorne had started work there when he was about sixteen years old, more than a half century before Kintner arrived. "He was head of the masters' association at the yard and really a powerful guy; whatever he wanted got done."

Before seeing the shipyard commander, Rickover closeted himself alone with Whitthorne for a half hour. Those who looked into Whitthorne's glass-enclosed office could see the two men shouting and pounding their fists upon Whitthorne's desk. The words were not audible. But when Rickover came out, his first words to Kintner were "OK, you're the new shipyard commander."

"After that, I got anything I wanted," Kintner told the authors. "I had to hold myself back from asking for more than I needed. . . ." Apparently Rickover had promised Whitthorne that if the yard did a good job on his submarines, he would get them more and more submarines to build. He kept his word; through 1972, when the last submarine was completed in a U.S. naval shipyard, Portsmouth built a total of ten nuclear submarines, while Mare Island had built seventeen. Whitthorne also kept his word: Mare Island built good submarines.

Thus, Portsmouth and Mare Island entered the nuclear era with help from Electric Boat. This gave the United States three nuclear building yards. The additional shipyard capability was needed.

The shipbuilding program of fiscal 1956—approved by Congress in 1955, the year the *Nautilus* went to sea—provided for eight combat submarines. That was almost as many as had been funded in the previous four years. Although the shipbuilding plan had been developed earlier, in August 1955, it would be carried out by a new Chief of Naval Operations who would have great impact on the fiscal 1956 program and would be a strong proponent of nuclear propulsion.

Arleigh A. Burke was jumped over ninety-two officers senior to him when President Eisenhower named him to become CNO. At age fifty-three, Burke was a very young CNO. He was a famous destroyer squadron commander (known as "31-knot Burke") during World War II, and he also became chief of staff to the fast carrier force, demonstrating his breadth. He was an ordnance specialist, and hence a member of the "gun club" that had long had major influence on the technical side of the Navy. He had coordinated the Navy's efforts to retain its traditional missions and prerogatives during the Congressional "Unification and Strategy Hearings" of 1949.

Burke had been to sea in the *Nautilus* in May of 1955, shortly before he became CNO. When he became CNO, the Navy had an *ad hoc* committee developing a long-range shipbuilding plan, the first such effort in almost a decade. The preliminary report, stressing the need to develop a number of new technologies, recommended that "as soon as practicable, nuclear propulsion be adopted as standard for all new submarines whose missions will derive tactical benefit therefrom," and that high priority be given to the development of nuclear propulsion for surface ships, specifically cruisers and aircraft carriers.

The final report was submitted to Burke as CNO in December 1955. Burke endorsed the report for planning purposes, although he also noted the tremendous costs. Burke was developing his own view of the future Navy. In a remarkably clear, concise statement of how he envisioned "The Navy of the 1970 Era"—almost fifteen years away—he told all major commands in a confidential report that "the Navy of the 1970 period, which we are aiming at," would include fifty missile-launching submarines with nuclear power, more than thirty surface warships with nuclear power, and almost seventy-five torpedo-armed submarines with nuclear power. This totaled more than one hundred and fifty nuclear ships—a building rate of more than ten nuclear submarines plus nuclear surface ships every year!

At one point four diesel-electric combat submarines and four nuclear submarines were to have been built in fiscal 1956. Three of the diesel-electric submarines were torpedo-armed boats, but the fourth diesel submarine, the *Halibut,* was to be armed with the Regulus guided missile for attacks against shore targets. The *Halibut* was to be built at Mare Island, where Ed Kintner was the "shipyard commander," at least according to Rickover.

Next to Kintner's office at Mare Island was the office of Commander William Heronemus, the design superintendent at the yard. There apparently had been some early discussion in BuShips about providing nuclear propulsion for the *Halibut,* but it was dropped, partly because of the considerable increase in cost* and the question of whether another nuclear plant could be available in time. Kintner and Heronemus went over the *Halibut* design and both felt that the S3W reactor plant that Mare Island would install in their first nuclear submarine, the *Sargo,* would work in the *Halibut.* After doing their calculations, Kintner called Rickover, who immediately gave his support and, armed with their data, reopened the issue in BuShips. Reportedly, Admiral Burke became involved in the discussions, and the matter was decided in favor of making the submarine nuclear-powered. Then the submarine design office of BuShips was brought into the picture and the "front end" of the *Halibut* was redesigned so that she had a larger missile hangar and other features to take advantage of nuclear propulsion.

This change meant that the fiscal 1956 budget would provide the Navy with three conventional submarines plus five nuclear boats. In addition to the *Halibut,* the nuclear submarines would be the third and fourth boats of the *Skate* class, plus a giant radar picket submarine, the *Triton,* and the first submarine to marry nuclear propulsion and the advanced "tear-drop" hull for high underwater speed, the *Skipjack.*

The Westinghouse-Bettis and General Electric-Knolls teams, turned free to work on more advanced plants for both submarines and surface ships, meanwhile had been hard at work. The smaller reactor plants for the *Skate* class and the *Halibut* had been scaled down from the *Nautilus* reactor, permitting smaller submarines. But even in the late 1940s Rickover had been thinking about a larger submarine plant, one that could develop twice the horsepower of the earliest reactors, or about 30,000 horsepower—enough to drive a submarine at perhaps thirty-five knots,

* *Official Navy cost information lists the* Halibut *as having a final cost of $44.6 million, while the Regulus missile submarine authorized the year before cost $22.1 million to build. However, the* Halibut *was significantly larger (5,000 tons versus 3,515 tons).*

faster than any submarine had ever gone and faster than most surface warships. The GE-Knolls team initiated development of such a plant under Rickover's direction. It would become the reactor that would be eventually installed in the giant submarine *Triton.*

Captain Ned Beach, who would become the first commanding officer of the *Triton,* observed later that "we were the prototype for the surface ship multiple-reactor plants then under design." The horsepower requirement could be met only with a two-reactor plant, the first ever installed in a submarine. In turn, this would dramatically increase the submarine's size.

How could a large submarine with high *surface* speed be employed? The mission requirement usually comes first in developing weapons, at least in theory. But the Rickover momentum was considerable, and the issue became one of finding a mission for the submarine, because in the killer role she would be too large and lack maneuverability to be effective. The solution was to make the *Triton* a radar picket submarine. This concept had been born at Okinawa in 1945, when Japanese suicide planes smashed into U.S. destroyers that were employed as pickets to give warning to carriers of Japanese aircraft. A submarine could detect approaching aircraft with radar and then submerge to escape attack.

The *Triton* would also be the world's largest submarine when built. Previously the world's largest submarine had been the *I-400* class of submarine aircraft carriers built by Japan. These were 5,220-ton ships that could carry three fully assembled floatplanes and parts for a fourth. The planes were launched while the submarine was on the surface. The *Triton* dwarfed even those craft. The nuclear submarine would be 447½ feet long (forty-seven feet longer than the *I-400*s) and would displace 6,670 tons submerged.

Even before the *Triton* was launched on August 19,1958, controversy was swirling over the $109-million submarine. Four months earlier the Navy had announced plans to take half of the fleet's radar picket submarines (SSR) out of service. The remaining five radar picket submarines would follow shortly. Although the Lebanese and Taiwan Straits crises delayed the disposal plan, the end of the SSR concept was obviously at hand. Improvements in surface ship radars and the development of radar picket aircraft had ended the usefulness of picket submarines.

Still another kind of controversy surrounded the *Triton.* According to Ned Beach, Mrs. Rickover was to have christened the ship. She was never invited to do so. Instead, Mrs. John M. Will, wife of a vice admiral who, like Rickover, had a reputation for hard work and getting the job done, christened the *Triton*. (When submarine force maintenance officer in Australia at the start of World War II, Will is said to have once found a pump at the bottom of a gold mine and two days later had it installed in a submarine.)

Rickover, apparently upset that his wife was not to christen the submarine—Ned Beach said, "the Navy reneged on its promise" to her—did not attend the launching. He had been at the six previous nuclear-submarine christenings. "I regret that I am not able to be present at the launching of the *Triton*, for I consider this to be a significant event in naval history," he said in a message to the president of Electric Boat. "The *Triton* will pioneer the submarine technology necessary for capital ships of the future to operate submerged."

After her ceremonious launching, the *Triton* was completed at Electric Boat, but behind schedule. During 1958–1959 emphasis at EB was shifting to the Polaris submarine program. The *Triton* was to have been commissioned in August 1959, but she did not even get under way until September 27. Finally, the Stars and Stripes were hoisted on the *Triton* and she was placed in commission on November 10, 1959. She would never serve as a radar picket and her career would be short.

The *Skipjack*, the eighth submarine authorized in fiscal 1956, was in many respects the most significant. In developing the smaller reactor plants for the smaller *Skate* class, Rickover had reduced horsepower. Rickover's staff and the Westinghouse-Bettis engineers sought to refine the *Nautilus* plant to keep its relatively high horsepower—some 15,000—while reducing its size. This was done, in part, by an intensive review of the older reactor to eliminate or reduce valves, piping, and other components wherever possible. The result was the S5W plant, which incorporated many of the lessons learned in the succession of Westinghouse-Bettis reactor plants, thus alleviating the need for a land-reactor prototype.

The first S5W plant was installed in a submarine hull incorporating the advanced "tear-drop" hull design, thus marrying two of the most significant submarine developments of the postwar period. The result was the *Skipjack*, the first "fast attack submarine." Built by Electric Boat, the *Skipjack* turned out to be the fastest United States submarine to go to sea for the next two decades. Official statements said only that nuclear submarines exceeded twenty knots submerged. The *Skipjack* was more than ten knots faster than that, with some press reports citing speeds as high as forty-five knots, an inflated but headline-making number.

Thus, the fiscal 1956 budget provided a large and, especially for Rickover, significant group of submarines:

3 *Barbel* class (SS)—the last diesel combat submarines built by the United States
2 *Skate* class (SSN)—standardized nuclear submarines
1 *Skipjack* class (SSN)—combining nuclear propulsion and the "tear-drop" hull shape
1 *Halibut* (SSGN)—the only nuclear guided-missile submarine
1 *Triton* (SSRN)—largest submarine constructed to that time

Rickover would often complain to Congress that the Navy continued to oppose nuclear submarines, preferring instead to build more submarines with conventional propulsion. But 1955—the year that the *Nautilus* got under way on nuclear power—was the last time that diesel submarines were asked for. Years later Rickover still would speak of Navy opposition to building nuclear submarines. But the 1956 budget, fully supported by the Navy, said otherwise. And, in 1956, in a rare moment of sympathy for the "real" Navy, he would tell Congress how he could understand the Navy's problems in funding nuclear ships and submarines: "You do have Admiral Burke over the barrel to this extent. Prices are going up seven percent a year on everything. The Navy gets a certain amount of money for ship construction in accordance with the President's proposals, and the Bureau of the Budget. The nuclear-powered ships cost a lot, but he [Burke] still has to meet today's problems and commitments."

The nuclear submarines were to some extent selling themselves despite some negative characteristics such as high noise levels and high costs. Their virtually unlimited high-speed endurance without surfacing led to numerous underwater feats. Even as the *Nautilus* was racing toward the North Pole in August 1958, the *Skate* was beginning her first polar cruise. Passing under the North Pole three times in August, she became the first submarine to surface through the arctic ice. The *Skate* returned to the arctic in March 1959, in the midst of the arctic winter, and again in July 1962, when she rendezvoused at the top of the world with the *Seadragon* in the first two-submarine operation under the arctic ice. In August 1960 the *Seadragon* traveled the fabled Northwest Passage across the top of North America, with an excursion up to the Pole. More U.S. nuclear submarines would follow these pioneers.

After the *Nautilus*' feat of being the first submarine at the top of the world, the most dramatic submarine operation was the remarkable cruise of the giant submarine *Triton.* Ned Beach had placed her in commission in November 1959. Early in the new year Beach was suddenly ordered to report to the Pentagon. Once there he was asked what shape his ship was in—and then: "Beach, you're about to start your shakedown cruise. Can *Triton* go around the world—submerged—instead?"

"The room swayed," Beach later wrote. "I had tried to imagine the reason for this Washington conference, and I must truthfully admit that the possibility that *Triton* might be asked to try a round-the-world mission had crossed my mind. I had even considered several full-of-confidence responses with which to answer such a request. But the actual situation hardly seemed appropriate to any of the replies I had thought of, and after a sudden nervous cough, I said, 'Yes, Sir!' That was all I could say."

Two weeks later, on February 16, 1960, the *Triton* slipped out to sea, operating under top-secret orders. Rickover, of course, had been involved with preparation for the voyage from a viewpoint of the power plant and, Beach remembers, immediately before departure gave him updated data on power settings for the *Triton*'s twin reactors. Following much the same route taken by Ferdinand Magellan in 1519, the *Triton* steamed south in the Atlantic, rounded Cape Horn into the Pacific Ocean, across to Magellan Bay in the Philippines, then south through Lombok Strait, across the Indian Ocean, around the Cape of Good Hope, up to the coast of Spain, and then back to the United States. The *Triton* surfaced off the coast of Delaware on May 10, 1960, having steamed 36,000 miles in eighty-three days and ten hours. Only twice had she come briefly to the surface, once to take off an ill sailor and once to take off a Navy information officer with film of the voyage. Both times the submarine merely broached her tall sail up out of the water and the man was transferred to a small boat sent out from a U.S. warship.

Rickover had no direct communications with Beach during the cruise, although the Admiral did advise Beach's wife that all was going well on their special operation. Ingrid Beach suspected, but did not know for certain, what the *Triton* was doing.

Beach's remarkable cruise had major political importance. As the *Triton* surfaced off the Delaware coast, a helicopter plucked Beach from her deck and flew him directly to the south lawn of the White House. There, amid pomp and cameras, the President, Dwight D. Eisenhower, whom he had served as naval aide, awarded Beach the Legion of Merit; the *Triton* was presented the Presidential Unit Citation. This time Admiral Rickover was in attendance.

Later in the day, riding in a White House limousine to the Pentagon, Beach caught sight of a newspaper. It gave him his first news about the American U-2 spy plane shot down over Russia on May 1. Only then did he learn that the remarkable voyage of the *Triton* was planned in preparation for the United States-Soviet summit meeting scheduled for May 16 in Paris. The *Triton*'s voyage was intended to help bolster America's prestige at the meeting. But Khrushchev walked out of the meeting after Eisenhower refused to apologize for the spy plane flight.

Five hours after Beach was pulled up from the *Triton*'s deck, a helicopter brought him back aboard, and he took the submarine into her home port of New London. Her voyage and those of the other early nuclear submarines focused more favorable attention on the nuclear-submarine program—and on its director, a man who now seemed immune to attacks from the nonnuclear navy.

"Rickover was always engineering-oriented," Beach later told the authors. "To him the two-reactor *Triton* was much more important than the follow-on *Skipjack* [and] *George Washington,* despite all the exotic stuff the *GW* had. We had [in *Triton*], of course, a surface-ship plant. . . ."

The *Triton*'s remarkable voyage was soon overshadowed by the Polaris submarine missile program. (See Chapter 24.) The *Triton* was, in Beach's opinion, never given a real opportunity to prove herself as a fleet picket or escort submarine. There were several proposals for using the submarine in special roles. Rickover himself later said that "as a matter of historical record . . . in 1954 I advocated building the *Triton,* the two-reactor submarine, to carry surface-to-surface missiles." The context was Senator Jackson asking Rickover about guided or cruise missiles. To Jackson's question of whether he had wanted the *Triton* to be used in the tactical-missile role Rickover answered, "Yes, sir." But the only weapon under consideration—or even available at that time—was the Regulus intended for land attack with a nuclear warhead.

The records available at the Navy's archives and elsewhere show no indication that Rickover ever considered a missile role for the *Triton.* Indeed, at a meeting with Admirals Burke and Mumma in November 1957, Rickover, according to the official minutes of the session, "advised strongly against" converting the *Triton* into a missile submarine.

Beach does recall how Walter Dedrick, at the time prospective commander of the nuclear submarine *Halibut,* wrote to NRB proposing that the *Triton* be considered for four alternative missions instead of the dying radar picket role. They were: advanced sonar scout for the surface fleet;

guided-missile ship; command and staff ship; and high-speed minelayer. Beach himself proposed that in whatever role she was employed the *Triton* also be fitted for the rescue and towing of future nuclear submarines disabled under the polar ice pack. He later used this idea in his exciting novel *Cold Is the Sea.*

Instead, the *Triton* was employed in general submarine operations for several years. She was large; as newer, faster and deeper-diving submarines joined the fleet, her inefficiency became more pronounced. As a one-of-a-kind ship she was also expensive to maintain. Finally, she was decommissioned in May 1969 and anchored in the "mothball" fleet—the first nuclear submarine of any nation to be taken out of service.

For fiscal 1957, the Defense Department asked for and the Congress funded another six nuclear attack submarines—five more of the high-speed *Skipjack*s, plus one of still another new design, the U.S.S. *Thresher*. As were submarines in the previous multiship *Skate* class, the lead *Skipjack* was built at Electric Boat, along with another of the class, the *Scorpion*. (The *Scorpion* was actually begun twice. Two months after her first hull plates were laid down, the submarine was reordered as the first Polaris missile submarine, the *George Washington*. Subsequently, another attack submarine was laid down at EB and completed as the *Scorpion*.)

Of the four other submarines of that class, the *Scamp* was built at Mare Island, the *Sculpin* and *Snook* at the Ingalls yard in Mississippi and the *Shark* at the Newport News yard in Virginia. Ingalls and Newport News thus became the nation's fourth and fifth nuclear submarine yards.

The sixth submarine of fiscal 1957 was the *Thresher*. While she had the S5W reactor plant of the *Skipjack*s as well as their "tear-drop" hull design, the *Thresher* was constructed of stronger HY-80 steel, which gave her a diving depth much greater than that of previous U.S. submarines. Inside, her arrangement was different: a large sonar dome in her bow, the optimum position for sound-detection equipment; her torpedo tubes in her waist (amidships), angled out at five-degrees. And she was far quieter than earlier nuclear submarines.

Of all these features, the most important was that she was quiet. A quiet submarine is harder to detect, and her own sonar is more sensitive to sounds of other ships. The job of making a submarine relatively inaudible is called "sound quieting" by designers and engineers. It is a difficult task. "Making them quieter," Rickover once said, "is a bigger job than nuclear power."

The pumps and steam turbines made earlier nuclear submarines very noisy. Some said, not really joking, that you could almost put your head underwater and hear the *Nautilus* several miles away. The noise was particularly bad when the submarines went fast. Vice Admiral John T. Hayward, head of Navy research and development in the early 1960s, told Congress about an exercise in which the *Skate,* going at twenty knots, could not get away from the fifteen-year-old destroyer *Abbot:* "When a submarine goes fast she cannot do much. . . . In this particular exercise the *Skate* went right through [under] the whole convoy and didn't even know it, trying to shake the *Abbot.*" The destroyer caught the *Skate.*

Sound quieting was a major undertaking in the *Thresher,* and Rickover is remembered as having opposed it. Rear Admiral James, Chief of BuShips at the time, said Rickover did not want changes made to the machinery. "He bucked it, and then washed his hands of it," according to James. There is little in the public record about Rickover's attitude on the greatly increased depth capability of the *Thresher.* While the submarine was being built he voiced some views to Representative George Mahon, a member of the powerful House appropriations committee, during the following exchange:

MAHON. Are you overdesigning these ships? I am talking now mostly about submarines. Are you putting on refinements that are really not necessary? You spoke of the *Thresher* diving to a very great depth.

RICKOVER. Yes, sir.

MAHON. How deep are you going?

RICKOVER. The World War II submarines were designed for [400] feet. Right after World War II we developed the present [classified]-foot submarines. Now we are going to [classified] feet. The reason is that the deeper a ship goes, the less is it possible to detect it. It can take advantage of various thermal layers in the ocean. It also is less susceptible to damage by various types of depth charges and other anti-submarine devices. The greater depth gives it greater invisibility, greater invulnerability. We would like to go deeper if we could, but a point comes where existing hull steel may not be able safely to withstand the greater pressure. . . . However, there is considerable military advantage, Mr. Mahon, to be able to go deeper; it is somewhat analogous to having airplanes which can fly higher.

Three years later the *Thresher* was lost. (See Chapter 19.) At that time Rickover took a different stand on the question of how deep submarines should go. During a hearing before the Joint Committee on Atomic Energy in 1964, Vice Admiral Lawson P. Ramage, a much-decorated submariner and at the time a Deputy Chief of Naval Operations, explained the reasons for going deeper, including more safety in certain situations. Rickover took issue with Ramage, declaring: "Sure, you can intuitively say—as Admiral Ramage said in the comparison he made—you would like to go deeper. It is good to have a machine that can perform better. However, I claim we have to be realistic and find out how important this is first, because right now we are incurring considerable expenses in building these ships [classified matter deleted]."

Admiral Ramage was quick to point out that Rickover had been present when the decision was made to make the *Thresher* a deep-diving submarine. In a statement heavily censored for security reasons, Ramage told of the meeting and of his point at the time—that "for safety reasons we did need the additional depth in order to recover from any operational casualty." According to Ramage, Admiral Burke, the CNO, then made the decision to go to the deeper depth.

Rickover could only protest: "That was only an HY-80 meeting—" referring to the steel used in the *Thresher*. But he then said nothing else as the Congressmen briefly heard from others on the need for greater submarine depths, and then moved on to other aspects of the *Thresher* disaster.

There is still another interesting aspect of Rickover's relation to the *Thresher*. In the complex of positions that he had ensconced himself in, Rickover had considerable influence on submarine design. For example, he essentially determined horsepower available, and this in turn influenced speed, which in turn related to hull design; the amount of generating power related to sonar capability and other systems; machinery weight and size affected how big the submarine could be and how deep she could go.

From about the late 1950s on, Rickover became a key participant in the design of U.S. submarines. He would later claim that he had "been involved in nearly all aspects of submarine design" since about 1933. This statement—often repeated by Rickover—is impossible to substantiate. In 1933, Rickover was executive officer of the submarine *S-48* in Canal Zone waters, and he certainly was not then involved in submarine design. He then served less than two years as Inspector of Naval Material in Philadelphia, where he may have inspected submarine components, but the design work was done in Washington and the submarine-building shipyards. His next four years were at sea and in the Philippines.

Finally, when assigned to the Bureau of Ships in Washington from August 1939 until 1945 he was involved with electrical equipment for surface ships and submarines but not with basic submarine design. Not until 1947, when he began work on nuclear propulsion, could it have been truly said that he had become involved in submarine design—but even then not "in nearly all aspects." Then, in 1963, testifying before a Congressional investigation in the *Thresher* disaster, Rickover would continually refer to the "systems under my cognizance," speaking only of the submarine's machinery spaces, and note, "I am not responsible for the hull . . ."—or the ballast system . . . or hull material . . . or . . .

Indeed, during the hearings into the loss of the *Thresher*, Rickover carefully pointed out to his Congressional supporters that he was not even responsible for the specific nuclear plant in the ill-fated *Thresher*. The following exchange then occurred with Representative William Bates.

> RICKOVER. Since the propulsion plant is intimately tied to the reactor plant in a new design arrangement, it has been worked out with the Bureau of Ships and with the shipyards that I am technically responsible to the Bureau for the whole propulsion plant of a new type. I had that technical responsibility for the *Enterprise,* the *Bainbridge,* and the *Long Beach.* It was the same for the *Nautilus* and the *Skipjack* but not the *Thresher.*
>
> BATES. Why didn't you have that responsibility for the *Thresher?*
>
> RICKOVER. The *Thresher* was essentially a *Skipjack*-type submarine except that all the equipment was mounted on a resilient mounting.

There followed a discussion of why the *Thresher* was, in Rickover's opinion, not a new class. The *Navy,* however, did consider the *Thresher* a new class. Her basic S5W reactor plant was the same as the *Skipjack,* but little else was the same. Her speed, depth and maneuverability differed significantly (the *Thresher* was slower, deeper diving, less maneuverable); the internal arrangements of the submarines were also different. Rickover himself, in other testimony before Congress, noted that the *Thresher* "is the first of the new deep-diving submarines," while virtually all Navy statements about the *Thresher* called her the "lead ship of the world's most advanced class of nuclear submarines." His responsibility was never publicly established.

The *Thresher*—built at Portsmouth—became the lead ship of a class of fourteen attack submarines completed through 1968. They were deep-diving and quiet, and they had excellent submarine-detecting sonars. But they were larger than the *Skipjack*s, and so their 15,000-horsepower S5W reactor could not drive them as fast. The same situation occurred in the next, larger *Sturgeon* class, of which thirty-seven submarines were completed through 1975.

New York Shipbuilding Corporation, which had built one of the last U.S. diesel submarines, participated in building these classes, as did the General Dynamics yard at Quincy, Massachusetts (formerly owned by Bethlehem Steel and, before that, by the Fore River Shipyard). These briefly brought to seven the number of yards in the United States building nuclear submarines. The entry of these yards into the complex world of nuclear-ship construction was not without problems. Rickover and NRB helped—and pushed—to the maximum extent. Rickover's trusted aide James Dunford even left the Navy in January 1961 and joined New York Shipbuilding to help them into the nuclear program. Of the four officers who had accompanied Rickover to Oak Ridge in 1946, Dunford was the last to leave the nuclear navy. Another NRB officer, Robert Laney, who had been with Rickover since late 1948, similarly retired to join the Quincy shipyard at Rickover's behest.

The tenure of some yards in building nuclear ships was not long. The yards had been brought into SSN construction partly because of the heavy commitment of other submarine yards to attack and Polaris nuclear submarines. Besides attack submarines, New York Shipbuilding built one nuclear cruiser and Quincy built two. But by the middle 1960s the last Polaris submarine had been ordered and attack-submarine construction was slowing down, leading to a surplus of submarine yards. New York Shipbuilding was also encountering management problems, which despite Dunford's efforts drove the yard out of business. At Quincy there was another kind of problem. The Quincy yard had built submarines almost from the start of the century into the early 1920s, but in the nuclear era it was oriented toward surface-ship construction. An Electric Boat engineer sent up to help organize Quincy's nuclear test group recalled that being assigned to submarine work at the yard was considered "punishment." At Quincy "if you screwed up on a surface craft they would send you to a submarine to work on. The tradesmen—the craftsmen—did not like to work on submarines. They didn't like to work in tight corners," he recalled.

The Ingalls yard in Mississippi, acquired by Litton Industries in 1961, continued producing *Sturgeon*-class submarines into the middle 1970s and carried out nuclear-submarine overhauls for a few more years.

As submarines were being mass-produced in the 1960s—fourteen were launched during 1963—it became impossible for Rickover to attend every keel-laying, launching and commissioning. He fully recognized the political importance of these events as Congressmen, industrial giants, and even Presidents waxed forth in speeches praising nuclear submarines and their "father." The biggest nuclear day came on June 22, 1963. On that Saturday the Mare Island and Newport News yards each launched a Polaris submarine, while Electric Boat slid both a nuclear attack submarine and a Polaris "boomer" into the water.

Rickover did go to sea on the initial diving trials of virtually every nuclear submarine. Sometimes he said *every one.* A question does exist, however, about the trials of the U.S.S. *Queenfish,* built at Newport News. Electric Boat built the lead ship of the *Sturgeon* class, but the *Queenfish* went to sea first. And she went very memorably.

To submerge, submarines are brought to a state of "neutral" buoyancy, and then are "driven" underwater by forward motion. The *Queenfish,* at sea for trials with Admiral Rickover on board, reached deep water and rigged for dive. She would not submerge. Rickover exploded. A short time later, a helicopter was summoned to take him off. The *Queenfish* returned to Newport News. Additional lead ballast was taken on board, and weights were redistributed. She again went to sea, but without Rickover.

Rickover's participation in the sea trials involved much ritual. First, he always tried to schedule them for Sunday. He would generally arrive early at the "local" airport—the nearest was often an hour's drive or more away—and be picked up by one of the officers from the submarine. When the car arrived in the yard, it went directly to the piers. There was no courtesy call on the shipyard commander. Moments after he stepped aboard the submarine the craft would be under way. There was rarely a greeting. His response to "good morning, sir," was a brief, rasping monotone: "OK, let's get under way."

He would be on the bridge, near his protégés, as the submarine swung into the channel and cautiously headed out to the open sea. He then descended into the submarine. One of his first acts was to proceed to the executive officer's stateroom (XOSR), shed his civilian clothes, and don a pair of khakis without any insignia of rank.

The submarine's crew had prepared for Rickover's being on board almost as carefully as they had prepared for the sea trials. There were special "arrangements" to "insure the Admiral's comfort" during the sea trial. The check list for his visits give insight into the Rickover style. The list of "arrangements" for Rickover's observing the Polaris submarine *George Bancroft*'s sea trials, for example, had twenty-eight items:

a. Full set of khaki available in XOSR with sox and belt. Shirt size 14–32; trousers waist 31, length 29. (1 short sleeve, 1 long sleeve—small)

b. Menu—no *special* meals, but insure Wardroom meals *include* proper diet. Fruit available—seedless grapes/apples/etc. (fresh orange juice)

c. Insure RM [radiomen] check out on Marine operator procedures. He will want to make ship to shore calls.

d. Have late airlines and train schedules available in XOSR desks.

e. Disconnect MC [loudspeaker] systems, buzzers, dial-X ringer in XOSR. DO NOT disconnect pantry call button.

f. Turn all MC speakers in WR [Wardroom] Country down to low, pleasant, but discernible level. He will make talk to crew and it should be heard in Wardroom.

g. Ship's force film badge and dosimeter. Doctor deliver personally.

h. Provide plenty of *George Bancroft* stationery, envelopes and pen available (must have right kind of pen and ink—check with CDR Martin) in XOSR desk.

i. Do not pull in shore phone connection until last minute when getting underway and then with CO's permission.

j. Have foul weather jacket (Blue & Heavy) available in XOSR with jacket patch (leather name patch) and *George Bancroft* patch. The jacket must be expendable.

And the list went on: at least five hundred plain white envelopes—so that he could write notes to key members of Congress, the Atomic Energy Commission, and others; latest weather reports; blank message forms; yeoman available for the Admiral's stenographic needs; copy of local newspaper and Sunday's *New York Times;* and even dental floss in the stateroom's medicine cabinet—although the *Bancroft*'s list did not stipulate whether it should be waxed or unwaxed. The lists are handled as if they had top-secret information in them.

Emerging from the stateroom in his khakis, Rickover would prowl through every part of the submarine, giving particular scrutiny to the engineering spaces. There Rickover peered over the shoulders of officers and sailors as they went about their jobs with textbook precision. When he felt it was necessary he gave orders, in violation of the practice and tradition that, except to the commanding officer, no visitor on board—not even an admiral or commander in chief—tells a member of the ship's crew how to perform a technical function.

Rickover has explained to Congress, "Knowing the ship and its machinery intimately, I know what is possible, and so I do not become frightened easily. A number of nuclear ships would not have made successful trials had I not personally made the decision to keep on with the trials."

He then went on to tell how he tests the skills of the men he has trained in the environment of a submarine at sea: "I turn to the engineering watch officer and I hit him on the shoulder and say: 'You are dead. Get out of here.'

"I tap a sailor on the shoulder and say, 'You are in charge.' And the sailor takes charge and does very well.

"It is good for them. It is good for a young man, particularly a sailor, to get that responsibility and carry it through."

Sometimes, it was more than a drill. "On more than one occasion," Rickover once said, "I have been in a deeply submerged submarine when a failure has occurred in a sea-water system because a fitting was of the wrong material. But for the prompt action of the crew, I might not be here."

The submarine trials include a shallow dive and then deeper dive; sustained high-speed runs, and other evolutions. When the long day is over, the crew—exhausted both physically and psychologically—carefully bring the submarine back to the shipyard. Rickover, rarely with a compliment, hastens ashore—wearing the foul-weather jacket and khakis provided by the submarine; his own suit, cleaned and pressed aboard the submarine, is neatly packed for him to carry ashore. The waiting car speeds the Admiral to the train station or airport, and he is gone in the night.

Back at the shipyard the submariners know they have "survived" his visit. Quite probably they have also "passed," but, for the moment, the most important fact is that they have survived.

17 | All Major Combatant Vessels . . .

Congress could take pride in its efforts to build a nuclear Navy. But even as the Navy's all-nuclear Task Force 1 circumnavigated the globe late in 1964, in the traditions of Magellan and Theodore Roosevelt's Great White Fleet, Rickover's plans for a nuclear surface fleet had already fallen into disarray. Rickover had obviously envisioned a long line of all-nuclear carrier task forces to complement the growing nuclear submarine fleet.

Under the direction of Admiral Burke, the Navy was formally proposing that six nuclear carriers be constructed during the 1960s, with designs being prepared by the Naval Reactors Branch and other sections of BuShips for the *Enterprise*'s successors to be about 10,000 tons smaller, with only four reactors instead of eight, as in the "Big E." The Navy hoped that the smaller size and fewer reactors would reduce the cost of the new carriers, albeit at the possible loss of two or three knots in speed.

To escort these nuclear carriers, in addition to the *Long Beach* and the *Bainbridge,* the Navy proposed the construction of twenty-two nuclear escorts armed with guided missiles. These were numbers generated by Burke's OPNAV staff and were not ships dreamed up in the Naval Reactors Branch. Thus, if the Department of Defense and Congress would support these plans, by the end of the 1960s the Navy would have over thirty nuclear surface ships in addition to more than one hundred nuclear submarines.

Such a surface fleet, continually urged by Rickover before Congressional committees, would establish Rickover as the "father of the atomic surface fleet" in the same manner that he was bestowed the title "father of the atomic submarine." But here Rickover would fail. And thus any chronicle of the zigzag course of the nuclear surface navy becomes a chronicle of Rickover's failure.

There were ominous statements by Navy leaders on the subject of future nuclear surface ships even before the carrier *Enterprise* had been completed in 1961. The fiscal 1959 budget that went forward to Congress early in calendar 1958 had asked for $35 million to order reactor components for a second nuclear aircraft carrier. While the Navy had originally wanted complete funding of the second nuclear carrier, the Department of Defense had asked for a one-year delay in the funding of the ship.

In discussing the delay before a Congressional committee, Rear Admiral Albert G. Mumma, Chief of the Bureau of Ships, said that the Navy would "fight" for the carrier in 1960. But the Eisenhower Administration was becoming increasingly concerned over climbing defense expenditures and the need for strategic weapons—including the submarine-based Polaris missiles—to counter the Soviet progress in nuclear weapons. Still smarting from the Soviets' Sputnik exploits, the Administration felt that aircraft carriers were of secondary importance in the United States–Soviet strategic balance.

The Eisenhower Administration was not the only party having second thoughts about nuclear surface ships. In cutting from the budget the $35 million needed to start a second carrier, the House Armed Services Committee warned in a report that the nuclear-carrier program "must be restudied in the light of changing concepts of modern warfare." In addressing the Navy's plan for six nuclear carriers, the Committee report said that further funds would be withheld until the Navy and the shipbuilding industry could produce a nuclear carrier "in an efficient and economical manner." The committee then observed that "such an ability by the Navy and the shipbuilding industry has not been demonstrated."

The Navy's leadership made a halfhearted effort to gain a second nuclear carrier, but the views of the powerful House Appropriations Committee reflected the feelings of not only its chairman, long-time carrier opponent Clarence Cannon, but also other leading members of the House. Further, the start of the Polaris submarine program, a large nuclear attack-submarine program, and other cold war efforts were costing the Navy dearly.

No carrier was authorized in fiscal 1959—the first year without a carrier after seven consecutive budgets that provided for a supercarrier. CNO Burke and Secretary of the Navy Thomas Gates had wanted another carrier, nuclear if possible. Although later Rickover lore would say that the Navy and Defense Department did not want such ships and that Congress forced them on the Navy, neither the House nor the Senate would vote funds for the reactor components of a second carrier that the Navy had asked for.

When the fiscal 1960 budget went to Congress, the Eisenhower Administration did ask for funds for another supercarrier—but with oil-burning boilers, not nuclear reactors. Justifying the carrier as a ship for limited, nonnuclear war, the Navy's leaders told Congress that this eighth large carrier was needed and that its propulsion was a secondary consideration. Meanwhile, the still-unfinished *Enterprise* was creeping up in cost, to over $350 million by the spring of 1959. A conventional ship, it was pointed out, would cost some $120 million less. Stated another way, the Navy could build three oil-burning ships for the cost of two nuclear ships. If one considered the "life-cycle costs," that is, the costs of fuel oil and the tankers to support the carrier over a thirty-year lifetime, the nuclear ship became more attractive. However, at budget time the Administration and Congress tended to look only at immediate building costs, and a nuclear ship meant that other programs would have to be cut to fund the nuclear surface fleet. Polaris, other strategic programs and conventional Navy ships were causing major budget problems for the Republican Administration, soon to face an election.

Admiral Burke was asked in one committee whether, were he given an additional $120 million, he would spend it on nuclear propulsion for the carrier. The CNO responded that he would not; there were other programs that Burke would give higher priority for extra funds. But a carrier—any carrier—was the Navy's No. 1 priority.

As Congress debated the pros and cons of nuclear carriers—and carriers in general—Rickover became more vocal outside the Joint Committee on Atomic Energy, his traditional position of strength on the Hill. Perhaps his promotion to vice admiral in October of 1958 had made him more confident to enter the arena of Congressional debate and to argue more openly against official Navy positions. In response to a question from Michigan Congressman Gerald R. Ford, Rickover defended the need to buy nuclear carriers: "You know darned well that to buy an obsolescent ship is stupid. I do not care what arguments are given to you."

Support for Rickover came from several quarters, including nineteen Democratic Congressmen from New York, who issued a statement urging the Navy to build a nuclear carrier at the naval shipyard in Brooklyn, which would soon deliver its last large ship to the Navy. (Brooklyn was not qualified to build nuclear ships; all future U.S. large-carrier construction would go to the Newport News yard in Virginia.)

The debate raged in the House and Senate appropriations committees, the two committees that could vote or deny the funds for new warships. The House voted no funds for carriers in the fiscal 1960 budget.

The committee in which Rickover's real strength resided, the Joint Committee on Atomic Energy, did not have a voice in new ship construction at all. However, at the time, three members of the Joint Committee were also on the Senate subcommittee on defense appropriations—Richard Russell, John Pastore and Henry Dworshak. All three were pro-Rickover, pro-nuclear navy, and they had influence in Senate appropriations. The Senate, generally more "pro-defense" than the House, did have major opponents to aircraft carriers, among them defense watchdog William Proxmire. Still, the Senate voted full funding—$380 million—for a second nuclear aircraft carrier. Then, in the conference to work out differences in the moneys voted by the two houses, the conferees compromised by providing only advance funds for the nuclear carrier, to be fully funded the following year.

In a paper on Congressional actions in the procurement of nuclear ships, graduate student Frederick Neikirk has made an analysis of this decision that is most incisive: "While four members of the seventeen member House Subcommittee had served in the Navy, none of its members had shipyards in their districts, nor had any of its members served on either the Armed Services or Joint Atomic Energy Committees. The Senate Committee, however, had four members with shipyards in their states (three of which had already built either nuclear submarines or were building nuclear surface vessels), six members of the Senate Armed Services Committee, and three were members of the Joint Committee."

Thus, in fiscal 1960 there were no carrier funds except for the procurement of reactor components for the second nuclear carrier. The Eisenhower Administration refused to spend even those funds. As could be predicted, when the Eisenhower budget plan for fiscal 1961 was proposed to Congress there was a request for another conventional, oil-burning carrier.

It was becoming obvious that support in Congress for nuclear surface ships was dissipating. Not only were carriers opposed, but no nuclear escort ships were funded in fiscal years 1960 and 1962. Conventional surface ships were being built, as were nuclear submarines, with 11 approved for fiscal 1959, 4 for 1960, and 9 for 1961.

The 1961 budget request for an oil-burning carrier was defended by newly appointed Secretary of Defense Thomas Gates, who had previously served as Secretary of the Navy. Gates told Congress that the

Navy could buy four or five anti-submarine ships for the money saved in giving the new carrier conventional propulsion. Again, to Burke the Navy's No. 1 priority was getting a carrier—with any kind of propulsion. This debate occurred early in calendar 1961, before any of the first trio of nuclear surface ships had gone to sea. It was a large-deck carrier that was needed to support American interests in the Mediterranean and the Far East. With one exception, all naval officers who appeared before the Congressional appropriations committees backed this position. The exception was Rickover, who protested strongly.

Again the House Appropriations Committee refused funds for any carrier; the Senate opted for a carrier—with any kind of propulsion. The conference resulted in funding the seventh oil-burning supercarrier in fiscal 1961, the U.S.S. *America.*

In January 1961, John F. Kennedy led the Democrats back into the White House. His Secretary of Defense, Robert S. McNamara, immediately accelerated the production of strategic weapons, the land-based Minuteman ICBM and the submarine-launched Polaris. The latter missile would spur the construction of more nuclear submarines.

However, McNamara was against carriers. His early shipbuilding budgets were very large as he sought conventional as well as strategic forces to counter Soviet capabilities at various levels of conflict. No nuclear ships were asked in the early McNamara budgets and none was sought by the Navy. Indeed, Rear Admiral James, Chief of BuShips, told Congress that nuclear escorts were not only more expensive but also heavier and slower than their oil-burning counterparts. Now Rickover appeared before the House Armed Services Committee.

Rickover told the committee that the real difference between a nuclear and a conventional frigate (small cruiser) was not even the $35 million cited by the Defense Department. Of that, he explained, $8 million was for nuclear fuel, and fuel was never counted for oil-burning ships. The real difference was only $27 million (although that was still a significant amount considering that a conventional ship cost less than $70 million). For that difference, Rickover explained, the nuclear ship could steam 400,000 to 450,000 miles at twenty knots without refueling, while the conventional ship could go only 8,000 miles at the same speed. He also argued that the weapons and not the power plant determined the size of the ships and that the speed loss was only one knot for nuclear power.

His testimony led L. Mendel Rivers, soon to become chairman of the committee and a fanatic supporter of Rickover, to comment that for any ship of 8,000 tons or more "not to contain nuclear power . . . is just as much out of date as a crossbow and a sailing ship."

Rickover, with Rivers's support, was successful and the House voted in favor of *two* nuclear escorts in the fiscal 1962 budget. At the same time, the Senate Armed Services Committee was voting for seven conventional frigates. In the more important appropriations committees of the two houses, Burke came forth in support of nuclear ships but still put priority on numbers: "If we had to take a choice between seven conventional frigates and four frigates of the nuclear type, we would have to take the seven frigates because we need the ships so badly."

Finally, the Congress voted for a fiscal-1962 budget providing six conventional frigates plus one nuclear ship, the *Truxtun.* The latter would cost $135 million—*twice* as much as the conventional frigates, which averaged $69 million each. Thus, after a hiatus of two years, Congress voted another nuclear surface ship. There would be a four-year interval until the next.

McNamara brought the concept of systems analysis to defense management and planning. He considered each weapon in the context of what it contributed to a program goal and not the wishes of the individual services. For example, to McNamara the Polaris missile submarines were not a Navy program but a strategic program, to be considered with ICBMs and manned bombers and not with other Navy programs, such as attack submarines and amphibious ships. Then McNamara demanded to know how each additional dollar spent on a project enhanced its capability. This was to be the source of most opposition to Rickover's proposals for nuclear ships during McNamara's unequaled seven years as Secretary of Defense. His deputy for analysis, Alain Enthoven, a young economist, addressed the problem of buying nuclear ships this way:

"This real issue is one of clarity of understanding. . . . Take, for example, the statement 'Nuclear power for surface ships offers a major increase in effectiveness.' Precisely what does that mean? Does it mean 10 percent better or 100 percent better? When that sort of question is asked, a frequent answer is, 'It can't be expressed in numbers.' "

Enthoven—and McNamara—demanded that some quantitative value be placed on "better." According to Enthoven, "If nuclear power costs, say, 33 percent more for a certain type ship, all factors considered, then, no matter what the budget level, the Navy and the Secretary of Defense must choose whether to put the nation's resources into four conventional or three nuclear ships or, for a larger budget, eight conventional or six nuclear ships."

Although McNamara opposed nuclear surface ships, the Navy fared very well; between 31 and 61 new ships were funded in fiscal years 1963 through 1966, including an average of six nuclear submarines per year. There was never any question raised of building any diesel submarines.

The Kennedy-McNamara budget for fiscal 1963 did ask for another nuclear frigate or cruiser, this ship to be the first of a series armed with the long-range Typhon missile for fleet air defense. Because of the ship's giant radars, only nuclear power could provide sufficient energy without cutting back on the ship's range. With little discussion, all concerned committees in Congress voted the $190 million to build the first Typhoon ship. But problems with the radar system led to cancellation of the ship shortly thereafter, and the Navy continued to build only conventional escorts despite exhortations from Rickover.

Rather, Congressional attention was soon focused again on the nuclear-carrier issue. After the oil-burning *America* had been voted in the fiscal 1961 budget, the Kennedy-McNamara Administration proposed another conventional carrier for fiscal 1963. The Navy's leadership had originally wanted a nuclear ship but McNamara prevailed. Both Secretary of the Navy Fred Korth and the new CNO, Admiral George W. Anderson, supported this position on Capitol Hill, citing the lack of experience with nuclear surface ships (this was early 1962) and, more important, the increasing costs of nuclear ships.

Rickover fought this position, holding his self-serving meeting of the Joint Committee on Atomic Energy aboard the nuclear carrier *Enterprise* in late March 1962. Although some of those attending had major influence on the appropriations and armed services committees, the Joint Committee itself, while totally supporting Rickover, could have little influence on the outcome of ship decisions. The carrier voted for fiscal 1963 by both appropriations and armed services committees was an oil-burning ship.

The following year, as expected by many, the Administration did not ask for another carrier of any kind. Admiral Anderson explained to Representative Mahon that other ships had higher priorities in the fiscal 1964 budget and that there was another carrier planned for the fiscal 1965 budget.

Mahon, one of the most powerful figures in the Congress, then asked if Anderson wanted the next carrier to be nuclear or oil-burning. Anderson responded that he would hope to get a nuclear carrier. Secretary Korth indicated his agreement with the CNO. That, so it seemed, would end the discussion of nuclear ships for the year. But it was not to be.

With some influence from Rickover, Dr. Glenn Seaborg, Chairman of the AEC, sent a letter to McNamara advising him that advances in reactors warranted a re-evaluation of propulsion for the fiscal 1963 carrier, the building of which had not yet started. Seaborg was able to tell McNamara that reactor-core "lives" had almost doubled—to perhaps seven years—making comparisons with oil-burning ships more attractive, and that only four reactors would be needed. At the same time, the Navy's leaders were beginning to have an appreciation of the capabilities of nuclear surface ships based on operating experience with the *Enterprise* and her nuclear consorts *Long Beach* and *Bainbridge*.

There were also rumblings in Congress. Representative Craig Hosmer of California, a member of the Joint Committee, made a statement in the *Congressional Record* that included an editorial from the magazine *Navy* asking for more nuclear ships and concluding: "There is still time to make the carrier authorized last year nuclear powered. And it should be."

In response to these and other questions being raised, McNamara ordered funds for the 1963 carrier (designated CVA-67) to be held up while a series of studies relative to the ship's mission and propulsion were undertaken. The action upset many carrier supporters, who feared (correctly) that such a delay would jeopardize the plans for another carrier in fiscal 1965.

Even as the studies were being started, Secretary Korth and CNO Anderson wrote to McNamara on April 5, 1963, urging that all ships over 8,000 tons—including the CVA-67—be nuclear-powered. This recommendation, only six months after completion of the *Bainbridge*—the prototype nuclear frigate or destroyer—was a remarkable move on the part of the Navy's leadership.

While studies were being continued, the Joint Committee on Atomic Energy, urged on by Rickover, joined the foray. On March 1—before the studies were completed—committee chairman John Pastore wrote to McNamara of his concern that there were no nuclear ships in the budget. Pastore noted: "I understand that it is still possible to consider the installation of a nuclear-propulsion plant on the aircraft carrier authorized in the fiscal 1963 shipbuilding program CVA-67. I would hope that every consideration will be given to the installation of nuclear propulsion in this carrier."

Pastore was answered by Dr. Harold Brown, McNamara's deputy for research and engineering,* who replied that "this question has also been of increasing concern to the Secretary" and that the issue was still under review. The CVA-67 was a frequent topic of discussion in the Pentagon, on Capitol Hill, and in the press during the summer of 1963. On September 26, Secretary of the Navy Korth again urged McNamara to build the ship with nuclear propulsion. McNamara replied to Korth that the Navy's own studies were not yet completed and, not yet himself convinced of the advantage of nuclear propulsion, he was ordering the CVA-67 to be built with conventional propulsion to avoid further delay.

That same day, October 9, Chairman Pastore wrote to McNamara that since he had not received a substantive response to his March 1 letter, he would hold formal hearings into the matter. A few days later Korth resigned as Secretary of the Navy in protest over McNamara's decision.

Amid this tension, the Joint Committee began its hearings into "nuclear propulsion for naval surface vessels" on October 30. It was an odd sort of hearing, because the committee could neither authorize nor vote funds for ships. In some respects it would be like the hearing aboard the nuclear *Enterprise* a year before—there would be unending words of praise for nuclear propulsion and almost unending words of praise for Admiral Rickover. But holding the hearing in the Capitol would bring more attention to the issue, with Secretary McNamara and many other officials participating—men who had not been aboard the "Big E" when she cruised off Cuba.

When the session was called to order, there were eleven members of the Joint Committee present (of the eighteen Senators and Representatives on the committee). The Defense delegation was led by Paul H. Nitze, as assistant secretary, who had just been appointed to succeed Korth as Secretary of the Navy, and young Harold Brown, who had received his Ph.D. in physics at age twenty-two. McNamara would attend a later session of the hearing. A member of the Defense Department group was a captain named Elmo R. Zumwalt, an aide to Nitze. Korth and just-appointed CNO David L. McDonald led the large Navy delegation, while Chairman Glenn Seaborg headed the AEC contingent. Rickover, of course, attended wearing both of his "hats," being listed twice, as a representative of the Navy and of the AEC. But in the official listing of

* Dr. Brown later served as Secretary of Defense under President Carter.

witnesses by affiliation, published by the committee, he was considered to be a representative of the AEC.

Korth led off the witnesses, expressing his support for making the CVA-67 a nuclear ship. Next came Rickover. His opening words were familiar to all in the room, although few outside the Navy realized their lack of accuracy: "It was this committee that forced the construction of the *Nautilus*. . . . Even after our success with the *Nautilus,* the Navy did not want to build additional nuclear-powered submarines. It was the Joint Committee that forced more nuclear submarines."

More impressive were the skippers of the first three nuclear surface ships—Wilkinson, de Poix and Peet—who paraded to tell in detail how "nuclear power is better." Possibly the most articulate spokesman, however, and in some ways the most credible because he was not nuclear-trained, was Vice Admiral John T. Hayward. An aviator and longtime supporter of Rickover, he had commanded the *Enterprise* task force in the Cuban quarantine. Hayward, a Navy participant in the Manhattan Project, had held the top research and development job in OPNAV as well as sea commands. His arguments for nuclear surface ships were most persuasive.

The hearing continued the next day, with a final session on November 13, when McNamara appeared as a witness. It immediately became apparent that for the cost of nuclear propulsion he was using dollar numbers that were different from those of the Navy. The numbers put forward by Navy witnesses varied; McNamara cited a $163 million difference—$94 million in ship costs, $32 million for the reactor cores (the equivalent of seven years of fuel oil), and $37.5 million for another squadron of airplanes. The last item—almost a quarter of the nuclear costs—was included because a nuclear carrier was larger, with room for another dozen jet aircraft. But counting that against the nuclear ship costs was like saying that a nuclear ship had room for another hundred rounds of ammunition, and hence bullets to fill that space should be included in nuclear costs.

In general, McNamara's testimony was unconvincing. He stressed that he was not certain about the viability of carriers for the Navy's future missions, especially against future Soviet threats. And thus, he reasoned, cheaper carriers should be purchased. "There are two circumstances I think you can anticipate developing between now and 1970," he explained. "One is more Soviet nuclear-powered submarines. The other is greater Soviet capabilities for long-range reconnaissance and long-range attack. These latter capabilities endanger an aircraft carrier substantially. . . . Therefore, it raises still further doubts whether you should put $160 million more into it today as opposed to putting it into escort vessels or submarines or something of that kind."

Expressing concern over the increasing Soviet submarine fleet—including nuclear-powered undersea craft—McNamara said he wanted larger numbers of ships to combat them. Then followed one of the few truly meaningful exchanges of the entire three-day session. Representative Craig Hosmer of California, a key Rickover supporter, responded: "The vulnerability of the argument if you should carry that to its extreme [is that] you should not have any Armed Forces at all because they will be destroyed."

"Carrying this argument to the extreme," McNamara responded, "means that you buy the forces that are most effective and you buy enough of them so you can oppose the opponent's pressures and oppose them successfully."

Hosmer countered on another tangent, telling McNamara, "I don't think you are in a position . . . of anticipating of what you will [need] to meet [the threat] ten or twenty years hence."

"Of course we do," answered McNamara. "We anticipated when we determined the balance of force we are buying today; we tried to look ahead and see what circumstances we will face and what is the proper balance of force in relation to those circumstances."

He continued, "I think every naval officer that you have asked the question, whether he would rather have more conventional or fewer nuclear ships, when you phrased it as coldly as that, said he wanted more conventionals. Numbers of ships are important."

Several issues were not raised in the hearings. For example, the Navy was keeping carriers deployed on a continuous basis overseas in the Mediterranean and Far East, reducing the need for high-speed, trans-ocean transits. And, nuclear ships required more highly trained people than conventional ships, and so personnel costs were considerably higher over the nuclear carrier's thirty-year-plus service life.

McNamara's strongest argument was probably his desire to buy "maximum defense" for every dollar spent. Thus, rather than buy one nuclear carrier, he would buy one conventional carrier and one conventional destroyer—which would give the nation more weapons at sea per dollar spent. But he also held out the hope that the Navy could produce smaller, cheaper nuclear power plants that would allow the purchase of large numbers of ships with nuclear propulsion in the future.

After the three days of hearings, the Joint Committee concluded that "nuclear propulsion provides significant advantages for surface warships" at minor cost, and that, specifically, the CVA-67 should have nuclear propulsion.

President Kennedy did not play an active part in these later discussions of propulsion for the ship. Obviously, at some earlier stage he had reviewed the budget, and such major issues as nuclear aircraft carriers would have come to his attention. But, according to his naval aide, Captain Tazewell T. Shepard, Jr., around this time Kennedy asked him about the nuclear-power issue. At a time when White House military aides had substantial influence and were not merely the social aides they would become, Shepard prepared a paper for the President. It recommended that the CVA-67 be given nuclear propulsion. Shepard recalled having professed that nuclear surface ships, coupled with very high-speed ships which rode on a bubble of air, "could provide the United States with a quantum jump over the Soviets, making their increasing efforts to build a surface [naval] fleet and merchant marine obsolete." He passed the paper to President Kennedy, who placed it on his desk on November 20, the day before he flew to Texas and a rendezvous, on the twenty-second, with martyrdom.

A short time later McNamara ordered the CVA-67—the *John F. Kennedy*— with conventional propulsion. The Secretary of Defense was, in the final analysis, the President's executive for military matters, and the Joint Committee's authority was in reality limited to nuclear matters related to research, safety and training.

As feared by some, the debate helped to destroy the long-range plan for a new large carrier every other year and there was no carrier of any kind in fiscal 1964, 1965 and 1966. Similarly, with the cancellation of the Typhon missile project, no missile frigates were asked for in fiscal 1965 or 1966. Congress rebelled, somewhat, by voting long-lead funds for another nuclear frigate in 1967, but McNamara delayed spending those funds for almost a year. By that time the debate over nuclear surface ships was being affected by another influence—the experience of the war in Vietnam.

From the outset, aircraft carriers were in action, in the Tonkin Gulf incident in August 1964 and, even before that, flying reconnaissance planes over Laos. Subsequently, carriers became a prime instrument of U.S. military force in Vietnam. The carrier *Enterprise* was the first nuclear warship ever to participate in a combat action. The "Big E," under her third commanding officer, James L. Holloway III, arrived off Vietnam on December 2, 1965. At that time the record for combat sorties or flights from a carrier in one day in the war was 131 from the oil-burning *Kitty Hawk*. The second day in the Gulf of Tonkin the "Big E" flew 137 combat sorties, and a week later the ship flew 165 in one day. "The tons of bombs that have flown off this ship would stagger you," Holloway said at the time.

The counting of combat sorties, like the counting of bodies, was one of the many ways in which McNamara's analysts judged the effectiveness of U.S. forces in Vietnam. The Navy cooperated, pushing the carrier commanders to launch more sorties, a factor then publicized by the Navy and by Rickover despite the subsequent revelation that the numbers of sorties had little relation to the damage inflicted on the enemy in Vietnam.

The value of carriers in the Vietnam War during 1964–1965 helped to gain McNamara's approval of a Navy plan to build three additional nuclear-powered carriers. That decision was based in part on the Navy's studies that showed how, on a peacetime basis, fifteen carriers were needed to continuously keep two in the Mediterranean and three in the Western Pacific. During the Vietnam War over half of the Navy's carriers were at sea at any given time.

Another factor influencing the carrier decision was further improvement in reactor technology that would permit two giant reactors to propel a 90,000-ton carrier compared to eight in the *Enterprise* and four proposed for the *Kennedy*. According to Rickover, the parts of the carrier's two-reactor plant "would be the largest ever manufactured for the naval nuclear propulsion program. . . . In some cases they are accurate to one hundredth of an inch. . . . These are the most difficult heavy equipments that have ever been made." The "dry" weight of the two reactors, that is without water or steam in them, would be 1,000 tons—as much as the light displacement of the first ship Rickover served in, the four-stack destroyer *La Vallette*.

More impressive from an operational viewpoint, the initial fuel cores for the new carrier's reactors would power the ship for at least thirteen years. Technology had thus advanced significantly, making a nuclear carrier in the fiscal 1967 budget more "cost effective"—to use McNamara terminology—than it would have been four years before, when Rickover had demanded a similar ship.

The first of these McNamara-era nuclear carriers would be the U.S.S. *Nimitz,* built by the Newport News shipyard. Rickover made certain that, through the auspices of the Navy and the Atomic Energy Commission, Senator Jackson, assisted by the late Admiral Nimitz's son, was the principal at the keel-laying for the *Nimitz*. Although a Navy affair, only two naval officers were listed in the program for the *Nimitz* ceremony—Captain Gerald Sargent, the chaplain who gave the benediction, and Rickover. Rickover, of course, wore civilian clothes.

With the *Nimitz* (funded in fiscal 1967) under construction, the fiscal 1968 budget request asked for reactor component funds for a nuclear carrier to be requested the following year. When McNamara went before Congress in February of 1968—shortly before leaving office—the first item of business was the capture by North Koreans of the spy ship *Pueblo* less than a month before, with eighty-three Americans on board. The nuclear carrier *Enterprise* was nearby in Japanese waters at the time but was unable to influence events. Next, McNamara went into a discussion of the Vietnam War and the Administration's proposal to immediately raise the American troop level to 525,000 men. Eventually McNamara got to the Navy's programs. He reiterated his plan to build three *Nimitz*-class nuclear carriers. But, he noted, "The estimated cost of the *Nimitz* has risen twenty-eight percent over last year's estimate ($544 instead of $428 million). . . . The price of the next CVAN promises to be at least as high as the *Nimitz*." He then explained that he was delaying this second ship for one year in order to study means of reducing costs and because of "exceptionally long-lead times required for nuclear components."

A year later, in early 1969 when the fiscal 1970 budget went to Capitol Hill, there was a new President, Richard M. Nixon, and a new Secretary of Defense, Melvin Laird. After representing a Wisconsin district in the House for sixteen years, in January 1969 he became the first former Congressman to head the Department of Defense.

The fiscal 1970 budget, actually developed by the outgoing Johnson Administration, asked for the second *Nimitz*, estimated to have a total cost of $510 million. This new ship would be named *Dwight D. Eisenhower* in honor of President Nixon's former superior. Congress promptly voted approval for this ship, which would give the Navy a total of three nuclear carriers by the middle 1970s. And the House Armed Services Committee tried unsuccessfully to include long-lead funds for still another nuclear carrier.

Although the Defense Department did ask for long-lead funds for the fourth nuclear carrier the following year, Laird announced that the moneys would not be spent until completion of a new round of studies into carrier requirements. The Navy's leadership, concerned over the wearing-out of older carriers that the nuclear ships were meant to replace, was upset with this action. Congress responded and in an unusual move the Senate and House Armed Services committees held a lengthy hearing on the "CVAN-70 Aircraft Carrier." For six days members of both houses, in session under the gavel of Senator John Stennis, heard a parade of Navy witnesses telling of the need for the additional carrier. And there was no question that the carrier would be nuclear-powered— another 90,000-ton giant of the *Nimitz* class.

Significantly, except for General Earle Wheeler, chairman of the Joint Chiefs of Staff, the witnesses all represented the Navy or Congress; there were no Defense officials. Rickover appeared, alone, not accompanied by either AEC officials or his own lieutenants, a rare setting for him. His two prepared statements—one on the need for aircraft carriers, and one on the need for nuclear propulsion—were models of well-reasoned, carefully researched papers, drawing extensively on the lessons of World War II. There was no question in Congress or the Navy that the next carrier should be nuclear.

When the overall testimony was published—it covered 758 single-spaced pages—it provided a remarkable analysis of modern aircraft-carrier issues. The final report—a five-page document—called for immediate spending of the long-lead funds for the CVAN-70. Of nine members of the Senate and House on the joint committee, only Senator Stuart Symington, a former Secretary of the Air Force and long-time carrier opponent, asked that the spending decision wait until the Administration and the National Security Council completed their review.

Such "recommendations" could not force the Nixon Administration to start work on the ship, and the next year, in March of 1971, when Laird took the fiscal 1972 budget to Capitol Hill it was the same story: both the *Nimitz* and *Eisenhower* were behind schedule (they would join the fleet in 1975 and 1977, respectively); and they were costing more than previously estimated. And, Laird told Congress, he was not yet prepared to order the ship in fiscal 1972; possibly, he said, he would do so in 1973 or 1974.

At last, Laird asked for advanced funding for the third *Nimitz* in the fiscal 1973 budget, which the Navy estimated would cost almost one billion dollars. The following year the ship was requested by the Administration and fully funded by Congress. With this ship, by the early 1980s the Navy would have twelve postwar carriers, of which four would be nuclear-propelled, plus the three older *Midway*-class ships.

No sooner was the third *Nimitz* authorized than it became evident that the total number of carriers would still decline because the older ships were wearing out faster than they could be replaced. The continued need for large numbers of carriers, even after the Vietnam War ended, led the Defense Department to come forward with a proposal to build several small carriers, of about 55,000 tons, with oil-burning propulsion. The Pentagon said it believed that several such ships could be built, each for about one-half the cost of a *Nimitz*. The Ford Administration had proposed to build one of these smaller ships in fiscal 1979 and one in 1981.

When President Carter took office, his Secretary of Defense, McNamara-protégé Harold Brown, instead announced he would seek funds to build only one of these "mid-size" CVVs, and that one not until fiscal 1980. The response by the Navy and Rickover was immediate and vitriolic.

Rickover told Congress, "For the foreseeable future, the aircraft carrier will be the principal offensive striking arm of the Navy in nonnuclear war. No other weapon system under development can replace the long-range sustained, concentrated firepower of the carrier air wing." He continued to tout the advantages of carriers and attacked the nonnuclear ships. He warned that as the number of carriers in the U.S. Navy decreased it was important to procure the largest and best available—that is, nuclear.

The Navy's leadership was, on this occasion, in full agreement with Rickover. In unity the top Navy officials had considerable influence on the Congress. The House proposed building a fourth *Nimitz* type—at a cost of over two billion dollars. The Senate, however, called for building another oil-burning ship, a duplicate of the *Kennedy*. Ironically, probably the strongest proponent of a large carrier in the Senate was Gary Hart of the Armed Services Committee. A decade earlier Hart had been campaign manager for George McGovern in a Presidential thrust that was based in large part on an antimilitary stand. But Hart, like many others, had come to understand the flexibility and capability of sea-based tactical aircraft. He was not, however, convinced that the nuclear propulsion of the *Nimitz* was worth the perhaps half-*billion*-dollar increase over a *Kennedy*.

The Senate-House conference agreed on building the fourth *Nimitz* and the ship was duly funded by Congress. But Carter stood opposed. Many observers believed that Secretary of Defense Brown simply wanted no carrier at all, while those with less opinion of the Carter-Brown team even suggested that the CVV was a "red herring"—an idea put forward that would result in such congressional indecision that no carrier would be built. Carter, pressing forward with the era of détente and emphasizing the NATO buildup in Europe at the expense of other forces, vetoed the entire fiscal 1979 procurement budget in order to kill the fourth *Nimitz*.

The mood of Congress was obvious, but Brown again proposed an oil-burning, medium-size carrier for construction under the fiscal 1980 budget. With little debate, the Congress again authorized and funded a $2.4 billion *Nimitz*. This time President Carter approved the budget. After a hiatus of six years, there was approval for another nuclear carrier—the fifth such ship. Each carrier, with some ninety aircraft and six thousand crewmen, represented the most complex and powerful warship built until that time. Admiral Rickover had influenced the decision to build each ship and, through selection and training of the key officers and enlisted men, the operation of each ship.

The construction of missile-armed frigates (called cruisers after 1975) to escort the nuclear carriers followed an even more convoluted course of action. Congress had substituted a nuclear ship—the U.S.S. *Truxtun*—for one of seven oil-burning frigates in the fiscal 1962 budget. After that, the difficulties with the Typhon antiaircraft missile system had halted the planned construction of additional nuclear frigates, and McNamara, concerned about the increasing Soviet submarine threat to Allied use of the Atlantic in wartime, had concentrated on building smaller, oil-burning anti-submarine escorts. (Congress was voting an average of eleven of these 4,000-ton ships every year in the middle 1960s.)

McNamara proposed additional oil-burning frigates to escort the nuclear carriers. Rickover as well as some other officers openly fought for nuclear ships before Congress. During the fiscal 1967 hearings, Rickover's testimony contained interesting—and highly objective—appraisal of the need for missile escort ships:

> In order to carry out his responsibilities, the Chief of Naval Operations certainly must have *real* ships, not *paper* ships. In order to get real ships, he must ask for ships that he thinks he can get. The record shows that the Secretary of the Navy and the Chief of Naval Operations have stated repeatedly their arguments for building a new nuclear-powered frigate and have stated that they want a number of such ships. Thus far they have not been granted approval for any of them.

Then, with an unusual degree of understanding of the "real" Navy's problems, Rickover continued:

> As much as I favor nuclear propulsion in our major surface warships, I agree that two conventional destroyers that are built are

worth far more to the Navy than an infinite number of nuclear frigates that are not built.

This was a strange statement from the man whose dogmatic callings for what *should* be built—always nuclear ships—probably had cost the Navy many oil-burning aircraft carriers and frigates during the 1960s. These Rickover statements coincided with those of the Navy's leadership. Addressing the same issue a year later, Secretary of the Navy Paul Nitze, in answer to a question in Congress about why he gave priority to conventional over nuclear escorts, answered: "I did not list the DLGN as being a matter of overriding concern, because my view . . . is that the important thing for us . . . are the two DDGs conventional destroyers which are in the budget."

Secretary Nitze and the Chief of Naval Operations were assisted in their arguments for more nonnuclear ships by the efforts of a brand-new rear admiral, Elmo R. Zumwalt. A new Systems Analysis Division had been established in OPNAV and Zumwalt's command of a cruiser-destroyer flotilla was prematurely terminated to make him the first head of the division. His first important effort, in response to McNamara's demands for more quantitative rationale from the Navy for more surface ships, was the Major Fleet Escort Study.

According to Zumwalt, "The study did not deal directly with propulsion systems, but since it recommended a very large building program that would ultimately bring the Navy's total number of escorts to a minimum of 242, and since a nuclear-powered escort—a DLGN like the *Bainbridge*—costs two-and-a-half times as much as a big, high-performance destroyer and five times as much as a relatively austere patrol vessel that is entirely adequate for many purposes, the study did come down by implication on the side of conventional propulsion for most escorts."

Rickover immediately opposed the study, in Zumwalt's words, with efforts that "were both overt and covert." One member of Zumwalt's study team was Captain Forrest Petersen, an aviator scheduled to command the nuclear carrier *Enterprise*, the top aviation command of the time. "As soon as Rick got wind of the way the study was going, two or three months before it was officially complete, he made it implicitly clear to me . . . that unless support for nuclear propulsion turned up somewhere in the study, Pete could kiss *Enterprise*—which meant his career—goodbye."

With some fancy footwork, Zumwalt and his colleagues developed the "need" for a supplement to the study that would address warship endurance; in the supplement, nuclear propulsion could be addressed, and very favorably. "Ironically," added Zumwalt, "although we bent the supplement in Rickover's direction as far as our professional scruples allowed us to . . . it still made a case for nuclear propulsion that was *underwhelming.* Rickover wanted something like twenty-five DLGNs. The supplement said that from sixteen to nineteen *could* be justified—with all sorts of questionable assumptions." (Zumwalt's emphasis)*

Petersen went on to command the *Enterprise,* and to hold several three-star positions before retiring in 1980. Rickover went on to criticize the Major Fleet Escort Study. He told the Joint Committee that the question of nuclear escorts should be answered separately from such analysis. Again, Rickover sought to divide his navy and all criteria for funding it from the rest of the Navy. But he did find one valid use for such studies. During the Revolutionary War, he reminded the Congressmen, in the Battle of Springfield in June 1780, the local troops ran out of cannon wadding. The Reverend James Caldwell, according to Rickover, "carried from his church an armful of hymnals by the theologian Isaac Watts. He urged the troops: 'Now put Watts into 'em boys. Give 'em Watts.' "

Noting that "in every war we have to fight with the weapons we have, I suppose in the next war, we'll be exhorting our sailors: 'Now put the Studies into 'em boys. Give 'em Studies,' " said Rickover—and he added, "This is one supply of ammunition that is inexhaustible."

Eventually yielding to Congressional pressures, McNamara allowed the funds voted by Congress in fiscal 1966–1967 for another nuclear escort to be released for use. This ship, designated DLGN-36, was a 10,000-ton warship. McNamara sought to have subsequent nuclear escorts built much smaller. At Rickover's urgings, Congress funded a series of six of these large nuclear escorts through 1975 albeit at irregular intervals. Yet despite Rickover's appeals, Congress was voting many more large oil-burning destroyers than nuclear ships. And, both Congress and the Navy were losing interest in nuclear ships as their costs increased at a faster rate than the costs of conventional ones, and nuclear-trained personnel were becoming harder to retain.

Still, Rickover argued for more nuclear ships. He told Congress in 1973 that "for the nuclear frigate program the future remains bleak. Two years ago the Navy long-range program for these ships called for building more than twenty. The Department of Defense has now eliminated any nuclear frigates beyond those under construction from their long-range plan."

* *At that time there were only four nuclear escorts in existence.*

Again Rickover played with the facts. There was not then a formal Navy *program* for twenty DLGNs—just the annex added to Zumwalt's Major Fleet Escort Study, in large part to keep Pete Petersen in good standing with Rickover. Again, Rickover was pointing to the Defense Department as the enemy when he sought support from the Navy. But as CNO, Zumwalt would not support the DLGN program. Instead, he sought many smaller conventional escort ships. The Secretary of Defense in 1974–1975, James Schlesinger, agreed. Noting the increasing costs of nuclear ships, Schlesinger told Congress that "if we are to procure the large numbers of ships that will be needed to maintain a force of even 200–225 surface combatants, it is evident that the bulk of them must come from the 'low' (nonnuclear) side of the spectrum."

Rickover fought back. In the hearing rooms of Congress he sought support of his nuclear program and won approval of the so-called Title VIII law that all future carriers and cruisers would be nuclear-powered. Even with Title VIII, Rickover still had to fight Defense and the Navy. Zumwalt tells the story this way:

> Rickover made a crafty and determined effort to get $244 million of construction money allocated to two of his guided missile frigates (DLGNs). Since that would have meant not building at least eight and probably ten patrol frigates that the Navy badly needed, I fought him tooth and nail. Rickover's repertoire of wiles ranged all the way from the almost sublime one of trying to slip the delivery date of the desperately needed third carrier by more than a year so that Newport News would be able to make room for DLGN work to the totally ridiculous one of getting himself invited to the Schlesingers' for dinner so he could make his pitch to the Secretary in the privacy of his home on the day after Christmas.

Schlesinger called Zumwalt to discuss Rickover's appeal. Zumwalt agreed that $100 million be given to the DLGN program to start another ship if the money was added to the budget and not taken from other programs. "I also urged that Rickover be made again to pledge active support to the conventional-ships program," according to Zumwalt's autobiography, *On Watch*.

When Schlesinger told Rickover about the "deal," Rickover reportedly said, "In other words you are blackmailing me," to which Schlesinger replied, "Yes." Rickover accepted the $100 million but continued to fight against funds for the so-called low-mix ships, the small carriers and anti-submarine ships wanted by Zumwalt.

The ninth nuclear escort ship, the DLGN-41, was funded by Congress in 1975 and the following year's Defense proposed another nuclear escort. That ship, the DLGN-42, would, it was estimated, cost $368 million, reflecting an increase of $25 million per year in DLGN costs every year since 1970. But the program ran aground as plans were being discussed for a much larger (17,000-ton) "strike cruiser" with nuclear propulsion for the 1977 budget.

That ship, whose cost would be more than twice that of a DLGN, would have an advanced radar/missile control system called Aegis that promised to revolutionize fleet air defense. Its high cost was due to the Aegis system (including missiles) and nuclear propulsion.

But the strike cruiser was not to be. As budget presentation time approached, the estimated cost for the first ship was $1.5 *billion*. This approached the cost of a nuclear carrier. Thus, with up to four such ships being proposed to escort each carrier, this meant an investment of perhaps $6 billion to protect a nuclear carrier that cost only about $2 billion.

Admiral Zumwalt had become CNO in 1970. Much to Rickover's chagrin, Zumwalt directed efforts to determine whether the Aegis radars and the missile launchers would fit in a smaller, nonnuclear destoyer. The answer was yes—Aegis could fit (with some reduction in missiles) in a ship of only 9,000 tons. The aircraft-type gas-turbine engines, which Rickover had earlier opposed in fear they would funnel development funds away from nuclear and steam plants, helped to make such a small ship feasible. Finally, Navy planners settled on a nonnuclear destoyer of some 9,000 tons to carry the Aegis—with the same armament as the nuclear strike cruiser of almost twice the size and cost. (The Aegis destroyer actually carries more guns than the planned strike cruiser.)

The feasibility of putting Aegis in a much smaller, nonnuclear destoyer helped to ring the death knell for future nuclear escort ships. At the same time, the Navy's leadership was becoming highly concerned about the reductions in the size of the post-Vietnam fleet. For example, just before the Vietnam buildup, the Navy had 240 cruisers and destroyers in active service; by 1976 there were only 95 such ships. World War II-built ships were being retired and relatively few new ones were being built. The result was too few ships for the Navy to carry out its assignments. In this austere environment the Navy needed many new missile escorts.

A third factor was working against nuclear surface ships: contractual problems with the Newport News shipyard. Rickover and others blamed the problems on the yard: poor management, false claims for more money, refusal to follow orders. The Newport News firm—the largest shipbuilder in the Western world—put virtually all of the blame on one man: Rickover. (See Chapter 22.)

Admiral James Holloway, the third skipper of the *Enterprise,* succeeded Zumwalt as CNO in mid-1974. He, too, fully understood the advantages of all-nuclear carrier task forces—Rickover had often quoted his letters on the subject before Congressional groups. But as head of the Navy, Holloway also understood the trade-offs between numbers of ships and the costs of individual units. He told Congress, "In planning for the future, a stable long-term shipbuilding program is the key to achieving the necessary capabilities to maintain a margin of superiority over the Soviets. Most *importantly* this plan must be affordable within the defense budget guidelines." J. William Middendorf, the Secretary of the Navy at the time, was even more outspoken, telling the same committee, "We should have an all-nuclear Navy, but I suspect it would be a pretty small Navy. The trouble is, the realities are such that we just couldn't get the number of ships we require."

Rickover reacted strongly, pointing out to Congress that Holloway had become CNO a month before Title VIII became law and that Holloway "recommended, and the Navy adopted his position, that the Navy build eighteen nuclear-powered strike cruisers in lieu of the previously proposed mix of sixteen nonnuclear and eight nuclear ships with Aegis." Then, according to Rickover, the Defense Department cut the Navy's 1977 budget and " 'persuaded' the Navy to recommend . . . a nonnuclear ship with Aegis."

But Rickover missed the point: Holloway might well have got the nuclear strike cruiser or, as was soon put forward, the smaller, nuclear DLGN-42 with Aegis. However, the cost to Holloway would have been an exchange ratio in which he would lose at least two nonnuclear Aegis ships for every nuclear ship that was built. Holloway was supporting a shipbuilding program that had what he considered a minimum number of carrier-escort ships. In 1976, midway through Holloway's four-year tenure as CNO, another Rickover-selected officer became President of the United States, Jimmy Carter. Although he took a public stand in favor of building nuclear submarines, Carter's Secretary of Defense, Harold Brown, soon deleted all nuclear escort ship and carrier construction from Defense planning.

Admiral Rickover continued to exhort Congress to fulfill the requirements of Title VIII—to build all "major combatant vessels . . ." with nuclear propulsion. But it was too late. The world situation had demanded that the United States have a larger Navy. To many Congressmen, even key Rickover supporters, as long as the ships were American it did not matter that their engines derived their energy from JP-5 aircraft-type jet fuel rather than nuclear fission.

In 1980, during the Iran and Afghanistan crises, a three-ship U.S. task force steamed from the Mediterranean, around Africa, and into the Persian Gulf—a distance of some twelve thousand miles—at an average speed of twenty-five knots. All three ships were nuclear-powered—the aircraft carrier *Nimitz* and the missile ships *California* and *Texas* (formerly the DLGN-36 and -39, respectively). Their rapid transit once again demonstrated the unsurpassed mobility of nuclear warships. That same year, however, Navy leaders began discussing with Defense officials and the Congress their plans for a new class of surface missile ships to be built during the later 1980s and 1990s. About fifty destroyer-size warships were being planned. They would be oil-burning ships. There was no consideration of their having nuclear propulsion. There was not even a discussion of a "mix" of both oil-burning and nuclear ships. For the foreseeable future, except for aircraft carriers, the nuclear surface fleet was dead. But Admiral Rickover wasn't; he was still on active duty, dedicated to building a nuclear surface striking fleet and more and larger nuclear submarines.

18
Yesterday's Visionary

"Nuclear propulsion has not improved submarines, but has made them an entirely new kind of warship," Rickover once told a Congressional committee. Rickover was right.

The nation's forty-one Polaris missile submarines provided the most flexible portion of the American strategic force—and the weapons most likely to survive. Nonnuclear strategic-missile submarines were feasible, and the Soviets built twenty-two, labeled the Golf class by Western naval intelligence,* but they were far inferior to nuclear-missile submarines that could remain submerged for longer periods and never had to raise a snorkel tube above the surface of the water to charge their electric storage batteries.

Similarly, nuclear propulsion made "attack" submarines a "new kind of warship." The attack submarines—or SSN, in Navy parlance— are armed with torpedoes for attacking enemy submarines and surface ships. Because of their covert operation, they are highly useful for surveillance and for intelligence gathering off enemy coasts. In the last role they quietly penetrate enemy waters and make visual observations (through their periscopes, at night with infrared lenses) and intercept radar and radio transmissions. Nuclear propulsion enhanced the attack submarine's capabilities in all of these roles.

By the 1960s the production of nuclear submarines had a high priority, especially the strategic Polaris submarines, which were accorded the "Brick-bat" priority,† the nation's highest. Attack submarines, while not

---

* One diesel-electric–propelled Golf-class missile submarine sank accidentally northwest of Hawaii in 1968; portions of that submarine were salvaged from a depth of 17,000 feet by the Central Intelligence Agency's Glomar Explorer in 1974.
† The Brick-bat priority was developed in the 1950s as the highest national priority for defense programs. Its assignment was approved personally by the President. Brick-bat, which was assigned to the Polaris program and a few other defense efforts, meant that the efforts had first call on scarce materials and manufacturing facilities.

while not given that top priority, also were being produced at a prodigious rate. For example, during the seven-year period that the forty-one Polaris submarines were funded, thirty-two SSNs were also authorized—more than all combat submarines funded in the previous seven-year period (sixteen) and more than in the succeeding seven years (twenty-nine). Indeed, the fiscal 1963 program, the first defense budget fully developed by the Kennedy-McNamara team, asked Congress for eight attack submarines—the most ever proposed by any administration in one year. The Congress, predictably, voted funds for all eight SSNs.

With the massive Polaris building program under way, these SSNs more than filled all available shipbuilding ways at the seven yards engaged in nuclear-submarine construction. The Navy's submarine community, whose leadership did not yet consist predominantly of Rickover-trained nucs, had worked hard to convince McNamara of the need for large numbers of nuclear attack submarines.

McNamara's fiscal 1964 and 1965 budgets asked for six SSNs per year, followed by only four in the 1966 request to Congress. The Congress voted six SSNs in every one of these years. With an expected submarine service life of perhaps twenty-five years, that meant that the Navy was building toward a fleet of one hundred and twenty-five nuclear attack submarines. Then the planned procurement of SSNs began to decline, in large part because of the escalation of the Vietnam War, which was taking funds away from new ship construction in favor of replacements for aircraft losses, troop costs, and buying bombs and ammunition. At the same time, McNamara's assistants in the Department of Defense began questioning some of the advanced submarine programs being proposed by Rickover.

The experimental *Nautilus* and *Seawolf* reactor plants had been followed by the smaller, less powerful plants for the *Skate*-class attack submarines. These undersea craft were in turn followed by the six submarines of the *Skipjack* class. These were fast submarines, with their 15,000-horsepower S5W plant driving the streamlined submarines at speeds above thirty knots.

This speed of the *Skipjack*s brought a new dimension to naval warfare. Writing in the Naval Institute *Proceedings* in 1959, Commander R. A. Weatherop observed, "In the future, even in moderate weather, it is possible that destroyer-type ships may not have the speed advantage to run down nuclear-powered submarines." In another *Proceedings* article,

Seadragon skipper George P. Steele wrote, "The nuclear submarine is as detectable by active sonar as is any other submarine, but her great sustained speed and depth can be used to pass through today's detection zone in a very brief period."

The "next generation" SSN, the *Thresher,* which was laid down in May 1958, was deeper-diving, quieter, had vastly improved sonar, different internal arrangement—and was slower. Rickover's same S5W reactor plant was used although the *Thresher* class was much larger, with a submerged displacement of 4,300 tons (compared to the *Skipjack*'s 3,500 tons) and was twenty-eight feet longer. Thus, the same reactor plant was pushing a larger, and hence slower, submarine.

The lead ship of the next class, the *Sturgeon,* was laid down in 1963. Improvements in the crew's living spaces, changes in sonar and torpedo-control equipment, and other features drove the *Sturgeon*s up to a displacement of 4,650 tons and added another thirteen feet to their length. Use of the same S5W plant in these craft produced still slower submarines.

There was one, almost incongruous effort to build a smaller nuclear attack submarine in this period: the *Tullibee,* another attempt at developing a small, "hunter-killer" submarine that could lie in wait off Soviet ports and in narrow straits to sink Soviet submarines going to sea. (This was the same concept as the three K-boats built by the U.S. Navy in the late 1940s.) The *Tullibee* would have nuclear propulsion, but unlike other nuclear submarines built up to that time, she would have electric drive rather than a gearing arrangement with her turbines. Because the reduction gears and other equipment would be eliminated, the *Tullibee* would be a smaller and quieter submarine. And since the submarine was quieter, the *Tullibee*'s own sonar would be more effective. However, she would be slower.

The Combustion Engineering Company developed a diminutive, 2,500-horsepower plant for the *Tullibee,* with its S1C land prototype being installed at Windsor, Connecticut, and the similar S2C being produced for the submarine, which was laid down at the Electric Boat yard on May 26, 1958. During construction the size of the *Tullibee* increased considerably beyond initial designs, and her actual submerged displacement of 2,640 tons was about twice that initially planned.

Her small reactor plant could drive her at just over fifteen knots underwater, too slow in comparison with the contemporary *Skipjack*s. Although she had superior sonar and was relatively quiet, the *Tullibee*'s smaller size meant that she had few torpedo tubes and reloads, and her crew would be more cramped on long patrols. At commissioning, her crew of fifty-six officers and enlisted men was just over half that of a *Skipjack*-class submarine.

At the *Tullibee*'s commissioning ceremonies late in 1960, Navy development chief John T. Hayward said the submarine would be a "vital force" in the battle for undersea supremacy. But the increased capabilities and versatility of the *Thresher* class had ended all serious consideration of additional small killer submarines. Rather, the pattern was set for larger submarines to be succeeded on the building ways by still larger undersea craft.

Some officials in the Navy and in industry still felt that smaller nuclear submarines were feasible, would be less costly to build (hence more might be built) and could be more effective in some roles. One supporter of small submarines was Dick Laning, the first skipper of the nuclear *Seawolf.* One point Laning made was: "It's going to be harder and harder to recruit people for dull, routine jobs." That problem, coupled with the Soviet superiority in numbers of submarines, made smaller killer submarines necessary, in Laning's opinion. Laning—and others—felt that "people-saving equipment" was the answer. One project, initiated in the late 1950s, which might have made small nuclear submarines possible was SUBIC—for Submarine Integrated Controls. This project sought to produce submarine controls like those of a modern aircraft, in which three or four men controlled the entire "platform" and its weapons instead of the fifteen or twenty men normally on watch in a nuclear submarine (with more men being needed when the submarine was at battle stations). Smaller crews would reduce costs and permit the submarines to be much smaller. Automation was possible, it was felt, in the nuclear-machinery spaces, where virtually all automatic systems had manual backup. As one nuclear submarine officer told the authors, "Most manual actions in the engineering spaces are taken after automatic action has already been initiated."

One Navy-Electric Boat study indicated that future, highly automated combat submarines might have crews as small as ten or twelve men. Laning recalls that about 1956 he, Eugene Wilkinson (the first skipper of the *Nautilus*) and Rickover discussed the trends in submarine design—"quite objectively"—and concluded that increasing costs would kill any real increase in the submarine force, and that the number of people aboard the boats had to be reduced. "There were several good ideas, but *never* a systems approach—looking at the entire submarine, all of its machinery and equipment and all of the things a submarine had to do," said Laning. Rickover resisted efforts to automate the propulsion plant and its many related components. Safety was his primary rationale, but, also, it would mean fewer people—fewer nucs—and a smaller nuclear navy.

Several interesting prospects for automation were developed by the Office of Naval Research as well as concepts for advanced, lightweight reactors for submarines. After the *Seawolf* problems, Rickover halted further development of sodium-cooled reactor development in NRB. However, the Office of Naval Research continued looking into the subject. The ability of liquid metals and gas to carry more heat from reactor cores than pressurized water gave promise of smaller reactors. After the subject was raised at a workshop sponsored by the Office of Naval Research, Rickover is reported to have become furious. When the Chief of Naval Research, Rear Admiral M. D. Van Orden, personally delivered him a transcript of the conference, Rickover used profane language and threatened to recommend to Congress that the office, having outlived its usefulness, should be abolished. Plans for a second workshop to discuss lightweight reactors with industry were abruptly halted when Van Orden's boss, an assistant secretary of the Navy, was called by Rickover.

In 1971, Senator Howard Baker had asked Rickover: "You foresee no immediate practical use for the liquid metal breeder reactor concept for submarines?" Rickover responded, "Liquid metal reactor plants are simply too dangerous for submarine application. In the early days we did develop a liquid metal plant for the *Seawolf* because we thought it might weigh less and be more compact." Rickover then explained that it was replaced because it was "potentially too dangerous." He made no acknowledgment of developments in the intervening two decades that may have affected the efficiency and safety of sodium plants.

Baker then suggested, "In summary, you think the future of submarine reactor design is essentially an extension of an elaboration of present techniques and designs with the possible upscaling, speeding up and quieting down of our submarines."

"That is correct, sir," Rickover responded.

The Department of Defense once planned to interview scientists at universities to get their views on the potential of lightweight nuclear reactors for ship propulsion. But these efforts were thwarted by Rickover's appeal to Congressional committees to have such "interference" with his work halted. He similarly deterred naval reactor research by industry. The result of Rickover's determined efforts to stop all nuclear-ship-propulsion development outside NRB has had the result of destroying any possible base for advanced nuclear-propulsion developments other than those he conceived and sponsored. After extensive interviews with individuals in the Navy and nuclear industry, *Science* magazine writer Deborah Shapley observed, "As a result of years of technical censorship of Navy research by ... Rickover ... the Navy today sponsors no significant research on lightweight, small reactors which many researchers believe have the potential for revolutionizing naval shipbuilding by enabling the construction of smaller but more powerful nuclear powered vessels."

Rickover himself has been innovative in his own way. Major quieting features had been provided in the *Thresher* and *Sturgeon* classes, which, according to several observers, Rickover had opposed strongly. Laning recalls Rickover saying that "making nuclear submarines quieter is a bigger problem than nuclear propulsion." But efforts were made to reduce the machinery noises of existing submarine propulsion plants, and two reactor plants were developed by Rickover in an effort to reduce noise.

First the *Narwhal,* laid down in 1966, had an S5G natural-circulation reactor. At low speeds the reactor used natural convection—the rising of warm water—instead of pumps to move the pressurized-water coolant through the reactor. At higher speeds pumps were still needed, but the submarine was quieter when slow.

Second was the *Glenard P. Lipscomb,* with electric drive. Laid down in 1971, the *Lipscomb*'s plant used electric drive instead of geared turbines, removing another principal source of submarine machinery noise. (The *Tullibee* had been an earlier—and smaller—attempt at this concept.) Both newer submarines are large, the *Narwhal* displacing 5,350 tons and the *Lipscomb* 6,480 tons, more expensive than their contemporary SSNs and, while the *Narwhal*'s speed is perhaps thirty knots, the *Lipscomb* is several knots slower.

In the late 1960s Rickover simultaneously urged the Navy and the Department of Defense to build two new designs, the quiet (slow) *Lipscomb* type with electric drive and the fast SSN-688 class with a more powerful but noisier S6G reactor plant. Rickover had initiated both classes, the latter based on a new, 30,000-horsepower reactor—twice the power of the earlier S5W—in an effort to return the high speeds that had been lost since the *Skipjack* class of a decade earlier. But the larger SSN-688 plant would mean a still larger submarine (even with weapons and sonar remaining essentially the same size). In turn, the larger SSN-688 hull would produce more drag; such a submarine would only be a few knots faster than submarines of the previous *Sturgeon* class.

These designs, initiated by Rickover, raised questions in the Navy and the Department of Defense: Was the *Lipscomb* or the SSN-688 worth the additional cost compared to a *Sturgeon*? Should both quiet and fast submarines be built? If so, how many of each? How should they be employed?

There was a submarine "desk" on the OPNAV staff (OP-311), a captain's position, which was the Chief of Naval Operations' adviser on submarine matters.* But there were several other Navy offices in the Pentagon involved in fleet planning and budget matters. Rickover sometimes did not work with those. In 1967, in an effort to better deal with the Department of Defense's systems approach to military forces, the Navy had established a division of systems analysis (OP-96). Its first director was Rear Admiral Elmo R. Zumwalt, Jr., who had declined to enter the nuclear navy after his classic Rickover interview. He later recalled that the SSN-688 had been "sprung upon me as a fait accompli when I was director of the Division of Systems Analysis, the office where all concepts for new weapons systems were supposed to be worked up first. Somehow Admiral Rickover had gotten the work done elsewhere and without my knowledge. I protested, but my immediate boss, Vice Admiral Ephraim Holmes, approved the concept anyway."

Thus, there was Navy planning and Rickover planning; the Navy would gear its plans and proposals to meet Defense Department budget restrictions and Navy analysis of future requirements. Rickover would not. Rickover contended that both quiet (*Lipscomb*) and fast (SSN-688) submarines were needed. There was opposition from both the Defense Department and the Navy. The large attack-submarine building programs of the middle 1960s had been reduced to five SSNs in fiscal 1967 and only three boats in fiscal 1968. Both Defense and the Navy asked whether the more expensive, quiet *Lipscomb* or faster SSN-688 were worth their high costs compared to a *Sturgeon*. Or would the nation be better off applying the cost difference to buy more *Sturgeons*?

All these factors led the Department of Defense to delay approving the electric-drive and SSN-688 submarines. This decision in turn led Rickover to prevail upon the Senate Armed Services Committee and the

---

* *The office would be elevated to Deputy CNO for submarine warfare (OP-02) in 1971 and made a three-star position; a short time later Eugene Wilkinson became the first nuclear-trained officer to hold that position. All his successors would also be nucs.*

Joint Committee on Atomic Energy to hold special hearings on the nuclear-submarine program. From those hearings he could espouse his views and debate Dr. John Foster, who had succeeded Harold Brown as Director of Defense Research and Engineering.

Still another issue that would be debated was whether any nuclear attack submarines at all would be built beyond 1970. The Navy and Defense Department had agreed on a goal of one hundred and five submarines in the fleet, sixty-eight of which would be SSNs. With the fiscal 1969 program, the Navy would have sixty-eight submarines. Rickover announced that the Defense Department planned no more nuclear submarines after that. Secretary of Defense McNamara had actually stated, "If our continuing study of the ASW [Anti-Submarine Warfare] problem should indicate that additional SSNs are required, we can add [more]."

In response to Rickover's claim that after 1970 no attack submarines were planned, Dr. Foster explained that there were no plans to build anything beyond 1975. That was as far as Defense five-year planning went. "It simply means that we have not yet authorized them," he said.

Senator John C. Stennis opened the Senate hearing before a subcommittee of the Armed Services Committee, on March 13, 1968, by announcing: "I have no preconceived conclusions as to the need for additional submarines, frigates or any other weapon system. I am not trying to prove anything. We just want to get the facts and I think this is the way to do it." But, as Rickover, Foster, and others spelled out their positions, some Senators seemed less objective. The following exchange between Stuart Symington and Foster was highly indicative of Congressional attitudes. Symington asked, "But Admiral Rickover wants it, doesn't he?"

"Yes, " said Foster, "I understand he wants it."

"And he has had some experience in the submarine field, hasn't he?"

"He certainly has, sir," Foster agreed.

"Don't you think," Symington asked, "if he wants it, and has had experience, and feels so strongly about it, as he has so expressed to this committee, that you are not risking too much of your engineering judgment by giving him one submarine to prove his point? . . .

"I don't mean to belabor this, but we went all through this kind of argument on nuclear carriers some sixteen years ago in this committee—the same type and character of reservations, hesitation, and discussion. It worked out that Admiral Rickover was right, all the way. He is perhaps the world's foremost authority on nuclear submarines, and not just an operator. He also has engineering talent.

"With the Vietnam War costing eighty million dollars a day, and with us talking about victory or defeat in a future battle like Midway, are we in such terrible shape if we risk, and have, one new submarine?"

When able to respond, Foster observed that while Rickover was indeed an expert engineer, "He has claimed no expertise in other aspects of the boat," and he called attention to Defense's concern for the over-all combat capability of the submarines. With respect to the high costs of the Vietnam War, Foster observed, "It may be because we are spending so much money on the war we ought to consider spending less in other areas."

More significantly, Foster pointed out to the committee that the "characteristics of this boat are not fully defined," and that the Vice Chief of Naval Operations had hastily called a panel together to discuss the operators' view of what Rickover was independently proposing.

After only one day, chairman Stennis lectured the Secretary of the Navy and the CNO—"I just can't conceive of the U.S. Navy coming out second-best in anything as important as the submarine fleet." After four days of hearings, Rickover's views seemed to carry the argument.

Three months later, in June, before the Joint Committee, the debate was more vehement. Early in the hearing, while explaining his position, Foster stated, "I believe the United States has today what are the best submarines in the world. I believe the Navy feels that way. I think Admiral Rickover would support that."

Rickover interrupted: "No, I would not support that. You have used my name twice now on things with which I don't agree. I would rather talk for myself." When he did have the floor, Rickover attacked the Defense Department:

"For several years we have not been able to get permission to build even one new-type submarine. The major reason for this is that our Defense Department headquarters believe we will be able to . . . [classifed matter deleted]. In consequence we are devoting our time to making studies—the standard Department of Defense way of keeping you occupied when they don't want to do anything. . . . Dr. Foster's office is now virtually responsible for designing submarines. . . . We are essentially working for them, and we can do little on our own; we can't get anything done. . . . The Department of Defense contribution has become that of increasing lead times by two years or so. That is the major contribution they are now making to new submarines, as far as I am concerned."

Rickover did have one positive comment: "Dr. Foster helped me to get the electric-drive submarine approved in the Department of Defense two years ago. I must in all fairness make this point."

Again and again Foster tried to make clear the Defense Department's objections: "I am not particularly concerned about the propulsion plant. I am very much concerned about the rest of the submarine." So much of the remainder of his testimony was classified that the authors could not fully comprehend his position. But the testimony from the June 21 hearing clearly shows that the Defense Department's concerns were not being answered and that Rickover was still carrying the day with the Joint Committee.

The Navy's ability to determine its own forces was being diminished by the Department of Defense at almost a steady rate since Robert S. McNamara became Secretary of Defense in 1961. In the opinion of many Navy leaders and planners Rickover exacerbated this process.

Rickover won his battles. The electric-drive *Lipscomb* was built and is successful. She is quieter than steam-turbine submarines, but slower, several knots slower, and she was much more expensive to build. Only one was built.

The SSN-688-class high-speed submarines, later named *Los Angeles* class, were also built. They are faster than the previous *Thresher* and *Sturgeon* classes. Although the exact SSN-688 speed is classified, Admiral Rickover's testimony before Congress indicates that the submarines are about five knots faster than their predecessors. To achieve that speed the SSN-688 class has a 30,000-horsepower reactor plant, about twice the power of the widely used S5W plant. Comparative costs are difficult to ascertain, but, according to Navy data, in fiscal 1978 dollars the last *Sturgeon* to be built cost $186 million while a production SSN-688 cost an estimated $343 million. The actual SSN-688 was higher because of additional inflation during its construction period. Thus, more than three *Sturgeons* could have been built for the cost of two SSN-688 submarines.

Explaining the SSN-688, Rickover told Congress that he saw the need for the submarine as an escort for carrier task groups and to counter advanced Soviet submarines. However, it is unlikely that in 1964—when he began development of what was to become the SSN-688—Rickover had knowledge of the capabilities of the Soviet submarines that would emerge a few years later. While the Soviets had a large submarine fleet, they still had far fewer nuclear units than the U.S. Navy, and their overall quality of submarines—and crewmen—was inferior. Rather, it appears that Rickover was concerned about the loss of speed as U.S. submarines had grown larger while still powered by the S5W plant.

Meanwhile, the Navy's management of attack submarines was changing. Heretofore attack-submarine design and construction was managed by the Bureau of Ships (which became the Naval Ship Systems Command). In late 1968 the Navy set up a separate project manager in the office of the Chief of Naval Material to direct construction of the advanced submarines. Rear Admiral Paul L. Lacy, Jr., the project manager, was a veteran nuclear-submarine skipper.

But in 1970 Rickover attacked "the Navy's" management of the SSN-688 program. His complaints to Congress led one of his supporters to explain that Rickover "says that most of the technical personnel previously involved in submarine work are widely dispersed [in Navy offices] where they act as advisors with no real responsibility or authority, or they have been transferred to other work, and the once-capable Bureau of Ships has become a center for court managers who rely on charts, progress reports, management studies, cost-effectiveness comparisons, improvement-program approaches, while neglecting the technical details. . . . They are aping the systems set up several years ago within the Department of Defense. It is well to remember that no number of gardening books will make plants grow in drought."

Navy officials took another view of the situation. The assistant secretary for research and development, Dr. Robert Frosch, said, "Admiral Rickover has the problem of building the reactor system and the propulsion system for the submarine. That is his sole and complete responsibility." The assistant secretary for installation and logistics, Frank Sanders, said, "I think the [Rickover] statement is not as solid as it might appear on the surface." And the head of the Ship Systems Command, Rear Admiral Nathan Sonenshein, said that "the strength in the submarine design field . . . which I think was being addressed here primarily, has not diminished."

In trying to clarify the matter, Representative Chet Holifield, a Rickover supporter, said that Rickover "is looking at one segment of the program, which is manageable in the way he is managing it. He has proven that by his record of accomplishment. But when you have . . . five or six areas and coordinate them, then this becomes a different, a more complicated problem and cannot be handled in the way he handled the nuclear-propulsion area of it."

"Precisely," answered Frosch.

Rickover's attacks on the way "the Navy" managed the SSN-688 program kept up undiminished, essentially until September 1976, when Vice Admiral Clarence R. Bryan became head of the Naval Sea Systems Command. Bryan, an EDO, was a submariner and nuclear-trained. And he gained a reputation as a "Rickover man" during his tenure as head of Navy shipbuilding, which lasted until 1980.

After the lead SSN-688 class submarine in the fiscal 1970 budget, there was an increasing rate of authorizations—four SSNs in 1971, six in 1973, and five in 1974. Elmo R. Zumwalt, who had become CNO on August 1, 1970, was willing to push for five SSNs annually during his first years as CNO and then cut back to two per year to provide funds for the advanced ships that he was planning. The net result would be more SSN-688s than the existing Navy long-range plans provided. Zumwalt contends that Rickover agreed to the plan but then, according to Zumwalt, Rickover "not only did not help me but continued to work actively against me." Zumwalt also sought to clarify exactly how many attack submarines the Navy should build. Rickover and OP-02 (Wilkinson) supported the five-per-year rate. But the Navy's analysis office (OP-96) looked at the over-all Navy forces available for various missions and determined a need existed for about eighty SSNs. The number of ninety SSNs was then put forward by Zumwalt as his official goal—a building rate averaging three and a half per year.

Rickover and Wilkinson objected. The issue was pushed up to Secretary of the Navy John Warner, who had taken that post in May of 1972. In what was described as a "stormy session," Zumwalt and Rickover stated their cases to Warner. Rickover, according to Zumwalt, using "foul language and making personal attacks against the commander from OP-96 who did the analysis," argued to preserve a goal of one hundred and twenty-plus SSNs. Warner decided in favor of Zumwalt. The goal of ninety SSNs was established.

But no sooner was the issue of SSN force levels resolved than Rickover sought to produce a faster and larger attack submarine, at the time called "the mid-1970s design." Rickover proposed developing a still larger submarine plant—one producing some 60,000 horsepower, or twice that of the *Los Angeles*. There would be a speed increase of several knots albeit with a larger and much more expensive submarine.

Zumwalt immediately opposed the project. The cost of developing the reactor and building a new, larger class of SSNs would force the Navy to cut back on other programs. Rickover began selling the ship in Congress as a weapon to counter the growing Soviet fleet of modern surface warships. The new submarine would have anti-ship missiles that it could fire, while submerged, to attack Soviet surface ships, in addition to anti-submarine weapons. Calling the proposed craft the "tactical cruise missile submarine," Rickover explained to the Joint Committee that "the military potential of a nuclear submarine capable of firing a cruise missile* has not been understood by the U.S. Navy. In my opinion," he said, "one of our most urgent military requirements is the development of a new design high-speed nuclear submarine capable of firing tactical cruise missiles." A few days earlier Representative Robert L. F. Sikes in a House hearing had asked Rickover: "Would you say this is the No. 1 need in submarine development today?" Rickover responded: "Yes, sir, the need for this submarine is clear and urgent."

Rickover's view was not shared by Zumwalt or by the Navy as a whole. Despite Rickover's description of his new submarine as primarily a tactical cruise-missile ship (critics began calling it a "submerged battleship"), Zumwalt was sidestepping this issue by directing that the new Harpoon anti-ship missile be made small enough to fit into existing submarine torpedo tubes. Thus, every SSN could replace some torpedoes with anti-ship missiles, alleviating the need for a new class of cruise-missile submarines.

However, the main justification for SSNs was the anti-submarine role. Here Rickover argued that the additional few knots of the 60,000-horsepower submarine would make it much more effective in submarine-versus-submarine battles. Despite his criticism of such studies, he commissioned a private research corporation to perform a one-million-dollar analysis of SSNs to demonstrate the superior effectiveness of the faster submarine. But his arguments were not convincing to Navy and Defense planners. It could be demonstrated that tactics, sonar effectiveness, and torpedo performance could also affect underwater battles, in many cases giving the edge to SSN-688 and earlier submarines. Zumwalt directed that the Rickover-sponsored study not be released until colored pages were added to each section telling OP-96's viewpoint of the issues.

The SSN-668 construction rate declined rapidly despite Rickover's effort on Capitol Hill—only three submarines each in fiscal 1975, 1976 and 1977, and then down to one per year. Opposition to the SSN-688 class was increasing. The submarine was large, at 6,900 tons submerged some half again as large as the previous *Sturgeon* class and sixty-eight

---

* A cruise or guided missile is a small aircraft-like weapon, using wings or fins for lift, is powered most or all the way to its target, and can have a varied flight path. A ballistic missile is like a bullet that has power only during the initial phase of its flight and travels a "straight" ballistic trajectory to its target.

feet longer. Yet the two classes had similar weapons and sonars as well as most other features. The SSN-688 had about five knots more speed in return for the increases in size and cost.

A Defense Department study completed in 1976 pointed out that the high cost of submarines would not permit the Navy to sustain a force of even ninety SSNs. The study, by Robert Chapman, noted that unless the cost-and-performance relationship could be improved there would be a major decline in SSN-force size. At three boats a year only some seventy-five would be available by the 1990s. A retiring Navy captain, William L. Bohannan, who had commanded the *Sturgeon* and served in several other nuclear submarines, said that SSN-688s could not be built efficiently, that is, with minimum labor and maximum use of advanced technology, because of their design. He said that future submarines could be smaller, cost less, and have smaller crews—perhaps only thirty men each—if technology was properly used.

Meanwhile, the cost of nuclear submarines was soaring ($597 million each in fiscal 1981). President Carter's Secretary of Defense, Harold Brown, was planning to build only one per year in the early 1980s. The Navy's leadership—nuclear and nonnuclear—was concerned about the general drop in planned shipbuilding under the Carter Administration, including the decline in submarine construction.

In May 1978 the Senate Armed Services Committee published its authorization bill, stating that the "committee is concerned that the high cost of the SSN-688-class attack submarine, coupled with probable fiscal constraints, will cause a decline in the submarine force levels. . . . The committee requests the Navy . . . to prepare and submit to the Congress . . . a comprehensive study and evaluation of all options . . . includ[ing] evaluations of lower cost, lower capability nuclear propelled submarines *and the use of non-nuclear* submarines for some missions. . . ." (Emphasis added) The Senate wording became part of the defense authorization bill.

At the invitation of CNO Holloway, Dr. D. A. Paolucci, a retired Navy submarine officer, in 1977 had proposed an analysis of submarine requirements to objectively determine the best requirements for future attack submarines. The OPNAV submarine community dissuaded the CNO from pursuing that effort. But the following year—aided by the Congressional interest—Paolucci convinced Dr. David Mann, the Assistant Secretary of the Navy for research and engineering, of the need for such an effort. Mann, less encumbered than the CNO, initiated the study to examine the benefits of again building *Sturgeon*-class submarines, with updated equipment, as well as other SSN options. Secretary of the Navy

Graham Claytor said, "It has become clear that we need to expand the Navy's options in the nuclear-submarine building program." Alternatives to the *Los Angeles* were being sought, according to Claytor, "to avoid letting future critical decisions be made by default."

Rickover protested. Dr. Paolucci was asked to leave the study group. Admiral Rickover's office and the Deputy CNO for Submarines were to participate in an "advisory" capacity. The Submarine Alternatives Study was completed in mid-1979.

While the study results remained secret, Rickover soon commented publicly on the report, providing an indication of their thrust. The study was totally a Navy effort under Dr. Mann; still, Rickover cited it as demonstrating "again the Defense Department disposition to produce voluminous expensive studies to support the pollyannish notion that cheaper is better."

Apparently the Mann study acknowledged that the *Los Angeles* was the "best" SSN that the United States could construct at the time. But it also raised the option of building cheaper, albeit less capable, SSNs in greater numbers than *Los Angeles*-class submarines. In his criticism, Rickover pointed out, "The Navy is perfectly capable of designing and building cheaper submarines, just as Detroit could design and build cheaper automobiles. The question is, will these cheaper versions serve the purpose for which they are intended?"

Obviously there is a reply to this which while not really a parallel does carry logic. Detroit was forced to build cheaper automobiles because of foreign competition, the gasoline situation of the late 1970s, and political-economic realities. Chrysler's concentration on larger (more capable) cars in part led to that firm's catastrophic problems, while the "less capable" X-model cars were an overwhelming sales success—and much cheaper to operate.

His testimony about the Mann study, given to the sea-power subcommittee of the House Armed Services Committee, also included traditional Rickover clichés: "History is repeating itself. The situation today is not unlike that in the early days of the *Nautilus* when Navy officials, unable to appreciate the significance of nuclear powered submarines, pressed for slower, less capable diesel submarines." (The authors have found no documentary evidence to support this frequently stated Rickover thesis.) And, of course, "Therefore while some of the views I express today may be contrary to those of my superiors, I claim no superior wisdom."

But the critique of the Mann study that he gave to the sea-power subcommittee on October 29, 1979, did make references to his superior wisdom: "I have fought for years to make the Defense Department understand this. I am not sure they ever will." And, "I knew . . . I initiated . . . I convinced . . . At my urging . . . I had suggested . . ." In his thirty-five-page statement and forty-nine-page critique of the Mann study, Rickover sought to demonstrate his superior wisdom before the committee, all to the end of insuring that the *Los Angeles* class—and its larger successors—were continued on the building ways. The offical Navy position, as voiced by CNO Thomas B. Hayward, who had succeeded Holloway in 1978, agreed with Rickover's views, while the Deputy CNO for submarine warfare said simply that the Mann study was "on the shelf—a matter of record." Once more the submarine community began looking at an improved *Los Angeles* design—for a larger, slightly faster submarine that could be built, it was claimed, for the same cost.

That view was not universal in the Navy. Many officers—nuclear and nonnuclear—were expressing the view that to continue building such large SSNs would result only in fewer being built, reducing overall Navy capabilities. This view was also held by Secretary Brown, who provided funds for the Navy to begin development of a smaller SSN, possibly a few knots slower, that would be cheaper, so that more than one submarine per year could be built. The technology, it was claimed, was available. Reportedly, the Electric Boat yard—the West's largest submarine builder—was developing a scheme to apply improved construction techniques and other features to the building of a smaller SSN that would be a few knots slower than a *Los Angeles,* but would carry more weapons and cost only two thirds as much as the larger undersea craft. (A senior Congressional staffer who sought information on this project was told by Rickover that it was none of his business; the staff man did not represent a committee that was particularly pro-Rickover.)

Many individuals, inside and outside the Navy, submarine-qualified and not, were putting forth proposals for lower-cost but still-effective submarines, including nonnuclear ones. Mann himself visited the West German yard building advanced diesel-electric submarines and appeared to have been impressed with such craft, while Senator Gary Hart, from the land-locked state of Colorado but one of the strongest supporters in Congress for a larger, more technologically advanced Navy, put forth a plan to build diesel attack submarines as well as nuclear ones.

The thought of the United States returning to the construction of diesel-electric submarines—to complement the nuclear attack boats—was raised in several quarters in the late 1970s. Hart and others proposed the idea on Capitol Hill in response to the high costs of the *Los Angeles* class, which, they felt, eventually would lead to fewer and fewer nuclear submarines. Several naval officers also raised the issue in private and in the pages of the *Proceedings.*

During this same period the Office of Naval Research compiled a report on "Proposed Future Submarine Alternatives." Included were suggestions for new types of reactor plants that could lead to smaller or more efficient nuclear submarines—gas-cooled reactors, liquid-metal–cooled reactors, gaseous-fueled reactors, and fusion reactors, as well as improved methods of converting nuclear power to propulsion, such as gas turbines, semiconducting motors, and magnetic hydrodynamic systems. The report sought only to describe submarine alternatives "that should be seriously explored if the United States is to maintain submarine tactical and strategic superiority over the Soviets."

When Rickover saw a copy of the draft report he immediately demanded that it be withdrawn from circulation. It was. A short time later the first nuclear submariner to head the Office of Naval Research was appointed.

But NRB was making progress itself in several areas, perhaps most notably that of reactor-core life. The first reactor core installed in the *Nautilus* when she was built drove her 62,562 miles, more than half of them while the submarine was submerged. On her second core, which lasted four and a half years, the *Nautilus* traveled 91,324 miles, most of them submerged. In 1969, Rickover told Congress that the submarine core then being produced would last 400,000 miles. He later told a Congressional committee that cores for the *Los Angeles* class—presumably the 400,000-mile cores—"will have the energy equivalent to over one million barrels of oil. [They] will last for ten to thirteen years of normal ship operation. We are designing cores to last longer than that. My ultimate objective is to design a core that will last the life of a ship."

Rickover has been the man who knows it all, including how many submarines the United States needed and where submarines fitted in the over-all fleet. When his superiors and Navy strategists argued for a balanced force, Rickover went to Congress with one of his picturesque statements:

> The value of submarines is forgotten now in a desire to have what is called a balanced Navy. The Navy's idea of a balance is like a chicken-horseburger sandwich: one horse, one chicken. The Navy

has many surface ship officers who see promotion and command opportunities denied them if we get more nuclear submarines. The nuclear submarines now constitute nearly one-third of the striking
forces of the Navy; however, they comprise about five percent of the
personnel. Since the voice you have in the Navy Department depends on the proportion of people you have, you can see why submarines are not strongly supported. The problem in getting more
submarines is not based on their importance to our defense needs; it
is these other considerations that count.

Members of the Congress and the public see it clearly. But I
cannot get it seen clearly in the Navy. There is a hidden fight going
on all of the time against submarines.

The alleged fight was not slowing down the building of nuclear submarines. By the 1980s the Navy was encountering difficulties with suppliers of nuclear-plant components, shipyards that built nuclear submarines,
and the men who manned the nuclear undersea craft. The last had become a particularly critical factor in the 1960s and 1970s. The first crisis
came with the rapid rate of commissioning Polaris submarines in the
early 1960s, each with two crews of some one hundred and fifty men.
There were bottlenecks: Rickover's need to interview all officers and senior enlisted men, and the length of schooling.

For men going to nuclear submarines—officers and enlisted—there
was a year and a half of nuclear schooling plus a few weeks in submarine
school between being selected and actually reporting aboard a nuclear
submarine. For nonnuclear enlisted men, after their two months of recruit training, there was a further nine to twelve months of missile or torpedo classes, plus two months of submarine school. Thus, from the time a
man enlisted in the Navy to specifically serve in a Polaris submarine it
could easily be sixteen months until he reported aboard ship, and longer
if he was to be nuclear-trained.

At one point, according to an officer who supervised the assignment
of submarine-related schooling, the Navy recruited one hundred men of
the top "mental group" for assignment as machinists in the nuclear navy.
These were the highest-caliber men recruited, including several college
graduates. A few dropped out of recruit school, a few more from the basic
machinist's school, and others from nuclear training. After almost two
years of schooling, only seventeen actually reached nuclear jobs aboard
surface ships and submarines. Most of the others were still in the Navy,
serving as machinists, but highly overqualified for that role—they should
have been trained instead in electronics or in another high-skill field. But

Rickover had demanded that one hundred men enter the specific class.

His method of running his own personnel matters was described by Vice Admiral Smedberg, a former superintendent of the Naval Academy and then Chief of Naval Personnel. "Rickover," Smedberg wrote, "was one person in the Navy empowered to pick the talent he wanted and have it directed into his program at the expense of all our other programs. . . . I was the chief of all naval personnel, but at no time did Admiral Rickover ever acknowledge or feel that I had any business saying anything about the people in his program. . . . I issued the orders but he'd send me over the list of people and where they were to go." But it was Smedberg, not Rickover, who had to be concerned about the overall careers and retention of the men in the submarines as well as in the rest of the Navy.

The nature of the nuclear program made the officer situation even worse. For example, in 1969 there were more than fifteen hundred positions for officers with nuclear training in the Navy, with only one hundred and twenty-two of them ashore. This meant that after an officer had served two or three years at sea aboard a nuclear surface ship or submarine, there was no nuclear shore duty for him. He could be put in a nonnuclear job, but the overall shortage of nuclear officers at sea raised the temptation to keep him aboard ship—for another two or three years. This situation led to increased resignations by nuclear-trained officers.

The situation did improve, but almost ten years later Chief of Naval Personnel Vice Admiral James Watkins, himself a nuc who would later become Vice CNO, told Congress, "The nuclear submarine community continues to be plagued by a shortage of officers." Although enough officers could be then enticed into the nuclear ranks, they simply could not be retained. By 1980 the situation reached the point where Naval Academy midshipmen were being drafted into the nuclear navy to counter the shortages of new officers. This in turn led to increased attrition of first-class midshipmen who had been designated for nuclear assignment.

The Navy was encouraging officers from other warfare branches to transfer into nuclear submarines, but the reverse was not allowed. A number of submarine officers, unable to transfer out of the nuclear navy to another branch, simply left the Navy. This exodus occurred despite the fact that the Navy was paying nuclear incentive bonuses of up to $20,000 per officer for remaining in submarine service.

Originally, Rickover and the Navy had sought to have all officers aboard nuclear submarines nuclear-trained. But this became impossible, and the submarines, from a manpower viewpoint, were divided into the "forward end" (the control, weapon, and sensor spaces) and the "after end" (the engineering spaces). Officers in the forward end were sometimes nuclear-trained, but the captain and executive officer were always nucs; in the engineering spaces, all were nuclear-trained. Thus, in a *Sturgeon*-class submarine, in addition to the commanding and executive officers, there might be five other "front" officers, while there would be five officers assigned to the engineering department. In a missile submarine there would be another five nonnuclear officers. The nonnuc officers, regardless of their training or excellence, could *never* become skipper or exec of a nuclear submarine. Still, there were minimal problems; they were a "band of brothers," with some nucs and nonnucs being Annapolis graduates and having gone to submarine school together, or having gone to universities, and all had gone or would go to the submarine school at New London. They ate together and shared living space, and were all, by an act of Congress, "officers and gentlemen."

But in the enlisted spaces things were different. In a *Sturgeon* there would be about fifty enlisted men in the forward end of the submarine and forty-five in the after end. There were few nucs in the forward end, while all in the engineering department were graduates of the Rickover school. Those enlisted men in the forward end stood watches outside their own specialized area, loaded stores and weapons during replenishments, and the junior men had mess-cook duty—helping the cooks, cleaning up, and waiting on tables.

The nuc enlisted men never stood nonengineering watches, rarely—if ever—helped load stores and weapons, and never had mess-cook duty. Rickover didn't allow it. The result was that quite often a second-class petty officer from the front end would pull mess-cook duty, serving third-class petty officers from the engineering department who would never have such work. None of the engineering department sailors were less than third-class, because they had been promoted while in school, before going to sea. Some nucs who were held back at nuclear school to serve as assistant instructors or for other reasons might not go to sea in their first submarine until they were first-class petty officers. This, in turn, meant there were many senior petty officers in the back end with little or no leadership experience.

Problems invariably resulted. There were hard feelings aboard many submarines. Harsh words were sometimes said, especially when the craft was taking on stores or torpedoes or missiles. On rare occasions fist fights broke out. In 1980, enlisted re-enlistments hovered around fifty percent for first- and second-term retention, in part because of bonuses of $15,000 maximum for nucs shipping over and $12,000 for nonnuclear enlisted men. But there was no third-term bonus, and re-enlistments fell from a high of eighty percent down to twenty-three percent in the late 1970s.

A small percentage of the Navy's submarine force—especially enlisted men—is black. Except for Naval Academy graduates after 1980, submarine duty has been voluntary, and blacks did not volunteer. Aboard the submarines there seems to be little if any prejudice against the blacks; if they are on board, they are qualified. Period.

There were personnel problems in the nuclear navy, officer and enlisted. In 1980 the Navy had 8,061 nuclear-trained men at sea in submarines and 2,674 in surface ships. That was hardly enough to fully man the nuclear positions in all the ships and submarines. The men suffered from long tours at sea, in part because of the lack of shore assignments. In the senior enlisted positions the Navy had only sixty percent of the men needed.

The Reagan Administration, which came to the White House in January 1981, rapidly pushed pay and benefit increases for military personnel through Congress. Those increases and the continued high bonuses for nuclear-qualified submarine officers led to a retention rate of about thirty-three percent during 1981—the worst for any category of naval officer.

Navy officials would say only that the rate was better than the thirty percent retention that they had anticipated if compensation had not been improved. Obviously, something more than pay and benefits was pushing many of these highly skilled officers out of the submarine service. Even those selected for command would not always stay. Several commanding officers of nuclear submarines have asked out—an action that has not occurred on other types of ships.

Still, Admiral Rickover, who once said a submarine patrol of ninety days instead of sixty days "is merely a question of placing more food on board," has always been optimistic about the personnel situation: "Morale is pretty good. Even though the people have to work much harder and are at sea much longer, I think morale in the submarine service is probably as good as in any part of the Navy. We retain a greater percentage of officers than is the case with other Navy components."

The latter part of Rickover's statement was factually incorrect. The former part could be argued—as it has been to the authors by several young nuclear-trained officers who simply left the Navy after back-to-back sea tours aboard submarines, with no hope for any relief. They are all Annapolis graduates; they all wanted to remain in the Navy. But they were not allowed to do so without going back to sea in nuclear submarines.

According to Rickover, the key to the Navy's manpower problem was leadership—and only he understood what leadership was. Nowhere did he better articulate his views on leadership than in the January 1981 Naval Institute *Proceedings*. Complaining about the frequency of articles on leadership "by young, inexperienced officers," Rickover recommended a hiatus "for a decade or so" of such "sophomoric drivel." He said he knew what the principles of leadership were—"in the military service as they are in business, in the church, and elsewhere: a. Learn your job. (This involves study and hard work.) b. Work hard at your job. c. Train your people. d. Inspect frequently to see that the job is being done properly."

Any effort to change his training program—or even to examine it— was met with his advising Congress that "there are those who say that we do not need the degree of excellence we strive for in training our people and that we should cut back on the amount of time spent in this effort." No naval officer dared to bring down the wrath of a Congressional committee by suggesting any change in the manner in which nucs were selected, trained, or assigned.

Similarly, efforts by the Navy's leadership, at times even the staff of the Deputy CNO for submarine warfare, to raise new issues or question submarine design or construction procedures—or the application of new technologies and systems even to the nonnuclear portions of submarines—ran the risk of attacks from Rickover. His direct and continuous lines of communication with the captain of every nuclear ship and with his agents at every naval shipyard that served nuclear ships provided Rickover with an unending stream of messages and letters that could support—from the fleet viewpoint—his position on virtually every issue.

Testifying before the House Armed Services Committee in 1979 when the question of more *Los Angeles*-class submarines was raised, Rickover responded immediately:

I recently received a letter from the Commander of the submarine force of the Pacific which cites actual cases where the *Los Angeles* class submarines were superior to the less capable submarines in ways that could have been critical in a wartime situation. I would be happy to provide the committee with a copy of this letter. It is classified and will need to be reviewed for security in order to include it in the unclassified record. You will find, however, that this letter tells you what it means to have the *Los Angeles* submarine capabilities when you are at sea and not behind a desk.

Could any Defense official or admiral on duty in Washington take a different view? It was the Rickover view and it tended to prevail. And, the Rickover view had never changed, not since the *Nautilus*. But the world and the Navy had changed, and the result, to quote Dr. Paolucci, submariner and analyst, is that the view becomes that of "yesterday's visionary, who is today's conservative, and tomorrow's reactionary."

19

A Nuclear Submarine
Is Missing . . .

"Our nuclear submarines . . . are steaming, on the average, more than twice as much per year as do the diesel-powered submarines. I am told by the operating people they have been very reliable. We have had little trouble," Rickover told a subcommittee of the House Committee on Appropriations on May 11, 1961. Eleven days earlier he had gone to sea on the first sea trials of the U.S.S. *Thresher.*

"She is the first of the new deep-diving submarines," he told the Congressmen. "We went deeper than any U.S. submarine had ever gone before. We did not go to the full design depth because some of the instrumentation . . . was not working properly." The submarine returned safely to port, the faulty instrumentation was repaired, and the *Thresher* went back to sea to complete her diving trials without further incident.

Nuclear submarines, Rickover explained, were safe. Indeed, a review of more than two decades of Congressional hearings on nuclear ships shows there is little concern voiced by the solons about the operating safety of the submarines or their nuclear power plants. Rather, the only major questions asked were about the danger of radiation. And here was Rickover's most pointed response of any issue: "We must be very careful that no accident involving radioactivity occurs. We must constantly exercise rigid controls in selection and training of officers and men and in operation of the ships themselves." The "we" was not the Navy but the Naval Reactors Branch.

But there were operating problems with nuclear submarines and their propulsion plants. Reportedly, "*Nautilus* had once experienced an involuntary shutdown which took twenty-four hours to overcome, during which she had only steerageway on the surface and her diesel auxiliary engine, and . . . at one time or another every nuclear reactor built had scrammed [shut-down] unexpectedly, though usually not for serious cause. *Triton,* with two reactors, twice had had reactor difficulty during her epochal round-the-world cruise, a fact which had been kept out of the papers but had been duly reported to higher authority."

The author of those words was Captain Edward L. Beach, first commanding officer of the nuclear submarine *Triton,* which he took around the world almost entirely submerged in 1960. Those words appeared in Beach's novel *Cold Is the Sea*—which was based on fact.

Rickover and the Navy had built backup diesel-electric propulsion systems in all nuclear submarines. These backup systems were considered necessary in case the reactor plant was disabled or scrammed. The latter occurred when the reactor's safety features shut it down because the safety system sensed a problem in the plant.

Beach's novel explained the potential disaster from a scram or other shutdown. "Granted," he wrote, "because of the intensive training both crews had received, *Nautilus* and *Triton* had been able to effect repairs themselves and had suffered no permanent disability. But the next reactor scram might be less benign. If the reactor could not be restarted, if it happened under solid ice cover, as might be the case with a single reactor ship under winter Arctic conditions . . . things could become difficult."

On several occasions "things had become difficult." The reality of Beach's statements in his novel is not publicly known. But most submarines have experienced reactor scrams, some of which have put the submarines in precarious situations. The Polaris submarine *Von Steuben* suffered a reactor scram while the submarine's diesel engine lay taken apart for maintenance. Large amounts of electricity are needed for a reactor start, and the storage battery was soon exhausted without restarting the reactor. The submarine wallowed helplessly on the surface as, by flashlight, the crew tried to reassemble the diesel.

The exact amount of time that the *Von Steuben* was adrift has not been made public, but it was obviously for several hours—at least. Finally, the diesel was reassembled and started, and recharged the depleted battery for subsequent restarting of the reactor.

Arctic expert Waldo K. Lyon, who sailed in the *Nautilus* on the first voyage to the North Pole, recalled that while he was aboard the *Skate* in 1962 "on the way up through Baffin Bay, somewhere off Thule, we did have a flooding casualty, where a sea-water circulation line failed . . . when we were down some four hundred feet and sprayed sea water and started to flood the engine room. . . . In this case, we were able to surface, we didn't lose propulsion power." Once on the surface, where the water pressure was greatly reduced, the *Skate*'s crew was able to stop the flooding. Lyon also observed that there had been a "number of instances of flooding and casualties on board, but no losses" in several nuclear submarines during this period. A Soviet book on nuclear submarines listed no fewer than thirty-nine "accidents" involving U.S. nuclear submarines.* Many of these can be confirmed by reading the American press.

There were also casualties in diesel submarines, and two were lost at sea.† But nuclear submarines were potentially more vulnerable to casualties, because they traveled faster, meaning that a jammed diving plane or other mechanical or propulsion failure could more quickly result in tragedy. From the *Skipjack* (completed in 1959) on, the volume of each compartment of a nuclear submarine is so large that the flooding of one would sink the submarine regardless of what countermeasures were taken, and from the *Thresher* (1961) on, the nuclear submarines operate significantly deeper than previous submarines; as one goes deeper the greater sea pressure increases the potential danger from piping failures.

One nuclear submarine that suffered a major problem with her reactor plant was the U.S.S. *Thresher*. The lead ship of a new class of attack submarines, the *Thresher* was still on her sea trials when, on the morning of November 2, 1961, she slid into San Juan, the capital and principal port of Puerto Rico. Upon mooring, the *Thresher* shut down her reactor. It was customary for nuclear submarines in port to use shore power, brought aboard by cable, to provide heating or air-conditioning, lights, refrigeration, and startup power for the reactor.

But because no shore power was available at San Juan, the *Thresher*'s diesel generator was started up to provide electricity. Some seven or eight hours after the reactor shutdown the diesel broke down. The men on duty did not immediately realize the severity of the breakdown, believing that it was a clogged cooling system that could be quickly repaired. While sailors worked on the diesel, electricity for the submarine was provided by her electric storage battery.

As it became obvious that the diesel could not be repaired quickly, the decision was made to restart the reactor. But it takes several hours and considerable electricity to restart a reactor after it has been closed down. Before the reactor could be brought to self-sustaining reaction condition the *Thresher*'s electric battery was depleted. What electricity

---

* See Appendix E.
† Two U.S. diesel-electric submarines have been lost at sea since World War II: the Cochino because of a battery fire in the Arctic in 1949, and the Stickleback from a collision off Hawaii in 1958. Their only personnel losses were one civilian from the Cochino and six sailors from another submarine who drowned while taking aboard Cochino survivors in rough seas.

could be drawn from the battery had been used in the effort to start up the reactor and keep vital instruments working. There was no electricity available for lights or ventilation.

Slowly the temperature in the submarine began going up. The reactor plant—a form of steam boiler—keeps its heat for several hours. This, coupled with the closed confines of the *Thresher* and the warm Caribbean night, sent the temperature inside the submarine's machinery spaces soaring—90° ... 100° ... 110° ... and on up to approximately 140 degrees. According to the men in those spaces, it seemed as if the submarine had plunged into hell itself.

But the men kept working, trying to repair the diesel generator and start up the reactor. Four sailors would later receive Navy Commendation Medals for their work that night. Some men had to be ordered out of the spaces as they began to suffer from the heat and irritants in the air. For some ten hours there was no power in the *Thresher* except for the dying electric battery.

Commander Dean Axene, the skipper, returned aboard just as the battery finally ran down, ending all possibility that the *Thresher* could restart her reactor without outside help. He was now concerned that the high temperatures and humidity inside the submarine would damage electrical equipment and force all of his crew to evacuate. Fortunately, the diesel-electric submarine *Cavalla* was moored alongside. With cables borrowed from another ship, a connection was made between the two submarines, and the *Cavalla* started up her diesel engines to provide electric power across to the *Thresher*. With this electricity—from a conventional submarine—Axene was able to restart the *Thresher*'s reactor.

"We could have gone to sea at six the next morning without any trouble," Axene said later. After her ordeal at San Juan, and some time spent there cleaning up the ship, the *Thresher* continued her trials.

The nature of the reactor plant, its long startup time and demand for large amounts of electricity, like its susceptibility to an inadvertent shutdown—a scram—could create situations that were potentially very dangerous.

From her continued trials in southern waters, the *Thresher* headed back north, to the Portsmouth Naval Shipyard, where she had been built. The *Thresher* was the first nuclear-submarine class whose lead ship had been built at Portsmouth. The Electric Boat yard had built the lead ships for the previous nuclear-submarine classes. After minor maintenance and repairs, the *Thresher* returned to sea in early February 1962 to continue tests, trials and exercises.

That spring the Navy decorated seven officers and five civilian engineers for their contribution to development of the *Thresher*. At ceremonies in Washington on the morning of April 23, Secretary of the Navy Fred Korth presented the Legion of Merit award to five of the officers, two of them rear admirals: Robert L. Moore, Deputy Chief of the Bureau of Ships, and Armand M. Morgan, formerly Assistant Chief of BuShips for ship design and research. Moore, briefly, had been designated by Rickover as his own successor many years before. Morgan had served with Rickover as a junior officer in BuShips before the war and had gone on to have a key role in the design of nuclear submarines.

The official Navy announcement of the awards said, "The design and operating characteristics of these submarines reflect a number of advances in submarine construction. The *Thresher* and successors can dive deeper, run more quietly, detect targets at greater distances, and fire more potent weapons than any previous attack type submarine." Admiral Rickover was not among those cited for the development of the *Thresher*.

The *Thresher*, meanwhile, continued to establish an enviable record in extensive tests and exercises until July 1962. She then entered the Portsmouth Naval Shipyard for a major overhaul prior to undertaking operational assignments. While in the yard, Commander Axene was relieved as commanding officer and ordered to command a Polaris submarine being built at Newport News Shipyard in Virginia. Axene protested: "I was unhappy with the orders and wanted to stay with the *Thresher*. I felt the overhaul was unfinished business, and I wanted to turn the *Thresher* over to my relief as an operating unit." But the Polaris program had top national priority and there was a shortage of experienced submarine skippers. Axene left the *Thresher*. His relief was Lieutenant Commander John W. Harvey.

Harvey, like Axene, was a Naval Academy graduate, although Harvey had first attended the University of Pennsylvania for a year on a scholarship. He liked and had played football, as had Axene. Their professional careers had crossed before; Axene had been in the original *Nautilus* crew, and shortly before he departed he had welcomed Harvey aboard as reactor-control officer. Wes Harvey had made the transpolar cruise in the first nuclear submarine and had returned to the arctic as executive officer of the *Skate* in 1962.

At 3:45 on the morning of April 9, 1963, the *Thresher* rested at Pier 11 of the Portsmouth Naval Shipyard. It was a cold, damp morning. Inside the *Thresher*, preparations were being made for going to sea, and Lieutenant Commander John S. Lyman, the engineer officer, began the four-hour countdown required for starting up the S5W reactor plant. Two hours later he requested permission to pull the first control rods from the reactor's core, to reduce the number of neutrons being absorbed and permit fission to begin. Harvey gave his approval. At 6:15 the reactor went critical, reaching the point of self-sustained nuclear fission.

At 7:30 Harvey was notified that the propulsion plant was ready to "answer all bells"—to produce as much power as needed to propel the *Thresher* to sea and into the depths. A short time later the *Thresher* cast off and swung into the channel of the Piscataqua River. On board were twelve officers and ninety-six men of the submarine's crew, a submarine-force staff officer, three officers and thirteen civilians from the shipyard, a specialist from the Naval Ordnance Laboratory, and three civilians from firms with equipment on board. In all, one hundred and twenty-nine men were aboard the *Thresher* as she went to sea the morning of April 9, 1963.

East of Boston the *Thresher* rendezvoused with the submarine rescue ship *Skylark,* a 205-foot Navy tug and salvage ship. Perched on her fantail was the McCann rescue chamber, a bell-like device that could be winched down a steel cable to the deck of a stricken submarine to rescue survivors. In its only real use, in 1939, such a diving bell had saved thirty-three men from the stricken U.S. submarine *Squalus.* (Twenty-six died when flooding compartments in the submarine were closed off to save other crewmen.) The *Squalus* had sunk in two hundred and forty feet of water. The chamber itself was designed for use down to eight hundred and fifty feet. The *Thresher* could operate much, much deeper.

Rather, the *Skylark* was accompanying the *Thresher* more as a surface escort, to provide a communications link to the surface and make certain no ships would interfere with diving trials after her nine-month overhaul. The only means of communication between the submerged *Thresher* and the *Skylark* would be the UQC, or underwater "telephone," a primitive sonar-type device. The quality of communication between a surface ship and a submarine varies as sea conditions and the distance between the ships change. Also, as there are differences in water density and temperature, the sound waves are distorted and deflected, with garbled transmission being a normal occurrence.

On April 9 the *Thresher* conducted shallow diving tests over the continental shelf, a narrow plateau of submerged land off the Atlantic coast. The shelf is about six hundred feet deep at its maximum, after which the bottom of the Atlantic falls off steeply, to more than eight thousand feet. The *Thresher*'s shallow dives over the shelf meant that a casualty could bring her to rest at no more than six hundred feet, well within the rescue capability of the *Skylark* if there were survivors in unflooded compartments.

During the night of April 9–10 the *Thresher*, her shallow tests completed, headed eastward, into the deep Atlantic. The *Skylark* wallowed along the surface, with the two ships again rendezvousing at 6:35 on the morning of April 10. The *Thresher* then proceeded to go deep into the depths, to the submarine's maximum operating, or test, depth. Some forty times before her overhaul the *Thresher* had been to that depth. The Navy classifies all information on submarine depths beyond four hundred feet, but, in view of subsequent statements by Navy officials, the *Thresher*'s test depth was obviously more than twice that distance.

In theory, U.S. submarines are designed to have a fifty-percent margin over their test depth. That means if a problem forces a submarine below its operating depth, it should be safe for half again that distance. After that, the tremendous sea pressure (445 pounds per square inch at one thousand feet) will force sea fittings and pipes to fail, and then rupture the steel pressure hull.

Commander Harvey took the *Thresher* into the depths. Through the precarious UQC communications link to the *Skylark* he advised that references to the submarine's actual depth would be in terms of the submarine's test depth. This avoided broadcasting the submarine's actual depths—just in case Soviet intelligence craft or submarines were in the area. The dive was slow and careful, halting periodically while the crew and specialists checked equipment and instruments.

There were routine communications checks. At 9:02 the *Thresher* asked for a repetition of a course reading from the *Skylark*. Ten minutes later the two ships made another routine check.

Then, "about a minute later," according to Lieutenant (j.g.) James Watson, the *Skylark*'s navigator, the *Thresher* reported: "Have positive up angle. . . . Attempting to blow up."

Others who were aboard the *Skylark* and heard the message would remember it differently. The commanding officer, Lieutenant Commander Stanley W. Hecker, recalled the voice over the underwater telephone as having said: "Experiencing minor problem. . . . Have positive angle. . . . Attempting to blow." Another man on the *Skylark* said the last message was: "Experiencing minor difficulty. . . . Have positive up angle. . . . Attempting to blow. . . . Will keep you informed."

The *Skylark*'s log—the official record—states that at 9:12 a "satisfactory" communications check was made. Subsequently, it showed, the submarine reported, "Have position up angle. . . . Attempting to blow up." Contrary to Navy procedure, the exact time of that message was not recorded.

Those aboard the *Skylark* then heard the sounds of air under high pressure—as if a submarine was trying to "blow up" by using high-pressure air to force water out of her ballast tanks. At 9:14 the *Skylark* told the *Thresher* she had no contact on the UQC. "Are you in control?" asked Hecker.

But nothing was heard from the submarine until 9:17, when there was a garbled message. To Hecker the message was unintelligible. To Watson it ended with the distinct words "test depth." Seconds later Watson heard a sound he remembered from his World War II service—"the sound of a ship breaking up . . . like a compartment collapsing."

The *Skylark* continued to attempt to communicate with the *Thresher*. There was no response. History's worst submarine disaster had occurred, and it was a U.S. nuclear submarine that had carried one hundred and twenty-nine men to their deaths.* The water depth where the *Thresher* was lost was 8,400 feet. Long before the submarine had hit bottom, pipes and fittings had given way, admitting high-pressure jets of water to several compartments; moments later the hardened steel hull began to pull, like taffy. The added weight of inrushing water pushed the submarine deeper at a still greater speed. Then the tremendous water pressure imploded the submarine—blew in the unflooded spaces. The compression created a flash of heat and light. All survivors inside the compartments—some were already dead or injured from the inrushing water and pressure—died instantly.

The remains of the *Thresher* rained down on the ocean floor.

By late in the afternoon of April 10, 1963, when the search for the *Thresher* was beginning, there were those at Norfolk and New London, and in Washington, who were fearing the worst. That night Admiral Rickover made several telephone calls. One was to the Office of Information, where he advised the naval officers on duty that he was available for any help that they may need from him. He also called Ralph K. James, Chief of the Bureau of Ships.

"He called to remind me on that occasion," said James, "that he was not the submarine builder, he was simply the nuclear-plant producer." James said that it was the only time in his four-year tenure as Chief of BuShips that Rickover "was thoroughly dishonest." James continued: "Rickover went to great extremes to disassociate any likelihood of failure

---

* *Previously the worst peacetime disaster was the ninety-nine men lost (of one hundred and three on board) when the British* Thetis *sank in 1939.*

of the nuclear plant from the *Thresher* incident. I considered this thoroughly dishonest."

The Navy named a court of inquiry to look into the *Thresher* disaster. The court met briefly at New London and then moved to the Portsmouth Naval Shipyard, from where she had sailed on April 9 on her last voyage. One of the first witnesses was the submarine's first commanding officer, Dean Axene. He told the court: "There is no way for me or anyone else to know what happened out there, but it must have been associated with a flooding-type casualty. And the flooding would have been almost instantaneous, leaving such short time that the personnel could not react to let someone know they were in trouble." Other former *Thresher* personnel testified, as did a number of engineers, submarine experts, shipyard officers, men who were aboard the *Skylark* at the time, and Vice Admiral Rickover.

Clad in civilian clothes, Rickover arrived at the court of inquiry on Monday, April 29. Rickover first said that he would like to say something about the crew: "I and members of my group knew many of the crew members personally and were responsible for their selection, training and encouragement. We knew their problems. Everyone knows how I felt about the crew. It was a personal loss to me. We can only hope that in giving their lives to their country they contributed to our future safety."

Rickover then said the reactor plants used in submarines and surface ships were designed to minimize nuclear hazards. He declared that it was "physically impossible for the reactor to explode like a bomb." Such information was neither new nor important to the court. More to the points of concern, Rickover said the design provided for protection against corrosion by sea water. "In the event of a serious accident," he explained, "fuel elements will remain intact and none would be released."

Danger, he said, could arise only "if the fuel elements were to melt or the boundary [shielding] were to rupture." But, he added, "There is no reason to believe any radiological problems were caused by the loss of the *Thresher*." He also told the court that ocean-floor samples from the area showed the bottom to be free of radioactivity.

After twelve minutes of testimony in open session, the room was cleared of observers and Rickover continued his testimony on a classified basis, behind closed doors. His testimony is still closed, but some who were behind the closed doors with him have shared their reactions with the authors. One officer said, "I was damn impressed by his intellectual honesty. When the chips were really down, when lives were at stake, he acted intellectually humble.

"He said things like, 'I never thought of that' or 'I don't know' or 'Let me go back and talk to my people about that.' "

He spoke for ninety minutes. At the end of his testimony he asked if he could have a transcript, presumably so he could check his testimony. The rules of the court—unlike those of Congress—prohibited such privileges. When he left, he refused to speak to newsmen.

Rickover's testimony was not made public. However, his views of the *Thresher* disaster can be gleaned from his appearances on July 23, 1963, and on July 1, 1964, before a hearing of the Joint Committee on Atomic Energy into the loss of the *Thresher*. His testimony is heavily laced with deletions for reasons of security. Still, the start of his comments were in defense of the *Thresher*'s nuclear plant. Based on studies by the court of inquiry, he said,

> ... statements have been made that [classified] the ship lost propulsion. Such statements cannot, in my opinion, be substantiated and may cause us to lose sight of the basic technical and management inadequacies that must be faced and solved if we are to do all we can to prevent further *Thresher* disasters.
>
> It is not the purpose of my testimony here today to prove that the nuclear power plant did not contribute to this casualty. When fact, supposition, and speculation which have been used interchangeably are properly separated, you will find that the known facts are so meager it is almost impossible to tell what was happening aboard *Thresher* at the critical time.

Then, in a rare admission of the need for improvement, he added:

> When you do not know the specific failure which caused the accident, then the only thing you can do is to examine your designs, fabrication techniques, inspection criteria, training programs, and operating procedures to see if there are further improvements that can be made. There is much we can do and will do in the nuclear power area.

After that, Rickover's testimony was mainly a series of criticisms— against the frequent rotation of officers, particularly those who were concerned with the *Thresher*'s overhaul in the shipyard; the lack of adequate welding techniques of the critical piping that penetrated the submarine's pressure hull; the poor management and quality control in submarine construction; and the manner in which the Navy's leadership made decisions about submarine requirements.

Rickover was correct in his accusations; there were problems in all these areas. But he carefully steered Congress and the Navy away from consideration of the nuclear plant as having any part in the submarine's loss, at least with regard to NRB responsibility. He carefully stated that he did not have responsibility for the *Thresher*'s reactor plant, because it was not a lead ship . . . although he did discuss the sections of the *Thresher* "I was responsible for."

The line of demarcation between Rickover's responsibility and that of the rest of the Bureau of Ships was hazy and to some extent awkward. On June 20, 1963, the Navy published a news release on the conclusions of the court of inquiry. The first two paragraphs gave the Navy's opinion of what killed the *Thresher:*

> A flooding casualty in the engine room is believed to be the "most probable" cause of the sinking of the nuclear submarine USS THRESHER, lost April 10, 1963, 220 miles east of Cape Cod with 129 persons aboard.
>
> The Navy believes it most likely that a piping system failure had occurred in one of the THRESHER's salt water systems, probably in the engine room. The enormous pressure of sea water surrounding the submarine subjected her interior to a violent spray of water and progressive flooding. In all probability water affected electrical circuits and caused loss of power. THRESHER slowed and began to sink. Within moments she had exceeded her collapse depth and totally flooded. She came to rest on the ocean floor, 8,400 feet beneath the surface.

Admiral James, from his viewpoint as Chief of BuShips during the construction of the *Thresher,* had a somewhat more pointed conclusion. "I have my own opinion," he said in his memoirs, "because, of course, in the ultimate analysis I was the person responsible for building the ship.

"I feel from what I know of the inquiry in which I participated, what I know of the ship itself, and events that occurred up to that time, that a failure of a silver soldered pipe fitting somewhere in the boat caused a discharge of a stream of water on the nuclear control board and 'scrammed' the power plant."

Then, according to James, "Because of inadequate design of the nuclear controls for the plant, power on the boat was lost at a time where [*sic*] the depth of water in which the submarine was operating forced enough water into the hull that prevented her from rising again because they couldn't get the power back on the boat."

A related explanation of the *Thresher* loss can be gleaned from her final messages, inexact as the recollections of them were by men aboard the *Skylark*. "Experiencing minor problem" or "minor difficulty" would probably not apply to a pipe failure. For example, at one thousand feet flooding through a six-inch pipe would admit approximately 100,000 pounds of sea water in just one minute! Even flooding through a half-inch pipe would be serious because of the noise, the powerful spray, and possible difficulty in stopping the leak and, in some circumstances, of quickly locating the pipe. (A reactor shutdown also could have been caused by the water spray when one of the pipes failed.)

The "minor" problem or difficulty was more likely a reactor scram. With power available to escape from a critical situation the submarine would simply accelerate, angle upward its diving planes—the small, wing-like structures on the sail structure and stern—and come up to the surface. The reference to "up angle" in the message may have implied the submarine was attempting to "glide" up with the momentum that remained from the slow speed of the deep-diving trials. Obviously that was insufficient to bring up the submarine. Perhaps the diving planes were jammed, or there was simply not enough foward motion—because of the loss of power.

And, if the submarine could be propelled up to the surface, there would be no need to "blow up," to use high-pressure air to expel ballast water. Blowing up is a slower process. (The message "attempting to blow" indicates that there were problems with this system, in the same way someone driving a car who said, "I am attempting to put on the brakes," would indicate a problem with the brakes.) Subsequent tests demonstrated that the *Thresher* did not have sufficient high-pressure air capability to blow up from her test depth. (Also, a full blow may have created pressure and temperature drops that caused moisture in the compressed air to freeze and clog the strainers in the system.)

Regardless, a reactor scram or other shutdown was probably the initial "minor" difficulty or problem. Further evidence of this came, according to James, when, almost immediately after loss of the *Thresher*, Rickover reduced the time lag after a scram to restart of the reactor. "Ten seconds had been considered a reasonably short interval of time to allow restoration of power after a scram," James said. After *Thresher*, the interval was reduced to six seconds, James recalled.

But Rickover carried the day. His testimony to the Joint Committee on Atomic Energy investigating the *Thresher* disaster ended with his noting that BuShips "was not doing many . . . things" to correct deficiencies in the new nuclear submarines, but "we have been doing these things all of the time." The "we," of course, was Rickover and the Naval Reactors Branch. And, he would continually repeat such statements as: "While we do not know the specific cause of these losses [the *Thresher* and, in 1967, the *Scorpion*], there is no evidence that it was due to a problem with the nuclear reactors. . . ."

Fourteen days after the disaster, the Secretary of the Navy established a review group to examine all naval capabilities in the deep-ocean environment. Headed by the Oceanographer of the Navy, Rear Admiral E. C. Stephan, the group consisted of fifty-eight experts in oceanography, underwater engineering, and submarines, including Captain Leonard Erb, a former Polaris submarine commander. But no NRB representative was in the group.

The review group, which completed its work in March 1964, recommended that a major effort be made to improve the Navy's ability to recover personnel from sunken submarines, to investigate the ocean floor, to recover small objects (such as satellites) as well as to salvage submarines and permit men to work on the ocean floor down to at least the six-hundred-foot continental shelf, ostensibly for salvage operations.

The major portion of the rescue program would be the development of a fleet of small submersibles that in an emergency could be carried and launched by another submarine to rescue survivors of a stricken submarine—down to any depth where there would be survivors—that is, the collapse depth of the latest nuclear submarines.

An agency to develop these capabilities, designated the Deep Submergence Systems Project, was established in June 1964, initially within the Navy's Special Projects Office, home of the Polaris missile effort. The reason for this was the office's expertise in managing large, complex projects, and continued efforts by that office to assess and understand deep-ocean technology for advanced strategic systems. The man personally directing the deep-submergence effort was Dr. John Craven, an engineer and lawyer, who was chief scientist of the Polaris project. After the deep-submergence project was made an independent project office in the Naval Material Command, Craven was succeeded as project manager by a naval engineer, Captain William M. Nicholson, with Craven remaining as chief scientist of both the Polaris and deep-submergence projects.

One of the programs placed under the Deep Submergence Systems Project was the NR-1, a nuclear-propelled submersible for deep-ocean research and engineering. The NR-1 was the child of Rickover, conceived by him, nurtured by him, and then offered up to the Navy and to the nation.

From at least 1959, Rickover had some interest in the deep-ocean technology studies being undertaken by the Polaris project. He later appointed a member of his staff to keep him informed of Dr. Craven's efforts in this direction. Then, sometime in 1964–1965, Rickover decided to build the NR-1. Dr. Robert Herold, a student of the decision-making "elite" in the government, who served with the deep-submergence project, has observed, "In the bureaucracy it is very difficult for anyone to *decide* anything. It is particularly difficult when the elite in question has no authority with which to play the role of policy decider. If the hierarchal system acutally worked, it would be impossible for an elite of Rickover's formal status to decide on such a matter. But in Rickover's case 'decide' takes on an assuredness not common to other elites."

Rickover obtained support for the NR-1 from two quarters. First, in the Pentagon, Rear Admiral Wilkinson, who had commanded the *Nautilus* and had become head of the OPNAV submarine branch in late 1963, and Dr. Robert Morse, the Assistant Secretary of the Navy for research and development, gave him support. Then, Rear Admiral Levering Smith in the Polaris project was approached. All gave support to the rationale that the NR-1 was needed to help develop reactors that could operate in deep-diving combat submarines of the future.

Rickover's initial estimate of the cost for the nuclear NR-1 was $20 million, according to the recollections of Paul Nitze, who was Secretary of the Navy at the time. Nitze said that "suddenly you would get rumors that Rickover was working on some brilliant idea that you had never heard of and you would ask Rickover to come in and tell you about his new project." He called Rickover in to discuss the NR-1. Nitze said, "I was enthusiastic about it. . . . The issue was how much would it cost."

"He said he could build the whole thing for $20 million," Nitze recalled. "I said, 'Rick, I don't know if we can for that price.'"

"Oh no, I'm certain that I can for $20 million" was the response Nitze remembers, with Rickover pointing out that he was in the submarine-building business.

"Rick, I'm prepared to back you. What I propose to do is to estimate that it will cost twenty-five million." Nitze felt the twenty percent "hedge" was warranted and proposed it to Secretary of Defense McNamara at that price. The NR-1 was approved.

Funds for the submersible were provided from the Polaris project. That office tended to overbudget for submarine construction, and in that era of Congressional and public concern for strategic weapons, such funds were available for missile programs but not for research-and-development efforts, such as an advanced reactor. Rickover, according to Dr. Herold, "rationalized . . . that there was little real developmental effort involved. He stated that he was merely providing a platform to test a nuclear-power plant." Thus, the Special Projects Office provided the initial funds—$30 million—for the NR-1.

The arrangements were kept very low-key. Rickover did not wish to have the proposed submersible included in the normal review and justification process, which was bureaucratic, formal and often painful. As a result, neither Secretary McNamara nor Secretary Nitze had full knowledge of the NR-1 project, and each had some embarrassing moments before Congressional committees. At the same time, Rickover's secrecy upset some of his own supporters on the Hill, because he had not provided them with his usual behind-the-scenes previews of his plans. But, when testifying himself on the NR-1, Rickover was a most forceful salesman.

The NR-1 probably would not have been approved had it gone through the normal budget and program cycles, especially with the Vietnam War draining off resources. Rickover would get the NR-1, but his secrecy would cost him in credibility with many in Congress and in the press, as well as in the Navy. The first public knowledge—and to a wide extent first Navy knowledge—of the NR-1 came on April 18, 1965, in a press statement from the Texas White House. President Johnson announced that the Navy and Atomic Energy Commission were "jointly developing a nuclear-powered deep-submergence research and ocean-engineering vehicle."

There was no reference to military roles for the vehicle. Rather, the White House release told of the capabilities of the NR-1 that would "contribute greatly to accelerate man's exploration and exploitation of the vast resources of the oceans . . . enable scientists to examine firsthand an extensive part of the earth's surface for new sources of raw materials . . . and extend accumulation of commercially useful information on the habits of diverse species of marine life."

The overall responsibility for the vehicle was assigned—in the news release—to the Special Projects Office, with BuShips being responsible for its design, development, and construction. The final paragraph noted that the AEC's "Division of Naval Reactors, headed by Vice Admiral H. G. Rickover will be responsible for the design, development, and fabrication of the propulsion plant."

Although the Presidential statement had assigned responsibilities for the NR-1 to the *Navy*'s Special Projects Office and Bureau of Ships as well as the Atomic Energy Commission's Division of Naval Reactors (not the *BuShips'* Nuclear Propulsion Directorate), the NR-1 was never a program of the real Navy. It did not appear in the Navy's fiscal 1965 shipbuilding plans or budget (although in retrospect that is the program year in NRB and Electric Boat documents), and the NR-1 never appeared in the BuShips monthly reports of shipbuilding progress.

At the start of the NR-1, agreements were made among the participants—Craven, Smith, BuShips and Rickover—as to how the NR-1 would be handled, its management, funding and publicity. These agreements were carried over to the Deep Submergence Systems Project and to Captain Nicholson when he took command of that effort in 1965. He had already been involved in the NR-1, in his previous position with the ship design office of BuShips. There he had been told that the NR-1, which had not been through the usual preliminary design and development studies, showed potentially serious buoyancy and weight problems. The opinion was that "the NR-1 would probably sink the way she was originally laid out," Nicholson said. BuShips engineers were finally able to convince key people in the Naval Reactors Branch that there was a problem, and a major redesign took place.

Without fanfare, the NR-1 was laid down at Electric Boat in Groton, Connecticut, on June 16, 1966. EB was already constructing civilian research submersibles, small, battery-powered craft for deep-sea exploration. EB's most ambitious submersible was the eighty-ton *Aluminaut,* a private venture of the Reynolds Aluminum Company. Soon after her completion, Rickover rode in the *Aluminaut,* probably his only time in a non-Navy undersea craft. Rickover, according to EB officials, wanted to ride the *Aluminaut* in secrecy. He flew down to Miami, in his usual civilian clothes, and then traveled in a large sports fishing boat to a clandestine rendezvous with the *Aluminaut,* some thirty-five miles off the coast. The fishing boat communicated with the *Aluminaut* over short-wave radio in code to hide Rickover's identity, while the distinguished visitor sat in the cabin munching white grapes. After his dive in the *Aluminaut,* Rickover raced back to Miami, and then flew north, filled with more ideas for the NR-1.

His original concept was to use the most advanced steel available, the HY-80 used in the *Thresher* and later nuclear submarines, with a small reactor to give the NR-1 virtually unlimited endurance and an operating depth of some three thousand feet (considerably more than combat submarines with HY-80 steel, because of the craft's smaller size and absence of hull openings for periscopes, torpedo tubes, and other military equipment). For the NR-1, Rickover also planned to use existing underwater equipment, to hold down development and procurement costs.

In February of 1968, however, he began to explain to Congress, through the Joint Committee on Atomic Energy, that there were unforeseen problems in using existing equipment. Although submersible equipment such as lights and instruments were available that would work down to three thousand feet, they were not intended for the long-duration missions of the NR-1 but for battery-operated craft that would remain down only a few hours per dive. In response, Rickover said, he had increased the estimated costs of the NR-1 to $58 million. However, he quickly added, "before you consider this to be excessive, please remember that the six deep-submergence rescue vehicles which the Navy is buying cost about $30 million each. NR-1 displaces [four hundred tons]. One rescue vehicle displaces about [fifty tons] and is battery powered."

What Rickover did not mention was that the Navy's rescue vehicles were *the* most sophisticated submersibles ever built. They were fabricated of more advanced HY-140 steel, permitting them to dive deeper than the NR-1 (to thirty-five hundred feet, to allow for future submarine developments); they could be carried to forward areas in Air Force transport planes, then be taken to sea riding "piggyback" on nuclear submarines, and "flown" off to descend to a stricken submarine, "mate" with its hatches, and rescue survivors. In comparison to these rescue submersibles, the NR-1 design was relatively simple and straightforward.

The cost of the rescue submersibles increased significantly before they were operational in 1971–1972. But the NR-1 also increased in cost. Rickover apparently never again discussed costs of the NR-1 with Congress, but the Navy's files indicate that the NR-1 cost at least $99.2 million—$67.5 million for the actual submersible, $19.9 million for equipment and sensors, and $11.8 million for research, mostly related to the nuclear plant. In total, at least five times the original cost Rickover is said to have predicted.

There were problems with the NR-1. In briefing Navy and Defense officials as well as Congress, Rickover always said that the problems are "here," pointing to the forward, nonpropulsion portions of the NR-1. He told a House Appropriations subcommittee in July 1969, that

When I started looking in detail into the non-propulsion areas of the. . . NR-1 . . . I found that the Naval Ship Systems Command did not have even one person assigned full-time to the non-propulsion aspects of the NR-1, regardless of the fact that the NR-1 will be the deepest diving nuclear submarine ever built.

I wrote a rather forceful letter [Rickover continued] and I got two people assigned responsibility for the non-propulsion aspects of the submarine. I also discovered that had I allowed the NR-1 non-propulsion plant design to continue the way it was proceeding, failures would quite probably have occurred.

But Rickover was not in fact allowing anyone else to manage the nonpropulsion aspects of the NR-1. Captain Nicholson, manager of the Deep Submergence Systems Project, sent his representatives to meet with Rickover and other NRB personnel; often they were sent back with Rickover declaring they were not qualified to discuss the craft. Others reached what they thought were agreements with David Leighton, Rickover's deputy, on specific matters, only to have a "memorandum of understanding" subsequently sent from Rickover to Nicholson stating merely the position of the NRB as the outcome of the "discussions."

The problems with the "front end" of the NR-1 were considerable, "because Rickover had simply not considered that end at all," said Nicholson. "He was interested in the reactor, period. For example, there were three bunks forward for seven crewmen although Rickover spoke of thirty-day missions. . . . Controls were also a problem, as he demanded full life-cycle testing, that is running them for thirty-day periods as if the craft were at sea. This was a sound engineering decision, and it helped to insure reliable operation once the NR-1 was built. But this extensive test and development was not part of the original plan and it was expensive. There was nothing in the budget for that and we had to pay out of other deep-submergence programs."

Similarly, Rickover's plans to use existing lights, controls, and other equipment came to naught. Equipment designed for a few hours at deep depths could not survive for weeks at depth. Nicholson was faced with a massive—and unbudgeted—development effort. At the same time, although he had continuous access to Rickover and others at NRB, he had limited knowledge about what was really happening.

One of Nicholson's staff men from 1967 on was Commander M. Scott Carpenter, one of the nation's seven original astronauts, who had flown a three-orbit space mission in 1962. Nicholson sent Carpenter to Electric Boat to speak to a management group at the shipyard. Nicholson also told him to look at the NR-1 while he was there, because he was concerned that there was inadequate space for the crew during long underwater operations. Carpenter was uniquely familiar with confined operating and living conditions.

While Carpenter was in Groton, Nicholson received a distress call from Joseph Pierce, general manager of EB. "He told me that no one could go aboard without specific orders from Rickover and that he, Pierce, had orders specifically to keep Carpenter off the NR-1." Nicholson immediately called Rickover, but the Admiral was enroute to Hawaii and could not be reached. Carpenter returned to Washington without visiting the NR-1. Nicholson believed that Rickover, wanting total control of all visitors to his empire, especially feared that the publicity that followed the astronauts would draw unwanted public attraction to the NR-1 if Carpenter visited the craft.

"But there was a postscript to the affair," Nicholson told the authors. "A few evenings later, at a social affair, I met Mrs. Craig Hosmer, wife of the California Congressman." During the course of their conversation she asked if Nicholson knew Rickover—and then told him that Rickover had arranged for her to have a "complete tour of the NR-1."

Secrecy was the key word for all aspects of the NR-1. Indeed, the Deep Submergence Systems Project, trying to call national attention and support to the Navy's and the national deep-ocean efforts, could speak of the NR-1 only in the words of the 1965 White House release (except that Dr. Craven in a 1966 *Proceedings* article wrote that the NR-1, "initiated without fanfare, may be the most significant innovation in the technology of the sea bottom"). The Navy could use only "approved" words to describe the NR-1 publicly.

According to the agreement reached with Rickover at the start of the NR-1 project, he and only he controlled publicity concerning the NR-1. About a year before launching, Nicholson had his public-affairs officer begin developing a standard Navy plan for a ship launching—the schedule, speakers, invitations, and the like. However, Rickover, citing earlier accords, said that he and only he would run the launching. Nicholson's project and the rest of the Navy were prohibited from even announcing the date of the launching. He was told there would be no ceremony and no press. This led one Navy officer to tell a reporter, "How he intends to launch that thing with nobody seeing it is beyond us . . . he will probably do it at midnight."

Rickover responded to inquiries with "All I can tell you is what I told Congress—sometime in 1969." He sidestepped questions from the press about the NR-1 costing some five times as much as he originally estimated to Congress. Speculation by the press was increasing, and late one Friday afternoon, a week before the launching, Rickover called Nicholson to say: "I have decided to let you take care of the launching ceremony."

Nicholson and his public-relations staff went into an emergency weekend session with officials from Electric Boat to plan the affair. Invitation lists were made up, cleared with NRB, and then the invitations were hand-delivered. Press releases were written and cleared through Navy and Defense Department channels. Finally, on Friday, January 25, 1969, the Department of Defense announced that the NR-1 would be launched the following day, at 3:15 in the afternoon.

The one-page release said that Robert A. Frosch, an Assistant Secretary of the Navy, would deliver the principal address, and that Mrs. Robert W. Morse, wife of a previous assistant secretary, would christen the NR-1. A fact sheet attached to the release gave some information on the NR-1—and noted an "orginal" $30 million estimate—and then explained how the total costs had climbed to $99.2 million. Although it would be another seven months before the NR-1 would be completed and go to sea, the Navy would never release later cost data on the submarine.

As the NR-1 slid down her building way at Electric Boat, Rickover was not on the speaker's platform. Rear Admiral Edward J. Fahy, head of the Naval Ship Systems Command, introduced Dr. Frosch. "NR-1's original purpose," Frosch told the audience, "was to demonstrate the feasibility of nuclear propulsion for a deep-submergence research vehicle." He then spoke of the benefits that knowledge gained by the NR-1 would give not only to the Navy but also to mankind. There was no mention of the use of the NR-1 as a test bed for future, deep-diving military submarines.

On August 16, 1969, the NR-1 went to sea for the first time. In addition to her Navy crew of five, several Navy, Electric Boat, and AEC representatives were on board, as was Admiral Rickover. No one from the deep-submergence project was there. In a letter written at the time, Rickover forecast a fleet of small, nuclear-powered research submarines having unprecedented depth capability. In anticipation of such a fleet of nuclear submersibles, Rickover once said, "I am convinced that once this ship becomes operational, there will be a requirement for more of them. I had the foresight to name it the NR-1, with that object in view."

The NR-1 was successful. The craft has provided the Navy with an unprecedented capability for deep-ocean work. Although long portrayed as a scientific research craft, her main value, within the limitations of her operating depth, has been deep-ocean "engineering." Missions have included helping to maintain sea-floor equipment, presumably including the SOSUS sea-floor submarine detection devices, and in locating and recovering an F-14 fighter that rolled off an aircraft carrier and came to rest in almost two thousand feet of water.

Even as the NR-1 went to sea Rickover was laying the groundwork for the second nuclear research vehicle in his "fleet." By 1972, Rickover had the Naval Ship Systems Command officially supporting his efforts to build an NR-2. This would have the same small reactor as the NR-1, but would be built of HY-130 steel, which had at one time been intended for the *Los Angeles* (SSN-688) class of combat submarines, but was not ready. By using HY-130 in the NR-2, Rickover felt that the submarine could operate significantly deeper than her predecessor.

In Congress, Rickover's own secrecy over the NR-1 would come back to haunt him. For example, in an exchange with his staunch supporter Charles Bennett, chairman of the House Appropriations subcommittee on sea power, Bennett interrupted a Rickover statement on the NR-1, to ask: "We have only one?"

"We have only one," replied Rickover.

Bennett would also ask if the fact that the ship existed was classified. It was not. After listening to the NR-1's attributes, another Congressman asked if the NR-1 had any rescue capability, to which Rickover had answered; "No, sir, it does not." Interestingly, a decade before, when the nation and the Congress were closer to the *Thresher* disaster, Rickover had responded to the same question that the NR-1 "could approach a disabled submarine, examine it visually, and gain valuable information to aid in rescue operations. For example, NR-1 could guide a rescue vehicle to a disabled submarine. It could help locate it far better than any existing underwater vehicle."

Again unsaid was that with its slow speed the NR-1 was severely limited in its ability to respond to a submarine disaster; the rescue submersibles provide the only real rescue capability for modern submarines.

And in the same hearing—six years after the NR-1 went to sea—Rickover told the committee that the "construction cost for the NR-1 was $63.9 million." He understated the actual cost of the vehicle and avoided mention of the factors that drove the NR-1's cost up to approximately $100 million. In late 1976—almost simultaneously with the election of President Carter—Rickover formally asked Congress for $130 million to build the NR-2. The Navy, interested in the vehicle from the viewpoint of using the HY-130 steel, wanted the small submarine to provide important fabrication and operational information. To make this point, the Navy began referring to the NR-2 as a Hull Test Vehicle (HTV), which subsequently became its formal designation. But opponents—some in the Navy—felt that there were cheaper and easier methods of testing the steel than building a nuclear NR-2.

No NR-2—or Hull Test Vehicle—was funded by Congress either in 1976 or since then. Plans have been discussed to build such a craft in the late 1980s. American interest in deep submergence had dissipated. The Vietnam War had drawn funds away from the deep-submergence project, and the project's SEALAB III underwater-living experiment had been canceled when a Navy diver died at the outset. The project was later abolished as a separate, Polaris-type effort and absorbed by the Naval Ship Systems Command. And, in May 1968, the U.S. nuclear-propelled submarine *Scorpion* was lost with all ninety-nine men on board.

The *Scorpion* was returning to the United States from operations in the Mediterranean. She failed to arrive at Norfolk on time. For several months the Navy searched her predicted track, finally identifying her shattered hull off the Azores in water ten thousand feet deep.

Unlike the *Thresher*, the *Scorpion* had been traveling alone. There was no communication from her just before her loss, and her remains could not establish the cause of her loss. Whereas the *Thresher* was on diving trials after a lengthy yard period, the *Scorpion* was fully operational and had been operating in the Mediterranean for three months under an experienced commanding officer, Francis A. Slattery, who had previously served in the *Nautilus* and had joined the *Scorpion* in mid-1967.

The rescue submersibles then being built could not have helped the *Scorpion*, for, like the *Thresher*, she lay at a depth far greater than any at which her hull and crew could survive.

Accidents continue to occur to U.S. nuclear submarines, as they do to virtually all advanced-technology products. In 1978, for example, the submarine *Tullibee* was partly flooded and in danger of sinking when the craft's propeller shaft broke. The submarine—submerged at the time—lost propulsion and suffered some engine-room flooding, but was saved. Improvements from a viewpoint of safety are continually being made to U.S. nuclear submarines. Many of the ideas that Rickover had advocated much earlier have been incorporated in submarine design and construction, not so much through objective analysis and conscious decisions, but more because Rickover has remained while most of his critics have long since retired, and because their replacements in the submarine force and in the submarine engineering community have been Rickover-trained men.

Still in Congress, when the *Thresher* or *Scorpion* losses are remembered, as they were in the sea-power subcommittee in March 1975, Rickover is quick to remind his listeners, "While we do not know the specific cause of these losses, there is no evidence that it was due to a problem with the nuclear reactors. . . ."

The *Thresher* loss and the NR-1 effort had permitted Rickover to enter another area of endeavor, which could, someday, have great implications for the Navy and the nation. But in the late 1960s, the Navy and the nation were too involved with the Vietnam War, racial unrest at home, and a multitude of other problems. Rickover failed in his effort to build a fleet of nuclear research submarines.

ONE OF A KIND

Rickover: a compulsive, driven, fiercely competitive person, one of a kind, who relishes that role and will never give it up. A genius at managing people, who has discovered the singular ability to establish perfection as commonplace among those working for him, or with him, so that the smallest hint of either pleasure or displeasure from him carries 50 times the weight coming from anyone else. A man who fully realizes his strength comes from his self-effacement (which is more apparent than real), his willingness to knuckle down with anyone, high or low, on a technical matter provided only that the other party is expert on the thing at issue (this is both apparent and completely true). A man adept at flattering the Congress or the press, yet unusually susceptible to the most elementary flattery himself. A man self-serving to an unbelievable degree, devoid of appreciation of or sympathy for the differences in people, intent only on getting his job done as he and he alone conceives it should be done.

—CAPTAIN EDWARD L. BEACH,
"Life Under Rickover: Stormy
Duty in the Silent Service,"
The Washington Post, May 27, 1977

20 | A Day in the Naval Reactors Branch

The headquarters of the Rickover navy has always been Rickover's desk. The names of that location have changed—once Code 390 and then Code 1500, the bureaucratic designation of nuclear propulsion's place in the Bureau of Ships, and more recently Code 08 in its successor Naval Sea Systems Command (there was, briefly, a Naval *Ship* Systems Command in between); wearing his other hat, with another desk elsewhere, it has been the Division of Naval Reactors and Naval Reactors Branch—just NRB or NR to most—in the Atomic Energy Commission, which then became the Energy Research and Development Administration, and now Department of Energy. (With the creation of DOE, Rickover got another title, Deputy Assistant Secretary for Naval Reactors.)

But whatever its name, the place—and despite two desks, Rickover was only in one place at one time—"NRB" has had the continuity of the medieval Vatican. And it was a Vatican where each day had most of the ritual of the day before, a Vatican whose pope never changed, and many of the same bishops, monsignors, pastors and curates were the same as the day before.

Each day may bring an incident, some event that will denote the passage of time in a place whose founder has never left. That incident may make the day different from others, but it will be an incident that will merge into the history of NRB, and that history is a saga of constancy.

The original base of NRB was at Main Navy, one of a series of "temporary" Washington structures that had been housing Navy officers since World War I. The Chief of Naval Operations and his staff had moved, albeit reluctantly, into the Pentagon after World War II. The hardware bureaus, including the Bureau of Ships, had remained at the Main Navy "tempos" that fronted Constitution Avenue, just west of the Washington Monument. (One of the oldest temporary structures on earth, Main Navy and its companion structures were finally torn down in the summer of 1970 by order of Commander in Chief Richard M. Nixon, who had served at Main Navy as a lieutenant at the end of World War II.)

When the "Navy Group" headed by Rickover returned to Washington from Oak Ridge, the men were placed in quarters even more temporary than the principal Main Navy structure. Behind that building were jerry-built offices thrown up to house the rapid expansion of Navy headquarters in World War II. One of them, T-3 building, was where Rickover and his few assistants were put. Visitors could easily discern that the spaces once had included a ladies room, and this would become part of the Rickover legend. So would the offices themselves: yellow, flaking plasterboard walls (not painted since 1941, went the bitterly proud lament) ... battered desks ... no rugs ... tables and shelves weighed down with reports. Rickover once told a visitor, "If you set a fellow up at a fine desk with a rug on the floor and decorations on the wall, he's likely to start thinking he's a big shot." (There were no rugs in the Rickover apartment, either, but the reason given there was that he was allergic to wool.)

The Washington Monument's reflecting pool lay behind Main Navy. There members of Rickover's navy would sometimes steal away for a brief, furtive stroll. If Rickover was in town, they rarely got beyond the call of their master's voice. He would pull open the window of his small, cluttered office, and yell out for them to get back to work. That was supposed to be all they were to do. Work.

Rickover had found a home in Main Navy. He could do what he wanted there, relatively isolated from the Pentagon across the Potomac. In his frequent lectures to Congressional committees, Rickover inevitably personified and attacked "the Pentagon," as if there were something diabolical about the building itself. The Pentagon was that strange place with gold-braided uniforms, chains of command and, by Rickover's perception, the pulling of rank.

In the Rickover offices at Main Navy there were no uniforms. There were no symbols of status. There were no distinctions between naval officers and civilians. Among the officers themselves, rank had little meaning. A lieutenant might be a commander's boss. A new, low-paid civilian engineer might be giving orders to an officer who had just commanded a warship. The Navy did not visibly exist.

•

After the Main Navy building was torn down in 1970, NRB head-quarters was moved across the Potomac to a place called Crystal City. The new location was a mile from the Pentagon, to which it was soon connected by the Metro subway system and a complicated road network. Built from the 1960s onward, and still growing, Crystal City is a huge complex of apartment houses, hotels, stores and office buildings—many leased to the U.S. government.

Crystal City arose from a jumble of rail yards and warehouses when developers covered the area with concrete and then built high-rise buildings, also of concrete. Some of the buildings leased to the government are called "national centers." National Center No. 2—also known as the Zachary Taylor Building—houses parts of the Naval Sea Systems Command, the descendant of BuShips and the Bureau of Ordnance. Across the street is National Center No. 1—called the James E. Polk Building—which houses the Navy's Anti-Submarine Warfare Systems (ASW) Project Office. By a kind of sense of humor that is charming because it is unconscious, the Navy has placed the ASW project office across the street from the offices of the father of the nuclear submarine.

Most of the corridors and rooms of the National Center buildings have the bare, look-alike interiors of the typical government office buildings. Visitors can wander through most corridors without signing in, at least between 8:30 in the morning and 4:30 in the evening. But on the third floor of National Center 2, the two ends of the short elevator corridor stop at locked doors. At the west end of the corridor, between locked doors, is a thick glass window. A red-lettered sign is on the door: *Naval Reactors/Nav/Sea 08 Restricted Area Authorized Personnel Only NR/08 Receptionist Room 3N162 Keep This Door Closed.* The doors can be opened by keys or, apparently, by a release button pressed by someone behind the glass panel.

The people who work there keep secrets. But there has been a human side to the doings at NRB, and that human side, while revealing no secrets about nuclear reactors, does reveal how Hyman Rickover ran NRB and how he dealt with the people who worked for him.

"If you really want to get a big job done," he once said, "you do not need a large group of people. If you do, the first thing you know your time gets taken up arranging for baseball games, picnics, and Easter parties for your employees; worrying about their morale rather than getting them to do the job for which they are paid. People who are doing useful work do not need these trivia for satisfaction."

There was not much time for trivia at NRB, and there was not much documentation of the trivia. But the tales are many. What follows is one that is documented.

In November 1970, Chief of Naval Operations Elmo R. Zumwalt, Jr., sent to the fleet one of his famous "Z-grams." This one, Z-57, authorized among other things, "neatly trimmed" beards and mustaches. Nearly two years later, a lieutenant (junior grade) in NRB began wearing a beard. The officer, named Lamb, was ordered into the office of his civilian superior and told that, since he was wearing a beard, he also had to wear a uniform.

Lamb wrote to Rickover, saying, "This beard policy violates Z-Gram #57 since, while it allows beards, it discriminates against those who choose to wear beards. And it discriminates in such a way as to make the wearing of the uniform of the United States Navy a penalty rather than a privilege." Lamb refused to wear his uniform, and the matter was brought to the attention of Admiral Isaac C. Kidd, Jr., Chief of Naval Material, and ostensibly one of Rickover's bosses. As Kidd interpreted Z-gram 57, NRB's beard policy was in violation of Navy beard policy and Lamb could keep his beard. Lamb, meanwhile, requested a transfer.

But NRB decided to remove Lamb rather than transfer him. "I found it increasingly difficult to get work done through my superiors, . . ." he later wrote; "each letter, memo, or management response I wrote had to be reviewed by the entire chain of command," including Rickover.

Lamb's fitness report claimed that he had allowed his appearance to become "slovenly." Lamb, in his response to the adverse fitness report, said that when he asked his superior about that charge, "He stated that on several occasions he had noticed that my shirt collar was not buttoned and my tied not quite snugged up to my collar." The reporting period was from March 1 to August 31—a time that included Washington's near-tropical days.

NRB told the Chief of Naval Personnel that Lamb's beard had nothing to do with the case. His "declining performance and negative attitude in spite of repeated counseling," the letter to BuPers said, "were the sole reasons for the action taken by this command."

In his rebuttal letter to BuPers, Lamb wrote, "I am certain my fitness report was purposely made adverse so that my superiors would have an excuse to remove me from Naval Reactors and that the report and my expulsion are the price I must pay because I dared to protest an illegal

and repressive policy of VAdm. Rickover. . . . I am confident that this report will not affect my future, since my previous Naval records, my graduate school, college and high-school records and my achievements
throughout my life, demonstrate that I am not the man depicted in this
fitness report."

From the beginning, the days of NRB started at 8 A.M. and—in the
words of one of Rickover's former secretaries—the days ended "at five or
nine or ten or eleven or midnight or one A.M." For Rickover and those
who worked most closely to him, the days never ended at five. Within the
working hours—the definite hour of beginning and the movable hour of
ending—the days had a pattern. Memories of days of working usually are
memories of incidents. Workers might forget what they worked on, but
they will not forget how it was to work, how co-workers behaved, how the
boss behaved.

Two of Rickover's longtime secretaries—one a Navy Wave,* the
other a civilian—have shared their recollections, which spanned some
twenty years of service in NRB. From their reminiscences the authors
have put together a composite day of remembered events. The memories
of the two women, who worked at different periods of time, are amazingly
consistent. Both gave almost identical descriptions of Rickover's eating
habits, for example. And both had for their old boss a fondness that
shone forth even during the recounting of bitter or embarrassing moments.

It is three minutes after eight. One of the yeomen wonders whether
she should call Rickover's home. He is late. She decides to wait until five
minutes after—and then the door opens and he is striding in. He wears a
grayish-black suit, a white shirt, and a narrow maroon tie faintly decorated with small diamond shapes. The tie is tightly knotted. (There may
be a variation: a light-blue shirt and a navy-blue suit that he claims to
have bought in 1958.) He wears black shoes, black socks, and is hatless.

He enters his office. One of his three-to-six female yeomen and civilian secretaries (he calls them his "girls") has prepared his breakfast. Typically, it consists of a glass of warmed skimmed milk, part of which will be
poured over a bowl of oatmeal. He may also have a heated roll or a Danish and an orange that she has peeled for him. The food has been prepared in a small kitchen near his office.

He reads *The Washington Post* and *The New York Times,* turning the
pages rapidly. He will read, or at least look at, every page, including the

* *Female Navy personnel were designated by the World War II term Waves until 1972.*

sports sections, not because he is interested in sports but in case he might want to josh some sports fan about a favorite team. This is Monday and he has also brought in a copy of *TV Guide.* He hands it to one of the secretaries. He has circled in red the public-affairs shows, such as *Meet the Press,* from which he will want transcripts. (He does not watch television; he reads it.)

He begins dictating, and the yeoman remembers how it was the day she was interviewed by him. "I was in yeoman school and I had about three weeks left. Admiral Rickover's office called and said they needed a girl. I walked into his office, and he said, 'Do you take shorthand?' I said yes. He threw a pad and pencil at me and said, 'Take it.' He started out with fiercely long words, which I never thought I would ever get. I took them, though, read them back to him at a hundred percent accuracy, and he said, 'OK. I want you here the day you graduate from school.' I got there at four o'clock on Friday, and I had graduated at ten that morning."

He is about to dictate an answer to an electronics firm when he mutters his favorite obscenity: "Those bastards!" He reaches for a small rubber stamp and stamp pad. He carefully inks the stamp pad, presses it in the middle of the firm's letter, refolds the letter, and orders it mailed back to the firm. The stamp, in red ink, shows the rear end of a horse with the word *Bullshit* printed beneath.

He can get angry at his secretaries too. One has put a pile of "pinks" on his desk—flimsy pink carbon copies of all letters and memos she had typed the day before. This is standard procedure. He flips through them, finds an error, and suddenly yells at her to come back in. "If you're not going to do this job right," he shouts, "then get out!" Her eyes brimming, she returns to her desk. An hour later, he apologizes and puts a box of candy on her desk.

His phone seems to ring constantly. The conversations usually last less than a minute, and his side of them does not include a hello or a goodbye. He receives and makes many phone calls. They are all done hurriedly. Sometimes too hurriedly. On one occasion, returning a call to "Mr. Paine," he gets back to Seth Payne of *Business Week.* Skipping salutations, Rickover begins "Paine . . ." and he is speaking rapidly, so rapidly that it is some time before Payne can interrupt and tell the Admiral he probably meant to call Roland Paine of the Polaris Special Projects Office.

"You aren't going to quote me, are you?" he asks.

"Admiral, you haven't said anything worth quoting," retorts Payne, who is one of the few newsmen that the Admiral seems comfortable with.

His telephoning habits have led to similar mistakes with others, with Captain William Nicholson receiving tirades intended for Admiral John Nicholson and the like.

Rickover reads the pinks, dictates, phones and answers phones. A few aides enter for visits that last just about as long as one of his phone calls. Smokers snuff out their cigarettes before they enter. No one smokes in Rickover's office.

At precisely 11:25 he has lunch at his desk. Today it is a small piece of fish broiled in the oven with a little milk. With it he has a glass of skimmed milk and a small dish of cottage cheese with fruit. A few other similar meals have been recorded:

With author Clay Blair, while they were working on Blair's book about Rickover—a boiled egg, a cup of chicken broth, an apple, a Saltine.

With columnist Drew Pearson (in 1958, while Rickover was getting press support during a promotion fight)—a cup of consommé, one hard-boiled egg, soda crackers, and an apple, plus a glass of milk.

With Under Secretary of the Navy Paul Fay—a breakfast of oatmeal, peeled orange, and a Danish pastry.

With Secretary of the Navy John Connally—thin soup, crackers, cottage cheese, skimmed milk. (Connally later said that Rickover had "demonstrated his austerity.")

After lunch, he may spend some time interviewing midshipmen who want to enter the nuclear navy. Some of these interviews are different from those covered elsewhere in this book, for at times they involved the secretaries, and the interviews became entertainments for the people at NRB.

A midshipman reveals that he is in the glee club at the Naval Academy. It is the middle of July, and the midshipman is sent to each of the Admiral's girls and is ordered to sing a Christmas carol to each one.

In the midst of an interview, Rickover asks a midshipman if he thinks he is good-looking. Before the young man can answer, Rickover shouts for his secretary to come into his office. He calls the Wave yeoman "lieutenant" and tells the midshipman she graduated second in her class at Vassar. Because the midshipman thinks the Wave is an officer, he springs to attention. Rickover says, "Lieutenant, do you think this young man is good-looking?" The Wave nods. "And do you think he is fat?" Rickover turns to the midshipman and orders him to remove his shirt. "All right, lieutenant," Rickover says to the Wave. She puts her arms around the midshipman to judge whether he is big enough around the chest. If not, Rickover tells her, "Make out a fat letter." This is a letter, usually on AEC stationery, that is sent to the midshipman's mother or girl friend and signed by the young man. In it he promises to lose a certain amount of fat in a certain period of time. He adds to the letter, "I hereby promise Admiral Rickover that I will lose _____ pounds in _____ weeks and every week I will write him a letter informing him."

A midshipman is asked, in front of several people, "Do you always obey orders?" He says he does. Rickover gives him marching orders until he is heading toward the window. The midshipman marks time at the window, and appears to be planning to open it and jump when Rickover calls off the show.

Rickover also puts on entertainments at the expense of people he thinks are getting too proud of themselves. Once he has a secretary remove her wig and place it on the head of a commander, who is then forced to walk around all the offices of NRB and wear the wig for the entire day. Rickover once had a Wave he called the Georgia Peach and one he called Daisy Mae. When he discovers that the Peach has a good voice, he orders her to enter certain offices regularly, remove her shoes (because she stands on hallowed ground), and sing "My Hero" (to deflate egos that Rickover thinks are swollen).

It is 2:30 P.M. and people on the floor below Rickover's office hear *clump, clump, clump* above them. He has started exercising. He is walking at a fast clip—"his pants flapped in the wind because he was going so fast," a secretary recalls—and he is getting everyone else to keep pace with him. This may keep up for forty-five minutes.

For a very few, the day will end around five o'clock. But for those nearest to Rickover—about eighteen or twenty men—the day will go on until about seven or eight. Daisy Mae and the Georgia Peach take turns working late and on Saturdays. He will come in on Saturday at eight o'clock in the morning and stay at least until two o'clock if there is nothing pressing. Usually, something is pressing and so he stays later.

In the regular Navy, a new man is said to "come aboard" even if he is assigned to a billet in an office ashore. In the Rickover navy, a new man walks into an office where there is no semblance of naval tradition. This is a workplace, and from the first day the new man (except for secretaries, the newcomer has always been a man) knows that he is not really of the U.S. Navy. Instead of being handed standard Navy rules and regulations, for instance, he is handed whatever Rickover at that moment believes is necessary for the newcomer to have and know.

A man who reported for duty on Rickover's staff in 1968 was handed a packet of wisdom that included a speech by Rickover ("The Significance of Electricity"); a speech by a doctor who attacked the American Medical Association; an excerpt from a *Harper's* magazine piece on the high cost of medical care; a chart on common poisons and their antidotes; excerpts from *Social Technology* by Olaf Helmer, including a long-range forecasting study that predicted one hundred and twenty-six probable breakthroughs within the coming decades—from reliable weather forecasts and effective oral contraceptives to "centralized (possibly random) wire-tapping" and "mass-hypnotic recruitment of forces from enemy population."

The newcomer was never told what he was supposed to do with his packet of amazing facts from Rickover. But the implication was that the packet was an inspiration; he should try to be as broad-gauged as the giver. He was also expected to read and read and read. (More than ten years later, the onetime newcomer, now no longer working for Rickover, still had his packet of amazing facts in the library of his suburban Washington home.)

Each newcomer is given an "NRB Information File" and an "NR Junior Engineer Reading List," which are continually brought up to date. The information file issued to newcomers in March 1970 contained twenty books published or sponsored by the Naval Reactors Branch. Several of the books were in two or more volumes. These books included highly technical works, such as *Beryllium, The Metal and Neutron Absorber Materials for Reactor Control.* There was also a library of non-technical books: *The Art of Plain Talk,* by Rudolf Flesch; *Education and Freedom,* by H. R. Rickover; *A General Account of the Development of Methods of Using Atomic Energy for Military Purposes Under the Auspices of the U.S. Government 1940–1945,* by H. D. Smyth; *Introduction to Logic,* by I. M. Copi; *Physics for the Inquiring Mind,* by Eric M. Rogers; *Swiss Schools and Ours,* by H. R. Rickover; *The New World,* Volume I of *A History of the Atomic Energy Commission,* by Richard G. Hewlett and Francis Duncan; *Education for All Children,* by H. G. Rickover; *American Education—A National Failure,* by H. G. Rickover; *Around the World Submerged,* by E. L. Beach; *Nautilus 90 North,* by W. R. Anderson; *Death of the Thresher,* by Norman Polmar;* *The Atomic Shield* (Volume II of

---

* *After* Death of the Thresher *was published, the author was told that Rickover would have nothing more to do with him because of the indications that a reactor shutdown was the first in a series of incidents that led to the* Thresher's *loss.*

the AEC history by Hewlett and Duncan); *Admiral Rickover and the Atomic Submarine* [sic], by Clay Blair, Jr.

The information file also included eighty-five reports and papers, which, taken together, give the impression of a crash course in the background needs and struggles of Hyman Rickover and his atomic navy. There are Rickover letters to Senator John Stennis, chairman of the Senate Armed Services Committee, and to the chiefs of the Bureau of Ships. There are technical articles, speeches, editorials and Rickover memos on procedures for maintaining manuals, dealing with contractors and writing letters. Rickover memos included in this list show his relentless interest in writing things right: "Reduction in Correspondence"; "Preparation of Naval Reactors Correspondence in Which Action is Based on Reported Requests by Admiral Rickover"; "Accuracy of Stating Laboratory and Shipyard Recommendations"; and "Preparation of Subject Lines on Naval Reactors Memoranda and Letters."

The information file then lists five and a half pages of references to testimony by Rickover before committees of Congress. By 1970, the number of items of testimony was up to sixty-five. Rickover usually testifies at great length. Five to ten thousand words of testimony sometimes is but the clearing of the decks for the real action to come. By rough estimate of the authors (who themselves are students of Rickover's decades of testimony), the conscientious newcomer who decided to read all those hearings would have before him well over one million words.

The information file also listed fifty-eight Rickover speeches, starting with "Metallurgy in Atomic Power," a vintage 1955 item. Topics included education (repeatedly), nuclear power (also repeatedly), roles of the professional man, of the critic, travel ("Our Visit to Switzerland"), and excellence ("The Talented Mind"; "Investment in Human Resources"). A typical Rickover speech would be almost thirty minutes long. So the conscientious newcomer could expect about twenty-nine hours of Rickover to read.

And the newcomer still would not be through with the information he was expected to absorb, for the file went on to list "articles of general interest," which spanned the human condition from being a good worker—"How to Write Letters They'll Want to Read" and "How Seven Employees Can Be Made to Do the Work of One"—to understanding the Russians—"Russia's New Elite" and "Comrade Soldier." There are eighty-one articles, including that old-timer "A Message to Garcia."

The information file has twenty-six books and articles that the new junior engineer is expected to read within a month after arrival. The first eleven items on this mandatory reading list are to be consumed within two or three days. The Number One item is *Admiral Rickover and the Atomic Submarine*. Number Two is "Admiral Rickover's Gamble, the Landlocked Submarine," an *Atlantic* magazine article by Edwin Kintner. Then come technical manuals and statements on office procedures. This is followed by several selected articles, three speeches by Rickover, and four days of his testimony before Congress. The engineer must also read an article that offers "Some Lessons to be Learned" from the sinking of H.M. Submarine *Thetis*—a British craft sunk in 1939 while on trials because a torpedo tube had been improperly opened to the sea. Although one end of the submarine actually projected out of the water, ninety-nine men died in the accident.

The proffering of reading matter never stops. The education of an NRB staff member is continuous. Even Christmas mementos tend to reek of self-help. One of the most charming bits of education dispensed by Rickover one year was a poem by Felicia Lamport about the use of collective terms for beasts and birds: ". . . Skein's the word for geese in flight . . . Starlings join in murmuration . . . Foxes muster in a skulk. . . ." With the copy of the poem was a note: "The accompanying poem contains words descriptive of birds and animals in groups. By learning these words at Christmastime you and your children (if your wife has any) can become more interesting conversationists. (signed) H. G. Rickover"

Was there subtle irony or even rarer forms of humor hovering beneath the surface of that note? Perhaps. Rickover's sense of humor has often eluded his listeners and readers. And often he himself has drawn a hazy line between his natural, everyday sarcasm and his compulsion to educate his associates about the follies of government. In a 1968 memo, for instance, Rickover responded to a request for comment on a report with the observation that the report "puts me in mind of the review of D. H. Lawrence's *Lady Chatterley's Lover* which appeared in the November 1959 issue of *Field and Stream*." He then quotes the review:

> This fictional account of the day-by-day life of an English gamekeeper is still of considerable interest to outdoor-minded readers, as it contains many passages on pheasant raising, the apprehending of poachers, ways to control vermin, and other chores and duties of the professional gamekeeper. Unfortunately, one is obliged to wade through many pages of extraneous material in order to discover and savor these sidelights on the management of a Midlands shooting estate, and in this reviewer's opinion this book cannot take the place of J.R. Miller's *Practical Gamekeeping*.

"It is evident to me," Rickover wrote, "that the reviewer lacked comprehension of the *primary* occupation of the gamekeeper. . . . A cursory review of the subject report leads me to conclude that its authors, likewise, lack comprehension in the manner of accomplishing Research and Development. Therefore, I believe no useful purpose would be served by detailed comments on my part."

What Rickover either ignored—or failed to know—was that *Field and Stream* was itself making a joke. The review of *Lady Chatterley's Lover* appeared in a column entitled "Exit, Laughing" and it is preceded by a tongue-in-cheek note by the author of the column, Ed Zern, who said he was thinking about starting a book-review department in the magazine and had decided to use this one as "a test case."

Rickover has rarely told a story on himself, and once when he did, he became infuriated after learning that the joke had been published. He was in Bethesda Naval Hospital, recovering from a heart attack, when he told some officers visiting him that he had had a disturbing visit from a medical corpsman. The young enlisted man, obviously embarrassed, had come to ask Rickover's wishes for burial in case he died while in the hospital. Rickover asked about accommodations, and each time the corpsman listed one, Rickover asked for a cheaper one. Finally, he explained to the young man why a big, ornate cemetery plot was not needed. "I'll only be there three days, you see," Rickover said.*

His hospital audience roared at the joke—rare because it came from Rickover, even rarer because he had told it on himself. One of the officers spread the story, and one of his listeners sent the joke to a magazine, which published it with credit to the source. According to the legend surrounding the joke, that officer's career was forever clouded. Rickover in vain tried to learn which one of his bedside visitors had spread the joke.

The people who worked with him every day in NRB have been the ones who have been most exposed to Rickover's sense of humor.

Entering Main Navy on a wintry day, he slipped and fell to the sidewalk on Constitution Avenue. He tried to stride into NRB as briskly as was his habit, but he was clutching his arm and grimacing. Word had already reached NR that he had fallen, and medical corpsmen had been summoned on the double from the adjacent dispensary.

Rickover noticed the concern on everyone's face, and said, "I fell." He paused, looked around, and with the slightest grin, brought down the house with his next line: "I wasn't pushed, you bastards."

* *The same joke is credited to J. Edgar Hoover, whose enduring hold on the FBI has often been compared to Rickover's tenacity at NRB.*

He once let the rumor spread that he "stayed with a broad" on his trips to Newport News, Virginia, to check on ship construction. He stayed with the family of a Richard Broad, head of quality control at the shipyard. (Rickover was notorious about saving government money by accepting the spartan—often reluctant—hospitality of contractors, colleagues, and the families of colleagues.)

In Congressional testimony, his humor had the flatness that typified the surroundings. When Senator Howard Baker asked him if he ever thought of using a breeder reactor for submarine propulsion, he answered, "Not in a submarine, sir! I was asked the question one time at Oak Ridge.... I said, 'The Navy has found it more convenient to breed ashore.' " He once told members of the Joint Committee on Atomic Energy that the hearing beneath the surface of the Atlantic aboard the nuclear submarine *Skipjack* was "the deepest and fastest thinking session this committee has ever had."

And once, at least, Rickover even joked with an admiral in the real Navy. In a meeting at Pearl Harbor in the early 1960s, Rear Admiral Roy S. Benson, one of the Navy's top wartime submarine commanders, recalled Rickover's saying, "You and I get along very well, better than I do with several others. How do you account for that?"

Benson responded, "Each of us renders unto Caesar the things that are Caesar's, and unto God the things that are God's," to which Rickover asked, "Which one am I?"

Glimpses of such humor do not produce a portrait, but they do serve as bits for a mosaic. A few more bits for the mosaic:

One of the secretaries who talked about her boss said she still respected him and still remembered happy moments in NRB. "I had ten years that were most rewarding," she said. "But the last nine months, when Admiral Rickover suddenly took a violent dislike to me, were awful. When I left, they took up a collection—to which they would not let him contribute."

The other secretary has another kind of memory. She was only eighteen years old when she started at NRB. "I walked in, and he told me, 'While you're here I realize that you don't have your father, so I will be your second father. So, if you have anything that you want to ask me or anything that you need, then go ahead.' And there were many times that I relied on his judgment. When I left, I wrote a note and told him that he had helped me through many, many times, and that he was wise, and that I am sure that he helped. And the next day I got a dozen yellow roses."

One man who worked for Rickover and soon quit the Navy left this description: "As a matter of fact, all the time I worked for him he never said a decent word to me. . . . If he found no fault, he simply looked, turned around and walked away. However, if I made the slightest mistake, in one of the foulest and most obnoxious voices I ever heard, he would tell the other people in the area what a horrible disgrace I was to the Navy and that I ought to go back to the oldest and slowest and smallest submarine from which I had come."

Years later, that description—by Lieutenant Jimmy Carter—would intrigue a clinical pyschologist who studied the "emotional health" of institutions. From such descriptions of Rickover the psychologist would point to the admiral as an example of a "phenomenon that sometimes disrupts large organizations, the abrasive personality."

The diagnosis could not have surprised Rickover, who viewed himself as an abrasive that shaped men. "Life," he once said, "is a constant fight against stupidity"; and in his wearing down of those who opposed him, in his fight against stupidity, there would be one particular target: the admirals.

"I do know that you could easily get rid of half the admirals and you would have a more efficient Navy," he told a Congressional committee, and he added: "And you could include me. . . . I would be very willing for you to cross me off the list as an admiral if you will cross off some of the [other] admirals at the same time."

21 | Shooting the Admirals, Firing the Experts

In the 1922 Navy of Ensign Hyman G. Rickover there were fifty-eight admirals. In the 1980 Navy of Admiral Rickover—when he himself had been wearing admiral's stars for twenty-seven years—there were two hundred and sixty admirals. In his mind some of them resembled "carved figures on the bow of a becalmed ship, the faintly absurd emblems of movement for a regime that will not move."

Whatever Ensign Rickover thought of admirals, Admiral Rickover disliked them as a group and many as individuals. There seemed to stir in him an old tradition that resisted the idea of a Navy with many admirals. *Admiral,* as he used it, became a symbol that could be as derogatory as *Pentagon.*

"The Department of Defense," he said in 1970, "is in the same situation the British Navy was in the early 1700s. They found they had to shoot an admiral once in a while to keep the Royal Navy efficient."*

The United States Navy did not begin using the rank of admiral until 1862, when *rear admiral* was recognized. In 1864 *vice admiral* was adopted. In 1866, in special tribute, Civil War hero David Farragut was made an *admiral,* as was David Porter in 1870. When Porter died in 1891, so did the title until its resurrection in 1899 for bestowal upon George Dewey, the hero of Manila Bay.

So, Rickover, whose own youthful hero worship was inspired by events of the Spanish-American War, saw in his maturity a Navy that had somehow gone wrong. Not that the Navy was too big; he constantly

---

* Admiral John Byng in 1756 was dispatched to relieve the British garrison on Minorca. He engaged the French and then withdrew, leaving the British garrison to its fate. When he arrived back to England, he was court-martialed for not doing as much as he should have. He was put to death by a firing squad on the quarterdeck of his own flagship. He left this epitaph: "They make a precedent of me such as admirals hereafter may feel the effect of." It was Voltaire in Candide—not the British Navy—who made the execution of admirals plural, remarking that England occasionally shot an admiral "to encourage the others."

fought for a bigger Navy. Rather, the Navy was too top-heavy, too full of admirals.

Rickover's historical perspective has been unique. He knew an America that emerged from the Spanish-American War, and he was still on active duty in an America that was grappling with the aftermath of the Vietnam War. He had seen much across that span.

Often, though, his view was the view of a curmudgeon—churlish, angry, full of the rage of a man who saw a world that affronted him. "There is hardly a large organization in the country which has not gone down hill over the last quarter of a century," he said in 1971, sounding like an old, bitter man on a park bench. "Is the Post Office as efficient as it used to be? The Naval Academy? The Air Force? The Navy? The Bell Telephone Company? The U.S. Army? New York City? The University of California?

". . . I am trapped in a lunatic world where the inhabitants talk sage nonsense to one another. They want to be considered intellectuals without the equipment for it and, as such folk will, have devised a jargon so elusive and standards so arbitrary that there is no way of being found out. They know a little about everything; they have a smattering of ignorance. . . ."

But he was not an old man on a park bench. He was in a witness chair in Washington, D.C., telling the defense subcommittee of the House Committee on Appropriations how much money to give to the Department of Defense—"it seems that every day at the Pentagon is amateur night"—for the security of the United States.

These were not the words of a memoir; they were active words of a man who was there, still working, still trying to produce change. But, from hundreds of thousands of words he has addressed to Congress, what emerges at best are the sharp observations of a critic and, at worst, the carping of a chronic malcontent. He ruled the Naval Reactors Branch as a king, and the submarines and surface ships of the nuclear navy formed his empire. By 1981 those ships powered by the atom comprised more than one third of the Navy's warships. The rest of the Navy paid homage to that empire in various ways, one of them being the offering-up of most of their favorite sons—the top graduates of the Naval Academy, Officer Candidate School, and Navy ROTC.

Beyond the Navy, Rickover's empire had influence, as would any powerful neighboring empire, in the Department of Defense. His monotone voice, amplified by Congress, called for reform throughout the Defense establishment. And yet Rickover himself was no reformer. This was vividly demonstrated in 1973, when he experienced something rare for him on Capitol Hill—a colloquy.

Representative Joseph P. Addabbo, then a member of Congress for a decade, interrupted Rickover's testimony before the appropriations subcommittee to remind him that Congress had to look beyond Rickover's needs. "I have to be the advocate of the devil on this committee," Addabbo said, "because I represent people from the city [New York] who have many problems, who need housing and everything else. You give us a priority. Every admiral coming over here says, 'My program is the most important.' Tell us where we can get those dollars."

Rickover said he was only looking for more funds for research and development. He asked Addabbo if he thought the percentage Rickover already had was adequate.

"You are the master," Addabbo replied. "Tell us how much is adequate." The Congressman bore in. "Where do we get it from? Can you tell me where we can get it in the Navy? Where can we make offsetting reductions?"

Rickover backed off: "Sir, I am not in a position to tell you in specific detail what items should be cut."

"Why not? You are a specialist. We are the generalists. If you don't tell us, then we will have to look at what we see in black and white on paper."

"It is precisely because I am a specialist that I cannot speak to what should be done to reduce spending in areas I am not familiar with. . . . You are asking me to speak to this as if I were the Chief of Naval Operations or the Secretary of Defense. If I were to give you specific recommendations, I would be doing a disservice because I do not know the basis for all the other R&D [Research and Development] work. I can only give you my opinion in a relative way."

"You are a great research specialist," Addabbo insisted. "Tell us where we can possibly look to, where we can look to in research . . ."

"Unfortunately," Rickover said, "Congress generally approaches this kind of problem by using the meat-axe approach." He was back in the familiar role of critic.

But Addabbo would not let him get away. ". . . You people will not give us the priorities."

"Sir, I am not talking about appropriating more money. I am talking about priorities for where money should be spent."

Addabbo still would not let up. They sparred, and then the Congressman pressed him again: "You are coming before this committee on which we are sitting and saying, 'You have got to do it.' Let us know how to do it. Go off the record and give us your advice."

Rickover would not go off the record (a tactic he has used often, especially to attack other programs). Nor would he accept Addabbo's invitation to "tell us where that fat is" in the Pentagon. Rickover insisted that he could not tell them how to "run every aspect of the Defense Department. . . . Nor every aspect of the Navy. I cannot do that. With your permission, I would like to talk about frigates now."

The duel between the Admiral and the Congressman showed Rickover to be a surprisingly reluctant executor. "When Eurystheus noted the Augean stables were dirty," he pleaded, "was he then responsible for cleaning them? That is what you are telling me. If I am a messenger and tell you something, you expect me to go on and do the job even though it is someone else's responsibility."

In his wary insistence that he was only a messenger, Rickover ducked any responsibility for carrying out what he so often, so tirelessly advocated, an improvement in the efficiency of the Pentagon, "a kingdom of illusion." He seemed more interested in eliciting laughter than reform. His typical offering was fantasy: He would first classify "the Pentagon people as *A, B, C. A* does the work, *B* and *C* are given offices without secretaries, messengers, desks, rugs, telephones, typewriters, or water pitchers. They do get scratch pads on which to write letters to each other in longhand. The letters would be dropped in dummy mail boxes and there would be no collection. The only writing instrument they could use would be crayons—if they had a sharp object they might harm themselves. Also they could show up for work and leave any time they desired, and vacations would be unlimited. Their checks would be mailed to their homes."

There were several versions of Rickover's prescription for solving the ills of the Pentagon. For one Congressman he devised a single plan for removing two levels of the Pentagon's five stories. When Representative George Andrews asked him about one of his earlier dicta—"Several years ago, you told us that the best way to promote efficiency and economy in Government would be to fire 25 percent of the civilian employees in the Pentagon. Do you still hold that view?"—Rickover instantly responded, "No, sir. I was wrong. I would now get rid of at least 50 percent of them."

The Congressmen laughed, but inside the Navy there were men who did not laugh. There were, for instance, officers working for the Chief of Naval Material. Rickover said that their "technical contribution . . . could be fully covered in one small paragraph of a *Reader's Digest* article." It was at that level, where there were real people, not just faceless "Pentagon people," that his wisecracks hurt. Such gibes—from a naval officer, aimed at fellow officers—inspired enduring hatred of him in the wardrooms of the Navy. As a matter of fact, rarely did his testimony before Congress actually hurt an individual. But his testimony did create an atmosphere in which the Pentagon and, specifically, the Navy were made to look inept. If, as Admiral of the Hill, he sought primarily to preserve his nuclear navy, his secondary purpose was to challenge the leadership of the rest of the Navy.

The challenge had been perennially ignored. Rear Admiral Ralph K. James recalled that in 1959, soon after he became Chief of BuShips, he attended a conference of senior officers. "Present," he remembered, "were all the fleet commanders, Atlantic and Pacific, the CNO, all the heads of the OPs, the fleet-type commanders, two technical bureau chiefs, myself, and the weapons boss, Paul D. Stroop [Chief, Bureau of Naval Weapons].

"Throughout this very wonderful meeting of the senior officers, who reviewed Navy problems and discussed them, one problem that kept recurring for which there was no solution was Rickover—how he not only dominated the technical aspects of the nuclear program, but had then started to infiltrate himself into the personnel and training aspects of it to the exclusion of those people in the Navy Department who felt that that was their prerogative.

"Page Smith was then Chief of Personnel. He got up and made the most pusillanimous review of the Rickover problem . . . [and] concluded by saying, essentially, 'There isn't a damn thing we can do to him or about him, because he's got Congress on his side, and we'd just better live with it.' And that was the attitude throughout."

Admiral James remembered another meeting that was called specifically to review issues involving nuclear propulsion. The meeting, which was held at the Naval Air Station in Jacksonville, Florida, brought together senior naval officers—but, to James's surprise, no Rickover. "I found to my amazement," James recalled, "that here we were sitting there talking about nuclear-powered ships, which I was fully competent to talk about, but when it got down to the nitty-gritties, I felt Rickover's presence was vital, and I felt that it was a great discourtesy not to have him present.

"The group debated whether to extend him a delayed invitation or not. Finally, the Vice CNO [James] Russell, who was chairman of the meeting, concluded that, 'Yes, Rickover ought to be invited.' He arrived the next morning by air.

"Those silly little slights were typical of the reactions that the Line [officers] exerted in an attempt to control Rickover. I thought that forceful action by the Secretary or the CNO at the beginning could have done a great deal to channel his efforts in a way that would keep the Navy from having to bear the cross that Rickover has become."

Rickover apparently nursed those slights, and he was suspected of striking back in ways that added to his legend. Documentation of such Rickover reactions is either nonexistent or buried in the decades-high mountains of "pinks" and other papers that he has locked up in the files of his Naval Reactors Branch. In public documents, especially in Congressional hearings, glimmers of vengeance can be perceived—but only the targets can supply the revelation that they have been hit, and a confirmed hit is hard to find.

When Rickover has criticized or attacked his superiors or colleagues, he has usually done so in the relative sanctuary of a Congressional hearing room. Often there has been the ghostly wisp of a script about such attacks. Once, for instance, Rickover was testifying before the Joint Committee on Atomic Energy when his old friend Senator Clinton P. Anderson asked, "Can you tell me if the Navy is still conducting foreign officials on visits to our nuclear submarines?"

"Do you mean tours of the propulsion spaces, Senator?" Rickover asked.

"I mean tours of nuclear submarines by foreign officials. If you need to qualify your answer, please do so. I am interested in access by foreign officials to our nuclear submarines."

"You must make a distinction, sir," Rickover replied, "because there is no requirement for the Navy to report to the committee any visit which does not include access to propulsion spaces. Visits which include the propulsion spaces have been greatly reduced, thanks to the action of this committee. There have been very few of them."

Something definitely was coming. Anderson fed Rickover another question: "How about the ones they don't report?"

"Unless the visit includes a tour of the propulsion spaces, Senator Anderson, I would not necessarily be informed of it. So I cannot give you any figure. I do know, however, that such visits take place. I have just been informed today, in fact, of an impending visit to a nuclear submarine in Pearl Harbor by the Russian naval attaché."

"The Russian naval attaché took a tour of a nuclear submarine? A U.S. Navy submarine?" Anderson asked incredulously.

Rickover was not asked how he had been "informed." He told the committee that he had a list of the attachés. They included naval officers from the other Soviet-bloc countries. Rickover handed over the information. Scanning the papers, Anderson asked, "Who are these two American admirals? Why are they in this group? What does this mean—ACNO Intelligence?"

"He is the Assistant Chief of Naval Operations for Intelligence," Rickover answered. "He is the Navy's senior officer in the intelligence field."

"And he's taking the Russian attaché on this tour?" Anderson asked. "Why, this is preposterous! I simply can't believe it."

Anderson said he would get to the bottom of this immediately. But there was an element of play-acting to the exchange between the Senator and the Admiral. Both of them had to know that the ACNO for Intelligence, Rear Admiral F. J. Harlfinger II, was carrying out duties that were often more than met the eye; there was an element of serious gamesmanship to those duties. Rickover and Anderson would have to have been extremely naïve about the work of naval attachés if they did not know what was going on. Dealing with foreign attachés—especially those of the Soviet Union—was a delicate problem of give-and-take; to show the foreign officers just enough to encourage them to show your man in their capital a bit more. Harlfinger had good credentials for the job, having earlier been the first U.S. naval attaché to West Germany.*

Anderson wrote to Secretary of Defense Laird and demanded information on what the Navy had officially described as the "Seventeenth Annual Tour of Foreign Attachés accredited to the Department of the Navy." Anderson wrote, "The present case, in my view, raises fundamental questions concerning the current management of our naval attaché system."

That Anderson had made it a "case" seemed significant, for security "cases" had long been a Rickover obsession. He lobbied, with varying degrees of success, to restrict contractors from placing what Rickover believed to be classified information in advertisements in trade journals; he

---

* Harlfinger was a highly decorated nonnuclear submariner. He previously was head of the Submarine Warfare Branch (OP-311), the last captain to head the submarine "desk" in OPNAV. He later was promoted to vice admiral to direct all Navy command, control, communication and intelligence activities.

had claimed that Naval Intelligence was not providing sufficient security in shipyards and around nuclear submarine bases; he had even tried to get toy manufacturers to take models of nuclear submarines off the market. He seemed to resent that security and intelligence were outside his purview, that the other Navy had control of the Office of Naval Intelligence. By springing the "Russian visit" at a hearing, he had, once again, sent Congress off on a skirmish with the Navy.

Secretary of the Navy John H. Chafee answered Anderson's letter to Laird. Chafee pointed out that the Army and the Air Force conducted similar tours and that the Navy was following the lead of the other two services in inviting the naval attachés of the Soviet Union, Poland and Bulgaria. He then provided Anderson with some of the facts of life about attachés. An attaché from the Soviet Union gets from the United States the treatment that the United States expects its attaché will get in the Soviet Union. No reciprocity, no future tours; we want information, and they want information. It is an old story—an old game—for attachés, who are, in effect, overt spies. Then Chafee went into the matter of the visit to the nuclear submarine.

When the tour was being planned, he said, various major commanders were asked for suggestions for the itinerary. The Commander in Chief of the Pacific Fleet sent in his recommendations. These were incorporated into a document, dated February 26, 1971—and it was this document to which Rickover referred in the March 10 hearing. At that time, Rickover had said the "Russian visit" to the submarine would take place "tomorrow," for the itinerary, enclosed with the February document Rickover had acquired, showed March 11, "1100—Unclassified tour of Nuclear Submarine or tour of Pacific Submarine Display."

But what was scheduled, according to Chafee, was not what happened. "When the Eastern European Countries were included in the tour," he told Anderson, "the major commands were informed and certain revisions were made in the program. In Hawaii the unclassified tour of a nuclear submarine and tour of the Submarine Training Facility were deleted."

Rickover, attempting to deride the activities of Naval Intelligence, had got his facts wrong. The experience, however, did not chasten him. U.S. military and naval attachés being sent to nations with nuclear programs, especially the Soviet Union, as part of their preassignment briefings are directed to visit with Rickover for a chat or, more accurately, a lecture. He tells them that their purpose is to learn about foreign developments, not to give away U.S. secrets. Addressing at least one group, he repeatedly said to one of his officers in the room, "Have we got the pictures?"

The pictures—which he hands to each attaché—show an American attaché's wife being kissed by a Russian. "That's not what you are going overseas to do—not to get involved with the enemy. . . ."

But the picture, taken at a dinner in London, really shows an American woman—quite startled—being kissed in an offhand way at a social affair. (After handing out the photos, sometimes at least, he will ask, "Did they get the pictures? Do you have the pictures? Where are the pictures?")

Rickover has many enemies. Some exist only as labels: "members of the inner circle of the naval aristocracy," and "the pseudo-intellectuals," and, always, "the bureaucracy," where a "civil service clerk is like a nail without a head. You can stick him somewhere, and then there's no way to pull him out." (Laughter) Stringing the labels through his testimony, he has amused Congress and enraged the Navy and the Department of Defense. He even once made the modest proposal that Congress abolish the Air Force, giving the Strategic Air Command to the Navy, and Air Force space and missile projects to the Army.

We have chronicled Rickover on Capitol Hill, where so much of what he did was visible—and audible. But something deeper stirred in him when he went beyond advocacy to crusading. He was mad at people, and people were mad at him. He was a target. And he made targets of others. Sometimes his words suggested that he saw himself as a solitary, self-made man up against the entire upper class. He has said that he has tried to understand why unqualified officials find their way to high positions in the Navy and the Pentagon. "I have pondered over this phenomenon for many years," he said. "The only rationale I can come to is that everything in life has been easy for these officials. They have been carried along by family, by wealth, by friends, possibly by political considerations. In a position requiring technical expertise for the first time in their lives, they believe themselves capable of solving these problems by using the 'personality' methods that have previously gotten them by."

Rickover, of course, used "personality" in getting things done, but he apparently did not equate an essentially negative personality with what he saw as the positive personalities of the privileged class. He also seems to have included Congress in that assemblage of personalities of privilege.

A senior staff member of a major House committee recalled that when Rickover wished to respond to a Congressional inquiry or wished to get something from a Congressman, he would send to the Hill an officer from the Naval Reactors Branch—in uniform. The Congressional aide, used to working with representatives from the Department of Defense, the Army, Air Force, and nonnuclear navy, was always intrigued by the fact that Rickover, the man who never wore a uniform, would see to it that a uniformed officer represented him. No other service so blatantly proffered homage.

Often Rickover would create the situation where members of Congress were portrayed as siding with him against "them," and the "them" was the U.S. Navy and the admirals who ran it—men who were nominally, at least in organization charts, his bosses. This opposition was often initiated and fostered by Rickover despite his persistent posture of humility—"I must make it clear that I claim no superior wisdom. Further, my superiors have responsibilities and problems that are different and more onerous than mine; these responsibilities and problems may require different solutions than I propose. I make no claim that my views are right and theirs are wrong."

But after such introductions to his remarks, Rickover would then continue, berating the opinions of "the admirals" and the Defense Department's analysts. He rarely mentioned admirals by name in this context, with one significant exception, Elmo R. Zumwalt, Jr., the Chief of Naval Operations. When writing his memoirs, Zumwalt would devote a chapter to "the Rickover complication." He began the chapter with these words: "The fact that from the start of my watch to the end of it Vice Admiral, and then Admiral, Hyman G. Rickover was a persistent and formidable obstacle to my plans for modernizing the Navy did not at all surprise me. I had expected him to be." Zumwalt and Rickover would fight over many issues during Zumwalt's tenure as CNO—personnel, ships and shipyards, among others.

Zumwalt was not the first CNO to find Rickover a "complication." Admiral Arleigh Burke came to dislike Rickover professionally and personally. Burke was particularly upset by Rickover the man.

When Burke became CNO on August 17, 1955, the Rickover navy consisted of only the *Nautilus*. As CNO, Burke was a strong proponent of nuclear propulsion, and the nuclear navy obtained funds for building its first aircraft carrier, missile cruiser, missile frigate and Polaris missile submarines during his six years in the Pentagon E-ring. Burke tended to leave Rickover, a junior rear admiral, to his own interests. Burke, like all other CNOs, had innumerable issues—military, manpower, political, economic—to worry about; nuclear propulsion was one of many. But when Burke made the decision to push the Navy into the Polaris strategic-missile program, he turned away from Rickover and selected William F. Raborn, limiting Rickover only to the Polaris submarine power plant. (See Chapter 24.)

Rickover, of course, would have the last words. He selected the submarines' commanding, executive and engineering officers; and, long after Burke and Raborn would retire, Rickover would still be going strong as the head of the nuclear navy.

Burke was followed by three less notable CNOs: George W. Anderson, David L. McDonald and Thomas H. Moorer. All were aviators, all had served as junior officers in World War II, and all fought primarily to hold the status quo within the fleet—submarines and surface ships were important, but it was the aircraft carriers, the "measure of difference" between the U.S. and Soviet navies, that were the Navy's and the nation's most important military asset. They tolerated Admiral Rickover—or more likely he tolerated them. Rickover could build nuclear carriers for them, and those behemoths, in turn, would require nuclear-propelled escort ships. In the ten years of their stewardship, an average of almost five nuclear attack submarines (SSN) were built each year, enough for an orderly replacement of older, diesel-propelled attack submarines. But the trend was downward in the last two years of Moorer's term as CNO.

As the end of Admiral Moorer's term approached in the spring of 1970, interest in his potential successor intensified. The naval aviation community—or "union"—of which Tom Moorer was representative, still ran the Navy. Aviators were the most organized, articulate, and—in view of the cost of carriers and naval aircraft—the most powerful of the unions. And so several candidates were aviators, excellent men in the tradition of Anderson, McDonald and Moorer. These candidates were flag officers in their middle fifties, the age of the CNOs of the 1960s.

Elmo R. (Bud) Zumwalt, Jr., in 1970 was commander of the U.S. naval forces in Vietnam. He was a comer, having had several commands at sea, the first one being a captured Japanese gunboat he used to "liberate" Shanghai in September 1945, just three years after graduation from the Naval Academy. He had served as an aide to the Assistant Secretary of the Navy for personnel and manpower and later to Paul Nitze, who was Assistant Secretary of Defense for international affairs and the Secretary of the Navy from 1963 to 1965. Zumwalt's service afloat, his outstanding student record at both the Naval War College and the National War College, and especially, his duty with Nitze marked him as CNO potential after he had a bit more maturity and seasoning as a task force commander—and possibly fleet commander. In 1970, after all, he was just forty-nine, four years younger than Forrest Sherman and Arleigh Burke, who were the youngest CNOs when they had been appointed, both at age fifty-three.

But shortly after 11 A.M., on July 1, 1970, on the portico of sprawling Bancroft Hall, Zumwalt was sworn in as the Chief of Naval Operations, the nineteenth officer to hold that position since its establishment in 1915. Zumwalt would seek to change the Navy, more so than any CNO in peacetime before him. But on that sunny July morning in 1970 the U.S. Navy was in large part the nuclear navy directed by Vice Admiral Rickover. Thus, a CNO attempting to bring about change would be in conflict with the nuclear navy as well as the traditionalists of the nonnuclear Navy.

"I knew," Zumwalt wrote in his memoirs, "that [Rickover's] Division of Nuclear Propulsion was a totalitarian mini-state whose citizens— and that included not just his headquarters staff but anybody also engaged in building, maintaining, or manning nuclear vessels—did what the Leader told them to do, Naval Regulations not withstanding, or suffered condign punishment. In sum, I knew as soon as I was designated CNO that developing a productive working relationship with Rickover was among the toughest nuts I had been called upon to crack. In my exuberance over being chosen to head the Navy, I believed I could do it. I was wrong."

Zumwalt's most emotional struggle with Rickover did not involve submarines or fleets but the career of a single officer. He was Captain Charles O. Swanson, commander of the Pearl Harbor Naval Shipyard. Swanson was scheduled to be relieved of his command on June 1, 1973, a year after assuming charge of the shipyard. From his lofty post, Zumwalt had no notice of this until May 1, 1973, when he received a letter from Swanson's wife, Anne.

The letter went into detail about "a political battle" between Rickover and all naval shipyards. She felt that the one at Pearl Harbor had been singled out, along with her husband. She said that Swanson had flown to Washington in April and had been "made aware of the fact that many in NavShips [Ship Systems Command] knew that his relief had been selected, even was making plans to be in Pearl Harbor by 28 May, and that he, Chuck [Swanson], would be relieved on 1 June."

Mrs. Swanson said she was not writing to Zumwalt to intercede— "Chuck sees his usefulness as an active duty EDO at an end and plans to submit his request for retirement"—but she thought that Zumwalt's "interest in this might stem the possibility of further intimidation and further breakdown of morale within the EDO community itself."

Zumwalt began what would be a year-long combat with Rickover over Swanson. The CNO first ordered the Navy's Inspector General, Vice Admiral Means Johnston, Jr., to look into the case. Johnston talked to yard officials and workers, took about sixty hours of testimony, and interviewed the senior officers in the Pacific. He then went to see Rickover.

Afterward, Zumwalt's executive assistant met with Means Johnston and on June 21 wrote a memo to Zumwalt: "[Johnston] described Rick as terribly emotional and unstable. He said Rick screamed and yelled at him and was extremely upset. Rick is apparently worried about a Congressional investigation." What neither the Chief of Naval Operations nor the Inspector General of the Navy realized was that Rickover at that time *was himself* calling for an investigation of Navy personnel practices. Testifying on June 21 before a subcommittee of the House Appropriations committee, he said, "Every standing committee of Congress has an investigating function. . . . Why don't you find out how much money is being spent on [naval] personnel? Why don't you investigate the areas I have just mentioned?" (The topics ranged from allegations about the decline in the Navy's technical competence to what was wrong with "the Navy's so-called 'human goals' program"—one of Zumwalt's pet projects.) "I think it is high time Congress stepped in somewhere and performed its constitutional duties."

The memo to Zumwalt about the Swanson case also said that Rickover "reluctantly" allowed the Inspector General to see reports sent to Rickover by the head of inspection at Pearl Harbor, but Johnston "said that he was not allowed to copy the letters or take the letters out of the room. He could read the letters and take notes . . . and he was under observation during this day-and-a-half period. . . . Rick would call him periodically and have another tantrum."

Johnston's inquiry broadened into what inadvertently amounted to an investigation of the shipyard branch of Rickover's nuclear navy. Rickover had assigned inspectors who were part of what Zumwalt called an "un-American and autocratic" management system outside the yard's command structure. Zumwalt said he learned that the inspectors prowled the shipyard, "clipboards in hand, making notes on who was smoking or drinking a soda or talking with friends, on how much time workmen spent on lunch breaks or in the head, and of course on which supervisors were allowing such deeds to be done by their people. They even went so far as to invade the parking lot of a popular restaurant just outside the yard to take down license-plate numbers of the cars with shipyard stickers parked there, because Rickover did not approve of his folk eating lunch off base."

The Inspector General's report implied that the U.S. Navy did not know the practices and dimensions of the Rickover navy. The Pearl Harbor shipyard was but one facility policed by what Swanson called an "Orwellian system," complete with "Big Brothers." What is most amazing about the Inspector General's report is the wide-eyed incredulity about a system which, in 1973, had been in existence for almost two decades in naval and civilian shipyards. (See Chapter 22.)

The Inspector General found at the Pearl Harbor Naval Shipyard five naval officers and one Navy civilian employee "wearing AEC hats." The report said:

> They are all experts in the radiological field, probably the best the Navy has. Unfortunately, they work directly for Vice Admiral Rickover in his AEC hat and not for the Navy. My investigation revealed that instead of really helping the Commanding Officer of the Shipyard, Commander Taylor [head of the AEC group] was actually harrassing [sic] the Commanding Officer involving himself in every facet of management, and submitting reports (no copy to the CO) direct to Vice Admiral Rickover in his AEC hat. Vice Admiral Rickover then used this information in his NavShips-08 position to write official letters to the Commanding Officer. This procedure violates the chain of command completely and, furthermore, it constitutes a vicious spy system, alien to normally accepted tenets of Navy management. As a related matter, COs of submarines also are required to submit secret reports to Vice Admiral Rickover concerning yard performance. When one CO was asked if the reports were balanced, that is, did he include favorable comments concerning management, he replied in the negative, that only unfavorable comments were desired. Again the CO of the Shipyard is not provided a copy of these informal letter reports. My recommendation is that Commander Taylor and his staff be withdrawn from the AEC and put to work helping the Navy. Commander Taylor should report to the Commanding Officer of the Pearl Harbor Naval Shipyard. I would further recommend that all other AEC representatives in all other yards work directly for the Shipyard Commander.

None of the recommendations was ever carried out.

As for Swanson, he got from his superior, Rear Admiral Robert C.

Gooding, of the Ship Systems Command, what Zumwalt called "a vehemently adverse fitness report," which contrasted totally with the others he had received. Zumwalt would recommend to the Secretary of the Navy that the adverse fitness report be stricken from Swanson's record. But Zumwalt would wait until Secretary John Warner was succeeded by J. William Middendorf II. Warner, who would successfully run for election as a Republican Senatorial candidate in Virginia, had declined to oppose Rickover, because of the Admiral's strength on Capitol Hill.* Middendorf did accept Zumwalt's recommendation. Swanson remained in command at the shipyard until October 30, 1974, when he retired.

Zumwalt, in his memoirs, gave Swanson's career this epitaph: "The system, alas, does not forgive anyone who takes it on as vigorously as Charles Swanson did. If he had not fallen afoul of Rickover his ability almost certainly would have won him flag rank, and his Naval career might well have been a brilliant one. The Navy also lost much when Charles Swanson was compelled to leave it. It lost his ability. Beyond that it lost his integrity, a quality in shorter supply and of more worth."

So "the system" that was unforgiving was the *Rickover* system. In the unsuccessful struggle to retain one man, the Navy, personified by Swanson and Zumwalt, had found itself outside what had become the real system. Swanson had tried to run a shipyard according to what he thought "the system" was; he had been brought down because there was another, more powerful system, and it was controlled by Hyman Rickover.

Zumwalt was Chief of Naval Operations for the standard four-year term, from July 1, 1970, through June 29, 1974, when he was relieved in ceremonies at Annapolis by James L. Holloway. During those four years Zumwalt served three Secretaries of the Navy—John Chafee, Warner and, briefly, Middendorf—and three Secretaries of Defense. Most of the admirals on active duty in July 1970 had changed their position at least once, and many had retired by 1974. But three flag officers did hold the same positions after four years: Rear Admiral Levering Smith, head of the Polaris-Poseidon project, and Rear Admiral John D. Buckley, president of the Board of Inspection and Survey. Both had retired but remained on active duty in the same posts. The third was Admiral Rickover.

Although Zumwalt considered Rickover his biggest single problem during his four-year tenure as CNO, he had other problems as well. The United States was withdrawing from the Vietnam War, and he was faced

* *Warner received the nomination in 1978 and won the subsequent election. Zumwalt himself unsuccessfully ran for the Senate from Virginia in 1976.*

with material and personnel problems of that winding down; across the country and in the armed services racial problems were stirring; the nation was moving toward an all-volunteer force; the Middle East flared up again in 1973, this time with the threat of direct Soviet intervention; the size of the U.S. Navy was being drastically reduced in the early 1970s; and the whole process of Strategic Arms Limitation Talks was building up.

Zumwalt was a key player in all of these situations, while at the same time trying to introduce several new technologies into the fleet—ships that rode on bubbles of air, hydrofoils that flew over the water, cruise missiles, aircraft that took off and landed straight up and down, small aircraft carriers, and also new concepts, such as the "high-low" mix. This meant that the Navy would seek a carefully calculated "mix" of ships—some on the "high" side, such as nuclear-missile cruisers, but more on the "low" side, such as low-cost anti-submarine escort ships. Rickover opposed the high-low mix, although all Navy planning during the Zumwalt period and to some extent afterward was based on this concept.

Rickover did not cite Zumwalt directly as a villain. Rather, as he told a subcommittee of the House Appropriations Committee in 1973, "in the Navy today, there are officers and civilians alike making decisions about weapons who are unqualified and ignorant concerning the technology involved. They are men without experience who have much authority. . . . They make decisions seemingly like the Queen of Hearts in *Alice's Adventures in Wonderland:* 'Let the jury consider their verdict,' the King said. 'No. No!' said the Queen, 'Sentence first—verdict afterward.' "

Such oblique attacks against Zumwalt and the Navy's leadership were not lost on Congress. More to the point on the high-low concept, Rickover told how he believed that "in peacetime we should build our most difficult warships, because during peace we have time. It takes at least five years to build these complex ships."

"Assuming a war lasts five years," he continued, "we will not have time to build them after the war starts. The smaller, less complex ships can be built more quickly when there is the threat of war, like the submarine chasers and Eagle boats* of WorldWar I, and the destroyer escorts of World War II."

---

* *The Eagle boats were small, 200-foot, 615-ton anti-submarine ships built by the Ford Motor Company during World War I. Although 112 Eagle boats were authorized in March 1917, and they were designed for rapid construction, the first unit was not commissioned until October 28, 1918, two weeks before the end of the war.*

Rickover was correct—in theory. In practice, in the 1970s the U.S. Navy needed ships—in quantity as well as quality—even in "peacetime" because of America's overseas political, military and economic interests. The situation was exacerbated by the dramatic reduction of the U.S. fleet after Vietnam, from over nine hundred active ships in the early 1960s to some five hundred in June of 1973, when Rickover made his arguments for high-mix nuclear surface ships and large submarines. Zumwalt's successor, Holloway, kept many features of the low mix.

As the years passed and Zumwalt gained perspective on Rickover, the former CNO became bitter about Rickover's long-term impact on the Navy. "Rickover is paranoid," Zumwalt told the authors. "And he had turned the world into his asylum." Zumwalt once was quoted as saying that the enemies of the U.S. Navy were the Soviet Union, the U.S. Air Force, and Admiral Rickover. Later he was asked whether he still felt that way. He said he was not certain that he had ever made such a listing, but he would make one for the authors. He said he would rank the Navy's enemies as the Soviet Union first and Rickover second.

Zumwalt also came to believe that Rickover's infiltration of the Navy was so pervasive that the actual dimensions of the takeover are beyond measure. Commenting on a study of long-range planning in the Navy, he said that no such study could "accurately portray what has happened over the years as the force of Admiral Rickover's out-of-channel, executive branch-unsupervised, Byzantine, bureaucratic operation has perverted the process. Only when one has access to the files of his office can the true story be portrayed. As more and more offices of OPNAV became penetrated by his process, there was an increasing need for long-range planning to be done under the personal supervision of the CNO in order to keep it untainted by that process."

Rickover's independence was virtually unrestrained by Zumwalt during his watch as CNO. Zumwalt characterized Rickover as working for Congress and not recognizing "that he works for the President of the United States or the Navy."

Holloway was an aviator who had gone to the Rickover school before being given command of the carrier *Enterprise*. It was a tribute to Rickover's durability that the new CNO was born the year that Rickover graduated from the Naval Academy. Holloway was the son of the Chief of Naval Personnel who first worked out the arrangements that gave Rickover control over the manning of his nuclear navy. With this power, Rickover had given Holloway the *Enterprise*. (Rickover later told Congress, "When we built the *Enterprise*, the Navy was changing captains of aircraft carriers every year, in some cases every nine months, so this could be put in their records. It was nothing more than 'a brownie point' required by the system so they could be eligible to make admiral.")

Holloway had been CNO for scarcely two months when Rickover, in a speech before the National Society of Former FBI Agents, issued a detailed indictment of what was wrong with the Navy. "In my opinion," he said, "there has been no point in the past fifty years where the fleet has been in as poor condition as it is today. . . . The Navy is raising a generation of officers who believe that technical training is not essential and that they can rely on management techniques to make decisions." He focused his criticism on line officers—in contrast to engineering-duty officers like himself—who lacked the "technical competence" to man modern ships. He claimed he knew of a senior line admiral who was so ignorant of technical matters that he issued an order that said: "There will be no more rust."

He attacked the management of the Navy, the curriculum at the Naval Academy and the Naval War College, and many other aspects of the Navy, from the designing of warships to their maintenance and operations. "The loss of professionalism among the engineers and the interference of line officers in technical matters has resulted in ships of questionable design," he said. He made an exception of nuclear-powered ships "only because of my ability to insist upon the contrary."

After that speech, Rickover periodically appeared in Congressional hearings or on public platforms and made speeches or issued statements about the deplorable condition of the Navy. Criticism of Holloway was barely concealed. Once, for instance, Rickover circulated a memorandum that he said was based on a report by the Navy's Board of Inspection and Survey. The memorandum said that of fifty-one inspected ships, forty-nine had defects that "significantly degraded required operational capabilities associated with the mission and primary mission areas of the ships."

What had prompted Rickover's attack on Holloway's Navy seems to have been Holloway's resistance to an all-nuclear navy. Here was an officer, picked and trained by Rickover, denying the basic tenet of Rickover's naval strategy. But Holloway was running an entire navy, and what he saw from his vantage point went beyond Rickover's nuclear-circumscribed horizons. What Holloway was seeing, for example, was Aegis, an extremely expensive, extremely sophisticated system for defending ships against missiles and aircraft. "In order to get the number of major surface combatants with Aegis," Holloway said, "we can't afford to have all nuclear power."

The Holloway-Rickover feud finally broke into the open in May 1976, when the CNO used one of Rickover's own techniques against him. Holloway went to Capitol Hill—not in person, but via a statement hand-delivered to several Senators. "The issue," said Holloway's message, "is which advice should the Congress follow: the advice of the CNO, the senior uniformed official responsible for the readiness of naval forces now and in the future—and whose views are supported by the Secretary of the Navy and Secretary of Defense and presidential decision—or the advice of Adm. Rickover."

Holloway, like Zumwalt before him, was reminding Congress that there was a chain of command and that the use of it was in the best interest of national security. But the word was passed on Capitol Hill that the Navy was out "to get" Rickover. A Congressman made a speech on the House floor accusing the Navy of mounting a "violent, unprecedented, and obviously inspired campaign" against Rickover. George C. Wilson, the Pentagon correspondent of *The Washington Post,* reported that Defense officials were seeing 1976 and 1977 as "the years to break Rickover's power." Rickover's critics and supporters agreed that the new wave of criticism stemmed not only from his traditional attacks on the Navy but also from his frequent sniping at civilians in the Pentagon and in the shipbuilding industry.

For years Rickover had been ridiculing analysts in the Pentagon and Navy. One of the most memorable of Rickover's well-staged outbursts against "sheepskin economists" and "instant experts" had come in 1967, when the Armed Services Committee asked Admiral David L. McDonald, the Chief of Naval Operations, "In the cost-effectiveness studies comparing nuclear and nonnuclear ships, what cost and what value is included for American lives?" McDonald replied that "human lives" did not get assigned "cost factors," because human life has an intrinsic value.

Having got "cost-effectiveness" and "American lives" neatly arranged as a backdrop, the committee called in Rickover and asked him to respond to the words of the man who was, theoretically, his boss.

"Cost-effectiveness suffers from a philosophical weakness, . . ." Rickover said. "The cost analysts live in a world of immutable abstractions. . . . They don't—and the types of studies they make render it impossible to—take account of human life. They do not believe that the good is as valuable as the profitable."

Eventually, "cost-effectiveness" went out of fashion and "systems analysis" came in, but Rickover continued his attacks on Pentagon studies. The Department of Defense, he said, "is constipated; it must be purged or it will become increasingly torpid. . . ."

Sent a stack of computer punch-cards and asked for a "peer rating" of Department of Defense laboratories, he returned the cards to the Pentagon with a letter saying he assumed that peer rating was analogous to the pecking order of fowl. He went on: "I am sure that eminent social scientists have advocated the training of humans by the methods derived from training pigeons—rewarding them with a grain of corn each time they fulfilled their norm. I have even considered replacing some humans with pigeons. On reflection I concluded this would not work; a number of those I had planned to replace with pigeons threatened to eat their replacements. . . ."

His permanent target, off and on the record, was Secretary of Defense McNamara. After his departure, Rickover criticized him more openly, once claiming that McNamara "and his whiz kids," with "their cost analysis and computer methods . . . managed to lose us the lead we had in nuclear submarines and allowed the Soviets to catch up with us to a dangerous degree. . . ."

The charge against McNamara reads well, but after even minimal scrutiny it is, at best, confusing. Did Rickover mean the qualitative or quantitative lead in submarines was lost to the Soviets? In 1961, the year in which McNamara became Secretary of Defense, the Soviet Union had 400 submarines and the U.S. Navy had 120 submarines; in 1968, when McNamara left office, the relative position of the U.S. submarine force had actually *improved,* as the Soviets had 360 submarines and the U.S. Navy had 160.

The quality of Soviet submarines and the number of nuclear units did increase during this period. Still, the McNamara budget proposals to Congress included an annual average of more nuclear submarines than any previous or later period. Although McNamara and to some extent the Navy delayed the electric-drive submarine (*Lipscomb*) and high-speed SSN-688 (*Los Angeles* class), the improved *Sturgeon* and *Narwhal* attack submarines were started during McNamara's term, as was the Poseidon submarine missile program.

Rather, Rickover's typically simplistic statement tends to ignore a basic difference in the U.S. and Soviet navies. The same year that he attacked the "massive irresponsibility" of McNamara, Rickover told a Congressional committee that "It is . . . clear that the submarine force has become the major element of their [the Soviet] navy." In contrast, the United States, with a need to *use* the seas rather than to deny them to an enemy, as was the Soviet situation, had a more balanced fleet—with aircraft carriers, surface warships, and amphibious ships, as well as a major submarine fleet.

"The DOD is not only drowning in words," Rickover said, "it is also settling in a swamp of half-ideas and fantasy. . . . [The] new school of thought in the 1970s is as sure of itself as were the old ones of the 1960s, which lost us our nuclear-ship supremacy; the 1930s and early 1940s, which left us ill prepared for World War II; and the 1920s, which accepted unpoliced disarmament. . . ."

There it was, the fundamental Rickover tenet: He, unlike the whiz kids and other new-breed analysts, could look down a long corridor of time past. And, because he had that perspective, he knew what was right. Ironically, it was because of his long view that his critics claimed he was monumentally wrong. As they saw his railings against Defense management, he had strayed far beyond his basic responsibility—building reactors for Navy ships—and in his zeal for an all-nuclear Navy, he had lost perspective rather than gained it. By continually looking back and urging others to do the same, he had lost sight of where the Defense establishment was going.

By the middle 1970s, Rickover's claim to overall expertise was consistently questioned in the Pentagon and even sometimes questioned in Congress. Once, after a diatribe against Defense management techniques, Rickover himself became the surprise target of criticism. Senator John C. Culver, an Iowa Democrat, said Rickover's testimony disturbed him because "it is absolutely unthinkable that, in the absence of system analysts' help and the independent view provided to the Secretary of Defense, we can get any kind of harmonization and rationalization out of the vicious service rivalry and bureaucracy, and that it is almost impossible for the taxpayer to ever conceivably fund the magnitude of the request for every conceivable kind of weapons system. . . . [The] priorities between defense and nondefense, as well as the internal priorities of this defense budget, require that very kind of tough-minded calculation."

"That is the function of the Office of Management and Budget," Rickover replied. "But certainly the management—I don't know whether I understand you. Are you saying that we must have systems analysts?"

"Absolutely," Culver said.

"You can get a housewife to do that, sir," Rickover insisted. "She can tell you where something costs more. It isn't very hard."

"That is not what they do," Culver said. "I think you are aware of that."

"Well, I know many housewives that can do a better job than the systems analysts."

"As you say, everyone is entitled to their own opinion," Culver said, apparently trying to end the dialogue.

"Yes, sir. I have been around and around. . . ."

But the virtue of having been around was no longer enough. As the Vietnam War wound down, Congress began taking a harder look at defense appropriations. Patriotism was no longer measured in how much money was handed over to the Pentagon. Politically, it was now less dangerous for conservative Congressmen to challenge the requests of the Department of Defense.

Rickover still had amazing immunity. He usually got what he wanted from Congress, and most Congressmen sympathetically heard him out when he launched into one of his diatribes. If there was one moment, though, when Rickover began to be a victim of the new trend—the "tough-minded calculation" Culver had mentioned—it came one day in 1975 when Rickover said he would rather command the Soviet submarine fleet than the American fleet. It was just one of those Rickover remarks, part of this shorthand for displeasure about numbers, performance, and what he always saw as obstacles. But Senator John C. Stennis, chairman of the Senate Armed Services Committee, was shocked. His committee had helped find the billions for the creation of those American submarines—and many of Stennis' own constituents had helped to build some of them, in the Ingalls Shipyard in Pascagoula, Mississippi.

For many Congressmen, Rickover's private war on shipyards would become an issue that at least privately set them against him. When he sounded off about shipyards, he was not merely criticizing a management philosophy or attacking nameless cost analysts in the Pentagon; he was focusing on the management of a single industry—shipbuiding.

As Rickover's denunciation of shipyards became more clamorous, one man challenged him in language as vociferous as his own. The man was an analyst. He was neither nameless nor faceless. His name was Gordon W. Rule, director of procurement control in the Naval Material Command from 1963 to 1976.

Rule had been an officer in the Navy during World War II, attaining the rank of captain. He returned to active duty in the contracts division of the Bureau of Ships during the Korean War. Then, as a civilian, he became director of procurement control, a post set up by Secretary Forrestal in 1941, with the responsibility of determining whether Navy contracts were prudent and in accord with applicable policies, laws and regulations. He was much cited by the Navy, and he wrote and donated to the Navy the book *The Art of Negotiation.* At times he was so outspoken that once he had been threatened with firing and had been temporarily demoted. He went to Congress for help and was supported by many there.

Rule was caustic, dogmatic, unflinchingly honest, arrogantly sure of himself and his cause. He seemed, in many ways, to be very much like Rickover. Or very much like the kind of man Rickover wanted in the Navy.

But Rule wanted Rickover out of the Navy, and he said so publicly in June 1976. "Here in Washington today," Rule told the Shipbuilders Council of America, "we have a group of government employees—including Assistant Secretaries of Defense and Navy and four-star admirals—working night and day and weekends in a sincere effort to carry out policy decisions of the Secretary of Defense and his deputy. In this same city of Washington today we have a second group of high-priced government employees whose loyalties are obviously not to the Secretary of Defense, working night and day to torpedo the carrying out of their decisions." The second group was the Naval Reactors Branch.

Rule said that Rickover "has made his continued presence in the Navy incompatible with sound management and military discipline. He has made himself a liability to the Navy and tragically has begun to destroy the very capability he helped to create.... If Admiral Rickover is permitted to continue his flagrant contempt for, and harassment of, both the Navy and the shipbuilders of this country, then I say to you, 'God help our Navy.' "

By the time Rule uttered his prayer for the Navy, Rickover's war with the shipbuilders had become what the Office of the Secretary of Defense called "a serious threat to our national defense." Several shipyards were threatening to stop all Navy work. Rickover had been complaining about the yards for years. But now it was a war.

He himself once said that there were shipbuilding claims against the Navy even before the *Monitor* and the *Merrimac.* Rickover's war with the shipyards also has a history, which began when he decided to put his own men in the shipyards and told them to tell him what was going on. He ordered his representatives to look for trouble in the yards—and when they found it, he told them, "Let me know, promptly."

Let Me Know, Promptly

From the time when he began building the *Nautilus*, Rickover had been determined to keep watch on the day-to-day work at the Electric Boat Company. He sent men from Naval Reactors to the yard with instructions to report any problems back to him. Workers and executives at Electric Boat understood. They were building a submarine at the edge of technology; they needed all the help and suggestions they could get.

But as more and more submarines and surface ships were launched, and as Electric Boat and then other yards—commercial and naval—gained experience, Rickover's "NR Representatives" increased, rather than diminished, in number. They became an on-the-site private investigation force answerable only to Rickover. He specifically told them that they were to report problems to him—but they were not to attempt to solve those problems by mediation. When word got back to him (as word always did) that these instructions were not being carried out, he would issue a memo on "Responsibilities for NR Representatives at Field Offices." One such memo was reissued on March 27, 1962. It is characteristically thorough and in plain English. The emphases on certain words are Rickover's. The text of the memo follows.

> From time to time I note evidence that NR representatives at field offices such as a shipyard or a laboratory do not fully understand their primary mission.
>
> It is amazing to me how representatives new to these positions uniformly get themselves into the frame of mind where they conceive of themselves as intermediaries between NR and the contractor; that is, that their job is to judge who is right—NR or the contractor, and then to make the decision on their own, in many cases not even notifying NR. In this way the NR representative becomes, in effect, NR's boss. Subtle pressures by a contractor such as making the NR representative feel that he is "good" and that he really un-

derstands the local problems and NR does not, contribute to this feeling of euphoria and omniscience. This situation has led to numerous difficulties, to considerable delay in NR's becoming apprised of the actual state of affairs and to millions of dollars of additional cost to the Government.

Typical is a recent case where an NR representative decided on his own to countermand a technical order issued by me, but without notifying me in the premises. All NR representatives are, of course, encouraged to state their views to me at any time. The weekly Critical Items List is an excellent medium for this; telephone calls and letters are always in order. However, NR representatives do not have the authority to countermand my orders; in so doing they are placing themselves above the Headquarters office. It is *not* their job to assume my responsibility.

Another and more serious mistake arises when the NR representative decides what he should or should not report to me. Frequently he decides not to report things to me because he feels he can handle the matter better himself; he is afraid that by notifying me of the situation (which *is* his job), I will take ignorant, improper action and upset the "apple-cart." Here again the NR representative, instead of *representing* me, has become my *judge*.

Nearly all NR representatives have had inadequate experience to handle the important and complex tasks they face; I do not expect them to be able to make wise decisions on all matters by themselves. Unless they are continually alert they can gradually create a situation where they become too "chummy" with the contractor; they thus tend to become, in effect, a member of the contractor's organization and to share his responsibilities; very subtly and imperceptibly they get themselves in this frame of mind where they really cease to be NR representatives, but feel themselves, instead, to be part of the contractor organization. Since they have permitted themselves to become emotionally involved with the contractor, they feel that they owe a "loyalty" to his organization. Once they reach this frame of mind they become practically useless to NR, doubly so because I am relying on them to represent me to the *contractor,* whereas they are actually representing the contractor to me, or *judging* me, but without my being aware that this is the case; if I but know this, I could take the necessary action. As a matter of fact, under such circumstances it is better to have no NR representative at all, because I would not then be lulled into thinking the NR interests are being taken care of.

Frequently you must sit back and judge the *contractor* and his performance. Minor events or troubles are frequently clues that show up deficiencies in contractor management, in organization, in ability of personnel, in practices. This will require a great deal of clear thought, but can result in great improvements in the contractor's organization and the resultant performance of NR business. Let me know, promptly, of observations such as this.

Please bear in mind *always* that you are the *NR representative;* that you are to carry out the policies of *NR;* that you are not to *judge* NR, or to represent the contractor to NR. To achieve the status of a true NR representative requires the acquisition of God-like qualities; but you can try.

H.G. RICKOVER

One Godlike quality for an NR repesentative was prescience, for he had to foretell what bad news Rickover would want to know. "He wanted bad news," a former representative recalled. "He would always say, 'Don't tell me what's going on right. I only want to know what's going on wrong.' We were simply his spies."

A typical representative would spend every work day at a contractor's plant or shipyard. Rickover had his representatives watching over every major component, from reactor-core manufacturing to hull construction, from technical work in the AEC laboratories he controlled to the time that workers spent in cafeterias and rest rooms.

Rickover's key representatives, drawn from his Washington staff, began their work week by arriving at assigned sites—say the Bettis Laboratory near Pittsburgh or Electric Boat in Groton, Connecticut—on Monday morning. This usually meant leaving their homes on Sunday afternoon or night. They would work on the site all week long and return to Washington in time for a Saturday audience with Rickover at his headquarters. The typical meeting lasted about fifteen minutes.

In the late 1960s, when what is described here was common practice, there were about thirty such representatives.* Each was expected to call Rickover from the site on a regular basis. With that number of calls, plus the numerous other calls Rickover would be getting and making, it was not possible for a representative to speak for more than about one minute. Sometimes Rickover's cryptic questions would extend the call by another minute or so.

The representative usually got through directly to Rickover, who simply picked up the phone and said, "Go ahead." The representative

* The practices have continued through the years, but the number of representatives is not publicly known.

stated his name and locale and presented a problem, typically drawn from the Critical Items List. "If you had nothing to report," a former representative said, "you weren't doing your job." The problems passed on to Rickover covered technical matters, not kinks in the schedule. "You only had a minute," the representative remembered. "And in that minute he wanted a sense of the whole situation."

Rickover loved to tell the story of one representative who, while on the phone to Rickover, spotted smoke in a shipyard. Rickover hung up and immediately called the president of the shipyard. The call reached the president before the yard's own fire alarm went off.

As the eyes and ears of Rickover, the representatives had the freedom of the plant or yard. "The vendors were terrified of us," a representative remembered, using the official NRB word for contractors. To Rickover, they filled that legal definition of vendor, and he seemed to view them with the same suspicion that anyone from the days of Chicago's old Maxwell Street would show toward pushcart operators or curbside vendors. Rickover simply did not trust vendors. He often had good reason.

One part of a nuclear plant steam system, for example, has ninety-nine carbon steel welds. They must be X-rayed and certified by the vendor before acceptance by NRB. But NRB makes its own X rays. Such double checks have turned up incredibly poor workmanship: an acceptance of only ten percent of the welds in one case; a one hundred percent rejection rate in another. Theoretically, the Navy's inspection system should have been enough of a guard against such shoddy work. But Rickover, from the very first days of the building of the *Nautilus,* had insisted on his own standards of quality control, and he had ordered extreme actions—the firing of executives, special training of workers—to get what he wanted. Once he told a company to move its executive offices to the main floor of the manufacturing area so that supervisors could look out their windows and see how hard the workers were working. This was just what Rickover said he was trying to accomplish: get industry to know "what is going on in its plants." Administrators, he said, "are being judged by the size of the profits and not by the excellence of the equipment they deliver."

The bad habits of workers also bothered him, and his informers frequently passed on tales of sloth. He continually told Congress about workers who loafed on the job. At one shipyard, he said, his representatives found that workers had built shacks "equipped with heat, air-conditioners, seats, radios, coffee messes, and *Playboy* pin-up galleries."

There is no single cause to which Rickover's war against shipbuilders can be traced. He began fighting contractors during his World War II days in the electrical section of BuShips. Ever since then, for many a manufacturer, dealing with Rickover was a surrealistic conflict that whirled in a seemingly endless spiral. The process began with the examination of one topic, and then its sources, and then the sources of those sources, and so on, regardless of cost, regardless of manpower, or regardless of that inexhaustible Rickover commodity, time. He would spend hundreds of hours convincing a vendor of his guilt.

One manufacturer, when challenged by Rickover over the quality of a boiler, cited an authority, the American Society for Mechanical Engineers' Boiler and Pressure Vessel Code. The code, Rickover was told, did not require the manufacturer to deliver a product that was totally free of defects. In fact, the manufacturer, well aware of his tough customer's reputation, had alerted Rickover to a defect in the boiler. The manufacturer had examined the product voluntarily, using sophisticated ultrasonic techniques, and had discovered apparent defects in welds. Then, undoubtedly feeling virtuous, he had notified Rickover's office. The spiraling began.

The manufacturer was told the boiler was unacceptable, code or no code. The next step was to call in a code inspector, who ruled that the boiler was acceptable. But by then Rickover was personally joined, and the questions began, each one breeding others: Who is the inspector? Why is he provided by an insurance company? In what states are such practices incorporated into laws? How was the code drawn up? How are the inspectors trained? Rickover demanded that the code be amended. He also set forth recommendations for changing the administration of the code. He then turned to the insurance companies and demanded an investigation of their procedures and records. He examined report forms and decreed that they were not written the way he would like to have them written.

Ultimately, the case of the questionable boiler became at least part of the inspiration for a Rickover campaign against what he saw as irresponsible manufacturers. He began recommending closer government monitoring of code-writing committees. He began viewing most industry with suspicion. He began to question the fundamental tenets of the military-industrial complex. "No person or group can be depended on to police itself," he said in 1968. "No man can serve two masters: his own interest and the interest of the public. Men should not be placed in a position where they have to reconcile the two. It is the function of government to do so."

He was speaking heresy: patriotism could not be expected from private enterprise. Industry could not be trusted. The Federal Government must intervene in the free-enterprise system. Somewhere in that mind where cynicism and patriotism entwined, there was an anticapitalist—perhaps even a socialist. He abhorred greed, and this abhorrence frequently became the inspiration for a tirade against capitalism.

"As Ralph Nader and others, including myself, have said," he told a Congressional committee in 1971, "many large companies are effectively above the law in such areas as environment and antitrust because government officials are reluctant to challenge the politically influential industrial giants. But this is not the most serious problem. . . . The real evil that follows a commercial dishonesty so general as ours is the intellectual dishonesty it generates. . . . Today the management of a big corporation is a free-floating quantum of power, behaving however it likes, subject only to an occasional takeover bid and the generally ineffective regulation of government."

He said that if he were marooned on an uninhabited island he would not "choose as a companion a man who had devoted all his life to making money." He based this on the belief that "while industrialism can build a society which is rich, prosperous, powerful, even one which had a reasonably wide diffusion of material well-being, it cannot build one which has savour and depth, and which exercises the irresistible power of attraction to the inner needs of human beings. The sad fact about some of our industrialists is that they have never come to this realization. My objection to the Henry Fords and Andrew Carnegies of the world is not that they have been spectacularly successful in producing goods and making money, but that for them these were the principal aims of life."

The same Congressmen who would smirk at the idealism of Ralph Nader would sit and sagely nod at the paralleling philosophy being offered by their hero Hyman Rickover—"If our capitalistic system should die, perhaps the reason is because it gives too much scope for greed. In earlier days capitalism could rely on other elements in our society—especially the church—to point out that greed is not a virtue. Today, those other voices have largely fallen silent or sound confused. Unless government can reassert itself as an effective check over corporate greed, there will be no real counter to the power of corporate America."

He had a way of ending arguments with contractors who wanted him to ease up on his demands. "If you knew that your son had to serve on that submarine, would you design it my way or your way?" he would ask. Almost inevitably, he got it done his way. For Rickover, it was simply a matter of not trusting contractors' competency, consciences—or patriotism.

Once, when General Electric and Westinghouse both refused to bid on equipment for nuclear submarines, Rickover informed Congress and the Secretary of Defense. He also reminded the Secretary of Commerce that he had jurisdiction over a law that forced a company to do work that the government determined to be vital to national defense. The Department of Commerce refused to invoke the law, and Rickover said, "I am beginning to wonder whether the Department of Commerce represents industry to the U.S. Government rather than the U.S. Government to industry." He then passed this observation along to Congress, which threatened an investigation. GE capitulated and agreed to manufacture the equipment.

Another Rickover dispute involved submarine components that were manufactured by a Canadian firm. In one of his campaigns against the sharing of nuclear secrets with other nations, he declared that no foreign contractor could have anything to do with the building of nuclear submarines. Even as he spoke, a Canadian firm was selling to the Navy a top-secret component for a new class of nuclear submarines. Rickover remained inflexible, and there were fears that he would insist that the item—a high-pressure valve—not be installed in the submarines. His engineers prevailed, and he relented, but only after the intervention of the Department of State amid frantic communications between the two governments.

Rickover has been critical and suspicious of all vendors, but, as his power and his nuclear fleet grew, much of his criticism and more and more of his caustic comments concentrated on the yard where the nuclear navy had been launched—Electric Boat. Here, where Rickover and contractor, Navy and worker, all had shared in the glory of the *Nautilus*, here was where Rickover's war on American shipyards would begin.

Electric Boat was successor to the firm that had sold the Navy its first submarine in 1900, the *Holland*, and it had continued to build submarines, few in the years of peace, many in years of war, unspectacularly, until Rickover and his plans for a nuclear submarine appeared in 1950. EB at that time was headed by John Jay Hopkins, a lawyer who had started as a director in 1937 and ten years later became EB's president.

The yard itself in 1950 was under the eye of O. Pomeroy Robinson, who had started his career in 1915 in the machine shop of the New London Ship & Engine Company, an EB subsidiary, and had been general manager of EB since 1938.

In 1950, as the official account discreetly tells it in *Nuclear Navy*, "Rickover had seen an opportunity to bring new management talent to Groton." The new talent was Carleton Shugg, who had graduated from the U.S. Naval Academy as the No. 2 man of the Class of 1921. But Rickover was not bringing Shugg to Groton as a Navy man. He was a Rickover man, a supporter in the AEC bureaucracy, an administrator with Navy shipbuilding experience. When Shugg just missed being appointed general manager of the AEC, Rickover got him a key job at EB. Hopkins put Shugg in charge of construction.

Robinson was doomed. Rickover, getting ammunition from his representatives' reports, built a case against Robinson, and in November 1952 Hopkins abolished the post of general manager. Hopkins, meanwhile, was assembling what would become a major aerospace and defense conglomerate, General Dynamics Corporation. He made EB a division of General Dynamics, appointed Shugg division manager in charge of shipbuilding and moved Robinson into the corporate structure of General Dynamics as a senior vice president. Hopkins had done the reorganizing, but Rickover had cracked the whip that had forced the reorganization.

Rickover virtually ruled EB. When he needed men to build the prototype of the *Nautilus* reactor plant in the wasteland of Idaho, he got three hundred EB craftsmen, who moved from Connecticut to Idaho with their families. "I don't want you to leave the job behind when you knock off at the end of the day ," Rickover said in a speech to the transplanted workers. "I want you to spend your spare time figuring out ways of improving the work."

And they did. "I never saw men work like that before," Charles Farrell, EB personnel manager, said later, "and I don't know if I ever will again. We developed a technique of working relationships that was, in some ways, more revolutionary than the sub itself. The men threw away their clocks and worked up to fourteen hours a day, including weekends, when needed."

Some welds took three days to complete, and some welders had to be heroes. Commander Edwin E. Kinter, who became project officer of the prototype reactor after the death of Raymond H. Dick in January 1953, remembered two EB workers who volunteered to weld a virtually inaccessible valve. "They wore goggles to shield their eyes," he recalled, "but nothing to protect their faces from the molten, sputtering stainless steel, because welding masks had previously interfered with the required delicacy of the operation. They made the weld successfully, but they suffered such severe burns that they were hospitalized for a week."

One of the Idaho workers remembered bumping into Rickover while rushing into the prototype building. "I just about knocked him over, and then I saw who he was. He didn't wear a uniform. He was wearing that iron-gray suit he would wear for fifteen or twenty years. I was flustered and apologized, but he said, 'You have more right to be here than I do.' "

The EB worker was assigned back to Groton to help build the *Nautilus*. He eventually became a foreman and then a supervisor. "On that first sub," he said, "we were on a common level. When the *Nautilus* went to sea for the first time, Rickover was a happy man. He had a sense of humor. But he changed.

"We heard the stories about all the things he demanded when he went on sea trials—the khakis they laid out for him, the basket of white grapes, the free haircut by the steward. And we heard he was getting a tremendous temper.

"For him, to save his time, he had the sea trials on Sunday. Workers and their families used to go down to the docks and watch him come and board the submarine they built.

"I remember being down there at four A.M. It was for the trials of the *Ethan Allen* [built in 1959–1960]. He came along with the general manager, and I heard him turn to the general manager and say, 'Who are these people?' The manager said they were the workers. Rickover said nobody was supposed to be on the dock. He didn't want anybody there. After that, I never went back to see him."

By 1961, EB had launched seventeen nuclear submarines and had been the lead yard of every submarine type except the *Thresher* class. Some 10,000 people worked for EB, which was the second-largest employer in Connecticut. The excitement of building nuclear submarines had evolved into a routine for what had become only one of the divisions of General Dynamics. But Rickover had not changed since those hectic *Nautilus* days when he hauled executives out of their beds with predawn phone calls or ordered his representatives to crawl about the submarines on the ways, looking for trouble.

His rule remained absolute, to the growing resentment of EB executives and the frequent embarrassment of the Navy. In April 1974, for instance, an internationally known analyst from a private firm was visiting the Navy's Submarine School at New London to give a classified lecture to the officer class. He also addressed most of the base's enlisted men and women at a luncheon, where, significantly, beer was available.

The analyst's luncheon speech—on Soviet use of the sea—was followed by a lengthy question-and-answer period. Afterward personnel from the nuclear submarine *Glenard P. Lipscomb,* which was being completed by the nearby EB yard, got involved in a conversation with the analyst and invited him to visit the submarine. Several senior submarine officers heard this exchange, and one of them offered to certify the analyst's security clearance and provide transportation to the yard. That evening the analyst attended a reception at the home of one of the submarine officers and then had a quiet dinner with his firm's president, a retired Navy captain, in a small New London restaurant.

The next morning a Navy car arrived at the analyst's motel to take him to the shipyard. At almost the same moment he was called to the phone and asked to first visit an office at the base. There he was advised that he would not visit a submarine in the yard, but, if he desired, a visit to a nuclear submarine at the base could be arranged. The *Lipscomb* visit was canceled "because it would cause difficulties at the shipyard." Rickover's name was never mentioned. The analyst visited a submarine at the base and then returned to Washington.

As soon as he arrived, he was called by the Director of Naval Intelligence, Rear Admiral E. F. Rectanus. The analyst was advised Rickover had called Rectanus that morning, declaring that the analyst had "seduced a sailor in a bar" to get aboard a nuclear submarine in the yard and that Rickover wanted his security clearance taken away immediately. Moments later, Rickover called Admiral Zumwalt, Chief of Naval Operations, with the same demand.

Rickover apparently did not know that the analyst was working on two projects for Rectanus, one of them at the specific request of Zumwalt. In response to Rickover's accusation and demands, Rectanus was forced to conduct an investigation, even though the analyst had a top-secret clearance and was personally known by the CNO and Rectanus.

Still, he was an analyst—and analysts were high on Rickover's hate list. And he had been invited to visit the yard, which was a Rickover fiefdom. No one could tread that ground or approach its treasures without Rickover's personal and specific permission.

There was an investigation by Naval Intelligence. The report of that investigation was forwarded to Zumwalt, with the following, highly informal covering note. The analyst's name has been deleted here.

> From: Director of Naval Intelligence [and]
> Commander, Naval Intelligence Command
>
> Subject: (...)
>
> 1. Attached refers to the possibility of (...) "leaking" classified information. ...
>
> 2. I believe that significant damage may have been done to the unique and very beneficial relationship which has existed between (...) and the Navy to date.
>
> 3. With your concurrence, I intend to send the attached to ADM Rickover, even though it probably will not satisfy him.

Zumwalt's response was a single word, scrawled over the memo: *Agreed.* The analyst, cited by several CNOs and Secretaries of the Navy for his contributions to the Navy, retained his clearance.

A similar attempt by Rickover to rule EB as his fiefdom came in 1978 when union officials—members of the safety committee of the Metal Trades Council—filed a complaint about hazards in the area of the yard where a Trident submarine was being built. The regional office of the Occupational Safety and Health Administration held up the complaints because of previous difficulties that OSHA inspectors had encountered in getting clearance to enter EB's nuclear yards.

As is customary with Rickover, the dispute soon escalated to the highest level: Ray Marshall, Secretary of Labor, whose department oversees OSHA, met with Rickover. Marshall got only a memo telling him that Rickover would continue doing what he was doing. Rickover was said to have uttered as a prelude to the meeting: "I am the greatest engineer in the world."

And that has been the motto of the fiefdom. He rules. He decides. Others come and go. Years pass. Decades pass. He is there. He has never learned to trust the "other" Navy, the rest of the government, or the workers or management of EB.

An official at EB told *Fortune* magazine in 1976 that Rickover "runs this yard through sheer terror." His influence runs from the supreme to the sublime. He has had David Leighton, his principal lieutenant, participate in the contract negotiations with EB. Leighton, an employee of the AEC and not the Navy, astutely represented Rickover and made certain that NRB's views were incorporated in all contracts between the Navy and Electric Boat. At a lower level of importance, but highly indicative of his attitude, Rickover once demanded that EB executives stop giving away toy-store plastic models of Polaris submarines. "He screamed when he saw them," a BuShips employee recalled. "They were showing too much, they were violating security." EB stopped distributing them. But a short time later Rickover began asking EB for models to give away to his guests.

Rickover's deteriorating relations with EB were only part of the picture. The saga that began with a band of brothers building the *Nautilus* would become a chronicle of war between Rickover and the shipbuilding industry of America. In that war Rickover would make charges of fraud and incompetence, and the shipbuilders would make huge financial claims against the government. Shipyards would refuse to build ships for him. A federal judge would order a reluctant builder to go back to work on a nuclear ship that the yard had abandoned in a dispute with Rickover. Ultimately, shipbuilders' claims against the Navy—mostly the nuclear navy—would climb to more than $22.3 *billion.* Responsible industry executives and federal officials would accuse Rickover of jeopardizing the future of shipbuilding in the United States.

In the beginning, it was only changes. Admiral James, Chief of the Bureau of Ships from April 1959 to April 1963, recalled how Rickover's changes—"Meddling is a very tame word for what he did"—affected a submarine's total design. Although ship design was then the responsibility of Rear Admiral James M. Farrin, Jr., Rickover ignored him. "Rick," said James, "could go to suppliers [of reactor components] and get them to do design aspects of the submarine and assign contract responsibility to Electric Boat. He would award this under his funds for the propulsion system." Rickover could claim that his changes were only in the system he was responsible for. But the engine area encompasses about half the space of an attack submarine. So his changes would affect the distribution of weight and the overall weight of the submarine. The changes would also affect decisions on where to put other, nonpropulsion equipment.

Most important of all, the changes Rickover ordered would often have a drastic effect on the most critical consideration in ship design. This is an aspect of stability called metacentric height. The metacenter is the point of intersection between a vertical line passing through a ship's center of gravity and a vertical line through the center of buoyancy when the ship is slightly out of equilibrium. If the height of the metacenter above the center of gravity is thrown off by poor design, the ship may develop a permanent list or may even capsize.

Such highly technical matters, involving the heart of a submarine's design, frequently took second place to Rickover's ideas.

A ship is built, not assembled. The more complex the ship, the more organic the process of building it. The initial design cannot be complete; shipbuilders design as they go along, especially on a lead ship, the first of its class. Succeeding ships will be similarly subject to change. They will need individual adjustments, usually the result of practical matters learned in the sea trials, the operational experience of the lead ship, and changes in equipment. The gestation period of a warship—from idea to completion—may be as long as ten years. The "platform characteristics" for a ship—hull form, propulsion, speed, range—may be designed and constructed with relative ease. Its combat system—weapons, communications, computers—evolve so rapidly that whatever is envisioned at the design stages of the ship may not be what becomes part of the completed ship many years later.

Edward S. Ruete, a submarine-warfare analyst, once estimated what happens when a 200-pound sonar unit is added to a submarine. The new equipment needs more electrical power, more cooling water, a mast whose raising and lowering adds to the hydraulic system. There is also need for another man—plus "a bunk and a locker for him, a place for him to eat his meals, larger freezers to hold his food for 90 days, requiring a larger refrigeration plant, requiring . . ."

Besides the immense technological problem of envisioning what a proposed ship will be like, there is the political and economic problem of predicting what the ship will cost. About ninety-five percent of all modern naval shipbuilding has been paid for by negotiated purchase, not by sealed bid. The result is high costs, disputes over contracts—and, especially when Rickover enters the picture, accusations of profiteering and bad faith on the part of the vendors.

Rickover in 1978 came up with an example of how EB developed a minor claim. The example—it involves one hole, 1½ inches in diameter, 1¼ inches deep—provides an insight into the complexities of negotiating changes in blueprints. The Navy asked that the hole be drilled in a steel shield box on Trident submarines. No work had yet started on that portion of the submarine, and the total price had been worked out, on a man-hours-per-pound basis. (An estimated 88,500 man-hours, based on the rate of 0.096 man-hours per pound times 921,792 pounds estimated weight.) The Navy had asked that one hole be drilled in this mass. And for that hole, according to Rickover, EB had put in a claim for $7,000. "Obviously," Rickover wrote the Secretary of the Navy, "the company's bid price for the ship would not have been any different whether or not Electric Boat had prepared the original detailed drawings correctly to show the 1½ inch hole."

Such claims against the Navy, long a part of shipbuilding, have skyrocketed in recent years—and so has Rickover's antagonism toward shipbuilders.

It was an antagonism born of frustration, for nothing seemed to enrage Rickover more than the discovery of something that he could not control or, perceiving a need to change, could not change. In his professional life, he came upon two such phenomena: law and capitalism. These two irritants combined with great complexity in the building of a ship and in the paying for a ship. Rickover would plunge into the process with the zeal of a crusader. There was also a man Rickover would encounter within the Navy, a man whose intelligence and experience would influence many decision-makers as much as or more than Rickover's. This man was Gordon W. Rule.

Their first skirmish on record came in 1963, when Rule was the newly named director of the procurement control and clearance division in the headquarters of the Naval Material Command. His job, as he described it, was to determine whether "the business aspects of proposed Navy contracts were prudent and in accordance with applicable policies, laws, and regulations." In his first year on the job he asked Rickover to change the way he wrote contracts for the components of nuclear propulsion systems. Rickover refused, and Rule persisted. Their struggle went on, deep in the Navy bureaucracy.

One time Rule disapproved a $50 million Rickover contract on what Rickover saw as grounds that the profit to the contractor would be too low. After a flurry of correspondence, Rickover finally agreed to increase the contractor's profit. On the original contract, according to Rickover's figures, the profit would have been $1,147,023.00. He changed it—to $1,147,023.05.

In 1967 Rule spoke out publicly in a campaign to stop Rickover from bypassing the chain of command and "dictating types of contracts." In the speech, Rule recommended that official Navy boards of inquiry be convened to "investigate and determine responsibility for important programs that double in cost because of inadequate test programs, premature commitment to production, design changes, etc."

Rickover heard about the speech, discovered what he called "errors," and managed to get Rule rebuked by a rear admiral in charge of procurement. A few months later Rule was awarded the Navy Superior

Civilian Service Award. He seemed at times to be as durable as Rickover.

The Rickover-Rule was a strange feud. Both of them, in loyalty to the Navy and to taxpayers, were advocates of contract control and foes of waste in defense spending. But Rickover, the skeptic of capitalism, viewed profits as occasions of sin, and Rule, the working negotiator, viewed profits as an essential ingredient of contracts. Rickover disliked negotiation; Rule relished it. Rickover distrusted shipbuilders; Rule wanted to keep the shipbuilding industry viable.

Rickover had launched the nuclear navy at a time when there were seven yards, both Navy-operated and civilian-operated, where nuclear ships could be built. In 1967 the Navy ordered its last new ship from a naval shipyard. Meanwhile, the private yards were becoming divisions of conglomerates. Just as EB had become only a part of General Dynamics, Ingalls Shipbuilding Corporation became part of Litton Industries in 1961, and Newport News Shipbuilding and Dry Dock Company was acquired by the Tenneco conglomerate in 1968.

What had drawn the conglomerates to shipyards was a torrential cash flow. The Navy had a policy of making "progress payments" during the construction of a ship. Until 1970 these payments were made weekly. Since the shipbuilders usually paid their bills once a month, they had vast sums of money at their disposal for weeks at a time. Litton saw another advantage: submarines and other ships built by Ingalls would be, in the words of a Navy procurement specialist, "containers for the weapons systems which were being developed and marketed by its other divisions." Tenneco bought in because the conglomerate decided it would build its own liquefied-natural-gas tankers to carry gas that Tenneco would be buying from the Soviet Union. The company also foresaw a need for oil tankers because of Alaska's north-slope oil boom.

For Rickover, the appearance of the conglomerates meant that he could no longer call up a yard president or manager and bark orders. He might not even be able to find out who was in charge. Once he did manage to find the president of Litton, and told him of a claim that Litton had made against the Navy. "I suggested that he get a brand-new start," Rickover said, "and look over the history of this claim and do the proper, honest thing. Do you know what he did? He came right back and resubmitted the claim for just about the same amount."

But unlike the president of Litton, Rule was part of the Navy, and Rickover could move directly against him. That is what happened after Rule sent a memo to Admiral I. J. Galantin, Chief of Naval Material, in June 1969. As former director of the Polaris project, Galantin knew about managing major Navy efforts. Rule said that a "potentially dangerous contracting situation" was developing in existing and planned contracts with Newport News Shipbuilding.

Rickover responded to Rule's memo by writing a blistering one of his own to Galantin, theoretically Rule's boss as well as Rickover's. Actually, Rickover acted in total independence, if not contempt of Galantin. This became evident during the 1969 Christmas holiday season, when Rickover treated a message in Galantin's name as a joke. Galantin's deputy had sent a long, bureaucratic message throughout the command asking for suggestions on how to word a New Year's message. Rickover replied (with copies to at least twenty people in the command) that "Happy New Year" should be sufficient—and if Galantin wanted more perhaps he could add "inspirational thoughts," including a decree "that there be no more rust or cost overruns (cost growth)."

In his serious memo to Galantin, Rickover asked that Rule be kept from reviewing any contract involving nuclear propulsion—meaning anything under Rickover's direct control. Listing his disputes with Rule, Rickover mentioned one that had just come up: Rule's opposition to a contract with Newport News for two nuclear-powered frigates, the DLGN-36 and -37.

The building of these ships would produce the bitterest contract battle in the annals of American shipbuilding.

The cost of the guided-missile frigates had been embroiled in controversy since Congress authorized the ships in 1968. The dispute involved traditional antagonists: Rickover and his Congressional supporters versus the Department of Defense and its budget makers. But what made this dispute different—and what produced the crisis that Rule had foreseen in 1969—was the evolution of the fight from one between traditional foes to a war between Rickover and the Newport News shipyard, a war that would be fought not in the Congress nor in the Pentagon but ultimately in a federal courthouse.

Rickover wanted five frigates. The Department of Defense authorized the Navy to order only three. The individual ship price for five ships would have been less than the individual price for three ships because, as more ships are built, the costs diminish; theoretically, the cost of building the last ship is substantially less than the cost of building the first. So there would be a large difference between the per-ship cost in a three-ship contract and the per-ship cost in a five-ship contract.

Rickover's longtime associate David T. Leighton negotiated with

Newport News on a five-ship basis, but won from the shipyard a fixed-price contract for three ships with an option for two more at the five-ship price. He had, in effect, gotten Newport News to agree on a five-ship price even though the shipyard would probably build only three.

It was a tough bit of bargaining by a tough bargainer. "Leighton runs the negotiations," Rule told the authors, "while the designated Navy contract officer sits there doing nothing. Leighton's a very able man. He's worse than Rickover. He's diabolical." But the frigate contract, Rule publicly stated, was "patently unfair" and "a blatant example of failure to recognize the basic element of a good-faith negotiation, namely fairness. . . ."

Newport News delivered the first of the DLGNs, the *California,* in February 1974, a year and a half later than the original contract had specified. The second, the *South Carolina,* was completed in January 1975, twenty months late. Relations between Newport News and Rickover's nuclear navy plunged to new depths. Rickover fumed over the delays, and his representatives, more inquisitive than ever, prowled through the yard looking for problems. Word about Rickover's "spies" rapidly circulated up the ladder through the foremen to managers to executives and, ultimately, to Nelson W. Freeman, chairman of the board of Tenneco, the Houston-based parent company of Newport News.

Freeman looked into the situation and issued an order: "If he shows up, throw Admiral Rickover's ass out of the yard." But it was never Rickover who showed up; it was his corps of representatives. Seeing that nothing had changed, Freeman got in touch with his lawyer, Thomas G. (Tommy the Cork) Corcoran, boy wonder of Franklin D. Roosevelt's New Deal and, ever since, a highly influential Washington lawyer. Corcoran, only a year younger than Rickover, had been the target of Rickover's wrath for decades. Legend traces their earliest clash to World War II, when Rickover was running the BuShips electrical section and Corcoran was a wheeling-dealing Washington lawyer for defense industries.

In October 1973, Freeman, accompanied by Corcoran, took his complaints about Rickover directly to Admiral Zumwalt, the Chief of Naval Operations, and Deputy Secretary of Defense William P. Clements, Jr. Rear Admiral Kenneth Carr, a nuclear-trained officer who was Clements' executive assistant, was also present for the meeting.

In the conversation, as preserved in a Zumwalt memo, Zumwalt said that "in my view we were dealing with a problem in which, as a result of Admiral Rickover's management system, we were about to kill the goose that laid the golden egg"—a reference to threats by Freeman that unless

Rickover were leashed by the Navy, the shipyard might have to stop building ships for the Navy. Newport News was "golden" in that it is the largest and most flexible shipyard in the West.

At this point, according to the memo, Carr "stated that Admiral Rickover was only responsible for the nuclear part of [shipbuilding]," a statement that reflected the true-believer faith of a nuc. Freeman then "said that anybody that thinks that doesn't know how the system works."

"I gave my view," Zumwalt wrote, "that Rickover does get beyond nuclear power and does really run the entire shipyard involved in constructing a nuclear plant and indeed the Ship Systems Command with regard to nuclear ships."

Freeman also told Zumwalt and the others that when Newport News made a bid for a design of a nonnuclear ship, Rickover "blackmailed" the shipyard—presumably by threatening to pull nuclear work out of it—and the contract went to another firm. "Mr. Clements appeared puzzled at this," Zumwalt wrote. "I pointed out to him that Admiral Rickover's policy is to work against any non-nuclear-propelled large (war)ship. Mr. Freeman confirmed that Admiral Rickover was vehemently against non-nuclear-propelled ships."

Zumwalt's memo ends with this: "Mr. Corcoran made the point that there is nothing as dangerous as an old man with a dream, that Admiral Rickover is trying very hard to accomplish his vision for a nuclear-propelled Navy before he dies; but that he, Tommy Corcoran, sees much evidence on the Hill of great concern about the corners that Admiral Rickover is now cutting."

Rickover would try to make Corcoran pay for that statement to Zumwalt.

Troubles were also mounting at Litton Industries' Ingalls Shipyard, where shipbuilding was on a collision course with politics. Ironically, Rickover, Rule and Zumwalt would find themselves at times shoulder-to-shoulder in the long-running dispute between the Navy and Litton.

Ingalls had been building nuclear submarines since the late 1950s, but as an industry, Litton was new to shipbuilding. After the conglomerate took over the Mississippi company, it proposed establishing a new "automated" yard there. A state bond issue helped finance the new yard, and from the beginning politics was in the air. There was not only the matter of the yard being in the state of John Stennis, powerful chairman of the Senate Armed Services Committee. There was also the matter of Roy L. Ash, president of Litton. One of the founding officers of the California-based conglomerate, he was a friend and a financial backer of President Nixon.

Ash resigned as president of Litton in 1972 to become director of the Office of Management and Budget. When Ash was named, Rule openly criticized the appointment and raised the issue of conflict of interest. Rule was fired two days later as director of procurement control by his boss, Admiral Isaac C. Kidd, Jr., Chief of Naval Material. Rule's warning had been inspired, at least in part, by a confidential memo that Rickover had written to Kidd.

Rule mentioned the memo in testimony before a subcommittee of the Joint Economic Committee, chaired by Senator William Proxmire, and ultimately the memo was leaked. In it Rickover accused Litton of "misrepresentation, if not fraud" in a "grossly over-inflated" claim for $37 million in overruns on submarine construction. Rickover wrote, "Many elements in the claim appear contrived and are irreconcilable with facts contained in the company's own files." He said only $4 million to $7 million in extra payments "can be justified."

Zumwalt was also displeased with Litton because the shipyard was continually behind schedule in the building of nonnuclear ships. "Though Congress, particularly Proxmire again, did plenty of chewing on this situation." Zumwalt wrote, "most of the action was in backrooms where Ash and Litton's chairman of the board, Tex Thornton, exerted whatever pressure they could for even more time and money. The atmosphere of irregularity that surrounded the program thickened when Ash was made Director of the Office of Manpower and the Budget."

Rickover's use of the word "fraud" intensified the Navy-shipyards conflict. So did reports that he had intervened to block still another yard from building civilian ships. He was blamed for a Defense Department decision to deny a "defense priority" that the Todd Shipyards Corporation needed to build 400,000-ton ultralarge oil tankers at a yard the corporation was planning in Galveston, Texas. Shipbuilding officials said that Rickover did not want Todd to trigger a supertanker boom because other yards—such as Newport News—might stampede to that civilian market and avoid Navy contracts.

By 1976, more than $1.7 *billion* in shipbuilding claims had been filed against the Navy. (By comparison, the Navy's request for shipbuilding funds in fiscal year 1976 was $2.3 billion.) One of the largest—$894,305,-520—had been submitted by Newport News, which presented the claim in sixty-four volumes. The company said that it had taken one hundred and ten man-years to prepare the claim, and for this alone the shipyard wanted $2.7 million. The lawyers who labored on this included people who had once served as claims reviewers for the Navy. This so incensed Rickover that he complained to the American Bar Association (which he called the American Bar *Protective* Association) about "the matter of lawyers switching sides." His attitude toward lawyers—especially toward Corcoran—would tick like a time bomb through the claims proceedings.

Newport News's claims involved nuclear-powered cruisers, submarines, and aircraft carriers. But of the sixteen nuclear ships being built at the yard, both the company and the Navy began to focus their dispute on a single ship, the DLGN-41, now classified as a cruiser (CGN-41). This was one of the "option" ships—whose target price, criticized by Rule, had been negotiated by the hard-bargaining Leighton years before. Claiming that the Navy's unilateral invoking of the old option price was not fair and not contractually binding, Newport News stopped work on CGN-41 in August 1975. The Navy went to court, and a federal judge ordered Newport News to resume work.

The nuclear cruiser became a symbol of the Rickover-shipyard war—whose result, according to John P. Diesel, president of Newport News, could well be "the flight of shipbuilders, subcontractors, and suppliers from the business." In February 1976, Diesel took a step toward fulfilling his prophecy by notifying the Navy that his shipyard would stop working on the *Carl Vinson*, one of two nuclear carriers that Newport News was building, unless the Navy took a realistic view of the steadily mounting claims.

Rickover, apparently countering Diesel's threat, wrote a memo (which was leaked in three days) that called for the government takeover of shipyards "as a condition" for settlement of the claims. Rule, who long before had been reinstated in his job as Navy overseer of contracts, said the suggestion "confirms the complaints of Electric Boat and Newport News that Admiral Rickover is trying to run their plants." Rickover has also suggested a fifty-year contract under which the government could acquire a yard by lease if it judges that the contractor's performance is unsatisfactory "so that never again could warships be held hostage by that shipyard in a contract dispute."

Proxmire meanwhile set up hearings on the issue. His star witness would be Rickover. It was a time when Rickover supporters in the nuclear navy and in Congress were claiming that a concerted attack had been launched against their admiral by the Navy and the shipbuilders. As if in confirmation, the Shipbuilders Council of America, a strong lobbying group, was convening in Washington on the eve of Proxmire's hearings. And the Council's star was Gordon Rule. He did not disappoint his hosts.

> Admiral Rickover [Rule told the shipbuilders] has been carrying on undeclared war with the rest of the Navy and our nuclear shipbuilding contractors for many years. He and his office are primarily responsible for the breakdown in normal business relations with the nuclear shipbuilders. He has declared open war on our only nuclear surface shipbuilder [Newport News] and his irrational stream of correspondence indicates clearly that the Navy's relations with that shipbuilder are not just impaired. He has destroyed them.
>
> I suggest that Admiral Rickover wants the Navy's relations with this shipbuilder so completely destroyed that he can find an excuse to continue his retaliatory advocacy of Government takeover. . . . His attitude and philosophy toward private industry and his methods of operation are arrogant, autocratic, and totally foreign to our American concepts of simple decency and fairness. . . .
>
> Admiral Rickover, by his own actions, has made his continued presence in the Navy incompatible with sound management and necessary military discipline. He has made himself a liability to the Navy and tragically has begun to destroy the very capability he helped to create. . . . At the very least, he should be relieved of any and all influence or control over the contractual and business relations with our country's nuclear shipbuilders.

Rickover's answer, though he did not describe it as such, came five days later, when he testified before Proxmire. Speaking of what had happened to shipyards that had been taken over by major corporations, Rickover said, "The conglomerates wouldn't care if they were building ships or manufacturing horse turds. Their man goal is to make money, no matter how."*

As for suggestions that he stay out of contract negotiations: "They say that if any criticism is needed, it should be left to those whose job this is. But some of these people have ceased to be capable of self-criticism. Although these officials have great power to protect the taxpayers, they sometimes appear impotent when called upon to do so. It is as if Prometheus had become manager of only a match factory. . . . The recording Angel may occasionally shed a tear for a sinner, but I doubt he will do so for these officials."

Another witness was Deputy Secretary of Defense Clements, who,

* Rickover used the "horse turd" term again in 1981 when, in Congressional testimony, he attacked General Dynamics and Newport News.

two and a half years before, had been educated in the CNO's office about Rickover's campaign against shipyards. Clements had gotten another lesson in Rickover battle tactics only a month before he appeared at the Proxmire hearing. In May, while Clements was testifying before the House Armed Services Committee about his plan to settle much of the dispute, a letter from Rickover—opposing the plan—was already in the hands of at least one member of the committee.

Clements had planned to invoke Public Law 85–802, which authorized the President or someone named by him to "enter into contracts or into amendments or modifications of contracts . . . and to make advance payments . . . without regard to other provisions of law . . . whenever such action would facilitate the national defense." Clements argued that the shipyard crisis constituted "a serious threat to the national defense." He proposed a settlement of $500 to $700 million on claims which by then totaled $1.8 billion. Rickover's opposition to the plan and Proxmire's resistance to it were on record as Clements testified. He said that Rickover's attitude toward shipbuilders was "the very, very gut issue of what is happening," and remarked that Rickover's "horse turd" remark vividly showed his attitude.

(Rickover, in subsequent testimony, switched to another metaphor. "I note in the newspapers," he told Proxmire, "that you have been mixed up in garbage in New York City, and I think this will give you a further education in garbage—the garbage with which the U.S. Government must deal. I consider much of the claims problems to be garbage. . . .")

By July, Clements was desperate. Newport News was going into U.S. District Court asking to be relieved of the court-ordered continuance of work on CGN-41. Litton and Newport News had withdrawn earlier offers of settlement, Newport News president Diesel citing "the dogged interference by Admiral Rickover and his staff." Diesel suggested that work get started on the mammoth job of transferring the half-built *Carl Vinson* and the submarines, in various stages of construction, from Newport News to Navy shipyards on the West Coast.

Clements, who had never met Rule, called him on the morning of July 13 and told him that a Navy car would pick him up for a meeting in Clements's office that afternoon. When Rule entered the car he met for the first time the new Deputy Chief of Naval Material, Vice Admiral Vincent A. Lascara. A supply and budget specialist who had joined Rickover's staff in 1953, Lascara was the only veteran of long service in NRR to make flag rank. He also had been supply officer on the *Enterprise*, the pride of Rickover's nuclear navy.

Clements assembled twelve officers and civilians to discuss the Newport News crisis, especially the problems of the CGN-41. The other men at the meeting included Admiral Frederick H. Michaelis, Chief of Naval Material and second commanding officer of the *Enterprise*; Rear Admiral Kenneth Carr, the nuclear-trained officer who had been at the meeting in Zumwalt's office in 1973; Assistant Secretary of the Navy for installations and logistics Jack L. Bowers; and Rear Admiral Francis Manganaro, the Rickover-trained Deputy Commander of NavSea and chairman of the newly established Navy Claims Settlement Board. (It would eventually settle $141 million in Newport News claims on CGN-36s and -37s for $44.4 million. The board would be abruptly dissolved as it prepared to settle $544 million in Electric Boat claims.)

Clements bitterly recounted his three years of work to settle the mountain of claims against the Navy. Then, according to Rule's recollection of the meeting, Bowers and Michaelis began to recite what they were doing about the claims. They had not accomplished much. Glaring at them, Clements said, "That's the same happy horseshit you have been giving me for months, and I'm not going to listen to it any more."

When he had cooled down, he pointed to Rule and said, "I want you to listen to Gordon Rule here. He probably knows more about what we are talking about than any man in this room—and maybe more than all of us put together. And I want you to listen to him."

Clements gave Rule the job of settling the CGN-41 claim. But, Rule later said, "Never did I receive one bit of support from my Navy superiors [Michaelis and Lascara] or the office of general counsel of the Navy. On the contrary, the Rickover navy and their ever obedient lawyers roadblocked my every effort."

Rule brought together three other negotiators he trusted and began work. He met with Lascara daily and, according to Rule, Lascara then met with Clements. "I knew that the admiral was keeping the Rickover mafia fully advised of what I was doing," Rule recounted, "and I could feed him only what I thought necessary. I had a friend who sat with Mr. Clements every day in his Lascara meetings, and I would get feedback on whether Lascara told Mr. Clements what I had reported. It varied considerably."

On August 19 Rule requested and received a contracting officer's warrant that authorized him to settle the claims on behalf of the government. The next day he and Newport News reached an agreement. Ten days later Michaelis set up a special group, headed by Lascara, ostensibly to review the proposed settlement. "The ill-concealed control of this group by Admiral Rickover left me no alternative," Rule said. On October 7, using his warrant, he executed the agreement and delivered it to the shipyard: Newport News immediately went into U.S. District Court to have the agreement made into a court order that would presumably end the litigation between the shipyard and the Navy.

But the Navy—or what looked like the nuclear navy—had just begun to fight. Michaelis said he had "withdrawn" Rule's warrant, even though Rule was theoretically working for Clements, who had approved the settlement. Michaelis, according to a court affidavit, also called Charles E. Dart, executive vice president of the shipyard, and told him that the settlement document was "invalid" and should be returned to the Navy at once.

Clements wrote to Attorney General Edward Levi, asking that the Justice Department accept the settlement. Proxmire, taking his cue from Rickover's position on negotiations, wrote Levi to criticize Clements and Rule. Levi, ignoring the plea from Clements, sent the Justice Department into court to try to void the agreement. Judge John Mackenzie heard the arguments and issued his opinion on March 8, 1977:

> The United States utterly failed, until the appointment of Gordon Rule, to so negotiate in good faith. . . . We find the United States is fully bound to the compromise agreement negotiated on August 30, 1976 between Gordon Rule, for the Government, and the Shipyard. . . .
>
> The Justice Department attempts now to discredit the settlement worked out by Rule. It suggests that Rule did not act with the best interests of the United States in mind. We find nothing in the record to support this view. In fact, Rule was appointed by Clements because of his reputation in negotiating settlements with contractors. That segment of the Navy command which was upset at Rule's appointment, but was then unable to prevent it, now attempts to discredit his completed settlement. . . .

The Navy appealed, and the Fourth Circuit Court of Appeals in Richmond, Virginia, in February 1978 sent the case back to the District Court, saying that a trial should be held. Because the case would be long in settlement, the District Court held a hearing the following month and ordered work on the ship to continue, with the shipyard to be paid costs plus a seven percent profit until the trial. The Navy appealed this order—along with another court order to pay a specific $19-million bill that the shipyard presented on the basis of the seven percent order. The appeals are expected to continue for years.

About the time the Navy was appealing Rule's settlement of some $30 million, the Navy was preparing to settle a $544-million claim from Electric Boat for $484 million (although auditors had put the total Navy liability at $125 million) and a $647-million claim from Litton Industries at $447 million. For settlements of nearly $1 billion, the Navy had not chosen to go into court.

By 1978, Clements was no longer Deputy Secretary of Defense, and Rule was retired. But Rickover battled on, presenting to Congress what a spokesman for Electric Boat called in 1981 "Admiral Rickover's annual presentation of arbitrary, biased and inaccurate charges against the American shipbuilding industry in general and Electric Boat in particular." Rickover's 1981 tirade against Electric Boat came shortly after Secretary of the Navy John H. Lehman had accepted a report that said problems between the Navy and EB were being resolved.

Rickover's war against shipyards amounted to vague charges of fraud against all three civilian shipyards still capable of building nuclear ships.* The charges lost their vagueness in October 1978, when, at the request of the Justice Department, a federal grand jury began questioning some twenty officials of the Newport News shipyard. After long deliberation, the grand jury ended the investigation without returning any indictments. Later, a second grand jury was impaneled, with similar results. Then, in 1981, reportedly at the urging of Rickover, a third federal investigation was begun.

The war between Rickover and the shipyards seemed destined to go on forever—as did his crusade for what he saw as justice, a crusade that inevitably involved clashes with his other enemies: lawyers.

A lawyer who handled one small "Rickover case" told the authors of the frustrations in dealing with the nuclear navy. "My client had gotten a contract to produce dosimeters—individual radioactivity detectors—for use by crewmen aboard nuclear submarines. One of the requirements was that the dosimeter survive a six-foot drop to a steel deck. None of them could survive that test, even when the requirement was changed to a wooden floor. It was simply an economic and practical impossibility. Given the design Rickover demanded, the product could not be pro-

* The Navy took delivery of the last ship to be constructed in a naval shipyard in 1972. Subsequently, only the Ingalls, Newport News, and Electric Boat yards continued to build nuclear ships. The last from Ingalls was delivered in 1974.

duced. We tried to get out of the contract. But nobody wanted to go to Rickover and tell him that the device he wanted would not work. And so we had to go to court. But it all could have been handled without court action . . . if it weren't for the factor of Rickover's suspicions of contractors—and, I guess, their lawyers."

Rickover's hatred for lawyers, by his own account, borders on the irrational. He has called lawyers who prosecute claims for contractors "the ambulance chasers of the Washington bar." He has put his own bizarre observations about lawyers in the very depositions which lawyers were taking for him in the marathon CGN-41 cases. At one point, as Rickover told it, he was being subjected to what amounted to a total of forty hours of questioning by as many as eight lawyers at a time. Then, "when I came back to the deposition sessions after Christmas, I said to these lawyers, 'I suppose some of you were at church celebrating the Nativity of the Lord Jesus Christ and I am sure you heard in one form or another that all men should follow in His footsteps.' " He said this did not get any response from them, for they "kept right on with the harassment, with their attempts at entrapment." Then he told them, "What bothers me most about this is not your harassment, but we have intelligent people here with good minds who have been trained by society, and now you are really acting against society. To me this is a form of intellectual masturbation." He said that even that drew no reaction. Then he told them, "You can fool people on Earth, but if you do believe in God, do you think you are fooling the Lord Jesus Christ? . . .

"I have to go to these sessions and I have to be as respectful as I can to what I consider ghouls."

His preaching led him down three paths. He tried to get legislation that would have permitted the government (namely, Rickover) to hire outside lawyers to fight claims. The second path was a speech to a roomful of lawyers—a sermon, really. A lawyer present said it was the most incredible speech he had ever heard a public man make. And finally, he took the third path as an avenger who would bring down one of the ghoulish foes of righteousness, Tommy Corcoran.

Athwart the path to the outside-lawyer law stood Navy General Counsel E. Grey Lewis, one of the men who had been in the room when Rule was charged by Clements with the job of settling the CGN-41 claim. In a letter to the chief counsel of the Senate Armed Services Committee, Lewis wrote, "I believe what is really involved is the desire of Admiral Rickover to obtain his own law firm which he can then use against Newport News or any other corporation or person he chooses, or even against the legal positions taken by my Office or the General Counsel for the Department of Defense. . . . Admirals have come to me privately and told me they do not support hiring outside counsel. None of this opposition has been allowed to surface."

Lewis said that Rickover and Leighton had told him that they wanted a nationally known attorney "to show Newport News that the Navy meant business and to lobby in Congress. We assumed he wanted a person to counter Tenneco's Thomas G. Corcoran. Lobbying by the Executive Branch is prohibited by statute and I will have nothing to do with it. . . ."

In Rickover's speech before the New York Patent Law Association, he accused lawyers of "contributing substantially to the erosion of values and institutions on which our society is based." What happens to those values, he asked, "when signed contracts are broken with no moral stigma attached to those who break them; when people are driven, under threat of litigation, to pay sums they may not owe; when those skilled in thwarting justice are considered successful men? . . .

"In coming here I feel a bit like Eurystheus of Greek mythology. The Augean stables housed three thousand oxen and had not been cleaned for thirty years. Eurystheus did not have the wherewithal to clean the stables himself. But he did point out the problem to Hercules, who cleaned them by diverting two rivers. In similar vein, I can only hope that some of you will take on the herculean task of cleansing the legal profession. This is well worth the effort, even if you have to drown a few oxen in the process."

And finally there was the move to avenge the deeds of Tommy Corcoran.

Rickover read in *The Washington Post* an excerpt from *The Brethren*, a book about Supreme Court justices. The book accused Corcoran of attempting to lobby two justices in 1969, while a Corcoran client had a case pending before the Court. Rickover wrote to the District of Columbia Bar and asked for an investigation to "determine whether the behavior of Mr. Corcoran violates the legal profession's code of professional responsibility," and, if so, whether "appropriate legal action" is warranted. Copies of the letter went to federal officials and newspaper reporters.

Corcoran did not speak publicly about the charge in the book, which said that he had called on Justice Hugo L. Black (who was dead by the time the book was published) and Justice William J. Brennan, Jr. Both justices, according to the book's account, summarily dismissed Corcoran.

Rickover's request for a bar association investigation rekindled stories of his feuds with Corcoran. Rickover had testified in 1977, for instance, that "Corcoran lobbied extensively to prevent my reappointment." But, as Corcoran told it, he tried to talk old friends in the Navy out of dumping Rickover. "I said, 'Take him out of this construction business, but, please, promote him. Promote him to be the commandant at Annapolis. Let him redo Annapolis, let him be the teacher of the future Navy.' But do you know what the boys said to that? They said, 'Jesus Christ, we'd sooner do without ships!' "

Corcoran's lawyer, Robert S. Bennett, told the authors that Rickover's complaint was "thoroughly investigated" by the District of Columbia Bar's Board of Professional Responsibility, which had turned the case over to the Bar Council, an arm of the District of Columbia Court of Appeals. Three months after receiving Rickover's complaint, the Board sent Bennett a letter which said, "We have completed our investigation of this matter and have been unable to establish that . . . Mr. Corcoran . . . sought to communicate with a Justice of the Court in a manner which could be considered a violation of a Disciplinary Rule."

What Rickover tried to do to Corcoran did not hurt Corcoran's reputation as a superannuated wheeler-dealer, but the incident reinforced Rickover's image as a self-righteous zealot whose morality was sometimes tinged with vindictiveness. The image that had made the cover of *Time* in 1954 and had earned the label "father of the nuclear navy" had tarnished with age.

The *Carl Vinson,* the nuclear carrier that Newport News once threatened not to complete, was launched on March 15, 1980. John Diesel, the president of the shipbuilding company, had let it be known that he would not sit on the same platform with Rickover. Diesel was there at the launching. Rickover was represented by a letter, which was read aloud at the ceremony. "It was funny," a young woman who was on the platform said later, "but his not being there was more of a reminder of him than if he were just sitting there like the rest of us." And most of the press, in describing the launching, barely mentioned Rickover's absence. Some newspaper stories did not mention him at all.

23 | Meeting the Press

The dateline is "At Sea, Submerged." "Dear Ed," the letter, written in a firm hand, begins. "We are returning to New London, Connecticut from sea trials of the U.S.S. *Skipjack,* our first nuclear powered, streamlined, single screw attack submarine. The ship successfully met all her trials, surface and submerged, and attained the highest speed ever made by any submarine. I am writing you because I know how interested you are and in gratitude for the fine friend you have always been to me. I want you to know that your help and understanding contributed to the creation of this revolutionary submarine."

The letter is signed "Cordially H. G. Rickover."

"Ed" was Edward R. Murrow, the nation's premier television journalist in 1959, when Rickover wrote that letter. They had met in 1956—it was "Admiral Rickover" and "Mr. Murrow" then—and they had indeed become friends. Rickover would help Murrow's son, Casey, get into Yale, which Rickover's own son, Robert, attended. They wrote and talked about the problems of the world, about education (Murrow would write a foreword for one of Rickover's books on the subject), and about the Navy. Rickover would recommend books to Murrow—a sure sign of friendship, for, to Rickover, a book was a great bond.

There was also talk about a Rickover book, which, according to the notes kept by Murrow, would have been a sensation in the late 1950s—or the 1980s. "It should be an exposé which will touch the public," a note dated September 2, 1958, says. The note, which reads like a capsule of Rickover's basic philosophy, continues:

> . . . to be about the people involved in the government and how the government really works. It should be written in the third person, by a writer who must write about what he sees, not what people tell him, and it should set forth his and Rickover's conclusions. The book would be a source book, a case history, which would influence indus-

514

try. The writer must be cleared in order to gain access to the most important facts.

Rickover feels that the exploitation of weapons is the main element in defense today. It would take very little exploitation to bring about the enemy's defeat. We must get on top of the situation through men of science and through cultural sources. A lot of "baloney" is going on today in Washington along educational, scientific and technological lines. We cannot allow the present danger of false premises to continue. If the truth is brought out something might be accomplished. At present there is too much publicity to the point that no one really knows what is going on. Defense is not getting enough money from the government. There are too many people involved in government operations. Rickover thinks personnel should be pared to a minimum, with the top people really doing the work. We must try to stop the draining of profits by eliminating unnecessary people and jobs. In our efforts to gain maximum efficiency there must be people involved who have imagination, artistic temperament in every phase of operations and the thinking must not be narrow. If we value our opportunity to be free we must be selfish and prevent our destruction. Our industry is not efficient. Everyone is fooling himself and the public through over-optimistic advertising.

Another note says that Max Lerner was Rickover's first choice to be the writer, "although Rickover thinks a novelist would be ideal, as he is apt to have more insight into people." Two other writers were named: Robert Wallace, who had just written a glowing *Life* article on Rickover, and John Dos Passos, who was suggested by a Rickover aide.

At least one publisher looked into the prospect, but the book was never written. In addition to the Murrow-inspired efforts to write a biography of Rickover, another book was proposed by Commander Edwin Kintner, of Rickover's staff, who wrote an article on the *Nautilus* prototype reactor in the Idaho desert for *The Atlantic* magazine. After the article was published in January 1959, Kintner went to Rickover to seek guidance. "Goddamn it," Rickover roared, "why should I let you write my autobiography?" That was the last time someone in NRB is known to have considered such a project.

Rickover's own books on education may have evolved out of Rickover's correspondence with Murrow, which consisted of letters similar to the one from the *Skipjack*. The letters show Rickover engaging in the art of public relations—an enterprise that he might have called baloney but one which, at least early in his career, he practiced like a professional.

The letters were part of a ritual that Rickover performed when he went aboard a nuclear submarine for sea trials. In the Preface to his book *Eminent Americans,* Rickover stated that, since the *Nautilus* went to sea in January 1955, he had been responsible for directing the sea trials of all of the Navy's nuclear ships. "Because many members of Congress had given strong support in getting the *Nautilus* built, I decided that it would be no more than proper for me to send each of them a letter reporting what the ship had done. I remember writing some 80 letters in longhand during that first voyage. Soon I expanded the list of recipients to include all members of Congress and appropriate officials in the executive branch."

In the earliest days, Rickover would write numerous letters by hand, as he had written the one to Murrow from the *Skipjack*. As the submarine fleet grew, a new instrument was added: an electric memory typewriter. With its aid, Rickover could prepare hundreds of copies of his standard message: I am writing to you from aboard the. . . .

The letters went to Congressmen, who often passed them on to constituents in newsletters; to defense officials; and to newspaper reporters and columnists. Rickover and his nuclear navy continually won publicity through his letter writing. But the practice wore down from overuse, and, as sea trials of submarines became frequent events, the letters began to have the tone and appearance of "Dear Occupant" junk mail. What had started out as notes to influential people evolved into three-page, single-spaced form letters that extolled nuclear-powered ships.

Rickover's dealings with the press began in a sunburst of attention in the 1950s, when Clay Blair was the instrument of Rickover's first publicity campaign. It certainly worked, for there is little doubt that without sympathetic publicity Rickover would not have won Congressional support for his promotion and retention in the Navy. His subsequent promotions, through the 1950s and into the 1970s, also were accompanied, if not inspired, by publicity—often of the extravagant type usually reserved for prelates and revered statesmen. At that time the media, meaning a mix of print and electronic journalism, had hardly been invented. Virtually all that mattered was the major press: daily newspapers, weekly magazines, the wire services, and medium-size newspapers, reached through their Washington bureaus.

Through Blair, Rickover got coverage in *Time* and *Life.* Also through Blair, Rickover's causes were taken up by Blair's friend Lloyd Norman, who covered the Pentagon for the *Chicago Tribune* and later for *Newsweek.* Rickover, as a Chicago boy who made good, was a darling of the *Tribune*. A frequent recipient of Rickover's underseas letters was Bill Anderson, managing editor of the *Tribune*.

Rickover became a master at leaking news. He often testified in executive or secret session, and weeks or even months might pass before his testimony was cleared and published. By the time this happened, a Washington reporter of the 1960s remarked, much of it "is worn threadbare and has been leaked several times in the past through John Finney [of *The New York Times*] and Ted Sell [of the *Los Angeles Times*]. Rickover usually picks a holiday or slow news period."

A case in point was the handling of one of the crises involving Rickover's retention. On Monday, February 4, 1963, *The New York Times* reported that Rickover's "Congressional supporters . . . are rallying once again" to prevent his compulsory retirement. "Officially," the story said, "the Navy is declining to take a position on the admiral's future. Privately, however, high Navy officials . . ." The story, which was bylined by John W. Finney, had the effect of warning Rickover's friends to spring into action. It was published on a Monday, traditionally a day when the news is scant and a reporter has a good chance of getting an exclusive story prominently placed in the paper. Finney's story was on Page One.

The Navy, of course, on occasion leaked to Finney and to other leading Washington reporters. But the Navy rarely was able to get much coverage of its side of any story about Rickover. One old reliable, though, was Hanson W. Baldwin, military correspondent of *The New York Times*, a graduate of Annapolis (Class of 1924), and from 1969 to 1971 president of the Naval Academy Alumni Association. It was Baldwin, for example, who broke a story in 1963 about a Congressional resolution that would honor "the true fathers of the nuclear submarine program." Baldwin wrote, "Some naval officers feel strongly that Admiral Rickover has received some credit that rightfully is not his, and the resolution is viewed as an attempt to establish this." Baldwin reflected the feelings of the many anti-Rickover admirals in the Navy—just as Finney, a few months earlier, had reflected the feelings of Rickover's many friends on Capitol Hill.

The attempt to cut down Rickover's achievement got nowhere. The resolution was introduced by Charles S. Gubser, who said he wanted to give credit to Dr. Ross Gunn and Dr. Philip Abelson for their work on nuclear propulsion in the 1940s. Newspapers gave it little coverage. Gubser's colleagues acted as if the resolution were the plague, and the Navy's Office of Legislative Affairs, official watchdog of legislation affecting the Navy, announced that the Navy would not support the proposed legislation.*

Rickover could hardly do wrong in the press from the time of his being hailed by Time, Inc., in the early 1950s, up to the late 1960s. During that heyday, Rickover and his organization played the leak game better than most partisans in Washington. Lloyd Norman, looking back on his career as a Pentagon reporter, said there were several types of classic leakers: infighter ("determined to win regardless of the means"); show-off ("a braggart who likes to demonstrate how important he is in the Pentagon hierarchy"); the whistle-blower ("a zealot who is convinced that his agency ... is being mismanaged and only he has the right answers"); the partisan dissenter ("feels his organization is being zapped by the rival's more glamorous or impressive weapon system or military mission"); the true-blue good guy ("truly believes that an informed press is vital to a democracy"); the compulsive talker ("bubbly with the latest flash"). At various times, Rickover, his staff, and his Congressional supporters played every one of these roles.

Norman said he believed that "every service academy and war college should include a course in public and Congressional relations, with lectures and textbooks by Henry Kissinger and Adm. Hyman G. Rickover, both of whom are outstanding experts in those fields."

During the 1950s Rickover appeared at the National Press Club, the headquarters for most of Washington's influential newspaper and magazine correspondents. He was available for interviews, and he answered telephone inquiries from the press. He was also frequently sought out to make speeches. His speeches were incisive, studded with warnings, and often prophetic. "Our high standard of living," he warned in 1959, "makes such heavy inroads into our capital of nonrenewable raw materials that, because of it, we bequeath to future generations of Americans a diminished national inheritance. . . ."

He was often eloquent. "The ships, the submarines, and the missiles I have talked about are very expensive," he said in a speech in 1957. "But many of you may remember the famous picture taken that day in 1940 when the Germans occupied France—the picture of the man standing on the sidewalk crying. To what avail were the savings of millions of individual Frenchmen as the conquering troops tramped by?"

* The "work of Gunn and Abelson" became a rubric for "Rickover doesn't deserve all that credit in the press." When the authors first began working on this book, the rubric was also recited to us by anti-Rickover officers. The authors already had independent knowledge of the facts; see Chapter 6.

The speeches he gave were, in fact, so interesting that a Washington publisher decided to put them in a book. On October 29, 1958, M. P. Schnapper, executive director of Public Affairs Press, routinely asked Rickover for permission to quote from the speeches. Schnapper had published collections of speeches of other public officials, including Presidents Roosevelt and Truman. The assumption up to October 1958 was that the speeches of public officials were public property.

Rickover believed differently. He said that his speeches were his property. He officially copyrighted his next speech, bundled up twenty-two of the speeches he had given in the previous four years, and copyrighted them. He also began putting a copyright notice on his speeches. The notice said, "No permission needed for contemporaneous press use"—meaning that Rickover could get publicity from newspapers quoting the speech, but as soon as he uttered it, the speech became his personal property.

He had used many of his speeches on education as the basis for a book, *Education and Freedom,* which E. P. Dutton was about to publish. "If he had merely turned me down because he wanted a different publisher," Schnapper said, "I would have dropped the matter. But he said I had no legal right to even excerpt from them. He even ordered me not to use them. I decided this was a clear test of a practice I have seen before in Washington—of a Government official selling rights to his official writings. So I set out to prove the Admiral Rickover speeches were public property."

Secretary of the Navy Thomas S. Gates, Jr., told Schnapper that Rickover had obtained the copyright as a private citizen and that he did not "deem it proper . . . to render a legal opinion." A patent expert in the Office of Naval Research, however, ruled that a government employee held the rights to "original written or spoken material" and could copyright it as long as it "is not prepared at the direction of the official superiors of the author or as a part of his official duties."

The U.S. Copyright Office said it had no record of a government official ever having copyrighted a speech. The office also said that it had no power to decide whether Rickover's opinion was legal. Schnapper decided to find out by filing suit in U.S. District Court and asking for a ruling on whether a public official could copyright material which stemmed from his work as a public employee.

Soon after he filed suit, Schnapper received from Rickover's office an anonymous letter that said the most recent speech, which Rickover had pointedly copyrighted, had been "written during Government time, on Government paper, on a Government typewriter and reproduced on Government mimeograph machines. All clerks, including one warrant officer employed in that office, have served notice that they would tell the truth about the entire matter if required to do so in court."

No one had to go to court. U.S. District Judge Alexander Holtzoff dismissed Schnapper's suit, ruling, "No one sells or mortgages all the products of his brain to his employer by the mere fact of employment. The officer or employee still remains a free agent.

"His intellectual products are his own, and do not automatically become the property of the government. The circumstances that the ideas for the literary product may have been gained in whole or in part as a result or in the course of the performance of his official duties, does not affect the situation."

The judge said that when someone is hired to write something for the government, the material becomes government property and is in the public domain. But what Rickover had written, the judge ruled, "comprises literary products" that are "no part of his official duties."

Schnapper appealed, and the U.S. Court of Appeals in 1960 ruled that Rickover did *not* have a copyright on the speeches he made between 1955 and 1958. But the court, in a ruling written by retired Supreme Court Justice Stanley Reed, said that later speeches, which bore a copyright, were validly copyrighted. The court asked for further hearings. Again Schnapper appealed, this time to the Supreme Court, which in March 1962 sent the case back to the lower courts for clarification of a record too "inadequate to support a ruling." Finally, in 1967, eight years after the case began, Judge John Lewis Smith in Washington District Court upheld Rickover's copyright and ruled that government officials could copyright speeches and writings done on their own time. Smith said that Rickover made the speeches as a "private citizen," had prepared them "in the privacy of [his] own home," and the speeches "were handled as private business from start to finish." The speeches had been duplicated in Navy offices, the judge noted, but these were "purely mechanical operations."

Rickover, who had kept his record of charitable contributions to himself, reluctantly announced that he had donated to children's charities about $20,000 in fees for speeches and magazine articles, along with book royalties. "I have never taken one penny for my interest in the schools. I have given it all away," he said. His donations went to an Italian orphanage, organizations aiding crippled children, the United Nations International Children's Emergency Fund, and CARE.

In 1972, when another book came out under his name, Rickover made an unusual arrangement. The 316-page book was a compilation of biographies of the forty-one men after whom Polaris submarines were named. In his submerged-at-sea letters, Rickover had sketched the lives of the submarines' namesakes. The *Chicago Tribune* called one of them, an essay on George Washington Carver, a "short classic." From these sketches evolved longer profiles, for which his wife, Ruth Masters Rickover, had done the research and helped with the writing. She died before the book was published. It was dedicated to her in these words:

> This book is a memorial to my wife, Ruth Masters Rickover, who gave me unmeasurable assistance in preparing the text. She was at once the most human and intelligent person I ever knew, the greatest influence on my life and work.
> To borrow from Tibullus: *"Tu mihi curarum requies, tu nocte vel atra lumen, et in solis tu mihi turba locis."**

Then, in explaining his wife's role in the book, Rickover stated, "During the past 4 years I have devoted virtually all my spare time to this task. Had it not been for the devoted efforts of my dear wife, who did most of the research for these essays, I could not possibly have completed this task while carrying out my official duties as a naval officer."

Congress authorized a Congressional printing of 12,000 copies of *Eminent Americans: Namesakes of the Polaris Submarine Fleet* and stipulated that Rickover could publish his own commercial edition. But, saying he wanted students to be able to afford the book, he had it published by the Government Printing Office and sold for $1.25. He did not receive a penny in royalties.

While print reigned as the master medium, Rickover got along with the press. He was rarely criticized. Editorials against his copyright stand were noteworthy for their restraint. Mostly, in an era when newspapers and magazines were the principal conduits for information, he was "good copy," a man who could get into print because he spoke words that made headlines.

The rising new medium of television confronted him, as it did many other public figures, with a need to change. His friend Edward R. Murrow had gently introduced Rickover to television, but the television of Murrow was not the television of the future. His "See It Now" show

---

* *"You are my consolation from sorrow, you are light in the black night, and at solitary times you are my tumult."*

had been powerful, live television. In 1954, his three-hour documentary on the tactics of Senator Joseph R. McCarthy had won him and CBS high praise from everyone except McCarthy supporters. Murrow's television was never bland, and it was always journalistic.

"I know you never watch television," Murrow wrote Rickover on November 22, 1960, "but you might care to look at Harvest of Shame, our Migrant Labor show on this Friday between 9:30 and 10:30 P.M. I believe you will not find it a waste of time." There is nothing in Murrow's correspondence to indicate that Rickover watched the show. He did believe that television was a waste of time, and he never gave it much time or thought.

Rickover's first appearance on a television panel interview program came in 1960 when he was the guest on NBC's "Meet the Press." The show's regular panel member was Lawrence E. Spivak, famed for his sharp and penetrating questions. The other members of the panel that Sunday were Ernest K. Lindley of *Newsweek,* Chalmers Roberts of *The Washington Post,* and James Reston of *The New York Times.* Rickover tried to keep the questions channeled toward education, and the questioners mostly cooperated. His answers were usually long and full of details, the kind of responses that may look good on paper but do not hold a television audience. And he did something that one was not supposed to do on television, especially in those days—he criticized TV.

He never did feel comfortable on television. His appearances were rare. In an age when advocates of every hue and subject were taking their pleas and images to the tube, Rickover remained essentially a pre-TV man. He could have masterfully staged video events (what historian Daniel J. Boorstin called pseudo events). But he chose not to, probably because of his contempt for the medium, a contempt that was greatly inspired by his belief that television harmed young minds.

There was a touch of the showman about the way he handled events that he could control. Retired submariner Richard Laning recalled how Rickover maintained his underdog image, for the benefit of the press. "Whenever there was a commissioning or other major event," Laning recalled, "the Secretary of the Navy would get together a group of VIPs and have a Navy plane made available to fly them to wherever the event was taking place. Apparently on several occasions the Secretary of the Navy would invite Rickover, and Rickover would respond that he had to go up early and would go in his own way.

"The Secretary would then fill up the airplane with VIPs and the press. At the last minute, Rickover would get word to him that he needed space on the plane for himself and other officers. This would then force the Secretary either to get an extra plane or to say he didn't have room. Rickover would then claim he was a martyr because there wasn't space for him. This helped build up the mystique."

In the 1970s he was still good at catching a headline, especially through his Congressional testimony. But often his were the words of a man whose impatience with the world sometimes made him sound heartless. Once, when he was in Charleston, South Carolina, for a ceremony honoring his friend Congressman L. Mendel Rivers, a newsman asked Rickover whether it was true that several workers in the Charleston Naval Shipyard had suffered heart attacks because he was demanding that they work harder. Rickover said that he had just had a heart attack himself and had been told by his doctor to exercise. He made headlines in the Charleston papers by then suggesting that perhaps the shipyard employees should work harder to avoid heart attacks.

One of his pet peeves was the publication of what he felt was too much information in technical magazines. Testifying about this, he remarked that he had made a form of censorship part of his contracts with suppliers. "My contract," he told the Congressmen, "says simply: 'Get Government approval for any advertising.' I solved my problem very easily. . . ."

A Congressman pointed out that he was "bucking the whole publication system, newspapers and everybody else. They will scream to high heaven. . . ."

"That doesn't bother me at all," Rickover said. "I just let them scream."

This is the technique he has used on many occasions when something he did not want published was something that the Navy or some other government agent did want published. What follows is the anatomy of a proposed 3,000-word article on "Safety Aboard U.S. Nuclear-Powered Ships." The article had been requested by the United States ambassador in Rome, apparently because he felt a need to give the Italian press reassurances about visits of U.S. nuclear-propelled ships in Italian ports.

Late in 1977: U.S. Information Agency contacts the Chief of Navy Information, Rear Admiral David Cooney, for recommendation of a qualified author. He suggests several. One is contacted and accepts.

January 19, 1978: Cooney arranges meeting with the author and

Captain John Drain, OP-616, Head of Ocean Affairs Branch, Politico-Military Policy Division. With Cooney present, Drain answers several questions about nuclear-propelled ships.

February 15: Author delivers to USIA a manuscript that has been reviewed for accuracy and security considerations by two nuclear-quali-fied submarine officers he knows. On an unofficial basis, a copy of the manuscript is given to Cooney. The USIA, as an agency of the govern-ment, meanwhile, formally submits the article to the Navy for security-policy review. Although Naval Intelligence finds no security violations, about two dozen "accuracy" and "policy" changes are made in the man-uscript. These changes included spelling out "A-sub" when the term ap-peared, deleting references to the *Thresher* and *Scorpion* losses, chang-ing "nuclear-propelled" to "nuclear-powered," deleting large sections of the description of how reactors work, and deleting (for "policy" reasons) a quote from Oliver Cromwell that "a man-of-war is the best ambassador."

Mid-April: Though no security problems have been found, the issues of clearance and who will approve, or "sign off," for the Navy have not been settled.

Then, for five months there was no progress at all. The author was led to believe that no one in the Pentagon wanted to broach the subject to Rickover's staff, for his approval—or at least nondisapproval—was re-quired. The article simply waited, as did the USIA and the ambassador in Rome.

September 27: Admiral Cooney delivers to International Communi-cations Agency (USIA's name has changed in the interim) a manuscript that has "cleared Navy and DOD security review. Please note there have been many amendments made to the article along the way."

October 3: The author, noting that "the changes made reflect a com-bination of Rickover and Department of Defense 'policy' changes," feels that the article lacks "credibility as well as honesty to anyone familiar with the subject." He asks that the rewritten article not be published with his byline.

The situation is very different when Rickover *wants* something pub-lished. Or when he wants to write something. He forced his will on liter-ary projects, such as *Eminent Americans,* the way he attacked any other kind of project. He used the full resources available to him, tried to con-trol every aspect of the project, and took drastic steps against any critics. All of this happened when he took on the project of finding out why the battleship *Maine* blew up in Havana harbor on February 15, 1898.

The project began one day in 1974, when Rickover read a newspaper story that raised questions about whether the explosion that destroyed the *Maine* had been the work of a mine. One of his first calls went to Vice Admiral Edwin B. Hooper, Director of Naval History. Hooper recalled picking up the phone and hearing Rickover merely say, "You're an ordnance expert. Would a mine exploding under a ship set off a magazine explosion?"

"I replied," Hooper said in his memoirs, "that I did not know." They discussed the technicalities of such an explosion, and then, a little while later, Rickover called again to ask whether Hooper had any historical records about such explosions. For days afterward there were other questions: What did Hooper know about the court of inquiry that looked into the sinking of the *Maine?* How did he evaluate the members of the court? And, finally, will you publish a manuscript on the subject?

Rickover was writing a book on the sinking of the *Maine.*

At Rickover's request the naval attachés of the Spanish, British and French embassies obtained documents from their nations' naval archives. At Rickover's request the Director of Naval Intelligence had the Spanish and French documents translated. At Rickover's request the Director of Naval Telecommunications, the Director of the top-secret National Security Agency, the Archivist of the United States, and specialists in the National Archives searched for, found, and then deciphered messages that the American naval attaché in Madrid had sent, in code, to Washington on the eve of the Spanish-American War.

Rickover called upon several historians, in addition to Hooper. The president of the Naval War College got from his archives the war plans the United States had drawn up for war with Spain. Two experts in international law were recruited from the George Washington University Law School. The curator of naval history at the Smithsonian Institution contributed information on mines and mine-laying techniques around the time of the sinking of the *Maine.* An expert on American diplomatic history reviewed the manuscript. Eight members of Rickover's staff, in his words, "took the time to read parts of the manuscript and gave useful suggestions."

What Rickover needed most were experts who could, in effect, hold a modern court of inquiry on how the ship was sunk. He was seeking definitive information that would indicate whether the ship was sunk by a mine or by an internal explosion. For this key research he turned to Robert S. Price, a research physicist at the Naval Surface Weapons Center at White Oak, Maryland, and Ib S. Hansen, assistant for design application in the Structures Department at the David W. Taylor Naval Ship Research and Development Center at Cabin John, Maryland. Hansen came to the *Maine* project as an expert on battle damage, Price as an authority on interpretation of underwater photography. (Among his Navy projects had been an analysis of the wreckage of the nuclear submarine *Scorpion*.)

The two men examined the official records of two inquiries, one that followed the sinking in 1898 and one held in 1911, after a cofferdam had been built around the wreckage, which was then extensively photographed. They concentrated on an investigation of the damage and what caused it, but they also ranged into such areas as questions as to the absence of dead fish after the explosion (interesting but inconclusive) and the feasibility of placing a mine near the *Maine* (unlikely; the ship was well guarded).

Their exhaustive investigation, which Rickover called the Hansen-Price analysis, was the heart of the 173-page book. Published as one of the book's three appendixes, the twenty-three-page analysis offered this conclusion:

> We have found no technical evidence in the records examined that an external explosion initiated the destruction of the *Maine*. The available evidence is consistent with an internal explosion alone. We therefore conclude that an internal source was the cause of the explosion. The most likely source was heat from a fire in a coal bunker adjacent to the 6-inch reserve magazine. However, since there is no way of proving this, other internal causes cannot be eliminated as possibilities.

In the book itself Rickover accepted the analysis, but ranged into other issues, such as the failure of the original board of inquiry to call technical witnesses and the unlikelihood of objectivity amid calls for war and shouts of "Remember the *Maine!*" He ended by adroitly making the sinking of the *Maine* a parable for our time:

> In the modern technological age, the battle cry "Remember the *Maine*" should have a special meaning for us. With almost instantaneous communications that can command weapons of unprecedented power, we can no longer approach technical problems with the casualness and confidence held by Americans in 1898. The *Maine* should impress us that technical problems must be examined by competent and qualified people; and that the results of their investigation must be fully and fairly presented to their fellow citizens.
> With the vastness of our government and the difficulty of controlling it, we must make sure that those in "high places" do not,

without most careful consideration of the consequences, exert our prestige and might. Such uses of our power may result in serious international actions at great cost in lives and money—injurious to the interests and standing of the United States.

As he had with his speeches decades before and with his book *Eminent Americans*, Rickover copyrighted *How the Battleship* Maine *Was Destroyed*. But this was a greatly different case. The book was printed by the United States Government at Navy expense. Although Rickover asserted to the U.S. Copyright Office that the book "was not written as part of my official duties," he had drawn in other government workers who would not have been as readily available to a freelance writer as they were to a four-star admiral. Hansen and Price said that they did most of their work on the book on weekends, but they conceded that some of the work was done on government time. The implication of the copyright was that their analysis was part of a protected book and, as such, could not be excerpted for publication as could a typically uncopyrighted government document. This time, there was no Schnapper to raise legal questions.

Admiral Hooper, in his memoirs, said that when he read the manuscript at Rickover's request, he suggested that it be published by the Naval Institute Press (the nonprofit publisher closely connected with, but not a part of, the Navy) or by a commercial publisher. Rickover said no. So, Hooper, with a "favorable impression of the book as a solid historical work and a major contribution," suggested to his Naval History advisory board that it be published by the Navy. The board accepted the suggestion, and Hooper in January 1976 simultaneously sent the manuscript to the Government Printing Office and notified Admiral James Holloway, the Chief of Naval Operations. Holloway concurred.

Hooper, acting in an editorial capacity, suggested some changes in the manuscript, and Rickover accepted them; they had a good working relationship. Hooper said, "The book is, I believe, historically first class. Some Spanish primary sources were used that have not to my knowledge been used by any other work. . . ."

The Navy said that $14,000 had been paid to the Government Printing Office for 2,000 copies of the book. The GPO printed 7,500 more and put the book on sale in August 1976 for $5.70. The price was based on the amount of money needed to recover $42,500 in printing and mailing costs.

The Naval War College, which had been one of the institutions that had aided Rickover, publishes a *Naval War College Review*, "in order that officers of the Navy and Marine Corps might receive some of the educational benefits available to resident students at the Naval War College." The *Review* does not generate much heat, but its Fall 1977 issue did, for in it was a review of Rickover's book by Graham A. Cosmas, a historian with the Marine Corps. He called Rickover's analysis of the *Maine* disaster "useful but limited," and concluded, "Another study remains to be done on the human elements in the situation—the men and institutions responding to the crisis. The definitive account of the fate of the *Maine* remains to be written."

Soon after publication of the *Review*, Vice Admiral James Stockdale, president of the Naval War College, received a letter from Admiral Rickover on Navy stationery. Rickover said he wanted to raise two points: "the qualifications of the reviewer [of the *Maine* book], and the function of the *Naval War College Review*." The reviewer, Rickover wrote, did not have the necessary technical background "to evaluate most of the technical points raised. . . . The major flaw he finds is that I did not write the book that *he* thinks I should have written. This is a fallacy common in most reviews, and a major reason why they are of so little use. . . .

"What appalled me when I first began to study the loss of the *Maine* was how little first-rate historical scholarship has been spent on the subject. . . . Perhaps, to paraphrase, history is too important to be left to 'professional' historians."

He then leaped to his next point: what kind of publication would allow Cosmas to write a review that suggested there might be something lacking in a book by H. G. Rickover?

> The *Naval College Review* purports to be a learned journal. A true learned journal can be an important source of information to those who have heavy demands on their time. From my experience, such a journal is no better than its reviews; and institutions are no better than their journals.
>
> Why is it necessary to have the *Review* at all? There are several publications already covering the same fields with greater specialization. . . . In these days when the government is attempting to reduce paperwork, do away with superfluous employees, and save money, eliminating the *Review* would be a noteworthy, precedent-setting action by the War College.
>
> I assume this letter will be published in the *Naval War College Review*. [It was.]

The Naval War College itself had long been a target of criticism fired off periodically by Rickover, who was never reluctant to stray beyond his own field of nuclear engineering. Two years before his book was published he had sent his deputy William Wegner to the Naval War College to "review the course of instruction" and make recommendations. Wegner's report, after a two-day visit, went on for page after page about what was wrong with the Navy—and former Secretary of Defense McNamara and former CNO Zumwalt. Wegner had thirty-three recommendations, including one that questioned whether there should be a Naval War College.

By the 1970s, Rickover had little direct dealing with the press. The publicity fallout from the *Maine* book, for example, was handled through the office of the Chief of Information. Cooney would talk to Rickover and then relay Rickover's words to reporters. The press, Rickover said in 1973, "often acts simply as a mirror. The irrational blathering of a fool is considered 'news' at the time of his blather. The more violent and impossible the speech, often the larger the headline and the more space it gets."

But if he disliked and distrusted the post-Watergate press, he hated television. "No one sitting through these nightly TV shows," he said in 1973, "is likely to make the mistake of thinking that he is participating in a flowering of American national culture. He is taking part in the surrender of the will to the conception of society as a captive mass audience. . . . First attracted and then corrupted by the deliberate employment of superficial and meretricious modes of entertainment, this mass audience becomes acquiescent to dishonest and fantastic commercial claims."

Holiday weekends are slow for television—except for sporting events—and the Labor Day weekend is the slowest of all. Weeks before this dullest of Sundays, a producer for the panel show "Face the Nation" in 1979 contacted Admiral Rickover and asked him if he would be a guest. Rickover said that he would appear only if the questions were limited to his great interest, American education. The producer agreed, though the combination of Rickover, Labor Day, and education must have been a sobering contemplation. But by the time Labor Day neared there was a possibility that Rickover could make news—by "blathering." President Carter, his onetime protégé, had just vetoed an appropriations bill that included funds for a nuclear carrier. Surely Rickover would understand if the assembled reporters strayed from the dull topic of education and asked him about his reactions to the carrier veto. Rickover did *not* understand, and the reporters and the viewers were treated to the spectacle of Rickover fuming.

Rickover steadfastly refused to talk about anything but education. The reporters sparred with him, and when he seemed to be determined to filibuster on the subject, George Herman of CBS News could stand it no longer. He broke in.

". . . and, as you well know," Rickover was declaring, "as the Talmud says, the world is upheld by children who study—"

"I'm not sure who knows what the Talmud says," Herman interrupted in an exasperated tone.

"That is far more important than any of these, which I might call, stupid questions that you want to ask me," Rickover said.

A few minutes later, Herman and Rickover tangled again. Herman accused Rickover of taking over the interview.

"That is correct," Rickover said, "and I will stop doing it when we talk about education."

"That's sort of a demand, I take it."

"It's not a demand. I'm here," Rickover angrily responded. "I'm not here—I'm here voluntarily. Now, if you wish to terminate this discussion, that's perfectly all—"

Herman broke in: "Do I understand you to be saying that you will not entertain—or will not attempt—to answer any questions except on education?"

"Haven't I already made that clear?"

"I think probably you have. Yes, sir."

The Admiral and the reporters calmed down for a few more minutes as Rickover got his way and a short dialogue on education developed. Then, remarking on a question from Herman, Rickover said, ". . . you may do some good for this country, for the people of this country, in getting off these pseudo-political questions and getting onto a real subject."

"I thought," Herman said, "that's what I was doing when I asked you about why the Navy is planning these—"

Rickover then soared off into something approaching a stream of consciousness: "No, you know, a suspicion enters in my mind. You know, my opinion of CBS and the other public networks is, they're advertising agencies, and all that counts with them is what will sell advertising. That's the whole function of this program. It has a sponsor. And that's why, instead of showing this program in Washington, there's a new football—professional football coach in Washington. My God, that's the biggest event in many years around here; naturally, the parents who look at advertisements, possibly, for beer or deodorants would much rather see—much rather see and hear the football coach talk than to be concerned about the education of their children. And yet, right here in the District of Columbia, we have one of the poorest educational systems in the United States, despite the fact that we're spending about as much money as any—as anywhere, and there are more functionally illiterate children proportionately, probably, than most other places, and yet the parents are not—the parents would rather hear the football coach."

(The show was being blacked out in Washington in favor of a pre-game interview with the new coach of the Washington Redskins, Jack Pardee.)

Shortly afterward, Rickover again fumed, this time in response to a question about the state of the nation.

"First," Rickover began, "the Government and the country today is more complex than any society has ever been. I have grave doubts that a democracy consisting of 218 million people can run as a pure democracy, yet we are trying still to run it that way. I have very grave doubts about it, and the reason is not the number, the reason is this football game. People are not—people are only—now have a pretty good life and everybody is taken care of. HEW spends 181 billion dollars a year, and in many cases there is no real incentive for people to work any more, and that's a natural human tendency, so why should they work when they can get handouts? And I—my opinion, and I'm not talking about the money part of it, but what impact it has on the character of our people and how they live and what they consider important.

"Now, let's get back to the Presidency because that's part of it. Now, as you may know from your history, even the Lord Jesus Christ only batted ninety-one and a half percent in choosing followers, but we expect the President of the United States to be pluperfect, even more perfect than the Lord, and we don't understand. We put a man on a job with little power, little authority, and we expect him to do everything that every citizen wants, and yet we have problems which appear are not even being solved either by business, by the press, certainly by the commercial TV stations, or by Congress, and . . ."

In his crusade against his enduring enemy—stupidity—Rickover wielded the printed word, warning his country of perils, chiding her for shortcomings, denouncing her frivolous ways. When he heard in 1980 that a Navy contractor was holding a party in the building that housed the Naval Reactors office, Rickover ripped off a memo and managed to have it leaked, just as he had been managing for so many years. The contractor had enticed Navy personnel to the party by inviting another

Rickover enemy—football. In his memo of outrage, Rickover said, "If, in fulfilling its responsibility for acquiring and maintaining ships and weapons, the Navy needs assistance from the Redskins, and cheerleaders, the Navy is in worse shape than I thought."

He was a man who knew his priorities, who knew what his country needed, who knew his enemies—and her enemies. But, in an age when words were being eclipsed by images, he was rarely being heard or seen. His memo to his superiors in the Navy said: "Make every effort to . . . cancel the party." The party went on.

IN THE PRESENCE
OF MINE ENEMIES

"It is still incredible to me that a missile can be successfully and accurately fired from beneath the sea. Once one has seen a Polaris firing, the efficacy of this weapons system as a deterrent is not debatable," wrote John F. Kennedy on November 19, 1963, shortly after he had watched an underwater missile launch from the nuclear submarine *Andrew Jackson.*

"Our best naval guns had a maximum 40 kilometers, while American Polaris missiles had a range of more than 2,000 kilometers. . . . This was a painful realization. . . . We made a decision to convert our Navy primarily to submarines. We concentrated on the development of nuclear-powered submarines and soon began turning them out virtually on an assembly line. . . . Thus we fundamentally changed the strategy and composition of our Navy," wrote Nikita Khrushchev in his memoirs.

The navies—American as well as Soviet—that built those submarines were the enemies of Rickover. Still, he was able to build support on all of their efforts; those who made the American strategic-missile submarines and used his reactors, and those who made Soviet submarines that could best be countered by more American nuclear submarines.

24 | The Highest National Priority

"No military significance" were the words used by President Eisenhower to describe the consequences of earth's first artificial satellite, which the Soviet Union placed in orbit on October 4, 1957. There had been ample warning—in Soviet speeches and the press—that such an event was about to take place. Still, the United States government was taken by surprise when the 184-pound Sputnik was placed in orbit. A month later there was even more consternation as the Soviets launched Sputnik II, which weighed 1,120 pounds.

The implication of the Sputniks was considerable. The satellites announced the tremendous efforts being put into missile boosters and guidance by the USSR. It would be several years before the United States would be able to boost a large payload into space. The Sputniks were the latest demonstration of intensive and continuing advanced-technology efforts in the Soviet Union.

Beneath the surface calm, the Eisenhower Administration quickly began looking at potential ways to ensure continued American superiority in strategic weapons—those that could strike the Soviet homeland and thus deter a Soviet missile strike or other overt aggression. One of the United States missiles looked at was Polaris, a strategic missile that was scheduled to become available on Navy surface ships and submarines in 1963—six years away—or later. Could development of the missile be accelerated, and could nuclear submarines be designed and built at a rapid rate to take the Polaris missiles to sea?

Chief of Naval Operations Arleigh Burke turned to his Polaris project manager, Rear Admiral William F. Raborn, and directed that he further speed up the Polaris schedule. Then, in a technological effort that in some ways was comparable with the Manhattan atomic-bomb program, Raborn put the Polaris missile *system* to sea—in nuclear submarines—only three years after Sputnik.

535

Late in World War II, the U.S. Navy had pushed the development of guided or cruise missiles, that is, missiles that have aircraft-type jet engines and wings or fins to provide lift and control. Discussions after Germany's defeat had centered on bombarding Japan from ships with American-built V-1 missiles carrying high-explosive warheads. After the war, the U.S. Navy successfully fired "Americanized" V-1 missiles called Loons from submarines on the surface. This led to development of the Regulus I, a surface-launched guided missile that could carry a nuclear warhead against land targets almost 600 miles away at a speed of about 600 mph. A more advanced missile, the ramjet-propelled Rigel, was being developed with the same range, but with a speed of about Mach 2—twice the speed of sound, or well in excess of 1,000 mph. But because it had technical problems and complex launching arrangements, Rigel was canceled in favor of the Regulus and the improved Regulus II with turbojet engines.

Regulus I became operational in the middle 1950s and was carried in several aircraft carriers, cruisers and submarines. Two fleet submarines of World War II vintage were converted to carry two Regulus missiles each, and three new submarines were built to carry four or five Regulus missiles each. One of the latter boats was the nuclear-propelled *Halibut*. From the late 1950s until 1964 these submarines were in the Pacific, with one or two continuously on patrol off the Soviet Siberian coast, their missiles targeted against military installations. (At the same time, the U.S. Air Force was installing land-launched cruise missiles, the Matador and the Mace, in Europe and on Taiwan.)

Throughout this period the Navy had been examining ballistic missiles, weapons that used rocket thrust to push them up to several thousand feet, after which, like a bullet, they would follow a ballistic trajectory to a distant target. The Navy and the Army tested German V-2 ballistic missiles. One was even fired from the aircraft carrier *Midway* in a dramatic but inconclusive and almost disastrous test.

Ballistic missiles held little promise for shipboard use; their size made them difficult to handle (the V-2 was 46 feet long), and their large quantities of volatile liquid fuel—the V-2's liquid oxygen had to be stored at minus-297 degrees Fahrenheit—were dangerous to handle aboard ship. Still, some Navy men thought the problems could be solved, and a handful believed that there could even be a marriage of nuclear submarines and ballistic missiles. While the Regulus flew like a jet airplane, it was vulnerable like one; but a ballistic missile could not be shot down after launching.

Advocates of what would come to be called the Fleet Ballistic Missile (FBM) made no headway until the advent of thermonuclear weapons, first detonated by the United States in 1952 and by the Soviet Union in 1953. In response to these weapons, President Eisenhower in 1954 established a committee to study future weapon developments and their strategic implications. The committee came to be called the Killian Committee for its chairman, Dr. James R. Killian, Jr., the president of the Massachusetts Institute of Technology.

The FBM advocates presented their case to the Killian Committee through then-Commander E. P. (Pete) Aurand, the Navy's liaison officer to the committee (and later naval aide to Eisenhower). The Killian group—officially the Technical Capabilities Panel of the President's Science Advisory Committee—endorsed the development of American ballistic missiles and recommended, among other projects, the sea-based ballistic missile. Such a statement would have significant impact in the middle 1950s, since the National Security Council in 1955 gave ballistic-missile programs the very highest national priorities.

Rickover's position on sea-based ballistic missiles at this time is difficult to ascertain. He told a Senate committee that his early proposals for *guided*-missile submarines were blocked by the submariners, who let it be known that they would accept cancellation of new submarines rather than let them be armed with missiles. Such a position has been impossible to substantiate; indeed, after the war the submariners were pushing hard for submarine-launched guided missiles to help justify more undersea craft. A different view of Rickover's position comes from political scientist Vincent Davis, a student of the Navy's leadership in the postwar period: "Rickover . . . opposed an expanded emphasis on FBM R&D [Research and Development] because he was fearful this might siphon away funds from his continuing work on nuclear submarines."

Other officers, in Davis' opinion, had "simply and honestly" studied the issues and had come up with an answer opposite to the one reached by the FBM enthusiasts when confronted with the agonizing age-old decision as to how much present and proved naval combat capability should be sacrificed for the development of an improved but future and highly expensive capability. Another argument heard in the Navy passages of the Pentagon was that Navy development of a long-range strategic missile would put the Navy in competition with the Army and Air Force, both of which had ballistic-missile programs underway. Those who came down against the FBM included the Chief of Naval Operations, Admiral Robert B. Carney.

But in the summer of 1955 two seemingly unrelated events finally put the Navy in the ballistic-missile business. First, acceleration of the Air Force's Atlas ICBM program led to the award of a contract for the missile's inertial-guidance system to General Electric at Syracuse, New York. The inertial guidance would "tell" the missile where it was during a flight of several thousand miles independent of the earth's spin and other terrestrial factors. Second, on August 17, Admiral Arleigh Burke became the Chief of Naval Operations.

Burke immediately called to Washington Captain George H. Miller, formerly head of the OPNAV Strategic Studies Branch and at the time commander of a destroyer squadron. Miller already had a reputation as a forward-looking strategist, having gained wide attention with his prize-winning *Proceedings* article, "Strategy of the Future—A Second Look." Miller had argued in his article that the United States was giving insufficient thought and effort to strategic problems, in contrast to the development of weapons.

Miller joined the CNO inner circle, which included Lieutenant Commander Frank A. Manson. Manson was a public-information specialist who was employed by Admiral Carney and then Burke for special research, especially into policy and weapons, writing major policy speeches, and liaison with Rickover.

Shortly after Burke became CNO, Manson was visited by Samuel Ingraham, who, as a lieutenant, once had worked for Burke. Ingraham, now with General Electric in Syracuse, told Manson of the Air Force contract to GE for Atlas missile guidance and said he felt that the technology could be applied directly to sea-based ballistic missiles. Manson informed Miller of the discussion, and Miller passed on the word to Burke.

A few days later, Burke flew to Syracuse. He heard enough in a briefing there to be convinced that an Atlas-type guidance system could make it possible for a submarine to launch a missile that could strike a target more than a thousand miles away. Back in Washington, Burke found strong support from Rear Admiral John H. Sides, head of the important Guided Missiles Division of OPNAV (then OP-51). Sides was influential in overcoming opposition from other flag officers.

Burke directed that planning begin for development of an FBM. He also asked the committee on undersea warfare of the National Academy of Sciences to look at the increasing threat from Soviet submarines. In the subsequent study, scientists considered missile submarines, and Dr. Edward Teller told of the rapid advances in making nuclear warheads smaller, permitting them to be fitted in torpedoes and missiles launched from submarines. The scientists strongly urged that the Navy build a solid-fuel ballistic missile with a weight of eight to fifteen tons that could carry a nuclear warhead to targets 1,000 to 1,500 miles away. (Moscow is 1,100 miles from the open sea.)

In response to Burke's efforts, Secretary of Defense Charles E. Wilson directed the Navy to join the Army in development of the Jupiter, a land-launched ballistic missile. At first the Navy objected, because of the Jupiter's volatile liquid fuels. The Navy preferred a more stable, solid propellant, but the time and cost required to develop solid-fuel missiles was too great. So the Navy reluctantly joined the Army, with the goal a Jupiter FBM for launching from *surface* ships.

On October 17, 1955, the Navy established a Special Projects Office for the development of the missile and shipboard-launch devices. The office had nothing to do with the ships the missiles might be fired from. Burke set up the office as a separate effort, apart from the Bureaus of Aeronautics and Ordnance, which directed other missile programs. He had the office report directly to him and the Secretary of the Navy.

A captain briefly directed the office until December 1955, when Burke named Rear Admiral William F. Raborn as director of special projects. Burke later said that he looked at the records of all the admirals and most of the captains in the Navy in his effort to select a director. "I realized that he didn't have to be a technical man. He had to be able to know what technical men were talking about. He had to get a lot of different kinds of people to work. . . . I wanted a man who could get along with aviators because this [program] was going to kick hell out of aviators. They were going to oppose it to beat the devil, because it would take away, if it were completely successful in the long run, their strategic delivery capability.

"It would be bad to have a submariner," Burke continued, "in that because it first was a surface ship [weapon]; submariners were a pretty close group and they would have wanted to do things pretty much as submariners had already done . . . besides they were opposed to ballistic missiles."

And Burke even had problems with surface officers, because "they didn't know much about missiles or strategic [matters]."

Red Raborn, from the Class of 1928, had served in surface ships before becoming an aviator in 1934. He later saw combat aboard carriers in the Pacific. Raborn had no post-Annapolis technical training, only one year at the Naval War College. Burke selected him, however, "because he has the driving ability, he's got a lot of energy, he's full of enthusiasm, and he can persuade people. He can get things done. He was a man who would appreciate other peoples' capabilities. . . . I wanted somebody to direct people who could develop the ballistic missile. . . . *In other words I didn't want a Rickover in there."* (Emphasis added)

Then, Burke went a step further and gave Raborn a letter of extraordinary authority, what became known as Raborn's "hunting license." It was Burke's personal endorsement of the FBM and Raborn—"I gave Admiral Raborn this letter because there was a lot of opposition within the Navy too—not opposition—there was a lot of difference of opinion. A lot of people thought this cannot be done . . . so I gave Admiral Raborn this letter and said to other people: 'Give this man what he wants and we'll restrict him to fifty people—fifty managers—fifty people directly under him. He can choose anybody he wants but he can't have very many, and that was to keep it small, so that each one of those people would be good or would be contributing.' "

And, said Burke, "I also told him, in the same letter, that there are many cutoff points on this thing—many things that you have to do—that you have to be able to do. If you reach a stage where you cannot do this thing, we will kill the project."

Raborn rapidly organized a highly effective and, for the time, highly innovative management team. In 1957 then-Captain Levering Smith became technical director. Smith was a Naval Academy graduate who had specialized in ordnance engineering and had extensive experience with missiles and rockets. (In 1965 he became head of the Special Projects Office and held that post for the next twelve years.)

The Special Projects Office immediately made it clear that the Navy would switch to a solid propellant as soon as technology permitted. The Army saw no threat to its liquid-fueled Jupiter missile, because most experts felt solid fuels were not practical for the foreseeable future. Reportedly, no less an authority than Wernher von Braun, the famed German rocket engineer who was now working with the Jupiter team, was quoted as saying that the farthest east that the Navy could hope to strike with a solid-fuel missile fired from the Atlantic coast of Europe would be the Simplon railway tunnel in Switzerland, a very improbable target for the U.S. Navy.

With Raborn heading the Navy team, the Army-Navy cooperation was excellent. The Army even changed the Jupiter's dimensions to ease shipboard handling. The Navy's Bureau of Ships was requested to develop plans for converting the relatively fast, 22-knot *Mariner*-class commercial cargo ships to carry the Jupiter and to "consider" the feasibility of designing a submarine to carry the missile. The missile—called Jupiter-S in its naval version—was initially 44 feet high and 120 inches in diameter and would weigh some 80 tons. (The earliest Polaris missile was only 28½ feet long, 54 inches in diameter, and weighed 15 tons.)

The Bureau of Ships, looking into the design of a nuclear-propelled submarine to carry the Jupiter, estimated that to carry four of the missiles a submarine would have to displace about 8,500 tons. This was more than twice the size of the *Nautilus* and *Seawolf*.

According to AEC historians Hewlett and Duncan, "under unwritten orders from Admiral Burke," Raborn and Rear Admiral Mumma, the Chief of BuShips, "excluded Rickover from all the preliminary studies." All three officers believed that Rickover's participation at such an early stage would lead to his domination of Polaris and threaten the excellent relationship that Raborn had with BuShips.

During the summer of 1956, the Atomic Energy Commission, noting that the Navy was the only service taking advantage of small-warhead development for missiles, estimated that even smaller nuclear warheads, compatible with a solid-propellant FBM, could be available by 1965—and possibly as early as 1963. The Jupiter's nuclear warhead weighed 1,600 pounds. The warheads being developed by AEC would be only a fraction as heavy, about 600 pounds, also with an explosive force of one megaton, the equivalent of one million tons of TNT.*

Because solid propellants had less thrust than comparable liquid fuels, the smaller warheads would be needed for the FBM. This meant a timetable of nine years—or just possibly seven—for Raborn's team to develop the missile and build the launching ships and, possibly, submarines.

With this timetable and warhead forecast, Levering Smith's ordnance experts felt that they could develop an FBM with a range of 1,000 to 1,500 miles. Actually, the lesser range was too short to strike Moscow—the "centroid" of all targeting studies—and many other key targets.

In August 1956, the Navy ended its participation in the Army's Jupiter program. Raborn and Smith were now going for the ultimate—a solid propellant missile that would be launched from a submarine. Late in 1956, Secretary of the Navy Charles S. Thomas reaffirmed the highest Navy priorities for the FBM, now named Polaris for the star constellation. Significantly, Thomas assigned the Special Projects Office responsi-

---

* By comparison, the atom bomb dropped on Hiroshima weighed 8,900 pounds and was the equivalent of 13,000 tons of TNT (13 kilotons); the Nagasaki bomb weighed 10,800 pounds and produced a 23-kiloton explosion.

bility for the entire FBM "system," including the submarines. Previously, the development of any kind of Navy ship or submarine had been the responsibility of the Bureau of Ships and its predecessor technical bureaus. Now the Special Projects Office would have over-all direction of the design and construction of FBM submarines, while using BuShips' technical sections to perform the actual work.

The mission of the Polaris FBM was spelled out in a then-classified study, "Introduction of the Fleet Ballistic Missile into Service," which stated: "A small FBM capability will permit penetration of the limited number of targets, such as Moscow, whose defenses will be difficult to penetrate with other weapons. . . . Very highly defended population or industrial targets should be specified by CNO as the target of the initial FBM capability. A large fraction of the targets of naval interest are more suitably attacked by aircraft, or air-breathing missiles. . . ."

Finally, the study spelled out a planned 1965 force to consist of six FBM submarines, each with three to ten missiles, with a goal of keeping two or three submarines at sea simultaneously from 1963 onward.

By the spring of 1957, Special Projects—in collaboration with the preliminary-design section of BuShips—had developed the basic characteristics of a submarine to carry the solid-propellant Polaris missile: submerged displacement of some 6,500 tons, an over-all length of 350 feet, a hull diameter of 32 feet, with a modified-*Albacore* design and a single propeller shaft.

The submarine would be able to carry *sixteen* Polaris missiles. With a warhead of almost a megaton in each missile, this would mean that a single submarine would have a destructive power equivalent to that of all the conventional explosives used by all sides during the entire Second World War. The missiles would be stowed in a vertical position within the submarine—like a forest of missile tubes. This would permit some at-sea maintenance on them.

Members of the Special Projects Office told the authors how the number of missiles per submarine had been derived. Some planners wanted as many as possible—16, 20, 24, or even more; for each missile added there would be a relatively small proportionate increase in the submarine's size and cost. Others felt that there were limits, possibly not too finite, as to how many missiles could be crammed into a reasonably sized submarine and still leave room for the power plant, living space, control equipment, ballast tanks, fire-control and navigation systems, and a thousand other items. The deadlock was reportedly solved when everyone concerned wrote the number of missiles he wanted on a scrap of paper. These were then added up and divided by the number of participants in the poll. The answer was sixteen.

Admiral Rickover's first official exposure to the Polaris submarine design came on April 16, 1957, when the Naval Reactors Branch in Bu-Ships formally received the submarine's description. The documents said the submarines would be nuclear-propelled, have an advanced hull design, and thus have a single screw, with a specified submerged speed. The S5W plant being developed for the new *Skipjack* and *Thresher* classes would be suitable for the submarine.

Rickover objected to the single screw for FBM submarines. He declared that the submarines would be too large and too important to rely on a single propeller shaft. Rickover wanted the submarine to have two screws. To many involved in the Polaris program, this was Rickover's first effort to gain influence in the development of Polaris. The only twin-screw nuclear plant that could be applied to Polaris submarines was the twin-reactor plant of the *Triton,* which was not yet launched. If applied to the Polaris submarine, the *Triton* plant would significantly increase the submarine's size and cost. If a new twin-screw plant was initiated for the Polaris program, Rickover would gain immense influence in the program. One of Rickover's key supporters in the ensuing debate was Rear Admiral John T. Hayward, just appointed to the new post of Assistant CNO for Development.

The Submarine Warfare Branch (OP-311) had recently decided that the single-screw S5W plant was suitable for attack submarines and did not want to reopen that issue. The decision held that Polaris would have the one-screw plant. (A single-screw submarine would have an "outboard" emergency propeller rod that could be cranked down in an emergency for a "come home" capability.)

Rickover apparently did gain one concession. The requirement for the Polaris submarines to operate under the arctic ice pack was deleted from their characteristics. (Two years later, however, Rickover would still tell a Congressional committee that the Polaris submarines "will be able to hide out under the polar icecap.")

During this period, Burke was financing the Polaris program entirely out of existing Navy budgets. At the same time, he was fighting for continued construction of nuclear attack submarines and funds for the Navy's first nuclear-propelled surface warships. Burke's task became more urgent when, on August 3, 1957, a Soviet SS-6 missile rocketed several thousand miles from its launch pad to impact in Siberia. Five weeks later, the Soviets orbited Sputnik, the first artificial earth satellite.

The White House and Congress expressed great concern about this evidence of a potential Soviet leadership in strategic arms. Politically, these events became the basis of the "missile gap" issue in the 1960 Presidential campaign.

Less than three weeks after Sputnik, in response to White House interest in accelerating U.S. strategic programs, Secretary of the Navy Thomas S. Gates put forward a plan drawn up by Burke and Raborn that proposed accelerating Polaris so that the first submarine would be at sea by December 1960 with a 1,200-nautical-mile missile. The AEC estimated that a suitable warhead could be available by 1960. Under Gates's proposal, two more Polaris submarines could be ready by 1962 and a 1,500-mile missile by mid-1963, instead of 1965.

But could a Polaris submarine be built in just two years? And another full year would be required for sea trials and missile tests. The *Skate*-class submarines, smaller and less complicated, were taking two and a half years to build. Engineers at Electric Boat did not believe that a new missile submarine could be built in so short a time. But could an existing submarine design, already under construction, be modified to carry Polaris?

On the building ways at Electric Boat was the hull of the third submarine of the *Skipjack* class, the U.S.S. *Scorpion,* which had been laid down on November 1, 1957. On the drawing boards, the 252-foot *Scorpion* was cut in half and lengthened by adding a midsection a fraction under 130 feet: forty-five feet were added to provide space for navigation and missile-control equipment, then a 75-foot section for the two rows of eight missile tubes, and another 10 feet for auxiliary machinery. The additions would make the submarine not quite 382 feet in length. Submerged displacement would be 6,700 tons.

On December 20, Secretary of Defense Neil McElroy approved the acceleration of the Polaris program to put the first operational submarine to sea by the end of 1960. Then, using funds "borrowed" from other programs, on the last day of 1960 the Navy reordered the *Scorpion* and a not-yet-started attack submarine at Electric Boat as Polaris submarines; they were later to be named *George Washington* and *Patrick Henry,* respectively. Not until the following February 12 did President Eisenhower sign the appropriations act that funded the three Polaris submarines. A month later, the third submarine was ordered from the Mare Island Naval Shipyard in California. The fiscal year 1959 budget, which took effect on July 1, 1958, funded another six Polaris submarines, but only three could be ordered in the summer of 1958, one each of the *George*

Washington design from Newport News and Portsmouth, and one improved submarine, the larger *Ethan Allen,* from Electric Boat.

Thus, by the summer of 1958 six ballistic missile submarines, or SSBNs in Navy parlance, were being built. This provided the base for further Polaris expansion into a strategic force.

Strategically, forty-five to fifty SSBNs would be needed to keep some thirty submarines "on station," at sea with their missiles targeted against the Soviet Union. The number forty-five had been developed in OPNAV through an analysis of the demographic and industrial centers of the Soviet Union. The studies also determined various submarine deployment schedules, basing sites and overhaul cycles.

Because SSBNs enjoyed the highest naval and national priorities, construction of attack submarines slowed down—as did construction of the giant radar picket *Triton,* whose future was now in question, for the radar picket submarine was no longer in vogue.

Equal priority was being given to the Polaris missile. The first Polaris test firing from Cape Canaveral occurred on September 24, 1958. The missile failed and had to be destroyed early in flight. Three weeks later a second Polaris was test-fired. It too failed. On December 30, the third Polaris was fired. It failed. On January 19, 1959, the fourth test Polaris was fired. It failed. On February 27 the fifth test Polaris was launched. It broke apart shortly after leaving the ground. Not until April 20, 1959, was the sixth Polaris test missile able to make the first successful flight.

Burke, Raborn, Smith, and others running the program were upset but not discouraged. They knew their work was sound, but they were rushing the program, probably at a rate faster than any other major advanced weapon development since the atomic bomb a decade and a half earlier.

Although Burke had hoped to keep Rickover out of the decision-making process for Polaris, the Naval Reactors Branch was inevitably drawn into the submarine construction program. And, of course, Rickover—using his AEC hat to ensure that safety considerations were always foremost in the minds of Polaris submarine skippers—became involved in Polaris personnel selection and training. Further, each submarine would have two complete crews, designated "blue" and "gold." While one crew would be at sea for a sixty-day patrol, the other would be on leave or in training in the United States. Then, when the submarine came in, the crews would switch, and the submarine could rapidly return to sea.

The first three Polaris skippers, named in late 1958, were Commanders James B. Osborn, Harold E. Shear and William E. Sims. All had been submariners during World War II, but none had served in nuclear submarines. Coming into the nuclear program as commanders, they were rather senior members of the submarine community, and now they would become nucs, the winning combination for flag selection. Osborn eventually reached rear admiral and Shear full admiral.

Meanwhile, their submarines were being rushed to completion. The *George Washington* was christened at Groton on June 9, 1959. At the ceremonies, Wilfred J. McNeil, an Assistant Secretary of Defense, noted that the submarine "incorporates into a single weapon system most of the great scientific developments which have so revolutionized warfare—the nuclear warhead, the ballistic missile, nuclear propulsion, inertial guidance for navigation, as well as radical developments in hull design and ship control." The submarine, he continued, "adds an entirely new dimension to our naval power."

This was from an official of the Eisenhower Administration, which was refusing to spend the funds for three additional Polaris submarines voted by Congress in the fiscal 1959 budget, and which had asked for no additional FBM submarine construction in the fiscal 1960 budget. Meanwhile, the Navy was discussing a goal of some forty missile submarines, and considering the installing of Polaris missiles in surface warships.

Finally, in July 1959, the Administration gave the Navy permission to build the three more, already funded submarines; one was ordered from Electric Boat and two from Newport News. The following January, presenting his final defense budget to the Congress, the President requested three Polaris submarines for fiscal 1961 for a total of twelve FBM submarines. Again there were charges of a "missile gap," and Burke, questioned by Congress, said that six submarines could be built in 1961 and then the Navy could produce one Polaris boat per month starting in 1962. Congress voted funds for five more Polaris submarines instead of the three requested.

The *George Washington* began her test firings of Polaris missiles in July 1960. Two missiles were fired on July 18 as the submarine cruised submerged off the Florida coast. Moments after the second, Admiral Raborn sent a message to the White House: POLARIS—FROM OUT OF THE DEEP TO TARGET. PERFECT.

The *George Washington* went to sea on the first Polaris "deterrent patrol" on November 15, 1960, steaming in the Norwegian-Barents Sea area with sixteen nuclear-tipped missiles. Before 1960 was over she was joined at sea by the *Patrick Henry* with another sixteen missiles.

As these submarines were being completed, President Eisenhower suspended the law that limited the number of full admirals and vice admirals that the Navy could have and, at the recommendation of the Secretary of the Navy and CNO, promoted Raborn to three-star rank.

On January 20, 1961, the Democrats returned to the White House. John F. Kennedy, the onetime torpedo-boat skipper, was in the executive mansion less than two weeks when he approved the immediate construction of the five Polaris submarines Congress had voted earlier. Then, in his budget request, Kennedy asked for another ten Polaris submarines for fiscal year 1962. These would boost Polaris strength to twenty-nine boats. The last nine would be of the *Lafayette* class, larger than the earlier boats, and deeper-diving.

Also, development was accelerated on more advanced missiles. The Polaris A-2, with a range of 1,500 nautical miles, became operational in 1962, followed by the Polaris A-3 in 1964. The latter missile had multiple warheads. As the missile flew toward its target, three separate "bombs" would be dispensed to strike in a cluster at a single target to inflict damage over a larger area and compensate for shortcomings in accuracy.

During the Kennedy-McNamara Administration, ballistic missiles had a high priority, in part as compensation for a cutback in U.S. bomber programs (including aircraft carriers) and the Air Force's land-based strategic cruise missiles. The fiscal 1962 budget provided ten submarines, fiscal 1963 another six, and fiscal 1964 six. Secretary of Defense McNamara held the program to forty-one submarines carrying 656 missiles. All named for "famous Americans" (including one native Hawaiian and one South American), the last of the forty-one submarines was completed in 1967.

Secretary NcNamara explained his holding at forty-one submarines in terms of seeking a "mix" of Polaris missiles and the new, solid-propellant Air Force Minuteman ICBM, twenty of which were in place by the end of 1962. "If there were no cost differential," McNamara said, "I think we would probably select more Polaris because it is probably at least in the short run more invulnerable than Minuteman."

By 1967, when the last Polaris and Minuteman missiles were deployed, the term "Triad" was evolving to describe the U.S. strategic deterrent forces: submarine missiles, land-based ICBMs, and land-based manned bombers.

The Polaris program was a remarkable "peacetime" construction effort—forty-one submarines in seven and a half years. More remarkable was the short development time for the solid-propellant missile and the many components of the Polaris FBM system.

The construction program caused delays in the attack-submarine effort, with four of the seven submarine construction yards building both types. But despite charges to the contrary by Rickover and others, the authorization of attack submarines did not suffer too greatly because of the FBM program. For example, during the seven-year period that the forty-one Polaris submarines were funded by Congress, an additional thirty-one attack submarines were voted. During the next seven years (fiscal 1965–1971) with no FBM submarines to draw off funds, only twenty-nine attack boats were authorized.

From the viewpoint of what had become the nuc community, the Polaris boats added more prestige, responsibility, and people to the Naval Reactor Branch's empire. A *Thresher*-class submarine had a crew of 12 officers and 108 enlisted men; a Polaris submarine had two crews, each with some 13 to 15 officers and 130 to 140 enlisted men. Polaris submarine skippers were generally commanders, a grade senior to the attack-submarine skippers. And all commanding officers would be nucs. Thus, through the men who would take the strategic-missile submarines to sea, Rickover would gain influence over the Polaris and its successors—even though Admirals Burke, Raborn, Mumma, James (who succeeded Mumma as Chief of BuShips in 1959) and others had stopped Rickover from having a major influence during the initial development of the FBM program.

Rickover had made major efforts to gain influence, if not control, on at least three occasions. First, there was the question of developing a new, twin-screw plant for the submarines. Next, when the second class of SSBNs was about to go to sea, led by the *Ethan Allen* in 1961, Rickover expressed concern over the adequacy of the testing of valves and other components of the new submarines. He recommended that the boats be limited to less than their designed operating depth until there was more diving experience with the *Thresher,* also completed in 1961, the first of the deep-diving submarines.

A late-night meeting in the Pentagon was recalled by one officer who attended; the participants included Admirals Burke, James, Rickover and perhaps a dozen other officers from their staffs. Finally, after a lengthy debate, Burke said that he had "had enough" and would announce his decision the next morning. The next day, Saturday, in his office, Burke expressed his confidence in the recommendations of James and Rear Admiral Armand Morgan, head of ship design in BuShips, and the *Ethan Allen* was cleared to operate at her full-depth capability.

The third effort by Rickover to influence the development of Polaris came with the speedup of the SSBN construction rate in the early 1960s. Each submarine required two large crews—simply too many men to be processed by Rickover's time-consuming interviewing of officers and key enlisted men. Several times the Ballistic Missile Committee—whose members included the Secretary of the Navy and key assistants to the CNO—tried to get the question of SSBN personnel selection and training on the committee's agenda. Rickover objected, usually at the last minute, and managed to get the Secretary to have the subject dropped. Finally the Vice CNO, Admiral James Russell, who when Chief of the Bureau of Aeronautics had been an early FBM supporter, personally took on the issue and succeeded in getting Rickover to speed up the selection process and stop trying to have a direct impact on the submarine production schedule.

One is inevitably drawn into comparisons of the nuclear-propulsion program under Rickover and the Polaris project under Raborn, and the styles of their leaders. But such comparisons have limited meaning and value. The nuclear-propulsion effort did have high-level Navy backing from the outset. Both Vice Admiral Mills and General Groves, through January 1947, when the Manhattan Project was succeeded by the Atomic Energy Commission, gave full support to nuclear propulsion. Subsequently, Chiefs of Naval Operations, beginning with Admiral Nimitz— largely through the efforts of Commanders Beach and Grenfell—also backed the project. Still, the nuclear-propulsion effort was undertaken without any national priorities and during a period of fiscal austerity in the Defense establishment, especially in the Navy.

In sharp contrast, Polaris was brought to fruition in large measure because of national priorities for accelerating the development of strategic weapons. Within the Navy, Raborn had the immediate and personal confidence of the Secretary of the Navy and the Chief of Naval Operations. Burke and later CNOs suffered Rickover's authoritarian role, his untouchable Navy-AEC bureaucracy and, always, his direct Congressional influence.

If Polaris is to be compared with any modern technical effort, it must be compared with the Manhattan Project to develop the atomic bomb and, to a lesser extent, the national space program that landed a man on the moon in 1969. All three had in common the driving force of

Presidential support, the prestige of top national priorities, and sufficient funding (Polaris at least in its later stages) to ensure that, with astute leadership, they would be successful.

A more practical and more important way to compare the nuclear-propulsion and Polaris efforts is to note what happened to them after the development process was completed. When Polaris was ready for sea in 1960, it became a part of the fleet. Although the Special Projects Office continued to direct development of the improved Polaris A-2, A-3, and then Poseidon missiles, such activities as Polaris crew training, submarine modernization, justification for further missile development, and port visits were the responsibilities of the CNO staff, the Bureau of Ships and its successors, and the fleet commanders. Indeed, Raborn left the program in 1962, and was relieved by a submarine officer, Rear Admiral I. J. Galantin.

Rickover—who in theory at least was responsible only for the nuclear plant—continued to exercise major control over all nuclear-propelled ships and submarines on an institutional and personal basis. Crew selection and training, design, construction and overhaul of nuclear ships remained activities under the overall jurisdiction of the Naval Reactors Branch, in fact if not in formal charter.

Raborn was not a technical specialist but a seagoing line officer, used to solving problems with organization, management, and even that nebulous trait "leadership." He knew how to get along with people and inspire them to reach a goal. He made E awards for excellence to contractors who met or exceeded requirements, and called all participants together to brief them on the total picture and how important each part was.

Rickover opposed all such recognition—of individuals or firms. He often told Congress how the Polaris program "handed out several hundred awards to private firms for the 'fine job' that had been done in the Polaris program. I happened to be at one of the companies that was late in delivering equipment to the Navy and in general doing a poor job for the United States."

Never identifying the firm, Rickover continued, "On the wall I saw the plaque they were awarded for their work in the Polaris program. I found out later that a secretary in the Navy office had contacted the public-relations man of that company: between the two of them they decided that the award was in order. This incident gives you an insight of how such awards are made."

In reality, all such awards were personally approved by the head of

Special Projects. More important, Special Projects—through hundreds of contractors—delivered the Polaris submarines and missiles several years ahead of the initial schedules. Rickover's nuclear-propulsion program could not claim such a record. Indeed, one could probably argue that, except for the Polaris submarines, no nuclear-powered ship was ever delivered earlier than scheduled, and most were delivered later.

Raborn also developed a management tool known as PERT—for Program Evaluation and Review Technique—which was a series of spider-web networks showing when each part and component of the system came together with all the others. After Raborn and his key officers visited many corporations, they devised PERT as a means of demonstrating the importance of each item (and the person making it) to the overall Polaris program.

Rickover later observed, "Not too long ago the PERT system had a vogue in government and industry. . . . Nothing is heard of it today. A political scientist analyzing the Polaris program concluded after several interviews that PERT was a sham. It was simply used to get political and financial support." In a way, PERT was a sham. The political scientist referred to by Rickover discovered that "PERT did not build Polaris, but it was extremely helpful for those who did build the weapon system to have many people believe that it did."

Raborn, like Rickover, had to invent his own "system" to get Polaris built. But Raborn demonstrated that a complex, large, expensive and successful Navy program could be developed within the "Navy system."

The Soviet Threat

Admiral Rickover once told Congress that his discussion of the Soviet threat was the most important portion of his testimony—"information to enlighten the committee beyond what you will get from ... the intelligence people." Rickover's earlier testimony to Congress, in the 1950s, was almost devoid of discussion of the Soviet threat. Generally, he spoke of his programs and the capabilities of the nuclear-propelled submarines that he was building. Like most admirals testifying before Congress, he left descriptions of the Soviet threat to the intelligence specialists. But there was often some reference to reports that the Soviets were building nuclear submarines and more definite information that a nuclear ice-breaker was being built.

By the 1960s Rickover's testimony included more discussions of the Soviet threat, with increasingly detailed information on their surface ships and submarines. One found that his testimony on the subject was often better organized, more comprehensive, and more detailed than that of the Director of Naval Intelligence. And there were the more personal observations from his single visit to the Soviet Union and his limited discussions with Soviet officials.

There were probably several reasons for the increased attention Rickover gave to the Soviets. First, as most defensive advocates found, describing enemy progress was an effective means of "selling" one's own program; second, the Soviets were constructing nuclear submarines as well as the icebreaker *Lenin* by the late 1950s; and third, Rickover's trip to the Soviet Union with Vice President Nixon in 1959 established him in the eyes of many in Congress and the press as an expert on the Soviet Union.

Rickover's trip to the Soviet Union and Poland had its beginnings in an earlier trip by American industrialists to the Soviet Union, which in-

552

cluded a visit to the Admiralty shipyard at Leningrad where the *Lenin* was under construction. The Americans invited the Soviets to send a return delegation to visit shipyards in the United States.

The Russians arrived in June 1959, led by First Deputy Premier F. R. Kozlov. The Soviet delegation included Andrei Tupolev, top Soviet aircraft designer and a favorite of Party Chairman Khrushchev. Kozlov visited the New York Shipbuilding yard at Camden, New Jersey, where the nuclear-powered freighter *Savannah* was under construction.

In his purported autobiography, *Khrushchev Remembers,* the Soviet leader described Kozlov's visit to the unfinished *Savannah*: "He managed to crawl around inside it and examine it thoroughly. Naturally, the Americans showed us only what they wanted us to see, but Kozlov told me our engineers nonetheless noticed a number of interesting things." Kozlov also visited the newly opened atomic-power station at Shippingport, Pennsylvania. He was guided through Shippingport by Rickover.

During an exchange at Shippingport, Rickover told Kozlov that he was a submariner and involved in building nuclear submarines, to which Kozlov responded: "It would be better to build atomic surface vessels rather than atomic submarines because atomic submarines are for the purpose of destruction."

Rickover quickly responded, "Sure, all Soviet naval vessels have doves of peace on their masts."

Kozlov carried back to Moscow the invitation from Eisenhower to Khrushchev to visit the United States later in the year.

Rickover's trip to Russia and Poland in July of 1959 came at short notice as the Eisenhower Administration decided that the Polish-born admiral could demonstrate the opportunities of America, while also providing a well-known technical representative to Nixon's party, as Tupolev had done for Kozlov's visit. Rickover later described himself as "Mr. Nixon's scientific adviser when he visited Russia."

In Leningrad, the Nixon party was escorted to the Admiralty shipyard on Galernyi Island. There the Russians proudly showed Nixon and Rickover their still-building icebreaker *Lenin*, which would displace over 19,000 tons full load when completed. The Americans' one-hour tour of the ship did not include the three-reactor power plant.

Rickover protested. He wanted to see as much of the ship as Kozlov had been shown of the *Savannah* and of Shippingport. The Russians refused. After the Russians debated the matter, Kozlov, who was accompanying Nixon, agreed, and Rickover spent almost two hours inspecting the ship. "I got to see everything I wanted to see," Rickover told American reporters with the Nixon party. "The manager of the shipyard asked if I was satisfied and I replied, 'No, but I am pleased. I am never satisfied.' "

While Rickover crawled through the *Lenin*'s engineering spaces, the remainder of the Nixon party visited the former tsarist palace at nearby Petrodvorets. Rickover subsequently told reporters, "I believe I was the first American ever to have been to the *Lenin*'s engine rooms.

"I don't think it is any more advanced than our reactors," he continued. After listing the size of the comparative United States nuclear-ship program, Rickover added: "I think they realize that we are far ahead of them in the production of atomic-powered vessels."

Telling how the Russian engineers had answered his questions freely once he had permission to see the nuclear plant, Rickover observed, "I think they have done a fine and creditable job. The equipment is good, and although it is difficult to estimate its efficiency at this stage, the design is adequate for their purposes." (But a decade later, telling a Senate committee about his tour of the *Lenin*, Rickover would remark that the *Lenin*'s engineering plant "was a sloppy job.")

The *Lenin* went to sea on trials two months after Rickover's visit. The icebreaker, the world's largest at the time, was the world's first nuclear surface ship and the first ship to get under way with a multireactor plant. (The two-reactor *Triton* went to sea fifteen days later, on September 29, 1959.)

The Soviets had not yet displayed a nuclear-propelled submarine, but the *Lenin*'s reactors—which Rickover described as "similar to those we use in our naval units"—were a clear indication of the direction in which the Soviets were moving. Upon his return to the United States, Rickover immediately directed a clamp-down in BuShips of all information being released about U.S. naval reactors, criticized technical journals for giving away information, and scolded toy manufacturers for producing realistic models of U.S. nuclear submarines. In the opinion of one BuShips official, "Rickover felt their nuclear plants were too similar to ours."

Less than a month after visiting the *Lenin*, Rickover appeared at a special hearing before the House Appropriations Committee to describe his trip. Most of the lengthy session was spent on education. (See Chapter 27.) A day earlier, on August 17, Arleigh Burke had begun his fifth year as CNO with a news conference announcing that the Soviets had ballistic-missile submarines that could strike the United States with nuclear-tipped missiles. These were primitive Polaris-type weapons—which the United States was still developing—but with a shorter range. The submarines that carried these missiles were identified as being nonnuclear, diesel-electric craft.

Burke also said that he believed the Soviet Union was constructing nuclear-powered submarines. At the time the United States had four nuclear submarines in service (plus the *Seawolf* in the yard having her sodium reactor replaced), and a large number under construction. Rickover's comments before the special House hearing touched only briefly on submarines, and no reference was made to Burke's comments of the day before. The exchange on submarines was brief. Representative Phillip Weaver asked, "From your observations what progress have the Russians made, compared to ours, in the field of atomic submarine propulsion?"

Rickover responded, "I think unquestionably we are ahead of them. I dislike saying this because I am responsible for naval atomic propulsion, but as far as we know, the only marine propulsion plant they have is in the *Lenin,* and it has not yet operated at sea. We have had naval plants operating since 1953. Mr. Kozlov, when he was in the United States in July, told me that they are building atomic-powered submarines." The next comment began, "Getting back to the question of education . . ."

As Rickover spoke about Soviet education, the Soviets were completing their first nuclear-propelled submarine, which would be labeled "N," or November class, by Western intelligence. The nuclear submarine had its origins about 1947, according to Soviet sources. While the Soviets cite 1953 as the actual start of nuclear-submarine construction, it is not publicly known when the first November was actually laid down or launched. But the lead submarine was apparently completed sometime in 1959—four years after the *Nautilus.*

The November is a torpedo-armed SSN, approximately 360 feet in length and displacing about 4,500 tons submerged, significantly larger than the *Nautilus.* Like the *Nautilus* design, the November has a single pressurized-water reactor with steam turbines turning two propeller shafts. Early U.S. Navy intelligence estimates apparently gave the November a speed of just over twenty knots, somewhat similar to the speed of the *Nautilus.* But later observations indicated a submerged speed of at least twenty-five knots. This meant that the November's nuclear plant produces more than the approximately 15,000 horsepower of the *Nautilus* plant.

Perhaps the most significant aspect of the initial Soviet nuclear-submarine program was its size. Whereas the *Nautilus* and subsequent *Seawolf* were one-of-a-kind submarines, followed after a brief interval by the four-submarine *Skate* class, and then several more one-of-a-kind ships, the Soviets immediately began series production of three different classes of nuclear submarines. The fourteen November-class SSNs were completed by 1965; almost simultaneously came eight nuclear Hotel-class submarines, each carrying three short-range (300-mile) ballistic missiles in addition to torpedoes, while other yards were producing the first of thirty-four Echo-class nuclear submarines armed with anti-ship guided missiles.

By 1965 the Soviets had more than forty of these nuclear submarines at sea. The United States, spurred on by the Polaris program priority, had completed twenty-three attack and thirty-three Polaris submarines with nuclear propulsion, plus almost the same number of both categories under construction.

However, despite this apparent U.S. leadership in numbers of nuclear undersea craft, earlier in 1965 Marshal Vasily Sokolovsky, former chief of the Soviet general staff and a leading strategist, declared that there was virtual parity in the two nuclear submarine fleets. "We have no fewer of them," he said at a Moscow news conference in February 1965. "The difference may be one or two." This may have more accurately been an indication of the number of nuclear submarines at sea *and* under construction.

The Soviets could also boast that one of their November-class SSNs, the *Leninsky Komsomol,* reached the North Pole in the summer of 1962. Under the command of Captain 1/rank Lev Zhiltsov, the submarine successfully surfaced at the North Pole. The Soviet press reported that the submarine maneuvered under the Arctic ice "to detect and destroy 'enemy' nuclear submarines trying to approach Soviet shores." After the voyage, Khrushchev himself is said to have decorated Zhiltsov as a Hero of the Soviet Union in ceremonies at Murmansk on the arctic coast. Subsequently, the Soviets reported that another submarine of the November class remained submerged for almost fifty consecutive days while steaming some twenty-five thousand miles—a sustained speed of almost twenty knots. And in early 1966, a "group" of nuclear submarines was reported to have made a circumnavigation cruise, submerged. Those submarines sailed almost 25,000 miles without surfacing, "crossed the equator several times, sailed around South America, and visited Antarctic waters," according to Soviet statements.

Despite Soviet claims and accomplishments, American naval leaders in the early 1960s had mixed feelings about the Soviet nuclear-submarine effort. First, it was always useful to point to the Soviet threat—and nuclear submarines were definitely a threat—when asking for funds from Congress. Burke in 1961 spoke to Congress about "how it is going to be real rough" to build defenses against Soviet nuclear submarines, while his successor, Admiral George W. Anderson, in discussing Soviet nuclear submarines declared, "I only wish that I could say to you, 'Don't worry. We have it licked.' Regrettably, I cannot do so."

However, the other side of the coin was the attitude of American naval leaders that "ours are better." In late 1961, Anderson told a news conference that the Soviets were probably having "some problems" with their nuclear undersea craft and "it wouldn't surprise me if they lost some." In a similar vein, during the Cuban missile crisis in the fall of 1962, the Soviets operated six diesel-electric submarines in the Caribbean area and the U.S. anti-submarine forces were able to identify all of them and force some to come to the surface. This triumph, admittedly with no Soviet nuclear submarines in the area, and periodic engineering problems with their submarines, helped to influence the American perspective. Hanson W. Baldwin, the dean of American military writers, in a column in *The New York Times* in early 1963, began with, "Numerous breakdowns in Soviet submarines and the success of the Navy's detection methods have influenced in the last year United States estimates of Soviet submarine strength." Baldwin, a Naval Academy graduate, called the Cuban crisis a "deep sea laboratory" in which the U.S. Navy could test anti-submarine methods. He concluded by noting that "the Soviet Navy's primary role today still appears to be—as it was in the days of the Czars and for decades thereafter—a defensive role."

But Rickover consistently came down on the side of the Soviets being a threat—a valid threat to the West—with their nuclear submarines the most potent aspect of Soviet military power. This is not to say that Rickover perceived the Soviet efforts as being perfect. "The Russians apparently had a great deal of difficulty when their nuclear submarines first went to sea about 1958," he told a committee. Later Rickover would elaborate on the problems, saying, "There is reason to believe that the early classes of Soviet nuclear submarines may have experienced some technical difficulties in their nuclear power plants. This is inferred from the fact that the operations of these first-generation nuclear-powered submarines in the period 1960 to 1963 were generally limited to short-range excursions while invariably being accompanied by surface escort ships."

In April of 1970 the Soviets did lose a nuclear submarine, a November-class attack boat. She suffered propulsion failure off the coast of Spain. The submarine was able to surface and her entire crew apparently was removed to other ships before she plunged into the depths. Another nuclear submarine, a Hotel-class missile craft, also had propulsion problems in the North Atlantic in early 1972, but she was saved and was towed back to base, as was an Echo-class nuclear submarine in the Pacific in mid-1980. The pioneer *Lenin* also suffered a major radiation leak. Rumors persist that many crewmen had severe radiation exposure. She lay idle, "too hot" to board for several years. (The *Lenin* has since been returned to service.) The problem with the nuclear plants was overcome.

"They must have put a tremendous effort on solving this problem. . . . To accomplish this they have given nuclear submarine design and construction a very high priority—they made it a matter of national urgency," continued Rickover. This was the crux of Rickover's argument to Congress: The Soviets gave nuclear submarines their highest priority, and thus so should the United States. And, the increased priority for nuclear submarines must be carried out in the Rickover manner—with safety and the conservative approach being the principal guidelines.

By the middle 1960s there were intelligence indications of a new wave of Soviet submarine construction. On July 24, 1968, Rickover testified before the Joint Committee on Atomic Energy; his comments were heavily censored for security reasons: "Knowing something about the vast scope of submarine design and construction required . . . I consider this the most tremendous design effort undertaken in all of submarine history. . . ." And, as a portent of what was coming, Rickover added that "furthermore the Soviets have for some time had the largest nuclear submarine building and repair facilities in the world. . . . Yet, despite this, they continue to expand their facilities."

His next statement was in support of his own position: "What is our situation? For several years we have not been able to get permission to build even one new type submarine. The major reason for this is that our Defense Department Headquarters believe . . . that we are far ahead of the Russians qualitatively. . . ." He also declared, "Never since I have been in the Navy has so much of my time and that of my senior people been taken up by useless things as it has been by these numerous studies that have come out so frequently from the Department of Defense. . . . We have been subjected to this harassment for years by the Department of Defense and this is the chief reason we are falling so far behind in our technical work—why the Russians can get ahead of us."

When would the Russians get ahead? In 1968, he told the Joint

Committee: "Last year in testimony before Congress I stated that, in my opinion, the Soviet Union would surpass us in their nuclear submarines within five years. I still hold to this view, although I may have underestimated the Soviet advance."

In 1970–1971 the Soviet Union overtook the United States in numbers of nuclear submarines, each Navy having completed some ninety nuclear submarines of all types.* Soviet nuclear-submarine construction continued at an increasing rate, reaching a peak of seventeen nuclear boats being launched in 1970, after which the rate declined to a sustained level of approximately ten nuclear submarines per year plus a small number of diesel submarines. The major Soviet effort produced three separate types of submarines, with new designs being introduced in the late 1960s for the torpedo-attack (SSN), guided missile (SSGN), and ballistic missile (SSBN) roles.

The new Victor-class SSN was a high-speed submarine, significantly faster than the U.S. nuclear submarines built since the Skipjack class of almost a decade earlier. The Victor's thirty-knot-plus speed was probably not equaled until late 1976, when the first U.S. Los Angeles-class SSN went to sea. Production of the Charlie-class SSGN was undertaken simultaneously with the Victor. This was also a relatively fast submarine, carrying eight short-range missiles that could be fired against surface warships in addition to a large torpedo armament. These underwater-launched tactical missiles became a major concern for U.S. naval leaders.

The third new design to emerge in the late 1960s in series production was given the designation Yankee by Western intelligence. This was an SSBN, a strategic-missile submarine like the U.S. Polaris type. Greatly resembling its U.S. counterpart, the Yankee class had sixteen missiles, each carrying a large nuclear warhead, for attacking targets ashore.

Beyond three new production classes, about 1970 two other nuclear submarine designs emerged from Soviet yards (plus new diesel submarines). A guided-missile submarine dubbed Papa was launched at the inland Gorki yard while a low-lying, streamlined submarine called Alfa was launched at Leningrad's Sudomekh yard. Both the Papa and the Alfa obviously incorporated many new technologies and would be a long time undergoing trials and modifications.

As the Soviet nuclear force grew, Rickover observed that "there has not been an arms race; the Soviets have been running at full speed all by themselves." Addressing the technical characteristics of these subma-

---

* In 1971 the U.S. Navy also had 59 diesel-electric submarines in service and the Soviet Navy some 265 conventional submarines.

rines, Rickover observed that "Numerical superiority, however, does not tell the whole story. Weapon systems, speed, depth, detection devices, quietness of operation, and crew performance all make a significant contribution to the effectiveness of a submarine force. From what we have been able to learn during the past year, the Soviets have attained equality in a number of these characteristics, and superiority in some."

On another occasion, discussing the quality of Soviet submarines, Rickover quite bluntly expressed to a Congressional hearing the startling view that he would "rather have command of the Russian submarine force than the American submarine force." When an alarmed Senator asked him to explain his statement, Rickover said that he was making his choice on the basis of the number and types of submarines in the Soviet Navy. He then blurted out: "I am the longest-serving officer in the U.S. Navy qualified to command submarines. I am not just a technical person; I am qualified to command operating submarines." Again, the Admiral misspoke. What he said may have been technically correct in the 1930s, although he had never had a submarine command. In the 1970s as an engineering duty officer he was no longer qualified nor could he legally command a U.S. submarine.

An issue that continued to dog Rickover was that of the Soviet submariners—their "nucs"—their traditions and capabilities. On the eve of World War II the Soviet undersea fleet had been the largest, with some 180 submarines in September 1939 and over 200 when Germany invaded the Soviet Union in June 1941.* The performance of these submarines was very poor, in part because of the geographic limitations of the Baltic, with ice blocking them in winter and the Germans and Finns laying mines and erecting submarine barriers in summer. But poor leadership and training also limited the Soviet submariners.

In 1969, before a subcommittee of the House Committee on Appropriations, Rickover continued using the Soviet submarine threat as a key for unlocking Congressional support for his own programs. "As I emphasized earlier in my testimony, the rapidly increasing Soviet threat makes it essential that the United States get the new high-speed [SSN-688] class into the fleet as soon as possible."

The Soviet submarine threat was indeed increasing in the late 1960s with the Victor, Charlie and Yankee classes. Various improvements of each followed, with the Yankee's successors of the Delta series being the world's largest submarines when the first one went to sea in 1973. If these

---

* When the war began in Europe in September 1939 the German Navy had fifty-seven U-boats.

were the Soviet second generation, the long-delayed Alfa that had emerged from a covered building way at the Sudomekh yard in 1970 could be considered the third generation. The submarine is relatively small, only some 265 feet long with a displacement of about 4,200 tons, slightly larger than the older U.S.S. *Skipjack* design. The Alfa introduced many features to nuclear submarines: a high degree of automation permitting a crew of less than half that of other nuclear attack submarines; a titanium hull that gives her an operating depth estimated at some two thousand feet, much greater than any other combat submarine; and the fastest speed of any submarine in history—more than 40 knots submerged.

The first Alfa engaged in a long series of trials. There are reports that she was rebuilt at least once. Obviously, the incorporation of many advanced features in a single hull was difficult. But by the late 1970s the Soviets were sufficiently confident in the Alfa to order series production of the design. At least a dozen Alfa SSNs were being completed by 1980.

Also in 1980 the Soviet Navy was building a new guided-missile submarine with nuclear propulsion, the Oscar, and after completing almost seventy Yankee/Delta SSBNs—compared to the U.S. production of forty-one comparable Polaris undersea craft—launched the first of a new class of giant strategic-missile submarines called the *Tuyfun* (or "Typhoon"). This submarine had a submerged displacement of almost 30,000 tons, dwarfing even the U.S. Navy's Trident missile submarines, which are 18,700 tons. This latest Soviet SSBN has twenty missile tubes.

When the first Typhoon was launched, the Soviets had exceeded the missile submarines permitted under the then-defunct but still observed SALT I agreement. Older Yankee submarines were being converted to attack boats, but the Red Navy could still claim sixty-three modern submarines in service with over 950 missiles; in comparison, in 1980 the U.S. Navy began dismantling the oldest Polaris submarines, so that by mid-1981 the Americans had only thirty-one SSBNs with 496 missiles.

In telling Congress about Soviet advances, Rickover said, "The Soviets continue to make rapid progress in the design and construction of nuclear submarines in particular, as well as the rapid expansion and improved capabilities of their surface combatant fleet. As a student of naval history, I am concerned that there has never in peacetime been anything comparable to the current growth of Russian naval power."

Rickover's emphasis on Soviet submarines was significant, for the Soviet Navy had long delayed the construction of nuclear surface ships. After the pioneer nuclear icebreaker *Lenin* was built, no more such vessels appeared for a decade and a half. In the 1970s the Soviets produced two larger nuclear icebreakers, one of which, the *Arktika,* on August 17, 1977, became history's first surface ship to reach the North Pole. A short time afterward, the Baltic yard, which had built the later icebreakers, launched the nuclear-powered battle cruiser *Kirov.* At 23,000 tons, the *Kirov* is the largest surface warship constructed by any nation since World War II, except for aircraft carriers. By comparison, the *Long Beach* was a 17,000-ton cruiser, while later U.S. nuclear cruisers reached a maximum size of 11,000 tons. And, reported under construction at Nikolayev near the Black Sea is an aircraft carrier of perhaps 60,000 tons, also nuclear propelled.

The Soviet naval effort has been impressive from a viewpoint of surface ships as well as submarines. A major factor—in some respects the most important—in this Soviet effort has been the same as in the U.S. Navy's nuclear program: the continuity of leadership. Admiral of the Fleet of the Soviet Union Sergei Gorshkov has been commander in chief of the Navy and a deputy minister of defense since January 1956. He had been specifically chosen by Khrushchev, who had met Gorshkov in the Black Sea region during World War II. Gorshkov can be credited with building the Soviet Navy in the past two and a half decades.

Unlike Rickover, Gorshkov is not a technological manager. His interests and responsibilities are broader, encompassing the entire Soviet Navy. Thus, whereas Rickover concerns himself with nuclear ships and their crews, with only passing interest in their actual operations and the remainder of the Navy, Gorshkov must be concerned with every ship, all naval personnel, and all naval operations plus the multitude of systems and activities related to them.

At the technical level it is difficult to identify a "father" of the Soviet nuclear-propulsion effort. The dean of Soviet submarine designers, B. M. Malinin, was an early supporter of nuclear submarines and was involved with their development when he died in September 1949. Khrushchev, in his reminiscences, gives credit for nuclear propulsion to academician I. V. Kurchatov. "He was the driving force behind our harnessing of nuclear energy. Thanks to him and atomic scientists like him, we were able to fulfill one of our fondest dreams, which was to have nuclear-powered engines for our submarine fleet." Kurchatov, a nuclear physicist, is generally given credit for having had a key role in development of the Soviet atomic bomb.

Within the Soviet Navy, several engineering admirals can be noted for long tenures in positions that contributed to the development of nuclear propulsion. Engineer-Admiral Nikolay Isachenkov directed Navy shipbuilding after the war and from 1952 to 1965 was deputy head of the Navy for shipbuilding and armaments, a position comparable to that of the U.S. Chief of Naval Material. He, in turn, was succeeded by his deputy, Engineer-Admiral Pavel Kotov, who continued to hold the post when this book went to press. But the credit for the vast Soviet submarine effort of the past two decades must go to Gorshkov.

Only Gorshkov among the world's living admirals has held active flag rank longer than Rickover. Gorshkov became an admiral in 1941 at age thirty-one, twelve years before Rickover donned his admiral stars. Both men greatly influenced their navies. Gorshkov has provided a fleet that has greatly influenced Soviet foreign policy. Rickover has influenced America far beyond its maritime interests.

26 | # The Ultimate Weapon
—Again

"As an ex-submariner, one who was in the initial program, I am personally biased. But I think that if there ever has been any one single weapon system that has insured our Nation's integrity and security, it has been the nuclear submarines, with a strategic weapon capability." At a White House press conference in early 1979, President Carter used these words to defend the Trident submarine program.

The President himself had to enter the debate because of the buildup of controversy over Trident. It had taken six years from the time Admiral Burke had made his decision to pursue a submarine missile until the first Polaris submarine went to sea. When President Carter spoke, the Trident had already been eight years in formal development and was still several years away from going to sea. The delays—and the problems that caused them—in the opinion of some participants in the Trident program could be traced to the fact that Rickover and Levering Smith had "captured" the Trident. Rickover had stated publicly that "the Trident submarine is not my brainchild." But he was having considerable influence on the program, in contrast to his lack of influence in the design of Polaris. Rickover tried to deflect any blame for the delays in the building of Trident. He insisted that the culprits were the systems analysts and the shipbuilders, the same men, he said, who were attempting to thwart his nuclear attack-submarine programs.

This time, there was no Arleigh Burke or Red Raborn to demand that Rickover keep his hands off Trident. And his hands were definitely on it.

By the middle 1960s the decisions had been made that would determine the size of U.S. strategic forces for the next fifteen years or more. Secretary of Defense McNamara had approved forty-one Polaris submarines, most of which were already at sea, one thousand Minuteman

ICBMs for the Air Force, and several hundred B-52 bombers. Under development was a new missile for the Polaris submarines, the Poseidon, which could deliver up to fourteen separate, albeit small, nuclear bombs on different targets within a given area. Thus, in theory at least, when the thirty-one newer Polaris submarines were rearmed in the 1970s they would each carry sixteen Poseidon missiles with a total of two hundred and twenty-four bombs per submarine. (Normally, however, only ten bombs would be provided to each missile in order to obtain more range—just over two thousand miles.)

Indications that the Soviet Union was itself developing a large ICBM and submarine-missile force, and possibly a defense against ballistic missiles, led McNamara, late in 1966, to initiate a study to determine whether the United States required more advanced strategic missiles than it already possessed and, if so, how they should be based—should the missiles be placed on land, at sea or under the sea, or on manned aircraft? The leading long-range strategic planners of the armed services participated in the study under the direction of Fred A. Payne, a "technologist" and former corporate vice president who had earlier served in the Department of Defense.* Thus, the study was made primarily of military men, not "systems analysts."

The senior Navy members of the study were Rear Admirals George H. Miller and Levering Smith. Miller, a leading naval strategist, had served in key OPNAV staff positions for CNOs Fechtler, Carney, Burke, McDonald and Moorer. He would soon become head of the new Navy Office of Strategic Offensive and Defensive Systems (OP-97), which was being set up to coordinate all Navy strategic forces. Smith was head of the Special Projects Office. Thus, active Navy officers representing both the OPNAV staff and the "hardware" side of the Navy participated in the study, which was called STRAT-X. No one from the Naval Reactors Branch participated. Decisions on specific propulsion systems would be made years after the basic concepts were decided by the study team.

The STRAT-X study examined a vast number of alternative methods of basing future missile systems, about 125 in all. These included fixed and mobile land-based missiles; afloat in surface ships or on barges in canals or inland waterways; in manned bombers; in submersibles that would crawl along the ocean floor; and in submarines. It was finally determined that submarine basing would be the least costly method and one that would also provide high survivability against a Soviet attack. Fi-

* Payne would also direct the Navy's Submarine Alternatives Study in 1979. See Chapter 18.

nally, the STRAT-X team decided to recommend four systems to the Secretary of Defense; two would be land-based and two sea-based, in keeping with the tradition of dividing resources equally among the U.S. military services.

Only one, the so-called Undersea Long-range Missile System, or ULMS, was approved for development. This system would later be named Trident.

From its inception, ULMS was envisioned as the eventual successor to Polaris and Poseidon. The principal difference between ULMS and the older Polaris-Poseidon missiles was that from the outset ULMS was to incorporate very-long-range missiles into submarines of rather conservative design, based largely on existing submarine technology, but with more quieting of machinery. The proposed submarine would not necessarily be deep-diving, would be able to spend long periods at sea, and would carry more than sixteen missiles.

Perhaps the most dramatic feature of one of the proposed ULMS designs was that missiles would be carried *outside* the submarine's hull, in a horizontal position. This arrangement would make it easier to provide new types of missiles for the submarine and would permit more flexible missile-firing techniques. For example, missiles could be released to "dwell" underwater before ignition, thus complicating Soviet attempts to locate the submarine when the missiles fired. External missiles also would mean a smaller submarine, fewer openings in the pressure hull, and easier ship handling and drydocking.

However, the longer missile ranges and advanced design concepts died rapidly as a result of arguments in the Navy that a shorter-range missile, perhaps a 4,000-mile weapon, could be developed more rapidly and be fitted into the existing Polaris-Poseidon submarines. There was also criticism that external missile tubes were too radical in idea, although the U.S. Regulus submarine missile and Soviet Shaddock-type missiles had been carried that way since the 1950s. The original ULMS design had specified a submarine 443 feet long with a submerged displacement of 8,240 tons, about the size of a later Polaris-Poseidon submarine but with more and longer-range missiles.

More and more additions and improvements were made. But most significant of all, Rickover pushed for a larger propulsion plant—a reactor that could develop 60,000 horsepower. This was the same plant size originally envisioned by Rickover to propel a large submarine with tactical cruise missiles. Zumwalt vetoed that attempt. But with the Trident program, Zumwalt felt that the need for additional U.S. strategic weapons was so great that he would have joined forces "with the devil" to add strategic missiles to counter the massive Soviet buildup.

The S8G reactor plant of the Trident is almost twice the power of the SSN-688 fast attack submarines and four times that of the reactor plant used in the previous attack submarines and all forty-one of the Polaris-Poseidon submarines. It has been difficult to fathom Rickover's rationale for the large reactor plant. Before his favorite forum, the Joint Committee on Atomic Energy, he would ridicule the original STRAT-X submarine concept—"The origin [of the Trident] was that we have a large submarine that could only make four knots and would most of the time rest on the Continental Shelf of the United States. That was the concept."

That was not the concept. Indeed, nuclear weapons—even "resting"—on the continental shelf were outlawed by international agreement. There had been earlier proposals for such weapons, dating back to the Polaris period. But what was most damning—and in the Rickover style—was his next statement. "That was dreamed up by the systems analysts."

As often happened, Rickover simply would not speak to the Navy and Department of Defense analysts or *designers* who were developing the Trident program. As one senior analyst in the Department of Defense told the authors, "We simply never knew his rationale. [David] Leighton would come and talk with us, and tell us what Rickover wanted or was planning. But never would he say why—what his reasons were." To the designers it was worse because the 60,000-horsepower plant was still in the design stage. How much would it weigh? What would be its exact location in the submarine? Its volume? Exactly how much power would it generate?

The internal, vertical missile-tube arrangement and the large reactor plant would drive up the size of the submarine significantly. By May 16, 1972, when Secretary of Defense Melvin Laird announced that the new weapons systems would be called Trident, the submarine had grown to a length of 560 feet with a submerged displacement of 18,700 tons. Although linear comparisons have limited value, it is still instructive to note that the Trident submarine with twenty-four missiles would have fifty percent more weapons that the Polaris-Poseidon submarines, but the Trident displacement would be more than one hundred percent greater.

With respect to numbers of missiles, Rickover said that he preferred sixteen, the same number decided more than a decade earlier—by lot— for the Polaris submarines. He also said that he did recommend approval of twenty missiles per submarine. Instead, the decision to have twenty-four in each submarine, he said, "was based on the cost effectiveness studies and recommendations of . . . systems analysts." Rear Admiral Levering Smith, whose office was primarily responsible for the Trident having twenty-four missiles, was certainly not a Department of Defense analyst. In time, Rickover would change his position on the number of missile tubes, especially when Trident critics would argue for smaller missile submarines, with fewer tubes and smaller reactors.

But the most controversial aspect of the Trident—after its size and cost—was the proposed 60,000-horsepower S8G reactor plant. Rickover told the Joint Committee that he planned to design the propulsion plant for the Trident "to be very quiet so as to make the ship difficult to detect. Almost equally important to quietness, in my opinion, will be a high speed capability," he said. "This capability will be important for breaking contact with the enemy if the ship is detected and will also insure that the ship has adequate power for control and for recovery from casualties."

Here was perhaps the major flaw in Rickover's logic about the Trident submarine. At slow speeds a submarine can be quiet, very quiet. But as speed increases, the submarine gets noisier. Some of the noises are from internal machinery—which can be quieted, but at great cost and increase in submarine size. At high speeds there is also noise generated by the submarine's propeller turning and the movement of the submarine through the water. This was the basis for the controversy between the quiet but slow attack submarine *Lipscomb* and the fast but relatively noisy SSN-688.

In many cases, when a submarine is detected at long ranges its best ploy is to go very slowly and hence quietly. If the submarine speeds up to evade its pursuer, more noise is generated. At long detection ranges, however, escape may be possible by a fast submarine. Could a Trident escape from a fast, thirty-knot-plus Soviet submarine? Such Soviet submarines were operating from the late 1960s onward, and about 1980 the 40-knot *Alfa* entered service. But the die was cast, and the Navy and Defense Department reluctantly agreed to the large-reactor design. Rickover thus won and became personally involved with the Trident submarine design—so much so that Representative John McFall of California even suggested they label it the *Rickover* class. Rickover objected: "Don't do that, please. I need support in the Defense Department."

"The ULMS, or Trident, as it was later called," according to George Miller, the senior naval officer on the STRAT-X study, "gave us an opportunity to develop a highly effective and survivable strategic deterrent." He continued, "Building more land-based ICBMs would be like 'setting up the artillery in the village square.' That is, if the enemy attacked your land-based strategic weapons, he would also kill millions of Americans at the outset.

"But an increasing reliance on sea-based missiles—with two-thirds of the earth's surface as an operating base—would mean that the enemy's efforts to destroy your submarines or surface ships would not rain down nuclear weapons on the United States." And Admiral Miller noted that "when the next-generation ICBM—the so-called MX missile—was proposed in the late 1970s for basing in the United States, a senior Air Force general actually said it would be a 'sponge' to absorb missiles—forcing the Soviets to spend money on many more attack missiles to fire at the ICBMs—*based in the United States.*

"As the Trident turned out," Miller told the authors, "the submarine was too big and the missile range was too little, and the whole program was too late." The submarine was too big mainly because of the 60,000-horsepower reactor plant.

Late in 1971 the Secretary of Defense approved development of the Trident underwater giant. Political opposition came immediately, principally from members of Congress and the Air Force; the latter saw the advanced submarine competing for resources with new land-based missiles. In Congress the opposition was strong—a marked contrast to the situation in the Polaris days, when the solons consistently voted all funds asked for missile submarines and then some. When the Defense Department and Navy went forward in 1973 to request the first Trident in the fiscal 1974 budget, there was, in CNO Zumwalt's words, "the most dramatic legislative struggle I took part in, and I am sure the most significant as well . . . the Senate, in the course of considering the military authorization bill, came within two votes of cutting that year's funds for Trident . . . by more than half."

The Navy team that went up to Capitol Hill to argue for the Trident was led by a strange triumvirate—Zumwalt, Rickover and Secretary of the Navy John Warner. All were intelligent and persuasive, but rarely did all agree on any issue. Zumwalt, enjoying great popularity on the Hill at the time, argued for Trident on the basis of the Strategic Arms Limitation Talks with the Soviets. The Moscow summit meeting in May 1972 between Brezhnev and Nixon had frozen Soviet superiority in numbers of land- and sea-based strategic missiles and submarines. Zumwalt, a close observer of the strategic scene as well as the U.S.-Soviet naval balance, felt that the inferiority in American missile numbers had to be compensated for with advanced long-range weapons. The Trident start was approved by Congress, with the lead submarine funded in the fiscal 1974 budget.

For planning purposes, the Navy scheduled ten Trident submarines to be built at an annual rate expressed in Pentagonese as 1-3-3-3. There were to be ten Trident submarines by the early 1980s, when the first ten Polaris submarines were to be retired after about twenty years of service. The first Trident was ordered from Electric Boat on July 25, 1974. At that time delivery of the submarine was specified as April 30, 1979. But there was a footnote to that date in the official Navy schedule: "In the recognition of the high national priority assigned to the Trident program the contractor has promised to use his best efforts to support a Dec. 1977 delivery date for the lead ship." This clause, inserted into the contract at Rickover's insistence, forced the Navy to buy many of the Trident's components at an accelerated pace. The early purchases did not offset the effects of inflation, because manufacturers, in order to meet the deadline, claimed higher costs and charged premium prices. Thus, at least a portion of the surge in the cost of the Tridents can be traced directly to Rickover's speed-up clause.

The cost of the Trident submarine increased drastically during the first submarine's long gestation. In the fiscal 1974 budget the price tag of the submarine was $780 million. That did not include Atomic Energy Commission costs for some reactor components and the fuel core, nor did it include the actual missiles the submarine would carry. Gordon Rule, head of the procurement and clearance division of the Naval Material Command, took one look at that first contract and rejected it "as being the most imprudent contract the Navy has ever proposed to execute." He said that the contract, which had options for three additional Trident submarines, was improper for a new class of ships with so many unknowns. Over Rule's objections the contract was awarded.

Rule's early warning signal was picked up by Representative Les Aspin, a member of the House Armed Services Committee, a former Department of Defense budget analyst, and a major critic of the Navy. In August 1974 Aspin wrote a "Dear Charlie" letter to Representative Charles Bennett, chairman of the committee's subcommittee on sea power. Aspin asked Bennett to undertake an investigation into Rule's charges. Aspin also asked for an investigation by the General Accounting Office.

Bennett asked Rule for more information. Rule provided an analysis of the problems, topped off by an opinion: "Just as Admiral Rickover recently castigated the Navy for line officer intrusion into engineering activities of the Navy, it is suggested it is high time that Admiral Rickover be politely but firmly informed that although his views are always welcome he must no longer dictate to the Navy the type of contract...."

Rule said that there had been no real competition between Electric Boat and its only rival, Newport News Shipbuilding, because the "desire and intention has been to award the first four Trident ships to EB and any attempt to obtain competition from the only other shipbuilder capable of building Tridents had been cosmetic window dressing. In short, the Navy continues to play games with itself, with the DOD, and with the Congress, in this case, to appease Admiral Rickover's desires...."

The case was virtually closed as far as Bennett was concerned. He wrote back a "Dear Mr. Aspin" letter saying that his subcommittee had already received testimony indicating that the Navy believes "the contractual arrangements were in the best interests of the Government." Bennett enclosed snips of testimony—still marked "confidential"—that included the words of Joseph Pierce, vice president of General Dynamics, the parent company of Electric Boat: "I feel we have ended up with a very satisfactory contract . . . with a delivery date that we feel can be met...."

At the same time, EB was getting another class of submarines and another set of problems. This was the SSN-688 class (later *Los Angeles*). The lead submarine would be built at Newport News. Then that yard and EB would share in construction of additional submarines. The plan, which Rule and others traced directly back to Rickover, produced what a Congressional report would call "a classic example of what can happen when the Navy accelerates a ship construction program without the benefit of sound design data." By 1977, with eighteen SSN-688s under contract at EB and thirteen under contract at Newport News, claims for $814 million had been made against the Navy. At that time, only one of the submarines had been delivered.

"The Navy continues to request funding from Congress for construction of complex ships that have not been designed, . . ." said the report of a subcommittee of the House Appropriations Committee. "The Trident submarine in the fiscal year 1974 budget fell into the same category."

With the Tridents and SSN-688 class being built side by side at Electric Boat, it becomes difficult to distinguish their separate problems. There were design changes—thousands of them—to both classes. The

Navy claimed there was not an inordinate amount; EB claimed there was. Rickover put the blame squarely on EB's workers. "For many years," he said, "there was been a large amount of loafing at Electric Boat. I have personally observed this problem in both shops and ships during my inspections, and recently I have received reports that loafing is so bad that some workers do not even make the effort to appear busy."

Many old-timers at the yard agreed with Rickover, but others suggested that management should share the blame. During the turmoil over Trident and the SSN-688s, EB had three general managers in three years. In a single year, one hundred and eighty of the top three hundred management positions changed hands. "The criterion for advancement," a disgruntled manager said, "is 'Who has made it twenty years and hasn't offended Rickover?' "

The third of these general managers was P. Takis Veliotis. He was in some respects like Rickover—foreign-born, a proud, hard-working, dedicated problem solver, who did not like to be coerced. Veliotis had not been approved by Rickover, as had several previous EB executives. As one EB official told the authors, "In a shipyard you were either Rickover's adversary or his slave." As a "slave," if you were high enough, you might receive a letter from Rickover spelling out your acceptance of Rickover's control of shipyard affairs. You were expected to sign the letter. Veliotis would not sign his letter from Rickover. Indeed, he quickly began to stand up to Rickover in the yard and in Congressional hearings.

The countdown thus began in 1977 for a confrontation between the contractor and the Navy—just as it was simultaneously happening at Newport News. EB announced that it would halt work unless the government paid the money EB said it was losing on the contracts that once had seemed ideal. Just before the deadline, the Navy agreed to increase the price it was paying for the submarines and to speed up the cash flow.

While Rickover, the government contracting agents and EB's management argued over schedules and payments, in Washington the Trident program also encountered stormy seas. The initial plan had called for ten submarines to be authorized in a four-year period. Then more would be requested. Although there was no "ultimate" goal—at least not one that would be stated for the record by Navy leaders—it was obvious that some twenty-seven Trident giants would be needed by the early 1990s when the last of the Poseidon boats reached their twenty-fifth year of service. That was an average of more than two Tridents per year. That number of Tridents would almost provide the six hundred and fifty-six submarine missiles available throughout the 1970s.

Inadequate budgets and efforts to continue a balanced—or compromise—mix of strategic-bomber aircraft (the B-1) and land-based missiles (the MX), as well as Trident, caused a loss of support for the submarine program. Soon the first ten boats were stretched out—in paper plans—to six years and then to seven. Even that schedule was not to be. And the lead submarine, named *Ohio,* was far behind schedule.

On November 29, 1977, the Navy's Trident program managers, Rear Admirals Albert L. Kelln and Donald Hall, both nuclear submariners, announced that the lead submarine had increased in cost from $780 million to almost $1.2 *billion*—a fifty-percent increase. And they explained that the lead submarine was still three years from completion. Asked why the program was delayed, Admiral Hall could state only that Electric Boat has "not stated a reason, they have just indicated that they would not make the contract delivery date." Asked about the higher costs, the answer was also vague: "It's primarily associated with the longer construction period, the stretch-out of the program...." The blame was being put on Electric Boat.

Admiral Hall did give some indication of the problem when he said, "I'd like to emphasize that this ship is over twice as large as any submarine we've built before. The technology is extremely advanced, and we're pushing it both in the missile and in the submarine area." The words seemed to be more like those of Gordon Rule than those of a member of the Rickover team. But Rule had retired in 1976 and his voice, at least from an official viewpoint, was at last stilled.

The Kelln-Hall press conference also demonstrated the confusion in the management of Trident, as indicated by the subsequent denials of some of their statements from Electric Boat, clarifications by the Navy, and more questions from Congress and the press. The Navy did not have an over-all Trident manager. For a brief period, from 1967 to 1971, the Director of Navy Strategic Offensive and Defensive Systems (OP-97) had full responsibility for Trident (then ULMS) development. At that time the name of the Polaris-Poseidon office was changed from Special Projects Office to Strategic Systems Project Office to reflect its subordination to OP-97. Miller, the first head of the office, was succeeded by a submariner, Rear Admiral James Osborn, who had been first commanding officer of the *George Washington.* Submarine—that is, nuclear-submarine—influence increased, and soon the Trident program was shifted to the new Deputy CNO for submarines.

The Navy's attempt to get all strategic programs together was thus short-lived. Today there is a Strategic Submarine Division and Trident

Program Coordinator (OP-22) in the office of the Deputy CNO for sub-marine warfare (in 1977 that was Kelln's job); nuclear and political mat-ters affecting Trident are under the Deputy CNO for plans, policy and operations; the Director of Studies and Analysis (OP-96, the office Zum-walt had set up) is in charge of strategic studies. On the hardware side, there is the Special Projects Office to handle missile development; a sepa-rate Trident Project Office (in 1977 under Hall) to handle most subma-rine matters, with other functions still under the Naval Sea Systems Command. In that command resides Rickover, responsible—at least on the organization chart—only for the submarines' nuclear plant. Ob-viously, he had considerably more rank and clout than any other flag offi-cer involved in the program.

Trident was in trouble, and everyone knew it. There had been one Trident authorized in fiscal 1974, two in 1975, one in 1976, one in 1977, two in 1978, and then none in 1979, a total of seven submarines in six years. The plan had been ten Trident submarines authorized in four years. (In the Polaris era, forty-one submarines had been authorized in a similar period.) Congress resumed funding Trident submarines in fiscal 1980—at a rate of one per year.

Meanwhile, alternative solutions to the missile-submarine problem were being sought. As an interim measure, from 1979 onward, twelve Poseidon-armed submarines were rearmed with missiles designed for the still-building Trident submarines. More significantly, in the early 1970s Secretary of Defense James Schlesinger had asked the Navy to look into the possibility of a smaller Trident submarine. Perhaps new Poseidon-type submarines could be built, smaller than the Trident ships and carry-ing only sixteen missiles, but at much less cost. Rickover immediately counterattacked. He told the Joint Committee in 1975, "The cost of the Trident has gone up because of inflation and stretchout of the program. I assure you that I think we are on the right course. I think if we stop now and change over to another submarine ballistic-missile program it will cost us more money, more money than we would save."

Then Rickover added, "I believe we should consider a smaller ship as a follow-on to the Tridents. The reason we are not pursuing that course now is because the development funds were cut out last year."

Representative Mike McCormack of Washington asked about smaller and faster missile submarines. Rickover responded, "It is true that a faster submarine is better from the standpoint of evading attempts at being destroyed, but you need a balanced high-speed capability against cost and other factors for the Trident. Suppose you have a number of

[new] Tridents that carry sixteen missiles instead of twenty-four, the cost per missile would go up quite a bit because you would need more submarines to get the same total number of missiles to sea."

Rickover thus contradicted his earlier statements that Trident submarines had to be fast (hence the 60,000-horsepower plant) and that he really preferred only sixteen missiles per submarine.

McCormack, who had been seated on the Joint Committee only since 1970, pressed further: "Supposing you had a much smaller submarine with external missiles . . . nothing but a portable, submerged, missile launcher, but which would go faster—"

Rickover interrupted: "No sir, that is not practical. When you decide to have atomic power, you inherently require lots of space and weight for shielding and other purposes." Forgotten were the U.S. and Soviet cruise-missile submarines of the 1950s and the original ULMS concept. Most of the remainder of the exchange between McCormack and Rickover was off the record—for security reasons.

Meanwhile, delays in the Trident program and cost increases continued. After the government settlements with Electric Boat, the Navy schedules showed November 30, 1980, as the delivery date for the *Ohio*. In March of that year it was announced that the ship would not be commissioned until February 1981. This meant the *Ohio* would be under construction for more than six and a half years. The remaining submarines—with eight on order by mid-1980—were also behind schedule, on the order of two years each.

The result of the slippage and the reduced rate of Trident authorizations caused the Navy to look into the possibility of retaining the Poseidon submarines for up to thirty years. With the Trident building rate and a twenty-five-year service life for the older submarines (some rearmed with sixteen Trident missiles), the total strategic submarine force could fall to about fifteen submarines, with 360 missiles, available in the early 1990s. A harbinger of such a shift came in 1980–1981 when the ten oldest Polaris submarines were taken out of service, reducing the force for the first time since 1967. Their retirement was to have been offset in part by the new Trident submarines. But, without the Tridents, by late 1981 the United States had thirty-one nuclear-powered missile submarines with 496 missiles, while the Soviets had about sixty-three modern missile submarines with more than 950 missiles.

Even if all the planned Trident submarines join the fleet by the early 1990s, those fifteen submarines will not all be at sea at one time. Assuming that at most ten are simultaneously at sea, the Soviets will have only that many to hunt. The hunting will be easier than it had been in the past, even though each Trident submarine armed with 4,000-mile missiles aimed at Moscow would be sailing in a much larger ocean area than Polaris submarines had sailed in.

While the Trident submarines are quiet, at least at low speeds, their large size increases their vulnerability to other forms of detection in comparison with smaller submarines. These include the magnetic, underwater wake, heat, and other "signatures" created as the submarines cruise underwater.

Another problem related to the Trident submarines' size involves simply getting them out of the Electric Boat yard to sea. The yard is almost four miles up the Thames River from Long Island Sound. In the 1970s, when the issue was raised that the river was not deep enough for the giant submarines, Electric Boat and Navy spokesmen said they could solve the problem by not fully loading the submarines when they left the yard, thus reducing their draft or depth. But in 1980 the Navy announced that the channel to Long Island Sound was being dredged, an action that "enlarges the margin of safety and allows greater flexibility in scheduling transits" between the yard and the sea. The government reported that it cost four million dollars to dredge the channel.

The *Ohio* finally left the EB yard on her initial sea trial early on the morning of June 17, 1981. The submarine got under way at 4:32 A.M., in part because of Rickover's belief that an early start would deter press coverage. But the first Trident submarine, the largest and most expensive undersea craft ever built in the United States, was too big a media event. As Rickover arrived at the yard that morning his car was mobbed outside the EB gate by newsmen and photographers. He screamed at them through the closed windows and tried in vain to wave them away. Then, seeing that EB photographers were inside the yard, he drove away from the *Ohio*. Minutes later a closed Navy van pulled up to the submarine's gangway. Sailors climbed out of the van holding up mattresses to shield Rickover from the cameras as he lunged aboard the submarine.

Once inside, after the submarine was at sea, he reportedly barricaded the captain's stateroom with mattresses to evade the EB and Navy photographers on board. One New England newspaper in describing these scenes compared Rickover to Greta Garbo. (The Navy—i.e., Rickover—immediately embargoed all official Navy and EB photographs of the *Ohio* on trials. Although much of the media suffered from this ploy, a

General Dynamics/EB ad and the next issues of *Time* and *Business Week* magazine promptly published commercial photos of the sub at sea.)

The *Ohio* successfully navigated the channel down the Thames River and into Long Island Sound, and then out to sea. However, she encountered problems when a part—provided by Westinghouse—was found to have been left ashore. While Rickover fumed, the *Ohio* lay idle until the part was brought out by tug. More important, the submarine was late, two to four years behind schedule, depending upon which schedule one cared to cite. The other Trident submarines were also coming along late.

Smaller Trident submarines, with either sixteen, or even twenty-four, tubes (the latter with smaller reactor plants and some equipment removed) would, in the opinion of some experts, be less vulnerable. Although the cost per missile carried would be more in a sixteen-tube submarine, the smaller size of that craft would most likely mean less cost, which would be more palatable to Congress. Dr. David Mann, Assistant Secretary of the Navy for research, said in 1979 that he believed that a new Trident submarine, capable of carrying twenty-four missiles, could be designed with a displacement of only 15,000 tons and could be built for about thirty percent less than the cost of the *Ohio*-class submarines. There was also a proposal put forth to adapt the *Los Angeles* SSN to carry Tridents by adding a new center section with sixteen missile tubes. This would create a significant advantage: the missile and attack submarines would have the same kind of reactor plant and other systems, thus simplifying maintenance, logistics and training.

Rickover pushed in every way possible for a continuation of the existing Trident line. The increasing costs of the lead ship *Ohio* and the delays in her completion were frustrating. Indeed, the Navy in 1981 could not even make total cost estimates for that ship. (In the fiscal 1981 budget a Trident submarine's cost was estimated at $1.5 *billion* each. The *actual* cost of the lead Trident submarine would not be known until the mid-1980s, when the first three ships had been completed, because of the nature of their multi-ship contract.)

All of this was further complicated by the Navy's legal problems with Electric Boat, the only yard building the Tridents. The delays at EB were not only with the Trident submarines but also with the *Los Angeles* class (with EB blaming both the Navy and the lead yard, Newport News, for those problems). The situation was so bad that in 1978 Rickover told a Congressional committee, "From my personal knowledge of the rate at which ships are built I would not award Electric Boat any more at this time. I don't say that you should not authorize one [Trident submarine] and appropriate funds for it . . . but I would not at this time award any new ship of any kind to Electric Boat."

This was the same firm to which Rickover had gone to build the *Nautilus* after he encountered bureaucratic problems at the Portsmouth naval shipyard and he had gone to EB for most of his new submarine designs. Representative Jack Edwards of Alabama, seeking clarification of Rickover's views on putting another Trident at EB asked, "And your 'no' is based in great part on the fact that you don't think in the near future that the Electric Boat yard can handle the construction of that Trident; is that correct?"

Rickover responded: "I will repeat what I said: Certainly not for two years would I put anything, even a barge, into Electric Boat. Two years from now I would see what the situation is."

After a brief additional discussion about the question of how long the period is from authorization to awarding of a contract, Edwards made the following remark: "We assume all your answers are honest answers." Rickover replied, "Thank you, sir."

A final factor complicating the Trident effort was President Carter's thrust for nuclear-arms reduction. When he became President in January 1977, he almost immediately asked the Joint Chiefs of Staff for an opinion on the possibility of eventually reducing the U.S. strategic forces to some two hundred submarine-launched missiles. That would amount to eight Trident submarines. His subsequent decision not to build the B-1 long-range bomber, along with delays and indecision on the MX, the advanced land-based ICBM, and the strategic cruise missile, were coupled with a slowdown in the Trident program.

The last Ford budget message to Congress had proposed the construction of eight Tridents in the next five years; under Carter and Secretary of Defense Brown, the five-year plans were cut back to six Tridents and then to five.

Still, Rickover's influence could be felt. At a White House press conference on March 30, 1979, in response to questions about Trident cost overruns and the feasibility of smaller submarines, President Carter defended the existing design—"to change from those two designs [Trident and *Los Angeles*] because there have been cost overruns, based primarily on natural inflation that has occurred, and an improvement in design during the construction phase, I think would be an error. So I don't think we will terminate those programs and change the design. I think they are very adequate, and I am very proud of what they have already done and what they will do in the future."

At that time the Trident had not yet been to sea. Several of the *Los Angeles* class were operating, and Rickover and President and Mrs. Carter had taken a cruise in the lead ship in May of 1977.

In his budget statement to Congress in late January 1980, taking into account the continued Soviet strategic buildup, the Soviet invasion of Afghanistan, and the declining capability of the U.S. armed forces through inflation and personnel problems, Secretary Brown announced that for the next few years the Carter Administration would build one SSBN per year through the middle 1980s, and then increase the rate to three ships every two years. He used the designation SSBN in part to distinguish the ships from the Tridents, for he continued: "Funds are programmed to support concept and design studies leading to a follow-on, less expensive SSBN. This SSBN could either be a re-engineered Trident design or a new design of a 24-tube SSBN with tubes of the same size as the Trident SSBN." To many observers, this meant that the end of the Trident existing "super submarine" program was in sight—barring Rickover's being able to directly influence a Presidential decision.

Brown, who in the Kennedy Administration had served as Director of Defense Research and Engineering and then as Secretary of the Air Force, had been a frequent opponent of Rickover. In the research job, he had been one of "those analysts" whom Rickover had described as an enemy of his and the nation. And as head of Carter's defense establishment, Brown was still an enemy of Rickover. But it was not Brown who was delaying the Trident. The causes of that delay predated the Carter Administration and continued after Mr. Carter and Dr. Brown left office in January 1981. At that time the lead Trident submarine, originally hoped for delivery in December 1977, was *planned* for completion in late 1981.

As the Carter Administration was leaving office, Rickover and Secretary of the Navy Edward Hidalgo were at war over the Trident. Rickover had written Hidalgo a memo critical of Electric Boat, and the memo had appeared in a defense industry trade paper. The memo predicted that "the Navy will again be confronted with omnibus claims" from Electric Boat, which will try to blame the Navy for cost overruns. Hidalgo left no doubt about who had leaked the memo. He said that such predictions were "completely irresponsible" and "provocations."

Speaking at the launching of the attack submarine *Baltimore* at

Electric Boat on December 13, 1980, Hidalgo suddenly veered from his prepared speech to say, "Those who do not wish us well would do well to understand that we are going ahead and will succeed not only in spite of, but because of, their opposition and because of their irresponsible criticism. They want us to fail. We shall not fail."

Hidalgo did not mention Rickover by name. He did not have to.

The Rickover-Hidalgo conflict was widely known in Washington, especially on Capitol Hill. Although many in the Navy considered Hidalgo a "lightweight," appointed by President Carter to put a person of Mexican descent in a key position, Hidalgo stood up to Rickover. As a result, several important members of Congress began questioning the actions (and antics) of Rickover.

Rickover bombarded Hidalgo with a series of memos denouncing Electric Boat. In one, he told the Secretary of the Navy: "I understand you and Mrs. Hidalgo will be Guests of Honor at the launching of the *Boston* at Electric Boat. Considering the problems at that yard, laudatory comments about the yard or Electric Boat management would be inappropriate and detrimental to Navy efforts to deal with the serious technical quality problems now being uncovered."

Each of the memos was a classic example of what an officer, even a flag officer, does *not* write to the Secretary of the Navy. The memos, for example, demanded a response about "the action you take in this matter." During Hidalgo's fifteen months in office, he received some 150 memorandums from Rickover. Often Hidalgo received his copy of the memo at the same time that—or after—copies went to Congressional supporters of Rickover. Hidalgo has said that he acknowledged the first memo and no others.

The issues behind the delays in the Trident program had become so complex and convoluted, with so many charges and countercharges, that on April 1, 1981, the Navy announced that it would not award a contract to Electric Boat for the ninth Trident submarine, which Congress had funded the previous year. Such a move—the Navy not awarding a contract for a high-priority strategic missile submarine—was unprecedented. The Reagan Administration's Secretary of the Navy, Dr. John Lehman, even raised the possibility of constructing Trident submarines at another yard.

At the same time, the Navy declined to take up an option for EB to build three additional Los Angeles-class attack submarines. Only one other yard in the United States was engaged in building nuclear submarines at the time, Newport News. But there was trouble there too. In January 1981, immediately after Secretary Hidalgo left office, Rickover caused a reopening of the federal investigation of the yard. Hidalgo had played a key role in settling the Navy-Newport News claims and now that Rickover had outlasted another Secretary of the Navy, he was again on the offensive. And in his attacks against EB and Newport News, he again advocated government takeover of the civilian yards or reopening the naval shipyards to submarine construction.

Reading Rickover's testimony before various Congressional committees at the time indicates that he believed that he, and only he, could solve the shipyard problem. His statements almost tended to avoid the main issues—the overall problems in the design and management of the Trident program—a program considered by some authorities the most important U.S. military undertaking of the time, with some of those authorities blaming most of the problems on a small, critical, outspoken man with a high-pitched voice, who never wore a uniform anymore.

HE NEVER WEARS
A UNIFORM

"He has two suits and he saves the blue one for good," one of Admiral Rickover's secretaries once observed. "I have never seen him in his uniform. I think that is why in the whole three floors of Naval Reactors no one wears a uniform. He does not hate it, but he wishes that he would not have to wear it. Therefore, he wishes it upon his people that they do not wear it."

He never explained why he did not wear a uniform. To the Navy, the explanation was simple: He hated the Navy, and he showed his feelings in the most obvious way. But there was another explanation. He never wore a uniform because he believed he was *more* than a naval officer, more than an admiral.

He had enemies to fight—stupidity, sloth, inefficiency, and the ultimate foe, time itself—and he fought these on his own, without the symbols of uniform and rank. His private wars took him beyond the Navy.

27 | Admiral of Education

The only mention of Hyman Rickover in the 1964 edition of the *Encyclopaedia Britannica* is on page 259 of Volume 20, where he is cited for his work, not as a submarine builder but as a critic of education. In an account on secondary education, the *Britannica* quotes a book that launched Rickover on a quixotic crusade against the citadels of American education. The crusade would also present the Navy with a chance to solve its Rickover problems by making him the educators' problem. For he could have become the U.S. Commissioner of Education.

Rickover had an inner vision of what was wrong with American schools and how they could be changed. He transformed his vision into that book, *Education and Freedom,* and two others, and into thousands of words in speeches and testimony before Congressional committees. But his campaign to improve American education, unlike his campaign to build a nuclear navy, was a failure. Nothing was changed. Nothing was built. Although the voice that had cried out in 1959 was still crying out twenty years later, hardly anyone heard him. Fewer responded.

Rickover, who had begun speaking about education in the middle 1950s, did not call for radical change until 1958, when, testifying before a subcommittee of the House Committee on Education, he urged "pretty much a complete revision of our entire primary- and secondary-school system." By then he was beginning to see better brands of education elsewhere.

In 1959, after his return from a brief visit to the Soviet Union with Vice President Nixon, he presented to the House Appropriations Committee, in spoken and written testimony, a "Report on Russia." Virtually the entire report was devoted to a comparison between schools in the United States and schools in the Soviet Union, which "produces a much larger talent pool than we obtained through our public-school system." He often established his credentials by remarking that he had spoken about education with Soviet Premier Nikita Khrushchev. When he said this during a rare appearance on "Meet the Press" in 1960, one of the panel reporters, James Reston of *The New York Times*, asked, "Have you ever talked with the President about it?"

"No, sir," Rickover replied.

"What about Mr. Fleming [Arthur S. Fleming, Secretary of Health, Education and Welfare]?"

"No, sir."

"Anybody in the government at all?"

"No, sir."

As Reston's question so bluntly demonstrated, no one in the Eisenhower Administration seemed particularly interested in hearing Rickover's views on education. Even in Congress his supporters seemed impatient when he would talk about education; they wanted to hear his fire-spitting words on the Pentagon, the Navy, and other exciting subjects. Representative Clarence Cannon, lavishly introducing Rickover as he began his report on Russia, said that "the destiny of world civilization may rest upon weapons initiated by Admiral Rickover." Cannon went on in this way for a while and then said, "Admiral Rickover has a hobby. He is deeply interested in education. . . ."

Admiral Rickover did not have any hobbies. As he would write in *Education and Freedom,* "For ten years I have hoarded my small amount of leisure"—he worked seven days a week, he said—"and invested it in an effort to understand what went wrong with the American dream of universal education and how we might put it right again."

There before the Congress, though, as he talked about education in the Soviet Union, he seemed to know the way to put America's schools right again. "I have in my hand, " he said, "the Russian ten-year school examination that will go into the record." The examination, which he said was given to Soviet students after they had completed ten years of education, covered fifteen pages of the record, beginning with algebra and ending with chemistry and physics problems.

"I hope that American parents and teachers will look at these exams," Rickover said, "and realize that our children are being shortchanged. I hope they become angry enough to force their school boards to improve the curriculum, to improve the teaching, and to stop wasting the time of our children with fun subjects and other matters unrelated to education."

He suggested that the examinations be used "in setting our standard diploma examination, at least to the extent that we would not wish our children to know less than the Russians. . . . In the technological race we are in with the Russians, I fear that our children will indeed need to learn as much as European children of equal mental aptitude have learned for many, many years. . . ."

The race with the Russians had been inspired by the Soviet launching of Sputnik on October 4, 1957. The early Soviet space successes had given America an inferiority complex. How could the Soviets outdo the Americans in technology? One of the answers came from Rickover and others in a back-to-basics education movement. Soviet children, they argued, received a better, more technological education than pampered American pupils did. Out of their arguing—and lobbying by educators of many hues—came the U.S. National Defense Education Act, passed in 1958. The law authorized the spending of $480 million by the federal government for "strengthening science, mathematics, and foreign language instruction."

By the time Rickover testified in 1959, the debate was still raging, the fears were still high, and Representative John J. Rhodes could say, without expecting anyone to smile, "I cannot imagine what kind of pills they feed these [Russians] children to make them so brilliant. . . . You are not saying we should change our whole way of life because of this?"

"No, sir, we should not, . . ." Rickover replied. "The function of the home and of the church is to train our youngsters. Children, when they are born, are little savages. The training they get in the home and in the church, if it is good, will prevent them from becoming big savages when they are twenty years old; we have plenty of big savages in this country."

Education's mission, according to Rickover, was to continue the traditional three Rs. He said that a "child's home and church develop in him manners, personality, good character, and devotion to ethical and religious principles." Responding to this, a writer in the National Education Association's *Journal* wondered how long it was "since he's seen some of the homes which pass their parental failures into our public schools."

Quite suddenly and without professional background, Rickover had become an expert on education and on the transformation of savage babies into worthwhile adults. He seemed to resent the time he had to give his crusade. "I have to take off time from my real work to be there," he testified. "I do not have a minute's time." But he said he was not making a sacrifice. "I am doing it because it is my duty to do it."

Beyond the desperation of the race with Russia there was something deeper in Rickover's vision. He was seeing the coming of technological

America, and in it would be a new kind of man, the technical expert. "Today he is still subservient to nontechnical leaders in government and industry, " he wrote in *Education and Freedom*, "and his work is hampered and sometimes destroyed by men in whom is vested great power but who cannot understand the realities of the new, artificial, technological age. But the 'verbal' men are on the way out; the men who can handle the intricate mysteries of complex scientific and engineering projects are on the way in."

In that description of the technical man, a man so hampered by his political leaders, could easily be seen the shade of Hyman Rickover. And in his warnings could also be seen his vision of technological America: "Unless we abandon false 'democratic' clichés which interpret democracy as enthronement of the commonplace and obstruction of excellence, we may find that we have traded democratic freedom for a mess of pseudo-democratic mediocrity."

Pessimistic as he was about the clichés of democracy, he was fascinated by the efficiency of the Soviet Union, whose educational system "produces exactly the sort of trained men and women her rulers need to achieve technological supremacy the day after tomorrow." In that land of practical education there were "no comfortable home playrooms, and back yards to play in; no juke boxes; far fewer movies; hardly any distracting radio or TV programs; and of course, no hot rods." Children in the Soviet Union "are imbued with a love of intellectual adventure through books in which the hero is a scientist or engineer who does valiant deeds that will benefit the country—not, as in so many of our books, and even more on radio and television, a cowboy or space cadet."

Rickover was sincerely convinced that we needed a spartan society to cope with the Soviet challenge. His was one of many voices of warning in those days of Sputnik and cold war. And his was not the only military voice. Dr. Fred C. Schwarz, leader of the Christian Anti-Communism Crusade, who numbered John Dewey and "liberals" among his foes, spoke at the National War College, ran seminars at military establishments, and was endorsed by military officials. When the American Civil Liberties Union protested the use of the Glenview (Illinois) Naval Air Station as the site for a Schwarz crusade, Secretary of the Navy William B. Franke did order an end to official sponsorship of such movements, but Schwarz appeared again two months later. Similar anti-Communism campaigns were held at other naval installations during the late 1950s and had the backing of the chief of naval aviation training.

In the rhetoric of the cold war, education was equated with defense.

A member of the staff of the Chief of Naval Operations spoke at the National Education Association's annual conference in 1957. "Whether an 'all-out' shooting war or an interminable 'cold war,' " he said, "World War III will confer victory upon the cause which most successfully mobilizes its brain power. The country's institutions of higher education have then, in fact, become the keystone of the arch of its defensive strength." Rickover had picked up that theme and taken it to Congress, apparently with the blessing of his commander in chief. Soon after the launching of Sputnik, President Eisenhower had urged educators to examine the failing of American schools in comparison with the success of the schools in the Soviet Union.

"I felt at that time almost certain that Admiral Rickover had talked to Ike," William Carr, then executive secretary of the National Education Association, told the authors. "I was surprised at how quickly and fiercely that idea came out." In his autobiography, Carr wrote of the post-Sputnik reaction against public schools—and remarked, "There was no serious criticism of the Pentagon or of the White House. There was no criticism of the rocket manufacturers or of the universities."

The United States launched its first satellite, the 31-pound Explorer I, on January 31, 1958, and Carr was quick to point out that of the sixteen major technicians responsible for Explorer I, fifteen were graduates of American public high schools. But Congressmen were listening to Rickover and other critics, and the NEA was often the critics' target.

In the educational profession itself, the NEA led the response against Rickover. It could hardly be called an attack. "There was a feeling of uneasiness about his criticism," Carr recalled. "He meant well for the Republic. It was just too bad we had to be his target. We were lobbing back hand grenades against his heavy artillery. The NEA did not declare war on the Admiral."

Neither did the NEA nor any other educational group openly challenge the issue of a military man stepping outside his area of responsibility and attacking what historically had been a civilian-controlled, locally administered public service—the primary- and elementary-school system. In the atmosphere of the time, Rickover could speak out with impunity against Communism and its threats to America. But he was doing more. He was telling Congress that we could learn something from the Soviet Union's emphasis on education. In Congress at least, Rickover's criticism began to go off track when he tried to make American society less appealing than Russian society.

Congressmen who supported Rickover the engineer and admiral had trouble supporting Rickover the educator and extoller of the Soviet system of education. No voices were raised against him in Congress, but the Congressmen were not stirred to carry out his reforms. The Soviet school examinations would not be picked up for use in America. It was well enough to cry the alarm about Sputnik, but it was going too far to suggest that the Soviet Union was doing most things right and we were all wrong. He received no endorsement of his criticisms when they were linked to the Soviet way of life. No one in Congress was as attracted as Rickover was to a life where there was "no need for attractive stores, for service industries, for advertising."

Rickover was rarely wrong in his assessment of Congressional moods, but he was wrong this time, and his rare blunder resulted in an even rarer Congressional event. A critic of Rickover was summoned before Congress, specifically before the House Appropriations Committee subcommittee that watched over HEW. Its chairman was John E. Fogarty, who especially disliked Rickover's upbraiding of HEW's Office of Education. Fogarty called before his subcommittee U.S. Commissioner of Education Dr. Lawrence G. Derthick.

In his testimony, Rickover had launched a tirade against the Office of Education for espousing the tenets of John Dewey. Under that influence, Rickover said, children were not being taught about "what the Greeks did and the Romans did and what the Church did in the Middle Ages and what was done during and after the Renaissance.... We have discarded much of the heritage of Western civilization." He also charged that the Office of Education had "fallen down on the job of alerting this country to the Russian educational menace."

Derthick told Congress that his agency had not only sent three missions to the Soviet Union in the previous two years but also that since 1955 it had issued 141 publications on education in other countries. Derthick, himself an expert on education in Germany, pointed out that Rickover had received his copies of the Soviet tests *from the Office of Education.*

Derthick said that he had been on one mission that had visited about one hundred Soviet schools, interviewed teachers, principals and education officials, and were given textbooks, which were later analyzed by American experts. Derthick then politely compared the educators' research with Rickover's:

> It is certainly no reflection on Admiral Rickover that he missed some of the significant facts about the Soviet educational system. . . .

For example, he said, "I had the opportunity to talk to the Ministers of Education in both Russia and Poland, and with other education officials."

Our experience with these people leads me to understand how, in their enthusiasm for their Communist system, they would paint glowing pictures, some of which are in marked contrast to the conditions actually seen by experienced, qualified educators.

The "top salesmen of Soviet schools," Derthick said, misled Rickover about the apparent lack of administrative personnel in Soviet schools, in contrast to what he regarded as an excess of administrators in American schools. "Our study showed exactly the reverse to be true," Derthick testified. "We were astonished to see in a single school medical, supervisory, administrative and service personnel, in addition to classroom teachers, that in number and variety are far beyond what one finds on the central staff of many of our good-sized school districts."

Rickover had also said there was a lack of organized sports in Soviet schools. "Actually," Derthick said, "we found athletics to be one of the chief interests of the Soviet people. When we visited the superintendent of schools in Moscow, for example, we found his outer office filled with cups, trophies, and other awards earned in competitive athletics with the schools of other cities."

The Office of Education, Derthick said, rejected the idea that the American school system should be redesigned to resemble the Soviet Union's system. "A school system," he said, "reflects the kind of society that gives it support. Our desire to protect the individual rights, freedoms, and opportunities of our people is so different from the aims of the Soviets that we could not possibly imagine patterning our schools after their system."

The professional response to Rickover's criticism came in the September 1959 issue of the *Journal of Teacher Education*. Because the author, Richard I. Miller, was connected with the NEA and because the article was later reprinted by the NEA's "Defense Commission," the article was considered to be the unofficial NEA response. Miller concentrated on a series of Rickover's speeches, and on his "Russian Report." The speeches themselves had been the core of *Education and Freedom*, and so the article also had the effect of analyzing much of what was in the book.

Miller's scheme was to take a generalization by Rickover—"rubbish and trash" in the curriculum, for example—and then refute it with a specific response buttressed with information drawn from professional sources: Curriculum development is often "the direct result of community and business interests. . . . the rapid growth of driver education [for example] has been encouraged by large automobile insurance companies, in some cases. " Such information, known to professional educators, is not usually known to a critic who attacks such "trash" as driver-education courses.

Miller did not deal harshly with Rickover. The educator looked at the Admiral and found that among the many critics of the time Rickover stood apart as "the only government or military figure of national prominence to take time and effort to look into education." Miller concluded that Rickover and educators were in agreement on placing immense value on education.

When the Kennedy Administration came into office, the Department of Defense lost its tolerance for military men who took positions on non-military subjects. On May 26, 1961, at a press conference on public-information matters, Secretary of Defense McNamara announced a policy: "In public discussions all officials of the Department should confine themselves to defense matters. They should particularly avoid discussion of foreign-policy matters, a field which is reserved for the President and the Department of State."

Rickover's speechmaking and book writing on education went on, but no longer was the stress on how much better the Soviet schools were. His wife, Ruth Masters Rickover, a linguist and an intellectual in the European tradition, began to help him gather information on another foreign school system, Switzerland's. At the same time, he sharpened his arguments for what would be the centerpiece of his educational philosophy, the setting up of national educational standards.

The book, *Swiss Schools and Ours: Why Theirs Are Better,* was published in 1962. The book was copyrighted by the Council for Basic Education, a traditionalist organization that did not align itself with teachers or conventional educational groups and was devoted "to the maintenance of quality in American education." In the American educational spectrum, the Council was of the right, just as advocates of John Dewey and the Columbia Teachers College were of the left.

Thus, the spectrum put Rickover on the right. John A. Stormer, author of *None Dare Call It Treason,* was able to quote Rickover's criticism of Dewey as a springboard for an attack on "progressive" education, the NEA, and even the National Defense Education Act (because it "provided money for trained counselors and testing programs"). The book, which was published in 1964, was a phenomenally popular attack on a host of Americans—ranging from President Eisenhower and John Foster

Dulles, to President Kennedy and people associated with the National Council of Churches and the Parent-Teachers Association. They were collectively charged with failing the nation in the cold war against Communism. The book went through twenty printings and sold 6.8 million copies in less than a year. There are few heroes in Stormer's book. In a scant reference, Rickover is made one.

In the debate on the future of education came charges from the left that the anti-Dewey forces were elitists intent on building an authoritarian, undemocratic society. Advocates of Dewey considered themselves pragmatists who wanted to teach children the skills needed to solve problems in a changing world. Out of this came a theory that confronted Rickover when he launched his attacks. The "progressive" theory held that education should be a force to change society, that schools could be social instruments. Sputnik challenged that view and gave the "traditionalists," represented by the Council for Basic Education, an issue. Rickover became a major champion of the traditionalist view.

In *Swiss Schools* he summarized beliefs that dovetailed with those of the traditionalists:

> American education has been dominated for almost half a century by "progressives" who want schools to be child- rather than subject-centered. On the grounds that to be democratic the school must let the child determine what he wants to study, the progressives have allowed less academically talented youth to shun the difficult subjects that make up basic education and to substitute easy life-adjustment and vocational know-how courses. . . .
>
> Progressives look upon the school as society in miniature and seek to transfer democratic theory and practice from the adult world of politics to the child's world of education.

Rickover carried this message to many podiums as a lecturer—and as a witness testifying in Congress, for he usually laced his reports on nuclear power with his opinions about American education. He was listened to, and his opponents even conceded that he helped to make them take a harder look at their progressive curricula.

His books, particularly *Swiss Schools,* did not fare as well as he did. Much of the Swiss book was devoted to an exhaustive analysis of curricula from kindergarten to university, and a history of higher education on the Continent. Sometimes there were three or four footnotes to a page. He devoted a 24-page appendix to "a mathematics-science, type-C maturity school in Basel" and used thirteen pages for a mathematics examination, complete with diagrams.

He praised the Swiss system, which set national standards that, in effect, regulated curricula. "The Swiss solutions may not be suitable for us," he wrote. "Nevertheless they show that democracy and federalism *can* be combined with national standards that preserve and enhance the quality of education." Ironically, it was this concept—essentially, direct federal involvement in education—that almost simultaneously brought him to a crest and brought him down.

The year 1962 saw not only the publication of the book but also a serious threat to his continuance in the Navy. President Kennedy, through Secretary of the Navy John Connally, extended Rickover beyond statutory retirement as a stopgap. The Navy, though, wanted him out. And there was a way to do it without antagonizing Congress: President Kennedy could appoint Rickover U.S. Commissioner of Education.

The idea lived for weeks, if not months, in the circle of Kennedy's advisers, and word of it was deliberately leaked to educators, including the NEA.

From Secretary McNamara on down through the hierarchy of the Defense Department and the Navy, Rickover was a target for involuntary retirement. He himself seemed to be cooperating by seeking the commissionership. Some time in 1962—the exact date is unknown—submariner Richard Laning was told by Rickover that he might try to become Commissioner of Education. He also said he was going to write another book on education, this one comparing the U.S. system with that of England.

In February of 1962 he spoke to the Navy Doctors' Wives Club luncheon at the National Naval Medical Center, in Bethesda, Maryland, where he had recently been a patient. After talking about education, he asked for questions, and according to reports from many of the 220 women there, he liberally sprinkled his answers with insults. Several women reported that he said that most American mothers were not capable of educating their children. When a woman questioned him about an answer, he responded, "I can see I can't satisfy you. . . . You appear to be a woman no one can satisfy." He criticized the Parent-Teachers Association because all its members did was "worry themselves with school lunches," and he said that there was not one secondary school in the United States that could compare with secondary schools abroad.

Once more there was embarrassment for the Navy, this time heated by officers' wives scorned. President Kennedy would make friends in the Pentagon and in the Navy if he did name Rickover U.S. Commissioner of

Education. But he would make few friends among educators, and more importantly, he would lose friends in Congress.

Rickover had been advocating national scholastic standards without looking beyond the issue to the political mine field it represented. Just as he would zealously advocate nuclear-powered ships without seeing the total needs of the Navy, so he did not see in this educational advocacy the beliefs of his traditional political supporters. Or at least it appeared that he did not see. His statements on education shed no light on his own political beliefs. He seemed to be looking on educational problems as an engineer would look upon technological problems—no political context was necessary.

What Rickover was advocating was a national board or commission that would establish educational standards. As he would prescribe at length in his next book, *American Education—A National Failure*, Congress would set up a "National Standards Committee . . . composed of men of national stature and eminence," which would "act as an educational watchtower announcing danger when it saw it approaching." The committee would also "formulate a national scholastic standard . . . which would make us internationally competitive and would also respond to our specific domestic needs."

The committee would set the standard (an engineer's concept) by means of examinations. Here are Rickover's thoughts on the examinations:

> No one would have to take them, but those who passed would receive national accreditation. The Committee would in no way interfere with established institutions now granting diplomas or degrees. . . .
>
> [The Committee's] job would be to draw up national examinations going deeply into a candidate's true knowledge and intellectual caliber—on IBM-graded multiple-choice tests. . . . The Committee might provide one set of examinations at the level appropriate for a high school graduate who aspires to enter a first-rate college; another set of examinations at the level of students who may wish to prepare for a semiprofessional or technician's job but not requiring a bachelor's degree . . . another for graduates of various types of colleges, especially those bound for the teaching profession. I stress again that no one would need to take these examinations; but those who did pass them successfully would obtain national certification—perhaps the notation U.S. National Scholar—stamped on their regular diplomas or degrees.

The "National Standard" and the "U.S. National Scholar" were nothing less than federal involvement in local education. Rickover's proposal came at a time when die-hard integrationists raged against federal regulations enforcing racial equality. Firms with federal contracts had been told to report how many black employees they had or risk the loss of contracts; the Justice Department had gone to court to stop segregation in hospitals built with federal funds; U.S. marshals and federal troops had enforced the desegregation of the University of Mississippi. And to this Rickover would add federal intervention in local education.

"I never did understand Rickover," a nationally known educator told the authors. "He operated in an educational vacuum. 'National standards' in political terms is anti-states' rights. Some states have said that setting their own standards *is* a right. He didn't understand what he was saying. We don't have one educational system. We have fifty, or fifty-seven if you count the territories. Every one is different. Congressmen know that. They're politicians. They don't want people coming into their states and telling them what to do. He didn't understand that."

But if his old Southern friends were shocked, they kept their peace. On the other hand, some educators and liberal legislators and federal officials saw merit in what he was proposing. Sterling M. McMurrin, U.S. Commissioner of Education, said that Rickover's "impact on American education has been very, very good for education." And President Kennedy was trying to get Congress to pass legislation giving federal aid to elementary and secondary schools. When McMurrin announced his resignation in July 1962, Kennedy directed Secretary of Health, Education, and Welfare Anthony J. Celebrezze to start looking for a new Commissioner of Education.

Three educators of that era recalled the reports of Rickover's imminent appointment. "Several names were floating around," an official of the National Education Association remembered. "and his was one of them. We couldn't believe it." Another NEA staff member of the time said, "He was a candidate. He definitely was." The White House confidentially passed names through the NEA to get reactions. Although the memory of Rickover's name lingers, there is no NEA record of the reaction except a general reminiscence of shock.

Francis A. J. Ianni, now a professor of anthropology at Columbia Teachers College, worked for NEA at the time. He recalled hearing "new rumors every day. . . . Some of the suggestions got rather outlandish. Admiral Rickover, for example, at one point was presented as the most likely candidate." There was also talk, Ianni remembered, that Rickover had solid support from officials of the Massachusetts Institute of Technology, where in 1949 he had initiated courses in nuclear engineering for officers he selected.

The consensus was that Rickover finally lost out because he was not an educator. The post had always gone to a professional educator, and President Kennedy's advisers apparently saw no reason to establish a new precedent. Liberals' support for Rickover's national-standards proposal, however, indicated that ideologically Rickover was acceptable.

By the late fall of 1962 Rickover was no longer a candidate for commissioner. The choice was Francis Keppel, dean of the Harvard Graduate School of Education and a backer of Rickover's national-standards proposal, which, Keppel said, "would be useful to parents, to schools and everybody else."

That was the high point of Rickover's career as a critic of education. His third and final book on the subject, *American Education—A National Failure*, was subtitled *The Problem of Our Schools and What We Can Learn from England*. The idea of comparing our system with that of another country was no longer new. The book itself had a makeshift quality—502 pages, including eight "annexes." One annex was a reprint from the Michigan State Press. Another included handwritten examinations by British students. Others were from Congressional testimony. One chapter was reprinted from *Swiss Schools*. One 94-page section contained 102 footnotes.

But a reader of the book could learn, inversely, what Rickover's critics had been saying of his proposals, for he responded to criticism by putting it in quotes within his sentences: "I would like to register a protest against being accused of wishing to 'militarize American education' or turn it into 'education for the elite.' . . . I have never urged that we 'educate the best and shoot the rest.' . . . The educational concepts I support are not 'archaic, fossilized or medieval' nor do I advocate that we return to . . . 'the Athenian master-slave state.' . . . I am not 'out to destroy democracy' nor am I indifferent 'to the broader human values.' I have never advocated that 'technical education replace the humanities.' On the contrary, I keep pleading for more science and humanities. . . ."

He was not the wild-eyed crypto-fascist that some of his critics conjured up. He was a man so narrowly focused on what he was advocating that he was innocent of the political consequences of doing things his way. In a way, he would have been an ideal U.S. Commissioner of Education, for he would have been the consummate bureaucrat—the man who performs tasks thoroughly but does not lift his gaze above the task to see the policy and the total picture. Nowhere in his writings was there any indication of sensitivity for blacks or other minority groups, not because he was a bigot, but because he was a pragmatist. His plan would ultimately take care of the best and the brightest, and if there were blacks and Hispanics and poor kids among them, that was the way it was supposed to be.

"My creed is a simple one," he honestly wrote. "Every American child, wherever he may live, whatever may be his religion, race, social origin, every child should get an equal opportunity at school to become educated up to the highest level he is able to reach. That is as far as we can go.... You can't carry equality into areas where rights must be *earned.* Our political rights were earned by earlier Americans in the past. But the right to a good education must be earned by everyone for himself."

He never stopped talking about education and he never stopped getting into trouble over it. In 1963, speaking at the convocation of the Fund for the Republic, Rickover said of women in the PTA: "They're an infernal nuisance, and ought to stay home and take care of their husbands." Later, he came as close as he could to apologizing. "I really didn't mean this," he told a friendly columnist, Drew Pearson. But, he added, "I'm glad my remark sparked discussion of the role of the PTAs.... I just don't want the PTAs to get engrossed in refreshments and fund-raising."

Rickover did not like the way of life of male parents, either. (But he could not have been thinking of the ones in the Naval Reactors Branch.) "Parents make a good living without themselves having had a particularly rigorous education, and often without having to work very hard. If the father works a five-day week, if he wastes his leisure time, if he goes on long vacations, how can he expect to convince his children they ought to go to school six days a week and for more than 180 days a year?" he said in rambling commentary at a hearing.

He continued to give Congress the benefit of his thinking on aspects of education.

On equality: "In a society blinded by the equality myth, talent is no longer deemed necessary; mediocrity will suffice. In an affluent society, the alienated who clamor for power are largely untalented people who cannot make use of the unprecedented opportunities for self-realization, and cannot escape the confrontation with an ineffectual self."

Education as a mirror: "Defects in our educational system are reflections of weaknesses and shortcomings in our national life.... The danger lies in confusing explanation with justification. Because racial discrimination can be explained historically is no reason for viewing it in any other light than as an abomination. So with defects and weaknesses in American education. To explain them is not to condone them."

On college disorders: "Most of the agitation in colleges is not by students who are studying hard subjects such as engineering, mathematics, law, medicine, science, history. It is usually by those in the social sciences—a field which requires no hard study, no exact answers, and in which everyone's opinion, young or old, appears to have equal value."

On corporal punishment. Asked, "How about that old adage, Admiral, 'Spare the rod and spoil the child?' " Rickover answered, "You apparently haven't the latest books on child upbringing. Nowadays, one year the books tell mothers to feed their babies by the bottle and spank them; next year they are instructed to feed them at the breast and never say 'no' to them. Take your choice. . . . Babies are appealing little creatures, but, truth to say, barbarian, self-centered, and the world's worst tyrants if you let them have their way. Raising them means guiding them toward more mature and responsible conduct. I was like that."

"There was no way in God's world that he would be taken seriously by educators," a senior NEA official told the authors, recalling the days of Rickover's crusade. "In education, everybody thinks he or she is an expert. It's what everybody has experienced. We've got a million critics because people speak from their own limited experience. Admiral Rickover spoke from that, and also out of his experience in the military. He was feeling frustration. The armed forces were inheriting the products of public schools.

"Only public schools and the armed services have to take whatever comes to them. We can't say, 'You can't come here. You're too dumb.' We don't train elitists. He liked the English system, where kids get put on tracks. The English train elitists. Their government people are all alumni of certain schools. They are overt about their system. We have a different system—a different economic system, a different political system. We cannot be overt about elitism. But that was his perspective—elitist."

There is a relatively objective way to gauge educators' declining concern about Rickover's criticisms: the *Education Index,* a cumulative list of important writings on educational subjects. The *Index* has six entries for "Rickover" from June 1957 to June 1959; five from July 1959 to June 1961; three from July 1961 to June 1963; two from July 1963 to June 1964; and none from then through June 1966. "By 1964," an educational researcher said, "Rickover was gone."

The 1974 edition of the *Encyclopaedia Britannica,* under "Rickover, Hyman G(eorge)," carries a picture of him in uniform and devotes nearly a column to his work in nuclear power. The article ends, "In the 1960s he was prominent as a critic of the U.S. educational system."

28

From Shippingport
to Three Mile Island

Thanksgiving Day 1957 was the first real day off that Captain Joseph H. Barker, Jr., had had in a long while. For months he had been regularly working holidays and weekends as well as nights. Barker was the project officer for a nuclear reactor that had been initially planned to power an aircraft carrier and was now destined to be the power source of America's first large-scale nuclear power plant. It was being built in Shippingport, Pennsylvania, and it was a little behind schedule.

At about 9:30 A.M. Thanksgiving Day morning, Barker got his first call from Admiral Rickover. Some electrical circuit difficulty had come up at the Shippingport site. Would Barker call Shippingport, look into the problem, and call back? Barker did. A little while later, the phone rang again. "It would be the site calling to give me information and tell me Rickover called and wanted something," Barker remembered. "And then I would call Rickover. Then I would call the site. And then the site would call me again.

"The calls kept coming, and I started keeping track. All sorts of comments were relayed from Washington to the site and vice versa. All day long. My wife was in tears. Finally, she and my mother and sons went out to the movies. On the twenty-third phone call, at 11 P.M. that night, Lawton Geiger in Pittsburgh told me he thought the exercise was over. He was going to bed, and he advised me to do the same. But it was too late then to eat Thanksgiving dinner."

Barker had been used to such days and could later laugh about it. In his recollections there was a grudging respect and admiration for Rickover, and happier memories of accomplishment at Shippingport. The building of that pioneer nuclear plant was a remarkable event in the lives of Barker, Geiger, and hundreds of others; it was a remarkable chapter in the history of nuclear power; and it was another remarkable case study of how Rickover got things done. He was an officer in the U.S. Navy, yet he would direct the creation of a civilian power plant. He would also help to launch the nuclear-power industry and would institute practices in that industry which would still be debated by investigators of the Three Mile Island accident twenty-two years later. He himself would become involved in that debate.

The roots of this Shippingport project were entwined in the roots of nuclear-carrier plans, which dated back to 1950, when Admiral Forrest P. Sherman formally asked the Bureau of Ships "to explore the feasibility" of building a nuclear-powered aircraft carrier. Rickover's group followed through almost immediately with a proposal for a prototype, land-based carrier reactor. When Sherman died in July 1951, the key supporter for a nuclear carrier was lost. But, according to the authoritative *Nuclear Navy,* Rickover, marshaling "new forces for his cause," soon "established a close relationship" with Atomic Energy Commissioner Thomas E. Murray and Senator Brien McMahon, chairman of the Joint Committee on Atomic Energy.

Rickover's moves would lead him not only to Shippingport but also to Capitol Hill. It was at this precise point that he began making his first influential connections beyond the Navy. Still a captain, still relatively unknown, his promotion fights ahead of him, Rickover had begun a process that he would refine in years to come: When the Navy—rarely—refused him he would invoke his connections in the Congress or the AEC; in the less common event that it was the AEC that resisted him, he would seek the support of the Congress and the Navy.

But this time the Navy and the AEC ultimately fell in line, endorsing Rickover's proposal for a land-based prototype reactor plant for future use in an aircraft carrier. The proposal, whose cost Rickover put at $150 million, next had to go through the budget-cutting gantlet set up by the incoming Eisenhower Administration. President Eisenhower had appointed Lewis L. Strauss special Presidential assistant on atomic energy. Strauss, a founding member of the AEC, would soon return to the commission as its chairman. A reserve rear admiral and a supporter of atomic energy, Strauss was also a hard-eyed pragmatist in a field full of visionaries.

The "atom" was still reverberating with the power of the atomic bomb. *Nuclear* was not yet as popular an adjective as the awesome *atomic.* An "atomic-powered" airplane under development was expected to fly 1,000 miles per hour. There were predictions that atomic power would be so cheap that electricity would cost virtually nothing. Gold and platinum could be extracted from the sea at such low cost that the once-precious metals would be used to line pipes and tanks carrying corrosive liquids. In President Eisenhower's inaugural parade was a weapon that would become a relic of the primitive era of the atomic age, the Army's 280-millimeter "atomic cannon."

On March 31, 1953, at a meeting of the National Security Council, Strauss recommended that the Navy's carrier reactor and the Air Force's atomic airplane be dropped from the budget. On April 22, at another NSC meeting, President Eisenhower accepted Strauss's recommendations. But the President said that this did not mean that he would turn down a proposal to make the carrier reactor a civilian project. Rickover thus had an opening, though he, a mere captain, was opposed by two powerful men: Deputy Secretary of Defense Robert M. Kyes and Robert LeBaron, Assistant Secretary of Defense for atomic matters. Both had told Rickover that the carrier reactor proposal was dead. Rickover appealed directly to Gordon Dean, chairman of the AEC, and got Murray to urge Henry D. Smyth, another AEC commissioner, to write to the President.

Smyth, a veteran of the Manhattan Project's bomb development work, wrote, "We are convinced that the pressurized light-water reactor, which is the heart of the planned large ship propulsion unit, offers a promising avenue of approach which must be pursued vigorously if the Nation is to get on with the job of attaining civilian power."

Murray next met with President Eisenhower on May 4 and lobbied for the transformation of the unbuilt reactor from carrier to civilian. Twenty-seven days later, Murray accompanied Rickover to the AEC's testing facility in Idaho, where Rickover gave Murray the privilege of being the first person to open the control valve of the *Nautilus* Mark I, the world's first operational nuclear power plant. (There was another first—the incident marked the initial use of the Rickover technique of awarding perquisites to men of influence.)

Rickover was also showing his genius for long-range planning. Commander Barker, who had reported to the Naval Reactors Branch in December 1952, was assigned in early 1953 to the Pittsburgh Area Office of the AEC. This office occupied space adjacent to Westinghouse's Bettis Laboratory. An officer in the Navy's Civil Engineer Corps, Barker was quite knowledgeable on matters relating to large-scale construction. By luck or by shrewd anticipation of events, Rickover had in place a man who could coordinate the building of a power plant. And he had a facility that was coming more and more under his direct control. Bettis had been created by Westinghouse in an act of faith inspired by Rickover's conversion of Gwilym A. Price, president of Westinghouse, into a true believer in atomic power.

The other major AEC reactor development facility, the Argonne National Laboratory near Chicago, was outside Rickover's sphere of influence. Rickover, moving toward his role as director of a civilian enterprise, had been focusing on Bettis. The two contrasting laboratories reflected a similar split in the ranks of high-level officials of the AEC. Rickover, with his converted carrier reactor, was on an independent track. On the conventional track was Stuart McLain, chief of the AEC's production reactor branch, who was developing a potentially competing reactor through Argonne.

The choice of one of the two approaches would be made by Lawrence R. Hafstad, director of reactor development and no fan of Rickover. At that time, a popular theory in the AEC held that it was possible to build a reactor that could fulfill three separate functions: power a ship, power an electrical generating plant, and function as a production reactor—a reactor that produces fissionable material for use in nuclear weapons. Neither Hafstad nor Rickover believed in the three-purpose-reactor theory, but they differed greatly in their respective attitudes toward the way public utilities should participate in nuclear projects. Rickover would presumably develop the civilian reactor the way he was developing submarine reactors: he was the man in charge; private industry did what he told it to do.

The capitalists were assembling. Walker L. Cisler, dynamic president of the Detroit Edison Company, had come forward with promises of a coalition of companies that would foster a reactor industry in America. Cisler, a Cornell engineering graduate, had been president of a large utility company since 1951. In that same year he had been given approval by the AEC for a "design phase" of a commercial reactor. The work should be done, at no government expense, by Detroit Edison and Dow Chemical.

Cisler was an adherent of the breeder reactor—a type radically different from Rickover's. Electric power from a breeder reactor became a reality when Experimental Breeder Reactor No. 1 lighted four 200-watt light bulbs at the AEC's National Reactor Testing Station. The date was December 20, 1951, long before the construction of Rickover's Mark I reactor prototype at the same Idaho site. EBR No. 1 was the creation of Walter Zinn of Argonne Laboratory.

A breeder reactor produces more fuel than it consumes. When the uranium atoms in the fuel bundle split, the released neutrons are not "slowed down" or "captured," as in the nonbreeder. Instead, neutrons "breed," in the sense of increasing their atomic weights so that uranium atoms become plutonium atoms. In about four years a fuel bundle consisting of 2,200 pounds of uranium can produce about 3,000 pounds of plutonium. The plutonium can then be used as fuel for a power plant— and it, in turn, will continue to breed.

Previously, utility executives had only dreamed of such things. Coal did not breed; oil did not breed; natural gas did not breed. Here was a fuel that would eventually cost nothing, or practically nothing. Cisler easily rounded up supporters from utilities that included such major companies as Consolidated Edison of New York and Philadelphia Electric. But Rickover was concerned about the inherent problems of the breeder's product. Plutonium, the deadliest substance made by man—little exists in nature—has a half-life of 24,000 years. That characteristic increased the problems of waste disposal. And its potential use in nuclear bombs increased the problems of keeping it out of the wrong hands.

Lines were being drawn. On one side Rickover, Murray, Bettis Laboratory, Westinghouse. On the other Zinn, Strauss, Argonne Laboratory, Cisler and his utilities. The Navy was not officially involved. Unofficially, the Navy was getting rid of Rickover, who would have been retired in June 1953 if the Navy system had worked. But he actually was on the verge of being promoted to rear admiral through the efforts of Congress. (The announcement would be routinely made by President Eisenhower in July.)

Behind the lines were others. W. Sterling Cole, chairman of the Joint Committee on Atomic Energy, was basically against the Navy's taking over a project that Cole thought belonged to free enterprise. James M. Dunford, one of the Oak Ridge originals, was an assistant to Murray; still a Rickover loyalist, Dunford kept communications open between Murray and Rickover. Members of Congress, led by Senator Henry M. Jackson and Representative Sidney R. Yates, had worked to get Rickover his promotion; they would work to get him the reactor.

Cole had questioned Navy involvement in what had been envisioned as a civilian industry. His questions raised another one about any government participation in the production of civilian electric power. President Eisenhower, like Strauss, was suspicious of federal intrusion into areas reserved for private enterprise, and one of the most sensitive of these areas was electric power. Eisenhower, who once called the Tennessee Valley Authority "creeping socialism," in 1954 would get into political trouble by trying to circumvent the TVA. He contracted with the Dixon-Yates syndicate to build a private-enterprise power plant on the Mississippi River; later, under pressure, he canceled the contract.

Strauss saw himself as having a mandate to uphold the Atomic Energy Act's specific pledge that "free competition in private enterprise" would be the route for the development of nuclear power in the United States. He was bothered by the image of a naval officer heading the epochal civilian project. And so was Cole, who, although supporting the converted-carrier-reactor proposal, wrote to Strauss—now AEC chairman—on July 8, 1953:

> Any advantage which . . . might be gained from a demonstration of the interest of the United States in peaceful application of atomic energy might . . . be impaired if administration of the program results in too heavy emphasis on the Navy aspects of the objectives. Such impairment might result from Navy direction, extensive Navy specifications, and the inevitable "leaked" [news] articles referring to aircraft carrier reactor prototypes. . . .

The day after he received Cole's letter, however, Strauss chaired a meeting of the AEC, which approved the assignment of the reactor to Rickover. What had been officially known as the CVR ("CV" being the Navy's designation for aircraft carrier, and "R" meaning reactor) became the PWR for "pressurized-water reactor." Hafstad, as director of reactor development (and one in a long line of Rickover's theoretical bosses), sent a teletype to the AEC offices responsible for Argonne and Bettis. The specifications for the PWR were given in the message, but they were not attributed to their source, Rickover's Naval Reactors Branch. The message said that Westinghouse would be the principal contractor and the Naval Reactors Branch would be responsible for the project.

Nearly a month later Strauss got around to answering Cole:

> [This] reactor will be as you described it . . . "a completely civilian version." No compromise or [hybrid] is planned or needed . . . no naval engineering will be introduced into this design if it would cause any delay or increase the cost or affect the economical functioning of this reactor for its primary purpose as a central station powerplant. . . . there will be no subordination of the primary civilian power objective to military considerations.

·

What seemed to influence Strauss was not admiration for Rickover but a sense of urgency. The Eisenhower Administration needed a demonstration of what was then referred to as "the peaceful use of the atom." The Administration feared that the Soviet Union might build a power reactor and win new friends from countries that had been looking to the United States for nuclear leadership. England and France, along with Canada, Norway and Australia, were all working on nuclear power plants. The Administration wanted America to be first—but not at a price that would strain the budget. Since Rickover had already done a great deal of work on reactors, his approach was a good investment.

Strauss was not then, nor would he ever be, a supporter of Rickover. Their fights were many, although Strauss did remember them with some fondness. In his memoirs, Strauss wrote of Rickover: "His personality was astringent—some even found it abrasive, though I did not—and his job was to him the most important assignment in the whole world, taking precedence over any other enterprise of anyone else whatever. . . . Toes trodden in the process were merely casualties in the path of achievement."

Significantly, it was Rickover's champion on the AEC, Commissioner Murray, who, in a speech on October 22, made the announcement about the Commission's plan to build a reactor. Referring to concern "about the psychological effect of a Navy man in charge," Murray said that "the only Navy aspect which the admiral will bring to this work is his title."

This was not what happened. Already at work on the PWR was Commander Barker of the Navy's Civil Engineer Corps, and the new Rear Admiral Rickover had assigned Commander Roddis, then functioning as Rickover's deputy, and Commander Roth directly to the PWR project. Many of the other key men were naval officers. They were all being paid by the U.S. Navy, not the AEC. When Roth, who would soon leave Rickover, asked why NRB was going to build a civilian reactor, he recalled that Rickover told him, "Civilian power plants mean nothing to me. But if it gets built by Westinghouse and I'm not allowed in, then the next thing we know Westinghouse would be in NR [Naval Reactors]." Rickover also believed that a new federal agency might be created and he would lose control of the reactor effort that was already under way.

A few months after Murray's announcement, Rickover again showed his attitude toward industry. On a train trip he happened to encounter David E. Lilienthal, the former head of the TVA who had become the first chairman of the AEC back in 1947. In his journal, Lilienthal later etched a perceptive portrait of the Rickover he saw in July 1954, at a time of incredible toil and tension—*Nautilus* launched but still untried; the radically powered *Seawolf* on the ways; the civilian reactor without a site. Lilienthal wrote:

> There is a kind of Chinese, or in any case, an oriental, repose or immobility in his expression which is strange, considering that what he says is usually severely condemnatory of others and extreme. . . . [He said] with a quick look, "Are you cleared?" I didn't particularly care for the way he framed the question, but said, no, and added that this made things easier for me. "Doesn't make them easy for me," he said. And he started off full tilt: the *Nautilus* at New London had her nuclear engine in her, will go off on a trial cruise this summer—figures on how far she can cruise, at how many knots, without surfacing. . . .
>
> I congratulated him on all this, but went on to say that while there were unique advantages presumably, in a nuclear-powered sub, most of the talk and professions about land-based civilian electric power plants, from the atom, seemed to me hopelessly optimistic and unrealistic. . . . The talk about having economic power, competitive with other forms of electricity, in a few years, such as one ran into all the time, seemed to me showed undue optimism, and a failure to appreciate the difficulties. . . . To my surprise, instead of rearing back and letting me have it—as I expected and almost counted on—his little gray face grew very sad. He couldn't agree with me more; why do people say things that don't make sense, and mislead people? And so on.

Lilienthal asked Rickover why he thought any work should be going on at all on nuclear plants. "Two reasons," Rickover replied. "Prestige, and the need to begin development of every resource we have, since we are chewing up our natural resources at a remarkable rate." Then, Lilienthal said, Rickover "launched into a violent attack on industry, particularly big industry, for using up our minerals, etc., 'for things that aren't needed.' "

The announcement about the civilian reactor mentioned three possible sites: Oak Ridge; Paducah, Kentucky; and Portsmouth, Ohio. In or near each place was an AEC facility. But when utility firms failed to flock to the AEC, formal invitations were issued, and it was obvious that the three proposed sites represented wishful thinking. Rather, the reactor would be built where some utility wanted it built. Of nine proposals, one stood out, financially, for the government. It came from the Duquesne Light Company of Pittsburgh.

Duquesne offered to put up $5 million toward the cost of the reactor; pay for the steam produced; build and operate the electric generating plant; operate the reactor after the AEC built it; and provide the site—at Shippingport, a small town on the Ohio River, about twenty-five miles west of Pittsburgh. Near there, by luck, Rickover had people and a friendly facility, Bettis.

The summer was spent in negotiation between Rickover and Duquesne and between Rickover and contractors. Ground was finally broken on September 6, 1954, when President Eisenhower, in Denver, waved a wand containing neutrons. This activated a fission detector, which closed a switch, sending current to Shippingport and turning on a device on an unmanned bulldozer, which started up and chugged around the site as a robot ground breaker. That was the last time any work was done at the site without Rickover's direct supervision.

"The quality control was unbelievable," Barker recalled. "We were dealing with huge pipes—some of them eighteen inches in diameter. And welds that had hardly ever been tried before. We had to set up a school for welding stainless steel. Welds were inspected again and again. One weld that turned out to be bad was deep in the system when we found it. No one could get at it. But somebody knew about a midget who was a welder and did jobs just like this. He lived in Texas. We found him and flew him up. We lowered him on a rope. He took out the bad weld and put in a beauty. We paid him $100 an hour, and it took him nearly a week, working inside that pipe."

At the very beginning Rickover had stipulated the most important construction requirement: "Safety must be an overriding feature." He insisted upon safe practices for the power reactor as rigorous as those for his submarine reactors. But this was a different kind of reactor. It was called a "seed and blanket" design, developed by Alvin Radkowsky, a physicist who had worked for Rickover in NRB since 1948. The design lessened the need for weapons-grade fissionable material, somewhat simplified the reactor's mechanical controls, and eased future refueling procedures. The reactor was essentially two reactors in one—the self-sustaining "seed" and its somewhat subcritical "blanket." Neutrons "leaked" from the seed into the blanket and enabled the blanket to produce. Thus the seed, in effect, controlled the blanket. The system used a relatively small portion of enriched weapons-grade uranium and a large amount of natural uranium. The heart of the reactor consisted of nearly 100,000 fuel elements encased in zirconium, the metal that NRB had developed for the *Nautilus* reactor. Under development in 1948, zirconium had cost $300 a pound to produce; by 1957, the cost would be only $12.50 a pound.

Rickover had taken on a task which even for him was formidable. He had responsibility for the building of a new kind of reactor, for the unprecedented linking of it to a utility company electric generating plant, and for getting the job done by the end of 1957—a politically imposed deadline based on the Eisenhower Administration's Atoms for Peace program. He also guaranteed that the plant would produce "at least 60,-000 kilowatts of useful electric energy"—enough to supply the needs of a city of 100,000 or a city of 50,000, depending upon the relative enthusiasm of AEC press releases.

Much of what was done at Shippingport was precedent-setting. For example, Barker (recently promoted to captain) coordinated the production of what was probably America's first environmental-impact assessment. With the aid of meteorologists from the U.S. Weather Bureau and sanitary engineers from the U.S. Public Health Service, information was compiled on the possible effects of an accident at the plant on the Ohio River and surrounding areas. Special permits were obtained. Regulations worked out then eventually became state laws. Information on reactors was declassified, and the Manhattan Project tradition of secrecy ended. Inestimable technical information was developed and diffused through thousands of publications.

The building of Shippingport also introduced Rickover and American industry to each other. Submarine work, up until Shippingport, had been virtually handcraft. Rickover, like the manager of a small machine shop, was able to keep an eye on just about everything that was going on. But, first at Shippingport and later at the shipyards building the nuclear navy, Rickover learned that not all men worked as hard as the men in NRB worked. He met contractors whose livelihood did not entirely depend upon pleasing Rickover and the Navy; he discovered that the speeding-up of union workers means costly overtime; and he saw budgets wiped out by what would come to be called cost overruns. Reluctantly, angrily, he had to go to the AEC and ask for more money than he had expected he would need. Soon he would start making public speeches about the declining American work ethic.

Although Rickover kept Barker stationed in Washington, the project officer made one hundred and seven trips to Shippingport, the frequency, length and intensity of the trips increasing as the deadline—December 1957—neared. (Barker made fifty-two other trips while on the Shippingport assignment.) "I always had shirts and a razor in my desk in Washington," Barker remembered.

Rickover went to the site often, and his routine was generally the same: He would fly from Washington to Pittsburgh late in the afternoon. Barker, Geiger, or others would meet him at the airport and drive him to Bettis or the site, discussing problems in the car—"we were a captive audience." At the site Rickover would prowl around, asking questions, sending the vice presidents of contractor firms to the construction shacks for firsthand answers, checking on the welders' school, inspecting details, issuing orders. In the darkness, long after day's end, and after an awful meal in the cafeteria, Rickover would be driven back to downtown Pittsburgh, still asking questions all the way, and, along with his aides, would be put aboard the midnight train to Washington. He and his companions got some sleep on the train; they would be calling the site from Washington early the next morning.

Barker had known Rickover since their days together aboard the battleship *New Mexico* in the middle 1930s. "He was the assistant engineer officer, and he put up signs that said, 'When not in use, turn off the juice,' " Barker remembered. "You got to paint a red E on the stack as an award for engineering efficiency. It was based on the amount of oil you used. With him aboard, the *New Mexico* got three annual engineering Es in a row." They had also met briefly on Okinawa, where Barker had watched Rickover driving his men at the ship-repair facility.

But even the *New Mexico* and Okinawa had not prepared Barker for the frenzy at Shippingport, where time was so compressed that, looking back, he thought it seemed incredible that the project not only was finished on time but was finished at all.

One particular facet of the project especially captivated Barker, who began the project more comfortable with large objects than with atoms. The large object he was most fond of was the reactor containment vessel, which was formed of manganese-molybdenum carbon steel plates and forgings. Stainless-steel cladding had been roll-bonded to the plates. These were the thickest-clad plates ever roll-bonded in the United States. The vessel's shape was cylindrical, but jutting from the bottom of the cylinder was a hemisphere from which projected large fittings for eighteen-inch pipes. The top of the cylinder was open but flanged to receive a dome. The vessel weighed 153 tons, was 25 feet high, had walls 8⅜ inches thick, and was extremely awkward to move.

The vessel was built in Chattanooga, Tennessee, and transported to Shippingport on an oversize flatcar. Before the actual vessel was moved, however, a dummy was sent over parts of the route. When the train passed through tunnels at normal speed, the dummy swayed and sometimes scraped the tunnel walls. So, when the real vessel was carried, the train slowed down. Through one tunnel the clearance was two inches.

Arriving at the site, the vessel had to be lifted by a crane rated at being able to lift only 125 tons. Before entrusting to the crane the job of hoisting the 153-ton vessel, the crane had been given increasing loads to lift, and when it did not buckle at 165 tons, it was given the job. (Barker, decades later, still did not like to think what would have happened if the crane did buckle. He had no choice.)

Riggers found that there were no lifting attachments on the vessel. So, lifting lugs were designed to fit the bolt holes in the flange at the top of the vessel. The crane lifted it off the flatcar and slowly raised it to a vertical position. Barker, standing by a window, was on the telephone to Rickover in Washington. As the vessel rose toward the vertical, Barker reported the progress to Rickover: "Ten degrees angle . . . twenty degrees . . ." The crane suspended the vessel several feet above its final support, fifty-five feet down in a deep chamber. It was then transferred from the crane to a special suspension frame. The vessel hung there, while the plant took shape around it, from October 1956 to February 1957, as thermal insulation and shielding were added. It was then lowered deeper onto its permanent support, and the reactor core—heart of the plant—was inserted.

By the time the reactor vessel was delivered, Rickover had got authority from the AEC to put the site on a sixty-hour week, not the kind of sixty-hour week he and his NRB men put in, but one in which overtime was paid. He had pulled in workers from the Naval Reactor Facility at Idaho Falls, Idaho, and Electric Boat at Groton, Connecticut. The work force numbered about 750.

"Progress measurement tools" theoretically kept track of workers. When work fell behind schedule, the "tools" helped pinpoint the cause, and, as *The Shippingport Pressurized Water Reactor,* the official history of the construction effort, gently puts it, supervisors could "promptly initiate corrective action." One measurement tool was the number of welds and weld-man-hours, correlated with the number of feet of pipe installed. In the nuclear portion of the plant, there were 80,000 feet of pipe with 25,000 welds. A weld on a stainless-steel pipe, 18 inches in diameter with 1½-inch walls, for example, would take 150 man-hours.

•

Atomic progress beyond Shippingport was easier to measure. The atom had become a plaything of politicians and visionaries. They were envisioning the atom at work in the air and on the sea. Two projects—an atomic-powered airplane and an atomic-powered merchant ship—shimmered with hope and promise. The pipes and vessels of Shippingport had a harder gleam, and that was where Rickover could be found. He did not build dreams.

But in 1955 a dream was flying. A huge, modified B-36 strategic bomber flew with a small nuclear reactor on board. The aircraft was conventionally propelled with six piston and four turbojet engines. The reactor was used only to conduct experiments on radiation in flight. Forty-seven reactor flights were made without incident. Although the Air Force contended that the plane flew only over "unpopulated" areas with the reactor operating, such a flight plan was impossible from a practical viewpoint. Between 1956 and 1957 a single aircraft turbojet engine was actually powered—on the ground—by a nuclear reactor at the AEC test station in Idaho. This lashup was tested for 150 hours.

By June 1959, when Representative Melvin Price, chairman of the research and development subcommittee of the Joint Committee on Atomic Energy, gave a dismal report on the atomic airplane, the project was all but dead. Secretary of Defense Charles E. Wilson said the atomic-powered plane reminded him of a "shite-poke—a great bird that flies over the marshes, that doesn't have too much body or speed to it, or anything, but can fly." President Eisenhower wondered if the plane would ever get off the ground. (President Kennedy killed the atomic airplane shortly after taking office.)

Although he did not champion the atomic-powered airplane, President Eisenhower, as part of his U.S. Atoms for Peace program, did get the world's first atomic-powered merchant ship under way. Revealed in a speech in 1955, the N.S. *Savannah** was conceived as a civilian-built, civilian-run ship that would carry the message of peaceful atoms and free enterprise. Unlike Shippingport, the *Savannah* would not be dependent upon a naval reactor—or Hyman Rickover. Eisenhower had wanted the *Savannah* as a demonstration of peaceful uses of the atom, and a reactor developed by an admiral—possibly from one used for an atomic submarine—might not demonstrate American sincerity. The *Savannah* was designed as a combination cargo-and-passsenger ship, with staterooms for

---

* *The N.S. [for nuclear ship] Savannah was named after the first ship to be powered by steam on the open sea. Built in New York in 1818, she carried an auxillary steam engine, which she used for eighty hours on her twenty-seven-day maiden crossing of the Atlantic.*

sixty guests in addition to her crew. Top speed was to be twenty knots, and that was exceeded in service.

Mrs. Richard Nixon, wife of the Vice President, presided at the *Savannah*'s keel laying on May 22, 1958, at the New York Shipbuilding Corporation's yard in Camden, New Jersey. (Mrs. Eisenhower would christen the ship just over a year later.) The *Savannah* was the yard's first nuclear ship; the nuclear freighter would be followed by a nuclear frigate, the *Truxtun,* and several nuclear submarines before the yard went out of business in the 1960s.

About May 1959, a few weeks after Admiral James took over as Chief of BuShips, Rickover told him that the *Savannah*—then a year on the ways—was being run by a bunch of amateurs, could cause a major catastrophe, and should be stopped. James, as coordinator of shipbuilding (both naval and merchant), looked into the project. He decided it was "a hell of a good thing . . . to develop a competitive ship reactor plant," and he told Rickover so.

Representative Herbert C. Bonner, chairman of the House Merchant Marine and Fisheries Committee, along with other members, at first supported the idea. But criticism from Rickover lessened Congressional support, and Bonner later ridiculed the *Savannah,* calling it "a sideshow ship . . . a carnival ship . . . a Mississippi riverboat." The building of the ship, directed by a star-crossed bureaucratic mating of the Maritime Administration of the Department of Commerce and the AEC, was a nightmare of technical problems. The ship's reactor, although it eventually proved feasible, was a one-time phenomenon; to the shock of the Naval Reactors Branch, no prototype was built. At one time, John A. McCone, who became chairman of the AEC in July 1958, called upon Rickover to, as he put it, "send my people to review the design of the plant and make recommendations on how to straighten it out." Only some of the recommendations were accepted, Rickover said. He never hesitated to criticize the *Savannah* or civilian nuclear-powered ships in general.

The *Savannah* was not finished until 1962, and labor troubles kept her in port for a year. When at last she did sail off on her peaceful mission, she was a success. She made five transatlantic crossings and thirty port calls in fourteen countries. In 1965 she was chartered for $1 a year to a company that sailed her commercially to twenty-five countries.

But, primarily because of her design and crew costs, the ship was too expensive to operate and could not compete with other merchant ships. In 1970 she was retired and presented to the city of Savannah as a museum of the Eisenhower Peace Center. Her nuclear core was removed, but radiation lingered on.

During a Congressional hearing in 1979, Assistant Secretary of Commerce Robert Blackwell was asked about the radiation. "We take readings every day," he said. "It is not a threat to the area or to the inhabitants, but frankly I wouldn't want it in my neighborhood."

Shippingport was built on time. On December 2, 1957, exactly fifteen years after Enrico Fermi and his team of physicists at the University of Chicago produced the world's first sustained nuclear chain reaction, Hyman Rickover and his driven work force produced criticality in the nation's first reactor devoted to the powering of an electrical generating plant. At 12:39 A.M. on December 18, the main generator was synchronized with the reactor's steam-driven turbine. Joe Barker was there. He then spent a few hours on an army cot in the field office.

Ten days later, the plant made a continuous 100-hour power run at 60,000 kilowatts of electric power, and the Duquesne Light Company had a nuclear power plant to operate. But weeks before, Rickover had insisted on limiting Duquesne's authority. Acting on his own, Rickover told Philip A. Fleger, chairman of Duquesne's board of directors, that the reactor would not start up until Duquesne signed an agreement that, as Rickover later stated it, "at any time the plant was operating one of my representatives could be present in the control room with authority to shut the plant down if he thought it was not being operated safely."

After some arguing, Fleger reluctantly agreed, and from the first day of operation on, Rickover has controlled Shippingport through the presence of his representatives. Twice a representative has shut down the plant.

The "whole reactor game hangs on a much more slender thread than most people are aware," Rickover said a few months before the Shippingport reactor went critical. "There are a lot of things that can go wrong and it requires eternal vigilance. All we have to have is one good accident in the United States and it might set the whole game back for a generation. We do not want that to happen."

It did happen in March 1979, and Rickover once more had given advice that had gone unheeded. It happened near Harrisburg, Pennsylvania, at Three Mile Island.

29

Danger: Radiation Hazard

The "event" at Three Mile Island became the worst accident ever to strike the nation's nuclear-power industry, and it was having the effect that Rickover had predicted. Members of the Nuclear Regulatory Commission were holding marathon meetings that would begin on the day of the accident, March 28, 1979, and go on almost continually until April 1. One of the commissioners, John F. Ahearne, former Deputy Assistant Secretary of Energy, got a call from Admiral Rickover.

Ahearne later told the other commissioners that "the Admiral also informed me that any service that we want of anybody in the Navy should go to the Admiral—"

Most of the commissioners' deliberations were taped; the transcript at this point noted "(Laughter)" and Ahearne continued: "Even the Chief of Naval Operations."

"Do you want a carrier?" NRC chairman Joseph M. Hendrie jocularly asked.

"Let's not knock it," said Commissioner Richard Kennedy. "You will recall that the Admiral's program works."

Kennedy spoke prophetically. The heart of the crisis at Three Mile Island was a gas bubble that had built up in the core of the new reactor in Unit 2 at Three Mile Island, on the Susquehanna River eleven miles from Harrisburg. About 150 miles to the west was the Shippingport reactor that Rickover had built nearly twenty-two years before. What Rickover and his Naval Reactors group had learned from that reactor would not be handed down to the NRC—men who, in the words of Hendrie, were "operating completely in the blind." That was never the way Rickover worked. He had insisted that he have his own man at Shippingport, and he had got his way. In the records of the NR group was a complete chronicle of everything that had happened there. Now, as the NRC

616

began its investigation of Three Mile Island, the commissioners realized they had little information about that plant.

Rickover sent no aircraft carrier, but he did send men from the Naval Reactors offices in Pittsburgh and Schenectady, and the Knolls Atomic Power Laboratory's emergency action coordinating team. Members of the team worked on assessing the bubble. Would it explode? The team's answer was no. They based their answers on solid facts, not on speculation. While they went about their work, Hendrie was complaining that he could not tell the governor of Pennsylvania what was going on at Three Mile Island. "His information is ambiguous," Hendrie said, "mine is nonexistent."

The discussion about Rickover came on April 4, when the crisis was easing off. In an atmosphere not as tense as it had been a few days before, the commissioners were giving each other minor, telephone-calling chores. Hendrie begged off. "No, no. I'm sorry," he said. "I've gone into a close-coupled communication with Admiral Rickover and that is all I can handle. You're going to have to continue to do the governors." The commissioners laughed.

"You've got one state," said Commissioner Victor Gilinsky.

"I do Pennsylvania and the Admiral," Hendrie insisted. Ahearne, who had got the original call from Rickover, asked the chairman, "Did I trip that off on you?"

"What's that?"

"The Admiral," Ahearne explained.

"Yes," Hendrie said, and again the commissioners laughed.

"You called the Admiral?" Commissioner Peter Bradford asked Ahearne, who replied, "No. The Admiral called me."

"That was a mistake," Hendrie remarked. "If he'd called the Admiral, that would have been all right. . . ."

Gilinsky asked Ahearne if he had ever called Rickover to thank him for a recent trip to an undisclosed, Rickover-controlled installation. Gilinsky reminisced.

"Well, when I went on my trip," he recalled, "I came back and I called him to thank him, and I told him how fantastic all this was, a tribute to his genius, and he said, 'Cut the crap, Gilinsky. How are you going to use what you learned?' (Laughter)

"So I said, 'Well, we have a kind of different mode of operating—' "

"Most of our plants are sort of stable," Kennedy broke in, apparently in a gallows-humor reference to Three Mile Island.

Gilinsky continued his interrupted sentence: "—'and I'll have to think how this applies.' He [Rickover] said, 'Think, think, think. That's all you guys do. When are you going to get off your ass and do something?' " (Laughter)

Thus did Rickover flit in and out of the deliberations over Three Mile Island. (Later, he would complain to the commissioners that he had not been thanked for what his men did.) The transcript gives only a glance at Rickover's relationship with the commissioners, but at least the transcript exists as proof that he was working behind the scenes during the crisis. Publicly, he kept distance between himself and Three Mile Island.

Testifying before the energy research and production subcommittee of the House Committee on Science and Technology two months after the accident, he gave no hint of his involvement. He told the subcommittee:

> Since the incident at the Three Mile Island site, I have been asked by many people to comment. There are several reasons why I have not done this. First, all the facts are not in, and it would be presumptuous on my part to make judgments on such a highly complex subject when I do not have the facts. Second, there are significant differences between the design and operation of naval reactors and plants such as the Three Mile Island plant. I want to weigh all aspects of the incident and see if there is anything from it I can learn and incorporate into the naval program. That is the way I have always operated.
>
> Another important aspect is the legal issue involved. It is yet to be decided who will pay all the various costs for the incident. It would not be appropriate for a government employee such as myself to be issuing pronouncements on the incident when there may be litigation.

This extraordinarily cautious statement came from a government employee who was involved in litigation amounting to billions of dollars in his disputes with shipyards. He never hesitated to speak out about shipbuilders and shipbuilding problems, and in fact he rarely hesitated to speak out about anything. As for not having the facts, he had access to all the information that the NRB's teams had obtained and produced in their work at Three Mile Island. And he obviously could get whatever other information he wanted.

Rickover's strategy through the years had been to keep the controversial and hazardous side of nuclear power as far from him and his operations as possible. His actions emulated the redundant signs posted around nuclear sites: *Danger: Radiation Hazard.* For Rickover, the danger was politically complex. Because he had built the first commercial power reactor in the United States, he had become the leading pioneer of the nuclear power industry. But he did not speak about the industry with characteristic bluntness.

In July 1979, when he was called upon to testify before the President's Commission on the Accident at Three Mile Island, he was relatively mild; his criticism was oblique rather than direct. For example, one of the problems that had been pinpointed at Three Mile Island was the "hassle factor"—the disorienting effect produced by a control room suddenly filled with flashing lights and blaring alarms.

Rickover told the Commission, "It is unusual for my plants to operate with any alarms for an extended period of time; extended operation with several alarms is unheard of." In similar low-keyed vein he lectured the Commission on the proper design and maintenance of a nuclear reactor.

Although he reiterated his oft-made recommendation that a government representative be kept in nuclear power plants, he did not say it with the vigor he had used as recently as 1975. Speaking then about his insistence on keeping NRB people at Shippingport he said, "I do not think you can depend on self-inspection alone any more than you can depend on every individual to properly report his income tax if there was no one checking up on him. I do not think that is in accord with human nature."

Rickover has done his best to keep the eye of Congress and the public away from problems. His standard statement on radiation exposure, for example, has been that "since 1967 no civilian or military personnel in the Navy's nuclear-propulsion program have exceeded the quarterly federal limit of 3 rem ["roentgen equivalent in man," the standard unit of radiation exposure] or an annual radiation exposure limit of 5 rem. . . ." Five rem is the equivalent of about 166 chest X-rays.

Like most officials connected with nuclear power in and out of the Navy, Rickover would not voluntarily mention accidents. One in particular involved the executives who had competed with Rickover in the 1950s for the honor of building the nation's first commercial power reactor. At that time, Walker L. Cisler, president of Detroit Edison, was forming the Power Reactor Development Company, whose proposed breeder reactor would produce electricity and plutonium, which would be sold to the United States government.

Rickover never associated himself and NRB with Cisler and the reactor company, and thus kept himself from being involved in what became a potential national disaster. The breeder reactor, which was built by Cisler and his group of utilities and other companies, was named the Enrico Fermi Atomic Power Plant. After long delays caused mostly by a United Auto Workers Union campaign against it on safety issues, the reactor was finally built and went critical in August 1963. But not until 1966 did the reactor begin a prolonged operation that was to gradually raise its power output from 1,000 kilowatts to 200,000 kilowatts. (By comparison, Shippingport produced 60,000 kilowatts.)

On October 5, 1966, the reactor was seemingly on its way toward a 100,000-kilowatt goal. Then, at 3:09 P.M., the radiation alarms began going off. The containment building was evacuted. Controls had malfunctioned. Part of the reactor core had melted down. The reactor was scrammed—an emergency shutdown. Officials, fearing a catastrophe, privately discussed the evacuation of Detroit.

Engineers spent months trying to determine what went wrong with Fermi. Finally the reactor was repaired and started up again in July 1970. But two years later, when the time for relicensing Fermi came up, the Atomic Energy Commission refused to do so. The AEC gave the reason that the reactor's owners did not appear to have sufficient financial resources available for sustained operation. The nation's first breeder reactor was sealed up forever.

Rickover himself does not appear in the dismal record of Fermi. But a longtime associate, Milton Shaw, publicly endorsed Fermi even after the partial meltdown. "The breeder reactor," he said, "is the world's hope for increasing energy to meet the world's needs, because it can make more fissionable fuel than it consumes." Shaw, who had worked on the Shippingport reactor and had been on Rickover's NRB staff from 1950 to 1961, was at the time in the AEC's reactor development division.

The AEC continued its commitment to breeder reactors, announcing plans to build an experimental one on the Clinch River on the Oak Ridge Atomic Reservation in Tennessee. The AEC said the Clinch River reactor would be the "first pure demonstration breeder reactor in the United States." The Fermi reactor—the actual "first"—was ignored as a bad memory.

The Clinch River reactor would also have a checkered history, which would directly involve both Rickover and a former U.S. Navy officer who had been briefly in the nuclear navy, Lieutenant Jimmy Carter.

Jimmy Carter's own nuclear career included personal exposure to reactor radiation. The incident occurred in 1952 in Chalk River, Canada, a village about two hundred miles northwest of Ottawa. Candidate Carter briefly mentioned the incident in his campaign autobiography, but neither he nor Rickover ever publicly revealed the extent of U.S. Navy participation in the incident.

The Canadian government built an experimental reactor, the NRX, at Chalk River in 1952. The reactor went out of control—due to problems with instruments and an operator's error—and thousands of gallons of "heavy," highly radioactive water had to be flushed out of it in an attempt to stop the chain reaction. Some of the fuel melted down. The installation was evacuated, except for a reactor crew. Ordinary water was then poured into the reactor to cool the melted fuel.

The emergency was over in hours, but the cleanup took months. Radiation was so intense that the Canadian workers had already absorbed or would absorb all that they could safely take. Canadian officials asked for help, and the AEC sent decontamination crews from Idaho, Electric Boat and the Knolls Atomic Power Laboratory (the same one that would respond to Three Mile Island). The contingent from Knolls included Lieutenant Carter, then in training at the prototype *Seawolf* reactor.

Carter and the other Americans were drilled first on a mock-up of the damaged NRX reactor. Then, in teams, they rushed into the reactor building, and did their job—in ninety seconds, the maximum time allowed. "We had absorbed a year's maximum allowance of radiation" in those ninety seconds, Carter later wrote. For months afterward, members of the Chalk River group had to have their feces and urine examined for signs of radioactivity.

Records of the U.S. participation at Chalk River remained vague and scattered until 1962, when a report was prepared by the U.S. Naval Radiological Defense Laboratory, an installation outside the nuclear navy's jurisdiction and then under the command of a Rickover exile, Captain Eli Roth. The report showed that men "were assigned to the operation in groups of ten to twenty for a one-week period. During this week they were to accomplish as much 'hot' work as was feasible." Navy men were allowed to be exposed to a higher level of radioactivity than were civilians.

•

The records of every nuclear reactor in the United States—except one—are available for examination in the public documents room of the Nuclear Regulatory Agency, 1717 H Street, N.W., in Washington. The only exception is Shippingport. Designated a "naval reactor," the civilian central power station has not deposited its records in the room. Rickover has held Shippingport's records almost as closely guarded as he has held the records of his submarine reactors. The latter are legally classified secret, in the interest of national security. Shippingport's records are theoretically open. But Rickover has kept personal control of all Naval Reactors Branch records, including Shippingport's.

He has been extremely sensitive to any reports of radiation exposure or breaches of safety. He apparently has investigated such claims or charges, even outlandish ones. Reacting to rumors that cancer had killed members of the crew of the *Nautilus,* for example, Rickover in 1978 quietly ordered a check of each of the ninety-six officers and enlisted men of the first crew. They were all alive and well, according to Rickover, who revealed the survey in 1979. The record certainly indicated that Rickover had been conscious of the need for vigilance. The "field of radiation effects has been one where insufficient effort has been expended," he said in 1978, "and an analysis on a nationwide scale is long overdue."

But he would not voluntarily reveal problems, he would not countenance the intrusion of outsiders, and he would not delegate authority. "I have always been personally responsible for everything that might happen in the nuclear navy," he said in 1976. "I still do that because I am responsible for this program from the womb to the tomb."

Rickover has particularly feared that an accident in one of his reactors would destroy public confidence in nuclear power. So intense has this fear been that Rickover has prohibited the appearance of nuclear submarines in many foreign and United States ports, especially New York City and Boston. He thus put himself in the position of insisting that nuclear power was safe—and insisting that his nuclear ships were not safe, at least in public-relations terms.

The issue surfaced in June 1961 with the release of Congressional testimony that Rickover had given the previous year. He had told the Joint Committee on Atomic Energy that nuclear submarines should not enter populated ports unless there was a military need or the national interest demanded such deployment. By that time, the Navy had sent nuclear submarines to La Spezia, Italy; Bremerhaven, Germany; Portsmouth, England; and Sydney, Australia.

These visits were for good will and crew recreation, the Navy maintained, and these purposes constituted military needs. The visits, although technically made under the orders of the Chief of Naval Operations, had been cleared by the Reactors Safeguards Committee, an advisory group to the Atomic Energy Commission and, at least in naval matters, absolutely under the control of Rickover.

But Rickover claimed that the clearance orders were being ignored. He told the Joint Committee that the Navy's "operating forces" did not heed his warnings that "they must not move these ships around the way they were accustomed to move conventional ships." He said that even though Admiral Arleigh Burke, Chief of Naval Operations, had "issued instructions to the Navy that there must be an actual military or national necessity before a nuclear ship can go into a populated harbor . . . the spirit of this order is not always lived up to fully. . . . What if something happens and you irradiate a city and you are called upon to prove there really was a military necessity? What are you going to say?"

Those were questions that the nuclear industry did not like anyone to ask in public—especially before Congress. But Rickover was asking them because, as an engineer, he knew the realities of nuclear power. So did a scientist. Edward Teller, who led the development of the hydrogen bomb, endorsed Rickover's warnings. Rickover the engineer knew that he himself, in what he controlled, could come near perfection, although he could not achieve it. But as that control went beyond him and into the hands of what he called "the Navy," he feared the results.

Rickover made a distinction between operating bases—such as the submarine base in New London and the naval base at Norfolk, Virginia—and "populated ports" like New York. There were certainly people living in New London, Norfolk, and the other American ports used by nuclear submarines and surface ships. But if those places were "irradiated" by a nuclear accident, Rickover at least would understand (as perhaps others would not) that the accident had happened where the nuclear ships *belonged*. An officer once stationed at the naval base in Charleston, South Carolina, said that if it were necessary to declare a nuclear emergency there, the first warning call would be not to the mayor of Charleston but to Rickover.

Rickover had worked out a bureaucratic arrangement that forced the Navy to get permission from the Reactors Safeguards Committee before a nuclear-powered ship could enter a U.S. or foreign port. No one in the Navy put this to an absolute test until 1962, when John W. McCormack, the Speaker of the House, let it be known to the Navy that he wanted the new nuclear-powered carrier *Enterprise* to pay a Fourth of July call on his home town, Boston.

Senior Navy officers decided to make a test of the Rickover rule by simply notifying him that the *Enterprise* would be sent to Boston on July 4. Nothing was heard from him until Rear Admiral Lawson P. Ramage, Assistant Chief of Naval Operations for fleet operations and readiness, happened to be discussing the forthcoming visit with a member of the Atomic Energy Commission.

Ramage, without revealing the identity of the commissioner, said in his memoirs that he told the AEC official, "This is a brand-new ship and a brand-new crew, and furthermore, as I gather from what you say and I know from personal knowledge, you take as many VIPs as you can possibly take out on it to witness these trials. So what is the safety problem?

"Well, obviously, he had no explanation for that and," Ramage recalled, "it just exposed the fallacy of this whole thing."

But the commissioner apparently reported the conversation to Rickover, who had a staff man, Theodore Rockwell, call Ramage and ask if the *Enterprise* truly was scheduled to go to Boston. Ramage told him she was.

Less than half an hour later, Ramage was summoned to the office of Secretary of the Navy Fred Korth, who asked him, "What's going on here?"

Ramage told him, adding that McCormack had already lined up radio and television coverage. "So," he argued, "if we turned around and said it was unsafe to send the *Enterprise* into Boston, it would be all over the papers and if this occurred, then what chance do we have of ever deploying the *Enterprise* to the Mediterranean? All the countries in Europe would say this is a real bomb and we don't want it over here. And you might as well take this brand-new ship that has never been deployed and put it in the back channels and forget about it. . . . This is ridiculous just over this foolishness."

Ramage said that Korth then told him to go over and talk to the man.

Rickover, according to Ramage's recollections, was at first civil— "and then all of a sudden he started going up the pole and he was just ranting and roaring that I had violated all the regulations and agreements and stuff. And I said, 'Look, come on back down and let's talk about this particular situation.'

"He sobered up for a minute or two and then he'd go off again. But obviously he was just so mad that we had embarrassed this Commissioner and really exposed the foolishness of or the lack of real criteria or the reluctance to give us [the official Navy] anything to go on. If we had been able to understand what was going on, or [if] he had given us some logical explanation or rationale for all this, I am sure there would have been no problem."

Ramage said he got nowhere with this argument, or with an insistence on the operational Navy having the clear right to send ships where it wanted to send them. Next, Vice Admiral Charles D. Griffin, Ramage's boss, was dispatched to see Rickover, but he was not able to change Rickover's mind. Finally, under threat that the issue would be taken to the White House, Rickover asked for time to contact the Joint Committee on Atomic Energy. "About five minutes later," Ramage said, "he came back and said, 'I contacted everybody on the committee and they said it is all right.' It was some means of saving face."

The *Enterprise* did go to Boston for the Fourth of July, but in other years other ships did not always go where the Navy wanted them to go.

Nuclear-propulsion plants are safe. There has never been an accident aboard a nuclear submarine or surface ship that endangered the crew. That is the claim, oft repeated, that Admiral Rickover has used to justify his rigorous selection and training of the men who sail nuclear ships, and for his own omnipotent position. He is essentially correct.

But two factors appear relevant. First, naval nuclear plants have not been totally safe. The reactor scram in the *Thresher* appears to have initiated the series of events that led to her tragic loss. Radioactive material has leaked from nuclear submarines, although this was not fully revealed until the late 1970s. And there have also been belated revelations about the exposure of shipyard workers to radiation. Such facts at least raise questions about Rickover's claims. Second, the reactors were neither the first nor the most dangerous nuclear possessions of the Navy.

Since 1950 the Navy has had nuclear weapons at sea. Initially, they were bombs kept aboard aircraft carriers. Later, nuclear weapons were placed aboard cruisers, destroyers, escort ships, and of course, submarines. By the late 1960s there were several thousand tactical nuclear weapons in the fleet, plus 656 Polaris and Poseidon strategic missiles with nuclear warheads. (The number of nuclear weapons in the fleet has since declined significantly.)

Unlike reactor plants, the weapons were designed to explode. None of the Navy's nuclear weapons—or many thousands more held by the Air Force and Army—has ever exploded accidentally. Some Air Force weapons dropped from a B-52 bomber after a mid-air collision over Palomores, Spain, and others from a B-52 that crashed off Greenland, did leak radioactive material. The Navy's safety record with its several thousand nuclear weapons has been at least as safe as Rickover's record with nuclear reactors. And that record has been achieved without centralized, authoritative control that preempted normal military lines of command. Rather, the Navy's nuclear-weapons program, which includes an extensive personnel selection and training effort, is carried on within the normal Navy channels.

Rickover's stress on safety and continual warnings of disaster have produced a reaction he had not expected. His admissions of fear naturally prompted the media, particularly around nuclear-ship ports, to keep careful watch over his ships. So, for example, when there were rumors of a spill of radioactive water in the Thames River at the New London submarine base, the local newspaper, *The Day*, tried to find out what had happened. The spill occurred on December 29, 1971, when reactor-coolant water was being transferred from the nuclear submarine *Dace* to the submarine tender *Fulton*. The connection between the ships somehow parted, and five hundred gallons of water spilled into the river. Word of the incident was passed to Rickover and other Navy officials, but there was no public announcement.

Word soon was passed in New London too—rumors of a "nuclear incident" spread around the city, and *The Day* was making inquiries. But not until January 8 was *The Day* able to make a full report on the spill. The Navy said that the water was only slightly radioactive and contained "less than the applicable limits set by Federal and international agencies." Unofficially, the Navy said that there had been "a few" such leaks in the past.

By Rickover's own figures, 1971 had not been one of the nuclear navy's best years for disposing of radioactive liquid waste. In 1971, the total of radioactive water "discharged within twelve miles from shore from all U.S. Naval nuclear-powered ships and their support facilities" was 1,089,000 gallons. The amount the year before was 2,571,000. The water, according to Rickover, was drinkable and only slightly radioactive. Obviously concerned about the amount of water being dumped, Rickover managed to cut the total down to a reported 289,000 gallons in 1972 and to less than 25,000 in 1973.

Rickover's position on nuclear safety had become increasingly complex by the late 1970s. He issued warnings regularly, but his statistics always showed that there was nothing to fear. He attacked corporate greed, but did not focus on corporations building civilian power plants. He wanted to keep nuclear ships out of populated ports, but he had nothing to say about electric-power reactors near cities. He insisted on training for every man who worked on his reactors, but he did not make such demands in the civilian industry and did not offer to share his training facilities with civilians. He liked to make speeches and testify before Congress, but he did not like the way the media "distorted the facts and the issues." (He himself described the New London spill in these words: "... a hose broke, spilling a few gallons of pure water into one of our most polluted rivers.") As a result of his ambiguous statements on nuclear safety, he found himself in 1978 on familiar ground—a Congressional hearing room—but experiencing the decidedly unfamiliar sensation of being interrogated by an unfriendly Congressman.

His appearance had been caused by publication in the Boston *Globe* of findings of Dr. Thomas Najarian, a blood specialist at the Veterans Administration Hospital in Boston. Najarian said that a study he made had indicated that workers in the nuclear area of the Portsmouth Naval Shipyard had a leukemia rate four times the national average.

About 1,400 workers at Portsmouth are exposed to radiation as part of their job. Portsmouth stopped building submarines in 1971, but since then the yard had been overhauling and repairing nuclear submarines. In the conflict over radiation exposure, it was singled out—as "a guinea pig," Rickover said—but it was not the only such yard, nor was it the biggest. Similar work went on at naval shipyards in Norfolk, Charleston, Puget Sound, Mare Island, and Pearl Harbor, and at private yards.

The *Globe*'s story, published on February 19, 1978, was based both on Najarian's report and on answers to questions the newspaper had asked of officials at the shipyard. Among the answers was one that said that a radiation-exposure study was being made, not by the National Cancer Institute, but by the Department of Energy. The only reasonable explanation for the Department of Energy stepping into a medical evaluation field was that Rickover was operating under his DOE hat. But this was not immediately brought out.

The *Globe*'s story led to a hearing by the subcommittee on health and the environment of the House Committee on Interstate and Foreign Commerce. Najarian was called before it to expand on his study. Later, Rickover was called. He began in his traditional fashion, by rattling off statistics and explaining that all was well. There was some sparring between him and a couple of Congressmen—one called him "a difficult witness"—and then Representative Paul G. Rogers, chairman of the subcommittee, said, "All right. Now, have there been any over-exposures at Portsmouth? You tell us evidently there have not."

"Yes, there have been," Rickover admitted, "and I will give you the figures. Prior to 1963, fourteen Portsmouth Naval Shipyard workers exceeded the quarterly radiation exposure limit. . . . No one had exceeded the cumulative lifetime limit. No one has been injured from an accident involving radiation exposure."

And so it went, specific questions and specific answers. Rickover, no longer hostile, was his usual model witness, with facts at hand, with detailed information on the radiological monitoring and training at Portsmouth. Then Rogers changed the line of questioning to find out how much time Rickover spent working for the Navy and how much for the Department of Energy. Rogers seemed baffled by how Rickover managed to hold down two jobs. After all these years, someone in Congress was asking Rickover for details about his two-hatted job.

"Well," Rogers said, "I just wanted to be clear in my mind how that [Rickover's doubled-up staff] operates. So, you operate your office in the Navy, but you have this position that you hold with Energy."

"I have an office in the Energy building, too; we operate in both places." Rickover began to bristle.

"Well, that is what I am trying to say. You also have a staff there?"

"No," Rickover said, without his usual *sir*. "One staff."

"One staff," Rogers repeated, "and [some] are on the Energy payroll and others on the Navy's."

Rickover agreed, and added, "Some are military, some are civilian. I do not know who they are."

"Who does know?" Rogers asked.

"I guess we have a record," Rickover said.

Rogers suddenly flared up, saying, "Well, I would hope so, Admiral. I do not want to appear to be absurd, but you are talking now to a committee of the Congress and we are asking how you operate. Now, I would hope you would be responsive."

"Yes," Rickover said, and this time he added, "sir."

Eventually, Rogers ordered Rickover to give him information on the staff—"I want their names, their salaries, and who pays them; and their duties"—because Rogers also wanted to know why the Navy had decided to have the Department of Energy conduct a radiation study at Portsmouth. It did not sound quite right to the Congressman.

The Congressman had a right to be suspicious. Rickover had not told the committee all that he knew about conditions at Portsmouth. While he was testifying on February 28, 1978, he had in his files a report, marked *Official Use Only—Noforn* [not to be distributed to foreigners], that was dated December 30, 1977, and was signed by H. G. Rickover. The thirty-seven pages of the report showed a naval shipyard far different from the one Rickover had described in his testimony.

He had told the Congressmen, "To the best of our knowledge, ability, and to the best scientific evidence we have, we do not see a problem."

But the report he had signed said:

> The shipyard has not placed sufficient management attention towards the training of radiological control technicians. As a result 80 percent of the technicians taking a written NAVSEA [Rickover's Navy billet, Naval Sea Systems Command] prepared radiological controls examination failed to achieve a passing score.
>
> The shipyard has experienced seven high radiation area incidents in 1977. This number is excessive compared to the number of such incidents experienced by other organizations performing radioactive work associated with Naval nuclear propulsion plants.
>
> Numerous deficiencies have occurred during the performance of radioactive work which resulted in additional radiation exposure to correct. These deficiencies have contributed to the shipyard exceeding its 1977 radiation exposure goal [of 561 man-rem] by over 170 man-rem. . . .
>
> In 1977, six personnel in the shipyard received radioactivity on their skin compared with twelve in 1976. [Rickover had testified, "No one has been injured from an accident involving radiation exposure."]
>
> In 1977, the shipyard experienced nineteen total radiological control incidents compared to thirty-six in 1976. Although this demonstrates improvement, only a few other shipyards performing radioactive work associated with Naval nuclear propulsion plants experienced more radiological incidents than Portsmouth in 1976.

The existence of the report was revealed by the Critical Mass Energy Project, a Ralph Nader organization. "Most unsettling," said a Critical Mass letter to Secretary of Defense Harold Brown, ". . . is Admiral Hyman Rickover's apparent failure to be completely candid with the Congress and the public. This is particularly distressing given the Admiral's noted integrity and his previous reputation for precision and forthrightness."

Why did Rickover hold out on Congress? His own answer, in a letter to the subcommittee, was simply that he did not tell about the report because no one had asked him about it. But another answer lay deeper, in that place where Rickover the engineer kept his doubts and worries. "I am not a proponent of nuclear power or of any other energy source," he said in a speech in 1979. "All alternatives have their own limitations; none are without risk."

Knowing those risks, aware that "the decision whether we should have nuclear power is a political one," he tried to find some ground on which he could make his stand. The ground once had been all his own. When he controlled all there was—the *Nautilus*—he stood on broad, firm ground. And the ground was firm at his enduring Shippingport, where he got his demands and where he kept his demands alive, decade afer decade. But while the *Nautilus* and Shippingport remained monuments to his tireless efforts, the nuclear fleet expanded, the nuclear industry grew, and his own ground became narrow.

For one brief moment it looked as if there could have been a third monument. He had proposed in 1964 the use of a new kind of breeder reactor to power giant pumps that would help to deliver water from northern to southern California, a gigantic aqueduct project. The idea vanished in a year, lost in a host of issues that had nothing to do with engineering—money, politics, free enterprise versus government controls.

He did not give up on the reactor, which became known as the water-cooled breeder reactor. It grew out of research at his Shippingport reactor. He continued to urge it, while simultaneously urging President Carter to reject the Clinch River version of the breeder. The latter would breed plutonium. Rickover's would use thorium as a fuel and breed an isotope of uranium, U-233. The isotope, like plutonium, can be used to make a bomb. But the cost of extracting the material from the Rickover breeder would be enormously higher than the relatively cheap technique needed to get plutonium, which, Rickover feared, if the breeder reactors were widely used, might fall into possibly unfriendly hands.

The Rickover breeder had little support. Back in 1969, Representative Craig Hosmer on the Joint Committee on Atomic Energy, while asking Rickover about the water-cooled reactor, remarked about "the charge that nobody in the utility business has any interest" in it.

"Nobody in the utility business was interested in Shippingport either," Rickover responded. "I was forced to have forums—meetings which the utilities demanded—and they all took cracks at what we were trying to do at Shippingport. So what does that prove? It just says that the utilities have suffered from a failure of imagination the way the Navy and the Department of Defense did when we were first working on nuclear-submarine development."

Despite the lack of interest, Congress has continually dispensed money to support the light-water reactor. "It's only $15 million or so a year," said a man who had been following the process for years. "And it's worth it to keep him from making a nuisance about it." In May, 1980, however, the Government Accounting Office, in response to a Congressional request, looked into the Rickover reactor and, on March 25, 1981, issued a little-known report that criticized the management of the reactor, publicly revealed for the first time the extent of its cost overruns, and recommended that the water-cooled reactor be made to prove that it does indeed breed.

The GAO report said that the Department of Energy had planned to have information on the reactor's "breeding potential" by 1978 but that such information was not likely until 1989. The report also said that, while the original estimate of the project's total cost was $91.5 million, the total cost is now expected to be $968 million. "Thus," said the report, "since 1965, the expected costs of the program have increased by $876 million, more than a nine-fold increase." Inflation was believed to be responsible for only 19 percent of the overrun.

The report questioned the assignment of this one reactor to Rickover, as Deputy Assistant Secretary for Naval Reactors, when all over civilian nuclear reactor development was the responsibility of the Deputy Assistant Secretary for Nuclear Reactor Programs. The report does not answer this question. The GAO said that it had learned that the DOE itself had not, through its Inspector General, reviewed the Rickover reactor program, apparently because of his tight control of it.

The GAO routinely circulated a draft of the report so that DOE officials could comment on the findings. The draft—and the later, published report—said that the reactor operations should be ended in January 1982 so that proof-of-breeding experiments could be carried out and a decision made about continuing the project. On the very day that the draft was being commented on, Rickover's Naval Reactors notified the DOE Division of Nuclear Reactor Programs that his reactor would be operated for three years *beyond* January 1982. That self-reprieve was Rickover's answer to GAO.

His breeder reactor may have escaped some criticism because the Clinch River breeder reactor, by 1981, was looking even worse: nine years behind schedule with a cost overrun estimated to be as high as 700 percent. In the Congressional furor over Clinch River, little notice was given to Rickover's breeder at Shippingport. Nor was industry giving it much notice. The GAO surveyed the industry and said in the report that forty-eight percent of the respondents "felt that the program should be reduced or terminated."

One reason the breeder has had little support, said someone who had known Rickover for decades, is that "he just doesn't understand that you just don't sell a product to the utility industry, or, for that matter, to any-body else, on the basis of 'Poppa knows best: You buy it. Here it is and I'll give you a report on it when I get around to printing it.' " The assessment came from Lou Roddis, who joined Rickover at Oak Ridge in the earliest days, helped work on submarine and Shippingport reactors, and left Rickover to become a pioneer in the nuclear-utilities industry, a leader in that industry, and president of Consolidated Edison of New York.

"He had very little impact after 1960 on the civilian power program," Roddis said. "Utilities were interested in reliability, price, general economics, safety, all these things." As such plants as Shippingport and Fermi were built, the learning continued. Not until 1964, when Westinghouse and General Electric entered the field, Roddis said, did the utility companies see that projects could be built at relatively acceptable prices. "After 1962," he added, "the impact of the Navy on the whole utility business has been almost entirely one of people, either in the operating or the design area"—Rickover's people, but not Rickover.

Rickover said in 1975 that the Navy was supplying about sixty percent of the people who worked in the nuclear-power industry. By 1976 the Navy had saved the civilian nuclear-power industry an estimated $2.5 billion in training costs.

In the industry the ex-nucs are sometimes called "Rickover's children." They have been trained well, but in the civilian power plants they no longer are in the closely monitored control rooms they knew in Rickover's nuclear navy. Men trained by the Navy were among the operators at Three Mile Island. Aware of this, Rickover in his testimony before the President's Commission on the Accident at Three Mile Island, said, "It appears that some in the civilian nuclear industry and, perhaps, the NRC [Nuclear Regulatory Commission] have been placing undue reliance on the mere fact that a person has been involved in the naval reactor program." But he pointed out that "under present laws and regulations it is not even possible for a prospective employer to determine whether an individual . . . performed satisfactorily or not."

Rickover is reputed to have gone beyond his formal statement to say, "We send the industry our dropouts." But records of his actual testimony were not made available by the NRC, which did release records of other testimony.

For Rickover, the nation's first nuclear-power plant is a monument to his will. At Shippingport he could watch over a reactor the way he wanted to, as unchallenged by utility executives as he had been unchallenged by admirals. At Shippingport he could stand on his narrowed ground and look back to what had made him the engineer who strove to make things work perfectly—always knowing that this was never to be. His doubts and his fears were the part of him that was the unexpected humanist.

"Science, being pure thought, harms no one; therefore, it need not be humanistic," he once said. "But technology is action, and often potentially dangerous action. Unless it is made to adapt itself to human interests, values and principles, more harm will be done than good. Never before, in all his long life on earth, has man possessed such enormous power to injure himself, his human fellows, and his society as has been put into his hands by modern technology."

That technology, he said, "can have no legitimate purpose but to serve man—man in general, not merely some men; future generations, not merely those who currently wish to gain advantage for themselves; man in the totality of his humanity. . . ."

Down deep, even deeper within the man who spoke this, there was humanity that he rarely let others see. Much . . . most, and yet not all . . . of his life was spent at work—"Man's work begins with his job," he often said.

There was a part of him that was not merely his work.

30 | The Admiral at Home

On a summer's day in 1953, Ruth Masters Rickover had just performed the familiar ritual of getting her husband off on a trip. He was Rear Admiral Rickover now, and momentarily peace had come into their lives after months of turmoil over his promotion. She was sitting in the tiny garden she had created behind the apartment house they lived in on upper Connecticut Avenue in Washington, D.C. She was "watching a hummingbird buzzing ecstatically among the white and pink hollyhocks," she would later write. "The zinnias were coming along splendidly and there would soon be many tomatoes for the salad bowl." Then—

"A most indignant young man appeared on the scene. 'You've just got to come upstairs, Mother, and tend to that phone. It's ringing and ringing and I have to do my Morse Code practice. I just can't be bothered with all those characters crying for Daddy.'

"I sighed and got up, thinking how completely our life had become enslaved to those pesky nuclear reactors. They'd elbowed their way into the family and become its most important members. . . ."

Such a glimpse into the private life of Hyman Rickover is extremely rare. Even rarer is an insight into how Ruth Rickover fitted into that life. Hyman Rickover would say of her, "She was at once the most human and intelligent person I ever knew, the greatest influence on my life and career." He has otherwise publicly said little about her.

Both her sketch of that interrupted summer's day and his short testament to her appear in *Pepper, Rice, and Elephants,* a book that was begun in 1954 but was not published until 1975, three years after her death. The book tells of the travels of the Rickovers—Ruth and George, as she called him—through Southeast Asia in the late 1930s. The book is far more than a travelogue. It is the work of a woman who is both indomitable ("became thoroughly blasé about cobras") and perceptive (in French-administered Laos: "I think it was a mistake that the French did

634

not know the native languages, for this lack made them too dependent on their interpreters").

She herself learned Malay before she set out on her journey. And, when traveling alone, she chose to stay as close as possible to the culture she so sensitively explored. Her book reflected her honest mind.

Once, on a train, she met a "tall, attractive North Chinese gentleman." They began conversing in French, and she realized that an attitude she had was changing. "Although I got along well with Orientals on our trips and made friends with many," she wrote, "I never could understand how a white person could marry into their way of life. Marriage, to my mind, is such a close relationship that it can't possibly succeed unless both partners have similar backgrounds, education, and attitudes toward life. . . . But here, for the first time, I met a Chinese who was attractive and who treated me with positively Gallic chivalry. I kept forgetting that he was not a Frenchman, and could quite well imagine that a white woman might fall in love with him."

She did not note that she herself had fallen in love with a man whose background was greatly different from hers. They were an oddly matched couple: son of an immigrant, daughter of a socially prominent family; product of Chicago public schools, scholar trained in European schools; ensign's commision from Annapolis, master's and doctorate from Columbia. She was a linguist who spoke with a slight European accent. He spoke English in a flat, nasal midwestern twang. She was Christian, he was Jewish, in an age when that difference mattered greatly.

He was as committed to nuclear energy as other men had been committed to the cathedrals of her Europe, her spiritual heartland. She would write of his nuclear power, "All I know is that there are problems in developing nuclear reactors—difficulties often arise in the middle of the night, resulting in the telephone ringing at all hours and making the lesser members of the family resentful."

That lesser member of the family never again showed her resentment. Her frank words appeared in the Foreword. She then began her journey back into time, a time when she and her husband "witnessed the end of an era that has since been swept away." Conceived in the late 1930s, written in the 1950s, her book hauntingly resounds with tragic place names of the 1970s—Saigon, Hanoi, Hue, Laos, Cambodia. They were places of peace then, but, as the book's last paragraph prophesied, "We came away from these people recognizing that their future would be troubled, for the tide of change was sweeping them toward social and political problems to which there could not be any easy solution. . . ."

Throughout her travels she had kept shorthand notes which she then worked into a diary. She took out the diary in the summer of 1953, "checked facts and added bits of history," and began writing. Except for doing research for her husband and offering sharply critical suggestions to him about his writings, she had done little of her own work for several years.

That young man who had suddenly appeared in the garden was Robert Masters Rickover, then going on thirteen. Since his birth at Georgetown University Hospital in Washington on October 11, 1940, she had been a housewife and mother. But her interest in international law continued, and she would remain what she had been when Rickover first met her—an intellectual steeped in the European tradition of scholarship.

Around the time she was writing her book, Clay Blair was writing *The Atomic Submarine and Admiral Rickover.* Blair submitted the manuscript to both Rickovers, but particularly remembered the reaction he got from Ruth Rickover—"She was an absolutely super-intellectual. She went over it very carefully, editing it, making changes." Blair, on a visit to the Rickovers' apartment, briefly met young Robert. "As I remember," Blair said, "he was making his own TV set. He was obviously a genius."

Around the time that Robert entered his teens and was attending nearby Alice Deal Junior High School, the Rickovers thought about moving so that their son could have a room of his own. But, when a second apartment became available in their building, they decided to rent that and move Robert into it. So the family lived separated lives—mother and father in their apartment and son on another floor in the eight-story apartment house.

Their apartment house at 4801 Connecticut Avenue stands among many that line the upper reaches of the broad avenue, a major traffic artery that runs from the heart of downtown Washington, through Washington's affluent Northwest quadrant, and crosses the District line into Chevy Chase, Maryland. Residents of those old and stately apartment houses traditionally have been called cliff dwellers because most of them have lived in the buildings for decades. Little about the neighborhood has changed since before World War II. Even Washington's new Metro subway system has veered away from upper Connecticut Avenue because the cliff dwellers did not want the changes that the Metro would bring.

The Rickovers certainly qualified as cliff dwellers. They moved into 4801 around the time that Rickover was assigned to BuShips on the eve of World War II, and they never moved away. Their apartment was large and spartanly furnished. There were no rugs, because, Rickover told visitors, he had an allergy to wool. He may have been joking, for he also had an allergy toward spending money on what he deemed to be nonessentials. The principal furniture in most of the rooms was bookshelves, filled with his ever-growing collection on a variety of subjects from history and biography to science and technology, and her books, in several languages, on international law and European cultural history.

Rickover periodically invited workers from the Naval Reactors Branch to cocktails and dinner. Ever since a drinking episode as a young officer (when he sounded off to a senior officer), Rickover rarely if ever drank. But he served liquor, and guests remembered him as a courteous host, quick with compliments to the ladies and eager for conversation on virtually any subject. He kept shop talk to a minimum, but tensions of the office day did not magically dissipate in the evening at 4801. It was still dinner at the boss's place.

Rickover had long since ceased considering himself a Jew, and keeping a kosher house was but a memory of the days in Lawndale. He told people he was an Episcopalian. Alvin Radkowsky, the senior physicist at NRB, was an Orthodox Jew. In an office where the six-day work week was routine, Radkowsky refused, because of his religious beliefs, to work on Saturdays. Nor would he travel on the Sabbath. Once when the Rickovers had the Radkowskys and other couples for dinner, he served them ham. The Radkowskys ate only the vegetables that evening.

Sometime after he married Ruth Masters, Rickover left the religion of his birth in a formal, straightforward way by writing a letter about his decision to his parents in Chicago. He is said to have lived for years without their forgiveness. Eventually, however, the hurt eased, and Rickover frequently visited his parents.

In his Congressional testimony, he often made allusions to Jesus, although he also cited the Talmud occasionally. That he was Jewish by birth was well known, and charges of anti-Semitism often arose during his promotion fights. While one was going on, Admiral Arleigh Burke, the Chief of Naval Operations, was startled to be told that three rabbis were waiting outside his office. He asked that they be shown in but warned that he could spare little time to hear entreaties about Rickover. "But all they wanted to tell me was that in their opinion he was not Jewish," Burke remembered.

Rickover may have left Judaism, but he did not abandon religion. In 1974, he gave a Congressional committee his personal view of religion:

•

Religion is one area that merits a more sympathetic under-standing by modern intellectuals. For religion has not so much de-clined as it has changed. It is true that religion no longer has direct influence on the large corporate structures that have emerged in the last 400 years, such as government, business, labor, the military, and education. It has had to relinquish many of its "mysteries" to the ex-planations of rational science. . . .

What has not changed are the basic functions of religion: Sup-plying a faith or meaning for coping with the questions of the human condition; providing for a feeling of belonging, in the broadest sense. . . .

If we are to regain some of these certainties of our life, we must understand and incorporate the most universal and worthy ideas of our past and our present existence. . . .

It makes little difference what particular religion a man follows. The important thing is that he live up to its precepts.

But, trying to harmonize his attitude toward religion with his feelings about morality, he spoke of religion more pragmatically. "We are now living on the accumulated moral capital of traditional religion," he said. "It is running out, and we have no other consensus of values to take its place. This is partly so because man can now obtain on earth what pre-viously was promised him when he reached heaven."

To him, morality was forever entwined with toil. When a Con-gressman asked him for his concept of man's purpose in life, he re-sponded with quotations from Voltaire and William James—and then Rickover added, "Man's work begins with his job, or profession. Having a vocation is always somewhat of a miracle, like falling in love." This was one of his favorite quotations—and one of his own authorship. It was one that expressed most eloquently the totality of his obsession with work.

The most efficient way to get from 4801 Connecticut Avenue to work was by car—as a passenger, not a driver. And that was how Rickover traveled. He belonged to a car pool, but he was the only member without a car.

Men in that ever-changing car pool can still recall, decades later, how they were exploited in the service of Rickover's decision to be effi-cient. He used the time in the car as work time, quizzing driver and fellow passengers on projects, rifling through his inevitable file of pinks, and, if he found something wrong, shouting at the perpetrator, particularly if he was in the car. "One morning," Joseph Barker remembered, "it was snowing real hard, and I was driving. He started going through the pinks and yelling, and I couldn't stand it any longer. I just pulled over to the curb and stopped. I said I didn't want to get killed. He saw the point and stopped yelling, and we started up again."

Rickover's penchant for sudden trips snarled the plans and jangled the nerves of his involuntary chauffeurs. If, say, Barker drove into Washington but was ordered to accompany Rickover on an overnight trip to the Shippingport reactor site, that meant that Barker drove his car to National Airport, leaving his fellow passengers to find other means of getting home that evening.

Rickover came close to owning a car in the Oak Ridge days when he, Lou Roddis, Miles Libbey and Ray Dick decided to invest a modest sum of money in a revolutionary new car, the Tucker, which appealed to the engineers. The six-cylinder engine was in the rear, and the four-door, six-passenger sedan was rated at thirty-five miles to a gallon, even though it was as big as a Cadillac. The namesake of a supersalesman, the Tucker never went beyond the hand-crafted stage. After a grand jury investigation into Preston Tucker's promises made to investors, his would-be assembly plant shut down, and investors were left with their dreams.

Men who worked with Rickover could tell about his kindness as well as about his relentless demands for work. He once sent an officer on a trip knowing that his wife was ill and needed help at home. Without telling the departing officer he would do so, Rickover appeared at the man's home and cooked for the family. Now contrast that story with another: A man who worked for Rickover broke down and cried as he remembered, more than twenty years later, how Rickover had ordered him back from leave a day after he had gone home to care for a seriously ill wife. "I couldn't believe it," the officer recalled. "I had told him I had to spend several days at home. She was very ill. And in one day—his phone call. I could never forgive him for it."

Why did Rickover show inordinate kindness to one officer and act heartlessly toward another? Perhaps there is an answer in what else the second man recounted. "I got a transfer soon after that," he said, "and for months I would be walking down the halls of the Pentagon and looking over my shoulder, expecting to see him. I stayed out of his way. I had absolutely nothing to do with nuclear work after that."

Was this man, in Rickover's eyes, a natural victim? And did Rickover purge such men from NRB by probing their weaknesses, by showing them only his harsh side? Perhaps. All that can be said is that there was no simple pattern, no guarantee that a worker's specific act would produce a specific Rickover reaction.

One reaction, however, seemed consistent. He was usually compassionate when personal tragedies struck people who worked for him. And his compassion went beyond NRB. When the *Thresher* and the *Scorpion* were lost, official letters of condolences were typed (sometimes with misspellings) and sent out to what the Navy called "the next of kin." Rickover wrote, in his own hand, letters to the widows of married men and the parents of unmarried men. Unlike the cold, impersonal official letters, the unexpected, handwritten Rickover letters became items that the survivors cherished.

But his compassion for those who mourned did not usually extend to those who merely wanted time with their families.

Time and again he would summon men to him on weekends and holidays. Time and again he would arrange schedules so that he and his workers traveled on weekends and that no time was wasted during normal workdays. He had a formal attitude about the work ethic, which he asserted many times in testimony and speeches—"Most of the work in the world today is done by those who work too hard; they comprise a 'nucleus of martyrs.' The greater part of the remaining workers' energy goes into complaining. . . ." If anyone was going to do any complaining, it would be Rickover, and his complaining often centered on workers who allowed their family life to take precedence over their work life.

Richard Laning, in a speech to a graduating class at the submarine school in New London, jocularly warned the prospective nucs that the designation of their submarines, SSN, meant not "attack submarine nuclear," but "Saturdays, Sundays, and Nights"—the non-days-off for nuclear submariners. This was standard operating procedure, Laning said, because the nuclear navy did not want "builders of nests and hatchers of eggs." Rickover heard about the speech, appropriated the phrase, and began using it in absolute seriousness. Questions about a prospective candidate's family life began appearing more frequently in Rickover's interviews.

Unmarried men were asked if they intended to marry; married men were asked whether they had or intended to have children. In the early nuclear days, when candidates were coming from the fleet for nuclear submarine training, a lieutenant commander who had commanded a nonnuclear submarine appeared for the Rickover interview. As the officer recounted the session later, Rickover quickly asked, "How many children do you have?"

"Four," the officer replied.

"What do you do when you come home from your ship?"

"Well, knowing my wife has had a pretty full day, I usually help her with dinner, do the dishes, clean up, and put the kids to bed."

"Oh. You're another one of these goddamn nesters."

The lieutenant commander was unable to respond. He swallowed his anger, and the interview continued. He was accepted—with the proviso that he spend at least forty hours a week, in addition to his regular duties, preparing for nuclear-power school. He would have no time for nesting. Rickover did not want nests.

In the world according to Rickover, tax deductions for dependent children would be eliminated "beyond some set number, perhaps three," and a tax penalty might be added "for any children in a family after the first four." As his personal belief in the transcendental nature of work spread beyond his own life and his own office, his philosophy collided with Navy policy, which called for rotating tours at sea and on the beach.

Admiral Smedberg, a former Chief of Naval Personnel, recalled in his memoirs, "I used to have his Polaris captains come to me and, almost with tears in their eyes, say, 'I can't take it any longer. I can't take it. I've been in command . . . for six consecutive years and I just can't take the pressure of being a commanding officer that much longer. I can't do it, and he [Rickover] wants me now to take out a new Polaris boat.' " Industry—particularly the nuclear industry—has profited from this, as bright young men, to save their marriages, have left the nuclear navy for civilian jobs. The practice even occurred in NRB itself, although many men spent their entire careers in Rickover's service and retired while he, twenty years their senior, stayed on.

As he preached work ahead of family, he practiced what he preached. He saw little of his own only child, Robert, but he was proud of his son's brilliant academic record. Ruth Rickover also had to endure the loneliness of a marriage to a workaholic. "He believes," Arleigh Burke once said, "you should put nuclear power ahead of your wife and everything."

She did not live the life of an admiral's wife. There were no white-glove receptions, no calling cards for receptions on the Washington military-political social circuit. The Rickovers were not part of the flag officers' community. If this bothered her, she did not complain. She had her studies, and she had her writings. When Robert was five, she was working for the Carnegie Endowment for International Peace, which in 1945 published her *Handbook of International Organizations in the Americas.*

She also wrote articles dealing with aspects of her special interest, international law. Her writings were intensely scholarly. A footnote might cite sources in three languages. Yet she might also digress into a personal allusion, as she did in an article on how international cooperation fostered European rail travel. She had traveled aboard European trains, and she had knowledge that went deeper than scholarship.

The Endowment aided in the formation of the United Nations World Health Organization, and one of the blueprints was a document written by Ruth D. Masters (who usually published under her maiden name). Her work at the Endowment continued into the late 1940s, but more and more of her time was devoted to Robert and to acting as an editor and co-author of her husband's continuous stream of writing. When her work was acknowledged, she was usually given credit for "assistance." One book by Hyman Rickover, *Swiss Schools and Ours: Why Theirs Are Better*, particularly bore the look of her scholarly approach and her firsthand knowledge of European education. In its review, *Newsweek* said, "Parts of 'Swiss Schools,' like some of Rickover's earlier works, actually were ghost-written by his wife. . . ."

Ruth Rickover rarely appeared in newsprint. She remained silent during Rickover's first promotion battle, when he was fighting compulsory retirement, but in 1958 she exploded in reaction to a double snub of her and her husband. Hyman Rickover had not been invited to a White House ceremony honoring Commander William R. Anderson, who commanded the *Nautilus* on her historic journey to the North Pole. And Ruth Rickover had been denied the honor of christening a submarine.

She allowed herself to be interviewed by one of Hyman Rickover's friends of the press, Ed Edstrom of the Washington Bureau of the *Boston American,* a Hearst newspaper. Edstrom's interview, widely circulated in Hearst newspapers, sizzled with angry words that made headlines. And in those words of a loyal wife could be seen flashes of life with Rickover—life with a man at war with "the bright and smiling smugness" of the official Navy.

She said that "up until the last minute" high-ranking Navy officials had not expected the *Nautilus* to work. "My husband had hoped for a quiet launching of the *Nautilus,*" she said, "but the press was tipped off by chuckling Navy officers that they should be sure to cover the coming fiasco. After it was a success, they tried to shove my husband under a rug while everybody else stepped in to take the glory. . . .

"You have no idea what it is like to work on the complex projects that my husband has conceived and carried through. But I know. He comes home to me at night, tired and discouraged, and I try to lift his spirit. When he first worked on the *Nautilus,* he could only hope and pray. It was only a gleam in his eye. When the launching was ready, he was worried because he knew of all the things that could go wrong. And now—now the Navy wants to pension him off to some little cow pasture. . . .

"I remember the day the Russians launched Sputnik I. My husband couldn't sleep for days. He worries and worries, but he is not even allowed to concentrate on his work. About three-quarters of his time is spent answering piddling notes and queries. . . .

"It is discouraging enough to encounter the ordinary failures you find in creative work. But when smug superiors throw every roadblock in your way, it is even worse. Supposing my husband had let his discouragement cause him to quit? Would we have the *Nautilus* today? This is a rapidly changing world. Some day I hope that the Navy will have officers who will understand odd officers with odd talents."

Mrs. Rickover was personally affronted by the Navy's decision not to allow her to christen a nuclear ship. This sacred tradition was at the time in the hands of the Navy; soon that too would come under Rickover's influence. But in 1958 the Navy selected the woman who swung a bottle of champagne against the bow of a warship on the ways, saying, "In the name of the United States, I christen thee ———." (The name would have been selected by the Secretary of the Navy, another perquisite that would change hands to a large extent.)

The Secretary also nominally selected the "sponsor," the woman who would christen the ship. In the 1950s, the honor usually went to a wife of a senior naval officer or a political official. The shipbuilder and the Chief of the Bureau of Ships often had a voice in the selection. In the Kennedy Administration, the tradition changed, and the wives of cabinet officers or high-ranking Democrats became sponsors. Around that time, Rickover also took the staging of christenings as one of his responsibilities.

When Mrs. Rickover was scorned, however, he did not have the power to do much about it. She and he had expected that she would christen the *Triton,* then the largest submarine ever built. But the honor went to the wife of an admiral who was a friend of Arleigh Burke. The Rickovers let it be known that Mrs. Rickover had been proposed as a sponsor eight times and had been inexplicably turned down eight times.

The day after the Hearst interview, the Navy announced that Mrs. Rickover had indeed been on a list to christen a nuclear submarine, but she just had not yet been given the invitation. The Navy declined to say which submarine it would be, but it obviously was not the *Triton*. The interview was published on August 14; the Navy claimed the existence of the phantom invitation on August 15; the *Triton* was christened on August 19. There was no shortage of submarines. The *Skipjack* had been christened on April 26, the *Seadragon* on August 16, and the *Robert E. Lee* would be christened on August 25. There would be no more launchings in 1958.

Ruth Rickover had said in the interview that she was "finished" with the Navy and would not be a sponsor. She had added that she had hoped that the "temporary bad management of the Navy" was only temporary. But, in fact, she never did christen a ship.

Admiral James, the Chief of BuShips, felt that the failure to give Mrs. Rickover the honor "became so obviously insulting that through my own efforts and those of Admiral Smedberg [Chief of BuPers] we got Mrs. Rickover invited to christen a new submarine. . . . Finally, when the invitation was extended, Rickover refused it, and I'm not sure that I wouldn't have done the same thing myself." Neither Ruth nor Hyman Rickover ever publicly acknowledged that invitation.

After the christening incident in 1958, Ruth Rickover vanished from the press. Robert, who had hardly ever appeared at all, completed his schooling with postgraduate work at Yale, began a career in banking and finance, and returned to Washington for occasional visits. Rickover became solidly entrenched after 1958, and although his battles did not end, neither he nor his wife ever again had to go to the press to plead his case.

At an age when other couples were settling into retirement, Ruth Rickover was the wife of a man still working a seven-day week. Her world became 4801 Connecticut Avenue. She continued to work with and for her husband, especially on biographies of namesakes of Polaris submarines. Rickover, who took great pride in these biographies, gathered them into a book, *Eminent Americans*. His wife helped him produce the book, which was published in 1972.

In January 1972 she was examined at the Naval Hospital in Bethesda, Maryland, a few miles north of Washington. She was diagnosed as suffering from atherosclerotic heart disease. On May 25 she collapsed after a heart attack at home and was taken to the Bethesda hospital, where she died that night. She was sixty-nine years old.

•

At about 5 A.M. on Thursday, November 16, 1972, a plane carrying Admiral Rickover from New London, Connecticut, landed at Washington's National Airport. Rickover had spent a long, taxing Wednesday at the Electric Boat yard, where the hostility toward him and his methods was steadily mounting. He walked rapidly away from the plane toward his office in the Crystal City complex, about a mile from the airport. . . .

He had been a walker for decades. Walking was a kind of exercise that made sense; it got you somewhere. When he was trapped in an office or in a hotel, he still walked—or, long before the word and act became fashionable, jogged. One time a fellow officer spotted Rickover walking rapidly up and down a hotel corridor, flapping his arms like wings. "Aren't you embarrassed?" the officer asked. "I'm staying alive," Rickover replied, and kept on walking in quick, jerky steps.

In the neighborhood around 4801 Connecticut he was well known as a fast walker. For one period he walked about four miles a day whenever he could. Gradually, through the years, he had cut down on his walking, but he never cut it out. He did believe that it was saving his life, for the exercise benefited his heart, and he had a history of heart trouble going back to at least 1961.

So, as he strode away from National Airport that November day in 1972, he was not doing anything new; a mile's walk would not ordinarily strain him. But he was even frailer than usual. Co-workers had noticed his decline since his wife's death. One of them said her death had devastated him. He had withdrawn even more within himself, and a man who had known and observed Rickover for years realized for the first time that he had never had any close friends. Death inevitably narrows a septuagenarian's circle of friends, but those who had any familiarity with Rickover's private life believed that for him there was no circle at all.

He reached his Naval Reactors office in the Crystal City building and began his day. He had to do two days' work in one, for he was scheduled to fly to Newport News, Virginia, the following day for a ceremony marking the laying of the keel of the nuclear submarine *Baton Rouge*. He had arranged to have the keel "authenticated" by Mrs. F. Edward Hébert, wife of the veteran Louisiana Congressman who was chairman of the House Armed Services Committee and one of Rickover's most loyal supporters on the Hill.

Rickover was scheduled to introduce Mrs. Hébert, one of many influential women and men that Rickover would place in ceremonies that began with the keel laying, continued through the christening, the commissioning, and the sea trials of each ship of the nuclear navy. He had become famous as a stage manager at these rites. "He never moved fewer than three people on a platform," one of his hand-picked guests remarked. But he would miss the ceremony for the *Baton Rouge*.

Some time after having walked the mile to his office, he collapsed, striking his head as he fell. Unconscious and bleeding from a head wound, he was given emergency treatment and taken to Bethesda. At first the Navy said he was suffering from exhaustion. But a few days later the hospital announced that he had had "a minor heart attack," was in the coronary-care unit and would be kept under treatment for a few weeks.

Rickover was well known in the hospital, one of the few Navy institutions he had never publicly criticized. Doctors, nurses, medical corpsmen, and his own NRB staff were ready for what would happen next—Rickover's suite would be transformed into an office, and he would insist on people bringing work to him, including, of course, the pinks.

The working-hospitalization tradition had begun in 1946, when, up from Oak Ridge for a hernia operation, he had labored from his bed. Rickover had similarly set up shop in Bethesda after a heart attack in July 1961. He conducted staff meetings, edited his writings, and in one of the rooms he had taken over, interviewed candidates for nuclear training. He soon recovered, and he became such a model of recovery that in 1964 the American Heart Association would present him with its Heart-of-the-Year Award for having "inspired people everywhere with new hope."

His hospitalization in 1972, because of his age and because of the obvious connection between stress and heart attack, was serious enough to warrant a change in his ways. But no change was apparent. The twelve-hour days continued. He did not slow down. And seven months later, he was back in Bethesda again, this time for what the Navy described as treatment for a respiratory ailment.

If he was aware of joining other men his age in the incontestable process of growing old, he rarely showed it. One day in 1973 he was testifying about the expensive Trident submarine when Senator Stuart Symington remarked, "I never thought I would see the day when a submarine would cost more than a carrier." Rickover bridled for a moment about what a carrier really cost, and twitted the former Secretary of the Air Force: "I never thought I would see the day when C-5A [the cargo plane] would cost $60 million."

"Neither did I," Symington said.

"You and I are getting old," Rickover said, "and we are old-fashioned. We don't realize the new economics."

"That is right," said Symington, who was seventy-two.

The following year there would be another Congressional dialogue that would have a touch of the joshing that goes on at a bachelor's stag dinner. Rickover was angrily testifying about Navy selection boards, and he asked Senator John Pastore, "Are you telling me that you are powerless to do anything about it?"

"What do you think?" Pastore asked.

"I do not think you are powerless," Rickover replied.

"You are supposed to be the father of the nuclear Navy," Pastore jabbed. "What have you done about it?"

"I am impotent," Rickover said.

Pastore brought the house down with his punch line: "All right. Don't say that now, whatever you do."

Representative Craig Hosmer interrupted the laughter to say: "He becomes the father of the nuclear Navy and then he gets married."

"Do you want to hear the reason for that?" Rickover asked.

"Don't tell me you had to," Hosmer exclaimed.

"I will," Rickover said. "When you meet a very charming, gracious, witty, intelligent, and beautiful woman, you must break the rules."

"Congratulations," Hosmer said.

A month before, on January 19, 1974, Rickover had married Navy Commander Eleonore A. Bednowicz, who was forty-three years old.

Rickover had met his second wife at Bethesda Naval Hospital while he was a patient and she was a nurse. She later was transferred to the Naval Training Center at Great Lakes, Illinois, near his home town, Chicago. Eleonore Bednowicz was commissioned an ensign in the Navy Nurse Corps in 1954. In a career that included duty at Navy hospitals from New York to Guam, she had risen in rank to commander in 1969.

When she and Rickover were married, their wedding plans were so secret that her superiors at the training center were not aware that she was going on leave to get married. No Chicago newspaper took notice of their marriage license, which they obtained on December 22, 1973. The Naval Reactors Branch found out when, without explanation, he gruffly ordered double accommodations for a forthcoming trip to London. NRB workers, accustomed to carrying out orders with a minimum of questions, could only assume that Rickover had a traveling companion in mind, but they did not ask who that might be.

The wedding was at St. Celestine's Roman Catholic Church in Elmwood Park, a Chicago suburb. They were married by the Reverend John

Powell, a Jesuit from Loyola University. News of the wedding was revealed after it took place. About twenty relatives of the bride and groom attended.

Commander Rickover retired from the Navy in the following November. She became interested in the hospice movement and served on the board of directors of the Hospice of Northern Virginia.

On September 30, 1979, the Navy celebrated a historic event: the *Nautilus,* the world's first nuclear-powered ship, had been commissioned exactly a quarter of a century before. The celebration was in the cavernous building that houses the Navy Historical Center at the Washington Navy Yard.

Vice Admiral Charles H. Griffiths, Deputy CNO for submarines, assessed the event: "The last twenty-five years will probably be remembered in history as the beginning of the nuclear age, and no doubt *Nautilus* will rank with the *Constitution, Victory, Mikasa,* and the rest of that select band of historic ships." He traced the operational history of the *Nautilus,* praised the men who manned her and the rest of the nuclear fleet, and then he said:

"One name will always be associated with the history of nuclear power. Over the entire life of the Navy nuclear-propulsion program Admiral Hyman G. Rickover has been its single, continuous thread of genius. He has made the Navy the world's foremost source of knowledge in the design, construction, and operation of nuclear power plants. His demanding leadership has molded the Navy nuclear power propulsion program. His technical leadership, open and frank exchanges with Congress, and dogged pursuit of excellence have had a profound effect on the entire Navy. His influence has reached into many areas of American life."

The man who was so officially and so historically praised was not there. He had not even responded to his invitation.

His appearance at the celebration would have been a surprise. He did not go to many events. Even for Hyman Rickover there were days and nights when he knew his age. A month before the *Nautilus* anniversary, he had been in Bethesda, this time for a hernia operation. His closest associates, men he had known for decades, were retiring from his service. He himself was almost alone of public men.

Few men born at the turn of the century were part of the American government in the 1980s. In the Congress there was none. On the bench of the Supreme Court there was none. In the Executive, that vast third branch extending from the White House through the Cabinet departments, the Armed Services, and innumerable agencies—in that multitude that numbered more than 4,500,000 people, a few hundred indomitable men and women in their seventies were still at work. Only one was a military officer on active duty, only one was in his eighties, working full time, indeed overtime. The cohorts of his age were long in retirement or had died. At least one was still at work—Jasper Holmes of his class at the Naval Academy was still writing and publishing. Scores of men whom Rickover had ushered into government when they were in their twenties and thirties now had completed full careers as civilians or as officers of the United States Navy and had long left the scene. Rickover was unique.

He no longer lived at 4801 Connecticut, and Naval Reactors Branch was no longer on Constitution Avenue. That was history, too. He lived near his work, for his apartment and the NRB were in the same complex of Virginia concrete known as Crystal City. Every morning, just before eight, a Navy car picked him up and took him around the block from his home, in the Buchanan House, to the building that housed NRB, National Center No. 2. The car pool was history, too. From their balcony at the rear of Buchanan House his wife could wave to him as he entered the office building. Then, in mid-1981, the Rickovers moved to The Representative, an expensive five-year-old condominium a mile from Crystal City on Arlington Ridge Road.

His personal life changed with his marriage to Eleonore Bednowicz, for she was more outgoing than Ruth, and the Rickovers attended more parties and dinners. The Navy had also changed; there were many nuclear ships. And the Navy's leadership had changed, with nucs in many key positions. But Rickover himself was largely unchanged. He was still fighting battles. Perhaps he was winning fewer, or perhaps he was simply fighting fewer of them. But he continued to do battle and he continued to shout.

THE MAN WHO SHOUTS

In ancient times a philosopher came to a city. He was determined to save its inhabitants from sin and wickedness. Night and day he walked the streets and haunted the marketplaces. He preached against greed and envy, against falsehood and indifference. At first the people listened and smiled. Later they turned away; he no longer amused them. Finally, a child moved by compassion asked, "Why do you go on? Do you not see it is hopeless?"

The man answered, "In the beginning, I thought I could change men. If I still shout, it is to prevent men from changing me."

I feel like that man as I talk to you today. I have fought for reform in the Navy for years. If I still shout, it is because I am afraid the Navy will not be able to meet the demands which will be placed upon it in the future.

> —ADMIRAL HYMAN G. RICKOVER,
> "The Role of Engineering in the Navy,"
> an address given before the
> National Society of Former Special Agents
> of the Federal Bureau of Investigation.
> Seattle, Washington,
> August 30, 1974

The Unaccountable Man

Some years ago a young man entered the inner sanctum of Admiral Rickover and stood stiffly at attention. After a few moments, Rickover looked up from his papers. He asked simply, "Are you the son of ———?" and he named a Navy admiral. The young man, who stood high in his class at the U.S. Naval Academy, answered, "Yes, sir."

"This interview is completed," Rickover declared.

The young midshipman would not—could not—enter the nuclear-power program. He could never aspire to command a U.S. Navy submarine or a surface ship powered by nuclear reactors. Thus was denied to him a large portion of the Navy, and a large amount of his opportunity to someday enter into the higher ranks of the Navy.

The decision, by Rickover, was firm. There was no appeal for the midshipman. For Rickover, there was no accountability for that decision.

At almost the same time, two hundred miles to the south at the Newport News Shipbuilding and Dry Dock Company, the largest ship-yard in the non-Communist world, work was coming to a halt on several nuclear submarines, a nuclear aircraft carrier, and two nuclear cruisers. These were critical programs at the time; the U.S. Navy had declined in the post-Vietnam period to less than half the strength of a decade earlier. Newport News was one of only two American shipyards producing sub-marines, and the only one at the time capable of building nuclear surface ships. The slowdown appeared as a step toward a total halt in the con-struction of those ships.

The president of Newport News, John Diesel, a respected American businessman; Gordon W. Rule, the Navy's financial watchdog; and the U.S. Fifth Circuit Court held one man accountable for the slowdown: Admiral Rickover. But neither the Navy nor the Deparment of Defense would hold him legally or professionally accountable.

653

On another occasion, when the nuclear submarine *Jacksonville* was on sea trials off the New England coast in January 1981, the craft went through a maneuver known as "quick stop" or "crashback." The maneuver is the end of the full-power submerged run, when the engines are put on full astern. If the submarine actually begins to move astern after stopping, the ship could be in an extremely dangerous situation; there is a possibility that the submarine will go out of control.

The speed changes were being ordered by Admiral Rickover, who stood in the small maneuvering compartment of the engineering spaces. But only someone in the forward navigation center could tell when the ship actually reached a full stop and when the engines should be set on "ahead" speeds. As the ship went through the crashback, Rickover hesitated a full minute before giving an order to go ahead. During that minute, the astern speed built up to more than nine knots, the submarine went into a stern-up attitude, and then plunged down about 70 feet.

According to the detailed report made to the Chief of Naval Operations, Rickover told the submarine's captain that he wanted to repeat the dangerous maneuver. He did so five times—even though the printed test procedures warned, "CAUTION—This test does not require the ship to go astern submerged." Other officers from the Naval Sea Systems Command, as well as the ship's officers, were concerned about the situation. One officer told an Electric Boat official on board that the situation should not occur but that nobody could control Rickover. Then, according to the EB official, the officer elaborated "that with a new ship and an inexperienced crew it was even more important that it should not be permitted to happen."

In his subsequent report, the EB official concluded: "It appears from observing this evolution that [the officers] will not override Rickover unless they believe the safety of the ship is in jeopardy. However, by the time they make such determination, the time available for recovery may be insufficient."

Six months later, the new submarine *La Jolla* went to sea on trials. Again Rickover hesitated during the quick-stop operation. The *La Jolla*, with 186 men on board, reached an astern speed of almost 12 knots before the hazardous situation could be corrected. Then, in gaining forward momentum, the submarine attained a down-angle greater than 40 degrees and descended 240 feet below the depth planned. This put the brand-new submarine in a precarious situation, deeper than she had yet been (although she was still above her safety margins).

Again, Rickover was personally in charge of the maneuver. And, again, he was unaccountable.

Some have tried to hold Rickover accountable. A few members of Congress have called him to answer specific questions and not slip into platitudes. Some have tried to be more specific. Vice Admiral William Smedberg, at the time Chief of Naval Personnel, and Admiral George W. Anderson, the Chief of Naval Operations, about 1962 "agreed that the time had come to provide for the possibility when there might come a showdown between the congressional supporters of Rickover and the Navy in Rickover's attempt to get increasing power in running the Navy."

After that meeting, according to Smedberg's recollection, "I took my chief yeoman and I sent him out to Admiral Lockwood, Admiral 'Fog' Low ... Admiral Earle Mills, who had been Chief of the Bureau of Ships, I think Admiral Mumma, who later was Chief of the Bureau of Ships, all of whom had been involved in the early days of nuclear power in the United States Navy."

The yeoman took the statements down in shorthand. Then, all that he and Smedberg had learned about Rickover—from the midshipmen interviews to answers to questions about how Rickover had risen to power—was put into a book.

"Now this book," Smedberg recalled, "put Admiral Rickover in quite an unfavorable light, through the testimony of the officers who watched Admiral Rickover in the early days of nuclear power in the Navy and who felt that his, in many cases, obstructionist tactics, which irritated the heads of Westinghouse and General Electric so much, really delayed progress in nuclear power more than should have been the case. This book is historically important to a historian who, some day, will want to do the full story of ... navy nuclear-power development. ..."

But the book has vanished. Smedberg said that he had locked it in his personal safe, but "I completely forgot about it when I retired. I left the Navy, and there the book was, in the safe.

"When next I began to worry about where it was and what it was doing, the Chief of Naval Personnel was Vice Admiral Jim Watkins, Jim being one of Admiral Rickover's nuclear submarine people. For obvious reasons, I didn't want to ask him to locate the book and turn it over to the Director of Naval History or the naval historian or whoever should have it. So I waited until he was relieved by Vice Admiral [Robert] Baldwin, wrote him a letter, told him about the book. He searched the safe and it's gone."

Although the record was lost, Smedberg remembered that the conclusion of the study was that Rickover had been put into the fledgling nuclear program "because they couldn't see his value in any other place in the Navy, so they thought they might put him in there. He kind of backed into that job."

Smedberg was correct. But there was one other key point: Mills had known that Rickover would strive toward a goal single-mindedly, without care about whom he insulted, cajoled, hurt, or helped. And Mills knew that the future of nuclear power was primarily to propel ships and that Rickover also understood that.

Rickover survived his critics in Congress and in the Navy and elsewhere because he did achieve his goal. When the *Nautilus* got underway on January 17, 1955, his methods were vindicated. He had earned the title of "father of the atomic submarine," a term that journalists began to use a short time later.

When the *Nautilus* went to sea, Rickover was a rear admiral. He would, under normal Navy policy, be reassigned to another position about that time, having been in the nuclear program of BuShips and the AEC for some eight years, or about twice the time an engineering duty officer would normally remain in one job. There was a brief flurry of activity by Rickover and his staff as they appealed to Congressional friends to support having the job made a civilian position. Thus, Rickover could retire and remain as head of the Naval Reactors Branch.

The Navy's leadership objected. A program manager working for a technical bureau had to be a naval officer. It had to do with accountability. Meanwhile, the Navy's leadership—the Secretary of the Navy and Chief of Naval Operations—continued to seek means and men to replace Rickover.

One of the earliest recorded efforts came about 1960, when Secretary of the Navy Fred Korth secretly summoned Captain Richard Laning, first skipper of the *Seawolf*, to Washington. "I gave my opinion that there were a lot of fine people in Rickover's program who could take over that program if given the proper backing, if Rickover died," Laning recalled. But he also said that "Rickover had done his best to keep these people away from the top job. . . . As people got to the point where they would be his Number 2 man, he would arrange it so they would resign and leave . . . and he would stay on."

Rear Admiral Ralph K. James, for four years, from 1959 to 1963, Rickover's "boss" as Chief of BuShips, observed that "anyone who began to challenge him in the preeminence in this field wasn't long for the program." Continuing on the subject of Rickover successors, James said: "He's arranged for the transfer out of the program, never to be reentered into it, any number of senior engineering duty officers who had tremendous technical capability, greater in many measures than Rickover ever possessed. Among these were Lou Roddis, Eli Roth, Ralph Kissinger and others."

Another officer seen as a prospective successor was Edwin E. Kintner, whom Rickover had sent out to Arco on a few hours' notice when there were problems with the *Nautilus* prototype reactor project. After thirteen years in NRB, Kintner realized that his naval career was nonexistent and decided to leave the Navy. On June 30, 1963, the last day of his naval service, Korth summoned him.

Korth, as Kintner recalled, said he had just learned that Kintner was leaving the Navy, that "there was no one else around with your experience in nuclear propulsion," and that "we want you to stay on." The Secretary went on to explain that a backup—and potential successor—was needed for Rickover. "I'm sorry I didn't know about this [retirement] sooner . . . we can cancel your release right now," Korth was remembered as saying.

But Kintner knew better—no EDO commander could succeed Rickover. Further, he had a commitment to a small firm in New England. Regardless, it was too late.

Kintner went to New England, and later Rickover twice asked him to return to NRB. The second time, after more than a year in the "outside world," Kintner returned to NRB to the vital job of supervising all reactor-core procurement. Then, several months later, one Saturday afternoon Kintner and Rickover were chatting, informally—"he was the most widely read and thoughtful person I know" is one reflection Kintner has on those talks. But that day Rickover mentioned John Crawford, a contemporary of Kintner, who had been in NRB until 1963. Rickover called Crawford "disloyal," indicating that he might have even had illusions of replacing him as head of NRB.

In a thoughtless moment as he was defending Crawford, Kintner mentioned his own meeting with the Secretary of the Navy a year and a half earlier. "Rickover was obviously upset," Kintner recalled. Suddenly there were "new circumstances . . . relations between myself and the Admiral immediately soured." Rickover made his remaining in NRB impossible. Six weeks later, despite the importance of his position and the outstanding contribution he had made as an officer and as a civilian, Kintner quit NRB.

Rickover's reference to Crawford in the conversation with Kintner does not square with the recollections of Crawford or former Secretary of the Navy Nitze.

In 1963, soon after becoming Secretary, Nitze had raised the issue of a successor with Rickover. But Rickover put Nitze off. Two years later, Nitze told the authors, "I came to the conclusion that we should prepare the way for getting a successor to Admiral Rickover by making him have a deputy. One of his ploys had been that he had no one to succeed him, and if he were to be removed, the organization would fall apart.

"I talked to Rickover, and he said he didn't need a deputy, and he did not know anyone who could do the job. I said to him, 'You choose a deputy. I order you to.' "

Nitze said Rickover recommended Captain John W. Crawford, Jr., a former member of NRB, who had left the Navy and taken a civilian job in New York. Nitze asked Under Secretary of the Navy Paul Fay to find Crawford and get him back.

In discussions with Fay and Nitze, Crawford remembered, "I made it abundantly clear that if your objective is to have a regular Navy officer as the deputy in Naval Reactors, then you should order me back to active duty. But, having been in that job before, I want you to know that, should you order me back to Naval Reactors, that does not make me a deputy as you know that job to be."

Crawford was politely confirming what Nitze and Fay already knew. Getting a deputy in name only would not change the situation. And so, what Crawford remembered as "a piece of paper" was drawn up. The paper, authorized by high officials, said that if Crawford did return as Rickover's deputy, he would be made a rear admiral. This extraordinary agreement was an indication as to how extraordinary the situation was.

Rickover had never allowed another flag officer in NRB. The piece of paper drawn up for Crawford virtually guaranteed that Rickover would have a rear admiral in place as a successor. The understanding was that when the first man of the U.S. Naval Academy Class of 1942 was selected for admiral, Crawford would also make admiral by personal action of President Kennedy. The arrangement had been approved by the Navy's judge advocate general. Fay, a Kennedy shipmate from PT-boat days, could speak with authority on the President's intentions.

Crawford was well qualified. He graduated Number 4 in the Class of 1942, had gone to work for Rickover after graduating from the Massachusetts Institute of Technology's graduate program in nuclear engineering, and later returned to MIT for a degree in physics. Besides serving with Rickover, Crawford had worked for three years as an NRB representative at the Newport News shipyard. He had also succeeded James Dunford as assistant to Atomic Energy Commissioner Thomas Murray, Rickover's major supporter on the commission.

After thirteen years in the nuclear program, Crawford had left in July 1963 and retired from the Navy as a captain a month later. If he returned to Naval Reactors, he would be the next senior naval officer to Rickover. But what the Navy wanted to happen did not happen.

Sometime after his meeting with Fay, Crawford got a call from Fay, who told Crawford that "the arrangement had fallen apart." Crawford, who would later become Deputy Assistant Secretary for nuclear energy in the Department of Energy, never found out what happened.

Other officers were also considered as backups—if not successors—to Rickover. Even after he had been "fired" by Rickover in 1950, Robert L. Moore, once designated by Rickover as a successor, had been mentioned several times. So had two admirals from the submarine community: Jim Calvert, of *Skate* fame, and, a more probable candidate, Dennis Wilkinson, the first commanding officer of the *Nautilus* and the *Long Beach*. Wilkinson, after serving as Deputy Chief of Naval Operations for submarines, had left the Navy in 1974. He was well known and well liked and, immediately after leaving the Navy, had entered the nuclear industry. In 1980 he was named to head the Institute of Nuclear Power Operations, the self-policing organization created by the utility industry after the Three Mile Island accident. Even at that time some in the Navy still thought he might make a suitable head of the Navy's nuclear-propulsion program.

Significantly, however, while Navy men and even some members of Congress still discussed a successor to Rickover, none seemed to use the term "replacement." For, despite Rickover's tarnishing reputation and declining political power, after the efforts of Paul Nitze in the 1960s no one seemed interested in forcing Rickover to leave the Navy. Perhaps it was because there were many nucs in top Navy positions; perhaps it was because the Navy had learned to better accommodate him as the lines between the nuclear navy and the real Navy had blurred. This seemed to be the case when even under his own nuclear-trained officers, with James Holloway as CNO and scores in lesser positions, the Navy did not seek an all-nuclear surface fleet.

Still, Rickover remained. He was the man who brought nuclear power to the nation, and he was the man who could keep the program safe and working.

Could other men have directed the nuclear-propulsion program?

The answer, obviously, is yes. Robert Moore had been named by Rickover at an early date as Crawford was later on; both were qualified to run NRB. Lou Roddis, a Navy Oak Ridge original, particularly demonstrated outstanding technical and management abilities, going on to become president of New York City's electric utility, Consolidated Edison. And Kintner had gone on to head the nation's fusion program in the Department of Energy.

All of these men were at about the rank of commander in the late 1940s. There were many others, who, as James remarked, could have taken over—without having "achieved their pinnacle of success by stepping over the recumbent bodies of their associates."

Rickover's unique contribution is often said to be that he pushed the Navy into nuclear propulsion, giving the nation the *Nautilus* at least five, ten, or—some observers say—even fifteen years before the submarine would otherwise have been built.* Eli Roth, in a speech before the Industrial College of the Armed Forces, has called this a case of "shortened lead time."

Recalling that in 1948 the only formal Navy nuclear-propulsion project was a heat-transfer effort at Westinghouse, Roth pointed out that by the summer of 1953 there was a full-scale submarine reactor operating in the desert at Arco, Idaho. Rickover's contributions to shortening that lead time were, in Roth's opinion, in five areas:

> *Vision.* This was a fundamental ingredient—the vision to see just how important and revolutionary a nuclear-propelled submarine might be.
>
> *Energy, drive, and singleness of purpose.* Rickover considered the job the most important thing in the world.
>
> *Selection and use of people.* He tried to get people smarter than himself for a particular part of the job to get done; he was ruthless in the use and misuse of people, with his apparent prime objectives of getting the job done *and* staying in control himself.
>
> *The two-hat system.* This was a masterpiece for cutting administrative red-tape; it let Rickover cite Navy rules that were being followed when he ran into trouble with the Atomic Energy Commission, and to cite AEC rules when he ran into trouble with the Navy.

---

* *In fact, the Soviet Union put its first nuclear submarine to sea within five years of the* Nautilus.

"It worked both ways—like the old shell and pea game—even when an action was improper by both rules," Roth said.

Training and education. Early in the program, before he had enough dollars to do other things, Rickover emphasized training—to the extent of making better physicists out of his engineers and better engineers out of his physicists.

Could these aspects of shortening lead time have been used by another officer to accelerate the nuclear-propelled submarine?

Smedberg and other officers who had watched Rickover in the early days would always believe that his "obstructionist tactics" had delayed progress. But a careful review of his entire nuclear-energy scene in the late 1940s leads to the conclusion that another officer probably could not have done what Rickover had accomplished.

In the immediate postwar years, the Navy was interested in the promise of nuclear propulsion, as were several industrial firms. But there was no concentrated program, and the real "villain" was the newly formed Atomic Energy Commission. It seemed that the AEC was, if not floundering, at least being excruciatingly slow in developing nuclear energy for power uses. "Decades away" was a term used at the time for the power application of the atom.

Rickover had left that Oak Ridge atmosphere with an intense sense of purpose, and once given the backing of Admiral Earle Mills, the Chief of BuShips, Rickover could both unify the Navy's scattered efforts and drive, badger, and coerce the AEC into action. It is doubtful that—given the circumstances of the immediate postwar environment—any other officer could have taken charge and moved the program as quickly and as well as Rickover.

He was unique in still another aspect. As he failed in his selection for admiral in the early 1950s, he appealed outside the Navy for support—to the Congress. This was not new; one of his quasi-heroes was William S. Sims, who as a young officer had found support for his gunnery innovations in President Theodore Roosevelt. (Sims had a distinguished career and later reached the rank of full admiral.) There had been others as well. But Rickover took the quest for extra-Navy support to an unprecedented level as he developed his special relations with Congress.

The basis of Rickover's Congressional support—indeed, the basis of his entire campaign against the Navy and the Defense Department—has been what he has labeled as stubborn opposition, from the outset, to nuclear submarines and, later on, to nuclear surface ships. Describing this situation to the House Armed Services Committee on April 18, 1967, Rickover revealed what he called the "philosophical aspect" of his problem:

"We have got somehow to drag the Navy into the Twentieth Century. From the beginning the Navy has opposed nuclear power. Were it not for this Committee, the Joint Committee on Atomic Energy, the Senate and the House Appropriations Committees and the Senate Armed Services Committee, we would not have nuclear submarines. It is a coincidence, but in 1948 when the Navy opposed nuclear submarines they had a study made by their cost-analyst experts. This study showed that a nuclear submarine would be worth 1.41 as much as a conventional submarine but would cost twice as much; the analysts therefore concluded it wasn't worthwhile."

This, then, is the basis of Rickover's support—that he, and only he, could recognize the value of nuclear propulsion, in 1948 and, two decades later, when he testified before the House committee, and still in 1980 when he testified with essentially the same words.

Had the Navy really been opposed to nuclear-powered submarines?

After several score interviews with key naval officers and civilians, after reading their memoranda and letters, and after reviewing the minutes and reports of the Submarine Officers' Conferences and meetings of the General Board, the authors could not find any opposition to the construction of nuclear-powered submarines. There is only one brief effort at restraint, that by then-Vice Admiral Robert Carney, who argued that a worldwide ban on nuclear propulsion should be attempted.

No other Navy opposition can be found. Questions? Yes. But opposition? No. In expounding his views on Navy opposition that day in 1967 to the House Armed Services Committee, Rickover would ably quote Bret Harte's Reverend James Caldwell ("Give 'em Watts!"), Alben Barkley, and Sir Thomas Browne, as well as a half dozen admirals who supported nuclear ships and submarines. But Rickover did not then, nor did he ever, so far as can be ascertained, quote a single admiral as opposing nuclear submarines or surface ships in that first decade of the atomic age.

Indeed, the record—which does *not* clearly speak for itself—states exactly the opposite. Beginning with the Tolman Committee set up by Manhattan Project director Groves, the Navy's Mills and Solberg were firmly convinced of the potential of nuclear propulsion. Similarly, Admirals Bowen (particularly close to Secretary of the Navy Forrestal), Styer and Momsen were all supporters of nuclear propulsion. Within the

OPNAV staff, Captains Grenfell and Beach and several lesser-known submarine officers were supporters of nuclear propulsion.

During the winter of 1946–1947 the Navy's Submarine Officers' Conference, the "wise men" of the submarine community, met to consider the future of submarine warfare and concluded, in part, "The development of a true submarine capable of operating submerged for unlimited periods, appears to be probable within the next ten years, provided nuclear power is made available for submarine propulsion." Earlier—in June 1946—the conference had recommended a building program that included nuclear submarines as well as conventional submarines that could be converted to nuclear propulsion when it was deemed feasible. Albeit premature, their recommendations revealed the true feelings of many in the submarine community.

In 1948, the Navy's General Board heard Admiral Momsen explain, "The atomic power plant uses as a source of fuel a concentrated radioactive substance, which has a very long life and which gives as much range as is needed." His qualifications were only that "the supply of such fuel is limited. . . . In addition, quite a bit of room is required for protective shielding and the submarine must be fairly large."

There were at that time no "systems analysts" in the Navy (nor in the newly established Defense Department) who argued against nuclear propulsion. Rather, within months of Momsen's presentation, which was an overall view of the entire U.S. submarine program, the General Board was also on record as favoring nuclear submarines. And Admiral Nimitz, the Chief of Naval Operations in 1946–1947, had formally endorsed nuclear propulsion for submarines in writing. (His successor as CNO, Admiral Louis D. Denfeld, gave priority to nuclear weapons development, partly at the urgings of Admiral Parsons, partly because delivering atomic bombs was the only viable role many saw for the Navy at the time.)

Beyond these admirals, there was one above all: Earl W. Mills. As Assistant Chief of the Bureau of Ships and a close associate of Groves during World War II and then as Chief of BuShips, until his retirement in November 1949, Mills more than any other in the Navy understood and pursued nuclear propulsion. After the war Groves wrote, "Personally, I am positive that the officer most responsible in the Navy for initiating the development of atomic propulsion was Mills." And, it was Mills who, frustrated by the inaction of the newly formed Atomic Energy Commission in the field of nuclear propulsion, attacked the AEC openly at the April 1948 symposium in Washington, and, finally, appointed Captain

Hyman G. Rickover as BuShips-AEC liaison to get the program moving.

It was the *Navy,* and not the commissioners of the AEC or even the members of Congress, that wanted nuclear propulsion.

Rickover was given the job to do by the Navy. Later, in 1951, when that same Navy decided that after directing the nuclear program for three years it was time to put a new officer in charge, Rickover balked. He astutely mobilized his men—dedicated and brilliant men—and used his own few contacts on Capitol Hill and elsewhere to fight the Navy. He succeeded.

The fight, however, changed Rickover. No longer did he have visions of promotion—possibly to the top engineering duty position, then a rear admiral and head of BuShips—before retiring in the late 1950s. He would now stay, for being head of the NRB was the only position that he could keep and that could keep him in the Navy. When he tried to keep the position as a civilian, Secretary Nitze and the CNO, Thomas Moorer, said no.

Rickover stayed. And he ensured that all Navy nuclear propulsion activities were directed from the offices of NRB. Efforts by Westinghouse or General Electric, or even the Navy's own Office of Naval Research, to look into alternatives or more advanced nuclear power projects were destroyed. Calls to corporation presidents were the first means he used to make certain such efforts by industry were stopped; later, when his calls were refused or not returned—or when GE and Westinghouse turned down his requests—he would testify in Congress about his problems with the firms. Any research not sponsored by Rickover would stop, abruptly. The same fate befell the Electric Boat yard, the West's largest submarine contractor, when it proposed some advanced submarine designs. The general manager of the yard at the time was Joe Williams, a retired vice admiral who had had a distinguished career in submarines. But it mattered not to Rickover; he strangled the proposal at birth. Even studies at the Office of Naval Research into advanced propulsion plants—nuclear and others—ran afoul of Rickover and were halted. In some cases, copies of internally distributed reports were recalled, locked up, or destroyed.

Such tactics may have produced results far more significant than anger and exasperation at Rickover's way of playing his game. General Electric, Westinghouse, Electric Boat, the Office of Naval Research, and a score of other research-oriented organizations look toward the future— in the case of industry, for business as well as for more altruistic motives. It is through these firms and some of the government research organizations that advanced technologies are developed. And these developments provide the technology for future military and often civilian progress.

But Rickover does not allow any party outside NRB to enter into his fiefdom. Science writer Deborah Shapley has quoted one naval expert as saying, "The father of the last technological revolution is in the ideal position to stamp out the next one." Rickover has stamped out the next technological revolution. As an example, Lou Roddis cites the Soviet development of the Alfa-class nuclear submarine, which can go faster and deeper than U.S. undersea craft, and yet is smaller.

Should Rickover have left the scene?

Laning has postulated that "when a revolutionary succeeds, he should be given five years and then shot. Or otherwise removed. Because they become then vulnerable to the politics of failure and they cease to advance. They rest on their laurels. I think that's what happened to Rickover."

The five years proposed by Laning—the five years after Rickover's success, the *Nautilus*, went to sea—would mean 1960, about the time when, in the view of several observers, the Navy's approach to submarine development did begin to become highly conservative. Later in that decade, when submarines designed in the early 1960s went to sea, the Soviets had more, faster, deeper-diving, and more heavily armed nuclear submarines than we had. The only clear advantages of U.S. submarines over their Soviet counterparts are quiet performance and the quality of certain systems.

Rickover had claimed that his designs could have prevented that situation—if only the Navy and Defense Department would have heeded him. The records do not clearly support him, especially when one considers that several major defense programs were initiated in that period. True, the McNamara era, 1961–1967, in general was hard on the Navy. But many submarines were built—more Polaris and attack submarines than in any similar period before or after McNamara. The harm done to the United States submarine effort, as several of McNamara's deputies expressed it, stemmed from the confusion over what Rickover and the Navy wanted submarines to do.

His changeover from the visionary to the conservative—if not to the reactionary—came to light with the loss of the *Thresher* on April 10, 1963. Rickover once told Congress: "My program is unique in the military service in this respect: You know the expression 'from the womb to the tomb'? My organization is responsible for initiating the idea for a project; for doing the research, and the development; designing and building the equipment that goes into the ships; for the operation of the ship; for the selection of the officers and men who man the ship; for their education and training. In short, I am responsible for the ship throughout its life— from the very beginning to the very end."

Another time before a Congressional committee, Rickover pointed out, "If you want to have real responsibility you must make a competent man responsible for the entire project and not let him say, 'Well, I'm here two years and if something goes wrong it was the fault of my predecessor.' I can never say that. . . . If anything goes wrong, I'm responsible."

But the night that the *Thresher* died, Rickover called Admiral James, Chief of BuShips, to point out that he, Rickover, was not responsible for the *Thresher*.

There is one interesting footnote to the question of when Rickover should have left the scene. It comes from Rickover, via the *Journals* of David Lilienthal, the first chairman of the Atomic Energy Commission. Telling of his conversation with Rickover in July 1954—before the *Nautilus* was completed—Lilienthal wrote: "In a revealing moment, as the train raced through the night toward the city of new light which had built the atomic bomb, Rickover responded: 'Maybe I ought to get out. You can stay too long for the good of the work you are doing; I have seen that happen. Maybe that is what is happening to me, right now.' " Then, according to Lilienthal's *Journal*, "The most troubled look went over his face at this point."

Rickover stayed on. And after building the *Nautilus* he tried to build the civilian nuclear power industry and he tried to change the American system of education. He failed, in both.

How could Rickover fail?

He was perhaps too idealistic, and many of his ideals far transcended those of his fellow Americans. To an ultramodern, cynical age, he sounded medieval with his warning, "It is a device of the devil to let sloth into the world." He preached patriotism and self-sacrifice to nodding Congressmen embroiled in scandals. He asked the Navy to man his ships with people whom society seemed no longer able to supply to the Navy—people who have "a purpose in life," who "put excellence in one's work and concern for what is right before personal safety."

His quest for authority, for a society that could somehow combine freedom and discipline, never ceased. "In our system of society," he complained, "no authority exists to tell us what is good and desirable. We are each free to seek what we think is good in our own way. . . . Perhaps the liberal tradition never really could believe that vice, when unconstrained by religion, morality and law, might lead to viciousness. It never really could believe that self-destructive nihilism was an authentic and permanent possibility that any society had to guard against. It could refute Marx effectively, but it never thought it would be called upon to refute the Marquis de Sade. . . ."

No one seemed to be listening. In 1979, his own organization began to tremble as five of his assistants retired. One had worked for him for twenty-three years and had been, like many before him, looked upon as a potential successor. Another had worked for Rickover for twenty years and, as Rickover told a Congressional hearing only months before the man's retirement, "I held him in my arms shortly after he was born."

That man passed from the scene and so had virtually all of Rickover's generation. But he clung on. As Captain Rickover he had done more than any other naval officer to build something no one had ever built before. As Admiral Rickover he tried to build a world for his creations, a world in which he fashioned even the people who would operate his creations. As Captain Rickover and the *Nautilus* became a memory, Admiral Rickover became a force in the Navy. They almost seemed like two men. "I liked him better as a captain than as an admiral," Dr. Edward Teller remarked in 1980. Teller had, with Mills, helped propel Rickover into nuclear propulsion, bringing pressure to bear on the AEC. He too was a man long on stage, but he had gradually withdrawn to the wings, often stepping out to speak but not to govern. "Yes," Teller replied when asked by one of the authors. "I think he should retire."

Rickover has never ceased to urge the best. It has become obvious over the years that his demands for excellence have far transcended the demands of most other parts of the American society, including the Navy. And coupled with his demands for excellence—at virtually any cost—he has also asked for the truth. His almost daily calls from his representatives in shipyards, for example, are to find out the problems. He wants the captains of nuclear ships to write him about their problems. He will not censure someone for telling of a problem—only for not telling him. That, too, is hard to find elsewhere in the modern American society.

He has asked why not the best of young men like Jimmy Carter, of his peers, of the Navy, of American society. He has preached and he has questioned what we are and where we are going. "Where do our goals and values come from?" he asks. "If we believe in a free society, what limitations, if any, are we willing to place on that freedom so that society may protect and maintain itself?"

These are the questions of a man who has reached a venerable age, a man who draws upon his own wisdom, shapes it into a testament, and then dispenses it in the hope that the next generation will benefit from his thoughts. But when the same man is simultaneously on stage as an activist, as a challenger, his words are rarely heeded, for he is of one generation speaking across another generation to yet a third. He is an angry, powerful man in his eighties, mocking the powerlessness of a midshipman in his twenties. After such an encounter, there is no inspiration but only more anger and frustration—on both sides. And thus does the philosopher feel even more convinced that no one is listening to him. Indeed, Rickover himself, testifying before a Congressional committee in June 1980, declared that no one asked his advice: "It is as if I simply do not exist."

But some people still listened to Rickover, mostly those who had to rather than, as in earlier days, those who wanted to. He was still trying to run the Navy and he still harbored hopes of influencing the nation. He was still controlling the careers of thousands. And he was still the unaccountable man.

Appendix A

RICKOVER CHRONOLOGY

June 15, 1875	Father Abraham (Eliachako) born		
July 14, 1876	Mother Rachel (Ruchal) born		
Aug. 24, 1898	Rickover born (according to school records)	*May 1, 1898*	Dewey's victory at Manila Bay
Jan. 27, 1900	Rickover born (according to Navy records)		
1904	Rickover comes to America with mother and sister Fanny		
1908	Family moves from New York to Chicago		
Sep. 1914	Enters John Marshall High School	*Aug. 1914*	World War I starts in Europe
		Apr. 1917	United States enters war
Feb. 1918	Graduates and is honored as mantle bearer	*Nov. 11, 1918*	World War I ends
June 29, 1918	Enters Naval Academy		
June 2, 1922	Graduates Naval Academy	*Nov. 12, 1921*	Naval limitation conference begins in Washington
Aug. 13, 1922	Reports aboard destroyer *Percival* at San Diego		
Sep. 5, 1922	Reports aboard destroyer *La Vallette* at San Francisco for duty		
June 21, 1923	Becomes Engineering Officer of *La Vallette*		
Sep.–Nov. 1924	Under treatment at Mare Island Naval Hospital		

669

Jan. 21, 1925	Reports aboard battleship *Nevada* at Bremerton for duty		
May 20, 1925	Transfers to hospital ship *Relief* and then to San Diego for treatment		
June 1925	Promoted to Lieutenant (j.g.)	*July–*	
Sep. 1925	Returns to *Nevada;* made Electrical Officer	*Sept. 1925*	U.S. Fleet (including *Nevada*) cruises to Australia and New Zealand
Apr. 28, 1927	Leaves *Nevada at Hampton Roads, Va.*		
June 1927	Reports Naval Postgraduate School at Annapolis		
June 1928	Promoted to Lieutenant		
1928–1929	Attends Columbia University; earns MS in Electrical Engineering		
Oct. 10, 1929	Reports to submarine *S–9* at New London, Conn.		
Jan.- *June 1930*	Attends Submarine School at New London		
June 21, 1930	Reports to submarine *S–48* at New London for duty		
March 1, 1931	*S–48* arrives at Coco Solo, Canal Zone		
June 1931	Becomes Executive Officer of *S–48*		
Aug. 4, 1931	Qualifies for submarine command		
1932	Marries Ruth Dorothy Masters in Litchfield, Conn.		
June 5, 1933	Detached from *S–48* (relieved as Executive Officer on June 2)		
July 5, 1933	Reports as Inspector of Naval Material, Philadelphia		
Apr. 13, 1935	Reports to battleship *New Mexico* at Los Angeles for duty as assistant engineering officer		
June 1937	Detached from *New Mexico*		
July 1, 1937	Promoted to Lieutenant Commander		

	July 7, 1937 — Incident at Marco Polo bridge near Peking starts conflict in China
July 17, 1937 — Becomes commanding officer of minesweeper *Finch* in Tsingtao, China	Aug. 11, 1937 — Japanese marines assault Shanghai
Oct. 5, 1937 — Relieved as commanding officer of *Finch* (departs ship October 24)	
Nov. 1, 1937 — Arrives at Cavite Navy Yard in the Philippines for duty	
1938 — Rickovers tour Southeast Asia	June 11, 1938 — U.S. gunboat *Panay* sunk by Japanese bombers
Aug. 1939 — Reports of Bureau of Engineering (soon to become Bureau of Ships) in Washington	Sep. 1, 1939 — World War II begins in Europe
Oct. 11, 1940 — Son, Robert Masters, born	Dec. 7, 1941 — Japanese attack Pearl Harbor
1945 — Heads special study team at supply center in Mechanicsburg, Pa.	
July 1945 — Becomes commander of ship-repair facility on Okinawa	Aug. 1945 — Atomic bombs dropped on Hiroshima and Nagasaki
Dec. 1945 — Becomes inspector general of 19th Fleet in San Francisco, supervising mothballing of warships	
	March 29, 1946 — Dr. Abelson completes study "Atomic Energy Submarine"
May 1946 — Assigned to Manhattan Project at Oak Ridge, Tenn. (initial briefings in BuShips)	
June 1946 — Arrives at Oak Ridge	June 4, 1946 — Submarine Officers Conference recommends construction of nuclear submarines
Nov. 1946 — Rickover addresses Submarine Officers' Conference	
	Jan. 9, 1947 — Submarine Officers Conference recommends major nuclear development program; Adm. Nimitz (Chief of Naval Operations) approves the next day
Aug. 19, 1947 — Dr. Edward Teller formally supports Rickover and a nuclear-propulsion program	
Sep. 1947 — Assigned to BuShips on staff of Adm. Mills	Dec. 5, 1947 — Adm. Nimitz formally recommends Navy nuclear-propulsion program to Secretary of the Navy

Apr. 1948	Adm. Mills (Chief of BuShips) attacks Atomic Energy Commission for lack of activity in naval nuclear propulsion		
Aug. 4, 1948	Adm. Mills establishes Nuclear Power Branch in BuShips under Rickover		
Feb. 1949	Additionally appointed to Division of Reactor Development in the AEC		
Jan. 1950	Discusses construction of nuclear submarine with Electric Boat Company		
July 1951	Passed over for selection to rear admiral by Navy board	*Aug. 20, 1951*	First nuclear submarine, U.S.S. *Nautilus,* ordered from Electric Boat Company
		June 14, 1952	President Truman lays keel for *Nautilus*
July 1952	Passed over by selection board for second time; must retire in mid-1953		
		Mar. 30, 1953	*Nautilus* reactor prototype goes critical at Arco, Idaho
July 1, 1953	Selected for promotion to Rear Admiral		
Oct. 1953	Placed in charge of Shippingport, Pa., power reactor program		
Jan. 11, 1954	*Time* cover story on Rickover	*Jan. 21, 1954*	*Nautilus* launched; christened by Mrs. Eisenhower
		Jan. 15, 1955	*Nautilus* underway on nuclear power for first time
Apr. 25, 1955	President Eisenhower announces nuclear merchant ship to be built separate from naval nuclear propulsion effort		
		Oct. 4, 1957	Soviets orbit Sputnik, first artificial earth satellite
		Dec. 2, 1957	Shippingport reactor goes critical
Aug. 1958	Rickover not invited to White House ceremony honoring *Nautilus;* represents President at New York ceremonies	*Aug. 3, 1958*	*Nautilus* reaches North Pole
		Aug. 19, 1958	*Triton,* first multiple-reactor submarine, is launched

Oct. 24, 1958   Promoted to Vice Admiral

June 9, 1959   *George Washington,* first laris missile submarine, launched

July 1959   Accompanies Vice President Nixon to Soviet Union

July 14, 1959   *Long Beach,* first nuclear face warship, is launched

July 21, 1959   Nuclear merchant ship *Sa nah* is launched

Sep. 24, 1960   First nuclear aircraft carr *Enterprise,* is launched

Nov. 8, 1960   Father, Abraham, dies

Jan. 27, 1962   Reaches statutory age for retirement from Navy

Apr. 10, 1963   Nuclear submarine *Thres* lost with 129 men

Mar. 10, 1968   Mother, Rachel, dies

May 1968   Nuclear submarine *Scorp* lost with 99 men

Jan. 25, 1969   Nuclear submersible NR-1 launched

May 25, 1972   Wife, Ruth Masters, dies

Dec. 3, 1973   Promoted to Admiral

Jan. 19, 1974   Marries Eleonore Ann Bednowicz

MAJOR AWARDS

Legion of Merit for duty as Head of the Electrical Section of the Bureau of Ships, from January 1941 to October 15, 1945 [sic]

Honorary Commander of the Military Division of the Most Excellent Order of the British Empire, for assistance to the Royal Navy while Head of the Electrical Section of Bureau of Ships

Letter of Commendation (with Commendation Ribbon) for duty at repair base on Okinawa from July 20, 1945, to November 26, 1945

Oak Leaf Cluster to Commendation Ribbon for duty with Manhattan District at Oak Ridge from July 4, 1946, to December 31, 1946

Gold Star in lieu of Second Legion of Merit for services as Chief of the Naval Reactors Branch, Division of Reactor Development, AEC, and Director of Nuclear Power Division, Bureau of Ships, from March 1949 to July 1952

Christopher Columbus International Communications Prize awarded by Genoa, Italy, in 1957

Congressional Gold Medal for achievement in atomic energy, April 1959

Distinguished Service Medal for being in charge of Naval Nuclear Propulsion program from January 17, 1955, to January 17, 1961

Gold Star in lieu of Second Distinguished Service Medal for Naval Nuclear Propulsion program from January 1961 to January 1964

Enrico Fermi Award from the Atomic Energy Commission for engineering and administrative leadership in the development of nuclear power, January 14, 1965

Honorary U.S. Naval Aviator, July 1970

Presidential Medal of Freedom for the development and application of nuclear propulsion in the U.S. Navy, June 9, 1980

OTHER AWARDS

World War I Victory Medal
China Service Medal
American Defense Service Medal
Asiatic-Pacific Campaign Medal
American Campaign Medal
World War II Victory Medal

Appendix B

U.S. NAVAL NUCLEAR REACTORS

PROJECT	SYMBOL	(OLD)[1]	STARTUP	INSTALLATION	NOTES
COMBUSTION ENGINEERING					
Submarine Reactor Small	S1C	(SRS)	1959	Windsor, Conn.[2]	2,500 shp
Submarine Reactor Small	S2C	(SRS)	1960	*Tullibee*	
GENERAL ELECTRIC					
Destroyer Reactor	D1G		1962	West Milton, N.Y.[2]	2 reactor plant; ~60,000 shp
Destroyer Reactor	D2G		1962	*Bainbridge, Truxtun, California, Virginia*	
Submarine Intermediate Reactor	S1G	(SIR Mk A)	1955	West Milton, N.Y.[2]	shutdown 1957
Submarine Intermediate Reactor	S2G	(SIR Mk B)	1957	*Seawolf*	shutdown 1959; replaced by S2Wa
Submarine Advanced Reactor	S3G	(SAR-1)	1958	West Milton, N.Y.[2]	2 reactor plant; ~34,000 shp;
Submarine Advanced Reactor	S4G	(SAR-2)	1959	*Triton*	shutdown 1969
Natural Circulation Reactor	S5G		1965	Arco, Idaho;[2] *Narwhal*	~17,000 shp
	S6G		1976	*Los Angeles* (SSN-688)	~30,000 shp
	S7G			West Milton, N.Y.[2]	
	S8G		1981	*Ohio* (Trident)	originally designed for 60,000 shp
Submersible Reactor	NR-1		1969	NR-1	

[1] *Symbols used prior to late 1955 are shown in parenthesis.*
[2] *Land prototype.*

PROJECT	SYMBOL	(OLD)[1]	STARTUP	INSTALLATION	NOTES
WESTINGHOUSE					
Large Ship Reactor	A1W	(LSR)	1958	Arco, Idaho[2]	2 reactor plant
Large Ship Reactor	A2W	(LSR)	1961	Enterprise	8 reactor plant; ~280,000 shp
Large Ship Reactor	A3W				
Large Ship Reactor	A4W		1975	Nimitz	2 reactor plant; ~260,000 shp
Cruiser Reactor	C1W		1961	Long Beach	2 reactor plant; ~80,000 shp similar to A1W plant cancelled
Single Reactor Destroyer Plant	D1W		—		
Submarine Thermal Reactor	S1W	(STR Mk I)	1953	Arco, Idaho[2]	shutdown 1981 (Nautilus); ~15,000 shp
Submarine Thermal Reactor	S2W	(STR Mk II)	1954	Nautilus, Seawolf (S2Wa)	
Submarine Fleet Reactor	S3W	(SFR)	1957	Skate, Sargo, Halibut	~7,500 shp
Submarine Fleet Reactor	S4W	(SFR)	1958	Swordfish, Seadragon	~7,500 shp
Submarine High Speed Reactor	S5W		1959	Skipjack, Thresher, Narwhal (S5Wa), Sturgeon, Dreadnought,[3] George Washington, Ethan Allen, Lafayette	~15,000 shp
BABCOCK & WILCOX					
Merchant Ship Reactor[4]	—		1961	Savannah	shutdown 1971; 22,000 shp

[1] Symbols used prior to late 1955 are shown in parenthesis.
[2] Land prototype.
[3] A complete S5W reactor plant was provided for Britain's first nuclear submarine, H.M.S. Dreadnought; completed in 1963.
[4] The Savannah was not part of the U.S. naval reactors program, but is included here to provide a complete listing of all U.S. ship propulsion reactor plants.

Appendix C

U.S. NUCLEAR-PROPELLED SHIPS AND SUBMARINES

SHIP OR CLASS[1]	NUMBER BUILT[2]	LAUNCHED COMMISSIONED	DISPLACEMENT[3] LENGTH	REACTORS	NOTES
Nautilus (SSN–571)	1	1954 1954	4,100 tons 320 feet	1 S2W	world's first nuclear-powered ship; decommissioned in 1980
Seawolf (SSN–575)	1	1955 1957	4,280 tons 337½ feet	1 S2G	original reactor plant replaced by an S2Wa in 1958–1960
Skate (SSN–578)	4	1957–1958 1957–1959	2,850 tons 268 feet	1 S3W or S4W	
Triton (SSRN–586)	1	1958 1959	6,670 tons 447½ feet	2 S4G	radar picket submarine; decommissioned in 1969

[1] SSN—nuclear-propelled attack submarine
SSRN—nuclear-propelled radar picket submarine
SSGN—nuclear-propelled guided-missile submarine
SSBN—nuclear-propelled ballistic-missile submarine
CGN—nuclear-propelled guided-missile cruiser
DLGN—nuclear-propelled guided-missile frigate
CVAN—nuclear-propelled attack aircraft carrier
CVN—nuclear-propelled aircraft carrier
[2] Number completed through January 1981.
[3] Submerged displacement given for submarines and full load for surface ships.

SHIP OR CLASS[1]	NUMBER BUILT[2]	LAUNCHED / COMMISSIONED	DISPLACEMENT[3] / LENGTH	REACTORS	NOTES
Halibut (SSGN–587)	1	1959 / 1960	5,000 tons / 350 feet	1 S3W	guided-missile submarine; decommissioned in 1976
Skipjack (SSN–585)	6	1958–1960 / 1959–1961	3,500 tons / 252 feet	1 S5W	high-speed submarines; Scorpion sunk in May 1968
Tullibee (SSN–594)	1	1960 / 1960	2,640 tons / 273 feet	1 S2C	attempt to build a small, "killer" submarine
Thresher (SSN–594)	14	1960–1966 / 1961–1967	4,300 tons / 278½ feet	1 S5W	deep-diving; delayed after loss of Thresher in 1963
George Washington (SSBN–598)	5	1959–1960 / 1959–1961	6,700 tons / 382 feet	1 S5W	carry 16 Polaris strategic missiles; decommissioned 1979–1980
Ethan Allen (SSBN–608)	5	1960–1962 / 1961–1963	7,900 tons / 410½ feet	1 S5W	carry 16 Polaris missiles; decommissioned 1980–1981
Lafayette (SSBN–616)	31	1962–1966 / 1963–1967	8,250 tons / 425 feet	1 S5W	built with 16 Polaris missiles; rearmed with Poseidon missiles; 12 submarines later refitted with Trident missiles
Sturgeon (SSN–637)	37	1966–1974 / 1967–1975	4,650 tons / 292 feet	1 S5W	
Narwhal (SSN–671)	1	1966 / 1969	5,350 tons / 314 feet	1 S5G	one-of-a-kind natural circulation plant
Glenard P. Lipscomb (SSN–685)	1	1973 / 1974	6,480 tons / 365 feet	1 S5Wa	one-of-a-kind turboelectric drive plant
Los Angeles (SSN–688)	13	1974– / 1976–	6,900 / 360 feet	1 S6G	large, high-speed submarines; 23 additional building as of Jan. 1981

Ohio (SSBN–726)	—	1979– 1981–	18,700 tons 560 feet	1 S8G	large submarines with 24 Trident missiles; 8 building as of 1981
Long Beach (CGN–9)	1	1959 1961	17,350 tons 721¼ feet	2 C1W	guided-missile cruiser; armed with antiaircraft and anti-submarine missiles
Bainbridge (DLGN–25; later CGN–25)	1	1961 1962	8,580 tons 550 feet	2 D2G	(as above)
Truxtun (DLGN–35; later CGN–35)	1	1964 1967	9,200 tons 564 feet	2 D2G	(as above)
California (DLGN–36; later CGN–36)	2	1971–1972 1974–1975	10,150 tons 596 feet	2 D2G	(as above)
Virginia (CGN–38)	4	1974–1978 1976–1980	11,000 tons 585 feet	2 D2G	(as above)
Enterprise (CVAN–65)	1	1960	89,600 tons 1,123 feet	8 A1W	carries approx. 90 aircraft; world's largest ship when built
Nimitz (CVN–68)	2	1972– 1975–	93,400 tons 1,092 feet	2 A4W	carries approx. 90 aircraft; world's largest ships; 2 additional ships under construction
NR–1	1	1969 1969	400 tons 136½ feet	1 ———— [4]	nuclear research submersible

[4] There is no formal designation for the NR-1 propulsion plant.

Appendix D

WORLD NUCLEAR-PROPELLED SHIPS AND SUBMARINES

Completed 1954–1980

Ship Type	United States	Soviet Union	Great Britain	France	China	Japan	Germany
Aircraft Carriers	3+	(+)	—	—	—	—	—
Missile Cruisers	9	1+	—	—	—	—	—
Strategic Missile Submarines	41+	75+	4	5	1	—	—
Attack Submarines	75+	95+	10+	(+)	—	—	—
Icebreakers	—	3+	—	—	—	—	—
Merchant Ships	1	—	—	—	—	—	1
Research Ships	—	—	—	—	—	1	—
Research Submersible	1	—	—	—	—	—	—

+ = Additional units under construction.

NOTES: Soviet submarine numbers are approximate. One Soviet and two U.S. nuclear submarines have been lost; several older U.S. and Soviet nuclear submarines are laid up in reserve, as are the U.S. and West German merchant ships. The Chinese nuclear submarine may not be fully operational.

Appendix E

U.S. DEFENSE-NAVY LEADERSHIP, 1947–1981

PRESIDENT	SECRETARY OF DEFENSE	SECRETARY OF THE NAVY	CHIEF OF NAVAL OPERATIONS	BUREAU OF SHIPS[1]
Harry S Truman Apr. 1945–Jan. 1953	James V. Forrestal Sep. 1947–Mar. 1949	John L. Sullivan Sep. 1947–May 1949	Chester W. Nimitz Dec. 1945–Dec. 1947	Earl W. Mills Nov. 1946–Feb. 1949
	Louis Johnson Mar. 1949–Sep. 1950	Francis P. Matthews May 1949–July 1951	Louis E. Denfeld Dec. 1947–Nov. 1949	David H. Clark Feb. 1949–Feb. 1951
	George C. Marshall Sep. 1950–Sep. 1951	Dan A. Kimball July 1951–Jan. 1953	Forrest P. Sherman Nov. 1949–July 1951	Homer N. Wallin Feb. 1951–July 1953
	Robert A. Lovett Sep. 1951–Jan. 1953		William M. Fechteler Aug. 1951–Aug. 1953	
Dwight D. Eisenhower Jan. 1953–Jan. 1961	Charles E. Wilson Jan. 1953–Oct. 1957	Robert B. Anderson Feb. 1953–May 1954	Robert B. Carney Aug. 1953–Aug. 1955	Wilson D. Leggett, Jr. Aug. 1953–Mar. 1955
	Neil H. McElroy Oct. 1957–Dec. 1959	Charles S. Thomas May 1954–Mar. 1957	Arleigh A. Burke Aug. 1955–Aug. 1961	Albert G. Mumma Apr. 1955–Apr. 1959
		Thomas S. Gates, Jr. Apr. 1957–June 1959		Ralph K. James Apr. 1959–Apr. 1963
	Thomas S. Gates, Jr. Dec. 1959–Jan. 1961	William B. Franke June 1959–Jan. 1961		

[1] *Bureau of Ships from 1940 until 1966; Naval Ship Systems Command until 1974, and subsequently Naval Sea Systems Command.*

PRESIDENT	SECRETARY OF DEFENSE	SECRETARY OF THE NAVY	CHIEF OF NAVAL OPERATIONS	BUREAU OF SHIPS[1]
John F. Kennedy Jan. 1961–Nov. 1963	Robert S. McNamara Jan. 1961–Feb. 1968	John B. Connally Jan. 1961–Dec. 1961	George W. Anderson Aug. 1961–July 1963	William A. Brockett Apr. 1963–Feb. 1966
		Fred H. Korth Jan. 1962–Nov. 1963		
Lyndon B. Johnson Nov. 1963–Jan. 1969	Clark M. Clifford Mar. 1968–Jan. 1969	Paul H. Nitze Nov. 1963–June 1967	David L. McDonald Aug. 1963–July 1967	Edward J. Fahy Feb. 1966–July 1969
		Paul R. Ignatius Sep. 1967–Jan. 1969	Thomas H. Moorer Aug. 1967–July 1970	
Richard M. Nixon Jan. 1969–Aug. 1974	Melvin R. Laird Jan. 1969–Jan. 1973	John H. Chafee Jan. 1969–May 1972	Elmo R. Zumwalt July 1970–June 1974	Nathan B. Sonenshein Aug. 1969–June 1972
	Elliot L. Richardson Jan. 1973–May 1973	John W. Warner May 1972–Apr. 1974		Robert C. Gooding June 1972–Aug. 1976
	James R. Schlesinger July 1973–Nov. 1975	J. William Middendorf II June 1974–Jan. 1977	James L. Holloway III June 1974–July 1978	
Gerald R. Ford Aug. 1974–Jan. 1977	Donald H. Rumsfeld Nov. 1975–Jan. 1977			Clarence R. Bryan Sep. 1976–Mar. 1980
James E. Carter Jan. 1977–Jan. 1981	Harold Brown Jan. 1977–Jan. 1981	W. Graham Claytor, Jr. Jan. 1977–Oct. 1979	Thomas B. Hayward July 1978–	Earl B. Fowler, Jr. Mar. 1980–
		Edward Hidalgo Oct. 1979–Jan. 1981		
Ronald Reagan Jan. 1981–	Casper Weinberger Jan. 1981–	John H. Lehman Jan. 1981–		

[1] Bureau of Ships from 1940 until 1966; Naval Ship Systems Command until 1974, and subsequently Naval Sea Systems Command.

Appendix F

U.S. NUCLEAR SUBMARINE ACCIDENTS

The following tables are taken from V. M. Bukalov and A. A. Narusbayev, *Proyektirovaniye Atomnykh Podvodnykh Lodok* [Design of Nuclear Submarines]. The only deaths known to have occurred in U.S. nuclear submarines in commission were in the loss of the *Thresher* and *Scorpion*, the latter having been lost after the Russian book went to press in 1968, and in the sinking of a Japanese merchant ship following collision with the U.S. nuclear submarine *George Washington* in 1981. (The later accidents have been added to the end of the table.) There have been shipyard deaths, as noted below.

YEAR AND MONTH OF ACCIDENT	NAME OF SUBMARINE	NATURE OF THE ACCIDENT	MEASURES TAKEN AND CONSEQUENCES OF ACCIDENT
		COLLISIONS AND NAVIGATION ACCIDENTS	
1959	*Skate*	Collision with submarine tender *Fulton*	Consequences unknown
1959	*Skate*	Collision with diesel-electric submarine *Cubera*	Propeller damaged
Oct. 5, 1959	*Seadragon*	Collision with a whale	Propeller shaft deformed, propeller damaged
April 1962	*Thomas Edison*	Collision with destroyer *Wadleigh*	Minor damage
May 10, 1962	*Permit*	Collision with cargo ship *Hawaiian Citizen 34* miles from San Francisco; submarine was surfaced	Damage to the outer hull

YEAR AND MONTH OF ACCIDENT	NAME OF SUBMARINE	NATURE OF THE ACCIDENT	MEASURES TAKEN AND CONSEQUENCES OF ACCIDENT
COLLISIONS AND NAVIGATION ACCIDENTS *(continued)*			
June 3, 1962	Thresher	Collision with a harbor tug while mooring	0.9-meter hole near the ballast tank below the waterline; put in for repairs
1963	Tinosa / John Adams	Collision while surfaced	Forward sonar dome damages on the *Tinosa*
July 1, 1964	Henry Clay	Run aground	Refloated an hour after arrival of two tugs at the accident scene
Jan. 11, 1965	Ethan Allen	Collision with cargo ship *Octavian* in the western Mediterranean; submarine was at periscope depth.	Slight damage
Oct. 13, 1965	Barb / Sargo	Collision during maneuvers submerged; 15 miles from Oahu Island	Forward end of one submarine damaged; mast, sale damaged on the other
Nov. 10, 1966	Nautilus	Collision with aircraft carrier *Essex* at periscope depth	Superstructure damaged
Aug. 8, 1967	Simon Bolivar	Collision with cargo ship *Betelgeuse*	Damage of moderate severity
FIRES AND EXPLOSIONS			
May 4, 1958	Nautilus	Fire in the turbine room due to the ignition of turbine insulation	Submarine surfaced and turbine room was ventilated; four hours required to put out the fire; one man killed
1958	Triton	Fire in the turbine room	Consequences unknown
Oct. 31, 1959	Triton	Explosion and fire in nuclear power plant	Four men received serious burns

Date	Ship	Accident	Consequences
June 14, 1960	Sargo	Explosion and fire in after end while shipping oxygen [in Pearl Harbor]	After end was flooded in order to stop the fire; there were casualties; repair continued for three months after the accident
Apr. 1962	Dreadnought (Great Britain)	Fire while the ship was moored to a fitting-out berth	Submarine sustained damages
Oct. 1962	Triton	Fire while the submarine was in repair	Three men killed, two received serious burns
May 1963	Flasher	Fire while fitting out	Three men seriously injured
May 1963	Woodrow Wilson	Fire while fitting out	Fire continued for three hours; three dock-workers were killed putting it out
June 2, 1964	Haddock	Fire while fitting out	
Dec. 20, 1965	Dreadnought (Great Britain)	Fire while the ship was in repair	Insignificant damage

ACCIDENTS INVOLVING POWER PLANT

Date	Ship	Accident	Consequences
1954	Nautilus	Rupture in secondary-circuit piping	Commissioning of the submarine was delayed several months
1956	Nautilus	Exposure of personnel due to defects in biological shielding	Submarine was docked for refitting; crew partly replaced
1956	Seawolf	Rupture of superheater pipes due to corrosion	
1958	Nautilus	Leak in main condenser pipes	Leak was eliminated after filling the condenser with a patented liquid used in the U.S. to repair leaks in automobile radiators
Mar. 1959	Skate	Leak in packing gland in stern tube of propeller shaft	Sealing is achieved by briefly reversing the direction of rotation of the shaft

YEAR AND MONTH OF ACCIDENT	NAME OF SUBMARINE	NATURE OF THE ACCIDENT	MEASURES TAKEN AND CONSEQUENCES OF ACCIDENT
		ACCIDENTS INVOLVING POWER PLANT (continued)	
Mar. 22, 1959	[no name given]	Leak in packing gland of main-condenser circulating pump	Pump was completely disassembled and reassembled. Repair took 7 hours. Submarine surfaced.
Aug. 15, 1959	Nautilus	Rupture in pipe (100mm) in cooling system with submarine operating at a depth of 120 meters	Emergency surfaced. Damage repaired in 2 hours
Apr. 1961	Theodore Roosevelt	Increased radioactivity due to incorrect disposal of radioactive waste from the primary circuit water demineralization system	Submarine decontaminated
Dec. 1961	Scamp	Propeller shaft breakdown	Submarine lost its propeller and was towed to Mare Island
		ACCIDENTS INVOLVING OTHER EQUIPMENT	
Aug. 1957	Nautilus	Two periscopes damaged while submarine was rising under ice conditions	Submarine surfaced and periscopes were repaired
Mar. 1959	Skate	Adjustable radio antenna damaged while submarine was rising under ice conditions	Submarine surfaced and antenna was repaired
1959	Nautilus	Leak in the fore end (presumably due to a faulty sea valve)	Emergency surfacing of submarine
Oct. 1959	Nautilus	Damage to electric cable while moored at base (sabotage presumably)	

Date	Name	Cause	Result
1959	Halibut	Intake of a large amount of water through the sea valve of one of the systems. Submarine began to plunge with a trim by the bow of 60°	Emergency surfacing of submarine
Apr. 1960	Triton	Rupture of pipe in hydraulic system	Hydraulic system switched to reserve line and damage repaired
1960	Patrick Henry	Launched missile struck the submarine	Partial destruction of the outer hull
1961	Ballistic-missile submarine (name unknown)	Rupture of pipe in hydraulic system due to failure of safety valve	According to press reports, at the time of the accident the submarine was close to a catastrophe
Apr. 10, 1963	Thresher	Most probable cause: intake of water into the pressure hull at a depth of 360 meters through a ruptured pipe	Loss of the submarine and all on board (129 men) at great depth

SUBSEQUENT U.S. NUCLEAR SUBMARINE ACCIDENTS REPORTED IN THE PRESS

Date	Name	Cause	Result
May 1968	Scorpion	Unknown	Loss of submarine and entire crew of 99 some 400 miles southwest of the Azores
April 9, 1981	George Washington	Collision while surfacing	Stricken Japanese merchant ship Nissho Maru sunk in East China Sea with loss of 2 crewmen; superficial damage to submarine

Sources

The following chapter notes are keyed to the Bibliography and Acknowledgments. NYT indicates The New York Times and USNIP the U.S. Naval Institute Proceedings. CS indicates Confidential Sources—i.e., interviews by the authors or correspondence and other documents that were made available to them and, at the request of the principals involved, are not cited.

1: THE UNBEATABLE MAN

17   Effort to remove Rickover: Nitze, Pastore, Zumwalt interviews; CS.

19   Selection board: Blair, Kintner interviews; Blair, *The Atomic* . . . ; Smedberg oral history.

20   Rickover on Okinawa: War Diary, Naval Operating Base, Okinawa (Navy Archives); Navy Judge Advocate General's report on typhoon that struck Okinawa Oct. 9, 1945; Duncan "Okinawa, Threshold . . ."; Barker interviews; citation for commendation for period July 20 to Nov. 26, 1945 (Navy file copy undated); "Having a vocation": Rickover, "Thoughts on . . ."; Leper colony: Rickover, *Pepper, Rice.* . . .

23   Class of 1922: *Roll Call*, U.S. Naval Academy Alumni Assoc. (1949 edition); Holmes interviews.

THE PROMISED LAND

25   Rickover's quotations: Rickover, "Thoughts on. . . ."

2: FATHER'S OCCUPATION: TAILOR

27   Historical background: Martin Gilbert, *Russian History Atlas* (New York, Macmillan, 1972); *Handbook for Travellers in Russia, Poland, and Finland* (London, John Murray, 1888).

30   Rickover family in Chicago: *The Sentinel's History of Chicago Jewry 1911-1961;* Abbott, *The Tenements* . . . ; Berkow, *Maxwell Street;* Rosenthal, "This Was . . ."; Simon Rawidowicz, ed., *The Chicago Pinkas;* Dr. Z. Ahams, *The Book of Memories* (New York, Farley, "Yidin," 1932); Blair, *The Atomic*

... ; "The Man ..." *Time;* Chicago *Daily News,* Oct. 18, 1974; Chicago *Tribune,* Nov. 10, 1960; Chicago *Sun-Times,* Sep. 3, 1958; death certificates of Rachel and Eliachako (Abraham) Rickover.

34   Rickover school days: records of John Marshall High School; recollections of Mrs. Lea Goodman, a classmate; *The Review,* John Marshall High School, February 1918, which includes Rickover's speech as "mantle bearer."

36   Representative Sabath: *The Sentinel's History of Chicago Jewry 1911–1961;* several CS.

37   Rickover enters Naval Academy: U.S. Navy, Bureau of Navigation, "Regulations Governing ..."; U.S. Naval Academy, "Register of ..."; U.S. Naval Preparatory School booklet, Werntz Special Collection, U.S. Naval Academy Library; Smith, Holmes interviews; U.S. Naval Academy, "Register of Candidates ..."; Blair, *The Atomic ...* ; several CS.

3: THE CLASS OF 1922

41   Routine at Naval Academy: Holmes, "A Youngster's ..." and Holmes correspondence and interviews; recollections of other members of the Class of 1922, in *Shipmate;* several CS; Blair, *The Atomic ...* ; *The Lucky Bag 1922* (yearbook of the U.S. Naval Academy); Alumni Memorabilia Box No. 7 (Alvan Fisher, Class of 1922), Naval Academy Library; Sweetman, *The U.S. ...*; Rosenberg, "Officer Development...."

47   Jews in U.S. Navy: Chaplain Samuel Sobel, *I Love Thy House* (Norfolk, U.S. Naval Station, 1962); Sweetman, *The U.S. ...* ; Lovette, *School of ...* ; U.S. Naval Academy, *Register of. ...*

51   Hazing at the Naval Academy: Sweetman, *The U.S. ...* ; Lovette, *School of ...* ; Holmes interviews; Alvan Fisher Memorabilia; *Shipmate,* Oct. 1979; several CS.

53   Kaplan-Olmsted rivalry: *The Lucky Bag;* Holmes interviews; Baltimore *Sun,* June 9, 1922; correspondence from Olmsted to friend in Annapolis; *Howitzer 1922* (yearbook of U.S. Military Academy); Alvan Fisher Memorabilia; contemporary news clippings; several CS.

4: STEAMING AS BEFORE

62   Rickover at sea: official Navy biography; logs of various ships, especially *La Vallette;* Blair, *The Atomic ...* ; Miller on World War I destroyers; Blackford, *Torpedo Boat Sailor. ...*

67   Rickover's recollection: Rickover testimony.

68   Milligan as Rickover hero: Rickover speech to National Society of Special Agents of the Federal Bureau of Investigation, Aug. 30, 1974.

69   Reeves as Rickover hero: Hays, "Admiral Joseph ..."; Rickover testimony.

72   Rickover aboard *Nevada:*   Blair, *The Atomic ...* ; log of *Nevada.*

75   Submarine service: logs of *S-9, S-48;* Ellsberg, *On the ...* ; miscellaneous files on submarine activities in Navy Archives; historical articles in *Dolphin;* weekly newspaper of New London submarine base.

80   Marriage to Ruth Masters: marriage license, Blair, *The Atomic. ...*

81   Rickover's relationship with Bennehoff: several CS.

83   Rickover aboard *New Mexico:*   Blair, *The Atomic ...* ; Barker, Schacht, Gillette interviews; log of *New Mexico.*

85 Situation in China: Boyden, "Changing Shanghai."
86 Rickover aboard *Finch:* Blair, *The Atomic* . . . ; log of *Finch;* miscellaneous files Commander in Chief Asiatic Fleet in Navy Archives; Rockwell correspondence; several CS.

5: ENGINEERING DUTY

90 Background on EDO: Furer, *Administration of* . . . ; Rickover speech to Society of Special Agents of the Federal Bureau of Investigation, Aug. 30, 1974.
91 *Canopus* and Cavite: log of *Canopus;* Rickover, *Pepper, Rice* . . . ; Blair, *The Atomic* . . . ; Rear Admiral Kemp Tolley, *Yangtze Patrol* (Annapolis, Naval Institute Press, 1971); Rickover testimony 1970; Harlfinger interviews; several CS.
96 Background on BuShips: Furer, *Administration of* . . . ; U.S. Navy Bureau of Navigation, *Navy Directory,* April 1, 1941; U.S. Navy, Bureau of Ships, "An Administrative. . . ."
97 Electrical Section: Blair, Cochrane, Fluke, Whitney interviews; "nucleus of martyrs": Rickover, "Thoughts on . . ."; U.S. Navy, Bureau of Ships, *Electrical Section. . . .*
100 Rickover aboard *California:* Wallin, "Rejuvenation of. . . ."
100 Visit to *Franklin:* Rickover testimony; log of *Franklin.*
103 British mine countermeasures: Blair, *The Atomic* . . . ; Lott, *Most Dangerous. . . .*
105 Rickover on engineering: see Chapter 4 reference notes, pp. 68–69.
107 Legion of Merit: citation for award Feb. 7, 1946; official Navy biography.
108 Rickover at Mechanicsburg: Fluke, James, Whitney interviews; Blair, *The Atomic* . . . ; U.S. Navy, Bureau of Ships, *Electrical Section* . . . ; James oral history; Rickover report on Mechanicsburg, 1945.
110 Rickover on Okinawa: Barker, Fay interviews; Hooper oral history; see Chapter 1 reference notes, pp. 20–22.

6: THE $1,500 COMMITMENT

115 President Truman's speech: *Public Papers of the President* (1945).
116 Rickover as inspector general: Blair, *The Atomic* . . . ; several CS.
117 Early nuclear research: Bowen, "Nuclear Energy . . ."; Gunn, "The Early . . ."; Laurence, "The Atom . . ."; Groves, *Now It* . . . ; Gunn, memorandum for the Director, Naval Research Laboratory, "Submarine Submerged Propulsion" (June 1, 1939); Abelson, Gunn interviews (for *Atomic Submarines*).
120 Early nuclear submarine research: Gunn, "The Early . . ." (also given as a portion of his testimony before the Special Committee on Atomic Energy, U.S. Senate, Dec. 13, 1945); Holmquist, "The Development . . ."; report by Abelson "Atomic Energy Submarine," Mar. 28, 1946; Groves correspondence (Navy Archives); Smyth, *Atomic Energy* . . . ; Rickover correspondence: to Vice Adm. Mills, June 4, 1947; to Mills, Nov. 12, 1946; Rickover memorandums "Nuclear Energy Propulsion for Naval Vessels," Aug. 20 and 28, 1947; correspondence, Chairman of the General Board to the Chief of the Bureau of Ships, Mar. 20, 1946; Chairman of the General Board to the Secretary of the Navy (April 4, 1946); Vice Adm. Cochrane to General Board (May 16, 1946); Abelson, Gunn interviews (for *Atomic Submarines*). The early nuclear submarine material is

based in part on research for Polmar, *Atomic Submarines;* that manuscript was reviewed by then-Capt. F. J. Harlfinger and then-Comdr. D. A. Paolucci.

125 Orders to Oak Ridge: Blair, *The Atomic* . . . ; Hewlett, *Nuclear Navy* . . . ; Libbey, Roddis, Roth interviews.

126 Rickover at Oak Ridge: Naval Reactor Branch files; Bowen, "Nuclear Energy . . . ; Hewlett, *Nuclear Navy* . . . : Libbey, Roddis, Roth interviews.

7: BUILDING THE *NAUTILUS*

135 Nimitz and nuclear submarines: Hewlett, *Nuclear Navy* . . . ; minutes of Submarine Officers' Conferences (1945–1946); hearings of the General Board; miscellaneous correspondence in Chief of Naval Operations and Secretary of the Navy files (Navy Archives).

137 Prelude to Rickover appointment: Hewlett, *Nuclear Navy* . . . ; Hewlett, *Atomic Shield* . . . ; hearings of the Navy General Board; files of Naval Reactors Branch.

142 Rickover startup of NRB: Blair, *The Atomic* . . . ; Hewlett, *Nuclear Navy* . . . ; Rickover testimony; Davis, Libbey, Roddis interviews.

146 Selection of Electric Boat: Hewlett, *Nuclear Navy;* Blair, *The Atomic.* . . .

150 President Truman's speech: *Public Papers of the Presidents* (1952).

151 Prototype reactor at Arco: Kintner, "Admiral Rickover's . . ."; Roddis, "The Nuclear . . ."; U.S. Navy, Bureau of Naval Personnel, "Principles of . . ."; Rickover, "Some Problems. . . ." A fictional view of the Arco prototype and its operation is found in Beach, *"Cold Is. . . ."*

153 Selection of Wilkinson: official Navy biography; Hewlett, *Nuclear Navy* . . . ; various newspaper articles.

8: THE TRUE SUBMERSIBLE

155 Launching of *Nautilus: NYT,* Jan. 22, 1954; Navy news releases.

156 Men in the Naval Reactors Branch: Hewlett, *Nuclear Navy* . . . ; Rickover testimony; Davis, Libbey, Roddis, Roth interviews; several CS.

157 Rickover versus Roth: Bureau of Naval Personnel files; Roth personal files; Roth, "Atomic Power . . ."; Libbey, Roddis, Roth interviews.

161 Description of *Nautilus:* Wilkinson, "Nautilus and . . ."; Anderson, *Nautilus 90* . . ."; Hewlett, *Nuclear Navy* . . . ; Navy news releases; Rickover testimony; Anderson interviews.

168 *Nautilus* polar cruise: Anderson, *Nautilus 90* . . . ; log of *Nautilus;* Lyon oral history; McWethy interview (for *Atomic Submarines*); Navy news releases; citations for enlisted men who received commendations; Lalor, "Submarine Through. . . ."

176 Snub of Rickover: various newspaper articles including Mrs. Rickover's statements in the Boston *Evening American,* Aug. 14, 1958; Anderson, *Nautilus 90.* . . .

9: PASSED OVER

183 Rickover's perspective: James interview; several CS.

183 Moore's career, plans: official Navy biography; Rickover memorandum to Chief, Bureau of Ships, Sep. 2, 1949; James, Moore interviews; several CS.

190 Selection board: Blair, *The Atomic* . . . ; Bureau of Naval Personnel memoran-

dum "Background—Rickover Case," Feb. 27, 1953; Holloway oral history; James, Moore interviews; several CS.

191 Launching the Rickover campaign: Blair, *The Atomic* ... ; Hewlett, *Nuclear Navy* ... ; Blair, "Brazen Prejudice ..."; Blair, Hingson, James, Kintner, Libbey, Thompson interviews; several CS.

192 Anti-Semitic incidents: Holloway oral history; Blair, Thompson interviews; several CS.

198 Save-Rickover campaign intensifies: *Washington Post,* Feb. 18, 1953, and various newspaper and news magazine articles; Amrine, "Fifteen-Day ..."; "Background—Rickover Case"; Hewlett, *Nuclear Navy* ... ; Blair interviews; several CS.

199 Writing the Blair book: Blair, Davis interviews.

201 Background on McCarthy: various newspaper articles; Congressional testimony.

203 Holloway on selection board: Holloway oral history.

204 Babcock & Wilcox approach: Lilienthal, *The Journals* ... (Vol. 3).

10: CONGRESS COMES ABOARD

207 Congressional shipboard visits: hearings of Joint Committee on Atomic Energy aboard the *Nautilus* (Mar. 20, 1955), *Skipjack* (Apr. 11, 1959), *George Washington* (Apr. 9, 1960), and *Enterprise* (Mar. 31, Apr. 1, 1962); Rickover testimony.

208 New promotion fight: Hewlett, *Nuclear Navy* ... ; Helfer, "He's No Team ..."; Blair interviews.

209 Snub of Rickover: Anderson, *Nautilus 90* ... ; various newspaper articles; Blair interviews.

214 Rickover's power in Congress: Navy news releases; various newspaper articles; Congressional testimony; Zumwalt, *On Watch;* Blair, Davis, Nitze, Zumwalt interviews; several CS.

218 Rickover's medals: Navy news releases; Congressional testimony. The Roosevelt-King letter on King's reaching age 64 is reproduced in Ernest J. King and Walter Muir Whitehill, *Fleet Admiral King, A Naval Record* (New York, W. W. Norton, 1952), facing p. 465.

219 Rickover's continued reappointment: Congressional testimony; Navy news releases; various newspaper and news magazine articles; correspondence between Secretary of Defense James R. Schlesinger and Representatives Melvin Price, George H. Mahon, and Senators John L. McClellan, John C. Stennis and John O. Pastore; Congressional testimony, especially Committee on Armed Services, House, "Full Committee Consideration of ... Resolution Recommending the Naming of the New Engineering Complex at the Naval Academy in Honor of Vice Adm. Hyman G. Rickover" (April 10, 1973); Shephard interview.

11: ADMIRAL OF THE HILL

222 Rickover in Russia: Nixon, *Six Crises;* Congressional testimony.

223 Rickover testimony: Congressional testimony; Miller, "The Ancient. ..."

224 Rickover's habits as witness: comparisons between transcripts of original testimony and printed hearings; several CS.

232 Nitze-Rickover dispute: Congressional testimony; Nitze, Zumwalt interviews; several CS.

236 Office of Legislative Affairs: Mack interviews; several CS.

238 Errors in testimony: Rickover testimony; various editions of *Jane's Fighting Ships* provide adequate data on Navy shipbuilding programs of the Roosevelt era; Grand Adm. von Tirpitz, *My Memoirs,* Vol. 2 (New York, Dodd, Mead, 1919); political role of Soviet naval leadership: assignments of Soviet flag officers are contained in various editions of the Central Intelligence Agency reference aid *Directory of USSR Ministry of Defense and Armed Forces Officials;* a review of military membership of the Presidium and Politburo is contained in *Admiral Gorshkov: A Modern Naval Strategist,* a report prepared for Director, Defense Research and Engineering (April 1974); Appendix D on Military Membership of the Central Committee notes that that body is "The highest political position to which a Soviet military officer normally can aspire," and identifies Marshals Zhukov and Grechko as the two exceptions who reached the Politburo. Of 396 members of the Central Committee in 1971 (including 155 nonvoting candidate members), eight percent were military officers including only one full member (Gorshkov) and two candidate members from the Navy.

242 Naming of nuclear ships: Congressional testimony; several CS. Submarines named after deceased Congressmen are: *Glenard P. Lipscomb* (SSN-685), *L. Mendel Rivers* (SSN-686), *Richard B. Russell* (SSN-687), and *William H. Bates* (SSN-680). The aircraft carrier *Carl Vinson* (CVN-70) was named for a living Congressman. (Mr. Vinson died in 1981.)

245 Passage of Title VIII: Congressional testimony; various newspaper articles; Rickover, "Nuclear Warships . . ."; Lewis, Lind, Lynch, Nitze, Zumwalt interviews; several CS.

12: OPERATION SEA ORBIT

250 Operation Sea Orbit: periodic reports Naval Nuclear Propulsion Program; Navy news releases; McKnew, "Four-Ocean Navy. . . ."

251 Early nuclear surface ship development: Congressional testimony; files of the Secretary of the Navy and Chief of Naval Operations (Navy Archives): Hewlett, *Nuclear Navy* . . . ; files of Naval Reactors Branch; Gunn, Strauss interviews for *Atomic Submarines;* various newspaper articles; Navy news releases related to nuclear-ship events (keel layings, reactor startups, etc.); Office of the Chief of Naval Operations booklet "Carriers Are Vital to the Atomic Navy" (1957).

257 Cruiser *Long Beach:* launching and commissioning booklets; "USS *Long Beach* . . ."; various newspaper articles, especially in *Navy Times.*

258 Carrier *Enterprise:* special Congressional hearings aboard the *Enterprise* (Mar. 31, Apr. 1, 1962); de Poix, "The Big . . ."; Kenney, "The Mighty . . ."; launching and commissioning booklets; various newspaper articles, especially in *Navy Times.*

258 Nuclear escorts for carriers: "USS *Bainbridge* . . ."; Neikirk dissertation; research notes of Friedman and Rosenberg for respective studies of naval problems; launching and commissioning booklets; Zumwalt, *On Watch.*

260 Nuclear ship problems: Comdr. Todd Blades in *USNIP,* December 1978 (comment on Chatham, "Leadership and . . ."); the Philadelphia Naval Shipyard newspaper *Beacon* of Apr. 27, 1962, shows the *Long Beach* at sea without her radars and describes the work to be done after her European cruise.

262 Nuclear warship activities: Rickover, "Nuclear Warships . . ."; the annual Congressional testimony of Adm. Rickover invariably contains excerpts of letters from the commanding officers of nuclear ships praising the advantages of nuclear propulsion.

13: A FASCINATING EXPERIENCE

269 No Christmas vacation: Barker interview; also CS.
271 Tomb interview: Cameron, "Admiral Rickover's ..."; several CS.
272 Delay wedding story: Beach, "Life Under ..."; trick chair: this gimmick and other ploys of the Rickover interview are described in Anderson, *Nautilus 90* ...; Calvert, *Surface at* ...; Steele, *Seadragon;* and Zumwalt, *On Watch;* several CS.
273 Interview of NROTC midshipman: the man himself and his father (both CS).
275 Statement on postinterview session: Barrett, official responses to questions to Chief of Naval Personnel; also CS.
275 Zumwalt experience: Zumwalt interviews; Zumwalt *On Watch;* Zumwalt memorandum written immediately after the interview headed "private—official" (undated).
285 Smedberg recollections: Smedberg oral history; Laning interviews; several CS.
287 Midshipman interview: interviews with midshipman quoted and with numerous other midshipmen at the Naval Academy (all CS); interviews with members of faculty of Naval Academy (all CS); various editions of *The Log.*
291 Midshipman essay: copy of original essay (author CS).

14: THE MEN CALLED NUCS

294 *Bennington* explosion: Rickover testimony.
295 Outline of training: Rickover testimony; Beach, *Cold Is* ...; Hewlett, *Nuclear Navy* ...; Laning, Libbey, Roth interviews.
297 Quotation from officer: Rickover testimony; naval bases as "clubs": Rickover testimony; several CS.
297 Initiation of "George": Hewlett, *Nuclear Navy....*
298 ComSubLant plan: Hewlett, *Nuclear Navy* ...; Laning interviews.
299 AEC letter: Congressional testimony; Hewlett, *Nuclear Navy....*
300 Details of nuclear power training: Rickover's 111-page statement before the subcommittee on Energy Research and Production, Committee on Science and Technology, House (May 24, 1979); various biographies cited in notes for Chapter 13, p. 272; Billones, Laning, M. Wade interviews; several CS who attended nuclear power training over a 20-year period.
305 Rickover on Naval Academy: Rickover testimony; academic standards: Schratz, "An Open...."
307 Information on superintendents: official Navy biographies of Calvert, Mack, McKee; Mack interviews; "Disneyland": Rickover testimony.
309 Rickover criticism of Naval Academy: Rickover testimony; Academy curriculum: Schratz, "An Open ..."; Mack, McKee interviews; athletic record: records of Naval Academy athletic office; Mack interviews; "policy statement": memorandum from CNO (Holloway) to Deputy CNO (Manpower), Director of Naval Education and Training, and Superintendent of U.S. Naval Academy on Naval Academy Education and Training Policy, Nov. 3, 1975.
311 Academy under McKee: McKee interviews; various edition of *The Log;* several midshipmen and members of the Naval Academy faculty (all CS).
312 Drafting of midshipmen: Barrett, Gammell in official responses to questions to

Naval Academy and Chief of Naval Personnel; Rickover testimony; Burke interviews; several CS.

315 Comments on Rickover: two senior submarine officers, nuclear qualified, holding important positions when interviewed (both CS).

15: THE DAY OF THE NUCS

318 Selection of early nuclear officers: Holloway oral history; official Navy biographies of early nuclear officers; various biographies cited in notes for Chapter 13, p. 272; also Beach, *Around the* . . . ; Anderson, Harlfinger, Laning, Zumwalt interviews; Raborn, K. Wade interviews for *Atomic Submarines.*

320 Experience of NROTC graduate: the officer himself (CS).

321 Structure of NRB: Rickover testimony; Hewlett, *Nuclear Navy* . . . ; James oral history and interviews; Libbey, Roddis, Roth interviews; several CS.

325 Swart incident: Adm. Swart confirmed the incident in an interview with one of the authors; however, the admiral, who was ailing, declined to be personally interviewed or go into detail; he died Feb. 7, 1981. James oral history and interviews; also CS.

325 James as Chief of BuShips: James oral history and interviews; Burke, Rosenberg interviews; Moore interviews and correspondence; Rickover-Farrin dispute: Farrin confirmed the incident in correspondence with the authors but said he did not remember the word "revolver" being used, which James and Moore did recall.

328 Rickover "back channel": Chatham, "Leadership and . . ."; Holloway oral history; Rickover testimony (with correspondence entered from commanding officers of nuclear ships sent directly to him on nonreactor subjects); Laning interviews; several CS.

329 Operational Reactors Safeguards Examination: Rickover statement (see notes for Chapter 14, p. 300); Billones, Wade interviews; several CS.

330 Beach recollection: Beach, "Life Under. . . ."

331 Incident reports: Rickover statement (see notes for Chapter 14, p. 300); text of "incident report" on author: copy of incident report; letter as "unauthorized literature": Billones; also CS; ASW device: Baker in *USNIP,* July 1978 (comment on Jones, "Some Thoughts . . .").

332 Stevenson and the *Finback:* various newspaper and news magazine articles; Navy news release of Oct. 2, 1975; Cooney, Taussig interviews.

334 Use of marijuana: Rickover statement (see notes for Chapter 14, p. 300); *Los Angeles Times,* May 4, 1977; data provided by Chief of Naval Personnel.

335 Barrett experiences: various newspaper articles; official Navy biography; several CS.

341 Carter and Rickover: Carter announcement speech delivered at National Press Club, Washington, D.C., Dec. 12, 1974; Carter, *Why Not* . . . ; Wheeler, *Jimmy Who?;* Fallows, "The Passionless . . ."; *Los Angeles Times,* Oct. 28, 1977; various newspaper and news magazine articles; Rickover testimony; Laning interviews; *O God Thy Sea* . . . : Shogan interviews. Rickover gave a similar plaque to President Kennedy (Shepard interview and others).

347 Criticism in *Proceedings:* Chatham, "Leadership and . . ." (and subsequent comment and discussion); Rickover, "Leadership" (and subsequent comment and discussion); discussions with editorial staff of *USNIP.*

350 Rickover's deputies retire: *Washington Post,* Aug. 7, 1979; *NYT,* Aug. 8, 1979. (The men declined to be interviewed for this book; one did write to the authors.)

16: BUILDING MORE SUBMARINES

353 Background on submarine construction: Rickover testimony; various editions of *Jane's Fighting Ships;* Hewlett, *Nuclear Navy....*

355 *Seawolf* design and operations: Hewlett, *Nuclear Navy* ...; Polmar, *Atomic Submarines;* Anderson, Laning interviews; Navy news releases; various shipyard newspapers.

359 Attitudes on nuclear power: Burke interviews; several CS.

360 Portsmouth shipyard: Moore, Roth interviews; Roth personal files.

360 Mare Island shipyard: Kintner interview; various editions of shipyard newspaper, the *Grapevine.*

362 Material on Burke: official Navy biography; Rosenberg, "Officer Development ..."; conversations with Burke, and Burke speeches over a 20-year period.

364 Nuclear submarine *Triton:* Beach, *Around the* ...; Beach, *Cold Is* ...; Beach interview and correspondence; Rickover testimony.

369 Nuclear submarine *Thresher:* Polmar, *Death of* ...; Harlfinger, Morgan interviews for *Atomic Submarines;* Rickover testimony.

374 Rickover aboard submarines: Plan of the day for submarine *George Bancroft;* several CS who were aboard submarines at the time of his visits.

17: ALL MAJOR COMBATANT VESSELS ...

377 Nuclear ship authorizations: annual posture statements of the Secretary of Defense and various Navy officials; Congressional testimony; Zumwalt, *On Watch;* various editions of *Jane's Fighting Ships;* Neikirk, "Congress and ..."; various newspaper articles.

381 McNamara and proposed carrier: Congressional testimony; Zumwalt, *On Watch;* Enthoven, "Systems Analysis ..."; Spitz, "Conventional Versus ..."; various newspaper articles.

385 Nuclear power for surface ships: Congressional testimony; files of Joint Committee on Atomic Energy; Nitze interviews.

388 Kennedy interest in nuclear carrier: Shephard interview.

388 Carriers in Vietnam: files of Deputy CNO (Air Warfare); various newspaper articles.

389 Decisions on nuclear carriers: Congressional testimony, especially before joint Senate-House armed services subcommittee on "CVAN-70 Aircraft Carrier"; annual statements of the Secretary of Defense and various Navy officials; files of Deputy CNO (Air Warfare).

394 Decision on nuclear ships: As above; also, Zumwalt, *On Watch;* Zumwalt interviews; files of Deputy CNO (Surface Warfare).

397 Strike cruiser controversy: Congressional testimony; Conversations with Secretary of the Navy J. William Middendorf and Adm. James L. Holloway III (CNO); Lind, Leopold, Doyle interviews; Zumwalt, *On Watch;* Friedman research files.

18: YESTERDAY'S VISIONARY

400 Nuclear submarine programs: Congressional testimony; Harlfinger, Paolucci interviews for *Atomic Submarines.*

401 Submarine speed: Weatherup, "Defense Against ..."; Steele, "Killing Nu-clear. ..."

402 Nuclear submarine *Tullibee:* Congressional testimony; various editions of the Naval Nuclear Propulsion Program; Laning interviews.

403 Submarine automation: brochures on submarine automation produced by Electric Boat and Norden firms; briefing at submarine control simulator, David W. Taylor Model Basin, Carderock, Md.; Laning interviews; discussions with technical staff members of Office of Naval Research (all CS).

405 Innovation in nuclear plants: Rickover testimony; Shapley, "Nuclear Navy"; various technical journals and newspaper articles; Laning interviews; several CS.

406 Office of systems analysis: Rickover testimony; Zumwalt, *On Watch;* several CS.

407 Debate on nuclear submarines: Congressional testimony, especially special hearings of the Joint Committee on Atomic Energy; Zumwalt, *On Watch;* Pao-lucci, Griffiths, Zumwalt interviews; several CS.

409 Debate over SSN-688: Congressional testimony, especially "Report on United States Nuclear-Powered Attack Submarine Program" by House Committee on Armed Services (1979); Zumwalt, *On Watch;* files and resource materials com-piled for Mann Study; Chapman, "Attack Submarine ..." (and subsequent comment and discussion); various newspaper articles; Lind, Paolucci, Zumwalt interviews; several CS.

415 Diesel-electric submarines: Van Saun, "Tactical ASW: A Case ..."; Van Saun, "Tactical ASW: Let's Fight ..."; material provided by Howaldtswerke-Deutsche Werft (HDW) shipyard; Lind interviews; several CS.

416 Rickover on balanced Navy: Rickover testimony.

417 Submarine personnel problems: Congressional testimony including annual posture statements of Chief of Naval Personnel; Smedberg oral history; various newspaper articles; conversations with several nuclear submarine officers and enlisted men.

19: A NUCLEAR SUBMARINE IS MISSING ...

423 Comments on *Thresher:* Rickover testimony.

423 Problems with nuclear submarines: Beach, *Cold Is . . .* ; Lyon oral history; vari-ous newspaper articles; Axene, Billones, Laning, Paolucci interviews; several CS; also see Appendix F.

425 *Thresher* startup problems: much of the *Thresher* material is based on previous research for Polmar, *Death of . . .* (which, in manuscript, was reviewed by Capt. E. L. Beach and Capt. D. A. Paolucci); citations for crewmen involved in emer-gency startup; Joint Committee on Atomic Energy hearing "Loss of the U.S.S. *Thresher*" (1964); Axene interviews.

427 Awards to engineers: Navy news releases.

427 *Thresher* change of command: official Navy biographies of Axene and Harvey; Axene interviews.

427 Last cruise of *Thresher:* Navy news releases and press conferences; log of *Sky-lark;* report of Navy Court of Inquiry; Axene, Paolucci interviews.

430 Rickover reaction: "Loss of the U.S.S. *Thresher*"; report of Navy Court of In-quiry; James interviews; several CS.

431 Cause of *Thresher* loss: Navy news releases; James oral history; Axene, James interviews; several CS.

435 Establishment of deep submergence project: Report of the Deep Submergence

Systems Review Group (March 1, 1963); Herold, "The Politics . . ."; Craven, Nicholson interviews.

436 NR-1 program and progress: periodic reports Naval Nuclear Propulsion Program produced by the Division of Naval Reactors (i.e., Adm. Rickover); various Rickover testimonies; White House press statement of Apr. 18, 1965; publications of Deep Submergence Systems Project; weekly NR-1 status report for DSSP management reviews 1967–1970; various issues of *General Dynamics News;* Craven, "Seapower and . . ."; Craven, Nicholson, Nitze interviews; several CS.

444 Loss of *Scorpion:* various newspaper articles; Navy news releases and press conferences.

444 *Tullibee* problem: *Boston Globe,* Aug. 16, 1978 (reprinted in *US IP,* Oct. 1978, pp. 124, 127).

20: A DAY IN THE NAVAL REACTORS BRANCH

449 Early home of NRB: Blair, *The Atomic* . . . ; Hewlett, *Nuclear Navy* . . . ; Anderson, *Nautilus 90* . . . ; Davis interview; personal recollections of one of the authors; several CS.

451 NRB at Crystal City: visit by the authors; Rickover testimony; interviews with Naval Academy and NROTC midshipmen (all CS).

452 Beard incident at NRB: correspondence of Lieut. (j.g.) Richard G. Lamb, USNR, to Chief of Naval Operations (Oct. 3, 1972) with First Endorsement by W. Wegner (Nov. 3, 1972), and related files and correspondence.

453 Typical day in NRB: constructed from Drew Pearson, *Diaries: 1949–1959* (New York, Holt, Rinehart & Winston, 1974); Blair, *The Atomic* . . . ; Davis, Roth, Laning interviews; several CS.

456 Information for newcomer: quoted and listed documents from official NRB reading lists. Note that book No. 14 is "Admiral Rickover and the Atomic Submarine," although the actual title of Blair's book is *The Atomic Submarine and Admiral Rickover.*

459 Rickover's sense of humor: Jokes about Rickover and attributed to Rickover are widely told throughout the Navy—even by nucs. Primary sources are Rickover testimony for several; "Lady Chatterley" review: Rickover memorandum to NavSea PMS-81 entitled "Special Audit Review of the Nuclear Powered Deep Submergence Research and Engineering Vehicle, NR-1 Project, Audit No. S00388."

462 Rickover as an "abrasive personality": Harry Levinson, "The Abrasive Personality at the Office," *Psychology Today,* May 1978, pp. 80–84.

21: SHOOTING THE ADMIRALS, FIRING THE EXPERTS

463 Rickover quotations and exchanges: Rickover testimony.

467 Meeting of flag officers: James oral history and interviews.

468 Rickover and naval attachés: Rickover testimony; several CS.

473 Background on Zumwalt: official Navy biography; Zumwalt, *On Watch;* Norman Friedman, "Elmo Russell Zumwalt, Jr.," in Love, *Chiefs of* . . . ; Burke interviews.

474 Swanson incident: Zumwalt, *On Watch;* Rickover testimony; Zumwalt interviews.

478 Rickover and "high-low" mix: Zumwalt, *On Watch;* Rickover testimony; Nitze, Zumwalt, Friedman interviews.
480 Rickover and Holloway: Rickover speech to National Society of Special Agents of the Federal Bureau of Investigation, Aug. 30, 1974; press release from office of Representative Samuel S. Stratton, June 3, 1976; Eaker, "Rickover May ...."; *Washington Post,* May 8, 1976.
482 Rickover and McNamara: Rickover testimony.
482 Comparison of U.S. and Soviet navies: Rickover testimony.
484 Gordon W. Rule: official biography; Rule interviews and speech, "Relations Between the Navy and the Shipbuilding Industry of the United States," to the Shipbuilders Council of America, June 2, 1976.

22: LET ME KNOW, PROMPTLY

486 Rickover memorandum: Reproduced from copy of NRB memorandum.
488 Rickover's representatives: Rickover testimony; several CS.
489 Rickover's attitude toward industry: Rickover testimony; several CS.
492 Electric Boat background: material supplied by Electric Boat; New London *Day* articles.
493 Rickover and Shugg: Blair, *The Atomic ...* ; Hewlett, *Nuclear Navy ...* ; also CS.
493 Rickover and Electric Boat: Kintner interview; EB employees and other CS; Schiller, "The Strange. ..."
494 Analyst's visit: Analyst's account, including copies of analyst's report, Director of Naval Intelligence's memorandum with Zumwalt comment, and NRB incident report on analyst's attempted visit to the submarine *Glenard P. Lipscomb* at the EB yard.
496 Dispute with OSHA inspectors: *Baltimore Sun,* Feb. 27, 1978; also CS.
496 Rickover "runs this yard": quotation from Cameron, "Admiral Rickover's ..."; plastic models: EB official and Navy information officer (both CS).
497 Changes in design: Edward S. Ruete in *USNIP,* Mar. 1980 (comment on Polmar, "The U.S. Navy: Attack Submarines"); Rickover testimony; James interviews.
499 First skirmish with Rule: Memorandum from Rickover to Chief of Naval Material, July 2, 1969; Rule interview; "nickel" contract change: Rickover testimony; Rule interview; rebuke of rule: Rickover testimony, including correspondence provided to committees by Rickover; Rule interview and Rule files.
500 Conglomerates and shipyards: Cole, *Procurement of ...* ; Rickover testimony; various newspaper and news magazine articles.
500 Memorandum to Galantin: Prina, "Rickover an expert ..."
504 Rickover and shipbuilding claims: This lengthy and complex story (which continued in the Navy and the courts when this book went to press) is based on: Rule speeches "The Rickover Navy" to the Greater Baltimore Chapter of the National Contract Management Association, Nov. 17, 1977; "Certain Aspects of Navy Procurement" to the Washington Chapter of the National Contract Management Association, June 21, 1978; "Is the Navy Disingenuous?" to the Symposium of the Mid-Florida Chapter of the National Contract Management Association, Feb. 15, 1979. Also, "Rebellion Rampart ..."; various editions of *Shipyard Weekly* from 1974 onward; various newspaper and news magazine articles; Congressional testimony, including that of Rickover, the Secretaries of the Navy, and Commanders of the Naval Sea Systems Command; digest of court

records; memorandum from Zumwalt to Nelson W. Freeman, October 1973; informal conversations with the following individuals from 1971 onward: Adms. Isaac C. Kidd, Jr., Frederick H. Michaelis, and Alfred J. Whittle, Jr., all Chiefs of Naval Material; Vice Adm. James H. Doyle, Deputy CNO (Surface Warfare); and William D. Houser, Deputy CNO (Air Warfare); James, Nitze, Rule, Zumwalt interviews; several CS.

510 Rickover and lawyers: Rickover letter to District of Columbia Bar (quoted in *Washington Post,* Dec. 21, 1979); letter from E. Grey Lewis to T. Edward Braswell, chief counsel of the Senate Armed Services Committee, June 4, 1976; Rickover speech "Lawyers Versus Society," Mar. 30, 1979.

23: MEETING THE PRESS

514 Rickover-Murrow friendship: correspondence between Murrow and Rickover, courtesy of Mrs. Murrow, from papers collected at the Fletcher School of Law and Diplomacy, Tufts University; *Rickover book:* letter from William Clifford, of Simon and Schuster, to Murrow, Mar. 6, 1958 (Murrow papers).

514 Rickover letters: Murrow papers; Rickover, *Eminent Americans.*

516 Rickover's early dealings with press: conversations with members of Washington press corps; Rickover-authored story carried by the Associated Press, Aug. 20, 1960; one of the authors' telephone conversations with Rickover in the early 1960s; Blair interview.

517 Rickover and Gubser: *Congressional Record,* Apr. 15, 1964, p. 7745; press release from Representative Gubser's office, June 11, 1964; letter from Rear Adm. C. B. Jones, Chief of Legislative Affairs, to Representative Carl Vinson, Chairman of the House Armed Services Committee, Apr. 27, 1964.

517 "Leaking" of information: Norman, "The Love-Hate. . . ."

519 Speech copyrights: various newspaper and news magazine articles; digest of court records; several CS.

521 Writing of *Eminent Americans:* Rickover, *Eminent Americans;* several CS.

521 Rickover and television: Murrow papers; transcript of "Meet the Press," Jan. 24, 1960.

522 Laning recollection: Laning interviews.

523 Rickover and the press: various newspaper and news magazine articles; Rickover testimony; several CS.

523 "Safety" articles: correspondence and other materials from Cooney, USIA, and the author of the article; author's notes from meetings involving Capt. Drain, Adm. Cooney, USIA officials, and author.

525 Rickover's book on *Maine:* Rickover, *How the* . . . ; Cosmas, Review of *How the Battleship* Maine *Was Destroyed* . . . ; letter from Rickover to Vice Adm. James B. Stockdale, President of the Naval War College, Oct. 19, 1977, published in the Naval War College *Review,* Winter 1978; Rickover testimony; several CS.

529 Rickover and the press in the 1970s: various newspaper and news magazine articles; Cooney interviews; conversations with Rear Adm. Bruce Newell, Chief of Information in 1980–1981.

529 Rickover on "Face the Nation": transcript of "Face the Nation," Sept. 9, 1979.

531 Rickover party complaint: memorandum from Rickover to Commander of the Naval Sea Systems Command, June 26, 1980, published in *Washington Post,* June 29, 1980.

IN THE PRESENCE OF MINE ENEMIES

533 Kennedy quotation: letter from Kennedy to Rear Adm. Levering Smith, Nov. 19, 1963.
533 Khrushchev quotation: Khrushchev, *Khrushchev Remembers, The Last Testament.*

24: THE HIGHEST NATIONAL PRIORITY

535 Origins of Polaris: Killian, *Sputnik, Scientists* . . . ; Sapolsky, *The Polaris* . . .; Davis, "The Development of Fleet . . ."; Polmar, "History of . . ."; various editions of "Polaris Fact Sheet" and "Polaris Chronology" [later both labeled "Polaris/Poseidon . . ."] published by the Special Projects Office, 1959–1970; Burke, Backus, Miller, Raborn, Smith interviews (some for *Atomic Submarines*).
541 Rickover exclusion: Hewlett, *Nuclear Navy* . . . ; Rickover testimony; Burke, Raborn, Rosenberg interviews.
542 Polaris development: Hewlett, *Nuclear Navy* . . . ; Sapolsky, *The Polaris* . . . ; Polmar, "History of . . ."; various editions of *Jane's Fighting Ships,* "Polaris Fact Sheet" and "Polaris Chronology"; Congressional testimony; annual posture statements of the Secretary of Defense, Secretary of the Navy, Chief of Naval Operations, and other Navy officials; Backus, Burke, James, Raborn, Smith, Miller, Paolucci, Harlfinger interviews (some for *Atomic Submarines*); Rickover opposition to deep-diving submarines: Rickover testimony, especially "Loss of the U.S.S. *Thresher*"; James interviews; also CS.
550 Rickover opposition to awards: Rickover testimony; Raborn, K. Wade interviews.
551 Rickover criticism of PERT: Sapolsky, *The Polaris* . . . ; Rickover testimony.

25: THE SOVIET THREAT

552 Rickover on intelligence: Rickover testimony.
553 Rickover's trip to Russia: Khrushchev, *Khrushchev Remembers, The Last Testament:* Rickover testimony, especially "Report on Russia by Admiral H. G. Rickover"; various newspaper and news magazine articles.
554 Soviet submarine progress: Minutes of Burke press conference, Aug. 17, 1959; Svyatov, *Atomniye podvodniye* . . . ; Bolgarev, "Submarines in . . ."; Volod'kovskiy, "Scientific and . . ."; Baldwin, "Soviet Submarine . . ."; Congressional testimony, especially Rickover and Directors of Naval Intelligence; various newspaper and news magazine articles.
555 Rickover's views on Soviets: Rickover testimony; Soviet nuclear propulsion programs: annual posture statements of the Secretaries of Defense, Secretaries of the Navy, Chiefs of Naval Operations, and other Navy officials; Wilson, "A Fast . . ."; Polmar, "Soviet Navy . . ."; Wilson, "Soviet Navy . . ."; Wilson, Soviets Launch. . . ."

26: THE ULTIMATE WEAPON—AGAIN

564 Carter statement: transcript of Carter press conference, Mar. 30, 1979.
565 Origins of Trident: Zumwalt, *On Watch;* Congressional testimony; extracts

from STRAT–X study report; Miller, Paolucci, Smith interviews; several CS.
566 Strategic weapon considerations: Miller, Zumwalt interviews.
568 Trident costs and problems: Congressional testimony; "Monthly Progress Report" of the Naval Sea Systems Command; Cameron, "Admiral Rickover's . . ."; transcript of Kelln and Hall press conference Nov. 29, 1977; transcript of Carter press conference Mar. 30, 1979; annual reports of Tenneco and General Dynamics, parent companies of the Newport News and Electric Boat shipyards, respectively; various newspaper and news magazine articles; Rule, Zumwalt interviews; several CS; strategic program management: Rosenberg, "OPNAV General . . ."; discussions with Rear Adm. James Osborn while OP–97, Rear Adm. Albert L. Kelln while OP–22; Miller, Paolucci, Zumwalt interviews.

HE NEVER WEARS A UNIFORM

583 Secretary statement: Transcript of interview with Rickover secretary.

27: ADMIRAL OF EDUCATION

585 Rickover comparisons of U.S. and Russian schools: Rickover testimony in "Report on Russia by Vice Admiral Hyman G. Rickover, USN" (1959); Rickover on "Meet the Press": transcript of "Meet the Press," Jan. 24, 1960.
588 Rickover on the technical man: Rickover, *Education and . . .*
588 Schwarz "crusade": Philip Horton, "Revivalism on the Far Right," *The Reporter,* July 20, 1961.
589 NEA and defense: archives of the National Education Association; Carr interview.
590 Derthick rebuttal: testimony before the House Subcommittee on Labor, Health, Education, and Welfare, Feb. 3, 1960.
591 Response to Rickover criticism: Richard I. Miller, "Admiral Rickover on American Education," *The Journal of Teacher Education,* Sep. 3, 1959.
592 National educational standard: Rickover, *Swiss Schools . . .* ; Rickover, *Education and . . .* ; Rickover testimony; newspaper and news magazine articles; Carr interview; several CS.
594 Rickover for commissioner of education: archives of the National Education Association; *The Reminiscences of Francis A. J. Ianni* (unpublished manuscript); Carr, Laning interviews; various newspaper articles.
594 Rickover on PTA and child care: Rickover testimony; newspaper and news magazine articles.
599 Rickover's influence on education: *Education Index* (New York: H. W. Wilson, 1963 through 1967); several CS.

28: FROM SHIPPINGPORT TO THREE MILE ISLAND

601 Barker Thanksgiving: Barker interviews and correspondence.
602 Carrier prototype reactor: Strauss, *Men and . . .* ; Hewlett, *Nuclear Navy . . .* ; Roth, "Atomic Power . . ."; Roth interviews.
602 Atomic predictions: various newspaper and news magazine articles.
603 Debate over carrier reactor: Strauss, *Men and . . .* ; Hewlett, *Nuclear Navy . . .* ; Barker interviews.

604 Hafstad and Rickover: Hewlett, *Nuclear Navy* ...; also CS.
604 Events leading up to reactor decision: Strauss, *Men and* ...; Hewlett, *Nuclear Navy* ...; Lilienthal, *The Journals* ... (Vol. 3); John G. Fuller, *We Almost Lost Detroit* (New York: Ballantine, 1976); Rickover testimony.
607 Announcement of nuclear plant: address of Atomic Energy Commissioner Thomas E. Murray, excerpted in *NYT*, Oct. 23, 1953; Lilienthal, *The Journals* ... (Vol. 3); "U.S. to Build Industrial Atom Plant," *Washington Star*, Oct. 22, 1953; Edward F. Ryan, "U.S. to Launch Atom Industry," *Washington Post*, Oct. 23, 1953.
609 Building the Shippingport plant: Barker interviews; *Shippingport Pressurized Water Reactor*, official history published by the Atomic Energy Commission in 1958.
613 Atomic airplanes: Gantz, *Nuclear Flight;* Congressional testimony.
613 *Savannah* program: Wirt, "A Federal ..."; series of technical reports on *Savannah* compiled for Atomic Energy Commission and Maritime Administration by the New York Shipbuilding Corp.; Will, "Administration Backs ..."; Rickover testimony; James interviews.
615 Start-up of Shippingport: Rickover testimony; Barker interviews.

29: DANGER: RADIATION HAZARD

616 Rickover and Three Mile Island: Transcripts of meetings of Nuclear Regulatory Commission, Apr. 14, 1979; Rickover statement before Subcommittee on Energy Research and Production, Committee on Science and Technology, May 24, 1979; various newspaper and news magazine articles.
620 Fermi reactor shutdown: see notes for Chapter 28, p. 604.
621 Chalk River incident: Carter, *Why Not?;* Laning, Roth interviews.
622 Survey of *Nautilus* crew: Rickover speech "Environmental Perspectives," Nov. 16, 1979; Rickover testimony.
622 Nuclear ship port visits: Rickover testimony; Ramage oral history; several CS.
625 Nuclear Navy's safety record: Rickover testimony; several CS.
627 Portsmouth radiation controversy: letter from Representative Paul G. Rogers to Rickover, Dec. 19, 1978; letter from Richard P. Pollock and Michael Bancroft of Critical Mass Energy Project to Secretary of Defense Harold Brown, Dec. 14, 1978; letter from R. W. Johnston, public-information specialist, Portsmouth Naval Shipyard, to Stephen A. Kurkjian, *Boston Globe*, Feb. 17, 1978; memorandum from Rickover to Commander of the Portsmouth Naval Shipyard, Dec. 30, 1977 (enclosing "Report of NavSea Inspection of Portsmouth Naval Shipyard's Radiological Control Performance 12–16 December 1977"); Critical Mass News Release, Dec. 17, 1978; undated "Response to Query" by Comdr. M. S. Baker addressing Critical Mass Energy Project statement on Rickover and Portsmouth Naval Shipyard radiation situation; Nordlinger, "Rickover Thwarts ..."; Pincus, "Rickover Agrees ..."; Rickover testimony.
632 Rickover and nuclear industry: Rickover testimony; Roddis interview; several CS.
633 Rickover on technology: Rickover speech "A Humanistic Technology," May 7, 1969.

30: THE ADMIRAL AT HOME

634 Mrs. Rickover: Rickover, *Pepper, Rice* ...; Barker, Blair, Davis, Kay, Roth, Schacht interviews; several CS.

634 Rickover and Mrs. Rickover: H. G. Rickover Foreword to *Pepper, Rice* ...; "The Man ...”; Blair interviews.
638 Religion and morality: Rickover testimony; Burke interviews; several CS.
639 Tucker car project: Libbey interview.
640 Rickover attitudes: Smedberg oral history; Burke, Burkhalter, Hays, Laning, Libbey, Roddis, Roth interviews; several CS.
642 Mrs. Rickover speaking out: see notes for Chapter 8, p. 176; James interviews; Mrs. Rickover's death: certificate of death; Rickover testimony.
645 Rickover's health: Rickover testimony; Navy press releases; various newspaper and news magazine articles; several CS.
647 Rickover and second wife: official Navy biography; marriage certificate; staff members of Bethesda National Naval Medical Center (CS); several CS.
648 *Nautilus* commemoration: Vice Adm. Charles H. Griffiths' speech at ceremony at Washington Navy Yard, Sep. 30, 1979; observations of one of the authors.

31: THE UNACCOUNTABLE MAN

653 Rejection of midshipman: CS.
655 “Book” on Rickover: Smedberg oral history; several CS.
656 Attempts to replace Rickover: James, Kintner, Laning, Nitze, Crawford interviews; several CS. (Fay, in response to written inquiries from the authors, said he had no firm recollection of the Crawford incident.)
660 “Shortened lead time”: Roth speech “A Case of Shortened Lead Time” to Industrial College of the Armed Forces, Washington, D.C., 1960.
662 Navy and nuclear propulsion: minutes of the Submarine Officers' Conferences; minutes of General Board meetings; report of Tolman Commitee; Hewlett, *Nuclear Navy* ... ; miscellaneous OPNAV files (Navy Archives); review of interviews conducted for this book.
664 Rickover and new developments: Shapley, “Nuclear Navy ...”; Laning, Roddis interviews; interviews with technical staff of Office of Naval Research (all CS).
666 Evaluation of Rickover: Rickover testimony; Lilienthal, *The Journals* ... (Vol. 3); review of interviews conducted for this book.

Bibliography

This book is based on three general sources: First, the words of Admiral Rickover, more than one million of them, which he has spoken before Congressional committees, ably supported by thousands of pages of prepared statements and supplementary papers. Second, interviews with, and the oral histories made by, scores of individuals—naval officers, enlisted men and women, and civilians involved with nuclear submarines, education, shipbuilding, the electric power industry, the Department of Defense, and many other parts of the American society. And third, the hundreds of reports and letters concerning Admiral Rickover and his various activities that reside in the Navy and National Archives, in libraries, and in the collections of the National Education Association, the Naval Academy, the Department of Energy, the Nuclear Regulatory Commission, and the private collections of several individuals.

Several books and articles were also used extensively. Among the most useful and the most professionally prepared are the three histories written largely by Dr. Richard Hewlett of the Department of Energy (nee Atomic Energy Commission). Those are: *The New World, Atomic Shield,* and *Nuclear Navy.* The last, written at the specific invitation of Admiral Rickover, provides a useful and accurate—albeit limited—account of the Navy's nuclear-propulsion program from 1946 until 1962. The large number of comments on nuclear propulsion and on leadership in the nuclear community—including a brief but important one on leadership by Admiral Rickover himself in 1981—in the Naval Institute *Proceedings,* have also been significant. The *Proceedings* is the professional journal of the U.S. Navy, and such comments are encouraged from personnel of all ranks, as well as civilians.

NEWS MAGAZINES AND NEWSPAPERS

Aerospace Daily
Beacon (Philadelphia Naval Shipyard)
Bulletin of Atomic Scientists
Chicago Sun-Times
Chicago Tribune
Day, The (New London)
Dolphin (Naval Submarine Base, New London)
Fortune magazine
General Dynamics News (Electric Boat Division)
Grapevine (Mare Island Naval Shipyard)
Ingalls News (Ingalls Shipbuilding Corporation)

Krasnaya Zvezda (Red Star)
Life magazine
Navy Times
Newsweek magazine
New York Times
Nucleonics
Our Navy magazine
Science magazine
Shipyard Bulletin (Newport News Shipbuilding & Dry Dock Company)
Shipyard Weekly (Shipbuilders Council of America)
Time magazine
Times, The (of London)
U.S. News & World Report
Virginia Pilot
Washington Post
Washington Star
Washington Times-Herald

SHIPS' LOGS*

Bushnell
Canopus
Charleston
Finch
Franklin
La Vallette
Nautilus
Nevada
New Mexico
Percival
Prairie
Skylark
S-9
S-48

ORAL HISTORIES

Vice Adm. James L. Holloway, Jr., Chief of Naval Personnel.
Vice Adm. Edwin B. Hooper, Director of Naval History.
Rear Adm. Ralph K. James, Chief of the Bureau of Ships.
A. P. Kenyon, civilian executive in the Bureau of Naval Personnel.
Dr. Waldo K. Lyon, Director, Navy Arctic Submarine Laboratory
Vice Adm. Lawson P. Ramage, Deputy Commander, Submarine Force, Atlantic Fleet, and Deputy CNO (Fleet Operations and Readiness).
Adm. Horacio Rivero, Vice Chief of Naval Operations.
Vice Adm. William R. Smedberg III, Chief of Naval Personnel.

NOTE: The authors are in debt to John T. Mason, Jr., Director of Oral History, U.S. Naval Institute, for his assistance in the matter of oral histories. Dr. Mason personally conducted most of these oral histories.

* A "log" is the official daily record of occurrences aboard a ship of the U.S. Navy.

CONGRESSIONAL TESTIMONY*

House Committee on Appropriations
    Report on Russia by Admiral H. G. Rickover (1959).
    Department of Defense Appropriations for 1959, Department of the Navy.
    _____ 1961, Part 7 [Nuclear Propulsion for Ships].
    _____ 1962, Part 6, Nuclear Propulsion.
    _____ 1964, Part 5, Procurement.
    _____ 1968, Part 6, Admiral Hyman G. Rickover.
    _____ 1970, Part 6, Testimony of Admiral Hyman G. Rickover.
    _____ 1970, Part 7, Secretary of Defense, et al.
    _____ 1972, Part 8, Testimony of Vice Adm. Hyman G. Rickover.
    _____ 1973, Part 9, Testimony of Vice Adm. Hyman G. Rickover.
    _____ 1974, Part 3, Testimony of Vice Adm. Hyman G. Rickover.
    _____ 1979, Part 6, Testimony of Admiral Hyman G. Rickover.
    Department of State, Justice and Commerce, the Judiciary and Related Agencies,
        Appropriations for 1980, Part 4, Department of Commerce (*Savannah*).
House Committee on Armed Services
    Appropriations During the Fiscal Year 1968 for Procurement of Aircraft, Mis-
        siles, Naval Vessels, and Tracked Combat Vehicles, and Research, Develop-
        ment, Test, and Evaluation for the Armed Forces, and for Other Purposes
        (1967).
    Report by Preparedness Investigating Subcommittee on the United States Sub-
        marine Program (1968).
    Trip to Knolls Atomic Power Laboratory, Sep. 28, 1970, made by the Subcom-
        mittee on Antisubmarine Warfare.
    Hearings on Nuclear Aircraft Carrier CVN-70 (1972).
    Hearings on Military Posture (Fiscal 1975), Part 2, Nuclear Navy—Title VIII.
    _____ (Fiscal 1976), Part 3, Seapower and Strategic and Critical Materials Sub-
        committee.
    _____ (Fiscal 1978), Part 4, Seapower and Strategic and Critical Materials Sub-
        committee.
    Hearing on ERDA Authorization Legislation (National Security Programs) for
        Fiscal Year 1978.
    Report on Nuclear-Powered Attack Submarine Program (1979).
House Committee on Armed Services, Intelligence and Military
        Application of Nuclear Energy Subcommittee
        Naval Nuclear Propulsion Program—1977
        Naval Nuclear Propulsion Program—1978
House Committee on Armed Services, Procurement and Military Nuclear Systems
    Subcommittee
    Naval Nuclear Propulsion Program—1980
House Committee on Government Operations
    The Efficiency and Effectiveness of Renegotiation Board Operations, Part 1
        (1970).
Joint Committee on Atomic Energy
    Atomic Power and Private Enterprise—December 1952.
    Naval Reactor Program and Shippingport Project (1957).

* *Only hearings and reports specifically on nuclear propulsion and nuclear power matters
are cited here.*

Report of the Underseas Warfare Advisory Panel (1958).
Review of Naval Reactor Program and Admiral Rickover Award (1959).
Naval Reactor Program and Polaris Missile System (1960).
Hearings on the Tour of the U.S.S. *Enterprise* and Report on Joint AEC—Naval Reactor Program (1962).
Nuclear Propulsion for Naval Surface Vehicles (1963).
Loss of the U.S.S. *Thresher* (1964).
Naval Nuclear Propulsion Program (1966).
_____ (1967–68)
_____ (1969)
_____ (1970)
_____ (1971)
_____ (1972–73)
_____ (1974)
_____ (1975)
_____ (1976)
Nuclear Submarines of Advanced Design (1968)
Nuclear Submarines of Advanced Design (2 parts; 1968)
Nuclear Propulsion for Naval Warships (1972)
Joint Senate-House Armed Services Subcommittee CVAN-70 Aircraft Carrier (1970)
Senate Committee on Armed Services
U.S. Submarine Program (1968)
Fiscal Year 1973 Authorization for Military Procurement, Research and Development, Construction Authorization for Safeguard ABM, and Active Duty and Selected Reserve Strengths, Part 5, Research and Development (1972)
Fiscal Year 1975 Authorization for Military Procurement, Research and Development, and Active Duty, Selected Reserve and Civilian Personnel Strengths, Part 7, Research and Development (1974)
Senate Committee on Armed Services, Preparedness Investigating Subcommittee Inquiry into Satellite and Missile Programs (1958)
Senate Select Committee on Small Business Patent Policies of Government Department and Agencies (1960)
Joint Economic Committee, Subcommittee on Priorities and Economy in Government, Part 1 (1977)

RICKOVER SPEECHES*

"Nuclear Power and the Navy," before the San Francisco Council of the Navy League, Chamber of Commerce, and Commercial Club, San Francisco, Oct. 27, 1955.
"The Never-Ending Challenge," at the 44th annual National Metals Congress, New York, Oct. 29, 1962.
"The Significance of Electricity," upon accepting the Prometheus Award from the National Electrical Manufacturers Association, Washington, D.C., Nov. 9, 1965.
"Who Protects the Public?" at the 50th materials engineering congress and exposition sponsored by the American Society for Metals, Detroit, Mich., Oct. 14, 1968.

* *Admiral Rickover has made some 65 major speeches since 1955. Those cited here are the principal ones used as sources in this book. Most of the others are repeats of the same material, based mainly on his Congressional testimony.*

"A Humanistic Technology," at the convocation on ecology and the human environment, St. Albans School, Washington, D.C., May 7, 1969.

"An Effective National Defense—Why?" before the Providence Rotary Club, Providence, R.I., Oct. 13, 1970.

"Energy—A Diminishing Capital Resource," at the annual meeting of the Pensacola Area Chamber of Commerce, Pensacola, Fla., June 8, 1972.

"The Role of Engineering in the Navy," before the National Society of Former Special Agents of the Federal Bureau of Investigation, Seattle, Wash., Aug. 30, 1974.

"Lawyers Versus Society," before the New York Patent Law Association, New York, Mar. 30, 1979.

"Environmental Perspectives," at the Puget Sound Naval Base Association's annual dinner, Bremerton, Wash., Nov. 16, 1979.

BOOKS

Abbott, Edith, *The Tenements of Chicago, 1900-1935.* Chicago: University of Chicago Press, 1936.

Anderson, William R., and Blair, Clay, Jr., *Nautilus 90 North.* Cleveland and New York: World, 1959.

Beach, Edward L., *Around the World Submerged.* New York: Holt, Rinehart & Winston, 1962.

_____, *Cold Is the Sea.* New York: Holt, Rinehart & Winston, 1978.

Berkow, Ira, *Maxwell Street.* Garden City, N.Y.: Doubleday, 1977.

Blackford, Charles Minor, *Torpedoboat Sailor.* Annapolis: U.S. Naval Institute, 1968.

Blair, Clay, Jr., *The Atomic Submarine and Admiral Rickover.* New York: Henry Holt, 1954.

Bukalov, V. M., and Narusbayev, A. A., *Proyektirovaniye atomnykh podvodnykh lodok* (Design of Nuclear Submarines), 2nd edition. Leningrad: Sudostroyeniye, 1968.

Calvert, James, *Surface at the Pole.* New York: McGraw-Hill, 1960.

Carter, Jimmy, *Why Not the Best?* New York: Bantam, 1976.

Cole, Brady M., *Procurement of Naval Ships* (monograph). Washington, D.C.: Industrial College of the Armed Forces, 1979.

Davis, Vincent, *Postwar Defense Policy and the U.S. Navy, 1943-1946.* Chapel Hill: University of North Carolina Press, 1962.

Dmitriyev, V. I., *Atakuyut Podvodniki* (The Submariners Attack). Moscow: Voyennoye Izdatel'stvo (USSR Ministry of Defense), 1973.

Ellsberg, Edward, *On the Bottom.* New York: Literary Guild, 1929.

Furer, Julius Augustus, *Administration of the Navy Department in World War II.* Washington, D.C.: Government Printing Office, 1979.

Gantz, Kenneth F., ed., *Nuclear Flight.* New York: Duell, Sloan and Pearce, 1960.

Groves, Leslie R., *Now It Can Be Told.* New York: Harper and Brothers, 1962.

Hewlett, Richard G., *Nuclear Navy 1946-1962.* Chicago: University of Chicago Press, 1974.

_____, and Anderson, Oscar E., Jr., *The New World,* Vol. 1 of *A History of the United States Atomic Energy Commission.* Washington, D.C.: U.S. Atomic Energy Commission, 1972.

_____, and Duncan, Francis, *Atomic Shield,* Vol. 2 of *A History of the United States Atomic Energy Commission.* Washington, D.C.: U.S. Atomic Energy Commission, 1972.

Khrushchev, Nikita, *Khrushchev Remembers, The Last Testament.* Boston: Little, Brown, 1974.

Killian, James R., Jr., *Sputnik, Scientists, and Eisenhower.* Cambridge: MIT Press, 1977.

Lapp, Dr. Ralph E., *The New Force; The Story of Atoms and People.* New York: Harper, 1953.

Lilienthal, David E. *The Journals of David E. Lilienthal*—Volume 3, *The Venturesome Years, 1950-1955;* Volume 4, *The Road to Change, 1955-1959;* Volume 6, *Creativity and Conflict, 1964-1967.* New York: Harper and Row, 1966-67.

Lockwood, Charles A., *Down to the Sea in Subs.* New York: Norton, 1967.

Lott, Arnold S., *Most Dangerous Sea.* Annapolis: U.S. Naval Institute, 1959.

Lovette, Leland P., *School of the Sea.* New York: Stokes, 1941.

Nixon, Richard M., *Six Crises.* Garden City, N.Y.: Doubleday, 1962.

Nosterenko, G. N., et al., *Primeneiye Atomnykh Dvigateley v Aviatsii* (Application of Atomic Engines in Aviation). Moscow: 1957.

Nicolson, Harold, *Peacemaking 1918.* Peter, Smith, 1919.

Olmsted, Gerald, ed., *The Lucky Bag 1922.* Annapolis: U.S. Naval Academy, 1922.

Pocock, Rowland, *Nuclear Ship Propulsion.* London: Ian Allan, 1970.

Polmar, Norman, *Atomic Submarines.* Princeton: Van Nostrand, 1963.

———, *Death of the Thresher.* Philadelphia: Chilton Books, 1964.

Rawidowicz, Simon, ed., *The Chicago Pinkas.* Chicago: College of Jewish Studies, 1952.

Rickover, H. G., *American Education.* New York: E. P. Dutton, 1963.

———, *Education and Freedom.* New York: E. P. Dutton, 1959.

———, *Eminent Americans.* Washington, D.C.: Government Printing Office, 1972.

———, *How the Battleship* Maine *Was Destroyed.* Washington, D.C.: Government Printing Office, 1976.

———, *Liberty, Science and Law.* New York: Newcomen Society, 1969.

———, *Swiss Schools and Ours: Why Theirs Are Better.* Boston: Little, Brown, 1962.

Rickover, Ruth Masters, *Handbook of International Organizations in the Americas.* Washington, D.C.: Carnegie Endowment, 1945.

———, *International Law in National Courts.* New York: Columbia University Press, 1932.

———, *International Organization in the Field of Public Health.* Washington, D.C.: Carnegie Endowment, 1947.

———, *Pepper, Rice, and Elephants.* Annapolis: Naval Institute Press, 1975.

Samuel, Herbert Louis. *Wars of Ideas.* New York: Carnegie Endowment, 1937.

Sapolsky, Harvey M., *The Polaris System Development.* Cambridge: Harvard University Press, 1972.

Smyth, Henry Dewolf, *Atomic Energy for Military Purposes.* Princeton: Princeton University Press, 1945. (The official report on the development of the atomic bomb under the auspices of the United States Government, 1940–1945.)

Steele, George P., *Seadragon.* New York: E. P. Dutton, 1962.

Stormer, John A., *None Dare Call It Treason.* Florissant, Mo.: Liberty Bell Press, 1964.

Strauss, Lewis L., *Men and Decisions.* London: Macmillan, 1963.

Svjatov, G. I., *Atomniye podvodniye lodki* (Nuclear Submarines). Moscow: Atomezdat, 1969. (Dr. Svjatov also translated the author's book *Atomic Submarines* for a Russian-language edition published in 1965.)

Sweetman, Jack, *The U.S. Naval Academy.* Annapolis: Naval Institute Press, 1979.

U.S. Navy, Bureau of Naval Personnel, *Nucleonics for the Navy.* Washington, D.C.: U.S. Navy, 1949.

———, *Principles of Naval Engineering.* Washington, D.C.: Government Printing Office, 1966. (Chapter 24, "Nuclear Power Plants.")

U.S. Navy, Bureau of Ships. *Electrical Section History.* Washington, D.C.: U.S. Navy, 1946.
U.S. Office of the Secretary of Defense, Historical Office, *The Department of Defense—Documents on Establishment and Organization, 1944-1978.* Washington, D.C.: Government Printing Office, 1978.
Wheeler, Leslie, *Jimmy Who?* Woodbury, N.Y.: Barron, 1976.
Westinghouse Electric Corporation and Duquesne Light Company, *The Shippingport Pressurized Water Reactor.* Reading, Mass.: Addison-Wesley, 1958.
Zumwalt, Elmo R., Jr., *On Watch.* New York: Quadrangle, 1976.

ARTICLES*

Abramson, Rudy, "Heavy Seas May Await Rickover," *Los Angeles Times,* Feb. 26, 1977.
"Admiral and the Atom, The," *Time,* May 21, 1956, 25-32.
"Admirals at Odds over Subsea Threat," *NYT,* Apr. 8, 1958.
Amper, Richard, "2nd Nuclear Carrier to Lose Its Priority to Atom Submarines," *NYT,* Dec. 29, 1957.
Amrine, Michael, "Fifteen-Day Runaround for Atom Sub Story," *Editor & Publisher,* Feb. 7, 1953, 12, 52.
Anderson, George W., "Our Nuclear Navy," *National Geographic Magazine,* March 1963, 149-50.
"Atom Carrier Delayed," *NYT,* Dec. 14, 1955.
"Atom Fleet Plan Gaining New Life," *NYT,* Jan. 15, 1961.
"Atomic Carrier Loses," *NYT,* Nov. 17, 1959.
"Atomic Carrier to Be Asked in 57," *NYT,* Dec. 12, 1955.
"Atomic Navy Is Pictured," *NYT,* June 6, 1955.
Auerbach, Stuart, "Adm. Rickover Assails the Legal Profession," *Washington Post,* Apr. 2, 1979.
Backus, Paul H., "Finite Deterrence, Controlled Retaliation," *USNIP,* March 1959, 23-30.
Baldwin, Hanson W., "Atom Propulsion: Score So Far," *NYT,* Aug. 9, 1959.
———, "M'Namara Faces Budget Decisions," *NYT,* Oct. 18, 1963.
———, "Nuclear Sea Power," *NYT,* Mar. 20, 1957.
———, "Rough Seas for Carriers," *NYT,* Jan. 26, 1960.
———, "Soviet Submarine Lag," *NYT,* Apr. 18, 1963.
Bamberger, Werner, "Drop in Shipbuilding Forecast by New Head of Naval Society," *NYT,* Nov. 19, 1960.
Barker, Karlyn, "Rickover Blasts Private Consultants," *Washington Post,* Aug. 21, 1980.
Beach, Edward L., "Life Under Rickover: Stormy Duty in the Silent Service," *Washington Post,* May 27, 1977, D-1.
Blair, Clay, Jr., "Brazen Prejudice," *Time,* Aug. 4, 1952, 18.
———, "The Dawn of Atomic Plenty: U.S. Contracts for a New Submarine," *Life,* Sep. 3, 1951, 18-22.
———, "What It's Like to Ride the *Nautilus,*" *Life,* May 28, 1956, 143-44, 146, 148.
Bolgarev, N., "Submarines in Modern War," *Voyenniye Znaniya* (Military Knowledge), Aug. 1959, 36-37.

* *NYT is used as an abbreviation for* The New York Times, *and USNIP is used as an abbreviation for the U.S. Naval Institute* Proceedings.

Bowen, H. G., "Nuclear Energy as a Power Source," *Mechanical Engineering*, American Society of Mechanical Engineers, Sep. 1946, 779–81.

Boyden, Amanda, "Changing Shanghai," *National Geographic Magazine*, Oct. 1937, 485–508.

Bracker, Milton, "Rickover Assails 'Yes-Man' Trend," *NYT*, Oct. 30, 1959.

Brown, Gordon V., "Arctic ASW," *USNIP*, March 1962, 53–57.

Bryan, C. R., and Wakefield, J. R., "The Effect of Weapons on Submarine Design," *Bureau of Ships Journal*, August 1964, 2–11.

Burke, Gerald Keith, "The Need for Trident," *USNIP*, November 1978, 32–41. Also see commentary by D. L. Holley, *USNIP*, February 1979, 26.

Cameron, Juan, "Admiral Rickover's Final Battle," *Fortune*, November 1978, 190–94, 196, 200, 202, 205.

"Carter to Sail Today in Sub with Rickover," *Washington Post*, May 27, 1977.

Casey, Phil, "Life's Better for Ex-Editor," *Washington Post*, Jan. 1, 1972. (Interview with Clay Blair, Jr.)

Chapman, R. M., "Attack Submarine Development—Recent Trends and Projected Needs," *USNIP*, August 1978, 97–102. Also comments by Lieut. R. E. Chatham, *USNIP*, October 1978, 87–88; L. D. Chirillo, *USNIP*, November 1978, 107–10; Capt. K. G. Schacht, *USNIP*, December 1978, 98–100.

Chatham, Ralph E., "Leadership and Nuclear Power," *USNIP*, July 1978, 78–82. (This essay won the Naval Institute's Vincent Astor Memorial Leadership Essay Contest for 1978.) Also comments by Comdr. John W. Asher III, and Comdr. P. W. Sparks, *USNIP*, October 1978, 81–84; Lieut. Harold C. Lowe and Vice Adm. Ray Peet, *USNIP*, November 1978, 113–14; Comdr. A. F. Campbell and Comdr. Todd Blades, *USNIP*, December 1978, 95–98; Comdr. R. N. Lee and Lieut. Thomas B. Salzer, *USNIP*, January 1979, 84–86; Lieut. John C. Morgan, Jr., *USNIP*, February 1979, 23.

Clark, David G., "SOSMRC: Steaming in the Desert," *USNIP*, February 1980, 97–99.

"Common Sense About Uncommon Carriers," *Saturday Evening Post*, Nov. 23, 1963, 96.

"Congress Report Scores M'Namara on Carrier Ruling," *NYT*, Dec. 22, 1963.

Corddry, Charles W., "Profile/Vice Admiral Hyman G. Rickover," *Navy*, Feb. 1970, 47–48.

Cosmas, Graham A., Review of *How the Battleship* Maine *Was Destroyed*, by Hyman G. Rickover, *Naval War College Review*, Fall 1977, 138–40.

Craven, John, "Seapower and the Seabed," *USNIP*, April 1966, 36–51.

Davis, Vincent, "The Development of Fleet Ballistic Missiles," *The Politics of Innovation: Patterns in Navy Cases* (Denver: University of Denver, 1967), 31–42.

———, "The Development of Nuclear Propulsion Units," Ibid., 23–30.

de Poix, Vincent P., "The Big 'E,'" *USNIP*, June 1962, 91–104.

Duncan, David D., U.S. Marine Corps, "Okinawa, Threshold to Japan," *National Geographic Magazine*, October 1945, 411–28.

Eaker, Ira C., "Rickover May Be Losing His 'Stranglehold' on Navy," *Navy Times*, June 14, 1976.

Eastman, R. S., "Nuclear Power for Combatant Surface Ships," *USNIP*, January 1963, 130–33.

Enthoven, Alain, "Systems Analysis and the Navy," *Naval Review 1965*. Annapolis, Md.: 1964, 98–117.

Fallows, James, "The Passionless Presidency," *Atlantic*, May 1979, 33–48.

"Fastest Submarine, The," *Time*, Sep. 3, 1951, 23–24.

"Fight for Survival of the Super Carrier," *Saturday Evening Post*, Nov. 2, 1963, 17–19.

Finney, John W., "A.E.C. Demands an Atomic Navy," *NYT*, Jan. 28, 1963.

————, "Air Force Warns B-70 Cutbacks Could Impair Retaliatory Punch," *NYT*, Apr. 12, 1961.

————, "Criticism of M'Namara Mounts," *NYT*, Nov. 17, 1963.

————, "Full Speed Astern," *Time*, Jan. 18, 1954, 20.

————, "Lawmakers Push for Atomic Fleet," *NYT*, Dec. 10, 1961.

————, "M'Namara Bars Nuclear Carrier Sought by Navy," *NYT*, Oct. 26, 1963.

————, "M'Namara Defers Navy Program for Atomic Fleet," *NYT*, May 6, 1963.

————, "M'Namara Faces Fight on Carrier," *NYT*, Nov. 4, 1963.

————, "Navy Chiefs Spur Atom Destroyer," *NYT*, Jan. 19, 1958.

————, "Navy Says Costs Ban Atom Fleet," *NYT*, Apr. 10, 1961.

————, "Navy to Keep Rickover in Post as Chief for Nuclear Power," *NYT*, June 22, 1963.

————, "Research Effort of U.S. Criticized," *NYT*, Nov. 6, 1963.

————, "Rickover Will Keep Nuclear Navy Post," *NYT*, Apr. 9, 1963.

Friedman, Ben L., "The Submarine That Saves Its Crew," *Naval Research Reviews*, January 1970, 23–24, 365–79.

Friedman, Norman, "Admiral Elmo R. Zumwalt, Jr.," *The Chiefs of U.S. Naval Operations* (Annapolis: U.S. Naval Institute, 1980).

"Gates Willing to Lose Some Ships to Get Funds for Atom Carrier," *NYT*, Apr. 18, 1975.

Grenfell, E. W., "USS *Thresher* (SSN-593) 3 August 1961–10 April 1963," *USNIP*, March 1964, 36–47.

Grimes, John, "Our Nuclear Navy," *Science Digest*, June 1956, 68–71.

Gup, Ted, and Jonathan, Neumann, "Rickover Makes Waves About Party by Navy Contractor in Va.," *Washington Post*, June 29, 1980.

Hays, John D., "Admiral Joseph Mason Reeves, USN (1872–1948)," Part 1, *Naval War College Review*, November 1970, 48–57.

Hayward, John T., Comment on "The Education of a Warrior," *USNIP*, April 1981, 21, 23.

Helfer, Harold, "He's No Team Man, But . . ." *Our Navy*, Mid-November 1958, 22–23, 34–36.

Henry, Neil, "Rickover's Nuclear Navy: Making Men Into Machines," *Washington Post*, June 16, 1981.

Hessler, William H., "The Biggest Warship That Ever Was," *The Reporter*, July 19, 1962, 30–32.

Holifield, Chet, "Naval Reactors Lead the Way in Overall Nuclear Power Advances," *Navy Magazine*, February 1970, 42–48.

Holmquist, Carl O., and Greenbaum, Russell S., "The Development of Nuclear Propulsion in the Navy," *USNIP*, September 1960, 65–71.

"Jackson Urges Navy to Speed Atom Power," *Aviation Week*, Nov. 28, 1955, 18.

Jones, J. D., "Some Thoughts from an Unrepentant Nuc," *USNIP*, November 1977, 86–87. Also comments by Capt. K. W. Estes, U.S. Marine Corps, *USNIP*, February 1978, 21–22; Comdr. Daniel B. Branch and Vice Adm. George P. Steele, *USNIP*, June 1978, 87–92; Comdr. J. Winsor Baker, Jr., *USNIP*, July 1978, 83; the June 1978 commentary includes a partial reprint of Adm. Steele's article "A Fleet to Match Our Real Needs" that originally appeared in the *Washington Post*, May 16, 1976.

Kenney, Nathaniel T., and Abercrombie, Thomas J., "Mighty *Enterprise*, World's Largest Ship," *National Geographic Magazine*, March 1963, 431–48.

Kintner, E. E., "Admiral Rickover's Gamble—The Landlocked Submarine," *The Atlantic*, January 1959, 31–35.

Kluttz, Jerry, "Rickover Tells of CSC Prying," *Washington Post*, Sep. 2, 1968.

"Korth Finds Cost Too High to Build Nuclear Carriers," *NYT*, June 21, 1961.

"Korth Urges All-Nuclear Line Fleet," *Aviation Week and Space Technology*, Nov. 4, 1963, 34.

Lalor, William G., "Submarine Through the North Pole," *National Geographic Magazine*, January 1959, 1–20.

Laurence, William L., "The Atom Gives Up," *Saturday Evening Post*, Sep. 7, 1940, 12–13, 60–63.

Lawrence, William P., "Superintendent's Report," *Shipmate*, October 1979, 17–20.

"Legislators Back Nuclear Cruiser," *NYT*, Jan. 26, 1956.

Lockwood, Charles A., "We're Betting Our Shirts on the Atomic Submarine," *Saturday Evening Post*, July 22, 1950, 26–27.

Lytle, Morton H., "Replenishing the Nuclear Navy," *USNIP*, October 1959, 56–61.

MacGregor, Greg, "Nobel Fete Told of Science's Role," *NYT*, Jan. 9, 1961.

McKnew, Thomas W., "Four-Ocean Navy in the Nuclear Age," *National Geographic Magazine*, February 1965, 145–87.

"McNamara Shifts Policy, Seeks Nuclear Power for Large Ships," *Aviation Week and Space Technology*, Apr. 15, 1963, 37.

Makansi, Antar, "Proud Ohio Surges to Sea as Rickover Plays Garbo," *Norwich (Conn.) Bulletin*, June 18, 1981.

"Man in Tempo 3, The," *Time*, Jan. 11, 1954, 36–39.

Miller, George H., "Strategy of the Future—A Second Look," *USNIP*, May 1950, 473–83.

Miller, Jonathan. "The Ancient Submariner," *The New Republic*, Nov. 12, 1977.

Mintz, Morton, "Attorney Corcoran Faces Ethics Probe," *Washington Post*, Dec. 21, 1979.

Morris, John D., "Budget Cuts Aim at Atom Carrier," *NYT*, Jan. 27, 1958.

"Naval Men Hear of United States Lead in Nuclear Ships," *NYT*, Oct. 29, 1960.

"Navy Gives Details of 3 Bonus Plans to Nuclear Officers," *Navy Times*, Aug. 23, 1976.

"Navy Makes a Promise," *NYT*, May 17, 1956.

"Navy May Build Atomic Carrier," *NYT*, Nov. 11, 1955.

"Navy Plans Work on Atomic Carrier," *NYT*, Oct. 17, 1965.

"Navy Requests URLs (Unrestricted Line Officers) to Enter Nuclear Field," *Navy Times*, Apr. 18, 1977.

"Navy Votes To Go All-Nuclear," *Business Week*, Apr. 13, 1973, 30.

"Navy Wants Atomic Powered Carrier," *Business Week*, Jan. 28, 1956, 30.

Naymark, Sherman, "Underway on Nuclear Power—The Development of the *Nautilus*," *USNIP*, April 1970, 56–63.

Nordlinger, Stephen E., "Rickover Thwarts Sub Safety Visits," *Baltimore Sun*, Feb. 27, 1978.

Norman, Lloyd, "The Love-Hate Affair Between the Pentagon and the Press," *Army*, February 1980, 14–20.

"Nuclear Carrier Is Urged," *NYT*, July 15, 1959.

Parke, Richard H., "Top Navy Award Given Rickover," *NYT*, Jan. 18, 1961.

Paolucci, D. A., "The Development of Navy Strategic Offensive and Defensive Systems," *USNIP* (Naval Review), May 1970, 204–23.

Patterson, Rachelle, "Rickover Denies Deceiving Panel about Portsmouth," *Boston Globe*, Jan. 10, 1979.

Philpott, Tom, "Rickover Backs 'Double Dip' Ban," *Navy Times*, Aug. 8, 1977.

Pincus, Walter, "Rickover Agrees on Need for Radiation Study," *Washington Post*, Mar. 1, 1978.

Polmar, Norman, "Soviet Navy Pulls Even in Nuclear Sub Might," *Washington Post*, Oct. 4, 1970.

———, "The Soviet Nuclear Submarines," *USNIP*, July 1981, 31–39.

———, "The U.S. Navy: Attack Submarines," *USNIP*, January 1980, 112–13 (especially the commentary by Edward S. Ruete, *USNIP*, March 1980, 11–12, 17, which provides a clear and concise explanation of the "how to build a smaller nuclear submarine."

———, and Paolucci, D. A., "Sea-Based 'Strategic' Weapons for the 1980s and Beyond," *USNIP* (Naval Review), May 1978, 98–113.

Prina, L. Edgar, "Rickover an Expert in Sarcastic Replies," *Joliet* (Ill.) *Herald-News,* Dec. 5, 1969.

Raymond, Jack, "Navy Advocates Nuclear Power in All Big Ships," *NYT,* Apr. 8, 1963.

———, "Navy Again Seeking 2nd Nuclear Carrier," *NYT,* Nov. 24, 1958.

———, "Navy Still Seeks Nuclear Carrier," *NYT,* Oct. 12, 1963.

"Rebellion Rampant in the Yards," *Time,* July 26, 1976, 62.

"Report on the Nuclear Carrier," *All Hands,* April 1960, 6–8.

Rickover, Hyman G., Comment on "Quarterly Marks and Promotion of Enlisted Personnel," *USNIP,* Mar. 24, 1934, 403–5.

———, "International Law and the Submarine," *USNIP,* Sep. 1935, 1213–27.

———, "Leadership," *USNIP,* January 1981, 82. Also comments by Lieut. Comdr. Barry J. Coyle, Electronics Technician 1/class John G. Hazard, Capt. Wayne P. Hughes, Jr., and Adm. H. E. Shear, *USNIP,* April 1981, 80, 83. Vice Adm. John T. Hayward, a longtime supporter of Adm. Rickover, has a critical view of his leadership commentary in "The Education of a Warrior," *USNIP,* April 1981, 21, 23.

———, "Management in Government," *Management* (U.S. Office of Personnel Management), September 1979, 16–19.

———, "Nuclear Warships and the Navy's Future," *USNIP,* January 1975, 18–24.

———, "Presentation of the Senior Mantle," *The Review* (John Marshall High School), February 1918, 22–23.

———. "Thoughts on Man's Purpose in Life . . . And Other Matters," *USNIP,* December 1974; abridged from Rickover's testimony before the House Committee on Appropriations, Subcommittee on Department of Defense, June 19, 1973.

"Rickover Details Pay Revamp Proposals," *Navy Times,* Feb. 6, 1978.

"Rickover Scores Atomic Ship Plan," *NYT,* June 26, 1955.

Rosenberg, Dr. David A., "OPNAV General Organization for Strategic Warfare, 1945–1972," unclassified appendix to Department of Defense study "History of Strategic Arms Competition, U.S.-U.S.S.R., 1945–1972," 1975.

———, "Officer Development in the Interwar Navy: Arleigh Burke—The Making of a Naval Professional, 1919–1940," *Pacific Historical Review,* November 1975, 503–26.

Rosenthal, Erich, "This Was North Lawndale," *Jewish Social Studies,* Vol. 22, 1960, 67–82.

Roth, Eli B., USN, "Atomic Power—Where Will It Pay First?" *USNIP,* October 1953, 1091–1101.

Ryan, Edward F., "U.S. to Launch Atom Industry," *Washington Post,* Oct. 23, 1953.

Schiller, Ronald, "The Strange Case of the Man Behind the Atomic Sub," *Look,* Mar. 10, 1953, 23–25.

Schratz, Paul, "An Open Letter (to Admiral Rickover)," *Shipmate,* April 1974, 19–22.

Shapley, Deborah, "Nuclear Navy: Rickover Thwarted Research on Light Weight Reactors," *Science,* June 18, 1978, 1210–13.

Shogan, Robert, "Rickover Provides Crusty Advice on Life," *Los Angeles Times,* Oct. 28, 1977.

"Sinking the Rickover Armada," *Los Angeles Times,* June 1, 1977.

Spitz, Allan A., "Conventional Versus Nuclear Power for CVA-67: A Study of Defense Management," Naval War College *Review,* April 1972, 3–14.

"Steam Pipe Fails in *Nautilus* Test," *NYT,* Sep. 19, 1954.

Steele, George P., "Killing Nuclear Submarines," *USNIP,* November 1960, 45–51.

Strong, James T., "The Opening of the Arctic Ocean," *USNIP,* October 1961, 58–65.

"The Man in Tempo 3," *Time,* Jan. 11, 1954, 36–39.

"Thomas Outlines U.S. Atomic Fleet," *NYT,* Oct. 30, 1956.

"2000-M.P.H. Plane." *All Hands* (Bureau of Naval Personnel), October 1958, 59–63.

"Unsinkable Hyman Rickover," *Time,* May 23, 1977, 16.

"USS *Bainbridge* (DLGN-25)," *USNIP,* July 1963, 90–103.

"USS *Long Beach* (CGN-9)," *USNIP,* Aug. 1964, 91–111.

"U.S. to Build Industrial Atom Plant," *Washington Star,* Oct. 22, 1953.

Van Deurs, George, "Oregon's Builders' Trials," *Shipmate,* July–August 1976, 27–30.

Van Saun, A., "Tactical ASW: A Case for a Non-Nuclear Submarine," *USNIP,* November 1978, 147–51.

———, "Tactical ASW: Let's Fight Fire with Fire," *USNIP,* December 1976, 99–101.

Vito, A. H., Jr., "Lone Carrier . . . Fact or Fancy?" *USNIP,* April 1962, 48–55. Also see commentary by Thomas D. McGrath and Norman Polmar, *USNIP,* April 1963, 121–22.

Volod'kovskiy, V. A., and Grach, S. P., "Scientific and Technical Progress and the Fleet," *Morskoy Sbornik* (Naval Digest), March 1971, 68–73.

Wallace, Robert, "A Deluge of Honors for an Exasperating Admiral," *Life,* Sep. 8, 1958, 104–106, 109–110, 113–114, 116, 118.

Wallin, Homer N., "America's New Dreadful Weapon," *Colliers,* Dec. 20, 1952, 13–17.

———, "Rejuvenation of Pearl Harbor," *USNIP,* Dec. 1946, 1520–51.

Weatherup, R. A., "Defense Against Nuclear-Powered Submarines," *USNIP, December 1959, 71–75.*

Wicker, Tom, "Korth Quits Post as Head of Navy; Nitze Appointed," NYT, Oct. 15, 1963.

Wilkinson, E. P., *"Nautilus* and *Narwhal*—A Unique Personal View," *Navy Magazine,* February 1970, 32–34.

Will, John, "Administration Backs Away from Nuclear Merchantman Shipbuilding Plan," *Navy Magazine* (Navy League), February 1970, 35–37.

Wilson, George C., "A Fast Soviet Sub Scares the Brass," *Washington Post,* July 21, 1968.

———, "New Submarine Proposals Challenge Rickover's Rule," *Washington Post,* May 21, 1979.

———, "Rickover Requests $130 Million to Build 2nd Nuclear Minisub," *Washington Post,* Nov. 5, 1976.

———, "Rickover's Team Begins to Dissolve," *Washington Post,* Aug. 7, 1979.

———, "Soviet Navy Has Faster, Lighter Sub," *Washington Post,* May 18, 1979.

———, "Soviets Launch Huge New Attack Submarine," *Washington Post,* Jan. 9, 1981.

Wilson, William E., "Graduates of the U.S. Naval Academy," *USNIP,* April 1946, 157–64.

Wirt, John G., "A Federal Demonstration Project: N.S. *Savannah,*" *Case Studies in Maritime Innovation* (Washington, D.C.: Maritime Transportation Research Board, 1978), 29–35.

Witkin, Richard, "Small Submarine Planned by U.S.," *NYT,* Apr. 1, 1959.

Zumwalt, Elmo R., and Bagley, Worth H., "Navy Enters New Shipbuilding Era,"

Navy Times, Jan. 29, 1979. This article was critically answered by John T. Hayward in "Is That Any Way to Build a Warship?," *Navy Times,* Apr. 9, 1979.

MISCELLANEOUS

Abelson, Dr. Phillip H., and others, "Atomic Energy Submarine," Memorandum to the Director, Naval Research Laboratory, Mar. 28, 1946.

Cosby, Millard A., "Polaris—Deep Deterrent?" (unpublished manuscript).

Ferguson, R. L., "The Nuclear Challenge," presented to Second Annual Conference on Liquid Metal Technology, Richland, Washington, Apr. 21, 1980.

Fuhrman, R. A., "Fleet Ballistic Missile System, Polaris to Trident," Von Karman lecture, Washington, D.C., February 1978. (Mr. Fuhrman is President of Lockheed Missiles and Space Company.)

Gunn, Ross, "The Early History of the Atomic Powered Submarine at the U.S. Naval Research Laboratory March 1939 to March 1946."

General Dynamics Corporation, Electric Boat Division, News Releases.

General Dynamics Corporation, Annual Report (various years).

Herold, Robert Cameron, "The Politics of Decision-Making in the Defense Establishment: A Case Study" (unpublished Ph.D. dissertation), 1969.

Holmes, W. J., "A Youngster's Log of the Midshipmen Cruise of 1919" (unpublished manuscript).

The Log, issues of 1976 through 1978, magazine published by midshipmen, U.S. Naval Academy.

Murrow, Edward R., Correspondence with H. G. Rickover (unpublished), courtesy of Mrs. Murrow. (The Murrow papers are collected at Tufts University.)

Neikirk, Frederick Richard, Jr., "Congress and the Procurement of the Nuclear Powered Surface Navy (1955–1963)" (unpublished M.A. dissertation), 1977.

Polmar, Norman, "Safety Aboard U.S. Nuclear-Propelled Ships" (unpublished manuscript), 1978.

————, "Supporting Study: US Strategic Missile Submarines," in Department of Defense Study "History of Strategic Arms Competition, U.S.–U.S.S.R., 1945–1972," 1975.

Rickover, H. G.; Dunford, J. M.; Rockwell, Theodore III; Barnes, W. C.; and Shaw, Milton, "Some Problems in the Application of Nuclear Propulsion to Naval Vessels," paper presented at the annual meeting of the Society of Naval Architects and Marine Engineers, New York, N.Y., Nov. 14–15, 1957.

Roddis, L. H., Jr., and Simpson, J. W., "The Nuclear Propulsion Plant of the USS *Nautilus* SSN–571," paper presented at the annual meeting of the Society of Naval Architects and Marine Engineers, New York, N.Y., Nov. 10–13, 1954.

Roth, Eli, "A Case of Shortened Lead Time," speech at the Industrial College of the Armed Forces, Washington, D.C., 1960.

Schacht, Kenneth G., "Forty Questions" (unpublished manuscript), 1980. (Questions asked about the Navy by a future midshipman.)

"Sentinel's History of Chicago Jewry 1911–1961" (unbound) (Chicago: Sentinel Press, 1961).

Shadrin, Nicholas George (pseudonym), "Development of Soviet Maritime Power," 2 vols. (unpublished Ph.D. dissertation), 1972.*

U.S. Atomic Energy Commission, Division of Naval Reactors and Naval Ship Systems Command, "The Naval Nuclear Propulsion Program" (various editions).

U.S. Atomic Energy Commission, semiannual reports (various editions).

* Dr. Shadrin was a Soviet naval officer.

U.S. Comptroller General, "Nuclear or Conventional Power for Surface Combatant Ships?" Mar. 21, 1977.

———, "The Department of Energy's Water-Cooled Breeder Program—Should It Continue?" Mar. 25, 1981.

U.S. Congressional Research Service, "Anti-Submarine Warfare (ASW): Some of the Issues and Some of the Programs," Sep. 12, 1979.

U.S. Naval Academy Alumni Association, *Register of Alumni* (various editions).

U.S. Naval Academy, "Register of Candidates for Admission to the U.S. Naval Academy as Midshipmen (1918 entries).

U.S. Navy, Bureau of Navigation, "Regulations Governing the Admission of Candidates to the U.S. Naval Academy," June 1918.

———, Bureau of Ships, "An Administrative History of the Bureau of Ships During World War II" (unpublished manuscript), 1952.

———, Booklets published for ship keel laying, launching, commissioning, and welcome aboard.

———, Deep Submergence Systems Review Group, "Summary Report," 1 March 1964.

———, General Board of the Navy, Hearings 1946–1954.

———, Naval Sea Systems Command, "Occupational Radiation Exposure from U.S. Naval Nuclear Propulsion Plants and Their Support Facilities," February 1979.

———, Naval Warfare Analysis Group, "Introduction of the Fleet Ballistic Missile into Service," 30 January 1957.

———, News Releases.

———, Office of the Chief of Naval Operations, "The Navy of the 1970 Era," Jan. 13, 1958.

———, Office of Naval Research, "Proposed Future Submarine Alternatives," 1978.

———, Submarine Officers' Conference, Minutes of various meetings, 1945–1950.

Acknowledgments

The following list includes many of the persons whom the authors interviewed or corresponded with on the subjects of Admiral Rickover and nuclear power. Others on the list provided material and research assistance to the authors, and several very kindly reviewed drafts of portions of the manuscript. In all, the authors spoke or corresponded with over two hundred individuals in the writing of this book. However, the following list is incomplete.

A large number of men and women—most of them in the Navy, the Naval Reactors Division of the Department of Energy, and the civilian power and shipbuilding industries—specifically requested that their names not appear as sources in this book. Also deleted are the names of a score of midshipmen at the U.S. Naval Academy and in Naval ROTC who have been interviewed by Admiral Rickover during the past two years. To those whose names do not appear the authors owe a special debt.

Dr. Dean Allard, head of the Navy's operational archives.
Capt. William P. Anderson, who, as commanding officer of the *Nautilus,* took her to the North Pole in 1958.
Comdr. Paul H. Backus, former executive secretary of the Navy Ballistic Missile Committee.
Capt. Joseph H. Barker, Jr., in NRB (1952–58) and project officer of the Shippingport nuclear plant.
Comdr. James Barrett, former Public Affairs Officer, Naval Academy; Public Affairs Officer, Navy Military Personnel Command (formerly Bureau of Naval Personnel).
Richard Bassett, Public Affairs Officer, Naval Sea Systems Command.
Capt. Edward L. Beach, first commanding officer of the *Triton,* naval aide to President Eisenhower, and author.
Lieut. August Billones, former nuclear submarine officer.
Clay Blair, Jr., author of *The Atomic Submarine and Admiral Rickover.*
Adm. Arleigh A. Burke, former Chief of Naval Operations.
Rear Adm. E. A. Burkhalter, submariner and Deputy Director of Naval Intelligence.
Robert A. Carlisle, head of Still Photography, Office of Navy Information.
Bernard F. Cavalante, Navy Operational Archives.
Edward L. Cochrane, Jr., son of former Chief of Bureau of Ships.
Rear Adm. David M. Cooney, Chief of Navy Information.
Capt. John W. Crawford, Jr., in NRB (1950–63) and selected by Secretary of the Navy Nitze to succeed Rickover.
Margaret "Dixie" Davis, secretary to Admiral Rickover (1949–60).

721

Vice Adm. James H. Doyle, Jr., former commanding officer of the *Bainbridge,* Deputy CNO (Surface Warfare).

Rear Adm. Edward Ellsberg, first in the USNA Class of 1912, a master diver and salvage officer, and author.

Rear Adm. Albert J. Fay, who served on Okinawa when Rickover was there.

John M. Fluke, innovative engineer who served in the electrical section of BuShips during World War II.

Gordon Freedman, ABC Television.

Dr. Norman Friedman, naval analyst and author.

Capt. Clark M. Gammell, Public Affairs Officer, U.S. Naval Academy.

Vice Adm. Charles D. Griffiths, former Deputy CNO (Submarine Warfare).

Vice Adm. Frederick J. Harlfinger, former Director, Submarine Warfare (OP-311) and former Director of Naval Intelligence.

Capt. James C. Hay, former commanding officer, Naval Submarine Base, New London, Conn.

Dr. Richard Hewlett, Historian, Department of Energy, and author of *Nuclear Navy.*

Comdr. James M. Hingson, former public-information specialist, Navy Department.

Capt. Wilfred J. Holmes (USNA Class of 1922), submariner, engineer, intelligence specialist, and author.

Rear Adm. Ralph K. James, former Chief of the Bureau of Ships.

Rear Adm. John D. H. Kane, Jr., Director of Naval History.

Dr. Robert Kay, who was in NRB.

Comdr. Edward E. Kintner, who was in NRB (1950–66).

Capt. Stuart D. Landersman, former Executive Director, Pacific Fleet Tactical Training, and surface warfare officer *par excellence.*

Capt. Richard B. Laning, first commanding officer of the *Seawolf.*

Professor Allan B. Lefcowitz, English Department, U.S. Naval Academy.

Dr. Reuven Leopold, formerly senior ship-design engineer of the Navy.

Dr. E. Raymond Lewis, Librarian of the House of Representatives.

Miles Libbey, one of the original Rickover Oak Ridge group, who was in NRB (1946–50).

William S. Lind, Congressional staff assistant.

Donald Lynch, Congressional staff assistant.

Vice Adm. William P. Mack, former Superintendent, U.S. Naval Academy and former Chief of Navy Information.

Patty A. Maddocks, Photographic Librarian, U.S. Naval Institute.

Dr. John T. Mason, Director of Oral History, U.S. Naval Institute.

Vice Adm. Kinnard R. McKee, submariner and former Superintendent, U.S. Naval Academy.

John Mercer, former enlisted submariner.

Rear Adm. George H. Miller, naval strategist and planner.

Rear Adm. Robert L. Moore, Jr., in electrical section of BuShips during World War II and at one time designated successor to Rickover as head of NRB.

Timothy S. Murphy, *The Day* (New London).

Capt. William M. Nicholson, former Project Manager, Deep Submergence Systems Project.

Paul H. Nitze, former Secretary of the Navy and former Under Secretary of Defense.

Comdr. Edward J. Ortlieb, former submariner and Navy personnel expert.

Dr. D. A. Paolucci, former submariner and defense analyst.

Mrs. Jane Price, assistant librarian, U.S. Naval Academy.

Fred Rainbow, Departments Editor, Naval Institute *Proceedings.*

Comdr. Carleton J. Robertson, submariner.

Capt. Joseph P. Rockwell, former commanding officer, U.S.S. *Finch.*

Louis H. Roddis, Jr., one of the original Rickover Oak Ridge group NRB (1946–55).

Dr. David A. Rosenberg, historian and biographer of Admiral Burke.

Capt. Eli B. Roth, early project manager of the Pressurized Water Reactor and in NRB (1948–56).

Gordon Rule, Navy contracts expert.

Jean Ruthoe, librarian, Nuclear Regulatory Commission.

Capt. K. G. Schacht, who served with Rickover in the *New Mexico.*

Rear Adm. Tazewell T. Shepard, Jr., naval aide to President Kennedy.

Robert Shogan, *Los Angeles Times.*

Capt. Robert B. Sims, former public affairs officer for the Polaris-Poseidon project and Deputy Chief of Navy Information.

Frank Slatenchik, former chief counsel, House Committee on Armed Services.

Capt. Roy C. Smith III, Editor, *Shipmate,* Naval Academy Alumni Association.

Capt. 1/rank G. I. Svjatov, Soviet submarine designer and strategic analyst.

Rear Adm. David S. Swart.

Capt. Joseph K. Taussig.

Hoyle A. Taylor, public-affairs specialist, BuPers.

Dr. Edward Teller.

Rear Adm. William Thompson, former Chief of Navy Information.

Capt. George W. Vahsen, former Commander, Naval Submarine School.

Capt. Kenneth Wade, former public-information officer for the Polaris-Poseidon project and former Deputy Chief of Navy Information.

Lieut. Michael Wade, former nuclear submarine officer.

Chancy Whitney, senior civilian engineer in the electrical section of BuShips during World War II.

James R. Woolsey, former Under Secretary of the Navy.

Adm. Elmo R. Zumwalt, former Chief of Naval Operations.

The authors have also drawn extensively on interviews and discussions with several persons who assisted in the writing of Mr. Polmar's previous books *Death of the Thresher* and *Atomic Submarines,* among them:

Dr. Philip Abelson, who designed the first atomic submarine power plant.

Rear Adm. Dean Axene, first commanding officer of the submarine *Thresher.*

Rear Adm. Roy S. Benson, former Commander, Submarine Force, Pacific Fleet.

Vice Adm. James F. Calvert, first commanding officer of the *Skate.*

Rear Adm. Lawrence R. Daspit, former Deputy Commander, Submarine Force, Atlantic Fleet.

Adm. Ignatius Galantin, former head of the Polaris project.

Vice Adm. Elton W. Grenfell, former Commander, Submarine Force, Atlantic Fleet.

Dr. Ross Gunn, former head scientist, Naval Research Laboratory.

Capt. Robert D. McWethy, planner of the first submarine polar cruises.

Rear Adm. Armand M. Morgan, former head of the Ship Design Division, BuShips.

Vice Adm. John H. Nicholson, who commanded the *Sargo* on her remarkable polar cruises.

Vice Adm. William F. Raborn, Jr., former head of the Polaris project.

Capt. B. F. P. Samborne, first commanding officer of the first British nuclear submarine, H.M.S. *Dreadnought.*

Rear Adm. Levering Smith, former technical director and later head of the Polaris project.

Rear Adm. Lewis L. Strauss, former Chairman of the Atomic Energy Commission. Hellmuth Walter, designer of the Walter closed-cycle submarine propulsion plant. Capt. Don Walsh, former deputy director of Navy laboratories and first officer-in-charge of the bathyscaphe *Trieste*.

The authors also received assistance in their efforts from researchers Constance Allen, Maria Hildeman, Beverly Polmar, Deborah Polmar, Dan Strets and Jill Shapiro.

Index

[Military officers are generally indexed at the highest rank appearing in the text.]

Abbot, 370
Abelson, Philip H., 119, 120, 121, 122, 125, 128, 135, 517, 518n.
Adams, Sherman, 171
Addabbo, Joseph P., 465–466
"Admirals' Revolt" (postwar unification controversy), 251, 362
Aegis weapon system, 480–481
  in *Long Beach* update, 346
  in nuclear ships, 346, 397, 398
  in gas-turbine ships, 346, 397
Ahearne, John F., 616–617
Aiken, George D., 244
Aircraft carrier debates, 250–257, 346–347, 377–381, 383–393, 398–399
Aircraft carriers, origins of nuclear program, 252–255, 260–264, 602, 606–607; *see also* Reactors
Aircraft nuclear program, 252–255, 602–603, 613
Air Force, 116, 133, 135n., 472, 536, 538, 547
  Rickover recommends abolishing, 471, 565, 569, 625
  Zumwalt lists as enemy, 479
  See also Aircraft nuclear program
Albacore, 354, 542
Alexander, Roy, 191
Alexander Hamilton, 333
Alice's Adventures in Wonderland, 478
Aluminaut, 438

America, 381, 383
American Education—A National Failure, 595–597
Amorosi, Alfred, 124
Anderson, Clinton P., 18, 166, 212, 216, 217, 218, 220, 244, 299, 468–470
Anderson, Adm. George W., 383–384, 473, 557, 655
Anderson, Robert B., 200, 203
Anderson, William, 517
Anderson, Capt. William R., 168–178, 210, 336, 357, 457, 642
Anderson, Mrs. William R., 176, 177, 210
Andrew Jackson, 533
Annapolis. *See* Naval Academy
Anti-Semitism
  in Russia and Poland, 27–28
  in Navy, 49, 64, 159–160
  in Naval Academy, 50, 51–53, 58, 59
  and Rickover, 189, 192, 194, 201, 213, 637
Arco. *See* National Reactor Test Station
Arctic, 63
Argonne, 61
Arktika, 178, 562
Ash, Roy L., 503–504
Aspin, Les, 570–571
Atomic Energy Commission, 125n., 127, 129, 131, 132, 137, 138, 143, 148, 150, 151

Atomic Energy Commission (*cont.*)
  attacked by Mills, 140–141, 142
  Rickover's position with, 237
  abolished, 245
*The Atomic Submarine and Admiral
  Rickover,* 33, 62, 205, 213, 458,
  459, 636
Augusta, 86, 87, 88
Aurand, Vice Adm. Evans P., 170,
  537
Automation in submarines, 403–405,
  413

Bagley, Adm. Worth H., 337
Bainbridge, 263, 285, 318, 320, 337,
  349, 377, 394
  design and construction, 260, 372
  operations, 264, 384
Baker, Howard, 404, 461
Baldwin, Hanson W., 517, 557
Baldwin, Vice Adm. Robert, 655
Baltimore, 579–580
Bancroft Hall, 41, 42, 43, 44, 47, 54,
  269, 338, 474
Barbel, 366
Barker, Capt. Joseph H., Jr., 156,
  639
  on *New Mexico,* 84, 611
  project officer at Shippingport,
  601, 603, 607, 609–612, 615
Barker, Midn. Joseph H., III, 269
Barnes, Willis, 156
Barrett, Capt. Ernest R., 335
Bartenbach, Cmdr. G. N., 239
Baten Ko. *See* Okinawa
Bates, William H., 242, 244, 372
Baton Rouge, 645–646
Beach, Capt. Edward L., 50, 138,
  153, 157, 188, 195, 200, 336,
  457, 549, 663
  author, 138, 195, 369, 424
  presidential naval aide, 156,
  170
  commands *Triton,* 319, 330–331,
  336, 364, 367–369, 424
  describes Rickover, 447
Beach, Mrs. Edward L., 367

Beardon, Machinist's Mate 1/class
  Richard T., 169
Bednowicz, Comdr. Eleonore Ann,
  647–648, 649
Behrens, Vice Adm. William W.,
  336, 337
Bennehoff, Lt. Comdr. O. R., 80
Bennett, Charles, 229–230, 443,
  570–571
Bennett, Robert S., 513
Bennett, Wallace, 244
Bennington, 294
Benson, Rear Adm. Roy S., 461
Beshany, Vice Adm. Phillip A.,
  337
Bible, Alan, 244
"Bird Hatcher," 270, 284, 640
Black, Hugo L., 512
Blackwell, Robert, 615
Blades, Comdr. Todd, 260–261
Blair, Clay, Jr., 19, 33, 39, 42, 88,
  104, 188–193, 195–196, 205,
  210, 213, 458, 516
  writes *The Atomic Submarine and
  Admiral Rickover,* 199–200, 455,
  636
Blizard, Everitt P., 124
Blue, Rear Adm. Victor, 218
"Bobby's War College." *See* Naval
  Academy Preparatory School
Bohannan, Capt. William L., 413
Bonner, Herbert C., 614
Boorstin, Daniel J., 522
Borden, William L., 197, 198
Boston, 580
Bowen, Vice Adm. Harold G., 118,
  123, 127–128, 135, 662
Bowers, Jack L., 508
Breeder reactors. *See* Reactors
Brennan, William J., Jr., 512
The Brethren, 512
Brewster, William J., 80
Brezhnev, L. I., 569
"Broom closet," 272–273
Broad, Richard, 461
Brown, Harold
  as Director, Defense Research

and Engineering, 264–265, 385,
407, 579
as Secretary of Defense, 346–347,
392–393, 398, 413, 415, 578,
579, 629
Bryan, Vice Adm. Clarence R., 345,
410
Buckley, Rear Adm. John D., 477
Buckley, William F., 195
Bureau of Ships
established, 96, 97–98
early interest in nuclear power,
120–134, 137
Nuclear Power Branch established, 142, 146, 147, 154
Burke, Adm. Arleigh A., 194, 314,
320, 326, 366, 378
as CNO, 167, 171, 255, 299, 362,
379, 381, 474, 554, 555, 557,
565, 623, 637, 641, 643
supports nuclear ships, 255–256,
258, 258, 362, 363, 377, 382
and Polaris, 256, 472, 473, 535,
538–549, 564
views on nuclear submarines, 359,
371
Burris, Capt. Harry, 96, 124, 125,
127, 130
Busch, Harald, 164
Bush, Vannevar, 139
Byng, Adm. John, 463n.
Byrd, Harry, 244
Byrd, Rear Adm. Richard E., 218

Caldwell, James, 395, 662
California (battleship), 75, 100
California (missile cruiser), 242, 399,
501–502, 508
Calvert, Vice Adm. James, 285, 336
as Superintendent of Naval Acad-
emy, 269–270, 307–308, 337
as Rickover successor, 659
Cannon, Clarence, 181, 256, 378,
586
Canopus, 89, 91
"Captain Hymo," 312
Carl Vinson, 505, 507

Carney, Adm. Robert B., 136, 155,
254, 255, 537, 538, 565, 662
Carpenter, Comdr. M. Scott,
440–441
Carr, Rear Adm. Kenneth, 502–503,
508
Carr, William, 589
Carter, Lt. James Earl, Jr., 667
as President, 220, 342–347, 350,
385n., 392–393, 398, 413, 529,
578–580, 630
Rickover interview, 267, 341–342
nuclear assignment, 357–358,
462–463, 621
defends Trident, 564
Carter, Mrs. James E., 243, 344, 345,
579
Carver, George Washington, 521
"Cat Futch," 333–334
Cavalla, 426
Celebrezze, Anthony J., 596
CGN-41 (Arkansas), 505, 508, 511
Chafee, John H., 470
Chalk River reactor incident, 621
Chapman, Robert M., 349–350, 413
Charleston, 62, 63
Chatham, Lt. Ralph E., 348–349
"Chicken-horseburger sandwich,"
416
Churchill, Winston S., 224, 239
Cincinnati, 344n.
Cisler, Walker L., 604–605, 619–620
Civilian nuclear power, 608–615,
630–633, 666
start of program, 157–158,
253–254, 603–607
See also Reactors, Shippingport,
Three Mile Island
Clark, Comdr. David C., 339
Clark, Rear Adm. David H., 147,
184, 186
Claytor, H. Graham, 413–414
Clements, William P., Jr., 502–503,
506–510
Cochino, 425n.
Cochrane, Rear Adm. Edward L.,
103, 104, 123

Cochrane, Lt. Richard L., 103
Cold Is the Sea, 369, 424
Cole, W. Sterling, 156, 176n.,
    605–606
Columbia University, 74–78, 80, 82,
    97
Combustion Engineering Co.,
    241–242, 402
Connally, John B., 219, 455, 594
Connally, Tom, 244
Constellation, 255, 261
Constitution, 241, 648
Cooley, Capt. Hollis, 118
Cooney, Rear Adm. David M.,
    523–524, 529
Corcoran, Thomas G., 502–503, 505,
    511–513
Cosmas, Graham A., 528
Costagliola, Francesco, 245
"Coventry," 51
Craven, John P., 435–438, 441
Crawford, Rear Adm. George C.,
    298
Crawford, Capt. John W., Jr., 156
    as Rickover successor, 657–660
Culver, John C., 483–484
CVA-67. *See John F. Kennedy*

Dace, 626
Dale, 184
Daniel, Rear Adm. Joseph C., 259
Daniels, Josephus, 51
Daniels Pile. *See* Reactors
Daniels, Midn. Worth Bagley, 51
Dart, Charles E., 509
David W. Taylor Naval Ship
    Research and Development
    Center, 526
Davis, Dixie, 200
Davis, Vincent, 537
DDG-47. *See* Aegis weapon system
Dean, Gordon, 150, 253, 603
Dedrick, Comdr. Walter, 368–369
Deep Submergence Systems Project,
    435–444
Delaware, 51
Dempsey, John J., 244

Denby, Edwin, 60
Denfeld, Adm. Louis D., 145, 146,
    147, 251, 663
Dennison, Adm. Robert L., 176n.,
    194
De Poix, Vice Adm. Vincent P., 337,
    386
    commands *Enterprise,* 261, 262,
    319
Derthick, Lawrence G., 590–591
Devereux, Brig. Gen. James, 193
Dewey (dry dock), 92
Dewey (frigate), 285
Dewey, Adm. George, 68, 92, 463
Dewey, John, 588, 590, 592, 593
Dick, Lt. Raymond H., 124, 127,
    134, 138, 156, 192, 194–195,
    198, 202, 493, 639
    briefs Blair, 190–191
Diesel, John P., 505, 507, 513, 653
Dirksen, Everett, 241, 244
DLGN-36. *See California*
DLGN-37. *See South Carolina*
"DOPE," 126
Dos Passos, John, 515
Doyle, Arthur Conan, 225n.
Doyle, Vice Adm. James, 345
Drain, Capt. John, 524
Dreyfus case, 213
Drug problems, 334–335
Dulles, John Foster, 202, 254,
    592–593
Duncan, Francis, 140, 192, 457, 458,
    541
Dunford, Capt. James, 124, 134,
    140, 156, 157, 160, 192, 373,
    605, 659
    at Zumwalt interview, 276, 277,
    278, 280, 281, 282
Dwight D. Eisenhower, 390, 391
Dworshak, Henry, 244, 380

Eberle, Adm. Edward W., 69
Eccles, Rear Adm. Harry E., 96
Edstrom, Ed, 642
Education and Freedom, 519, 585,
    586, 588, 591

Edwards, Jack, 578
Einstein, Albert, 48, 119
Eisenhower, Dwight D. (and Administration), 19, 49, 116, 153, 197, 200, 202, 204, 212, 214, 222, 242, 253, 254, 256, 325, 359, 362, 367, 368, 378, 380, 535, 537, 546, 547, 553, 586, 589, 592, 602, 603, 605, 607, 609, 610, 613
and *Nautilus,* 171, 175, 209, 210
on board nuclear submarines, 344n., 358
cuts defense spending, 378
delays spending nuclear carrier funds, 380
Eisenhower, Mrs. Dwight D., 155, 156, 176n., 614
Electric Boat, 114, 146, 146n., 147, 149, 154, 158, 159, 167, 188, 327, 360, 373, 374, 426, 488, 493–498, 500, 510n., 544, 546, 580–581, 612, 632, 645, 654, 664
and submarines (*q.v.*): *Nautilus,* 151, 155–156, 164, 186, 189, 212, 326; *Lafayette,* 218; *Glenard P. Lipscomb,* 243; *Seawolf,* 355, 560; *Skate,* 360; *Triton,* 365; *Skipjack,* 365, 369; *Sturgeon,* 374; *George Washington,* 369; *Tullibee,* 402; NR-1, 438, 441, 442; *Trident,* 570–573, 575–581
and studies, 403, 415
origins, 492
claims against, 508, 510, 571–572
Ellis Island, 25
Ellsberg, Rear Adm. Edward, 48–50
Emerson, George B., 124
Eminent Americans: Namesakes of the Polaris Submarine Fleet, 516, 521, 524, 527, 644
Engineering duty, as career, 90–91, 198–199
Enterprise, 296, 318, 336, 377, 378, 386, 507
Congressional hearings aboard,

220, 262–263, 383, 385
design and construction, 255, 258, 261–262, 372, 379, 389
commanding officers, 261, 298, 319–320, 337, 338, 394–395, 398, 479–480, 508
operations, 262, 264, 384, 388–389, 390
Boston port visit, 623–625
Enthoven, Alain, 382–383
Erb, Capt. Leonard, 435
Estes, Maj. K. W., 349
Ethan Allen, 494, 545, 548, 549
collision, 335
Evans, Lt. Comdr. Donald S., 88, 89

Fahy, Rear Adm. Edward J., 442
Farrell, Charles, 493
Farrin, Rear Adm. James M., Jr., 327, 497
Fast vs. quiet debate, 405–409. *See also Glenard P. Lipscomb;* GUPPY; *Los Angeles;* Trident
"Fat letter," 455–456
Fay, Vice Adm. Albert J., 110
Fay, Paul, 455
on Rickover successor, 658–659
Fechteler, Adm. William F., 186, 565
Fermi, Enrico, 118
Fife, Vice Adm. James, 193
Finback, 332–334
Finch, 20, 21, 86–89
described, 86
sunk, 89
Finney, John W., 517
Fisher, Alvan, 43
Fleet Ballistic Missile. *See* Polaris missile program
Fleger, Philip A., 615
Fleming, Arthur S., 586
Fletcher, Adm. Frank J., 83–84
Flood, Daniel J., 231–232, 240–241, 246, 305
Fluke, John, 102, 107, 109
Fogarty, John E., 590
Forand, Aime, 244

Ford, Gerald R.
  as President, 220, 293, 392, 578
  as Representative, 344n., 379
Forrestal, 255, 258
Forrestal, James V.
  as Secretary of the Navy, 123,
    128, 137, 662
  as Secretary of Defense, 139, 143
Foster, John, 407–409
Franke, William B., 588
Franklin, 100–101
Franklin D. Roosevelt, 115
Frazer, Midn. John L., 53, 55
Frederika, Queen, 167
Freeman, Nelson W., 502–503
Frosch, Robert A., 410, 442
Fulton, 626
Fulton, Robert, 189

Gallantin, Adm. I. J., 500–501, 550
Gallery, Rear Adm. Daniel Vincent,
    51
Gamow, George, 121
Gas-turbine propulsion, 228–229,
    233–236
Gates, Thomas S., 210, 325, 378,
    380, 519, 544
Gato, 352
Geiger, Lawton, 601, 611
General Board, 123, 148–149, 662,
    663
General Dynamics Corp., acquires
    Electric Boat, 146n. *See also*
    Electric Boat
General Electric Co., 75, 123–124,
    126, 127, 145, 147, 297, 298,
    322, 359, 363, 364, 492, 655, 664
  and sodium reactor, 124, 137, 141,
    143, 144, 146, 150, 355
  and destroyer reactor, 125, 130,
    137, 257, 259
  and breeder reactor, 130, 131, 144
George Bancroft, 375
George Washington, 242, 369,
    544–546, 573
Georgia, 243

Germany
  submarines: Rickover discusses,
    82–83; development in World
    War I, 239, 240; in World War
    II, 161–162, 165, 166; technol-
    ogy to Soviets, 142, 353
  military leadership, 235
Gilinsky, Victor, 617–618
Gillette, Rear Adm. Norman C., 84
Glenard P. Lipscomb, 243, 405–409,
    482, 495, 568
Glomar Explorer, 400n.
Gooding, Rear Adm. Robert C.,
    476–477
Goodman, Louis, 55
Gold Star, 88
Gorshkov, Admiral of the Fleet of
    the Soviet Union Sergei G.,
    562, 563
Grechko, Marshal A. A., 239
Grenfell, Vice Adm. Elton W., 96,
    138, 141, 194, 337, 549, 663
Griffin, Vice Adm. Charles D., 625
Griffiths, Vice Adm. Charles H.,
    345, 648
Groves, Maj. Gen. Leslie, 120,
    122–123, 124, 134, 240, 549, 663
Gubser, Charles S., 517–518
Gunn, Ross, 118, 119, 120, 121, 122,
    125, 128, 135, 251, 517, 518n.
GUPPY submarines, 147, 354

Hafstad, Lawrence R., 132, 133, 143,
    145, 157, 252, 604
Hagerty, James, 171
Haldane, Lord, 225
Halibut, 363, 366, 368, 536
Hall, Rear Adm. Donald, 573–574
Halsey, Fleet Adm. William, 116
*Handbook of International Organi-
    zations in the Americas,* 641
Hansen, Ib S., 525–526
Harlfinger, Vice Adm. F. J., II, 93,
    469
Harnish, Capt. William H., 319
Harriman, W. Averell, 343

Hart, Gary, 392, 415
Harter, Isaac, 204
Harvey, Lt. Comdr. John W.
427–430
Hayward, Vice Adm. John T., 254
supports Rickover, 264, 386
criticizes Rickover, 340–341
heads Navy research, 370, 403,
543
Hayward, Adm. Thomas B., 415
Hébert, F. Edward, 645
Hébert, Mrs. F. Edward, 645
Hecker, Lt. Comdr. Stanley W.,
429–430
Helena, 103
Hendrie, Joseph M., 616–617
Herman, George, 530
Herold, Robert, 436–437
Heronemus, Comdr. William, 363
Hershey, Maj. Gen. Lewis B., 17
Hewlett, Richard G., 140, 192, 457,
458, 541
Hickenlooper, Bourke, 244
Hidalgo, Edward, 579–581
Hinchley, John, 156
Hingson, Comdr. James M., 188
Hinshaw, Carl, 241, 244
Hiss, Alger, 202
Hitler, Adolf, 224–225, 235
Holifield, Chet, 18, 213, 220, 244,
246, 262, 410
Holland, 155, 238
Holland, John P., 155, 242–243
Holloway, Vice Adm. James L., Jr.,
194, 203–204, 298
Holloway, Adm. James L., III
commands *Enterprise,* 298, 388,
479
as Chief of Naval Operations,
311, 334, 337, 345, 346, 398,
413, 415, 477, 480, 527, 659
Holmes, Sherlock, 225
Holmes, Capt. W. J., 23, 44, 45, 46,
53, 649
Holtzoff, Alexander, 520
Hooper, Vice Adm. Edwin B.,
110–111, 525, 527

Hoover, J. Edgar, 17, 197, 214,
460n.
Hopkins, John Jay, 492–493
Hosmer, Craig, 244, 352, 384, 387,
630, 647
Hosmer, Mrs. Craig, 441
How the Battleship Maine *Was Destroyed,* 524–529
Hughes, Charles Evans, 61

Ianni, Francis A. J., 596
I-400, 364
Iltis, Theodore, 156
Ingraham, Samuel, 538
Introduction of the Fleet Ballistic
Missile into Service, 542
Isabel, 89
Isachenkov, Engineer-Adm. Nikolay
V., 563
Israel, Joseph, 47

Jackson, Henry M., 18, 19, 168, 198,
200, 201, 202, 203, 206, 212,
220, 221, 368, 390, 605
Jackson, Richard, 276, 277, 278
Jacksonville, 654
James, Rear Adm. Ralph K.,
109–110, 187
as Chief BuShips, 262, 325–327,
370, 467–468, 497, 548, 666
compares nuclear and non-nuclear ships, 381
on *Thresher* loss, 430–431,
433–434
on *Savannah,* 614
on Mrs. Rickover christening submarines, 644
on Rickover successor, 656–657,
660
Japan, submarine design, 364
Javits, Jacob, 213, 214
Jenkins, Thomas, 244
Jenks, Lt. Shepherd M., 173–174
Jews in Navy, 47–51
See also Anti-Semitism
John F. Kennedy, 242, 246, 389, 392

John F. Kennedy (cont.)
  debate over nuclear propulsion,
    384–388
Johnson, Edwin, 244
Johnson, Lyndon Baines
  as President, 17, 18, 219–220, 437
  as Senator, 214, 217, 220, 244
Johnston, Vice Adm. Means, Jr., 475
Joint Committee on Atomic Energy,
    156, 166, 176n., 194, 197, 198,
    206, 208, 209, 211–212, 220,
    238, 241, 242, 244, 245, 246,
    247, 252, 259, 295, 299, 352,
    371, 379, 380, 558–559, 568,
    574–575, 602, 613, 625, 662
  Rickover's first time before, 147
  meets on board nuclear ships,
    167, 207, 216, 220, 262–263,
    383, 385, 386–388, 461
  composition of, 244, 245
  abolished, 248
  hearing on *Thresher* loss, 432–435
Jones, Rear Adm. Claude, 105
Jones, John Paul, 181, 218, 318
  Rickover attacks upon, 340
Jordan, Hamilton, 343

K-class submarines, 354, 402
Kaplan, Capt. Leonard, 40, 47, 50,
    51, 53, 55, 58–59, 90, 107, 194
Kasatonov, Admiral of the Fleet
    Vladimir A., 238–239
Kaufman, Irving R., 201
Kaufman, Vice Adm. Robert Y., 345
Kefauver, Estes, 202
Keitel, Gen. Wilhelm, 235
Kelln, Rear Adm. Albert L.,
    573–574
Kempff, Rear Adm. C. S., 76
Kennedy, John F. (and Administra-
    tion), 242
  as Senator, 213
  as President, 219, 344n., 381, 383,
    388, 401, 579, 592, 593, 613,
    643, 658
  and Polaris, 533, 547
  considers Rickover for Commis-

sioner of Education, 585,
    594–595, 596–598
Kennedy, Richard, 616–617
Keppel, Francis, 597
Khrushchev, Nikita S., 222, 368,
    533, 553, 556, 562, 586
Khrushchev Remembers, 553
Kidd, Adm. Isaac C., Jr., 452, 504
Kiddler, 68
Kilday, Paul J., 244
Killian, James R., Jr., 537
Kimball, Dan, 191, 200
King, Fleet Adm. Ernest J., 49, 107,
    120, 148, 218, 317
  reaches retirement age, 219
Kintner, Comdr. Edwin E., 19, 152,
    156, 459
  at Arco prototype, 152, 493–494,
    657
  at Mare Island, 360–361, 363
  proposes Rickover biography, 515
  as Rickover successor, 657, 660
Kirov, 562
Kissinger, Henry, 518
Kissinger, Ralph, as Rickover suc-
    cessor, 657
Kitty Hawk, 255, 261, 389
Knolls Atomic Power Laboratory,
    124, 143
  See also General Electric Com-
    pany
Korth, Fred H., 219, 383, 384,
    385–386, 427, 624
  as Rickover successor, 656–657
Knowland, Bill, 244
Kotov, Engineer-Adm. Pavel G., 563
Kozlov, F. R., 553, 555
Kurchatov, I. V., 562
Kurrus, Engineman 1/class John B.,
    169
Kyes, Robert M., 603

L. Mendel Rivers, 243
Lacy, Rear Adm. Paul L., Jr., 410
Lady Chatterley's Lover, 459–460
Lafayette, 218, 547
La Guardia, Fiorello, 78

Laird, Melvin R., 220, 243, 390, 391, 470, 567
La Jolla, 654
Lamb, Lt. (j.g.) Richard G., 452–453
Laney, Robert, 156, 373
Langley, 46
Laning, Capt. Richard B., 121, 336, 342, 522–523, 594, 640, 665
  on Rickover interviews, 286–287
  commands *Seawolf,* 298, 356–358
  on automation, 403–404
  on submarine quieting, 405
Lascara, Vice Adm. Vincent A., 156, 507–508
Laurence, William L., 119–120
La Vallette, 61, 62, 63–69, 71–72, 389
Lawrence, D. H., 459
Leahy, Fleet Adm. William D., 69
Le Baron, Robert, 603
Leggett, Rear Adm. Wilson D., Jr., 204
Lehman, Herbert H., 161, 191, 193, 202
Lehman, John H., 510, 580
Leighton, Comdr. David T., 156, 236, 440
  in contract negotiations, 496, 501–502, 505, 512
Lenin, 261, 552–555, 558, 561
Leninsky Komsomol, 556
Lerner, Max, 515
Levi, Edward, 509
Levy, Commo. Uriah P., 47
Lewine, Frances, 212
Lewis, E. Grey, 511–512
Libbey, Comdr. Miles A., 124, 156, 190, 639
Libby, Vice Adm. Ruthven E., 194
Life magazine, 186, 187, 188, 189, 191, 212, 213, 515, 516
Lilienthal, David E., 142, 204, 607–608
  on Rickover's reflections, 666
Lincoln, Abraham, 241
Lindley, Ernest K., 522

Lipscomb, Glenard P., 235, 242, 243
Lockwood, Vice Adm. Charles, 122, 655
Long, Adm. Robert L. J., 337, 345
Long Beach, 276, 318, 319, 346, 377, 562, 659
  design and construction, 257–261, 372
  operations, 264, 384
Lorenz, Lt. Comdr. W. J., 78, 80
Los Angeles, 405–416, 421–422, 443, 482, 560, 567, 568, 571–572, 578, 580
  visit by President Carter, 344, 579
  alternative to Trident, 577
Lott, Arnold S., 104
Low, Rear Adm. Francis, 655
Lucke, Charles, 74
The Lucky Bag, 53, 54–58
Lyman, Lt. Comdr. John S., 427
Lyon, Waldo, 168, 172–174, 424–425

Mackenzie, John, 509
MacNeice, Louis, 224
McCarthy, Joseph R., 201–202, 204, 522
McCone, John A., 614
McCormack, John W., 213, 623–624
McCormick, Mike, 574–575
McDonald, Adm. David L., 385, 473, 481, 565
McElroy, Neil, 544
McFall, John, 568
McGovern, George, 392
McKee, Rear Adm. Andrew I., 96, 146
McKee, Vice Adm. Kinnaird, 82
  Superintendent of Naval Academy, 307, 311–312, 338
McLain, Stuart, 604
McMahon, Brien, 194, 197, 198, 211, 244, 250, 252, 602
McMurrin, Sterling M., 596
McNamara, Robert S., 233, 235, 257, 265, 381, 382–383, 392, 393, 395, 401, 436–437, 482, 529, 547, 564–565, 592, 665

McNamara, Robert S. (*cont.*)
  on firing Rickover, 17, 18
  opposes nuclear carriers, 246,
    384–387
  supports nuclear carriers, 289–391
  initiates STRAT-X study, 565
McNeil, Wilfred J., 546
McShane, Rear Adm. R. E., 147
McWethy, Comdr. Robert D., 168
Mack, Vice Adm. William P.,
    308–309, 310, 311
Mafia. *See* Rickover Mafia
Mahon, George H., 225, 234–235,
    370, 383
Maine, 524–529
Major Fleet Escort Study, 394–396
Makow, Poland, 27
Malinin, B. M., 562
Manganaro, Rear Adm. Francis, 508
Manhattan Project (Manhattan En-
    gineering District), 120, 122,
    123, 124, 125n., 126, 127, 129,
    131, 139, 141, 254, 603, 662
  compared to nuclear submarine
    program, 549–551
Mann, David, 413–415, 577
Manson, Comdr. Frank A., 538
Marshall, Ray, 496
Massachusetts Institute of Technol-
    ogy, 124, 537, 597, 658
Masters, Ruth D. *See* Rickover,
    Ruth Masters
Michaelis, Adm. Frederick H.,
    319–320, 338, 345, 508
Michelson, Lt. Comdr. Allen A., 48
Michigan, 243
Middendorf, J. William, 398, 477
Midway, 98
Mikasa, 648
Military Academy, 227–228, 310
Military Liaison Committee, 134,
    135n., 145
Miller, Rear Adm. George H., 538,
    565, 568–569, 573
Miller, Richard I., 591–592
Milligan, Robert W., 68–69
Millikin, Eugene, 244

Mills, Vice Adm. Earle W., 96–97
  in BuShips, 99, 104, 107, 108, 109,
    120, 125, 127
  as Chief of BuShips, 129, 130,
    131, 134, 135, 137, 138, 139,
    140, 141, 142, 143, 178, 183,
    254, 549, 655, 656, 661, 662,
    663–664, 667
  retires, 144
Mississippi, 345, 347
Missouri, 115
Mitchell, Brig. Gen. William, 70,
    213, 214, 218, 225, 319
Mitzler, Alfred J., 62
Momsen, Vice Adm. Charles B.,
    141, 663
Moore, Rear Am. Robert Lee, Jr.
  selected as Rickover successor,
    183–188, 659, 660
  role in nuclear program, 354, 355,
    326–327, 360, 427
Moorer, Adm. Thomas H., 270, 329,
    473, 565, 664
Morgan, Rear Adm. Armand M.,
    96, 142, 144, 427, 548–549
Morse, Robert, 436
Morse, Mrs. Robert, 442
Mumma, Rear Adm. Albert G.
  in nuclear program, 124, 125, 127,
    128, 131, 134, 142, 144, 145
  as Chief of BuShips, 209, 211,
    259, 323, 325, 359, 378, 655
  and Polaris, 541
Murphy, Charles J. V., 191
Murray, Thomas E., 151, 197, 252,
    602, 605, 607
Murrow, Edward R., 514–516,
    521–522

Nader, Ralph, 491, 629
Najarian, Thomas, 627
Narwhal, 405, 482
National Archives, 525
National Education Association
    (NEA), 589, 591, 596, 599
National Reactor Test Station, 149,
    151, 255, 258, 302, 322, 338,

339, 340, 341, 342, 343, 361,
493–494, 515, 603, 604, 612,
621, 657, 660
National Security Agency, 525
National Security Council, 229, 537,
603
National War College, 473, 588
Nautilus (1954), 69, 179, 183, 191,
194, 196, 198, 203, 207, 218,
238, 250, 269, 294, 297, 317,
328, 386, 401, 414, 422, 472,
486, 492, 515, 516, 541, 556,
603, 608, 610, 622, 630, 643,
648, 656, 657, 665, 666, 667
design and construction, 114, 150,
155, 157, 161–164, 186, 188,
189–190, 212, 217, 253, 255,
316, 326, 355, 358, 359, 360,
361, 555, 648, 660
officers and crew, 153, 167, 261,
295, 300, 318, 336, 338, 357,
403, 427, 436, 642, 659
launching, 155–156, 176n.
illustration, 163
trials and operations, 165–168,
168–179, 209, 353, 362, 366, 416
core (fuel) life, 167
Congressional hearings on board,
167, 207, 216–217, 262
problems, 171, 172, 369–370,
423–424
decommissioned, 178
Nautilus (Jules Verne), 113, 114
Naval Academy
entrance regulations, 37
Rickover at, 41–60, 74
Class of 1922, 20, 23, 37, 39,
41–60, 61, 88, 96, 107, 194, 479,
649
hazing in, 51, 52, 53–54
Jews and anti-Semitism in, 52, 53
Rickover attacks on, 305–311,
340, 480
Rickover "ransom note," 312
Naval Academy Preparatory School,
38–39
Naval Electronics Laboratory, 168

Naval History Division, 525, 527,
655
Naval Institute Press, 527. *See also*
Proceedings
Naval Intelligence. *See* Office of
Naval Intelligence
Naval Radiological Defense Labora-
tory, 161, 621
Naval Reactors Branch (NRB). *See*
Atomic Energy Commission;
Bureau of Ships
Naval Reactors Facility. *See* Na-
tional Reactor Test Station
Naval Research Laboratory, 118,
120, 128, 251, 355
Naval Surface Weapons Center, 525
Naval Telecommunications Com-
mand, 525
Naval War College, 82, 240, 340,
473, 480, 528–529, 539
help on *Maine* book, 525
review of *Maine* book, 527–528
Naval War College Review, 527–528
Naymark, Sherman, 156
Neff propulsion system, 117
Neikirk, Frederick, 380
"Nest-building," 284, 640–641
Nevada, 58–59, 72–74, 76, 77, 83
New Mexico, 83–85
New York City, 178
Nichols, Brig. Gen. Kenneth D.,
125–126, 129, 130
Nicholson, Harold, 81
Nicholson, Rear Adm. John H., 455
Nicholson, Capt. William M., 435,
438, 440–442, 455
Nimitz, 242, 346, 389–393, 399
Nimitz, Fleet Adm. Chester W.,
110–111, 115, 135, 136, 137,
138, 139, 145, 177, 251, 317,
549, 663
Nitze, Paul H., 215, 385, 394, 664
seeks to fire Rickover, 17–18, 659
supports gas-turbine propulsion,
232–236
on NR-1, 436–437
on Rickover's successor, 658

Nixon, Richard M., 202, 205, 210,
225, 344n., 504
trip to Soviet Union, 214, 222,
326, 552–555, 585
as President, 220, 221, 242, 390,
391, 450, 569
Nixon, Mrs. Richard M., 614
Norman, Lloyd, 200, 516, 518
NR-1, 353, 435–443, 445
NR-2, 443–444
Nuclear Navy, 192, 202–203, 602

Oak Ridge, Tenn., naval group at,
96, 113, 117, 120, 123, 125–134,
138, 143, 156, 192
Office of Legislative Affairs (Navy),
236–237, 309, 517–518
Office of Naval Intelligence, 142,
469–470, 524, 525, 552
Office of Naval Research, 123, 139,
404, 416, 519, 664
Ohio, 243, 567, 573, 576–577. *See
also* Trident
Okinawa, Rickover on, 20, 21–22,
23, 611
Olmsted, Ens. Jerauld L., 47, 53, 54,
57, 58, 194
Olson, Loren K., 262
On Watch, 215, 396, 474
Operation Sea Orbit, 249, 250, 377
Oppenheimer, J. Robert, 15, 117,
138, 197
Oregon, 68–69, 86
Osborn, Rear Adm. James B.,
545–546, 573

Paine, Roland, 454
Panay, 88
Paolucci, Dominic A., 413–414, 422
Parks, Rear Adm. Lewis S., 195, 196
Parsons, Rear Adm. William S., 20,
23, 123, 128, 135, 135n., 663
Pastore, John O., 18, 241, 265, 380,
384–385, 647
Patrick Henry, 242, 544, 546
Patterson, Robert, 123
Payne, Fred A., 565

Payne, Seth, 454
Pearson, Drew, 202, 455, 598
Peet, Vice Adm. Raymond E., 337,
386
commands *Bainbridge,* 264,
219–320
defends Rickover, 349
Pegram, George, 118
Pepper, Rice, and Elephants, 634–636
Percival, 62, 63
Percy, Charles H., 241
Permit, 335
PERT management tool, 551
Petersen, Vice Adm. Forrest S., 345,
394
Phelps, 284
Pierce, Joseph, 441, 571
Polaris missile program, 171, 218,
242, 256, 260, 263, 326, 329,
335, 337, 351, 373, 374, 375,
378, 379, 381, 382, 400–401,
424, 427, 435, 444, 454, 472,
477, 500, 521, 533, 535–551,
555, 556–565, 566, 567
proposed for cruisers, 258
start of program, 365, 537–540,
564
manning, 417–421, 548, 549, 550,
569, 573, 574, 625, 641, 644, 665
and Deep Submergence Systems
Project, 435–438
toy models of, 497
compared with nuclear submarine
program, 549–551
Polmar, Norman, 457
Port visits of nuclear ships, 178,
622–625
Poseidon missile program, 477, 482,
550, 565, 566, 567, 572, 573,
574, 575
Powell, John, 647–648
Prairie, 63
President Hoover, 92–93
Price, Gwilyn A., 604
Price, Melvin, 166, 220, 613
Price, Robert S., 525–526
Proceedings (U.S. Naval Institute)

articles by: Rickover, 82, 83, 421;
Bowen, 127–128; Roth, 158;
J. T. Hayward, 340–341; Craven, 441; G. E. Miller, 538
criticism of Rickover, 347–350
on effectiveness of nuclear submarines, 401–402
on diesel-electric submarines,
415–416
Proposed Future Submarine Alternatives, 416
Proxmire, William, 380, 504,
506–507, 509
Pueblo, 390
PWR reactor project, *see* Reactors

Queenfish, 374
Quieting of submarines, 369–370,
405. *See also* Fast vs. quiet de-
bate
Quiet submarine. *See Glenard P.
Lipscomb*

Raborn, Vice Adm. William F., 473,
535, 539–541, 544–551, 564
Radford, Adm. Arthur W., 337n.
Radioactive exposure, 626–628
Radkowsky, Alvin, 609, 637
Ramage, Vice Adm. Lawson P., 371,
624–625
Ramey, James T., 209
Reactors, 136–138, 140, 143–144,
149
aircraft, *see* Aircraft nuclear programs
advanced lightweight, 404–405,
416
breeder, 130, 140, 143, 604–605,
619–620, 630–632
civilian, *see* Civilian nuclear
power
core life, 167, 416
Daniels Pile, 124, 126, 128, 129,
131, 146
A1W/A2W/CVR (carrier), 157,
252–254, 255, 258, 602, 606–607
A4W (*Nimitz*), 389

D1G/D2G (frigate-cruiser),
259–260
SIR/S1G/S2G (*Seawolf*), 141,
143–144, 146, 149, 260,
355–359, 401, 404, 621
S1C/S2C (*Tullibee*), 402
S3G/S4G (*Triton*), 363–364, 368,
543
S5G (*Narwhal*), 405
S6G (*Los Angeles*), 405, 409
S8G (Trident), 411, 566–567, 568,
569, 574–575
S3W (*Skate, Halibut*), 360, 363
S4W (*Swordfish*), 360
S5W (*Skipjack*), 365, 369,
372–373, 401–402, 405, 409–410,
427–428, 543
STR/S1W/S2W (*Nautilus*),
143–144, 146, 149–150, 151–153,
162, 164, 361, 401, 493–494,
515, 603, 604
Reactor scram, 151n., 424, 434, 625
Reagan Administration, 420
Rectanus, Vice Adm. Earle F.,
495–496
Reed, Justice Stanley, 520
Reeves, Adm. Joseph M., 69–71, 83
Regulus missile, 355, 356, 360, 536,
566
for *Nautilus,* 166
for cruisers, 258
in nuclear submarine, 363
for *Triton,* 368–369
Relief, 73
Reston, James, 522, 586
Rhodes, John J., 231, 587
Richard B. Russell, 243
Rickover, Abraham (Eliachako), 27,
28, 29, 32, 34
Rickover, Fanny, 28, 29, 30
Rickover, Adm. Hyman G.
PERSONAL LIFE
emigrates to America, 25, 30
family and childhood, 27–35
question of birthdate, 29–30, 34,
37–38
school records, 30, 34–35

Rickover, Adm. Hyman G. (*cont.*)
   youth in Chicago, 31–37, 489
   "mantle-bearer" speech, 35–36
   religious preference, 40, 192, 635,
      637–638
   at Naval Academy, 41–60
   biography in *The Lucky Bag*
      (*q.v.*), 55
   at Columbia University, 74–75
   meets Ruth Masters, 75
   marries Ruth Masters, 80–81. *See
      also* Rickover, Ruth Masters;
      Robert Masters
   tour of Southeast Asia, 94–95
   other travels: Japan, 85; Burma
      Road, 96; Vatican City, 356;
      Soviet Union and Poland, 222,
      552–555
   health problems, 40, 71–72, 73,
      129, 143, 456, 460, 645–646
   wearing of uniform, 156, 205, 210,
      215, 216, 219, 322, 374, 450,
      453, 494, 583, 600
   marries Eleonore Ann Bednowicz
      (*q.v.*), 310
   at home, 636–637, 644, 649
   sense of humor, 460–461, 501
   NAVAL CAREER
   "father of atomic submarine," 15,
      374, 377, 647, 656 (claim dis-
      puted, 199, 517–518)
   promotion and retention issues,
      17–18, 19, 183, 187–205, 206,
      207, 218–221, 246, 268–269,
      350, 594, 605
   Okinawa, 20, 21–22, 110–111, 611
   commands *Finch,* 20–21, 86–90
   BuShips, 21, 22, 96–107, 326–327,
      354, 372
   commissioned ensign, 60
   La Vallette, 61–72, 389
   Percival, 62–63
   insults senior officer, 67–68
   Nevada, 72–74, 75, 76
   promotions: lieutenant (j.g.), 73;
      lieutenant, 75; lieutenant com-
      mander, 85, 86; commander,
   107; captain, 107; rear admiral,
      153, 605; vice admiral, 211, 214,
      219–220, 337, 379; admiral, 221
   saves sailor, 80
   postgraduate at Naval Academy,
      74
   at Columbia University, 74–75
   submarine duty, 75–81, 296, 371
   fails to get submarine command,
      81
   Naval War College course, 81
   Office of Inspector of Material,
      81, 371
   New Mexico, 83–85, 611
   changes to engineering duty,
      90–91 (EDO promotion poli-
      cies, 198–199)
   Cavite Navy Yard, 91–96
   heads BuShips electrical section,
      97–107
   Mechanicsburg, Pa., supply depot,
      108–110
   inspector general, Nineteenth
      ("mothball") Fleet, 116–117
   Oak Ridge, 125–134
   special assistant for nuclear mat-
      ters, 134
   proposes joint AEC-Navy nuclear
      program, 140
   BuShips liaison to AEC, 142
   reassembles Oak Ridge group,
      143
   first appearance before Joint
      Committee on Atomic Energy,
      147
   sets up land prototype reactor,
      149
   selects Electric Boat for *Nautilus,*
      146
   involvement in civilian nuclear-
      power program, 157–158,
      253–254, 257–261, 262–264,
      601–615, 630–633, 666
   snubbed by White House,
      176–177, 209, 210, 642
   chooses successor, 183–188, 326
   start of nuclear carrier program,

251–257, 262–264
start of cruiser-destroyer program,
    257–261, 262–264
excluded from Polaris program,
    537–551, 564
building of Shippingport reactor,
    609–612, 615
awards listed, 673–674
DEALING WITH CONGRESS
argues with Congressmen,
    240–241, 465–466, 483–484
"creature of Congress," 208
editing of testimony, 229–230
errors in testimony, 238–240,
    263–264, 366, 371–372, 386,
    414, 420–421, 470, 482, 560, 567
German translation, 224, 240
gets medal, 216–218
Report on Russia, 222–223
Rickover Lecture, 226, 244
use of quotations, 224–225
as witness, lobbyist, 147, 206–249,
    250, 309–310, 322–323, 325,
    329, 330, 346, 353, 366, 370,
    371–372, 376, 381, 385–386,
    391, 392, 393–394, 395, 398,
    400, 407, 409, 414–417, 421–
    422, 464–471, 478, 481–484,
    506, 507, 552, 554, 555, 557,
    558–562, 567, 574–575, 577–578,
    623, 627, 646–647, 665–666
See also Joint Committee on
    Atomic Energy; NR-1; Office of
    Legislative Affairs; Rogers, Paul
    G.; Three Mile Island
METHODS AND POLICIES
approach to shipbuilding: general
    practices, 149–150, 486–513;
    shipyard representatives, 476,
    486–489, 502; contracts and
    claims, 485, 490–513, 571–572;
    on building "horse turds," 506,
    507
Carter, relationship with as Presi-
    dent, 267, 341–345, 347
clashes within BuShips and Naval
    Sea Systems Command,

325–327, 360
emergence of "two navies," 161
"job offers," 212–213
"leaks" of information, 505, 517,
    518, 531
letters to supporters, 514, 516, 517
media: relationships with, 189,
    195–197, 212, 213, 330, 357,
    358, 454, 507, 516, 517, 518,
    521, 523, 529; criticism by,
    340–341, 347–350; Naval Reac-
    tors Branch, organization and
    control of, 156–157, 158–161,
    321–323, 327–332, 348–349, 360,
    361, 628–629
NR-1 program, 435–444
personnel: interviews, selection,
    training (nuclear), 179, 231,
    267–293, 294–323, 329–332,
    335–336, 417–421, 455–456,
    640–641; non-nuclear person-
    nel, 338–341
scope of responsibility, 665–666
sea trials, 165, 374–376, 442,
    654–655
Soviet attaché visit to nuclear
    submarine, 468–470
Three Mile Island, reaction to,
    615, 616–619, 632–633
Trident, relationship to, 564,
    566–581
work practices, 83–85, 93, 99–100,
    101–104, 106–107, 108–111, 117,
    199–200, 223, 322, 343, 449–
    462, 638–639
VIEWS AND OPINIONS
on admirals, 463–464, 466–467
on advanced reactor studies,
    404–405, 416
autobiographical comments, 23,
    651, 668
on disobeying orders, 232–235,
    321, 347
on education, 223, 235, 519, 529,
    531, 555, 585–600
on gas-turbine engine, 228–229
on golf, 71–72

Rickover, Adm. Hyman G.
    VIEWS AND OPINIONS (*cont.*)
    on John Paul Jones, 340
    on lawyers, 502–503, 505–506,
        510–512
    on leadership, 421
    "man who shouts," 651
    on Naval Academy, 305–311, 313,
        480
    on Naval War College, 480,
        528–529
    "nucleus of martyrs," 25, 102
    on oceanography, 289–290
    on officer rotation, 231
    on philosophy of life, 225, 633,
        638, 662
    on port visits of nuclear ships,
        178, 623–625
    on preference for Soviet subma-
        rines, 484, 560
    on primary duty to AEC, 321,
        385–386
    on PTA, 593, 594, 598
    on *Savannah,* 614
    on Soviet threat, 552, 557,
        558–562
    on submarines: automation,
        403–404; depth, 370–371; de-
        sign, 164, 166; extending patrols
        of, 420, 498; German, 82–83,
        239, 240; quieting, 369–370
    television: appearance on, 522,
        529–531; criticism of, 529
    on *Thresher* loss, 430–435
    WRITINGS
    books: *American Education—A
        National Failure,* 595–597; *Edu-
        cation and Freedom,* 519, 585,
        586, 588, 591; *Eminent Ameri-
        cans: Namesakes of the Polaris
        Fleet,* 516, 521, 524, 527, 644;
        How the Battleship Maine *Was
        Destroyed,* 524–529; *Swiss
        Schools and Ours: Why Theirs
        Are Better,* 592, 593–594,
        597–598, 642
    copyright dispute, 519–520, 527,
        592
    in *Proceedings,* 82, 83, 421
    speeches, 457, 518–519 (listed,
        710–711)
Rickover, Rachel (Ruchal), 28, 29,
    30, 32
Rickover, Robert Masters, 151, 190,
    514, 634, 636, 641, 642, 644
Rickover, Ruth Masters, 75, 82, 85,
    86, 151, 200, 202, 521, 592, 641,
    644, 649
    marries Rickover, 80–81, 637
    writings, 82, 94–95, 634–636,
        641–642
    ship christening controversy,
        176–177, 210, 364–365, 642–644
    in Southeast Asia, 634–636
    religion, 635
Rickover class, 568
Rickover Hall, 310, 221
Rickover "Mafia," 214, 215
"The Rickover Solution," 291–293
Ridgway, Ens. A. K., 63
Rivers, L. Mendel, 241, 381–382, 523
Robert E. Lee, 644
Roberts, Chalmers, 522
Robinson, O. Pomeroy, 146, 147, 493
Rockwell, Lt. Joseph P., 86–87, 89
Rockwell, Theodore, 624
Roddis, Comdr. Louis H., 113, 124,
    125, 129, 134, 137, 139, 140,
    156, 157, 199, 607, 639
    on civilian nuclear power, 632
    as Rickover successor, 657, 660
Rogers, Paul G., 627–628
Roosevelt, Franklin D., 69, 119, 139,
    219, 502, 519
Roosevelt, Theodore, 238, 377, 661
Roosevelt, Theodore, Jr., 60
Rosenberg, Anna, 201
Rosenberg, David A., 326
Rosenberg, Julius and Ethel, 201
Roth, Capt. Eli, 191, 621
    in NRB, 156, 157–158, 607
    breaking away from Rickover,
        158–161, 360

on Rickover's techniques, 161,
660–661
as Rickover successor, 657
Ruete, Edward S., 498
Rule, Gordon W., 484–485, 499–
504, 506–511, 570–571, 573
Run Silent, Run Deep, 138, 195
Russell, Adm. James, 177, 467–468,
549
Russell, Richard B., 244, 380

S-class submarines, 86, 93, 184
accidents, 49, 78, 79
S-9, 76
S-48, 76–81, 296, 371
Sabath, Adolph J., 36–37, 198
Saltonstall, Leverett, 199, 200, 203
Sampson, Rear Adm. William T., 68
Sandburg, Carl, 31
Sanders, Frank, 410
Sargent, Capt. Gerald, 390
Sargo, 176n., 328, 360, 361, 363
Savannah, 6, 613–615
Soviet visit to, 533
Scales, Rear Adm. Archibald H., 51,
52, 53, 57
Scamp, 369
Schacht, Kenneth G., 84–85
Schlesinger, James, 396, 574
Schnapper, M. P., 519–520, 527
Schwarz, Fred C., 588
Scorpion, 369, 544
loss, 444–445, 524, 526
Rickover letters to families, 640
Scram. *See* Reactor scram
Sculpin, 369
Seaborg, Glenn, 384, 385
Seadragon, 176n., 336, 360, 366, 402,
644
Seawolf, 260, 297, 298, 336, 342,
360, 401, 403, 541, 556, 608, 621
design and construction, 154,
176n., 188, 253, 355–357
operations, 358
reactor change, 358–359, 404, 555
See, Capt. Thomas Jefferson Jack-
son, 67

Selection boards, 19, 123, 153, 186,
190
Rickover passed over, 187, 192,
203
Rickover selected, 203–204
Senior Officer Ship Material Readi-
ness Course, 338–339
Seymour, Lt. Comdr. Philip, 66
Shapley, Deborah, 405, 665
Shark, 369
Shaw, Milton, 156, 620
Shear, Adm. Harold E., 337,
545–546
Shenandoah, 70
Shepard, Capt. Tazewell T., Jr., 388
Shepley, James R., 191
Sherman, Adm. Forrest P., 147,
186n., 251, 252, 253, 474, 602
Sherrod, Robert, 188
*The Shippingport Pressurized Water
Reactor,* 612
Shippingport reactor plant, 176, 254,
601–602, 609, 615, 619–620,
622, 630–631
construction of, 609–613
See also Civilian nuclear power
Shogan, Robert, 344–345
Shugg, Carleton, 493
Sides, Rear Adm. John H., 538
Sikes, Robert L. F., 412
Sims, Capt. William E., 545–546
Sims, Adm. William S., 661
Skate, 176n., 285, 307, 360, 363, 365,
366, 370, 401, 427, 544, 556, 659
problems, 424
Skipjack, 307, 336, 337, 363, 365,
366, 368, 372, 401, 402–403,
405, 425, 514, 516, 543, 544,
561, 644
Joint Committee on board,
216–217, 461
Skylark, 428–430, 434
Slattery, Comdr. Francis A., 444
Smedberg, Vice Adm. William R.,
285–286, 418, 641
on Mrs. Rickover christening sub-
marines, 644

Smedberg, Vice Adm. W. (*cont.*)
  missing report about Rickover,
    655–656
  on Rickover successor, 661
Smith, Gerald L. K., 201
Smith, Vice Adm. Harold Page, 467
Smith, John Lewis, 520
Smith, Rear Adm. Levering, 436,
    477, 540, 545, 564, 565, 568
Smith, Lt. Comdr. R. E., 262
Smithsonian Institution, 525
Smoot, Rear Adm. Roland N., 199
Smyth, Henry D., 603
Snook, 369
Sokolovsky, Marshal Vasily D., 556
Solberg, Rear Adm. Thorwald A.,
    120, 134, 135, 140, 145, 662
Sonenshein, Rear Adm. Nathan B.,
    410
South Carolina, 501–502, 508
Soviet Union, 346, 351, 353, 378,
    386, 388, 398, 429, 479
  submarine developments, 142,
    229, 386, 387, 393, 400, 409,
    416, 482, 538, 552, 554–563,
    566, 568, 665
  nuclear icebreakers, 178, 222, 261
  Nixon-Rickover visit, 214, 222,
    326, 552, 585
  leadership, 238–239
  military record, 240–241
  attaché activities, 468–471
  strategic arms, 544, 565
  officials visit *Savannah,* Shipping-
    port, 553
  nuclear submarine loss, 557–558
  education in, 585–591
  See also Arktika; Lenin; Sputnik
Spanish-American War, 68–69, 106,
    218, 335, 463–464
Special Projects Office, established,
    539. *See also* Polaris missile
    program
Spivak, Lawrence E., 522
Sputnik (satellite), 222, 223, 378,
    535, 543–544, 587, 590, 593, 643
Squalus, 428

SSN ("Saturdays, Sundays, and
    Nights"), 640
SSN-688. *See Los Angeles*
Steele, Vice Adm. George P., 336,
    402
Stennis, John, 345, 407–408, 484,
    503
Stephan, Rear Adm. Edward C.,
    435
Stevenson, Adlai, 197
Stevenson, Comdr. Connelly D.,
    332–334
Stickleback, 425n.
Stockdale, Vice Adm. James, 528
Stormer, John A., 592–593
Strategic Air Command, Rickover
    recommends transfer, 471
STRAT-X study, 565–569. *See also*
    Trident
Stratton, Samuel S., 221
Strauss, Rear Adm. Lewis L.,
    140–141, 141n., 176n., 197
  chairman, AEC, 155, 253, 254,
    602–603, 605–607
  opposes nuclear carrier, 253–254
Strike cruiser. *See* Aegis weapon
    system
Stroop, Vice Adm. Paul D., 467
Sturgeon, 373, 406, 412–413, 419,
    482
  design and construction, 402,
    405–406, 409
Styer, Rear Adm. C. W., 136, 138
Submarine Alternatives Study,
    413–415
Submarine Officers' Conference,
    135–137, 145, 146, 662, 663
Submarine speed
  fast vs. quiet debate, 405–409
  Trident speed, 574–575
  See also Glenard P. Lipscomb;
    GUPPY; *Los Angeles*
Sullivan, John L., 138, 139, 143
Swanson, Capt. Charles O., 474–477
Swanson, Mrs. Charles O., 474
Swart, Rear Adm. Robert L., 325,
    326

Swift, Wesley, 201
Swiss Schools and Ours: Why Theirs Are Better, 592, 593–594, 597–598, 642
Swordfish, 158, 159, 176n., 336, 360
Symington, Stuart, 391, 407–408, 646–647

Tactical Cruise Missile Submarine, 411–412, 566
Tang class, 147, 148, 153, 168, 354, 359
Task Force 1. *See* Operation Sea Orbit
Taussig, Capt. Joseph K., Jr., 334
Tautog, 332
Teller, Edward, 126–127, 128, 132–133, 197, 538, 623, 667
Texas (battleship), 218
Texas (missile cruiser), 399
Theodore Roosevelt, 242
Thetis, 430, 459
Thornton, Tex, 504
Thomas, Albert, 244
Thomas, Charles S., 255, 325, 541
Thomas, J. Parnell, 244
Thompson, Rear Adm. William, 194
Three Mile Island, 204, 315, 347, 602, 615, 616–619, 621, 632, 659
Thresher, 494, 543, 548
    design and construction, 369–373, 402, 405, 409, 425, 427
    loss, 370, 372, 423–435, 443–445, 524, 625, 665, 666
    Rickover letter to families, 640
Time Magazine, 29, 186, 187, 188, 189, 191, 192, 195, 196, 205, 206, 210, 513, 516, 577
Tirpitz, Grand Adm. von, 239
Title VIII, 246–247, 249, 396, 398
Tolman, Richard C., 120
    Tolman Committee, 120, 125, 134, 145, 662
Tomb, Rear Adm. Paul, 271
Trident missile program, 226, 243, 564–581, 646
    accelerated schedule, 570

defended by Carter, 564
    supported by Zumwalt, 566–567, 569–570
Triton, 319, 336, 363–369, 543, 545, 554
    circumnavigation, 367–368
    decommissioned, 369
    Mrs. Rickover and, 364–365, 643–644
Truesdell, Harry E., 62
Truman, Harry S, 115, 141n., 145, 148, 198, 200, 217, 347, 354, 519
    at *Nautilus* keel-laying, 150–151, 189–190
    and Rickover promotion, 161
    briefed by Rickover, 194
Truxtun, 382, 393, 614
Tucker automobile, 639
Tullibee, 402–403, 405
    accident, 444
Tupolev, Andrei, 553
Turnbaugh, Comdr. Marshall, 360
Twenty Thousand Leagues Under the Sea, 113, 122
Typhon weapon system, 383, 388, 393

Udall, Morris K., 241
Ultra program, 23
Undersea Long-range Missile System (ULMS). *See* STRAT-X, Trident
United States, 251

Vandenberg, Arthur, 244
Van Orden, Rear Adm. M. D., 404
Van Zandt, James E., 216, 244
Veliotis, P. Takis, 572
Verne, Jules, 113, 122
Victory, 648
Vinson, Carl, 325
von Braun, Wernher, 540
Von Steuben, 424

Wagner, Robert F., 177
Walker, Hank, 189
Wallace, Robert, 515

Wallin, Rear Adm. Homer N., 100, 195–196, 200–201, 204
Warner, John, 411, 477
Washington, Booker T., 33
Washington, Gen. George, 218
Washington Naval Conference, 60–61
Watkins, Rear Adm. Frank T., 176n.
Watkins, Adm. James, 338, 345, 418, 655
Watson, Lt. (j.g.) James D., 429–430
Watson, John H., 225
Watts, Isaac, 395, 662
Weaver, Charles H., 198
Weaver, Phillip, 558
Webster, Capt. Hugh, 286
Wegner, William, 156, 236, 529
Weinberg, Alvin M., 138
Werntz, Robert Lincoln, 38
Westinghouse Electric Corp., 126, 141, 143, 145, 146, 147, 149, 151, 152, 297, 322, 359, 363, 365, 492, 603–604, 605, 607, 632, 655, 660, 664
  large-ship reactors, 253, 254
  civilian reactors, 254
  small destroyer reactor, 260
  See also Reactors
Westland, Jack, 244
West Point. *See* Military Academy
Wheeler, Gen. Earle, 391
Whitney, Chancey, 99, 101, 106, 109
Whitthorne, Irv, 361
Whittle, Adm. Alfred J., 338
Wilkinson, Vice Adm. Eugene P., 114, 143, 153–154, 156, 386
  commands *Nautilus,* 164–165, 168, 318, 403, 436
  commands *Long Beach,* 261, 318
  selection to Rear Adm., 318–319

in OPNAV and Deputy CNO (Submarine Warfare), 336–337, 406n., 411
  as Rickover successor, 659
Will, Vice Adm. John M., 364–365
William H. Bates, 242
Williams, Vice Adm. Joe, 664
Wilson, Bob, 229, 230
Wilson, Charles E., 254, 255, 539, 613
Wilson, Charles H., 230, 248–249, 346
Wilson, George C., 481
Wilson, Rear Adm. Henry B., 57, 58
Wilson, Woodrow, 33
Wisconsin, 45
Wolfe, William C., 66
Wood, Lt. Comdr. Valentine, 67–68
Wyoming, 58

Yarnell, Adm. Harry E., 69, 86, 87
Yates, Sidney R., 19, 37, 198, 201, 206, 605

Zern, Ed, 460
Zhiltsov, Capt. 1/rank Lev, 556
Zhukov, Marshal G. K., 239
Zinn, Walter, 140, 604–605
Zumwalt, Adm. Elmo R., Jr., 215, 385, 495–496, 502–504, 529
  as CNO, 228, 236, 285, 307, 311, 337, 338, 397, 411–412, 452, 472, 473–479, 481
  Rickover interview, 275–285
  establishes Deputy CNO (Submarine Warfare), 336–337
  as Director, Systems Analysis Division, 394–396, 406, 574
  supports Trident, 566–567, 569–570

ABOUT THE AUTHORS

NORMAN POLMAR is an author, analyst and historian who has specialized in naval and military matters. For the past fifteen years he has directed or participated in major studies for the Navy, Defense Nuclear Agency, Army, Maritime Administration, and private shipyards and aerospace firms. At the same time he has been a prolific writer, producing several books and numerous articles on defense subjects. For ten years he was Editor of the United States sections of the annual *Jane's Fighting Ships,* the "bible" of the world's navies. He left that London-based publication in part to begin a new series of reference books for the U.S. Naval Institute, the Navy's professional society. As a writer and analyst he has been to sea in most types of warships, from the battleship *New Jersey* to PT-boats, and aboard several nuclear submarines. Studies and research have also taken him throughout Europe, to North Africa and the Middle East, and to the Soviet Union as a guest of the Academy of Sciences and Soviet Navy. His in-depth knowledge of naval and defense matters has led to his being a frequent witness before Congressional committees and his serving as a consultant to several members of the Senate as well as to senior civilian and uniformed officials of the Navy Department.

Mr. Polmar is a native of Washington, D.C., and a graduate of the American University.

THOMAS B. ALLEN is an author and editor. For more than fifteen years he was with the National Geographic Society as associate chief of book service. He edited several National Geographic books, including the million-plus best seller *We Americans.* He has edited and written for a score of the National Geographic books and is the author of *Vanishing Wildlife of North America.* He is also the author or co-author of three other nonfiction books: *Shadows in the Sea,* a definitive book on sharks; *The Quest,* a report on the search for extraterrestrial life; and *Living in Washington,* a guide to life in the District of Columbia. He is the author of two novels, *The Last Inmate* and *A Short Life,* the latter having been made into a television film. A former newspaperman in Connecticut and New York City, he has written news articles that have been syndicated in leading American newspapers. He has lectured on writing at the U.S. Naval Academy and the University of Baltimore, and teaches writing at the Writer's Center of Washington.

Mr. Allen is a native of Bridgeport, Connecticut, and a graduate of the University of Bridgeport. He served in the U.S. Navy during the Korean War.

Messrs. Polmar and Allen have collaborated on a novel that originated with research based on this book.